Indians of the Tulares

Adaptation, Relocation, and Subjugation in Central California

1771-1917

Dear Readers,

Pechanga established the Great Oak Press in order to provide an avenue by which Native voices and topics of significance and of importance to Native Americans could find their way into the contemporary discourse and become both a growing and permanent part of recorded knowledge.

As a publisher of scholarly and academic books, Pechanga's Great Oak Press is dedicated to working with the leading experts and also the up and coming experts in a wide range of fields, ranging from the arts to the sciences and from history to languages. Our focus, though broad in topics, is finely centered on publishing works of great importance that preserve and expand knowledge as well as encourage creative thought and intellectual exploration.

However, Great Oak Press is not focused solely on producing scholarly titles that only the academic and higher education community find accessible. Rather, Great Oak Press is committed to producing books of exceptional quality that literally begin with First Readers for children and will include works for the entire range that comprises the K-12 reading levels. After all, the health of society is directly related to its efforts at raising and educating its youth.

In this work, George Harwood Phillips, one of the first scholars of California Indian history to give both a voice and agency to California Indians, has assembled a remarkable study to continue in his tradition of exceptional works that shape an entire genre.

We thank you for your support.

Mark Macarro

Tribal Chairman of the Pechanga Band of Luiseño Indians

Indians of the Tulares

Adaptation, Relocation, and Subjugation in Central California

1771-1917

George Harwood Phillips

Combined into one volume, revised with additional chapters, *Indians and Intruders in Central California, 1769-1849*; *Indians and Indian Agents: The Origins of the Reservation System in California, 1849-1852*; and *"Bringing them Under Subjection:" California's Tejon Indian Reservation and Beyond, 1852-1864*.

A CIP catalog record for this book is available from the Library of Congress.

ISBN: 978-1-942279-05-1

Publisher: Great Oak Press, Pechanga, California

Printed in the United States of America

Contents

PART III: SUBJUGATION *255*

Illustrations

Maps

Tables

Preface

The three books that form this volume were written over the course of about fifteen years. Each book was designed to stand on its own, but each is set in the same region and each follows the previous one chronologically. Nevertheless, to establish cohesion and continuity, it was necessary to eliminate the background chapters in the second and third books and revise, condense, move, and combine others.

Some chapter titles have been changed as well. And because two original chapters have been added, the time frame has been extended. Therefore, even though the three parts in which the book is divided correspond to the three volumes on which it is based, it is far more than a sum of its original parts.

Reviews of the books upon which it is based were highly favorable, due in large part to those who assisted me in their preparation. Their support has been acknowledged in each volume and will not be repeated here. But those assisting me in the publication of this volume were Myra Masiel-Zamora, Thomas Maxwell-Long, and Lauren Kirschke Niezgodzki Their support has been most valuable. Since the publication of the first volume, books and articles have been published that have been valuable in what rewriting has been necessary. Important works by James Sandos, Laurence H. Shoup and Randall T. Milliken, Gelya Frank and Carole Goldberg, Thomas Maxwell-Long, Glenn J. Farris, Rose Marie Beebe and Robert M. Senkewicz, and Donald Cutter have been consulted.

INTRODUCTION

Ethnohistorical Considerations

In 1962 the British social anthropologist E. E. Evans-Pritchard encouraged his colleagues to consider the historical dimensions of the peoples they studied. Concerned with the structures and functions of tribal societies, most social anthropologists then paid only cursory attention to the change these societies underwent after contact with Europeans. This neglect could be corrected, Evans-Pritchard argued, only if documentary sources and oral traditions were used.[1]

Evans-Pritchard also had some advice for historians: "It is understandable that in the past they should have restricted their activities to European history, but it is no longer so in the world in which we live today. When, instead of adding to our knowledge of Charles the Bold and the Conciliar movement, they show more initiative and write histories of non-European peoples and cultures they will better appreciate how relevant to their studies is our own research." Rhetorically, he asked how many scholars then in England could write the histories of India, China, and Africa that dealt with the indigenous peoples of those regions.[2]

At the time he wrote, however, several British historians were investigating the histories of nonEuropean peoples, especially African peoples, and when their research appeared in print a short time later, the changes he called for were well underway.[3] And not all British anthropologists agreed they were ahistorical and unaware of the effect European colonialism had on tribal peoples.[4] According to I. M. Lewis, "the majority of monographs based on field research in the structural-functional tradition have included some excursions into history, however unsophisticated or unsystematic these may seem to the orthodox historian."[5]

Whereas anthropologists have expressed some interest in history and historical methodologies, until recently few historians have acknowledged that anthropology has much to offer them. An exception is Keith Thomas, who some years ago claimed that those studying Great Britain could gain much from an examination of the anthropological literature. "Where can one find a better explanation of the Divine Rights of Kings than in Evans-Pritchard's analysis of the kingship of the Shilluk of Sudan? Where is there a closer analogy with the medieval and Elizabethan world-picture than in the Tikopia conception of the future life…? The emphasis upon the binding force of oaths among the Kikuyu is reminiscent of seventeenth-century England, where the oath provided the sanction for almost every form of legal, official or ecclesiastical arrangement. The Cargo cults of Melanesia are obviously analogous with such millenarian movements as that of the Fifth Monarchy Men in England."[6] Thomas reasoned that the historian "familiar with the findings of the anthropologists is in a better position to ask intelligent questions of his material."[7]

More so than historians, anthropologists have identified the common ground shared by the two disciplines. William Fenton noted that, "it is the ethnologist's business to delineate patterns, forms, and processes of culture history. But such attempts at descriptive integration…are also characteristic of the work of the historian."[8] Alfred Kroeber understood that historians, like anthropologists, employ synchronic analyses. Occasionally they halt the "narrative flow in order to hold a…period steady while they review the state of institutions, arts, manners, attitudes, and values … in the country or area they are dealing with." Temporarily, "the pervasive regularities of human behavior" take precedent over diachronic developments.[9]

According to Robert Anderson, "historians are remarkably like anthropologists in their concern with culture studied holistically and comparatively. They typically study societies as integrated wholes even though they rarely use an explicit model of functional integration. Additionally, they usually make comparative assessments, even though they rarely use any systematic technique for comparison. One finds, as a result, much implicit theory in their work, and it merits looking into."[10] It would be inaccurate, in the words of Claude Levi-Strauss, to claim that, "the historian and the anthropologist travel in opposite directions. On the contrary, they both go the same way. The fact that their journey together appears to each of them in a different light—to the historian, transition from the explicit to the implicit; to the anthropologist, transition from the particular to the universal—does not in the least alter the identical character of their fundamental approach."[11] Marshall Sahlins wrote that "practice clearly has gone beyond the theoretical differences that are supposed to divide anthropology and history. Anthropologists rise from the abstract structure to the explication of the concrete event. Historians devalue the unique event in favor of underlying recurrent structures."[12] Even the sources used by anthropologists and historians are not as distinct as they may appear. Kroeber pointed out that, "ethnographic accounts are usually based not on search and exploitation of already extant documents, but on newly made documents resulting from face-to-face interviews and observations."[13] What does the historian do, Levi-Strauss queried, "when he studies documents if not to surround himself with the testimony of amateur ethnographers, who were often as far removed from the culture they described as is the modem investigator from Polynesians or Pygmies?"[14]

Although the basic kinds of sources used by anthropologists and historians have not drastically changed over time, the theories they employ and themes they develop often derive from the intellectual climate current at a particular time. Historians long have acknowledged that their views of the past are influenced by their perceptions of the present. But neither are anthropologists immune from the influences of contemporary life. As Evans-Pritchard explained: "What anthropologists inquire into, observe, and record, and the inferences they draw from their observations, also change from generation to generation."[15]

That many anthropologists and historians have been greatly influenced by the recent activities of non-Europeans is to state the obvious. As African, Asian, and Pacific peoples have achieved independence from their European colonizers, and as Native Americans, Australian Aborigines, Maoris, and other minority groups have sought more recognition and rights within their respective countries, interest has been generated regarding the historical interaction of intruding and indigenous peoples. In their investigations of interethnic relations, anthropologists and historians increasingly have employed the term "ethnohistory."[16]

Several decades have passed since 1966, when William C. Sturtevant, an anthropologist, concluded that ethnohistory is fundamentally the study of the peoples usually studied by anthropologists.[17] The same year, however, Gregory Dening, an historian, first wondered if "ethnohistory is only history writ polysyllabically" and then noted that "ethnohistory's prime concern is not with myth, legend or genealogy, or with historical reconstructions of illiterate societies, or with the origins of these societies. The ethnohistorian's prime concern is with the description of illiterate societies by literate observers at the time when contact between the two had not changed or destroyed the illiterate society. On every continent this period of contact and change has been caught in the journals and letters of explorers, administrators, traders and missionaries." To Dening, therefore, ethnohistory is defined by subject, time, and sources.[18]

In 1973 Kenneth C. Wylie suggested that the confusion over the term is "the result of a penchant to define ethnohistory as subject per se rather than as a methodology.... Ethnohistory is best defined as the use of ethnographic and traditional documentary evidence within a methodological framework, which combines the best analytical techniques of both history and anthropology. In a sense ethnohistory combines synchronic and diachronic explanations." Wiley insisted that "ethnohistory must make use rigorous use of all pertinent written documents along with equally precise and systemic use of whatever oral data are available. Neither the use of oral tradition nor documentary evidence alone can result in ethnohistory."[19]

Historian James Axtell concluded in 1981 that, "Historians and anthropologists now have no difficulty in agreeing that ethnohistory is essentially the use of historical and anthropological methods and materials to gain knowledge of the nature and causes of change in a culture defined by ethnological concepts and categories."[20] By claiming that ethnohistory draws upon the methods of history and anthropology but also is concerned with cultures defined by anthropologists, Axtell's definition bridges the gap between those claiming ethnohistory is a subject and those insisting it is methodology. Unlike Wylie, Axtell does not qualify his definition by insisting that an ethnohistory must contain oral evidence.

Shepard Kretch III, an anthropologist, noted in 1991 the changes anthropology had undergone since Sturtevant issued his definition: "For one thing, anthropologists are as likely today to study urban Westerners as they are exotic and remote peoples, who in any event daily become less exotic and inhabit less remote comers of the non-Western world. Furthermore, numerous works in history demonstrate an interest... [in] the history of peoples whose cultures and societies had once been the exclusive focus of anthropologists." Kretch concludes his essay by declaring that, "it may be ill-advised to continue to use 'ethnohistory' as we have used it in the past. Both anthropological history and historical anthropology substitute well for ethnohistory without stigma or illogic, and one's training in anthropology should not prevent one from writing anthropological history (or plain history for that matter), just as training in history should not preclude production of an historical anthropology."[21]

A few years later, historians Mellisa L. Meyer and Kerwin Lee Klein supported Kretch by noting that, "by the 1980s, many anthropologists not associated with ethnohistory had turned to historical interpretation. Many historians not associated with ethnohistory interviewed informants and used oral texts as historical evidence.... The transitions have generally emptied "ethnohistory" of its methodological content. The word no longer points to a method distinct from what other ethnographers and historians do."[22] But their insistence that the term be abandoned because it no longer defines a methodology distinct from those applied by historians and anthropologists presupposes that ethnohistory has been defined as a methodology. There is no agreement on this point. Moreover, because hundreds of articles, essays, reports, journals, and books use the term "ethnohistory" in one way or another, discontinuing the term is impossible.

That ethnohistory represents a synthesis of the two disciplines is advocated by some. Dening has suggested that it is a reaction to, even a rejection of, the old ways of doing things: "Ethnohistory is the bastard child of history and anthropology, born out of the snobbish reluctance of historians to be interested in anyone who was not white and did not wear a crown and born too out of the intransigent belief of anthropologists that to understand anyone they must be alive, in remote places and in dire danger of disappearing."[23] Others doubt that a hybrid discipline will emerge. Isabel McBryde, an historian, admitted that because of "its sources, methods, and aims," ethnohistory would always straddle other disciplines. But even though it should not necessarily be regarded as an independent entity in itself, its "contributions can still be real, individual and analytical."[24]

Because most scholars calling themselves ethnohistorians were trained either as anthropologists or as historians, their research usually is designed to fulfill the goals dictated by their respective disciplines. Anthropologists use written documents to corroborate the data gained from field work. Historians draw upon the cultural information produced by anthropologists to support the data derived from the written sources. As noted by Sturtevant, "when historians and anthropologists read each others' writings it is usually in search of specific data on a culture of mutual concern rather than through interest in the theory and method of the other field."[25] Regardless of the discipline in which they were trained, ethnohistorians, according to Bruce Trigger, "require not only all the skills of a good conventional historian but also a sound knowledge of ethnology, if they are to be able to evaluate sources and interpret them with reasonable understanding of the perceptions and motivations of the native people involved."[26]

Although anthropologists and historians may share similar goals, the gap between the two disciplines remains conceptionally wide. What Richard White, an historian, said about the writing of history might seem to some anthropologists haphazard and unscientific: "Practicing historians have long recognized that they write as if they are describing the world as it was, but what they are actually describing is the world they have created from the debris of the past. They interpret the traces that the past leaves in the present by using the intellectual tools they possess and following rules of their collective devising. The weight they give to certain kinds of evidence, the questions they ask, and the issues they explore are inextricably tied up with the concerns of their own society. Historians make maps of vanished countries. There are only maps; the past is gone and cannot be recreated."[27]

As viewed by Bernard Cohen, an anthropologist, the writing of anthropology might seem rigid and unrealistic to many historians: "The anthropologist posits a place where the natives are authentic, untouched and aboriginal and strives to deny the central historical fact that the people he or she studies are constituted in the historically significant colonial situation, affirming instead that they are somehow out of time and history.... The anthropologist follows in the wake of the impact caused by the Western agents of change, and then tries to recover what might have been. The anthropologist searches for the elders with the richest memory of days gone by, assiduously records their ethnographic text, and then puts them between the covers of their monographs a picture of the lives of the natives."[28]

Regarding the study of Native Americans, members of each discipline demonstrate strengths and weaknesses. On the one hand, historians have been trained to investigate intersocietal activity within large regions and thus conceptually are well prepared to examine Indian-white and inter-Indian relations over time. But many are methodologically ill prepared to understand the activities and behavior of nonliterate peoples. On the other hand, anthropologists are well prepared to investigate distinct, usually small-scale groups, but many lack the training necessary to fully appreciate the dynamics of multisocietal interaction, especially when Euro-American societies are involved. Trigger admitted that, "the anthropologist usually knows little about the complex economic and political relationships among the European powers who were in contact with the Indians."[29]

The two disciplines are restrictive in other ways as well. Because anthropologists of the American Indian tend to place the people they study in culture or linguistic areas, they often overlook processes of interaction. The Huron, for example, have been placed in the Northeast Culture Area, but they traded with the Cree, who have been classified as a subarctic people. Because historians of the Indian often present their data within time frames exclusively created to trace and analyze Euro-American activity, they often fail to understand that the historical watersheds occurring in Indian and Euro-American societies seldom intersected. The American Revolution may have ended British rule, but it did not end Cherokee independence.

Particularly detrimental in appreciating the importance of Indians in shaping postcontact North American history has been the widespread application of the frontier thesis. Formulated by Frederick Jackson Turner in 1893 and perpetuated by his many followers, the thesis relegates Indians to "the frontier," a vaguely defined area repeatedly penetrated by westward-moving whites.[30] As pointed out by Francis Jennings, this kind of history presents "only one side of the frontier.... The Indians who appear in it are cardboard figures set up to be knocked down. It cannot be anything else so long as the frontier is conceived as a line of separation constantly being pushed back."[31]

Modifying the concept of the frontier to encompass distinct cultures had been undertaken with some vigor. To Robin Wells, an anthropologist, the frontier is "a dynamic social network of a particular kind which covers an extensive geographical area and which links a number of culturally diverse societies.[32] To Jack Forbes, an historian, the frontier is a situation that involves "more than momentary contact between two ethnic, cultural or national groups."[33] Historians Leonard Thompson and Howard Lamar have conceptualized the frontier "not as a boundary or line, but as a territory or zone of interpenetration between two previously distinct societies. Usually, one of the societies is indigenous to the region, or at least has occupied it for many generations; the other is intrusive. The frontier 'opens' in a given zone when the first representatives of the intrusive society arrive; it 'closes' when a single political authority has established hegemony over the zone." Thompson and Lamar argue that although a zone closes with the end of the frontier phase, this does not result in a static relationship developing between ethnic groups. Instead, a "new structural situation has been created and subsequent relationships are relations of ethnicity and class within a single society, not a frontier relationship between different societies"[34] By identifying the frontier first as a zone of interpenetration and then by claiming the frontier opens and closes in a zone under certain conditions, these historians consider the frontier as both a place and a process. In this regard, Thompson and Lamar (and Forbes) have failed to overcome some of the concerns issued by Walker Wyman and Clifton Kroeber in an earlier publication. "Considering the great variety of frontiers," they wrote, "it is small wonder that historians have no fixed meaning of the term. They have considered it a place, or a process, or a situation."[35]

Because the "frontier" of one people is the "homeland" of another, the addition of "frontier," an elusive term at best, to the study of interethnic relations clouds rather than clarifies the issues under discussion. Alfonso Ortiz, an anthropologist, proposed that, "we dispense with the notion of the frontier altogether when talking about historical encounters between peoples...because it is possible to make so much mischief with this notion."[36] Much of this "mischief" is overcome by discarding the term and identifying the places where indigenous and intruding peoples meet as "zones of interaction." A zone may be defined as a place with geographical unity, indigenous cultural uniformity, and historical continuity.

An island, valley, river system, or coastal strip, may not be perfect geographical entities, but they can provide spatial frameworks in which to investigate interaction. Because most zones comprised more than one indigenous society, political unity may be lacking, but cultural similarities, such as common subsistence patterns, might be present. Whether different societies located in a particular zone shared a common culture and a territory with perfectly defined features, however, is less important than their sharing a common past with one another and with the intruders with whom they interacted.[37] Within this framework, the ethnohistorian might, perhaps should, begin with an analysis of the indigenous peoples as members of independent societies managing their own affairs and interacting with one another prior to contact. Such an analysis is crucial to understanding the degree of change the culture underwent after contact. It also allows for an appreciation of indigenous intersocietal relations that continued after contact. Whether peaceful or hostile, that interaction was sometimes of crucial importance in shaping the history of a particular zone.[38]

Obviously, the historical importance of the intruders becomes increasingly apparent as they impose their institutions upon indigenous peoples. Ironically, the institutions designed to subjugate them, such as a colony, reserve, reservation, or mission, offer the ethnohistorian the framework in which the activities of the confined can be studied. Confinement does not preclude responses that helped shape the structure, function, and history of the institution. But crucial to understanding confinement is an understanding of how and why the institution was founded in the first place. The options available to the confined depend on when and for what purpose it was created, on how well it was managed, and for how long it lasted. Although confinement obviously results in the indigenous land base contracting, some times to a fraction of what it once was, the situation usually remains fluid. Institutions of confinement may be expanded, abolished, or changed. The history of American reservation system has examples of all three processes. As Asian, African, and Pacific people expelled those colonizing them, their land bases expanded, in some cases, back to their original sizes.

The extent and availability of the cultural and historical evidence will determine to what degree the processes of interaction in a particular zone can be comprehended. Because some indigenous peoples have been extensively studied by anthropologists, ethnohistorians have access to an abundance of data regarding material culture, spiritual beliefs, social organization, and economic systems. Other peoples dispersed or disappeared before much information was recorded. In some cases, the oral traditions Indians have transmitted over time provide ethnohistorians with the values and viewpoints of the people being investigated. In other cases, so devastating was the intrusion that indigenes remember little of their distant past.

Ethnohistorians concerned with Indian-white interaction must rely heavily upon documentary evidence. Contrary to established opinion, those who left accounts of indigenous peoples did not always portray them in negative and stereotypical ways. Few appreciated or understood the cultures they observed to any significant degree, and many expressed their ignorance and bigotry in no uncertain terms. But others demonstrated concern and occasionally respect for the peoples they encountered. True, their descriptions often were determined by the relationship then existing between indigenes and intruders. Conflict is not conducive to objectivity, but even those repeatedly suffering from attacks often left behind more information than opinion.

Over the course of some five hundred years of Indian-white contact, a vast body of data has accumulated. Much of this evidence has either been ignored or employed to rationalize Euro-American expansion and conquest, but it exists nonetheless. The problem is not the amount of historical evidence; the problem is that much of it lies buried in bits and pieces in the diaries, journals, and reports that deal mainly with other matters. As any ethnohistorian will attest, it is much easier to write about those who produced the documents than about those mentioned intermittently in them.

Writing the history of a culture relying mainly on documents produced by another is, in the words of Trigger, "different from writing the history of a literate people who have abundantly documented their own activities. Admittedly, it may not be so different from trying to understand the history of illiterate peasantries or working classes in Europe using documentation produced almost exclusively by the state, the clergy, and the upper classes. Yet, in dealing with native people, there is the additional challenge of studying wholly alien cultures."[39]

The vast majority of North American historians, of course, are concerned with issues having little or nothing to do with Indians. But those studying the colonial period, western expansion, and particular regions that overlook Indian activity may be doing themselves a disservice. According to Trigger, "the price of ignoring native history has been not simply a one-sided understanding of relations between native peoples and Europeans. In some cases it has resulted in serious misunderstanding of the internal dynamics of European colonialism."[40]

The price of downplaying or overlooking Euro-American activity is equally costly to our understanding of interethnic relations.[41] At different times and places, Indians and whites interacted with such intensity that to ignore the latter is to trivialize the activities and influences of the former. As explained by Trigger: "If we are to understand the total situation, we must attempt to achieve a … dispassionate understanding of the motives of European groups … who interacted with the Indians."[42] Dening put it this way: "To know the native one must know the intruder…. In the ethnohistory of culture contact … we are concerned to write the anthropology and the history of those moments when native and intruding cultures are conjoined. Neither can be known independently of that moment. They are both changed by it and change all the subsequent moments."[43]

Maintaining a perfect balance between the activities of indigenes and intruders, it should be admitted, is difficult if not impossible to achieve, although the imbalance is partially corrected when interethnic relations are investigated within a zone of interaction. By selecting the lands of indigenous peoples as the spatial framework for the investigation, the ethnohistorian acknowledges their historical importance. Because those penetrating a zone were usually bent upon domination and exploitation, prominent figures in North American history-the explorer, missionary, trapper, and pioneer—are cast in a different light. The task of the ethnohistorian, however, is not to replace one set of "heroes" with another. It is, rather, to present an accurate description of the process of interaction and a careful analysis of the ramifications it produced in the different societies under investigation.

Most of the activity examined in this study transpired in the vast region the Spanish called the Tulares but now known as the San Joaquin Valley. Although comprising only half of the great Central Valley, it contains ample geographical unity to fulfill the territorial requirement for a zone of interaction. Because most of the Indian peoples residing in the zone spoke Penutian languages, because all subsisted upon the abundant wild plant and animal life, and because all were organized in relatively sedentary village communities, cultural similarity was extensive. Most importantly, the valley represents a zone of interaction because, more than other interior regions of California it was repeatedly penetrated by intruders—Spaniards, Mexicans, and Americans—beginning in the last third of the eighteenth century.

The coastal region from where most of the intruders came also constitutes a zone of interaction. Because Indians in this zone were first to experience the consequences of colonization, understanding aspects of its history is crucial to comprehending the nature of Indian-white interaction in the interior. The historical processes unfolding in the two zones further intersected when Indians from the coast fled to the interior to reorder their lives and later when Indians from the interior intruded upon the coastal lands occupied by the colonizers.

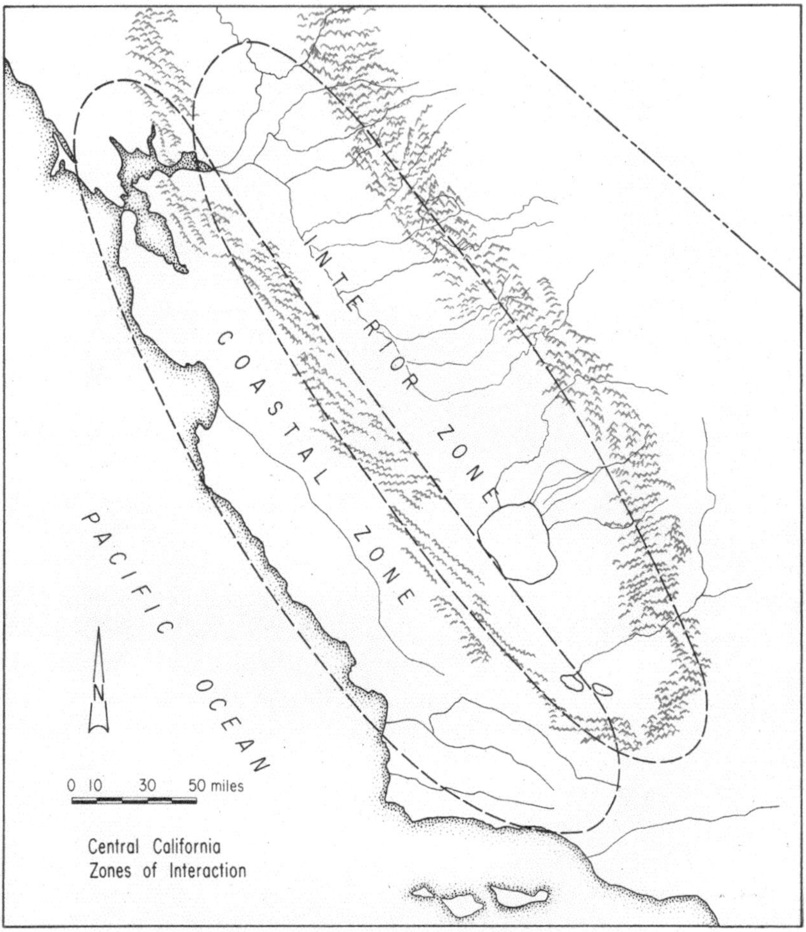

In short, just as geographical features rather than the concept of the culture area determined the spatial framework of this study, the dynamics of Indian-intruder interaction rather than traditional periods in California history (Spanish, Mexican and American) determined its temporal framework.

PART I

Adaptation

PART I begins with a cultural overview that acknowledges, if only briefly, the Indians' long pre-contact history and the variety and complexity of their institutions. Without some understanding of traditional Indian political organizations, it is difficult to comprehend the varieties of policies implemented by them, when parties representing several foreign nations entered their terriotories. This called for the application of archaeological and anthropological data, as well as data culled from the first-hand accounts of the foreigners. Contrary to common belief, the written documents produced by the intruders often provide as much insight into Indian life as into the lives of those who wrote them.

By placing the processes of adaptation undertaken by the Indians in a zone of interaction, the geographical framework of this study is delineated, setting the stage, as it were, for the arrival of new actors. With some exceptions, historians have overlooked this arrival, the San Joaquin Valley being of little interest until the beginning of permanent foreign settlements. As a consequence, they have overlooked important aspects of European colonialism and thus have failed to appreciate how Indian activity impacted foreigners themselves. An ethnohistorical approach corrects this neglect.

Part I ends not with the conquest of the Indians of the Tulares but with most of the interior still firmly in their control. In fact, some groups had adapted so successively to the changing circumstance that they were aggressively intruding into the coastal zone, the region where the intruders had established their institutions.

CHAPTER I

Indian Occupation

In old times water covered all this earth.... Chicken Hawk...was God's son. Every morning he would go around looking for the earth. First God made four ducks, two large and two somewhat smaller. He didn't like these as they were quite useless, just floating around on the water all the time. The ducks, however, kept diving down under the water to try to find the bottom. God thought it was time they all had some earth to live on; he asked Chicken Hawk to take care of the matter.

Chicken Hawk asked the ducks what they were doing. They told him they were trying to touch bottom. Hawk told them to continue trying, for if they could get some earth they could make the world. The two larger ducks tried again and came up exhausted. Then the larger of the smallest pair went down; he failed though he was nearly unconscious when he returned. Finally the very smallest black one went down. He went down, down, down: he thought he'd drown. He reached the bottom and seized the earth with both his hands. As he came up the rush of passing water washed all the sand out of his fists. When he reached the surface he was almost dead. Hawk picked him up, scraped the sand from under his fingernails. This he took to his father.

God told his son to take the sand and go far back toward the east, and as he traveled westward again to drop one grain of sand at a time. Chicken Hawk did this. As the grains were dropped they grew up into mountains which pushed the water westward to the place it now occupies. The ocean's home used to be where the Sierra Nevada Mountains are standing.[1]

This Yokuts creation myth shares much with the geologic record regarding the formation of the Central Valley. Some 140 million years ago the interior of California formed part of a vast shallow sea floor. Eventually, a batholith of crystalline rock emerged in the eastern portion of the sea, forming a mountain range. During the following ninety million years, residue from these mountains was transported westward down ancient streams to the sea, where it formed a sedimentary pavement on the floor. About fifty million years ago, the western edge of the sea floor warped into the geographical predecessor of the Coast Range. The peaks of this range remained above sea level for only a short period before again becoming part of the sea floor.[2]

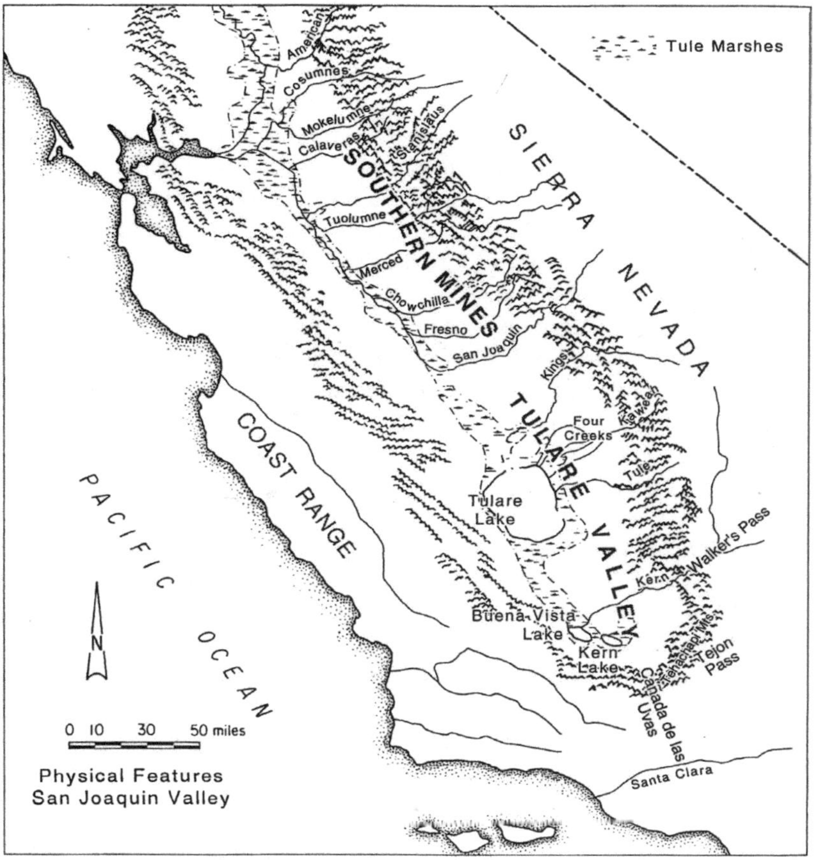

During the ensuing thirty-seven million years, the batholith evolved into a low plain that sloped to the west. Uplifting of several thousand feet on the eastern side of the batholith caused a steepening of the western plain, creating the Sierra Nevada. Between the mountains and the sea lay the Central Valley. The western edge of the valley was later formed when the Coast Range reemerged.[3]

Then God made one man and one woman for each tribe and put them where their home is now. At this time brothers and sisters married each other. God did not like this so he made a road so that the tribes could travel about and many among each other. Men began to walk on this road.... When they first met each other they'd ask each other who they were and where they were going. They were all friendly, asked one another to visit, and intertribal marriage resulted.[4]

The movement and interaction of peoples mentioned in the legend corresponds with the archaeological record, which postulates that Indians arrived in California in waves. The first wave probably occurred between 10,000 and 9,000 B.C.E (Before Common Era), resulting in the occupation of parts of the coast and the interior of southern California.[5] As members of the Paleo-Indian culture, the first occupants relied heavily upon big game for subsistence, in particular bison, mammoth, antelope, camelids, deer, sloth, and an early species of the horse. They hunted and trapped smaller game such as rabbits, hazards, and tortoises and probably collected and harvested much of the plant life as well. But as big game hunters, the Paleo- Indians are best known.[6]

Paleo-Indians arrived in California when North America was experiencing the last glaciation of the Pleistocene. As the earth began to warm, rainfall decreased and ground water evaporated. The grazing areas available to the large herds shrank dramatically. By the end of the Pleistocene (9,000 B.C.E), the large animals had disappeared and with them the Paleo-Indian culture.[7]

Then God dropped acorns, manzanita, and all seeds that were needed. In the spring the salmon came: they were dried and taken home.... The Indians moved about to gather acorns. Everything was free.[8]

The use of acorns, seeds, and fish referred to in the legend was the salient feature of the Archaic Culture, which followed the Paleo-Indian. The disappearance of the big game forced Indians to experiment with the environment, to develop a more varied economy. By about 3000 B.C.E, they had become dependent upon a variety of plant species.[9] It was during the Archaic, moreover, that Indians established permanent settlement in the northern reaches of the San Joaquin Valley. This occurred between 3500 and 2500 B.C.E.[10]

Those occupying the delta area, where the San Joaquin and Sacramento rivers converge, hunted deer and other small mammals for meat and hides and fished for salmon.[11] They gathered hard seeds from the grasslands and chaparral, grinding them on milling slabs. The mortars and pestles found at their sites suggest they also consumed acorns. The olivella and abalone shell ornaments located in graves indicate trade connections with coastal groups. Charmstones carved from steatite and other materials identify the delta people as the originators of spiritual beliefs that eventually spread throughout the Central Valley.[12]

By about 1700 B.C.E, settlements in the delta had increased in size and numbers, and Indians increasingly relied upon salmon and acorns for subsistence. They manufactured more milling tools than before and depended more heavily upon trade than had their predecessors. Instead of burying their dead in a horizontal position, as was the former tradition, they interred them with knees lifted toward the chest.[13]

Settlements continued to grow in the delta. By 500 C.E (Common Era), the acorn and salmon had become the most important food staples. Villages located along the San Joaquin and Sacramento rivers and in the delta contained large pit-houses and storage facilities. Indians manufactured from bones a variety of practical artifacts, such as awls, needles, and barbed harpoon heads.[14] Linguistic evidence indicates that these Indians were the ancestors of the Miwok. They spoke Penutian, a language stock that appeared in California about the time the delta first was settled.[15] The Penutian speakers who later spread southwards became known as Yokuts. Upon arriving at the southern end of the valley, they met Chumash Indians, who spoke a Hokan language.[16] Sometime after 1000 C.E, speakers of an Uto-Aztecan language crossed the Sierra Nevada from the east and settled in the western foothills, eventually becoming known as the Mono.[17] Other Uto-Aztecan speakers, the Kitanemuk, settled in Antelope Valley and later, about 1700 C.E spread into the Tehachapi Mountains.[18]

The occupation of most of the San Joaquin Valley and adjacent foothills indicates that the region contained an abundance of natural food resources. The animal life of the area probably had changed little when first observed by literate visitors. To be found in the interior, James Carson noted in 1852, were elk, antelope, black tail and red deer, grizzly and brown bear, black and gray wolves, coyotes, ocelots, California lions, wildcats, beaver, otter, mink, weasels, ferrets, hare, rabbits, gray & red foxes, gray & ground squirrels, kangaroo rats, badgers, skunks, muskrats, hedgehogs, and many species of small animals not here mentioned; swan, geese, brant and over twenty different description of ducks also cover the plains and waters in countless myriads from the first of October until the first of April, besides millions of grocus (sand hill crane), plover, snipe and quail.[19]

As reported in 1851 by an anonymous traveler to the Tulare Lake region, "The abundance of fish of all kinds in these waters is absolutely astonishing. The waters seem alive with them, and the variety is as great

Fishing for salmon in the southern Sacramento Valley, by J. R. Bartlett, 1854. (Courtesy of the Bancroft Library, University of California, Berkeley.)

as the quality of most of them is good. Pike, perch, bass, salmon, grout, eels, suckers, and many other kinds ... are caught with the greatest ease.... The quality of game which frequent these magnificent sheets of water, and build their nests and hatch their young among the tules, is immense. Large flocks of geese, swans, pelicans, cranes, ducks, teal and curlews, can be seen at every point."[20]

The kinds of food resources consumed by the Indians were determined by the ecological zones in which they lived. The lake peoples (Yokuts) relied heavily upon the fish and waterfowl found exclusively in this particular environment. The foothill peoples of the lower levels of the Sierra Nevada (Yokuts, Miwok, Mono) occupied an area containing a great variety of wild foods. Because they lived along streams or on ridges between streams, they had easy access to fish, but they also harvested the wild plants that grew in the woodland, grassland, and chaparral vegetation zones. The valley peoples (Yokuts and Miwok) tended to cluster along the San Joaquin River and its tributaries, fish being a most important staple. The delta peoples (Miwok) also relied heavily upon fish.[21]

The Indians hunted and trapped a variety of large and small game. In the foothills they stalked the Columbian black-tailed and California mule deer, and in the valley the tule elk and the pronghorn antelope.[22] With bows and arrows Indians shot them from blinds at lakes and waterholes and snared them in nooses placed along trails. They also flushed rodents and ground squirrels from their holes by smoke and water and drove rabbits into nets stretched over a wide area.[23]

Regarding all the plant life available to interior Indians, the acorn was perhaps the most important. Of the nearly twenty species of oak, Indians used nine as food, although some of these were of marginal

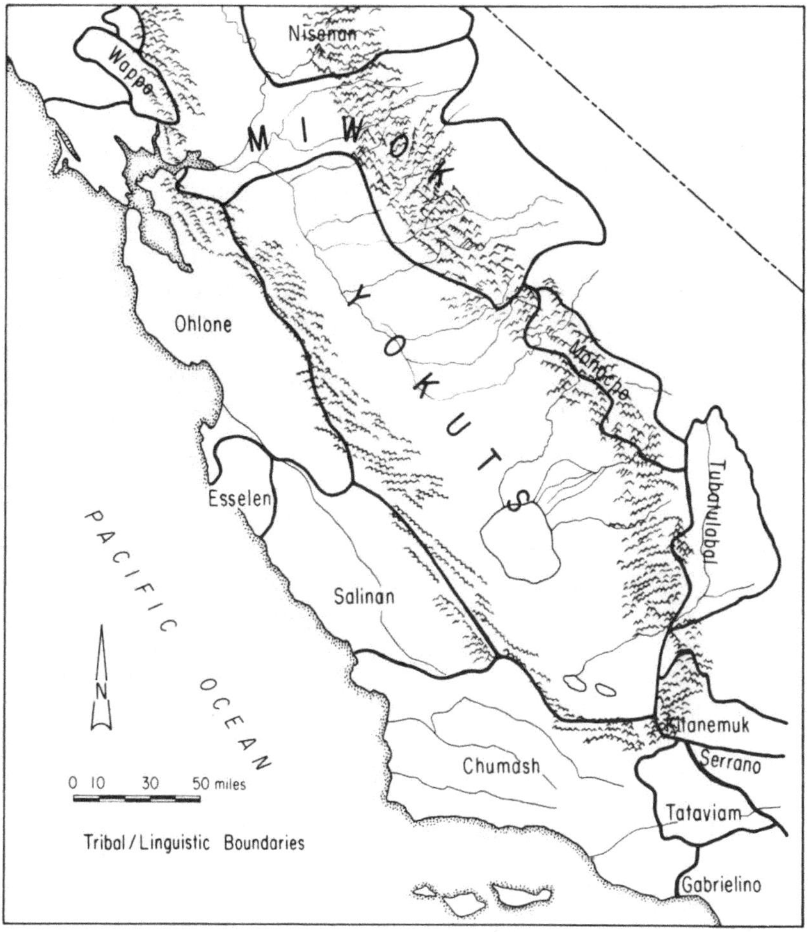

value. Especially important were the valley oak, blue oak, maul oak, and black oak, Indians preferred some species to others, but availability and abundance, not preference, often dictated which oaks were harvested. The valley oak was found not only throughout the valley floor but also in the foothills of the Sierra Nevada to elevations of about fifteen hundred feet. It failed to grow in dense stands and thus was not as numerous as some of the other species, but it produced a large crop. Every third year Indians could expect an abundant harvest from this specie. In a good year, one tree might produce five hundred pounds of acorns. On the dry, rocky hillsides in the Sierra Nevada foothills, between five hundred and two thousand feet, grew the blue oak. Smaller than the valley oak, the average blue oak produced only about 160 pounds of acorns per season. The maul oak was found in the Sierra Nevada between fifteen hundred and five thousand feet, its crop size averaging between 150 and 200 pounds per tree. Sharing the same habitat was the black oak, which produced between 200 and 300 pounds per tree in a good year. It was, moreover, a reliable tree, producing at least one good crop every two years.[24]

Harvesting, transporting, and storing the acorns were relatively easy tasks. Indians knocked the acorns from the trees with long poles and stored them in large baskets inside dwellings or in large wattle granaries on platforms built a few feet above the ground.[25] Before the acorns could be eaten, the tannic acid had to be removed. One method, probably the first devised, was to dry the unshelled acorns in mud for several months, thereby neutralizing the acid. Only when the technique of leaching was invented, however, did the acorn become a truly important staple. The nuts were shelled and then pounded into a meal. The meal was placed either in a basket or in a sand-lined hole in the ground. Hot water poured over the meal leached the tannic acid. Sometimes the meal was baked into a cake on a flat stone in a fire, but more commonly it was mixed with water in a watertight basket. Hot stones, continually added, kept the water boiling. The meal was either drunk or eaten with a spoon. Spanish clover, pond lily roots, mushrooms, tree fungi, and small seeds often were mixed with the meal to enhance its flavor.[26]

As recalled by an American settler, George Stewart, Indians made use of many plant species:

> "Several plants, such as burr-clover, sorrel, and Indian lettuce, and edible roots, were consumed in quantities without cooking. Leaves of a number of plants were boiled and eaten as greens. A kind of soup was made of the seeds of the peppergrass. Berries of various kinds were eaten fresh or dried. Some varieties known to be poisonous when first picked were cooked in a manner to render them harmless. The bulbs of many plants were eaten raw, but other kinds were cooked before eating. Fungi growing on oak, cottonwood, and willow trees were eaten fresh or roasted and were considered delicacies."[27]

The anonymous visitor to Tulare Lake observed Indians putting the

Gathering seeds in the San Joaquin Valley, by S. Eastman from a sketch by E. M. Kern, 1865. (Courtesy of the Bancroft Library, University of California, Berkeley.)

tules, or bulrushes, to good use, noting that, "the green roots are used for food, and when ground into pulp and baked into cakes, are very palatable, and seem to be nutritious." Tules were useful in other ways as well: "the dry roots serve for fuel; from the stalks baskets are made; while more than one Indian conceals his nakedness under a mat of them." No one could ask for "a better bed than a mass of fresh-pulled tules."[28]

As a source of medicine, some plants were indispensable. "The Indians, and particularly the women, had a remarkable knowledge of the medicinal properties of plants," Stewart recalled. "They prepared purgatives, emetics, poultices, decoctions of various kinds, and ate roots of some plants and leaves and stems of others for the beneficial effects of their juices.[29] The Chumash used a root that grew in the mountains. Called chuchupate or "plant of great virtue," the Indians, according to the Spanish explorer Jose Longinos Martinez, ascribed to it "a cure for all kinds of headaches by merely smelling it, and for pains in the stomach by chewing a little of it and swallowing the saliva."[30] The Chumash also believed that when worn or carried, the root would protect the individual from rattlesnakes.[31]

Of great spiritual importance to the Chumash and to the peoples residing in the southern San Joaquin Valley was a species of the hallucinogenic plant commonly called jimsonweed. Preparing the concoction took special skills, because the root was poisonous. The dose swallowed to induce a vision was only slightly less than the lethal amount. The age of the plant, the kind of soil in which it had grown, the size of the root, and the season in which it was harvested were factors the preparer took into consideration. Too strong to ingest late in the year, it was consumed by the Yokuts and Kitanemuk only during the winter and early spring. Those who took it attempted to make contact with a supernatural guardian, the dream helper, who would assist them in becoming more proficient at a particular task, communicating with the dead, viewing the future, overcoming unhappiness, or curing illness.[32]

Indians not only devised a variety of ways to procure and use the natural food and medicinal resources of California, but also consciously manipulated the environment to ensure that nature's supply would be available and accessible. Indians regularly burned brush, thus producing parkland environments, which lessened the likelihood of wildfires, increased animal and plant productivity, and improved the flow of springs.[33] Martinez noted that the Indians "have the custom of burning the brush, for two purposes: one for hunting rabbits and hares...; second, so that with the first light rain or dew the shoots will come up."[34] "At times," Stewart recalled, "when there was no danger of a prairie-fire large clumps of tall bushy weed were set on fire at the windward side, and hares, rabbits, coyotes, skunks, and other animals, as they ran out, were shot by hunters who had previously surrounded the place."[35]

Because of the abundance of wild plant and animal foods, Indians of the Tulares, although hunters, gatherers and fishers, lived a remarkably sedentary existence. Hamlets and villages were designed to be permanent. An American traveler, Stephen Powers, noted that the Yokuts resided in houses, "conical or wedge-shaped, generally made of tule, and just enough hollowed out within so that the inmates may sleep with the head higher than the feet, all in perfect alignment, and with a continuous awning of brushwood stretching along in front."[36]

The residents of every village constructed at least one temescal, or sweathouse. The Spanish explorer Francisco Garces described the temescal "as an underground room covered with sticks and grass after the manner of an oven; it has no more than one opening, which in some (cases) is in the roof and in others at the side. The hour of entering therein is either during the morning, or during the evening. When once the persons are inside, they kindle a fire; and ... they ... sweat until the earth grows wet; when indeed they can endure no more they climb out by means of their ladder of sticks and throw themselves into the river."[37] Bathing cleansed the body, but it also guaranteed good health and a long life.[38]

Living a healthy existence in a bountiful land, the Indians of California increased to over three hundred thousand by the time of European contact.[39] How a people relying exclusively on nature for subsistence could have grown so large confused some of the early visitors. Late in his life, J. J. Warner recalled a journey through the San Joaquin Valley during the winter of 1832-33: "The banks of the Sacramento and San Joaquin, and the numerous tributaries of these rivers, and the Tule Lake, were at this time studded with Indians villages of from one to twelve hundred inhabitants each. The population of this extensive valley was so great that it caused surprise, and required a close investigation into the nature of a country that without cultivation, could afford the means of subsistence to so great a community." His "close investigation" revealed a correlation between food resources and population density. Warner acknowledged the importance of fish, fowl, and game to the Indians but also realized that "the demand for food would have been but partially satisfied had they not brought the vegetable kingdom under contribution.... So great was the number of inhabitants, that no source from which subsistence could be derived in this most abundant and productive valley, was neglected."[40]

The densest populations were located near rivers and lakes. The Kings and Kaweah rivers and the Tulare Lake basin carried a population of over twenty thousand. Another seven thousand persons resided in the less-watered areas of the southern San Joaquin Valley. Some forty thousand

Yokuts lodges, by Stephen Powers, 1877. (Courtesy of the Bancroft Library, University of California, Berkeley.)

individuals settled along the San Joaquin River and its tributaries-the Fresno, Chowchilla, Merced, Tuolumne, Stanislaus, Calaveras, Mokelumne, and Cosumnes. Nine thousand persons occupied the delta area; another four thousand resided in the foothills of the Sierra Nevada. Thus, the population of the San Joaquin Valley and adjacent foothills grew to approximately eighty thousand.[41]

In important ways, population density was linked to the types of social organization Indians developed in California. Those who first arrived in the region were organized into bands. Most bands comprised fewer than one hundred persons, thus allowing all members to know one another intimately. As Indians improved their knowledge of procuring and processing wild foods, societies grew in size and density. The intimacy characteristic of band organization gave way to impersonal relationships, which forced Indians to erect a system of symbols that allowed the individual to act in prescribed ways to other members of the society. Kinship principles, in particular the lineage/clan system, provided this set of symbols.[42]

The areas most heavily settled contained Indians with the strongest kinship systems.[43] For example, the Miwok who resided along the rivers and in the delta possessed well-developed lineages. Comprised of males and their offspring, and called *nena*, each lineage was associated with either the land or the water moiety. An Indian belonging to a nena in the land moiety had to marry someone from a nena in the water moiety. Residence was patrilocal; wives left their natal settlements to live with their husbands.[44]

Apparently, the male members of each nena, along with their wives, resided in a single hamlet. Land immediately adjacent to the hamlet, usually containing a stream or spring, belonged to the nena and was used in common. The convergence of kinship organization and territory meant that the nena formed the basic political unit among the Miwok.[45] A headman governed the nena but acted only with the consensus of all adult male members, especially the elders. Regulating trade, directing relations with other groups, settling disputes, and teaching morality were some of his duties.[46]

Yokuts residing immediately to the south of the Miwok, especially those settled along the major rivers, probably employed the lineage as their basic political unit and thus differed little in this regard from their neighbors to the north. But those residing south of the San Joaquin River possessed lineages that lacked distinct territories and exclusive political functions. Many, if not most, of the southern Yokuts were organized into territorial units, each consisting of several lineages. Furthermore, unlike the Miwok lineage in which all members resided in a single hamlet, members of several lineages often resided in a single village. Kin, therefore, were diffused throughout the political unit.[47]

A chief governed each unit, and his duties were manifold. He authorized trading and food gathering expeditions, directed the intertribal mourning ceremony, sanctioned punishment, provided assistance to those in need, and advised individuals with personal problems. Assisting the chief were members of his lineage and those who formed a staff called the *wina'tum*. The staff served as an ad hoc police force during large gatherings, managed the distribution of food, and regulated ceremonies.[48]

A shaman also assisted in the regulation of the social order. Usually a friend and associate of the chief, he occupied an important position in Yokuts society. As both doctor and priest, the shaman administered to the sick by prescribing medicines for common ailments and by employing the supernatural powers he claimed to possess.[49] But if the shaman lost three patients he could be put to death by relatives of the deceased. Some shamans became famous beyond their own communities and traveled widely to serve the needy.[50]

Yokuts also traveled long distances to trade. A Spanish priest, Antonio Ripoll, remembered parties of twenty or thirty men and women arriving once a year along the coast with a thick sugar called *panocha*. Made from honeydew and sweet carisa cane and wild tobacco mixed with lime, it was chewed.[51] The Yokuts also provided the Chumash with herbs, seeds, salt from salt grass, and obsidian.[52] The Yokuts brought back to their villages a variety of products. While in the Tulare Valley, Father Francisco Garces spotted small baskets, knives of flint, and vessels with inlays of mother-of-pearl obtained from coastal peoples with whom "they carried on much commerce."[53] The Chumash also supplied the southern Yokuts with beads and ornaments made from a variety of shells.[54]

Yokuts seldom crossed the Sierra Nevada to the lands occupied by Paiutes.[55] But Owens Valley Paiutes sent trading expeditions west across the mountains. For salt, pine nuts, obsidian, rabbit-skin blankets, balls of tobacco, and buckskins, they acquired manzanita berries, baskets, and strings of shells. Paiutes who resided at Mono Lake also ventured westwards,

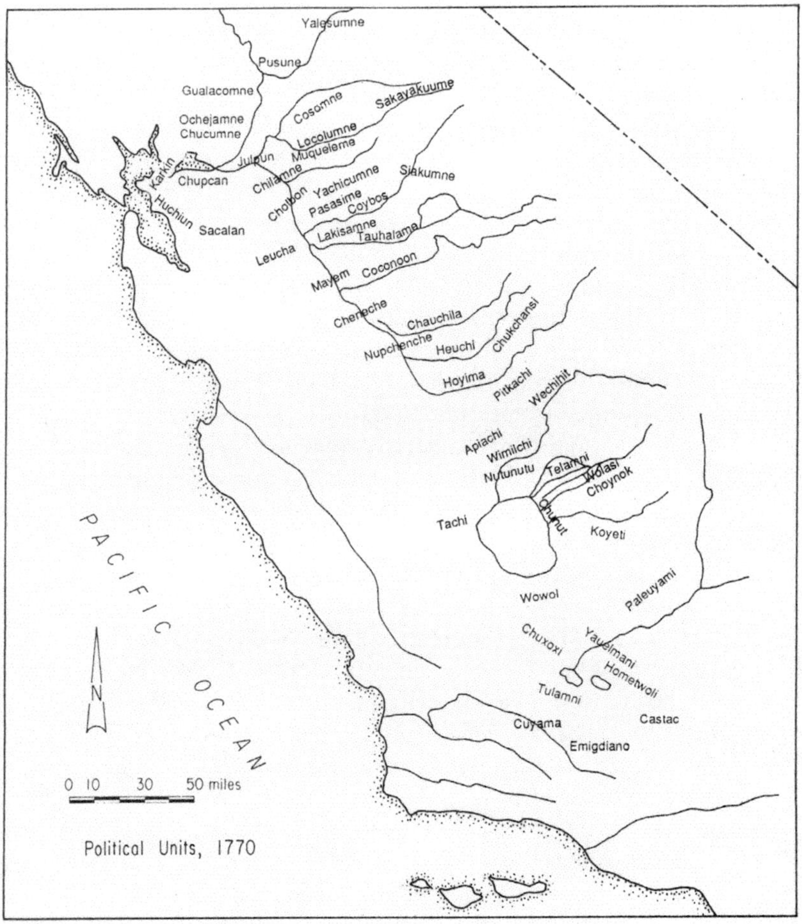

exchanging baskets, pine nuts, and salt for acorns, manzanita berries, and elderberries. The Paiute traders often wintered in the Yosemite Valley, where they married Miwok women.[56] The permanent establishment of Paiutes (the Mono) on the western side of the Sierra Nevada may have resulted from a trading expedition stranded because of early snowstorms.[57] The northern Yokuts living in the foothills of the Sierra Nevada supplied the Mono with acorns, willow-bark baskets, and shell beads. They received, in turn, rabbit-skin blankets, moccasins, rock salt, and *piñon* seeds.[58] The Mono rarely traveled across the mountains to trade but exchanged with neighboring Yokuts the products Paiutes brought to them.[59] They became, in effect, middlemen in a trans-Sierra economic system.

Perhaps the single most prevalent cause of intersocietal conflict resulted from economic competition. The intrusion by members of one group into another's territory to hunt, fish, or harvest was grounds for retaliation. Martinez noted that wars "always originate over the rights of boundaries or places where they gather seeds."[60] Along the eastern side of the San Joaquin Valley, where Uto-Aztecan speakers (Mono) and Penutian speakers (Yokuts and Miwok) shared common borders and the same food resources, battles often took place.[61]

Conflicts also erupted between coastal and interior peoples. In 1879 an Indian, Juan Estevan Pico, told Stephen Bowers about an ancient fight between Yokuts from the southern San Joaquin Valley and the Chumash from the Point Mugu area. A woman belonging to a Yokuts group had been unfaithful to her Chumash husband and was, along with her lover, condemned to death. Three times the Yokuts warned the Chumash that the execution would lead to war. As recorded by Bowers, "the man and woman were killed and their bodies burned according to the laws and customs of the Santa Barbara Indians. Four hundred Tejon [Yokuts] Indians at once set out to revenge the death of the woman by punishing the Magu [sic] people; but in the encounter they were badly defeated and left some seventy of their dead on the field."[62] Conflicts with other peoples were not far in the future.

CHAPTER II

Spaniards Enter the Valley

Spanish colonization of Alta California began in 1769 with the founding of a mission and presidio in the San Diego area. Although initiating a process that ultimately resulted in the establishment of twenty-one missions, four presidios, three pueblos, and a few privately owned ranchos, the Spanish military and religious personnel occupying San Diego represented an empire in steep decline. Because the monarchy lacked the men, money, and motivation to militarily conquer and effectively populate California, the task of bringing the region under the flag of Spain fell largely to Franciscan missionaries.[1]

The Franciscans arrived in the region with a well-developed colonizing ideology, which had taken shape over several centuries. Precedent, experience, and law dictated, at least in theory, how the Indians were to be treated. By persuasion and example, the missionaries would convince the Indians, whom they labeled gentiles, to abandon their traditional culture for a life that embraced Catholicism, agriculture, the Spanish language, and Iberian political institutions.[2] After a period of tutelage and baptism, the gentiles would become neophytes and would be transformed into loyal subjects of the king and dedicated believers in Christ. Ultimately, they would govern themselves in villages created from the missions. The Franciscans would then move on to other regions to begin the process anew.[3]

During the 1770s several Spanish settlements took hold along the central California coastline. In 1770 a presidio and Mission San Carlos Borromeo were established at Monterey among the Ohlone. In 1771 and 1772 Mission San Antonio de Padua opened in Salinan territory and San Luis Obispo de Tolosa in that of the Chumash. At the tip of the

San Francisco peninsula, Mission San Francisco de Asis and a presidio were planted among the Ohlone in 1776.[4] From these and subsequent settlements, Spaniards ventured into the San Joaquin Valley.

Two army deserters were the first to enter the interior.[5] Ordered to bring them in, Captain Pedro Fages passed through the Canada de las Uvas to Buena Vista Lake in early 1772. From the village of Tulamniu of the Tulamni (Yokuts), he explored the surrounding country. Unsuccessful in apprehending the deserters, Fages nevertheless gained important geographical and ethnographical knowledge. He noted, for example, that "in their villages the natives live in the winter in very large squares, the families divided from each other, and outside they have very large houses in the form of hemispheres, where they keep their seeds and utensils. They are people of very good features and of a superior height, and are very frank and liberal." He remained only a short time in the Tulare Valley before departing for the coast.[6]

Fages retuned to the interior in March. Accompanied by Father Juan Crespi and twelve soldiers, he departed the presidio at Monterey on the twentieth. As the party moved northwards along the east side of San Francisco Bay, it passed through the territories of several Ohlone groups, such as the Huchiun. At the Carquinez Strait, the Spaniards entered land controlled by the Karkin, from whom the name of the strait was taken. Crespi reported that "on the banks on the other side we made out many villages, whose Indians called to us and invited us to go to their country, but we were prevented by a stretch of water about a quarter of a league wide; and many of them seeing that we were going away, came to this side, crossing over on rafts, and gave us some of their wild food."[7]

Continuing along the southern shore of the strait, they "came to five large villages of very mild heathen, with pleasant faces, ... all with long hair which they tied with twine. We were well received by them all and presented with some of their wild food." Once past the strait to Suisun Bay, the Spaniards turned to the southeast, entering Miwok territory, where they encountered four Indians, who "shouted at us, making signs that we should go and receive a bow trimmed with feathers, the pelt of an animal, and arrows which they had thrust into the ground. The captain went forward with a soldier and received their presents. "Fages reciprocated with beads which pleased the Indians.[8]

While crossing a spur of Mount Diablo, they sighted the juncture of the San Joaquin and Sacramento rivers and proceeded there at once to take note of the land and waterways. On their way back to Monterey, the Spaniards passed through the Livermore Valley and came upon three small villages. "As soon as the heathen caught sight of us," recalled Crespi, "they ran away, shouting and panic-stricken without knowing what had happened."[9]

Early in 1776 Captain Juan Bautista de Anza, Father Pedro Font, and twelve soldiers traversed the same area Fages and Crespi had explored in 1772. As recounted by Font, a short distance from the entrance to the Carquinez Strait, "thirty-eight Indians came to us unarmed, peaceful, and very happy to see us. At first they stopped and sat down on a small hill near the camp. Then one came, and behind him another, and so they came in single file.... They were very obliging, bringing us firewood, and very talkative.... After they had been a while with us they bade us goodbye and we made signs to them that they should go and get us some fish with two hooks which I gave them. They apparently understood us clearly, but they brought us nothing and showed very little appreciation for the hooks, because their method of fishing is with nets."[10]

The next day a delegation of Indians arrived at the Spaniards' camp. Font described the ceremonial nature of the meeting:

> At sunrise the ten Indians came, one behind another, singing and dancing. One carried the air, making music with a little stick, rather long and split in the middle, which he struck against his hand and which sounded something like a castanets. They reached the camp and continued their singing and dancing for a little while. Then they stopped dancing, all making a step in unison, shaking the body and saying dryly and in one voice, "Ha, ha, ha!" Next they sat down on the ground and signaled to us that we must sit down also. So we sat down in front of them, the commander, I, and the commissary. Now an Indian arose and presented the commander with a string of cacomites [bulbs], and again sat down. Shortly afterward he rose again and made me a present of another string of cacomites and again sat down. In this way they went making us their little presents, another Indian giving me a very large root of chuchupate, which he began to eat, telling me by signs that it was good.[11]

The ceremony concluded, Spaniards and Indians set out for a nearby village. The Indians began to sing but were interrupted by Father Font chanting the *Alabado*, which he did every morning of the journey. Once he had finished, the Indians commenced singing again but this time "in a higher key, as if they wished to respond to our chant." Near the village, the Spaniards were greeted by three Indians carrying "Long poles with feathers on the end, and some long and narrow strips of skin with hair on, which looked to me like rabbit skin, hanging like a pennant, this being their sign of peace." Once in the village the Spaniards presented the residents with glass beads and received cacomites in return. Font wrote in his journal that the Indians "were apparently sad because we were leaving, and I was moved to tenderness at seeing the joy with which we were welcomed by those poor Indians."[12]

Passing beyond the Carquinez Strait, they spotted Indians in tule boats. Anza offered to trade beads for fish. The Indians ignored the offer until shown a colored handkerchief. Font recounted that he had not seen "in any other place Indians like these, so desirous of clothing..., for they preferred any old rag to all the glass beads, which others are so fond of."[13]

Turning southeastwards, the Spaniards encountered other Indians who also sought their possessions: "They showed themselves to be somewhat crafty and thievish, for as soon as one stolen thing was taken from their hands they stole another, and we did not have eyes enough to watch and care for everything. So we resorted to the expedient of putting them out of the camp and telling them goodbye in a good-natured way, but this did not succeed, and one of them even became impudent with the commander, who thus far had shown great patience with them. So, half angry, he took from the Indian a stick which he had in his hands, gave him a light blow with it and then threw the stick far away. Thereupon all departed, talking rapidly and shouting loudly, which I suspected was a matter of threatening."[14]

Close to the mouth of the San Joaquin River, the Spaniards entered a village of the Julpun (Miwok). Its houses "were not of grass and dilapidated like those we had seen during this journey, but rather large, round, and well made, like those of the Channel, and made of tule mats with a framework of slender poles inside, and with doors." Communication proved to be difficult, and initially the women feared to leave their houses. Finally, an Indian climbed to the top of the temescal and erected a long pole with feathers and a strip of rabbit skin. Font interpreted this to be a sign of peace. Spaniards and Indians exchanged glass beads for "feathers, little sticks, and other gewgaws esteemed by them."[15] From this village the Spaniards followed a branch of the San Joaquin River upstream, passing an abandoned settlement, to a tule swamp. Unable to cross the river to reach the Sierra Nevada, they retuned to Monterey.[16]

Later in 1776 three expeditions explored the same area. The first two, organized at the presidio of San Francisco, were to meet at Carquinez Strait on September 26. When the overland party failed to arrive at the designated time, the other sailed through the strait, stopping at villages of the Chupcan (Miwok) to trade tobacco for fish. The Spaniards explored the lower San Joaquin and Sacramento rivers before returning to San Francisco. The overland party, meanwhile, marched directly to the San Joaquin, following it upstream for several days. Indians the Spaniards met on the journey offered seeds and fish and were given beads in return. The third expedition explored the same general area in early December. It crossed the west and middle branches of the San Joaquin, land controlled by the Julpun, to the junction of the Mokelumne and Cosumnes rivers, where the Indians were described as brave and robust.[17]

Another Spaniard entered the San Joaquin Valley in 1776. In March, Father Francisco Garcés arrived at Mission San Gabriel from the Colorado River. With three Indian guides, he journeyed to a village in the Tehachapi Mountains. Named San Pasqual by Garcés, it was probably a Kitanemuk settlement. Most of the residents fled when the party approached, but returned when they realized that only one of the visitors was a Spaniard.[18] A previous encounter with Spaniards had not gone well. In February the Anza-Font expedition had passed along the coast on its way to Monterey. A total of 240 persons, including twenty-nine wives of the soldiers, formed the expedition. All were mounted, and they herded some three hundred head of cattle.[19] In April, Anza and twenty-one men returned by the same route.[20] They robbed the Kitanemuk of baskets of seeds and other valuables.[21] The Indians may have been on a food collecting expedition when contact was made.

Once he convinced the villagers he was a Spaniard who came from the east and thus "did harm to no one," Garcés was warmly received. Invited to the lodge of the village elite, he "recited the rosary ... of Maria Santisima, singing the hymn … with the Indian Sevastian and the two Jamajabs [Mohaves] who accompanied me from the beginning, and who already knew the Ave Maria.… A little while after the service began the wife of the chief arose, took a basket… of seed… and scattered it over the Santo Cristo I wore on my breast; the same did other women, and they even threw some of this seed … on the fire, in order that there should be a bright light. Having finished the praying and singing I seated myself by the captain and the rest of the elders of the rancheria, who had assembled as soon as I began the services. They smoked the tobacco that I gave them, and begged me to exhibit again … the breviary, compass-needle, and other little things, manifesting great delight throughout."[22] Apparently, Garcés and his companions tasted the jimsonweed, being given an extremely bitter paste to eat which caused two of his Indians to vomit violently. The villagers found this very amusing. Garcés noted in his journal that they drank this gruel "to cure fatigue, and consequently it is customary to offer it to all their guests."[23]

Accompanied by several Indians, including the leader of the village, Garcés passed into the San Joaquin Valley. At a village east of Kern and Buena Vista lakes, his guides and companions refused to go farther because they were near Indians who "were very bad, and no relations of theirs." But Garcés persuaded an old man to escort him to the Kern River where it exits the mountains. The current being too strong to cross, they followed the river downstream to a village where the inhabitants "were obsequious to us." Three guides from this village escorted Garcés to a crossing. The villagers held "a great feast over my arrival, and having regaled me well reciprocated to them all with tobacco and glass beads, congratulating myself on seeing the people so affable and affectionate. The young men are fine fellows, and the women comely and clean, bathing themselves every little while."[24]

Continuing northwards Garcés camped with Indians who "showed me every attention." On May 2 he and another guide reached a village where an old man persuaded the Spaniard to give him his crucifix. The following day Garcés visited a village of 150 souls, many of whom sought to kiss his Saint Christopher medal, The Spaniard was surprised when an Indian begged him in Spanish for paper to make cigars with. "I wondered much, and on questioning him he told me that he was from the sea where there were padres like myself.... When he took to kiss the Santo Cristo, he did so with great veneration, and set himself to preach to the rest. I had a suspicion that he might be some Christian who had just fled from the missions of Monte-Rey, since he made signs of shooting and of flogging."[25]

If correct in his assessment Garcés spoke with one of the first mission neophytes to settle in the interior. He also spoke with Indians from a village to the north who admitted killing two Spaniards who had mistreated their women. As recounted by Garcés, the Indians "had cut off the hands, had laid open the breast and all the body ... and scattered the remains."[26] Presumably, those executed were the deserters Fages had sought a few years before.

After baptizing a young boy who was near death and visiting a nearby village, Garcés, against the wishes of his hosts, decided to turn back. At a village where the residents also pleaded with him to stay, Garcés heard about a Spaniard married to an Indian woman who lived somewhere to the east. An Indian told the priest that the Spaniard "wore on the breast a certain round thing that I conceived should be some medal or reliquary, ... that he ... already had a little son; that he was of a good heart, and was much in request of all, living ... like the rest of the Indians."[27]

On May 7 Garcés was back on the Kern. A village downstream from the one previously visited caught his attention as an ideal site for a future mission. Although the Indians expressed friendship and provided him with game and fish, an old man refused to kiss his crucifix, asserting the "shells and tobacco were good, but that el Cristo was not, and that he held it in great dread." This rejection caused Garcés to question the feasibility of establishing missions in the interior. He envisioned "a scene of the highest felicity and docility shifting in an instant to one of mishaps and fatalities."[28]

Back in the village he called San Pasqual, Garcés again spoke with its leader, "intent upon persuading him that the Españoles were a good people; to which he would by no means assent." The Indian reminded Garcés that Spaniards had stolen valuables from his people. The following day Garcés departed for the Mohave Desert, having traveled in the Tulare Valley for over three weeks.[29]

As they explored the San Joaquin Valley, Spaniards sometimes intruded into inter-Indian affairs. In August 1790 Indians from the Chumash village of Najayalewa, located northeast of Mission Santa Barbara on the Santa Ynez River, killed three men and a woman who resided in or near the southern end of Tulare Valley. A large revenge party quickly formed, including eight Yauelmani (Yokuts) from the village of Loasu and thirty-nine Castec (Chumash). Evidently, the Indians formulated their plans at the Chumash village of Matapuan, whose leader, Tuchachana, commanded the party.[30]

At the same time the revenge party was forming, a Spanish military contingent was heading towards the Tulare Valley. On August 24 the commandant of the presidio at Santa Barbara had dispatched nine soldiers and an Indian interpreter to apprehend a neophyte, Domingo, who recently had fled from Mission San Buenaventura. Domingo's destination was a village in the San Emigdio area. The commandant feared Domingo would incite the villagers to attack Indians friendly to the Spanish. Five days later, the Spanish, supported by fifteen Indians from Najahalewa and a few others, made camp in San Emigdio. They explored the immediate area for precious stones. Two soldiers investigated a nearby gully, while nine Spaniards and three Indians searched for a vein near the trail they had followed. Two other soldiers remained in camp.[31]

Neophytes from San Buenaventura, in the meantime, had warned the Indians comprising the revenge party that Spanish soldiers were moving inland.[32] Some of the Indians wanted to avoid the Spaniards, but the leader of the village of Loasu sought revenge for the crimes committed many years ago by the two army deserters.[33] The Indians attacked the Spaniards in the gully but were driven off. But they killed the two guarding the camp and appropriated cloaks, ponchos, five shotguns, riding gear, and a horse.[34]

The Spaniards who had gone to search for precious stones returned to camp, buried the dead, and retreated to an area near Mission San Buenaventura, where they were joined by the two soldiers who had survived the attack in the gully. On September 1, the party returned to Santa Barbara. The commandant wrote to the governor, claiming that Domingo, the runaway neophyte, must have participated in the attack because only someone familiar with stock could have caught and saddled the horse the Spaniards lost.[35]

Whoever was responsible may have introduced the first horse to the Tulare Valley. The fight also represents the first significant violent encounter between coastal Spaniards and interior Indians, a point not lost on the commandant, who requested from the governor soldiers to punish the

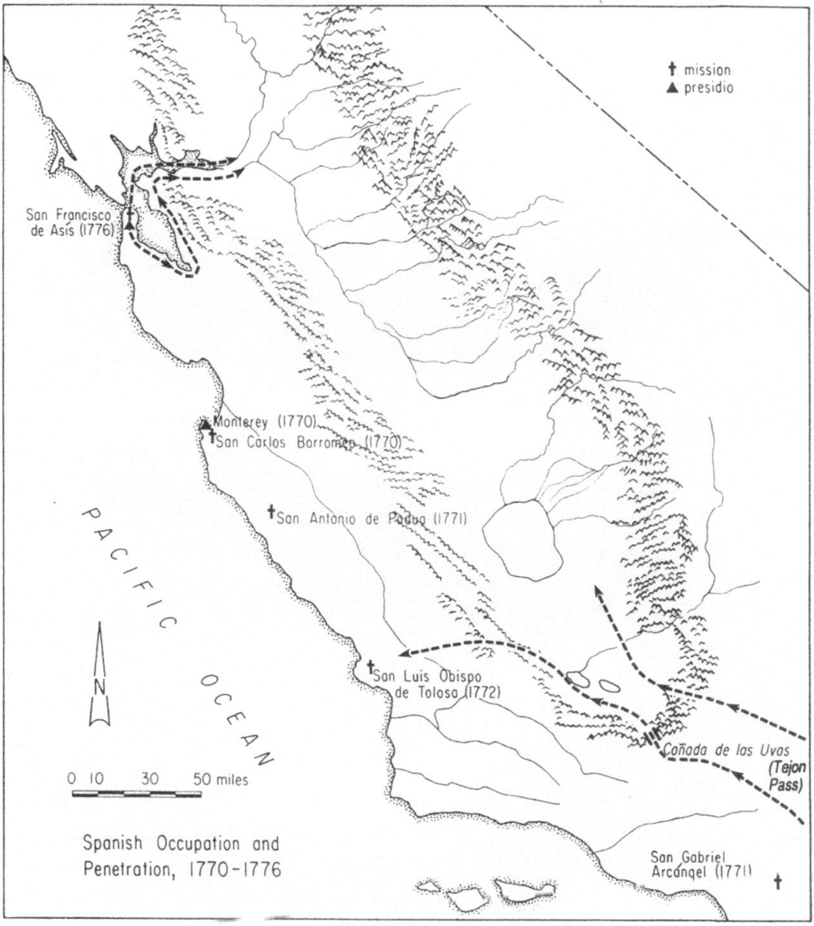

Indians. It would not be just, he reasoned, if "they get away without a lesson."[36] But the party entrusted to teach the lesson returned with only two prisoners, Soxollue and Samalla.[37]

In mid-September another Spanish contingent penetrated the interior, apparently to the village where the Indians had launched their revenge party. The Spaniards returned to the presidio at Santa Barbara with three prisoners who subsequently were released. Domingo turned himself in at Mission San Buenaventura and was promptly imprisoned at the presidio at Santa Barbara.[38] Interrogated by the commandant, Domingo claimed he had received permission to leave the mission to visit his mother and had not participated in the attack on the soldiers.[39] Domingo, Soxollue, and Samalla were absolved of all crimes and released.[40]

Because the Spanish increasingly relied on neophytes to assist in the apprehension of fugitives, disputes erupted between mission Indians and the so-called gentiles. In early January 1797, the priest at San Luis Obispo sent a party of neophytes into the interior to locate the wife of an Indian who had converted and resided at the mission. The Spanish suspected she had poisoned her baptized daughter who had died at the mission. Somewhere near the edge of the Tulare Valley, the neophytes captured the woman.[41]

On its way back to the mission, the party paused at a village, where two neophytes insulted an old man and his two sons. The three villagers killed one of the neophytes, Toribio, and burned his body.[42] On January 8 a military contingent was dispatched to apprehend the three, but it failed in its mission.[43] Later in the month, another party brought the old man and his sons to the mission, where they confessed to the murder.[44]

More troubling to the Spanish than gentiles murdering neophytes was gentiles protecting them. Thus, in July 1797, when it was reported that gentiles at a village north of San Jose were harboring runaways and encouraging neophytes to rebel, the Spanish responded immediately. On the fifteenth, three soldiers and twenty-five civilians contacted the Sacalan (Miwok). Sergeant Pedro Amador recorded what transpired: "Although we repeatedly told them that we did not wish to fight but only to take away the Christians, they admitted to no persuasion but began to shoot so as to kill one of our horses and wound two others. Seeing this opposition, we used our weapons in order to subdue them so that they would surrender. Some were killed, for they refused for two hours to give up. Finally, it was necessary to dismount and throw them back with swords and lances."[45]

The Spaniards captured thirty-two gentiles and neophytes. After explaining the purpose of his mission, Amador released the gentiles but kept the neophytes under guard. The following day the Spaniards surprised three Huchiun (Ohlone) villages, rounding up more fugitives. They returned to Mission San Jose with eighty-three neophytes and nine gentiles.[46] Soon Indians in the interior zone would encounter even more intruders.

CHAPTER III

Refuge

From the late 1770s to the late 1780s, Spanish occupation of the coastal zone increased dramatically. The pueblo of San José de Guadalupe and nearby Mission Santa Clara de Asîs were founded among the Ohlone in 1777. A presidio at Santa Barbara and Mission San Buenaventura were established among the Chumash in 1782. Missions Santa Bárbara and La Purísima Concepcion were opened in 1786 and 1787 respectively, also among the Chumash. In 1791, Mission Santa Cruz was founded among the Ohlone and Nuestra Senora de la Soledad along the Esselen-Salinan border. Four more missions were established in 1797: San José and San Juan Bautista among the Ohlone, San Miguel Arcángel among the Salinan, and south of the San Joaquin Valley, San Fernando Rey de España. But early in the nineteenth century several of the older missions ceased to grow. Mission Santa Bárbara achieved its maximum number of neophytes (1792) in 1803; La Pureísima (1520) in 1804; San Antonio (1296), San Luís Obispo (961), and Soledad (688) in 1805. Those missions soon experienced rapid population decline. The introduction of European diseases from which the Indians initially had no immunity accounts in large measure for this development.[1]

The decline of the coastal population forced the Franciscans to increasingly probe the interior for mission recruits. In late 1803, for example, Father Juan Martin of Mission San Miguel, accompanied by a soldier, journeyed to the village of Cholam of the Tachi (Yokuts), seeking from the local leader, Guchapa, children to take back to the mission. Guchapa refused, ordered the Spaniards out of his village, and told the priest that he was not afraid of soldiers. The following month, the commandant of the presidio at Monterey sent fifteen soldiers to the village. They returned in early January with Guchapa, his son, two other Indian leaders, and two neophytes. Guchapa negotiated his own release by promising to bring to the presidio all fugitive neophytes then in his village, He left his son as hostage.[2]

The following year Father Martin again sought children for his mission.

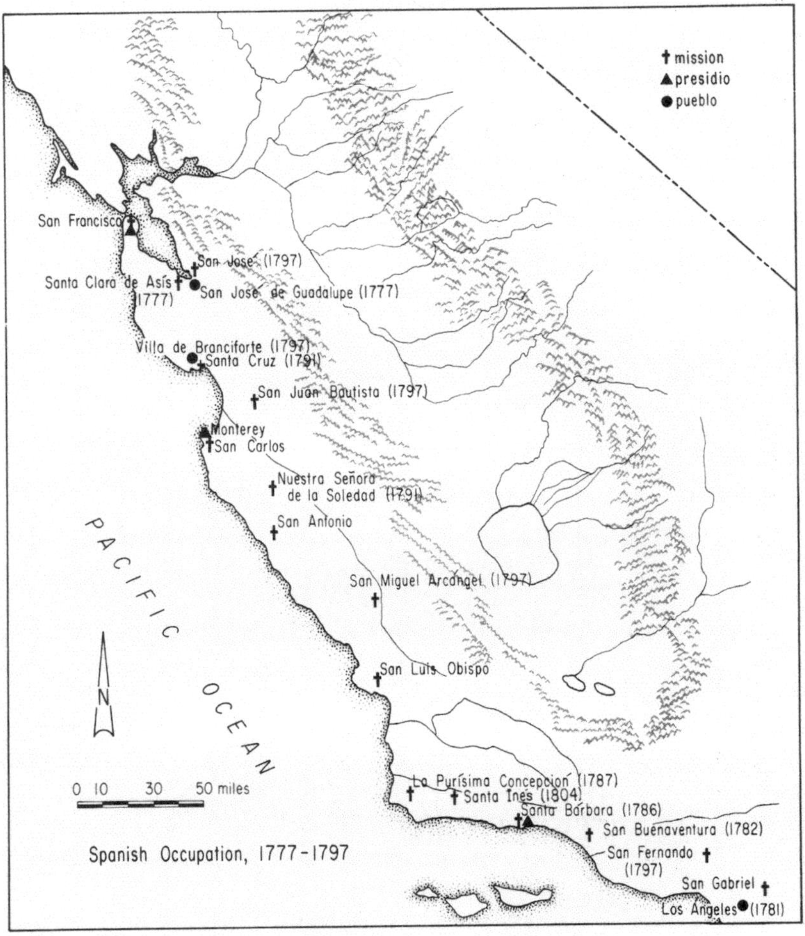

Informed by neophytes returning from Tulare Lake that gentiles in the area were willing to have their children baptized, the missionary, in the company of two soldiers, proceeded to the territory of the Wowol (Yokuts). At the village of Bubal, Martin was offered some two hundred children to take to the mission. Unsure whether all Indians approved of this, he sent for the headman, Chape, who was absent at the time. Chape returned at once and prohibited the release of the children; Father Martin retreated to his mission empty-handed.[3]

Even when successful incorporating Indians from the interior, the missionaries found it extremely difficult to keep them at the missions. In their biennial report of 1804, the Franciscans at San Miguel admitted that "it is the painful experience of the missionaries that such Christians, very much attached to their Tulare homes, leave the Mission, and in consequence lose the holy Mass and offend God, and hide in the Tulares region where they cannot be taken out without peril and without troops."[4] The missionaries did not exaggerate the dangers. In September and October 1804, Sergeant Luis Peralta twice entered the interior east of San Jose in search of fugitives and those gentiles who had murdered some neophytes. Nothing was accomplished in the first expedition but the second resulted in the capture of eleven fugitives and thirty-two gentiles. The captives were turned over to the priests.[5]

In January 1805 Father Pedro de la Cueva of Mission San José, accompanied by two soldiers and a few neophytes, journeyed into the hills south of Livermore Valley. The village of Asiremes was abandoned except for two dying neophytes who sought last rites. Continuing eastwards, the party experienced determined resistance from the Leucha (Yokuts), who killed three neophytes, including an Indian officer, and wounded the priest and a soldier.[6] Retaliation was swift. Fifteen civilians and eighteen soldiers marched to the scene of the fight, where they discovered the body of the Indian officer. By capturing two Indians whom they pressed into service as guides, the Spaniards located those they were searching for. In the ensuing fight they killed five and captured fourteen men and twenty-five women. A leader from a village on the San Joaquin River visited the Spanish encampment to proclaim his innocence regarding the attack on Father Cueva. Fugitives residing at several villages returned to their missions.[7]

Departing Mission San José in May 1805, Luís Argüello and twenty-two men traversed the region from Mt. Diablo in the north to the Pacheco Pass in the south encountering no hostile Indians. But they returned to the mission with twenty-two Indians—thirteen Christians and nine gentiles, six of whom were suspected of murdering a Christian Indian. Argüello, however, failed to capture Joscoui, a notorious rebel, who had fled his village before the Spaniards arrived. Those apprehended were turned over to the Fathers of Missions San José and Santa Clara, and apparently Argüello recommended leniency in the punishment of the six accused of murder.[8]

The priests at Santa Clara also had to contend with settlers in the nearby pueblo of San José, who were luring neophytes from the mission to work in their homes and fields. Once the missionaries alerted the governor to the situation, in 1807 he ordered the settlers to return the neophytes to the mission and to lash those twelve years and older twenty-five times each.[9] To make up for the loss of workers, the governor allowed the settlers to enter the San Joaquin Valley in search of replacements. Some Cholvons agreed to the terms offered them—thread, needles, blankets, glass beads, and flannels in exchange for harvesting wheat and hemp. The Cholvons returned to their villages after the harvest.[10]

Most expeditions into the interior sought souls not workers. In July 1806 Father Jose Maria Zalvidea and Lieutenant Francisco Maria Ruíz, supported by a few soldiers, departed from Santa Bárbara for the Tulare Lake region. The padre sought to promote friendship with the local Indians and to search for mission sites. The expedition stopped at several Chumash villages, where Zalvidea offered baptismal rites to a group of predominantly old women. Near the Cuyama River the Spaniards spotted a wild horse.[11] If yet to penetrate the San Joaquin Valley, wild horses soon would diffuse over much of the interior.[12]

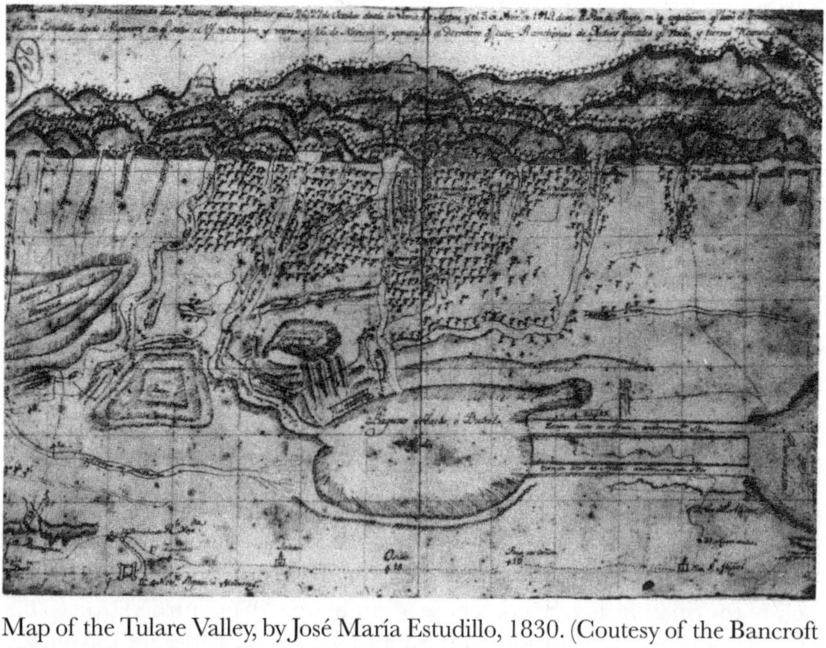

Map of the Tulare Valley, by José María Estudillo, 1830. (Coutesy of the Bancroft Library, University of California, Berkeley.)

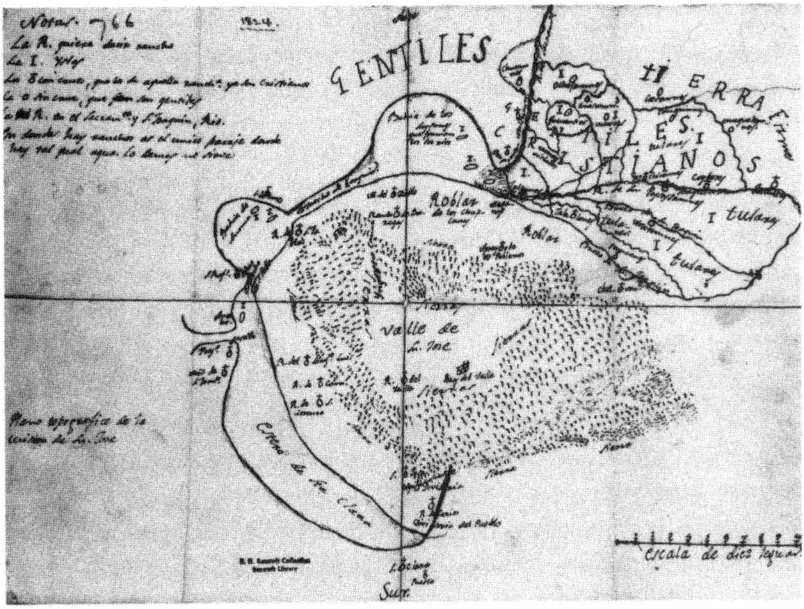

Map of Mission San José, neophyte and gentile villages, 1824. (Courtesy of the Bancroft Library, University of California, Berkeley.)

A few days later the Spaniards arrived at the Chumash village of Malapoa, where Zalvidea baptized an eighty-year-old woman, christening her Maria Rufina. At a nearby settlement he baptized five old women and an old man. At the village of Tulamniu, in the territory of the Tulamni (Yokuts), the missionary baptized another old woman.[13]

With several Indians, including the headman of Tulamniu, to guide them, the Spaniards departed on the twenty-sixth for the village of Pohalin Tinliu at the southern end of Kern Lake and in the territory of the Hometwoli (Yokuts). Unknown to the missionary and the soldiers, Tulamniu and Pohalin Tinliu were enemies. As the party approached the village, the residents fled to a nearby tule swamp. They returned a short time later, and Zalvidea negotiated a peace between the headmen of the two villages.[14]

A short distance from the village, the priest visited an "old woman, in a little hut, who was at her last breath, destitute of all human assistance. After having labored very hard to revive her, so that I might make her a Christian, I finally attained my desire and named her Maria Gertrudis: two hours after baptism she surrendered her soul to its Creator."[15]

Moving southwards the Spaniards arrived at the foothills of the Tehachapi Mountains, where they spent several days exploring the surrounding country. On July 29 Zalvidea and nine soldiers visited the village of Tacuyo, consisting of twenty-three inhabitants and located west of the Cañada de las Uvas. Zalvidea baptized two old men, whom he named Fernando and Ramon. On August 1 the entire party journeyed northwards, arriving at a village of the Yauelmani. According to Zalvidea, many Indians volunteered to be baptized but only if missions were opened in their land. The following day, the Spaniards turned back and a few days later arrived at Santa Bárbara.[16]

Shortly after Zalvidea and his party left the Tulare Valley, another expedition entered the interior. Commander Gabriel Moraga, Father Pedro Muñoz, about twenty-five soldiers, and a few neophytes departed Mission San Juan Bautista on September 21, 1806. Muñoz intended to spread the word of God and search for mission sites. On the San Joaquin River, the Spaniards met forty-two men of the Nupchenche (Yokuts) who presented them with fish. "I made them acquainted with the purpose of our visit," Muñoz recalled, "showing them an image of Our Lady of Sorrows. This they received with much satisfaction, appearing, according to their behavior, ready to enroll under the banner of the Divine Savior."[17]

The following day the Indians escorted the Spaniards to their village, which was situated on the east side of the San Joaquin River. Governed by Choley, it numbered about 250 inhabitants. According to Muñoz, "they all received my talk with pleasure and, having listened silently to the Divine Word, they begged to become Christians." He baptized a twenty- three old women and three old men, explaining to the rest that they must wait for a mission to be established in their territory."[18]

On the twenty-seventh the Spaniards re-crossed the San Joaquin and made camp in a spot infested with butterflies. They divided into three groups; one remained at camp, and the other two reconnoitered the areas to the north and northeast. Both parties encountered Indians on the Merced River, who fled at the first sight of the intruders. Found at one village, however, was a feeble and terrified old woman who managed the strength to plunge into the river. Rescued by one of the neophytes and treated kindly by the Spaniards, she overcame her fear. Muñoz gave "her as adequate a lesson as was permitted by the shortness of the time. I baptized her, she giving very clear evidence of the joy which filled her heart."[19]

Three days later the Spaniards encountered terribly suspicious Indians. The few who approached were given food, presents, and instructions to bring in their relatives. To the thirty Indians who appeared, Muñoz explained the benefits of Christianity. They asked for a mission and to be baptized. Proceeding to the Tuolumne the next day, the Spaniards found deserted villages, heavily used trails, but no Indians. On the Stanislaus, probably in the territory of the Siakumne (Yokuts), they discovered a village situated on steep cliffs. Between twelve and fifteen Indians descended to a narrow shelf but would not come closer because, they said, soldiers killed and captured people. Muñoz explained the nature of his visit, but "it was not possible to achieve a single baptism, although there were a great many old women to whom baptism might be administered, because they would not come down from their hiding places and it was too difficult for me to go up."[20]

Continuing northwards to the Cosumnes River, the Spaniards met "affectionate and affable" Indians but could not communicate with them because they had entered Miwok territory. And because he lacked an interpreter, Muñoz was unable to offer baptism. But the potential of the area did not escape his notice: "This river has excellent land for agriculture and grazing and has a good oak forest. In the mountains there is pine.... It has also much ash, willow, torote, and wild vines."[21]

Returning to the Stanislaus the Spaniards encountered forty armed Indians on the opposite bank. Carrying a flag made of feathers, three crossed to meet with the strangers, who convinced them their intentions were friendly. But the main body of Indians would not cross the river. The Spaniards departed for the Tuolumne the next day, one party making a side trip to the mountains, where it located many Indians but no site suitable for a mission.[22]

The expedition reached the Merced on October 7, terrifying twenty children, who "began to scream and throw themselves into the water to save themselves by flight." The party continued along the opposite bank and made camp in a meadow. Shortly, seventy-nine men from the village of Latelate arrived, presenting the Spaniards with seeds and fish. The Spanish reciprocated with food and presents.[23]

As recounted by Muñoz the following day, Indians and Spaniards met again: "On the morning of this day, carrying the image of Holy Mary of Sorrows (who was our patron Saint) we started out to pay a visit to the village, on account of the attention they had paid us. We were received with great joy. They laid out their mats on the ground for us to sit down upon. This matter attended to, we set forth the reason for our coming. They replied in a very pleased manner that they all sought baptism and the establishment of a mission. I baptized six old women and one old man who were present. Near Latelate was the village of Lachio, where Muñoz thought a mission and a presidio might be established. The wide meadows were perfect for raising crops and grazing stock."[24]

Heading eastwards before turning south, the expedition skirted the foothills of the Sierra Nevada, encountering no Indian settlements until arriving at the San Joaquin on October 11. Two days later a scouting party visited the village of Pizcache of the Pitkachi (Yokuts). Its leader, Sujoyucomu, told the Spaniards about a fight between Indians and soldiers

Ohlone Indians fighting a Spaniard, by Tomás de Suria, 1791. (Courtesy of the Bancroft Library, University of California, Berkeley.)

that had taken place on the east side of the mountains some twenty years before. The soldiers had killed many Indians, and the Pitkachi expected to be invaded from the east. Sujoyucomu was surprised the Spaniards had come from the west and demonstrated kindness. Muñoz baptized four old Indians, two men and two women.[25]

On October 16 the Spaniards arrived at the Kings River in the territory of the Wechihit (Yokuts). Upstream, a scouting party entered the village of Ayguiche, where it heard the same story about the fight on the east side of the mountains. The priest baptized eight women and one man at the village and twenty old women and two old men at three villages downstream.[26] A few days later the Spaniards entered the territory of the Telamni (Yokuts). At the large village of Telame, the missionary baptized twenty-two persons. On October 20 they visited another large village, Cohochs. Its residents welcomed the Spaniards, sought baptism, and asked for a mission. Returning to Telame, Muñoz baptized a little girl near death. He noted in his journal that "during the days which we spent at this place all the Indians showed themselves very much satisfied with having us in their midst, even to the extent of pointing out to us a spot appropriate for the establishment or foundation of a mission."[27]

On the twenty-seventh, the expedition penetrated the land of the Koyeti (Yokuts), where the inhabitants of a small village sought baptism. Muñoz could not perform the ritual because the Indians were too young.

The party continued southwards, arriving at the Kern on the following day and passing through the Cañada de las Uvas on November 1. During the forty-three days spent in the interior, Muñoz baptized 141 persons, all *in extremis*.[28]

The following year, 1807, Gabriel Moraga, with twenty-five soldiers, returned to the Tulare Valley. Intending to round up runaway neophytes and "to bring in others for the Padres to make Christians," as one soldier put it, the Spaniards met stiff resistance. Yauelmani attacked the party when it entered the mountains, killing two soldiers and stealing one hundred horses.[29] The acquisition of horses suggests that some Indians, by the early nineteenth century, had become skilled equestrians and that the animal had become a source of food and probably transportation.

Also seeking fugitives José Palomares and a few men departed the presidio at Santa Bárbara in late October 1808. At Mission San Fernando, Palomares obtained a list of runaways and enlisted the service of three Indians and a Spaniard, all of whom were familiar with the southern interior. Indians in the San Gabriel Mountains informed Palomares that ten fugitives, five of whom were on his list, resided in the southeast corner of the Tulare Valley at a village led by an individual called Quipagui. Palomares traveled to the Antelope Valley, capturing on the way an Indian, Macal, who apparently had participated in the fight against Moraga the previous year.[30]

The party crossed the Tehachapi Mountains, arriving near Quipagui's village. After a brief skirmish in which no one was hurt, Indians and Spaniards held a meeting. Quipagui told Palomares that the Christian Indians had fled either into the mountains or into the tule swamps. Palomares attempted to enlist the services of Quipagui in rounding up the fugitives. The Indian leader promised to help but only after it stopped raining. Before departing for Mission San Fernando, Palomares told Quipagui that the padres would pay him if he brought in the fugitives. Quipagui again promised his assistance, but the runaways were never delivered.[31]

In his report Palomares recomended that Quipagui "be removed from that place with all his village for many reasons. The first is because he has killed many unconverted Indians and is still killing them. He is the most feared Indian in that entire country. The other reason is that he gives refuge to Christian fugitives, and they know that neither Christian nor heathen will go to look for them there on account of the terror which he inspires. I would have brought him back with his people but the weather did not permit me to do so without running the risk of injury in capturing and securing them."[32]

Expeditions searching for fugitive neophytes and mission sites also entered the northern reaches of the San Joaquin Valley. In mid-August

1810 Padre José Viader, six soldiers, and four neophytes departed Mission San José. They journeyed north to Suisun Bay and then eastward to the San Joaquin River. Following the river into the territory of the Chulamni (Yokuts), Viader learned that fugitives from San José were in the vicinity. Unable to locate the Indians, the party continued upstream. On August 21 it arrived opposite a village led by Bozenats. Refusing to cross the Indians informed Viader that they harbored no fugitive Christians. Traveling a short distance the following day, the intruders encountered about thirty armed Indians on the opposite bank who also refused to cross. They ordered the party to leave and demonstrated an eagerness to fight. Residing with them, they acknowledged, were fugitive neophytes from Missions Santa Clara and Santa Cruz. A short distance upriver the party encountered hostile Indians on both banks. Six Indians on the near side fired arrows at a soldier and a neophyte interpreter. Those on the opposite bank also launched a volley of arrows, wounding a Spaniard. The soldiers returned fire, hitting at least one Indian. On August 24 the Spaniards headed back to the coast.[33]

Two months later Viader led another expedition into the interior. Twenty-four soldiers and about fifty neophyte auxiliaries invaded the territory of the Chulamni, secretly taking up positions near a village whose residents were conducting a ceremony. At dawn, October 21, they struck, capturing fifteen fugitives from San José and sixty-nine gentiles. Two of the runaways escaped, and fifty-one gentiles, all women, were released. The remainder were sent under guard to San José.[34]

Viader followed the San Joaquin upstream into the territory of the Mayem (Yokuts), where the residents denied sheltering fugitives from Mission Santa Clara. They promised never to allow Christian Indians in their village, but Viader did not believe them. Upriver the party halted near a village that Viader also suspected harbored fugitives. He sent word to the inhabitants that those Christians who gave themselves up would be pardoned. Shortly, six gentiles visited the priest, claiming that all the neophytes had returned to the mission and promising that henceforth none would be admitted to their village. Viader doubted the sincerity of the promise. The party reached the Merced River before turning back. At a village previously visited, Viader attempted to lure the residents into a trap, but "they refused to come out... They guessed right for they would have been taken captive. From this point, considering that the people of Mayem would also refuse to come out,... we turned west." The party arrived at Mission Santa Clara on October 27, 1810.[35]

Many neophytes also resettled at several villages along the lower Sacramento and San Joaquin rivers. In October 1811 Spaniards moving up a branch of the San Joaquin encountered at three villages neophytes who apparently resided there by permission of the missionaries at San

José. A short distance upstream, they arrived at a village of the Cholborn (Yokuts), where San José neophytes presented themselves. A priest baptized six old women and the baby boy of a neophyte. Crossing to the main branch of the San Joaquin, the expedition entered a village containing neophytes, and downstream, in the territory of the Coybos (Yokuts), encountered more neophytes from San José. The priest baptized a sick boy and an old woman.[36]

Continuing their journey the Spaniards approached a village prepared for war. Its residents had been told that all the Coybos had been killed. The Spaniards quickly explained their peaceful intentions and moved on. Downstream they reached the Sacramento River and passed several large villages, including one which contained a few neophytes from San José. The expedition returned to San Francisco on the thirtieth.[37]

Seeking fugitives Lieutenant Luis Argüello led ten soldiers from the presidio at San Francisco into the same region in 1813. At the mouth of the Cosumnes, three soldiers and one hundred neophyte auxiliaries from Mission San José joined his party. Shortly, Spaniards and auxiliaries confronted a fighting force of about one thousand men recruited from four villages. Apparently, the fugitives had warned their hosts that a Spanish military force soon would arrive.[38]

The Indians, as reported by Argüello, "attacked with such fury that all the valor of the soldiers was necessary in order to repulse them. This was accomplished by heavy fire, the hostile Indians maintaining their offensive for a long time and holding their position on all sides without perceiving the damage which their obstinacy caused then. They were confident perhaps in their own great number and the small number of soldiers and Indian auxiliaries with whom they were contending, as well as the advantages provided them by the terrain." After three hours of fighting, the Indians abandoned their positions. Most escaped capture by swimming to an island in the river or by hiding in the dense tule swamps. The intruders may have killed or wounded several Indians, but they failed to recover a single fugitive.[39] They also lost Julio, a neophyte leader at Mission San José, who was killed in the battle.[40]

In 1817 Argüello returned to the delta. With two priests and a contingent of soldiers, he sailed up the San Joaquin and into the territory of the Pasasime (Yokuts), According to Father Narciso Duran, these Indians "have been at the mission many times, and some of them have been baptized." Downstream, they met over one hundred Yachicumne (Yokuts) and Muqueleme (Miwok), "half of them painted and armed," but Duran convinced them he had come in peace. He noted in his diary, that "most of these natives live on the mainland, and one may visit them on horseback, if, perchance, it should be necessary to do so." A few days later the party sailed out of the area.[41]

Indians residing in the southern area of the San Joaquin Valley also experienced visitors from the coast. In October 1814 Father Juan Cabot, a sergeant, and thirty soldiers departed for the Tulare Lake, arriving at the village of Bubal on the southeast shore on the third. The villagers, evidently Wowol (Yokuts), warmly greeted the Spaniards with food and the headman allowed Cabot to baptize ill and old Indians. Departing this village of seven-hundred residents, the Spaniards rounded the lake to the village of Sumtache on the Kaweah River, also consisting of seven-hundred persons. Word that the Spaniards intended to kill them reached the village before Cabot arrived. The Indians prepared for battle, but in the ensuing skirmish only an old woman was killed.[42]

From this village the Spaniards entered the territory of the Telamni where a village was identified as a perfect site for a mission and a presidio. Continuing northwards to the Kings River in the territory of the Tachi, they arrived at a nearly deserted village. Having heard of the expedition, most of the one-thousand residents had hidden themselves in the dense tules and remained there for the two days the Spaniards occupied their village. But the thirty-six men and six women who met the Spaniards evidently were treated well, some exhibiting an interest in receiving baptism. Although the area contained good land for raising crops, it lacked wood and stone and thus was deemed unsuitable for a mission. With this important geographical knowledge, the Spaniards returned to Mission San Miguel.[43]

José Señan, the father president of the missions, noted in 1814 that "in the direction of San Miguel there exists a bounteous harvest of four thousand souls that can be gathered within the pale of the Holy Church and brought to a recognition of our sovereignty by founding a mission in the neighboring Tulare Valley." He strongly believed that the Indians "desire the establishment of a mission, and the place called Télame offers favorable conditions for its founding."[44]

Mariano Payeras, Señan's successor as father president of the missions, also argued for a mission being planted among the Telamni. "With this measure taken," he noted in his report of 1815-1916, 'the bird is attacked in its nest', conquest will be advanced for Heaven, and lands and subjects secured for the State." Many Telamni had recently died from an epidemic and "in their last anguish those unhappy ones sought the water of baptism and the bread of celestial doctrine along with material bread given daily from the hands of the Padres." But he was also aware that because the Tulamni were surrounded by hostile Indians no mission could be founded among them until the government established a presidio in the Tulare Valley.[45]

Spaniards returned to the area in November 1815. Sergeant Juan Ortega led thirty men, including a priest, from Mission San Miguel to the Kings River. On the northern edge of Tulare Lake, in the territory of the Tachi, they encountered two mounted Indians driving four horses. The Indians abandoned their animals and swam to safety across the Kings River. A saddle on one of the horses was identified as that used by a neophyte called Antonio, a fugitive from Mission Soledad.[46]

Antonio had convinced the residents of a Tachi village that if captured by the soldiers, they would be killed. Thus, when the Spaniards arrived on November 10, they found the village deserted. Three horses, one from San Miguel and two from Soledad, were recovered, however. Later in the morning, eight or nine Indians appeared. They told the intruders that Antonio and his companions had fled up the Kings River to the Nutunutu (Yokuts). But at the village where Antonio supposedly had taken refuge, the Spaniards found no fugitives. They proceeded into the territory of the Telamni. In recent years the population of the area had declined significantly. The few Indians who remained at one village offered the Spaniards presents and allowed the priest to baptize four very old women and a terminally ill man.[47]

Venturing southwards the party encountered fearful and suspicious Indians who had been told by fugitives from Mission Soledad that the Spaniards intended to kill them. When asked about the whereabouts of the runaways from Soledad, the Indians replied that two had gone to the village of Bubal of the Wowol to meet with two neophytes who were there by permission of their priest. Two other fugitives had joined the Tulamni. After instructing them to accept no more fugitives, Ortega departed for Bubal, where he and his men received a warm welcome. On November 15 they left Bubal to make contact with another expedition that recently had departed Mission San Juan Bautista.[48]

The goal of that expedition was to round up fugitive neophytes but also to recover stolen horses. Commanded by Sergeant José Dolores Pico, the Spaniards had on November 7 made camp on the west side of the San Joaquin River in the territory of the Cheneche (Yokuts). They assaulted a settlement on the morning of the eighth, capturing over sixty fugitives and gentiles and recovering seven horses. The soldiers released four men and twelve old women; a priest baptized an infant girl on the brink of death. From their captives, the Spanish learned that upriver among the Nupchenche were many horses and four fugitives: Justo, Damian, Severo, and Pedro Pablo. A corporal and fourteen men departed immediately to a village where they arrested the headman and a few companions. Most of the residents had fled into a tule swamp. The headman convinced the corporal that if released he would bring in the others. When the Indian failed to return, the corporal and his men rejoined Pico in Cheneche territory.[49]

Pico considered attacking a nearby village but concluded that "the Tulares were very much stirred up and it did not seem wise to do so." He sent fifty-four neophytes and gentiles to the presidio at Monterey under a guard of nine men, while he and the others proceeded southwards to a settlement at the mouth of the Chowchilla River. The villagers launched arrows at the intruders, who returned fire and killed two. The Spaniards retreated to a safe position, where they made preparations to storm the village the following day.[50]

The Indians made their own preparations and at dawn formed near the Spaniards' camp. Pico described the confrontation: "I told the interpreter to ask them what they wanted and they answered, to fight. Even after we had said to them that the officer in charge did not wish to do them any harm, they gave no heed, but began to fight. Seeing this I ordered them be fired upon. They then retreated to the interior of the underbrush. The troops dismounted at my command and fell upon them, killing three and capturing one alive. Of the dead, one was found to be a Christian of Mission San Juan and a leader in stealing horses. Of those who escaped some were seen to be wounded, and, according to the quantity of blood visible along the river, I considered that most of them must have died." A short time later, the Spaniards recovered one horse and captured two Indians, who told their captors that the dead Christian had been the most intent on killing them. That night Indians fired a few arrows into Pico's camp, none hitting its mark.[51]

The Spaniards followed the slough connecting the San Joaquin River with Tulare Lake into the territory of the Wimilchi (Yokuts). On one occasion, Pico warned several Indians not to "admit Christians or horses in their villages." On the fifteenth he met the expedition led by Juan Ortega, and two days later the joint command visited a Nutunutu village, where Pico delivered another lecture about neophytes and animals. The Spaniards followed the slough back to its juncture with the San Joaquin. On the twenty-third, they entered a village but managed to capture only a neophyte from Santa Cruz and eleven elderly gentiles. They discovered the remains of 238 recently killed animals, a large amount of meat that had been quartered and dried, and sixteen horses, most belonging to Mission San Juan Bautista. Releasing all the prisoners except the neophyte, the Spaniards returned to Cheneche territory, where they found deserted villages. They arrived at San Juan Bautista on December 2 with nine Indian prisoners.[52]

Early the following year, 1816, another expedition, consisting entirely of neophytes from Mission Soledad and led by an Indian called Socio, entered the Tulare Valley. Socio returned with several fugitives, but he left behind a woman because she had just given birth and two others because they were tending to sick children. Their husbands also were allowed to remain. Socio was unable to locate three fugitives-Marcos, Pastor, and Justo—who had found refuge in a village containing numerous horses. He managed to recover thirty horses but lost twenty when Severo and Pedro Pablo, the fugitives Pico had sought, raided his camp.[53]

Neophytes largely made up the expedition that entered the Tulare Valley in May 1816. Led by Father Luís Antonio Martinez, the force proceeded to a deserted Bubal. Although Chape, the headman, had taken most of his followers into the tule swamps, the neophytes managed to round up ten families. Shortly, Chape and seventy men appeared. He and Martinez exchanged gifts before the Spaniard departed. But upon his return from a visit to villages east of Tulare Lake, Martinez discovered Bubal had been relocated. He found the village but was met with a volley of arrows. The following day the neophytes entered the village and captured two women and a man. Martinez reported that "the village was burned and everything in it destroyed because the people in it had taken up arms against those who had treated them well."[54]

Loyal neophytes continued to penetrate the interior. In early December 1817 Odorico led a party from La Purísima to the Tulamni village of Tulamniu, located on the northwest bank of Buena Vista Lake. Odorico, called by Father Mariano Payeras "a worthy neophyte" who could be trusted, was to bring in his friend, Felipe Amuchu, a twenty-five-year-old fugitive.[55] Also to be apprehended were the parents of Amuchu, their second son, and two other men. Before the arrival of the neophytes, Taciats, the headman of Tulamniu, took his followers to safety across the slough connecting Tulare and Buena Vista lakes.[56] Evidently, the neophytes returned to La Purísima empty-handed.

In May 1818 Father Payeras informed Captain José de la Guerra y Noreiga, commandant at Santa Bárbara, that at Tulamniu were "many Christians of all the missions of this jurisdiction who are determined not to recognize their destiny. This is not to mention those from San Miguel, or those from San Luis [Obispo]. From this I gather that they are establishing in the interior a republic of Hell and a diabolical union."[57] By this time, at least thirty-three neophytes had resettled at Tulamniu.[58]

Guerra proposed to the governor that an expedition be mounted to round them up. He sought to recruit thirty men from Santa Bárbara and San Diego and to take with him Father Payeras. When some of the neophytes from Mission Santa Bárbara returned, however, the plan was cancelled.[59] In September, Payeras told Guerra that Indians from his mission remained with Taciats at Tulamniu and that the gentiles there no longer feared an expedition would be sent against them.[60]

Also troubling Payeras was the use of horses by interior Indians. In his 1817-1818 biennial report on the condition of the missions, he noted that "the Tulareños are today here and gone tomorrow—not on foot for they move only on horseback." The Indians stole the animals from the mission ranchos, so "No live stock is safe in all the Valley of the North; and worst of it is that after traveling with horses on the run through all the Valley of the Tulare and the mountains that surround it, they finally kill and eat the animals." Unless a chain of missions and presidios was established in the valley, fugitive neophytes would be incorporated into the "immense gentile population," and "there will arise a situation threatening the existence of the Province, and transforming into a new Apacheria a country which until recently has been the center of tranquility."[61]

In early July 1819 he complained to Father Guardia Baldomero López that "any small altar boy grabs horses; kills cattle; goes about the mission chain terrorizing; steals tame and castrated herds, taking and selling them in the Tular."[62] Later in the month, he sent a circular to the padres, noting that "in the Tulare (I am told by the Governor) both Christians and Gentiles make their journeys on horseback. Even the women are learning to ride. Fairs are held at which horses stolen from the missions are put up for sale."[63]

More despondent two months later, Payeras, in a letter to the governor, lamented that the spirit of insubordination "which is rampant in the world at large has reached the Christian Indians. A considerable number have withdrawn from the mild rule of the friars, and have become one body with the savages with whom they carry out whatever evil their heart and malevolent soul dictates. A contagion is general, and we must confess that the pagans are corrupted by the bad example and perverse suggestions of the apostates.... From day to day the danger of an attack from the united apostates and gentiles is growing."[64]

Of particular concern to the Spanish were the Muqueleme. In a letter to the governor, Father Narciso Duran claimed that the Muqueleme "give shelter to numerous Christian fugitives who are their friends and neighbors. We do not dare to demand their return, for the heathen are very refractory and according to the account of our Indians are disposed to fight and try to kill the Christians, the soldiers, the priests and others who may go there. It is said to be the common refrain of the wild Indians that they are still unbeaten, for they have many bows, arrows and horses."[65]

The Spanish expedition launched against the Muqueleme in October 1819 met stiff resistance. The Indians killed a neophyte auxiliary and wounded three or four soldiers. The Spanish killed twenty-seven and wounded twenty Indians and recovered forty-nine horses, but they returned to Mission San José without a single fugitive. Duran admitted to the governor "that this business is not yet finished."[66]

The same month the governor ordered Lieutenant José Maria Estudillo to undertake a reconnaissance of the Tulare Valley. Estudillo departed from Mission San Miguel on October 21 with a few soldiers, two Yokuts guides, and forty-one neophyte auxiliaries. The expedition arrived a few days later at Bubal. According to Estudillo, Bubal had provided more converts to Mission San Miguel than any other village.[67] By 1819 the missionaries had baptized at least thirty-seven Indians from this village.[68]

Estudillo found Bubal deserted. Apparently, in late September several residents had attended a fiesta at Mission San Miguel where they learned of Spanish intentions. They told the villagers the Spanish sought to apprehend neophytes and gentiles and would kill all who refused to return with them to the mission. Certainly not forgotten was the fact that Father Martinez had razed their village three years before. Estudillo, however, managed to capture forty-five persons, including a neophyte woman, Liberata, who had been given permission to return to Bubal. Understanding the importance of the village to Mission San Miguel, the commander treated the captives "with the greatest kindness." He dispatched five messengers into the swamp, and soon many Indians appeared, including Chape, the headman of the village. Estudillo released the captives and departed the following day.[69]

Proceeding east of Tulare Lake, the expedition entered the territory of the Koyeti. Tuckal, a headman, told Estudillo that his people had known for several days that Spaniards were coming. At another village Estudillo spoke with its headman, Joasps, and the leaders of seven villages who had arrived to attend a funeral ceremony. The Spaniard explained why he had come, and the headmen "assured me that they had among them no more Christians." Joasps told Estudillo that he and his people had never seen troops before, although they had heard about them. A few days later the expedition arrived in the territory of the Telamni, where Estudillo convinced the residents of a village to deliver two neophytes from San Miguel and to search for three more who were in hiding. "They begged me," he recalled, "to pardon them, for they were all either their sons or brothers. I exhorted them not to detain any Christian in the future even though he were a relative."[70]

Estudillo entered Tachi territory on November 1 but found a village usually friendly to the Spanish deserted. Its residents had taken seriously a warning issued by neophytes from Mission Soledad that the Spaniards had hostile intentions. Estudillo proceeded to the Kings River, where a Nutunutu envoy told him to remain in place. The Indian would inquire if the several headmen assembled at a nearby village would speak with him. Estudillo dismissed the envoy and marched into the village. He lectured the headmen about harboring fugitives and then crossed the river into Wimilchi territory.[71]

Traveling north of Tulare Lake on November 9, the party reached a village of the Cheneche, where neophytes from Santa Cruz, Santa Clara,

San Francisco, and Soledad resided. Recently three Indians-Pomponio, Bakazar, and Clareno-had arrived with twelve horses stolen from Mission Santa Clara. Estudillo found the settlement deserted and concluded that continuing to a village on the Merced River would be unproductive, because "it would have been already abandoned for many days by both natives and the renegade Christians who live with them. They would be hidden in the tules and swamps whose inviolability is a complete certainty, the more so since they carry nothing with them, and get about easily with their knowledge of the country." Estudillo returned to Monterey on November 16.[72]

The fatalism of Estudillo was countered by Father Payeras who clung to the notion that fugitivism could be overcome, and gentiles converted by founding a chain of missions in the interior. In 1820 he identified six locations for missions that began on the border with Baja California and extended to the Tulare Valley. Tejón, at the foot of the Tehachapi Mountains, was considered one of the best locations because it had "people, water, timber, and some pasture with a large area for ranchos."[73] The following year, the last of Spanish rule in California, Father Señan reported that another village, this one on the Kaweah River, had been added to the list.[74] Because a chain of inland missions was never established, the interior remained open to intruders who sought not Indians but its untapped wealth.

CHAPTER IV

Rebels, Trappers, Raiders, and Traders

In 1821, Mexico proclaimed its independence from Spain. In February 1824, the corporal of the guard at Mission Santa Inés flogged a neophyte visitor from Mission La Purísima, sparking an uprising in which the neophytes drove the missionaries and guards into a building at the rear of the church and set fire to several structures. The following day soldiers retook the mission, but many of the neophytes fled to La Purísima where the neophytes there also had risen.[1]

At La Purísima, rebels killed four Californios (Mexican residents of California), two of them travelers on their way to Los Angeles, but seven Indians may have lost their lives in the takeover. Subsequently, the rebels released all the prisoners they had taken, including Father Antonio Rodriguez, who chose to remain at the mission.[2] Mariano, Pacomio, Benito, and Bernabe commanded the rebels.[3]They built fortifications, cut loopholes in the walls of the church, and activated a canon that had been used only for ceremonial purposes.[4]

Once the uprising began at Santa Inés, neophytes dispatched a messenger to Mission Santa Bárbara informing Andres Sagimomatsse, an alcalde (neophyte officer appointed by the padres), that soldiers would arrive shortly to kill the Indians while they attended mass. The alcalde sent the women and children into the nearby foothills and a messenger to Mission San Buenaventura.[5] Indians at that mission, however, expressed no interest in participating in the uprising. Many years later, a Californio claimed the Indians at Santa Bárbara "were at odds with those of San Buenaventura. But for this circumstance the Indians of the latter Mission would have risen."[6] After a short battle with the Mexican guards, in which three Indians died, Sagimomatsse and his followers sacked the mission, appropriating money and clothing but disdaining wine, religious items, seeds, and furniture. They retreated to the foothills behind the mission.[7]

Troops arrived from the Santa Bárbara presidio the same day the neophytes fled, finding only four or five old women and a half-wit. They murdered an Indian wandering about on a mule and the following day killed four Indians who had played no part in the uprising. The soldiers also looted the houses of the Indians. When Father Antonio Ripoll sent messages to the rebels imploring them to return, they questioned why they would be treated differently than the four Indians the soldiers had murdered. They wanted to know what they would do at the mission "since the soldiers have robbed all our belongings."[8]

When two Indian workers from the presidio joined the rebels, spreading the rumor that soldiers were intent upon killing all the Indians and abolishing the mission, Sagimomatsse departed for the Tulare Valley.[9] Before leaving, he sent three messengers, Hilarion Chaaj, José Venadero, and Luís Calala, to contact interior Yokuts.[10] Padre Juan Cabot of Mission Soledad also dispatched Indian messengers to the interior. They visited several villages, warning the occupants not to join the rebels.[11]

Seeking to enlist interior Indians to their cause, the Purísima rebels sent sacks of beads to several Yokuts societies. The Tachi and Telamni refused the presents; the Nutunutu took the presents but did not join. The residents of Bubal and another Wowol village accepted the presents, some departing for La Purísima. Upon learning that the rebels had been defeated, however, they turned back.[12] On March 16 soldiers had surrounded Mission La Purísima. The Indian rebels opened fire with muskets and the cannon they had activated. The soldiers bombarded the mission with artillery. After a battle lasting two and a half hours and the intercession of Father Rodriguez, the rebels surrendered. Sixteen Indians and one Californio lost their lives.[13] Either before or after the attack, some of the La Purísima neophytes escaped to the interior.[14]

In the meantime, Sagimomatsse attempted to spearhead a general revolt among the Indians of the Tulare Valley. Apparently, he intended to attack Mission Santa Bárbara and perhaps the nearby presidio as well. Largely unsuccessful in his recruiting efforts, he did receive the support of the leader of a village located northeast of Buena Vista and Kern Lakes in the territory of the Paleuyami (Yokuts). Half of the fighting men of this village joined the rebels at their camp at San Emigdio.[15]

Before the arrival of Sagimomatsse at San Emigdio, local Indians had captured an American and a greatly disliked California who resided at San

Buenaventura. Coastal and interior Indians may have disagreed over the fate of the prisoners. According to Father Ripoll, the neophytes advocated leniency, the gentiles execution. Be that as it may, Indians killed both men.[16] On the whole, however, amicable relations were forged between neophytes and gentiles at San Emigdio. On one occasion, Sagimomatsse had twenty-five steers butchered and evenly distributed the meat among members of both groups. Not terribly concerned about their fate, Indians spent much of each day gambling with money taken from Mission Santa Bárbara and bathing in sweat houses. Initially, neophyte and gentile males freely exchanged married and unmarried females.[17] Sagimomatsse put a stop to this practice, however.[18]

Mexican civil and religious authorities greatly exaggerated the threat the rebels posed to the missions and pueblos. Padre Blas Ordaz, for example, believed the Indians were well armed and led by a Russian. He was convinced that neophytes from Mission San Fernando had joined the rebels and that those at San Gabriel were in a state of agitation.[19] Evidently, the neophytes at both missions had no intention of joining the rebellion.

In April a Mexican military force entered the interior. An indecisive battle took place on the eleventh in which soldiers killed four Indians and recovered thirteen horses.[20] A short time later, Padre Luís Antonio Martinez and a few soldiers visited two abandoned villages near San Emigdio where they found a horse from La Purísima and evidence that a large herd recently had been in the area. Martinez feared that the rebels had gone to the edge of the Sierra Nevada from where they would raid the coast with impunity.[21] Some of the rebels found sanctuary at the extreme end of the Tulare Valley.[22]

Soldiers, accompanied by Padres Vicente Francisco de Sarria and Antonio Ripoll, contacted the Santa Bárbara rebels near Buena Vista Lake on June 10. Because the Indians had taken refuge in a tule marsh, it was clearly in the best interests of the Californios to negotiate. Pablo de la Portilla, commander of the force, promised Jaime, a spokesman for the rebels, that upon surrendering the Indians would be pardoned by the governor. Jaime conveyed this message to his superiors. A short time later he informed the commander that the Indians were ready to return to their missions. They were, however, reluctant to turn over their weapons. After two conferences, Portilla allayed their fears.[23]

The surrender was jeopardized when a gentile and a neophyte from San Miguel erroneously informed the Indians that more troops were on their way. Immediately, several rebels fled the area, although most returned a short time later.[24] The surrender took place as scheduled. As recorded by an eyewitness, "Father Sarría said to them: 'Come along, come along for we have to sing the Corpus tomorrow.' ... That afternoon a great number of mission rebels came over to us; on the following day the Indians put together an arbor for the function of the Corpus which was celebrated right there in camp."[25]

On the thirteenth several Indians informed Portilla that their alcaldes had lost status during the uprising and suggested that new ones be appointed. The commander agreed, selecting Lazaro Huilamuit and Juan Pablo Aguilait, but he allowed Andres Sagimomatsse to retain his authority. The three Indian leaders joined twenty-five soldiers and a few vaqueros to search for horses and the Indians who had fled the previous day.[26] The party proceeded north along the edge of Buena Vista Lake to the village of Tulannniu, where fifty armed Indians surrendered. The village was in a state of confusion, because three Indians from San Diego had told the residents the Californios intended to murder them. The party located eighteen neophytes from Santa Bárbara; fifteen were retuned to the mission. The other three, along with seven neophytes from Missions San Diego, San Miguel, and San Luís Obispo, found sanctuary in a tule swamp.[27]

Portilla sent Lazaro Huilamuit and a few men back to Tulamniu, where four neophytes were found and brought to camp. And at the village of Halau, Jaime persuaded sixteen Indians from Santa Bárbara to surrender. Leaving Sagimomatsse and six other Indians in the interior to locate the neophytes still missing, the soldiers returned to the coast.[28] The military authorities executed seven Purísima neophytes for murdering the four Californios. They sentenced eight Indians to eight-year prison terms, and the ring leaders-Mariano, Pacomio, Benito, and Bernabe—to ten years each.[29] Portilla reported to the governor on June 28 that 163 Indians remained unaccounted for.[30] According to the padres' annual report of 1827-28, some of the Purísima neophytes were still at large.[31]

Discontented neophytes at other missions continued to flee to the interior. In December 1825 José Pico led a force of twenty-nine soldiers from the presidio at Monterey to the San Joaquin River. On the way, Pico captured Rustico and Canuto, fugitives from Mission San Juan Bautista who long had eluded the authorities. He also located fourteen neophytes Father Felipe Arroyo de la Cuesta had sent to apprehend the fugitives and captured sixteen men and twenty-three women and children, all gentiles. The fugitives and the male gentiles were sent to Mission San Juan Bautista. Rustico, Canuto, and the male gentiles were turned over to the corporal of the guard.[32]

Pico proceeded in an easterly direction, his destination being the Hoyima (Yokuts) who resided along the San Joaquin River just to the east of where it bends to the north. He sought a neophyte from Mission Soledad and another from San Juan Bautista. The soldiers attacked a village on January 5, 1826, capturing forty Indians but failing to locate the two fugitives. An Indian from San Juan Bautista was arrested, however. He was married to a gentile and had a small child. Pico released all the women and children but kept seven men, including the married neophyte.[33]

In the vicinity of the village Pico observed "fresh bones and hides of horses which the Indians had slaughtered." The following day he warned the Indians that if found again with "dead horses in their possession, they would be taken to a strange country and never see their own land again." On January 11 the soldiers overran a village of the Apiachi (Yokuts) and captured ten neophytes from Mission Soledad. Pico accused the villagers of recently killing and eating a horse and warned them that they would be severely punished if horses were again found in their possession.[34]

The following day the party arrived at the Kings River. A village, probably occupied by the Nutunutu (Yokuts), was situated on the opposite side. Pico persuaded an Indian leader to cross but only after considerable effort: "He stated that he had come only with great reluctance because he had never before seen any soldiers, but had only heard them talked about. I succeeded in winning his confidence and asked him if he had Christians in his village, to which he answered no. I asked if he had any horses and he said no. To this I could only reply that his own companions had told me that they had two horses. This argument he answered by saying that although it was true that there had been two horses, the latter had not belonged to his village but to some heathen at the village of Cauya. These individuals, on learning of our arrival, took flight and left the horses in their village."[35]

The Californios journeyed upstream, making camp a short distance from a village. Pico called upon its leaders to turn over all Christian fugitives but none was delivered. The following day Pico met with several leaders of another village. Initially, all denied harboring neophytes, but later that afternoon they turned over three fugitives from Mission Soledad. Fearing for their safety, the Californios retreated to a safe area.[36]

On January 14 they continued upstream, searching for five animals lost the previous day. Near a Wimilchi (Yokuts) village, Pico divided his command into small parties to scour the area for the animals and the Indians who stole them. When the parties reassembled, the soldiers reported killing seven Indians. They also turned over to Pico six captives who denied stealing the stock, blaming the act on their enemies, the Nutunutu. The soldiers discounted any chance of recovering the animals.[37]

A few days later Pico sent eleven soldiers with twenty-two Indian prisoners to San Juan Bautista. Pico and eighteen men traveled downstream, arriving at a village on January 20. As recounted by Pico, the Indians "were all on the other side of the river and all armed, both Christian and heathen. The Christians belong to Mission Soledad. I talked to these Indians and called for the chief but he would not come. They said they would not come over to where I was because they were afraid and because they already knew how we had killed seven of the heathen Guimilches [Wimilchi]." Rebuffed and unable to cross the river at that point, the Californios continued downstream to a better crossing and proceeded along the eastern shore of Tulare Lake.[38] On the twenty-second they arrived opposite the village of Bubal, now located on an island in the lake. Neophytes from Mission San Miguel presented papers from their padre giving them permission to be in the area. The headman of the village supplied the soldiers with food and offered assistance in fighting the Tachi, promising to drag them out of the tule swamps in the lake. Declining the offer Pico departed the following day for San Miguel.[39]

Having traversed a wide area, killed a few Indians, and captured several fugitives and gentiles, Pico's expedition was one of the most successful undertaken by the Californios. Later in 1826, however, Cosomne (Miwok) routed a force of Californios and neophytes from Mission San José. Evidently, the neophyte auxiliaries initiated the attack and suffered as many as thirty-four dead. The intruders retreated, abandoning the cannon they had employed against the Cosomne.[40]

In November, José Antonio Sanchez of the presidio at San Francisco led a punitive expedition, consisting of 21 soldiers, 21 volunteers, and 150 neophytes, against the Cosomne.[41] A padre at Mission San José, apprehensive that the recent victory would instill in the Cosomne even more confidence and defiance, financed the campaign with money, arms, and horses. Victorious this time the command killed forty-one Cosomne and returned to Mission San José with forty prisoners, mostly women and children who were enrolled in the mission. Because none of the prisoners was wounded, a visiting British naval officer "feared that the Christians, who could scarcely be prevented from revenging the death of their relations upon those who were brought to the mission, glutted their brutal passion on all the wounded who fell into their hands."[42] A subordinate reported that the mother of a boy of four or five was shot while attempting to save her son. This "furnished a subject of mirth of her executioners. Many such instances of wanton cruelty occurred, the blame of which we were told was to be imputed solely to the Tame Indians and their thirst of revenge."[43]

Not all the neophytes at Mission San José proved to be loyal supporters of the missionaries. In mid-May 1827, approximately four hundred neophytes fled to the interior.[44] Deeply troubled over such a large-scale defection,

Father Narciso Duran confessed to Ignacio Martinez, commandant of the San Francisco presidio, that he could not "get over the surprise of such an unforeseen occurrence by a people that appeared to be so peaceful and docile."[45] An alcalde, Narciso, had organized the mass desertion, and when sent to persuade the runaways to return, he remained with his followers. He sent messages to the neophytes at Missions Santa Clara, San Juan Bautista, and Santa Cruz to join him in the interior. Father Duran blamed American trappers then in the interior for the desertions. Neophytes informed him that the Americans had offered the Indians of San José protection if they would leave the mission.[46]

The trappers causing so much concern had arrived at the southern mission of San Gabriel Arcángel in late November 1826. Led by Jedediah Smith and guided by Spanish-speaking Indians, the twenty-man party crossed the Tehachapi Mountains early the following year and in February camped on the east side of Tulare Lake near a Wowol (Yokuts) village. "When I arrived," Smith recalled, "some mats were spread in front of the Lodges and I was invited to sit down. Grass seed was then brought in and poured on my head until I was nearly covered."[47]

Smith and his party trapped their way north, striking the San Joaquin where it exits the mountains and following it downstream to the Stanislaus. Smith saw few Indians along the river, noting in his journal that "the greater part of those that had once resided here … [have] gone into the missions of St Joseph and Santa Clara."[48] The Americans experienced no difficulties with Indians until arriving at the Cosumnes where they were attacked by a party of Muqueleme (Miwok). No injuries were inflicted, but the trappers were forced to withdraw to safe ground. The following day the Americans discovered the Indians had taken some of their traps and had formed on the opposite bank. Unable to cross to do battle, the trappers remained helpless until an Indian ventured too close to the bank and was shot dead.[49]

Smith led his men north to the American River and, seeking a route across the Sierra Nevada, followed the south fork deep into Nisenan territory. When Indians (perhaps Yalesumne) pressed too close, Smith "tried to convince them of my friendly disposition but to no purpose. Their preparations were still going forward and their parties were occupying favorable points around me." Smith ordered two of his best marksmen to foe at long range so "it might give them the idea that we could kill at any distance. At the report of the guns … two indians fell."[50] Unable to cross the mountains, the trappers returned to the Stanislaus.[51]

When word reached the coast that Americans were in the interior, Father Duran formulated his theory regarding the desertion of the four hundred neophytes. Writing to Lieutenant Ignacio Martinez on May 16, the priest claimed that "the Anglo-Americans sent several communications to people in that part of the country, offering them protection to abandon the mission and Christian obligations and return to their villages to live and die gentiles." Americans had visited the villages of the Muqueleme and Cosomne "and their stay brought about this inconvenience to this mission."[52] Duran may have been particularly concerned about the Cosomne joining the Americans because recently they had suffered greatly from a Mexican military invasion.

Regarding the Muqueleme attack on the trappers, Martinez claimed in a letter to Governor José Maria Echeandia that once the Indians realized the Americans were not Mexican soldiers they made peace.[53] His assessment was correct, because shortly after the encounter, Te-Mi, a Muqueleme leader, returned a horse and seven or eight traps the Indians had taken, and on a regular basis delivered to the Americans meal, raspberries, and other food in exchange for meat.[54]

When informed by a neophyte that Father Duran was troubled by the presence of Americans in the interior, Smith wrote to the priest on May 19, informing him that he and his trappers had attempted to leave California by crossing the Sierra Nevada but were forced to remain in the interior until the snow melted.[55] The following day Smith and two companions departed up the Stanislaus and successfully traversed the mountains. The rest of the party, under the command of Harrison Rogers, were to remain in camp until Smith returned with supplies.[56]

In the meantime Governor Echeandía instructed Martinez to locate the Americans and order them to leave the province. Martinez turned the task over to Sergeant Francisco Soto, who with about a dozen soldiers arrived at the trappers' camp in early June. Soto delivered to Rogers a letter from Luís Antonio Argüello, commandant of the San Francisco presidio.[57] Argüello chastised Rogers for remaining in Mexican territory and for attempting "to win the goodwill of these natives, while at the same time you survey the land and rivers. Moreover, you give notice to these same natives that all that Territory, as far as the Columbia River, is yours. You point out to them boundaries on the San Joaquin River and appoint captains with insignias, over whom you have asserted civil and political authority. The actions are too insolent, and in no way will our Mexican government view them with indifference."[58] Rogers penned a reply to Argüello. Neither he nor the United States had any designs on California; he had not communicated with Indians except those who came to his camp; he was willing to give himself up if so ordered.[59]

On his return journey Soto rounded up the neophytes who had fled from Mission San José and visited several villages of gentiles to ascertain if the Americans had attempted to influence them in any way. Soto told Argüello he had found no evidence the trappers had encouraged the neophytes to leave the mission. In a letter to Governor Echeandia, Argüello admitted there was little evidence to implicate the Americans but insisted they had come to California not to trap but to explore.[60]

In August, Smith returned to California. On the Colorado River, Mohave Indians killed ten of the eighteen members of his party, and when he reached the Stanislaus in September he found his trappers in a destiute condition. With three men he departed immediately for Mission San José where he was promptly arrested. He was later taken to Monterey, but in November Echeandia issued him a passport to leave the province, and at the end of December 1827 he headed north.[61] Smith took with him a large herd of horses an Englishman, William Garner, had purchased for him in Monterey.[62] Twenty years later, Garner recalled that Smith "bought three hundred and ninety seven head of horses and mules, of the best kind that could be found in the country; and only one horse amongst them cost as high as fifteen dollars–the average price he paid for them was about nine dollars."[63]

With the departure of Smith and his trappers, Mexican authorities could better concentrate on a much more serious problem–Indian stock raiders. In April 1828 soldiers and neophyte auxiliaries traveled to the San Joaquin River where it exits the foothills. On the twenty-sixth ten soldiers and fifteen auxiliaries crossed the San Joaquin and attacked a Hoyima village, killing three and capturing twenty-six Indians. According to the commander of the expedition, Sebastian Rodriguez, "we found 27 horses, … the flesh of which the Indians had been eating for three days, after the animals had been killed with arrows. In the brush there may have been 60 to 80 more horses." They burned all the remaining horsemeat, "not leaving the Indians as much as a quarter to eat."[64]

Upstream they found deserted villages. Rodriguez noted that "these three villages are all part of the tribe of Joyimas (Hoyima), and when horses are brought in they are divided up among the Indians who caught them, to be eaten at leisure." A scouting party discovered some Indians in hiding, and in the ensuing fight the Hoyima killed an interpreter and five other neophytes. The intruders captured five men, nineteen women, and thirteen boys and girls. Later, several other Indians also were taken, including two neophytes from San Juan Bautista and two gentiles, Selli and Salmi, apparently well-known horse thieves.[65]

The command then ventured north into the territory of the Heuchi (Yokuts). Although Delfino, a neophyte from San José, had spread the word that a military force was in the area, Rodriguez managed to capture eight gentiles and three neophytes from San Juan Bautista. On April 30 he sent a contingent into the territory of the Chauchila (Yokuts) to "catch either Christians or heathen, for these people are also horse eaters." No Indians were found. A few days later Rodriquez and his men returned to Mission San Juan Bautista with fifty-two horses and eighty-five neophytes and gentiles.[66]

In late May, Rodriguez again penetrated the interior, this time to Buena Vista Lake. The village of Tulamniu, located on the north shore, was deserted, its residents having been warned by a neophyte from Mission San Miguel that the soldiers intended to kill them. Shortly the headman appeared, and he told Rodriguez that the six Christians living in his village had fled to a tule swamp.[67] The contingent that entered the swamp returned with a few Indians; one informed Rodriguez that he would find horses and saddles at a village in the mountains near Santa Bárbara. When Rodriguez and fifteen men arrived at that village, the headman presented a document stating that he had authorization from a padre at Mission La Purísima to recover horses belonging to the mission. Unconvinced, Rodriguez confiscated eight saddles, five mules, and fifteen horses. On the way back to Buena Vista Lake, he collected eleven more horses.[68]

While Rodiguez was absent, the headman of Tulamniu turned over four of the six neophytes who had fled from the village, and upon the return of Rodriguez delivered the other two. And a leader of the Yauelmani (Yokuts), who resided on the east side of the lake, presented soldiers with twelve horses. Admitting that Christians resided in his village, he surrendered them a short time later.[69] Rodriguez proceeded to the village of Bubal. He demanded from the headman sixteen neophytes and apprehended nine gentiles to ensure delivery, but the headman located only two fugitives. Rodriguez then departed for Mission San Miguel, where he turned over to Father Juan Cabot forty-seven animals from Missions San Luís Obispo, La Purísima, Santa Bárbara, Buenaventura, San Fernando, and San Gabriel. Thirty-one neophytes and gentiles were taken to the Monterey presidio.[70]

Judged by the number of neophytes and animals recovered, the two expeditions conducted by Rodriguez were highly successful. But the Californios had little time for self-congratulation. Late in 1828, a party of neophytes departed from Mission San José, apparently with permission from the resident priests, to visit relatives. On November 9 Father Duran reported that most of the neophytes had returned except for the Lakisamne (Yokuts), whose natal villages were on the Stanislaus River. Duran identified Estanislao Cucunuchi as the ringleader.[71] Baptized in 1821 he was one of thirty-five Lakisamnes to receive the sacraments that year.[72]

According to a contemporary, Estanislao was "about six feet in height, with a skin nearer white than bronze. He was of slender build and an excellent horseman. His face was nearly covered by a beard." Born at the mission, he became a vaquero and mule trainer.[73] He also served as an alcalde.[74] From the Stanislaus River, Estanislao sent a message to Father

Duran announcing that his people were rising in revolt. He had no fear of the soldiers because they "are few in number, are very young, and do not shoot well." Duran notified the presidio commander that the rebels expected to be joined by neophytes from Missions Santa Clara, Santa Cruz, and San Juan Bautista. He emphasized that "everything depends upon capturing dead or alive a certain Estanislao from this mission and a person from Santa Clara called Cipriano."[75]

Sometime in late 1828 or early 1829, a sergeant and fifteen soldiers confronted the rebels in a dense thicket, where they received a barrage of insults. In the skirmish that followed, the Indians killed two and wounded six soldiers, including a sergeant who subsequently died in the pueblo of San José. Several Indians also may have died.[76] A short time later Estanislao and six followers apprehended two neophytes fishing on the San Joaquin River. As related by Father Duran, "Macario was relieved of the horses, his saddle, harness and clothing. An even more lamentable circumstance was that the companion, named Benigno[,] went over to the enemy." Estanislao sent Macario back to the mission with a message that soon the rebels would attack coastal settlements.[77]

In early May the Californios organized another military force. Commanded by José Antonio Sanchez and initially comprising nine cavalrymen and three artillerymen from the presidio at San Francisco, it was augmented at Mission San José with more cavalry, a few civilians, and seventy neophyte auxiliaries. The intruders sought to dislodge the Indians by bombardment, but the artillery piece was rendered useless when one of its wheels broke. The soldiers opened fire with their carbines but to no effect.[78]

The command made camp a short distance from the Indian stockade. Later in the day, when Estanislao appeared in the distance, Sanchez ventured out to talk with him. He promised the rebel that no harm would come to him if he returned to the mission. The following day Sanchez again called upon Estanislao to surrender, but the rebel replied that he would prefer to die in the underbrush. Thirteen leaders, all gentiles, came forward and told Sanchez they were afraid of Estanislao and Cipriano. The commander encouraged them to return to their villages, but they remained with the rebels.[79]

From several directions, Californios and auxiliaries attacked but withdrew after about three hours of fighting. The rebels killed two and wounded eight Californios. Eleven auxiliaries also were wounded. The Californios counted eight rebels killed. Concluding that further assault was foolhardy, Sanchez broke camp later in the day, arriving at Mission San José on May 10.[80] Left behind and in the hands of the Indians was Andrés Mesa. Estanislao summoned Indians from nearby villages to celebrate the victory and to witness the execution of the Californio. They hanged him by one foot from the branch of an oak tree and riddled him with arrows. His body and that of another soldier were then burned.[81]

Upon receiving a report of the campaign, the commandant of the San Francisco presidio ordered M. G. Vallejo to organize yet another expedition against Estanislao and Cipriano. He informed Vallejo that "The Indian rebels from Mission San José and Santa Clara have gathered together at the rivers, resolved to die rather than surrender. They are extremely insolent, committing murders and stealing horses, ... seducing other Christians to accompany them in their evil and diabolical schemes, openly insulting our troops.... They are relying upon the manpower of the wild Indians, on the terrain and positions which they are occupying." Vallejo was "to administer a total defeat to the Christian rebels and to the wild Indians who are aiding them, leaving them completely crushed."[82]

Vallejo departed from San José on May 26 with over one hundred soldiers and civilians and about fifty Indian auxiliaries from Missions Santa Clara and San José. At the site of the previous battle, he found the charred bones of the executed soldier but no Indians. When he set the thicket on fire, however, he received a volley of arrows. The Californios then opened up with their muskets and artillery. Vallejo ordered his cavalrymen to dismount and to probe the dense underbrush on foot. Waiting until the soldiers were nearly on them, the Indians launched their arrows, wounding three corporals. Before the Indians could cut them off from their mounts, the soldiers beat a hasty retreat. Probing the thicket the next day, the intruders discovered that the Indians had fled during the night. Before withdrawing, the rebels may have buried some of the dead in the trenches they had dug for defense.[83]

The command followed the Indians to the Tuolumne River and on May 31 surrounded a village of the Tauhalame (Yokuts). A resident of the village, who was captured the previous day, was sent to implore the rebels to surrender. Instead, he told them to retreat into a nearby thicket, because once captured they would be killed. The Indian returned to the Californios' camp and was immediately executed. A rebel, Matias, however, went over to the Californios. As recalled by Joaquin Piña, "Matias was told to speak to his compatriots and say to them that the troops were about to close in on them and that they should come out. Their reply was that they would not do this, they would prefer to die on the spot." The Californios and the neophyte auxiliaries then attacked. The rebels, protected in trenches, responded with volleys of arrows that forced the intruders to retreat. After the battle most of the Indians withdrew from the area.[84]

The following day the Californios captured three women, including a neophyte called Agustina. Enlisting her and Matias as guides, Californios and auxiliaries entered the thicket and discovered several bodies near the trenches. They also captured three more women, who were shot on the spot. The civilian entrusted with guarding Matias shot him as well. Except for the timely intercession of the commander of the expedition, Agustina and her two companions also would have been murdered.[85] As recounted by Piña, the retribution inflicted on the rebel Indians continued:

> "The Indian auxiliaries ... managed to find a Christian Indian from Santa Clara. After capture he confessed that he had been the one who had burned the bodies of the two dead soldiers who had been killed on the previous expedition under Don José Sanchez. On learning this the Indian auxiliaries ... began to beg the Commander for permission to kill the prisoner.... They were given this permission. So the Indian auxiliaries formed a semicircle, placed him in the middle, and four of them began to shoot arrows at him.... Finally seeing that he did not die a cavalry officer shot him in the head with his carbine.... From there they took him to an oak tree and hung him up."[86] The expedition returned to San José with eighteen horses Indians had stolen from the vicinity of Missions San José and Santa Clara.[87]

Once aware that Indian prisoners had been murdered, the governor of California ordered an inquiry.[88] The investigator determined that two males and three females had been killed by arrows but only one had died from gunshot. He identified a soldier, Joaquin Alvarado, as the murderer of a defenseless old woman and recommended he be sentenced to five years' additional service in Baja California.[89]

On the advice of Father Duran, the governor pardoned the rebel Indians, provided they return to their missions and by "Christian and industrious conduct" exhibit proof of their repentance. The governor had determined that "it is easier to control them when they are present than when they are absent."[90] Estanislao and many of the other Indians returned to Missions San José and Santa Clara.[91] Apparently, Duran allowed Estanislao to resume his duties and responsibilities as a vaquero, because in July he was back in the Tulares rounding up horses.[92] An apostate to the end, Cipriano died and was buried in the interior before the end of 1829.[93]

No sooner had the Estanislao rebellion been crushed than the Indians of the Tulares experienced different kinds of foreigners entering their territories. On January 31, 1830 a party of sixty traders from New Mexico, commanded Antonio Armijo, arrived at Mission San Gabriel. Their purpose in coming to California was to obtain mules.[94] William Garner, who had settled in California a few years before, recalled that the New Mexicans purchased many animals "at the low price of fifty cents each, and among them were some very splendid animals."[95] They lost some of their stock to Navajos on the return journey but arrived safely in Jemez, New Mexico, in late April, having been gone about five and a half months.[96]

Although the road to California (called The Old Spanish Trail) terminated at Los Angeles, sub-branches eventually extended over a wide area. As explained by J. J. Warner, who arrived in California in 1831, "Los Angeles was the central point in California of this New Mexican trade.... From thence they scattered themselves over the country from San Diego to San José, and across the Bay to Sonoma and San Rafael. Having bartered and disposed of the goods bought, and procured such as they wished to carry back, and what mules they could drive, they concentrated at Los Angeles for their yearly return."[97]

Following the New Mexicans into California were individuals representing several nationalities. In mid-1830 a trapping party, comprised mainly of Americans and a few French Canadians, camped at San Gabriel. Led by Ewing Young, the foreigners proceeded immediately to the San Joaquin Valley to trap for beaver.[98] But in July they became involved in a California-Indian dispute. Early that month Californios and neophyte auxiliaries from Mission San José traveled to the Cosumnes River, where they recruited Indian allies. From there the combined force proceeded into the territory of the Ochejamne (Miwok), who were suspected of harboring fugitive Christians. Their leader, Huyumegepa, admitted Christians were in his village but refused to turn them over. Fighting broke out, the Ochejamne wounding eleven of the auxiliaries.[99]

The Californios turned to the nearby Americans for help. Several volunteered, and in the ensuing fight, which lasted three hours, the combined force killed three and wounded nineteen Ochejamne. The Indian auxiliaries set fire to the village.[100] Kit Carson, a participant in the fight, recalled that "the next day we demanded the runaways and informed the Indians that if they were not immediately given up we would not leave one of them alive. They complied with our demands, and we turned our prisoners over to those from whom they had deserted."[101]

Shortly after this incident Young purchased horses and mules in the pueblo of San José.[102] Guarding these animals proved to be a difficult task, however. "Indians came to our camp during the night," Carson remembered, "frightened our animals, and ran off with sixty head." Twelve trappers, including Carson, located the Indians in the Sierra Nevada, "feasting off some of our animals they had killed. We charged their camp, killed eight Indians, took three children prisoners and recovered all of our animals, with the exception of six that were eaten."[103]

Although concerned about the intrusion of trappers, Mexican officials and missionaries concluded that the traders posed a greater threat. As early as March 1831 Governor Manuel Victoria informed his presidio commanders at Santa Bárbara and San Diego that "those who have been in the habit of coming to this territory from New Mexico are establishing trade relations with the wild Indians, Christian fugitives and actually some of the mission neophytes." The Indians rob the missions of horses and sell them to the traders, "who take the animals to their own country by various routes."[104]

William Garner claimed that the year following the arrival of the first caravan from New Mexico, "the wild Indians began to steal from the settlements."[105] Father Juan Vicente Cabot reported in February 1833 that his mission of San Miguel had lost 108 mules and many horses since the New Mexicans first came to California."[106] The same month, Father Vicente Pasqual Oliva of Mission San Gabriel alerted Governor José Figueroa to what he perceived to be a deteriorating situation: "The introduction of articles of commerce into this territory by natives of New Mexico has caused extensive robberies, both open and concealed. They sell, they trade, they induce the Indians to steal animals to sell."[107] Summing up the situation a few years later, a visitor to California wrote: "Many of these traders are honest men, but there are many who purchase a part of their horses at a fair rate from the owner, and then set out on the pretended return, when in fact, they only retire to the interior, where pasture, and game, is abundant; they, there, pitch their tents, and ... prevail on the Indians to supply them with as many horses as they wish."[108]

Local authorities attempted to curtail the activities of the traders. In January 1833 the legislative assembly passed an act prohibiting New Mexicans from buying mules and horses at prices other than those set by a justice of the peace. Receipts were required to document the legality of the purchase. Thereafter, officials in Los Angeles were to inspect the animals before the traders left New Mexico.[109] When a party of New Mexicans departed Los Angeles in January before submitting to an inspection, six Californios set out to bring them back. They failed to overtake that party, but on the Mohave River east of Los Angeles they encountered another with two hundred animals, most of them stolen. The Californios took the leader, Juan Jesus Villapando, to Los Angeles; his followers were to remain in place but the men who returned to the river found the camp deserted. The Californios overtook the New Mexicans in Tulare Valley, where they confiscated many horses, including one hundred head from Mission San Luís Obispo.[110]

On February 26 Governor Figueroa ordered a detachment of soldiers from the presidio at Santa Bárbara and a party of civilians from Los Angeles into the interior "in order to break up a union of the New Mexicans who, with pernicious intentions on the property of this territory, are gathering in the Tulares." If found in possession of stolen animals, the traders were to be brought, by force if necessary, to Los Angeles.[111]

Figueroa instructed the soldiers to treat fairly the Indians encountered in the interior: "In passing through the villages of the Indians, find the chief of the region, win his confidence, so that he will not be afraid or anxious, and declare that they may live in peace devoted to their labors. Be scrupulously careful in punishing the men under your command who transgress moderation in their dealings with the gentiles." The soldiers were to defend themselves against hostile Indians, but they "should be generous to their enemies when conquered, for more comes from good treatment than severity."[112] The Californios experienced no difficulties with Indians. They apprehended three traders and confiscated 430 animals taken from Missions San Luís Obispo and San Fernando. Found guilty and imprisoned, two of the traders later escaped and fled back to New Mexico.[113]

The arrival at Los Angeles in January 1834 of 125 New Mexicans caused Figueroa further concern. They brought with them a large quantity of woolen goods, including 1,645 *serapes*, 341 *fresadas* (woolen blankets), and 171 *colchas* (bedspreads).[114] Their entrance into Santa Bárbara the following month prompted a local resident to predict that the mules they could not purchase "they mean to take by force."[115] Upon learning that members of the expedition had departed to the interior to encourage Indians to steal horses for them, the authorities in Los Angeles sent a military detachment to their camp. They were to be escorted to Los Angeles, where they would remain until all members of the caravan assembled for the journey home.[116]

Foreigners entering California from the north also troubled the governor. In April 1833 he reported to the minister of war and navy that "the British and Americans, established on the Columbia River, make frequent incursions into this country on the pretext of trapping beaver and other quadrupeds. Scattering over various regions they identify themselves with the wild natives, following the same kind of life. They live in a wandering fashion with them and in this way become familiar and gain their confidence. From this has come rapidly one positive evil, namely that, influenced by these adventurers, the natives have dedicated themselves with the greatest determination to the stealing of horses from all the missions and towns of this territory."[117]

The month Figueroa wrote the letter, a party of neophytes from Mission San Francisco de Solano ventured to the mouth of the Sacramento, where trappers of the Hudson's Bay Company were camped. John Work recalled the meeting: "Four Indians came to the camp with some horses to sell in the evening. It appears that Indians are not allowed to make bargains whatever but that all must be done by the Priest or some of his deputies. The Indians dont [sic] seem to understand this arrangement. They say that... these horses are their own and neither the Priest or the Spaniards have anything to do with them. However in order to avoid trouble we declined buying any of the horses but two."[118]

While trapping on the San Joaquin River, the foreigners increasingly lost horses to Indians, and Work predicted he would "be obliged to go to war with these daring scoundrels." On July 13 his prediction came true. Eight Indians on horseback and nine or ten afoot, led by a "Spanish talking Christian," visited the trappers, who presented them with food and tobacco. While some of the Indians engaged the whites in trade, others attempted to steal their horses. In the ensuing fight, the trappers killed two Indians and drove the rest into a nearby tule swamp.[119] The Indians regrouped and before sunrise the following morning launched a counterattack. As Work described it, "the arrows were falling thick among us but it was so dark that the indians could not be seen." Although continuing their fire until after daybreak, the Indians succeeded in injuring only a horse. Apparently, the large size of the trappers' party discouraged the Indians from rushing the encampment. The whites, however, departed for Campo de Los Franceses at the juncture of the Stanislaus and San Joaquin rivers.[120]

On July 24 Work wrote in his journal that "the Indians are becoming troublesome and we are very short of ammunition, scarcely enough to defend ourselves." The following day, he sent eighteen men to a village, where some of its eighty to ninety residents were identified as participants in the recent encounter. According to Work "the Indians immediately turned out in hostile array, one who came ahead of the rest made signs that the chief was among those who were killed on the l 3th. – After the first fire from our people they fled into a dry channel of the river…, yet some were killed and several wounded, and the people took 18 horses but they are so miserably lean that they will be of very little service to us."[121] Another fight occurred the next day. Some of Work's men, searching for stolen horses near the Mokelumne River, encountered Indians who fired on them. The trappers chased the Indians back to their village and then into a swamp, killing and wounding a few. They razed the village of nearly forty lodges and confiscated twenty-one horses, four of which were identified as theirs. A short time later, the trappers journeyed north into the Sacramento Valley.[122]

Not long after Work's departure, Joseph Walker led a group of Americans into California, ostensibly to trap for beaver but also to acquire stock. On one occasion they exchanged a yard of scarlet cloth and two knives with some Indians for five branded horses.[123] Twenty-five horses also were purchased from two deserters from the Mexican army. The Americans obtained 315 horses and 45 head of cattle.[124] Zenas Leonard, a trapper who wrote an account of the expedition, failed to mention where and how the animals were obtained, but he acknowledged that "stealing horses is practiced more than any other kind of theft."[125] Many years later William Craig, another member of the expedition, admitted that stealing horses was their real purpose in going to California.[126]

Late in 1833 Ewing Young again entered California. On November 1 a party of Californios from San José encountered the trappers on the west side of the San Joaquin River. The Americans possessed a large number of horses the Californios claimed had been stolen from Missions San Fernando, San Gabriel, Santa Bárbara, and San Miguel. Young turned over twenty-seven animals but refused to surrender the rest, insisting they had been legally acquired. The Californios then moved into the territory of the Muquelenne (Miwok) and stormed a village. They killed twenty-two Indians, captured two fugitives from Mission San José, and recovered twelve animals. Back on the San Joaquin River, they met some French Canadians, probably in the employ of the Hudson's Bay Company, and confiscated three animals.[127]

A short time later Governor Figueroa ordered the military commanders of the presidios at Monterey, San Diego, and Santa Bárbara to launch monthly expeditions into the interior. Private citizens and missionaries were to provide the mounts for the soldiers. Stock was to be confiscated from anyone who could not prove ownership. Foreign trappers were to be ordered out of the province, and Mexican citizens were to be notified that they must obtain a license to hunt. Those in possession of stock in the interior would be regarded as thieves and would be held responsible for damage done by the Indians, "whom they incite to evil." Commerce was to be conducted in the towns and not in the interior with Indians. Those who disobeyed the order were to be regarded as smugglers and their goods confiscated.[128] Figueroa also defined his Indian policy. Indians were to be treated with "gentleness and charity," but they were to understand that stealing stock would not be tolerated. Those who ignored these orders were to be taken to the presidios for punishment. All Indians were under the obligation to reveal the identity of the thieves, "it being understood that if they do not do so they will be punished as accessories." Military commanders and property owners were to pursue the stock raiders and turn over prisoners to the proper authorities.[129]

Figueroa's instructions that Indians be treated humanely were ignored. On January 28, 1834 the Walker expedition encountered a party of Californios tracking Indians who had driven off three hundred horses from Mission San Juan Bautista. With the assistance of a few Americans, the Californios located the Indians in some timber and opened fire with artillery. Upon entering the camp, they found only a few feeble men and some women and children. Outraged at losing their prey, the Californios slaughtered the Indians and cut off their ears. According to Zenas Leonard, "their object in taking off the ears, was to show the Priests and Alcaldes, that they had used every effort to regain the stolen property."[130]

The murdering of Indians was not limited to Californios. In the summer of 1834 Ewing Young returned to California to acquire horses.[131] Several men joined his party in San José. Two were former members of the Walker expedition; three, apparently, were runaway sailors. While camped on the San Joaquin River, three of the newcomers, discovering the absence of Indian males at a nearby village, raped some of the women and stole valuable property. The following day fifty Indians from the village caught up with the trappers. Hall Kelley warned the leader not to seek revenge: "The chief gave a word of command, and they turned about and hastened from us; but he, himself, stood awhile, looking toward us as though he feared not death. Turning slowly upon his heel, he walked away. Two of the party started to follow. I begged they would not; they persisted, saying they would do him no harm. In fifteen or twenty minutes after this, I heard the reports of their rifles." The two men returned with the bow and quiver of the chief.[132]

For several days ten or twelve Indians pursued the whites, and on the American River stole several animals, which they gave to the residents of a village. The day following the theft, seven Indians from the village crossed to speak with the trappers. Five approached the whites with fish and seeds. "Standing in a semi-circle not more than ten feet distant from me," recalled Kelley, "their orator began to speak and explain as to their innocence." The Americans, however, were in no mood for explanations: "They seized their rifles and shot down those fine innocent, and to all appearances, upright and manly men.... I heard but a single groan. Two or three of the party, mounting their horses, hastened to murder in like manner the other two, and they were shot while fording the streams."[133]

Young and his men journeyed north through the Sacramento Valley with Mexican horses. Ninety-eight animals may have been purchased, but the fifty-six probably were stolen.[134] Regarding the activities of Young, Governor Figueroa informed the head of the Hudson's Bay Company at Fort Vancouver that "these adventurers forgetting the hospitality with which they were treated by the inhabitants of this territory committed the crime of robbing upwards of two hundred head of horses belonging to various Mexican citizens."[135] These citizens would soon discover that because the Indians of the Tulares were undergoing considerable cultural modification soon they would pose an even greater threat to their livelihood.

CHAPTER V

Cultural Modification

In August 1833 the national Mexican government passed a law secularizing the missions of California. In theory the law, implemented the following year, required the missionaries to relinquish secular control over the neophytes and to perform only religious duties until replaced by parish priests. As quickly as possible, the missions were to be converted into pueblos and their lands distributed among the neophytes. Each family head or adult male over twenty years of age was to receive thirty-three acres of land. Half of the livestock, equipment, and seeds of each mission was to be divided among the neophytes. Remaining land, animals, and property would come under the jurisdiction of civil administrators who would oversee the missions until secularization was completed. A few Indian pueblos were founded but functioned for only short periods, and most of the land promised to neophytes eventually fell into the hands of prominent Californios. From mission lands, private estates called ranchos were created. Throughout the 1830s and into the 1840s, however, most of the missions, although reduced in size, continued to operate.[1]

The secularization of the missions resulted in a massive land transaction, which saw the rancho replace the mission as the basic social and economic institution in the coastal zone. The transaction carried stipulations and responsibilities. The owners could not interfere with the Indians in the cultivation of their lands and could not alter the improvements they had made. The owners could not sell, alienate, or place any financial burden on the land. They were required to build and inhabit a house within one year. They could enclose the land, as long as roads were not affected. Some of the land was to remain undeveloped for the possible establishment of military posts. Judicial possession would be granted when a judge delineated the limits of the rancho. The limits would be identified by plants or fruit trees planted beside landmarks. Judicial possession also entailed a survey witnessed by neighboring rancheros, followed by a ceremonial act of possession by the grantee. The petition for the grant and the survey notes would then be submitted to the territorial legislature for approval.[2] Many neophytes found work on the ranchos, transferring their loyalty from the missionary to the ranchero.[3]

Other neophytes moved inland. Rejoining kin probably was the goal of some, but given the population disruptions caused by disease and warfare, many had no choice but to seek residence among alien groups. This required the host societies to make social adjustments that allowed for the incorporation of persons based on criteria other than kinship. Sixty-five years of colonization, however, had created loyalties and hatreds that often divided neophytes and gentiles. The English naval officer F. W. Beechey noted that "the wild Indians have a great contempt and dislike for those who have entered the missions, and they will frequently not only refuse to readmit them to their tribe, but will sometimes even discover their retreat to their pursuers. This animosity between the wild and converted Indians is of great importance to the missions, as it checks desertion.... The Indians, besides, from political motives, are, I fear, frequently encouraged in a contemptuous feeling towards their unconverted country men, by hearing them constantly held up to them in the degrading light of *béstias!* and in hearing the Spaniards distinguished by the appellation *gente de razón.*"[4]

Gentiles and neophytes, however, found ways to overcome this animosity. Writing in 1846, William Gamer concluded that the Indians who left the San Luis Obispo area "would not be well received by their relatives and friends in the Tulares, if they went empty handed, and having nothing else to take with them as a peace offering, thought that taking a quantity of horses would serve a double purpose, which is this: instead of having to walk from 150 to 200 miles and meet with a cool reception, or something worse, they would be able to ride that distance and have wherewith to make themselves independent when they got there."[5]

Not all Indians who trekked inland lost contact with coastal peoples. "The Tulares came once a year." recalled Stephen Fields, a resident of Monterey. "They bathed in the Monterey Bay and scraped their skin. They stayed about two weeks. The Tulares took back mussels and abalones."[6] To obtain trade items, groups from the interior, numbering between twenty and thirty males and females, often journeyed on foot to Mission Santa Bárbara. In exchange for a currency called ponga, consisting of mussel shells connected on strings brought to the coast by Indians from Santa Rosa Island, they provided tobacco, smoking pipes, and panocha, a thick sugar made from honeydew and the sweet carisa cane.[7]

Indians also journeyed to the coast to maintain ceremonial contact with the Chumash. Fernando Librado, a Chumash, recounted a visit, which took place after the September harvest at Mission San Buenaventura: "About nine or ten o'clock in the forenoon the entrance would begin.... It was made by the Tulareños. Their entrance was only a war display, for they came with their bows and arrows. It was very impressive. These Tulareños were not Christians, but came in the memory of the soul of Kakunupmawa and with their weapons to inspire respect. They entered running and dodging, but not singing. If a dog was running by they would swing around and pierce the dog with an arrow. After they had killed the dog, they would pick it up and carry it under their arms.... It was generally supposed that they ate the hindquarters of the dog raw."[8]

The rewards of employment also enticed Indians to the coast. There were "a good many Tulare Indians around here when I was a boy," recalled Juan Francisco Dana, born in San Luís Obispo in 1838. "They used to come over the mountains to trade with the Mexicans, and work as cooks, servants and general handy men."[9] James H. Carson noted that large numbers of Nutunutu and Tachi journeyed "to the settlements and towns during the summer and work, for which they get well paid; they then purchase blankets and clothing, and but few of them go naked in the winter season."[10]

Those who journeyed to the coast to trade were engaging in an economic process that long had been in place. But with the arrival of the trappers and especially the traders from New Mexico, interior Indians found new customers and therefore new opportunities to demonstrate their commercial expertise. Those located in Walker's Pass on the Kern River became especially active. Most likely Chumash refugees from Mission La Purísima, they traded with those entering and leaving the San Joaquin Valley. Zenas Leonard noted that they were "well acquainted with the rules of bartering for goods or any thing they wish to buy-much more so than any other tribe we met with."[11]

By the mid-1830s, they also had become active stock raiders. According to Leonard, they have "the habit of making regular visits to the settlements for the purpose of stealing horses."[12] On occasion their neighbors stole from them the horses they had taken.[13] The trade in horses extend throughout much of the San Joaquin Valley and beyond the Sierra Nevada, especially to Paiutes residing north of Owens Lake.[14]

The economic change experienced by many interior peoples altered traditional political relationships. An Indian told an American military officer in 1848 that the stock raiders who resided at the southern end of Kern Lake "have certain chiefs who divide the horses among their followers at regular periods."[15] While passing through the Tulare Valley in 1850, Eugene Upton learned that "nothing can be bought or sold except by the chiefs."[16] John Marvin commented on the complexity of Indian political organization: "The system of government which holds among the Indians, is far more complicated than would be generally supposed. In addition to the Alcaldes, Judges of the Peace, &., they elect Commissary, Generals, Chiefs of Divisions, &.,&., to all of whom certain duties and certain honors pertain, which are eagerly sought after. In an Indian village of 500 persons, more officers would be found than in any Spanish or American town of thrice the number of inhabitants."[17]

That neophytes gained political power among some interior societies is evident from the accounts of non-Indians penetrating the interior. José Palomares recalled entering the village of José Jesus, "chief of the tribe on the Tuolumne River. He was a Christian Indian, but fled the missions, and since he had excellent qualifications ... was named Chief.[18] Bennett Riley reported in 1849 that many "renegade Christian Indians who by their superior tack and intelligence have risen to a controlling influence among these Indians."[19] Marvin asserted that "a Mission Indian usually holds the office Alcalde in each tribe."[20] In 1850 a U.S. Army officer met a neophyte from Mission San Luís Obispo governing one hundred Tachi (Yokuts) at the southern end of Tulare Lake. To the east a neophyte from San Miguel ruled another Tachi village. The officer also visited two large villages in the Four Creeks area. A gentile called De-e-jah controlled one; Francisco, a neophyte from San Luís Obispo, was in charge of the other.[21]

Continual pressure from Spanish and later Mexican military incursions dramatically altered Indian societies throughout the San Joaquin Valley. Beginning early in the nineteenth century, large numbers of Yokuts and Miwok were incorporated into the missions located directly west of the valley. Between 1805 and 1832 nearly two thousand gentiles were baptized at Mission Santa Clara. Between 1811 and 1834 over five thousand were baptized at San José. Between 1816 and 1833, over one thousand received the sacraments at San Juan Bautista. Another one thousand gentiles were baptized at Santa Cruz, Soledad, and San Antonio between 1806 and 1838.[22] Areas most vulnerable to missionary influence became vacant. It was reported in 1816 that the Mayem (Yokuts) had abandoned their lands along the San Joaquin River and had moved to Mission Santa Cruz.[23]

The population loss of this magnitude produced profound ramifications within interior societies. For example, before the arrival of the Spanish, the Miwok had been organized into patrilineages called nena. The male members of each nena, along with their wives and children, tended to reside in a single hamlet. The convergence of kinship organization and territory was the salient characteristic of the nena. The disruption caused by the intruders, however, forced members of different nena to amalgamate into new political units in areas offering better protection. Hamlets gave way to village communities comprised of individuals not necessarily related by kinship or marriage.[24] Similar readjustments took place among the more politically centralized southern Yokuts, such as the Tachi, Wowol, Wolasi, Telamni, and Chunut.[25]

Some villages, such as Bubal of the Wowol (Yokuts), were relocated several tirnes.[26] Local terrain often determined where villages were reestablished. A French naval officer visiting California in the 1820s reported that the Indians usually construct their villages on "solid pieces

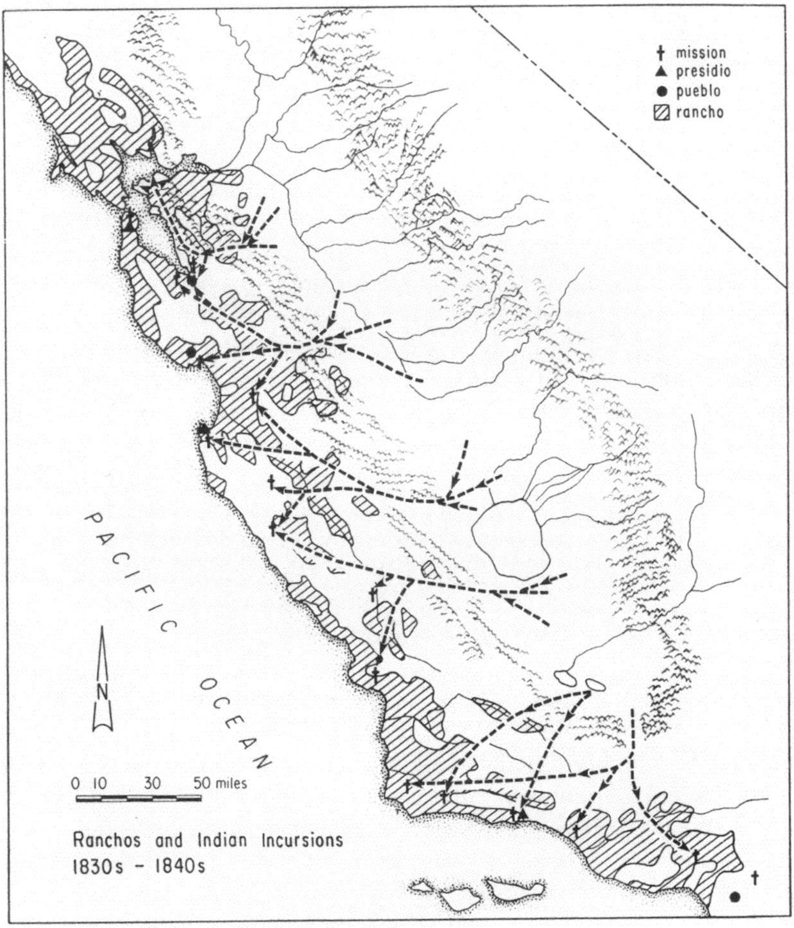

Ranchos and Indian Incursions
1830s - 1840s

of ground surrounded by marshes which the Spanish call tulares, from the great quantity of reeds … growing there. Thither the Californian riders cannot come with their horses."[27] The fertility of the soil may have determined the location of some villages. Many of the neophytes fleeing into the Tulare Valley and adjacent mountains took up small-scale farming. At San Emigdio, for example, a Californio met in 1828 an Indian named Francisco and some old women cultivating a garden.[28] The Indians Zenas Leonard observed in Walker's Pass "follow agriculture pursuits to some extent, raising very good crops of corn, pumpkins, melons."[29] In 1841 Indian leaders at a village in the Tehachapi Mountains petitioned the prefect of Los Angeles to grow crops. Their request was granted.[30]

Neophytes carried into the interior other aspects of Spanish culture, the Spanish language being the most obvious. Whites penetrating the San Joaquin Valley during the 1830s and 1840s encountered Spanish-speaking Indians from one end to the other. An American settler noted that even "the wild ones leaned Spanish, ... that being the language of the country, and everybody had to learn something of it."[31] John Marvin mentioned that "the Indians in Tulare Valley, and those among the mountains adjoining speak Spanish tolerably well."[32] According to Eugene Upton, many of the chiefs in the Tulare Valley spoke fluent Spanish.[33] Indians also incorporated Spanish words into their own languages. Terms for firearms and accessories such as *escopeta* (gun), *pólvora* (gunpowder), *balago* (lead) and *munición* (ammunition) were adopted by Nisenan-speakers.[34] The Southern Miwok borrowed *escopeta* and *pólvora* plus *puñl* (dagger), *cañón* (cannon), and *rifle* (rifle).[35] The Chukchansi (Yokuts) used *rifle* and *bala* (bullet), and the Mono (Paiute) *pistola* (pistol).[36] Words referring to animals and stock equipment were employed by the Miwok, including *caballo* (horse), *garañón* (stallion), *jegua* (mare), *mula* (mule), *ganado* (cattle), *freno* (bridle), *silla* (saddle), *cincho* (cinch), *espuela* (spurs) and *jaquima* (hacamore)."[37] The Nisenan adopted *mula*, *silla*, *espuela*, and *freno* as well as *reata* (lariat) and *corral*.[38] The Chukchansi and Mono borrowed *caballo*, *mula*, and *ganado*.[39] Religious terms such as *iglesia* (church), *dio* (God), *cruz* (cross), *misa* (Mass), and *diablo* (devil) were retained by the Miwok.[40] Nisenan used *alcalde* to signify an officer or official.[41] To the Nupchenche (Yokuts), *alcalde* referred to chief.[42] The Southern Miwok substituted *capitán* for chief.[43] *Vaquero* (cowboy) was adopted by the Southern Miwok, the Nisenan, and Mono.[44] The Miwok also borrowed *música* (music).[45]

Perhaps less obvious than the diffusion of the Spanish language was the introduction to the interior of European music and instruments. While visiting a village at the juncture of the American and Sacramento rivers in 1841, American naval officers heard songs suggesting a Spanish origin: "Their music was more in harmony than among the other tribes we have seen."[46] In 1855, at the southern end of the San Joaquin Valley, Americans witnessed the persistence of Spanish music. An army officer recalled that "while we were waiting for the dance, we were astonished as well as pleased by a band of Indian musicians. They were Mission Indians and had learned from the Priests to play. Three performed on the flute, one on the violin, one the triangle and another beat the drum."[47] An observer to the same event wrote that "some of the Indians, who had been at one time at the old Missions, were singing songs in a nasal tone very much like the intoning of the service by the old Padres, from whom they had undoubtedly acquired it."[48]

Many of the neophytes continued to dress in the style introduced by the missionaries. A British naval officer, while sailing up the lower Sacramento River in 1837, encountered Indians "clothed in shirts, jackets, trousers."[49] Edwin Bryant observed twenty or thirty Indians in the Sacramento Valley in 1846, some of whom were "dressed in white shirts and pantaloons, with the Mexican sombrero, or broad-brimmed hat."[50]

The Hispanicized Indians who took up residence in the interior also introduced newly acquired skills to the region. As early as 1780 Father Junípero Serra complained that an alcalde from Mission Santa Clara had fled into the interior "with considerable number of followers, among whom are those we most need, such as the blacksmith, a number of carpenters and day workmen."[51] In 1824 the Indian rebels from Mission Santa Bárbara sent word to Father Antonio Ripoll that "we shall maintain ourselves with what God will provide us in the open country. Moreover, we are soldiers, stonemasons, carpenters, etc., and we will provide for ourselves by our work."[52] Visiting the interior in 1842 a Swedish traveler observed Indians manufacturing "several little things." The neophytes "were all trades people, and exercised now their respective trades."[53] Another visitor, however, concluded that the neophytes "returned to their native plains and hills, vastly worse for all they have learned, since they have wants they cannot now satisfy, and are partially unfit for savage life."[54]

Some of their "wants" were satisfied by the traders from New Mexico, whose woolen goods they eagerly sought. Stock, of course, was the Indians' item of exchange and the raid their primary means of obtaining it. That neophytes planned and led many if not most of the raids is evident from the testimony of firsthand observers. Neophytes "are the leaders in the incursions for stealing horses and in all acts of hostility against the whites," declared an American in 1849.[55] John Marvin reported that mission Indians "commonly lead thieving parties to the ranches and towns for plunder."[56] According to an American naval officer "many of those who were once the best of Indian Christians are now the very worst of horse-thieves."[57]

The techniques developed to acquire and control horses indicate the raiders became experts in animal behavior. As recalled by William Garner, the Indians would open the gates to a corral, allowing the animals to slowly walk out by themselves. About half a mile from the corral, they would mount up and drive the animals at full gallop until daybreak, herding them "through the worst thickets and most intricate roads they can find, and turning round several times, for the purpose of deceiving their pursuers." Resting in a secluded spot for the remainder of the day, they would continue the journey that night."[58]

The raiders controlled the animals by launching arrows at those that broke from the herd. Two sticks tied crossways about an inch above the point of the arrow prevented it from penetrating deeply. Apparently, this technique worked very well, noted Garner. When struck by one of these arrows "the horse immediately takes his place again in the band and it is very seldom that the Indians are obliged to punish one unruly horse twice for that offense."[59]

In the event Californios gave pursuit, the Indians were well prepared to protect their recently acquired property. In his composite picture of a raid, Garner has most of the raiders dismount at a location on the trail that provided cover and protection while the others continued with the horses. If the pursuers were few in number, the Indians would leave their cover "and dispute the pass with their adversaries." More often they would "shoot their arrows from their hiding place at the first horseman that presents himself within their range. This method invariably checks the ardor of the horsemen, who seldom have the courage to advance, rather choosing to lose their horses than risk their lives in the dangerous pursuit." In the meantime, those with the horses "are driving on as fast as they can, well aware that their companions will follow them on foot, and find them in a short time in some preconcerted spot."[60]

The audacity of the stock raiders prompted Father Narciso Duran to report in late 1832 that the pueblo of San José and neighboring ranchos were "almost on the verge of ruin by reason of the incessant robberies of horses committed by apostate Christian Indians in league with gentiles.... Their unpunished insolence constrains us to foretell that, before many years, we shall see ourselves obliged to abandon our posts and reunite at one point for common defense."[61] So damaging had the raids become that Governor José Figueroa, beginning in November 1833, allowed civilians to capture stock thieves when encountering them "in the act or upon proof of crime."[62]

Civilians from San José entering the interior in late 1834 or early 1835, however, failed to distinguish between innocent and guilty Indians. They confiscated property and kidnapped seven boys. Fearful that abuses such as this would continue, Figueroa issued orders to the alcalde (mayor) of San José. When encountered on future campaigns Indians "who are defenseless shall not be molested, nor shall weapons be used against those who offer no resistance." Indians were to be pursued only when caught in the act of stealing and no expedition was to be undertaken without his permission. Figueroa ordered the alcalde to place the captured children in the care of the priests at Mission Santa Clara "so that they may be educated there or returned to their parents as may seem appropriate."[63]

Indian raids continued. In February 1835, the alcalde reported that recently Chauchila and Hoyima (Yokuts) had stolen "the rest of the horses which belonged to the pueblo." San José "is in a lamentable condition, having no way to round up its cattle scattered in the fields."[64] Late the following year local Californios complained to San José officials about the loss of horses. They were convinced that neophytes took the animals into the interior, sold them to gentiles, and then implored the padres to protect them from the civil authorities. As an example, they pointed to Mateo, a neophyte from Mission Santa Clara who had become an active stock raider. Recently he had turned himself over to the missionaries at Mission San José. They sent him to Santa Clara where he was secure from prosecution.[65]

In mid-August 1837 Indians stole one hundred horses from Rancho San Antonio, situated some twenty miles north of San José and adjacent to San Francisco Bay. Rancheros pursued the robbers to the San Joaquin River but recovered only thirty head.[66] Indians also targeted Rancho San Palo, located just north of San Antonio. On August 15 two Indian vaqueros arrived at the rancho supposedly to visit relatives. When informed by loyal Indians that the visitors intended to steal horses, local rancheros located the men and another Indian on the Strait of Carquinez. All three managed to escape, one by jumping into the water. Safely on the opposite bank the Indian broke into laughter while gesturing obscenely to his pursuers.[67]

Foreign immigrants, especially those who acquired grants in or adjacent to the San Joaquin Valley, also had to contend with Indian raiders. According to M. G. Vallejo, Governor Juan Bautista Alvarado believed the foreigners would "hold in check the vandal hordes who were threatening to wipe out all the wealth which had been accumulated in more than seventy years at the cost of great sacrifice of blood and money."[68] Burdened with the task of checking "the vandal hordes" was John Marsh. Originally from Massachusetts and recently converted to Catholicism, he purchased Rancho Los Meganos in 1837. Located about forty miles north of San José and near Mount Diablo, the rancho was extremely vulnerable to Indian raids. Its previous owner, José Noriega, had resided there only with the protection of between seven and ten vaqueros. Noriega never had received judicial possession of the property because the alcalde of San José feared to travel to the rancho where the transaction was to take place.[69]

In January 1838 Marsh drafted a plan, apparently for the governor, to halt the incursions of the Indian raiders, especially in the area where his rancho was located. He calculated that fifty men in the district were capable of bearing arms. They should be divided into two groups. Those over forty years of age would assemble twice a year, except in cases of emergency, to have their arms and equipment inspected. The younger men would undergo inspection on the first Monday of each month. Each militiaman would possess a weapon, one pound of powder, fifty balls, and two strong horses. The governor would appoint the captain, but the lieutenants would be elected.[70]

Marsh moved on to Los Meganos in late April and began life as a Californio ranchero. Residing on the rancho were some thirty Indians, many of whom were suffering from malaria. Marsh, who had received a license to practice medicine in California, gave them quinine and quickly gained their trust.[71] Vallejo recalled that the local Indians did not trouble Marsh "because upon various occasions he had cured some of the Indian women who were suffering from illnesses which the Indian doctors did not know how to cure."[72]

As with all rancheros residing in isolated areas, Marsh must have carefully chosen the location of his house. William Heath Davis recalled that most houses were built on "open ground, devoid of trees, generally elevated, overlooking a wide stretch of the country." This allowed the residents to "notice if any intruders were about the Rancho for the purpose of stealing cattle or horses."[73] Marsh constructed his house to withstand attack, cutting loopholes beneath the eaves to fire at Indian raiders. Two of his Indian vaqueros always slept in the attic to assist him in case of a raid.[74]

In the fall of 1838, upon returning from a visit to San José, Marsh found his house ransacked and most of his horses driven off. Later, he and several rancheros located those responsible in the Sierra Nevada; they killed eleven and recovered five hundred animals, many bearing Marsh's brand.[75] For their part in the campaign, John Marsh and seven other Americans gained the trust and respect of the Californios. Vallejo wrote in his memoirs that "aside from the pleasure I experienced upon receiving word of the defeat of the band of outlaw Indians headed by the neophyte Telmo, I was also very glad to see that American citizens whom the majority of Californians used to look upon with suspicion had shown themselves so inclined to make common cause with us against the Indians of the Tulare region."[76]

Joint efforts such as this, however, failed to deter the stock raiders. In mid-August 1838 a band of Muqueleme hit Rancho las Borregas, located near Marsh's estate. Led by Ambrosio, a former neophyte, the Indians killed one and wounded several Californios. A party of Californios pursued the raiders into the interior and captured Ambrosio. Brought back to Mission San José he was given last rites by a priest and shot to death.[77]

In January 1839 six Indians led by Yoscolo struck a rancho near San José, killing two persons and fleeing with, according to José Francisco Palomares, "much booty." Four or five soldiers, a few civilians, and one hundred Indian auxiliaries overtook the raiders a few miles from the rancho. As Palomares reported, the commander of the force, Manuel Peña, allowed the Indian auxiliaries to do all the fighting, but only one, Pedro, lost his life:

> So it was that the followers of Yoscolo succumbed to the many arrows that assailed them from all sides. Yoscolo died fighting, and, while he had the strength, he did not cease to do damage to his enemy.
>
> Peña's Indians had some wounded.... The soldiers had not fired a single shot.... When everything was over, Peña ordered them to cut off Yoscolo's head. An Indian took this work upon himself and brought it, dripping with blood, to the captain who, with his own hands, fixed it on the iron of his lance and so carried it to the mission. He ordered it nailed on a pole and put in front of the church, where it remained for two or three months. The bodies of the thieves remained unburied on the site of the battle...[78]

Palomares insisted that thereafter thefts of horses were less frequent in the jurisdiction of San José.[79] And for a short time the Californios took the offensive. In early July 1839, a force of eighty men, led by Captain Antonio Buelna, assaulted two villages on the Kings River. The Californios captured seventy-seven Indians, mostly women and children, one of whom was identified as a thief.[80] The prisoners were turned over to José Castro who put them to work on his rancho.[81]

Indian raids soon resumed. In late July, Indians stole animals from Mission Santa Clara, killing one person and wounding three others in the process. A few Californios and neophyte auxiliaries caught the raiders in nearby mountains. They killed one Indian and wounded two others.[82] In December, Indians struck twice in the vicinity of San José, carrying off considerable numbers of horses.[83] The pursuit party that formed consisted of fifteen soldiers and civilians and fifty-five neophytes. The expedition overtook the raiders, but sustained heavy casualties; the commander and six soldiers were wounded and three civilians were killed.[84]

In January 1840 Indians raided Rancho Pinole, situated adjacent to San Pablo Bay, and appropriated nearly all the saddle horses belonging to the owner, Ignacio Martinez. A party of Californios overtook the raiders, killed several, and recovered the stock.[85] But the Indians forced the rancheros to retreat, leaving behind a dead comrade, Felipe Briones. His body was recovered a short time later.[86]

Terribly concerned over the incessant attacks, Governor Alvarado ordered in July the formation of a force of twenty men to police the areas most frequently visited by the stock raiders. The men were to be divided into two squads. One was to be stationed at San Juan Bautista; it would patrol the region from La Panocha to Las Garzas. The other was to reside at San José; it would guard the area from Las Garzas to Mission San José. The commanders of each squad were to apprehend Indians suspected of wrongdoing and prevent those lacking passports from crossing the line they guarded. The volunteers would serve for three months; the program would then be reviewed.[87]

If ever activated, the militia failed to curtail the raids. Indians attacked Mission San Juan Bautista in January 1841.[88] In March stock raiders drove off two hundred head of horses within six miles of Monterey.[89] Indians struck Santa Clara the same month, killing an Indian vaquero but losing two men.[90] And in July, Indians ran off three hundred animals from the vicinity of San José. Charles Wilkes, an American naval officer, reported that the pursuing party "came to a village, and without any inquiry whether its dwellers had been the aggressors, it was set on fire, and reduced to ashes; some of the defenseless old men, who from their infirmities could not escape, were put to death, and forty or fifty women and children carried off as prisoners. This was not all: these prisoners were apportioned as slaves to various families, with whom they still remain in servitude, and receive very harsh treatment."[91]

The alcalde of San José told Wilkes that Indian stock raiders remained within striking distance of the pueblo, but pursuit was impossible because troops were unavailable.[92] For vastly different reasons, the American also sought an end to Indian raiding: "This constant foray on one side or the other keeps up a continual embitterment, and as long as the present imbecile government lasts, this state of things must every day grow worse, and will undoubtedly tend to affect the value of property, as well as to prevent [American] immigration, and settlement in the country."[93]

One kind of property already was affected. William Dane Phelps, visiting California in 1841, noted that once "the best horses were then to be had for 50 cents a piece. But there is now a scarcity, as the Indians on the frontiers for a number of years back have stole all the horses they could lay hands on."[94] The following year a French naval officer, M. Duflot de Mofras, wrote that "the supply of horses is now diminishing in California, for the Indians carry on endless raids, and almost every night hundreds are carried off to the Tulare Valley.... The value of horses has materially increased since these Indian depredations. At one time horses were sold like cattle; but today even a mule is valued as 10 or 15 piasters."[95]

Indian raids damaged the ranchos in other ways as well. In early June 1843 three Californios from the Monterey area petitioned the governor for assistance. Soon they would be forced "to abandon the ranchos ... since the overseers and those charged with running the ranchos no longer desire to remain upon them, because they no longer have any security of life." Even the campaigns the government launched against the raiders caused them economic harm. The horses and saddles the soldiers requisitioned often were not returned.[96]

The same year, Rancho Laguna de Tache, situated in the northern Tulare Valley, was granted to Manuel Castro. Immediately occupied by a few vaqueros, the rancho was imprecisely bounded in the south by the Kings River, on the north by a village of the Yokuts-speaking Nutunutu, on the west by the Laguna de San José, and on the east by the plains.[97] Individuals giving depositions in a land claims case in the mid-1850s commented on the Indian situation. According to José Rafael Gonzales it was impossible for Castro to occupy the rancho: "From the year 1833, until the time of the American emigration, there was a destructive war, always raging with the Indians east, west, north & south of the San Joaquin River: the Indians always making attacks on the settlers."[98] Juan B. Alvarado remembered the area being "infested" with hostile Indians "who were fighting and committing all sorts of depredations."[99] Vincente Prefecto Gomez said, that "Laguna de Tache was the headquarters of the Indians, and from there they sallied out to commit their depredations on the surrounding country."[100]

Ironically, the Indian raiders often had to drive the animals through areas teeming with wild horses. How many roamed the San Joaquin Valley is impossible to determine, but according to the descriptions of those entering the interior in the middle of the nineteenth century, the number was extraordinarily high. William Garner claimed to have seen "in the course of two days travel, forty thousand wild horses and mares."[101] James Carson concluded that the valley probably "contains a larger portion of wild horses than any other part of the world of the same extent. On the western side of the San Joaquin, they are to be seen in bands of from two hundred to two thousand. These bands are to be met with at intervals from Mount Diablo to the Tulare Lake. The traveller, in going from the mouth of the lake slough to the head of the lake.... can see the plains covered with these fine animals."[102] Apparently, horses did not diffuse south of Tulare Lake.[103] The animals left a favorable impression on the observers. Garner said that some were "as noble looking animals as ever I saw in my life."[104] Carson bragged that "the wild horse of the Tulares ranks amongst the finest of his species. He, unlike the common mustang to be found in the southern portions of America, is of fine size, unparalleled proportions, and as fleet as the wild winds he breathes."[105]

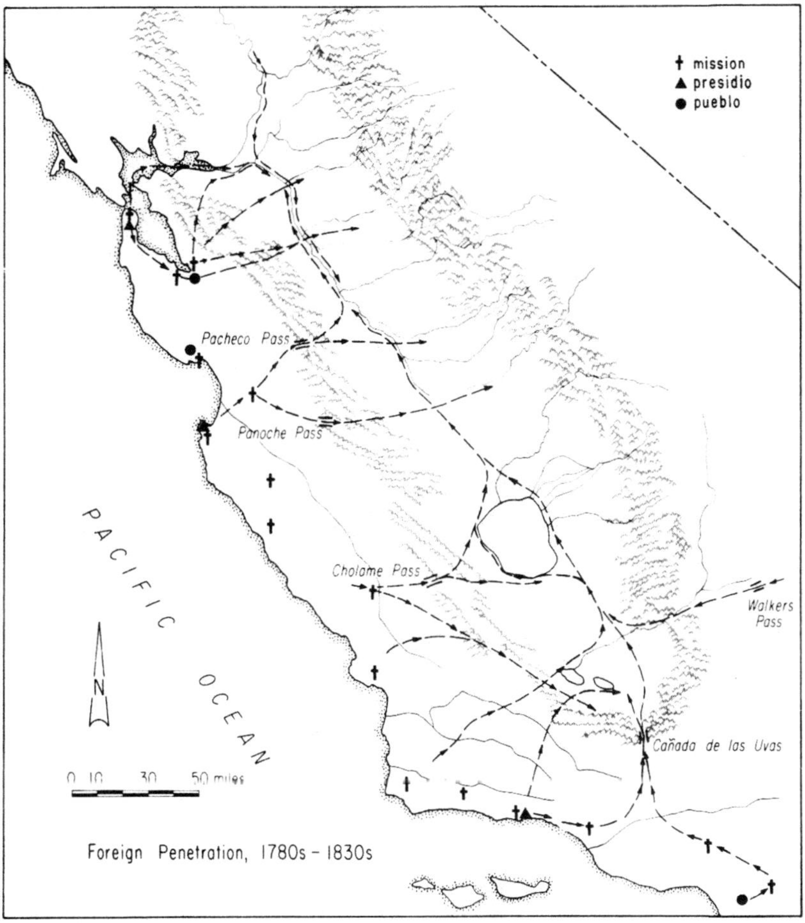

Why Indians raided for horses when large numbers roamed the interior puzzled Zenas Leonard. He thought, "it would be less trouble for them to catch wild horses."[106] Only by raiding, however, could Indians obtain domesticated mules and horses. Most likely the traders from New Mexico demanded such stock. They were easier than wild animals to herd, and they probably brought a higher price. William Heath Davis, who arrived in California in 1831, asserted that the Indians raided the ranchos for domesticated horses.[107] John Sutter, an immigrant from Switzerland, suggested that "it was easier for the Indians when they wanted tame horses to steal them than to tame them."[108] But not all domesticated horses were exchanged. Garner pointed out that the Indians kept the fleetest horses "for the purpose of hunting the elk, which abound in the Tulare Valley."[109] In 1830 members of a Mexican expedition spotted some thirty Indians chasing deer on horseback in the northern San Joaquin Valley.[110]

When stockowners were particularly vigilant or when fresh meat was in immediate demand, the Indians hunted and trapped wild horses.[111] In 1844, two American travelers reported that stock-raiding Indians residing on the San Joaquin River, some thirty miles from its mouth subsist "upon horse-flesh; some which they procure from the wild bands."[112] Regarding the Nutunutu (Yokuts), Carson wrote that they "kill wild horses and jerk their flesh."[113] While traveling near the Stanislaus River in 1841, John Bidwell and his men came upon a pile of bones; "We thought that an army must have perished there. They were of course horses that the Indians had driven there and slaughtered."[114] In 1845, a party led by John Fremont camped at a spot on the Mariposa River "whitened with the bones of many horses."[115] From the Mokelumne River to the source of the San Joaquin, a newspaper reported in 1847, Indians "have become so habituated to living on horseflesh, that it is now with them the principal means of subsistence."[116]

At the extreme end of the Tulare Valley, however, Indians developed other means of subsistence. During the early years of the nineteenth century, Indians fleeing the Spanish missions along the Santa Bárbara Coast and Mission San Fernando resettled at the foot of the Tehachapi Mountains near the Tejón Pass.[117] There they intermarried with the local Kitanemuk. Speaking a Takic language, the Kitanemuk occupied much of the Tehachapi Mountains and the Antelope Valley.[118] The arrival of the neophytes may have begun as early as 1824, when Chumash Indians revolted at Missions Santa Inés, La Purísima, and Santa Bárbara. Although most of those who fled to the interior returned to their missions, some, apparently from La Purísima, remained.[119] American trappers passing through the southern Tulare Valley in 1833 spent a night at a village comprised mainly of neophytes. Zenas Leonard, a member of the expedition, wrote:

> After we halted here we found that these people could talk the Spanish language, which we thought might be of great advantage to the company, and on inquiry ascertained that they were a tribe called the Concoas, which tribe some eight or ten years since resided in the Spanish settlements at the missionary station near St. Barbara, on the coast, where they rebelled against the authority of the country, robbed the church of all its golden images, & candle-sticks, and one of the Priests of several thousand dollars in gold and silver, when they retreated to the spot where we found them....They still retain several of the images which they pilfered from the church—the greater part of which is the property of the chiefs. —These people are seven or eight hundred strong, their houses are constructed of poles and covered with grass, and are tolerably well supplied with house-hold furniture which they brought with them at the time they robbed the church. They follow agricultural pursuits to some extent, raising very good crops of corn, pumpkins, melons &c. All the out-door labour is done by the females.[120]

The "Concoas" may be the Indians residing at the village of Takuyo on Tecuya Creek. It was located in the general area where some of the rebels found refuge. And with the breakup of the mission system in the late 1830s and early 1840s, more neophytes moved to the region.[121] Apparently, Chumash replaced Takic as the predominant Indian language of the area.[122]

The names of their villages indicate that the Tejón Indians, or Tejoneños, resided in an area long occupied. As recalled by Juan Coluco, a Tejoneño, his predecessors once lived in several apparently politically independent but socially connected settlements, some consisting of more than one village: Tinhw, Tsuitsan, Hoshtsiw, Laikiw, Nahantruw, Turuw, Tripohow, Yauliw, Santsiw, Kukukaw, and Posun Tinliw. The latter, meaning cave of the dog had perhaps the longest history of any of the villages.[123] Juan Dionisio, another Tejoneño, noted that Posun Tinliw had been occupied "from ancient times, long before my birth."[124] By the late 1840s the Tejoneños had consolidated into five settlements, some consisting of more than one village.[125]

A captain governed each settlement, his authority deriving not from his bloodline but from his character and abilities. Occasionally, when not performing up to expectations, captains were replaced by their followers.[126] Presumably, Vicente who became chief of the Tejoneños, was subjected to the same pressures. Although Vicente had never been baptized, Chico, his brother and the captain of Mumumpea, had received the rites in 1819 at Mission San Fernando, where he later served as an alcalde. Vicente and Chico resided in El Monte at Mumumpea, the most easterly and

TEJON INDIANS.

Tejón Indians. (From Williamson, Explorations and Surveys.)

largest settlement of Tejoneños. Mumumpea consisted of three villages. The most westerly settlement, Tinliw, was located in Tejón Viejo. Its captain, Zapatero, although born of Kitanemuk and Hometwoli (Yokuts) parentage at a village in El Monte, spent much of his youth at Mission San Fernando, where in 1834 at the age of ten he was baptized and where he learned the craft of shoemaking.[127] Martin resided at Laikiw, Francisco at Tsuitsaw, and Jose Antonio at Hoshtsiw.[128]

The villages were located on widely spaced patches of rich, damp soil that yielded limited but reliable crops.[129] As recalled by Dionisio, adjacent to the villages were "fields cultivated and irrigated by the native Indians."[130] At Tinliw, Guadalupe Isidro remembered, were "good fields, good ditches and plenty of water."[131] Maria Chololo noted that the Indians "cultivated and irrigated by means of ditches."[132] At the time of his arrival, Juan Coluco observed plots of land and Indians cultivating with the kind of hoe found at the missions.[133]

White men passing through the area occasionally commented on Indian farming. Abel Steams visited Tejón in 1848, recalling that the "Indians had some small fields."[134] The following year Benjamin Harris observed

Table I. Tejoneño Settlements

Village	*Location*	*Captains*
Hoshtsiw	El Monte de Caporal	José Antonio
Laikiw	El Paso	Martín
Mumumpea	El Monte	Chico
Tinliw	Tejón Viejo	Zapatero
Tsuitsaw	El Monte en Medio	Francisco

Sources: Adapted from Latta, *Rancho El Tejón,* 128-29; C. Hart Merriam, "Ethnographic Notes on California Indian Tribes III: Ethnographic Notes on Central California Indian Tribes," in Robert F. Heizer, ed., *Reports of the University of California Survey* no. 68, pt. 3 (December 1967): 429-36:, "Treay Made and Concluded at Camp Pensifer F. Smith, at the Texon Pass, State of California, June 10, 1851, Between George Barbour, United States Commissioner, and the Chief, Captains and Headman of the 'Castake,' 'Tejon,' and Tribes of Indians," in Kappler, ed., *Indian Affairs* 4:1102.

Indians preparing the land for cultivation near the Tejón Pass. Zapatero accepted the worn-out mule Harris offered but not to eat. He informed the American that his people were Christians and not mule-eaters. Unknown to Harris, Zapatero sent runners to potentially hostile villages to ensure that no harm would come to the American as he proceeded up the Tulare Valley. When Harris returned to Tejón a few years later, he spent a night with Zapatero, whose wife prepared biscuits, meats, and vegetables. The men talked until midnight about the relative merits of bows and arrows, rifles, and shotguns, agreeing that the rifle was the most effective weapon. "If a heart aglow with friendship, love, and kindness be the choicest jewel," Harris wrote in his journal, "then was good old Zap wealthy indeed, and I rich indeed in owning his esteem."[135]

In June 1851 Luis Bunnell and a few companions arrived at Tejón, where they obtained from Chief Vicente ears of corn and melons. To Bunnell "the vegetables seemed better than any we had ever before eaten. Vincente's [sic] system of irrigation was very complete." On another visit Bunnell wrote: "the watermelons and abundant supplies of vegetables were strong arguments in favor of a few days' rest for our animals and recreation for ourselves." Vicente impressed Bunnell with his knowledge of agriculture, "which was really considerable."[136]

In July 1853 Harry Edwards stayed with the Tejoneños for eight or ten days, the editors of a San Francisco newspaper reporting what he told them about the land and the people. The Tejoneños were "the most civilized in the country, supporting themselves by regular farming in which they are largely engaged. They inhabit a beautiful country, about twelve miles long by four wide, just in the lower corner of the Tulare Valley, where the Coast Range meets the Sierra Nevada. Their country is watered by clear and sparkling streams, running out the mountains in every direction, and so located that every foot of their land can be irrigated without any trouble. They turn these streams at will from one patch to another. When Mr. Edwards saw them, they had splendid crops of wheat, barley, Indian corn, watermelons, &c."[137]

The following month William P. Blake wrote that the areas around the villages were "well cultivated, water being brought from the creek by numerous acequias to irrigate the surface. In these fields, corn, barley, and melons were growing luxuriantly, and it was evident that the ground only required water to make it productive." That the Indians did not plow was to Blake proof of the soil's fertility.[138]

Although the Tejoneños introduced a new economy—irrigation farming—to the region, they supplemented their diet with wild foods. Labor was evenly divided between the men, who hunted and fished, and the women, who gathered the wild plants and seeds.[139] In the words of Dionisio:

> The women of these rancherias knew the plant products of all the surrounding country. There was individual ownership of certain oak trees which were noted for good or sweet acorns. The seeds of 30 or more species of wild flowering plants were assiduously gathered by the Indian women of the rancherias for preparing the native pinole. This pinole was made by toasting and grinding the seeds. The seed of each kind of plant had its own peculiar flavor. The different kinds of pinole were appetizing and delicious but it was much work for the Indian women to gather the small seed. They knew how and gathered them diligently. There were also several kinds of wild onion that were dug. The Indians also hunted certain medicinal herbs where they grew about the rancherias mentioned above. The Indians also knew certain plants which were delicious as greens and always gathered them about their rancherias.[140]

Perhaps Dionisio had in mind the wild grapes that grew in abundance near the Tejón Pass. Some of the creeks, wrote Blake, were "overgrown in places by thick masses of grapevine, loaded with long and heavy clusters of fruit." The berry was small and round with "a high color, yielding a juice of a rich claret-color."[141]

The men excelled at hunting. "There were antelopes and elk on the plains of the Tejón in early times, and the hills and mountains were full of bears and deer," recalled Dionisio. "Almost all kinds of animals were hunted and used for food by the Indians."[142] Maria Chololo remembered the "antelope drives on the plains between Kern Lake and the Tejón."[143] When food was scarce, the Tejoneños cut channels from streams to squirrel holes to flush out the animals. "The hills and plains are covered over with little ditches," wrote an American visitor in 1854. The labor expended "must have been incessant; and for so small a compensation!"[144] A taboo prevented at least one animal from being hunted for food. The Tejoneños would starve before eating the grizzly bear. They believed that humans acquired courage only after seeing it displayed in the bear and that every person killed by a bear immediately became one. To appease the spirits of the bears, the Indians deposited at certain spots arrows, beads, skins, and feathers of birds of prey.[145]

The Tejoneños retained other aspects of their pre-Spanish culture. The women manufactured "beautiful baskets or shallow trays, out of a round wiry grass, which they wind and weave together very dexterously," noted Blake. "The grass is stained with different colors, and is worked in so as to produce different geometrical figures. These baskets are highly valued, and are used to contain food after being cooked, or even to boil water in by means of hot stones, the weaving of the grass being so close that they are completely water-tight."[146] Although familiar with construction in adobe, the Tejoneños built their houses in the traditional fashion. Bulrushes were secured vertically to a wicker frame.[147] Occasionally, mud was plastered over the thatch.[148] Cultural life centered on six ceremonies, or feasts, the most significant being the mourning ceremony, usually held in October. A person of wealth and prominence sponsored the ceremony, providing food, clothing, beads, and baskets. Invited to the ceremony were Indians from neighboring villages who recently had lost close kin. Women mourners would bring offerings of clothes, beads, and food, but no more than two or three baskets each, because the sponsor provided most of the items. Once the objects were burned, the dancing began.[149]

Because the Tulareños and other Indians in the Tulare Valley had formed strong and resilient societies, Californios attempting to occupy their lands faced daunting challenges. In 1842, Governor Juan B. Alvarado granted Rancho San Emigido, located to the west of the Tejón region and consisting of four square leagues, to José Antonio Dominquez.[150] The following year, Governor Manuel Micheltorena granted to José Maria Covarrubias, patriarch of a prominent Santa Bárbara family, Rancho Castac, situated to the southwest of Tejón.[151] At the mouth of the Canada de las Uvas, Covarrubias and some twenty workers built several houses

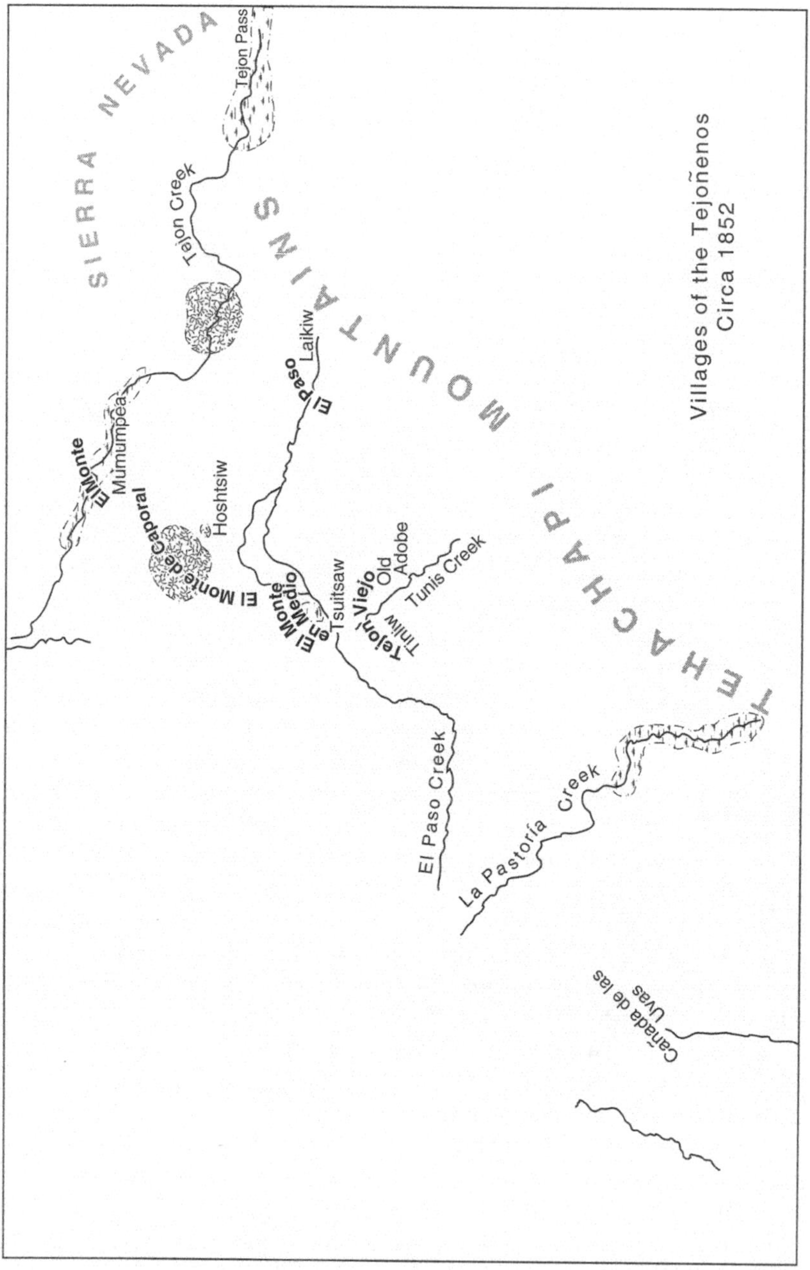
Villages of the Tejoñenos
Circa 1852
SIERRA NEVADA
TEHACHAPI MOUNTAINS
Tejon Pass
Tejon Creek
Laikiw
El Paso
Mumumpea
El Monte
Hoshtsiw
El Monte de Caporal
El Monte
El Medio
Tsuitsaw
Tejon Viejo
Old Adobe
Tunis Creek
Tinliw
El Paso Creek
La Pastoría Creek
Cañada de las Uvas

and a corral for horses, and planted small fields of corn, melons, and other vegetables.[152] In May 1843 José Antonio Aguirre and Ignacio del Valle sought twenty-two square leagues in the southern Tulare Valley. In their petition to the governor, they claimed that the area known as Tejón was vacant and that its occupation would be advantageous to the government. Other useful and industrious persons, they insisted, would find adjacent areas suitable for colonization. Granted in December, Rancho El Tejón extended from the Kern River in the north to the Tehachapi Mountains in the south, from the Sierra Nevada in the east to Tulare Lake in the west. The southern end of the grant encompassed the villages of the Tejoneños.[153]

Aguirre and del Valle never received judicial possession of Rancho El Tejón. On two occasions judges residing at Santa Bárbara refused to deliver the official papers to the two men at the rancho, because they feared the local Indians.[154] The grantees, however, persuaded Manuel Jacinto Fogo to manage the rancho. With the assistance of five Indian workers, Fogo built a house and a corral, tended a small herd of horses, and raised corn, beans, and some vegetables. He remained on the property from early July 1845 through August 1846, abandoning the rancho when the Mexican-American War broke out.[155] That month Juan Gullardo turned down del Valle's offer to manage the one thousand head of cattle grazing on the rancho because of the war and Indian hostility.[156] Earlier in the year two other ranchos had been founded adjacent to El Rancho Tejón. On April 21 Governor Pio Pico granted Rancho La Liebre to José Maria Flores, and on May 27 Rancho Los Alamos y Agua Caliente to Francisco Lopez, Luis Jordan, and Vincente Bottilier. The owners of the ranchos remained in Los Angeles.[157] In the northern reaches of the Tulares, however, foreigners entered the valley intent of remaining.

CHAPTER VI

Foreigners Establish a Foothold

In August 1839 a Swiss immigrant named John Sutter, nine white men, ten Hawaiians (including two women), a young Indian boy, and boat crews sailed up the Sacramento River into an area recently ravaged by smallpox. Sutter sought to establish a rancho deep in the interior.[1] About ten miles below the mouth of the American River, the party encountered members of the Gualacomne (Miwok). Late in his life, Sutter recounted the meeting: "The Chief Anashe ... was present with his people ... when I came up.... A few runaways from San José came forward, who understood Spanish well enough to interpret between us. Anashe, from the beginning, was inclined to be in favor of peace, and to make terms of friendship with me; the others, for some time remained treacherous." Sutter also mentioned that the Gualacomne "had become very much reduced by various diseases, and particularly have they suffered from the small pox, which had made terrible destructions amongst them prior to my arrival."[2]

Sutter and his men continued upstream to the juncture of the American and Sacramento rivers, where, recalled William Heath Davis, they encountered "seven or eight hundred Indians, men, women and children. We prepared ourselves for an attack, but our fears proved groundless. They came off to our anchorage in large numbers in canoes made of tule."[3] On the north bank of the American resided the Pusune (Nisenan), enemies of Miwok groups occupying the territory south of the river.[4] A large village comprised of remnants of the Ochejamne, Chucumne, Gualacomne, and four other societies was located on the south bank.[5] Known to the Californios as the Ochejamne ranchería (village), it was governed by Narciso, a former resident of Mission San José. Narciso took a liking to Sutter and assisted him in building the settlement called New Helvetia.[6] Sutter, in turn, employed the Indian as his alcalde.[7]

Evidently, Narciso was the Ochejanane chief Huyumegepa, who had repulsed a combined force of Californios and neophyte auxiliaries in mid-1830 only to be defeated a short time later when the Californios enlisted the aid of Ewing Young and his party of American trappers.[8] Not long after the battle, large numbers of Ochejamne entered Mission San José. Huyumegepa was baptized "Narciso" on January 18, 1831.[9] He was one of 268 Ochejamne baptized that year.[10] By the end of 1831, a total of 514 gentiles, the second highest number for any year, had received the sacraments at San José.[11]

In 1838, when smallpox struck the mission, 252 Indians were buried at San José.[12] Obviously, not all died from the disease, but the former rebel Estanislao was one of its victims.[13] Perhaps fleeing from the disease, Narciso and his Ochejamne followers may have removed to the juncture of the American and Sacramento rivers sometime during the year. According to Juan Bautista Alvarado, neophyte fugitives were moving up the Sacramento River about the time Sutter arrived.[14]

Situated near a large village of neophytes and in the midst of several Indian societies, Sutter survived by practicing astute diplomacy. As recalled by Heinrich Lienhard, Sutter "took gay-colored handkerchiefs, bags of Hawaiian sugar, and glass beads and left them near their camps where they could not fail to find them. In this way the resourceful captain gained the Indians' confidence and friendship; soon crowds of them appeared at his headquarters, now actually begging for gifts. Day after day, the dusky visitors grew more numerous, and by giving them presents for running errands it was not long before they were even bribed to work."[15] Sutter, however, had to maintain constant vigilance and occasionally fired his cannon to impress his neighbors.[16]

In the spring of 1840 Indians stole horses and cattle from New Helvetia, forcing Sutter to launch a retaliatory raid. A battle took place where the Feather River joins the Sacramento. Charles Wilkes reported that a village had once existed at the juncture of the two rivers, but it "was destroyed by Captain Suter [sic] and his trappers, because its inhabitants had stolen cattle.... The affair resulted in one of the Indians being killed, twenty-seven made captive, and the removal of the remainder beyond the limits of his territory."[17]

During the summer of 1840 Indians residing near New Helvetia withdrew en masse to an area about twenty miles away on the Cosumnes River.[18] From their new position they raided Sutter's settlement, killing cattle and stealing horses. In a punitive raid Sutter employed his cannon against the raiders, who numbered between two and three hundred. "The fighting was a little hard," he remembered, "but after having lost about 30 men, they was [sic] willing to make a treaty with me."[19] Many of the Indians returned to New Helvetia and became the nucleus of Sutter's work force.[20] The remainder abandoned their villages and joined neighboring groups.[21]

Sutter relocated Indians from several villages to his post, including the Pusune, who proved to be some of his most capable workers.[22] Indian prisoners, many of them children whose parents he had killed on his campaigns, also were brought to New Helvetia. According to a neighbor, Theodor Cordua, Sutter claimed the children "as payment for the cost of the war."[23]

On one occasion Sutter had to contend with Indians still attached to a mission. In early October 1840 a party of neophytes arrived at New Helvetia. The leader, Acacio, possessed a passport issued by José de Jesus Vallejo, the alcalde of the Pueblo of San José. Acacio sought permission from Sutter to trade with the Sakayakumne (Miwok) on the Mokelumne River. Granting the Indian's request, Sutter warned him not to take anything by force.[24]

Instead of proceeding to the Mokelumne, Acacia's Indians raided a village of the Yalesumne (Nisenan) located on the American River, where they killed five men and captured all the women and children. Most of the men were absent, many working for Sutter. Pulpule, the leader of the Yalesumne, initially suspected that Sutter was somehow involved, but Sutter convinced him that the kidnappers would be apprehended and the captives returned to their husbands and fathers.[25] The following day Sutter, twenty white men, and numerous Indians overtook the neophytes on the lower Sacramento River and rescued most of the prisoners, although a neophyte, Gerato, escaped with four women.[26] Sutter executed fourteen of the kidnappers on the spot.[27] He informed Vallejo about the affair, recommending that mission Indians not be allowed to journey into his region.[28]

Sutter could legally undertake military operations against Indians because he had been granted Mexican citizenship and endowed with civil authority for the administration of local justice, which included subduing hostile Indians.[29] In June 1841 he officially received a land grant of eleven square leagues, or nearly forty-nine thousand acres.[30] As in all Mexican grants, his contained provisions regarding the treatment of Indians: "He shall maintain the native Indians of different tribes on those places in the free enjoyment of their possessions without troubling them, and he may only reduce them to civilization through prudent measures and a friendly intercourse; he shall not cause them hostilities of any kind without previously obtaining authority from the Government."[31]

One of Sutter's "prudent measures" was to provide goods and services to neighboring groups. The gunsmith Sutter hired to repair his weapons also serviced those owned by Indians. On a regular basis Indians brought to New Helvetia animal skins to trade for gunpowder and other items such as handkerchiefs, blankets, and liquor.[32] Sutter acquired powder, lead, shot, beaver traps, and clothing from the Hudson's Bay Company located on the Columbia River.[33]

Not all visitors came to trade. In late 1840 or early 1841 three Indians—Antonio, Sixto, and Angel—offered to take Sutter to an American supposedly living somewhere in the Sierra Nevada. Sutter declined, writing instead a letter to the American and entrusting Angel to deliver it. A few days later Angel returned, claiming the individual was nowhere to be found. Sutter's suspicion that Sixto and Angel intended to kill him once they had lured him away from New Helvetia was thus confirmed.[34]

On March 1, 1841 Antonio and fifty armed Indians arrived at New Helvetia. Antonio sought from Sutter some of his Indian workers for an attack on an enemy group. Suspecting that their real intent was to kill him and destroy his property, Sutter disarmed the Indians and sent them away. But later in the month Antonio and nine companions returned to New Helvetia. Evidently, they attempted to persuade Sutter's Indian workers to join them in an attack on the settlement but changed plans upon learning that Sutter had discovered their intent.[35]

Eventually, Sutter arrested four Indians. Interrogated by Narciso, Sutter's alcalde, one of the captives accused Margin, Camilo, and Julian of plotting to attack New Helvetia. Speaking on behalf of his comrades Margin claimed they were incapable of doing harm because they had been raised in the missions. When Sutter threatened to kill them unless they told the truth, they admitted joining the conspirators but only under duress. They insisted that Antonio, Chupuhu, and Anashe had planned the attack.[36]

At the same time Sutter was punishing hostile Indians he was trading with peaceful ones. In March 1841 he purchased forty horses from Indian stock raiders. Because every animal was branded, Sutter knew he had acquired stolen property.[37] Concerned about Sutter's activities, late in the year M. G. Vallejo, commandant general of the northern frontier, sent Rudesindo Berreyesa to New Helvetia to gather information. He reported that Sutter had gathered around him many Indians, all of whom possessed good horses, and had issued numerous passports to foreigners, especially to trappers of the Hudson's Bay Company.[38]

By the beginning of 1842, Sutter had extended his jurisdiction down the Sacramento ten to twenty miles. At the village governed by Anashe, he employed thirty Indians to catch and cure fish for his settlement.[39] Sutter bestowed upon Anashe the title of El Capitan de los Pescadores.[40] A few years later these Indians were observed growing beans, melons, and corn.[41]

Horticultural Indians also established a settlement on the south side of the lower Cosumnes River, an area left vacant by Sutter's military campaigns.[42] Some thirty adult neophytes and twenty children occupied the area in 1841. They spoke Spanish, several being literate; they professed the Catholic faith, some wearing the cross and rosary.[43] Included in the group were a weaver, shoemaker, carpenter, and a tanner.[44] Within fenced fields they planted beans, corn, and melons and raised poultry and stock. And beginning in 1844 they grew wheat, mainly to trade to Sutter, who lent them horses at harvest time to thrash the crop.[45] He also furnished oxen and ploughs.[46] On a regular basis Sutter sent his own wheat to the settlement to be ground.[47] Ox-drawn carts transported produce and supplies to and from the settlement.[48]

Sutter also was dependent upon local Indian labor. He acknowledged that the Indians, working for very little, "make slavery wholly unnecessary here, and may be employed for all field and house work."[49] Visitors to New Helvetia described how Sutter recruited his Indian workers. According to William Dane Phelps, Sutter "tells the Chief how many hands he wants for the next week, and at daylight on Monday they are sure to be there."[50] John Frémont remarked that "on application to the chief of a village, he readily obtains as many boys and girls as he has any use for."[51] Lienhard recalled that the Indian workers "were furnished by the various chiefs, who acted as corporals, and to flatter their vanity he called them capitanos. They also received far better pay than the poor wretches who worked as common laborers, and had to slave two weeks for a plain muslin shirt, or the material for a pair of cotton trousers."[52]

A Swedish traveler observed a ceremony in which an Indian leader presented to Sutter a contingent of workers: "Only the Chief of these Indians came armed with bows and arrows. All others came unarmed, and after having gone through their customary graceful movements in file, in square, in flanges, and in body, the Chief made a long speech, which sounded very eloquent. At last he laid down his bow and arrows at the feet of Captain Sutter, saying, 'Take these, and with them penetrate my heart if I or my tribe betray the trust you now put in us and which we now solemnly promise to keep.' "[53]

The way Indians were treated at New Helvetia drew comments from visitors and employees alike. Lienhard admitted that he "had to lock the Indian men and women together in a large room to prevent them from returning to their homes in the mountains at night, and as the room had neither beds nor straw, the inmates were forced to sleep on the bare floor. When I opened the door for them in the morning, the odor that greeted me was overwhelming, for no sanitary arrangements had been provided.

What these rooms were like after ten days or two weeks can be imagined, and the fact that nocturnal confinement was not agreeable to the Indians was obvious."[54]

The Swede was outraged at the way the Indians were fed: "Several hundred Indians flocked in for their morning meal, before being led out for labor .... I must confess I could not reconcile my feelings to see these fellows being driven, as it were, around some narrow troughs made of hollow tree trunks, out of which, crouched on their haunches, they fed more like beasts than human beings, using their hands in hurried manner to convey to their mouths the thin porridge which was served to them."[55]

Sutter paid his Indian workers in merchandise. Phelps noted that "the only articles they now want is cotton to make shirts, and beads to gamble with.... Those who have distinguished themselves during the week he rewards with an extra string of beads, or a few needles and some thread."[56] Fremont wrote that the Indians "receive a very moderate compensation-principally in shirts, blankets, and other articles of clothing."[57] A kind of monetary system was also designed for the Indian workers. Each received a tin coin through which a hole was punched for every day worked. The number of holes indicated the value of merchandise to which the worker was entitled. At Sutter's store the Indians exchanged the coins for blankets and other items. To prevent the "currency" from falling into the hands of white men, it was accepted only from Indians.[58]

Sutter's efforts to keep his Indian workers under strict control were not always successful. When cattle were slaughtered Indians often appropriated the choicest cuts, and on occasion they stole bread from the bakery.[59] But Indians caught defying his authority were imprisoned and occasionally executed.[60] Wilkes reported that Sutter "has, according to his own belief, supreme power in his own district, condemning, acquitting, and punishing, as well as marrying ... those who are under him."[61] He often exclaimed: "I, Sutter, am the law."[62]

Convinced that the chiefs had too many wives while the young men had too few, he performed on one occasion a mass marriage. He had the Indian men and women form separate lines. Each woman then stepped forward to select a husband. Obviously, this was an effort to stamp out polygamy practiced by the Indians in his jurisdiction.[63] But Sutter failed to apply this moral standard to himself. Having left his European wife in Switzerland, he "acquired" a native woman while in the Hawaiian Islands and brought her to California. Later, he "gave" her to one of his Hawaiian workers.[64]

Sutter also took advantage of Indian girls. Lienhard recalled that "everyone knew Sutter was a typical Don Juan with women. In addition to the large number of young Indian girls who were constantly at his beck and call, there were also in the fort many young Indian loafers who rarely worked, but were fed and nicely clothed because their wives received special consideration from the master of the fort.... As he grew older Sutter seemed to prefer young Indian girls."[65] Sutter fathered several children, but evidently none lived for very long.[66]

Sutter also provided Indian children to several rancheros in northern California. In his memoirs, Juan Bautista Alvarado accused Sutter of giving to friends, twenty Indian children shortly after the founding of New Helvetia.[67] Cordua was highly critical of this practice. Children taken by Sutter in his Indian campaigns "became regular commercial objects because the inhabitants of the coast preferred the Indians of the Sacramento Valley as servants, and paid good prices for them. In this way a regular trade of human beings developed."[68] Sutter also provided Indian workers to rancheros on short-term contracts.[69]

The expansion of Sutter's authority and the success of his enterprise caused the Mexican authorities concern. Wilkes reported that "the present governor of the district west of New Helvetia, felt jealous of the power and influence that Captain Suter [sic] was obtaining in the country; and it was thought that had it not been for the force which the latter could bring to oppose any attempt to dislodge him, it would have been tried. In the mean time Captain Suter is using all his energies to render himself impregnable." The wall Sutter constructed around his buildings was designed to protect him from Mexican as well as Indian attacks.[70] Not without reason was New Helvetia called Sutter's Fort.

Californios also suspected Sutter of providing a sanctuary for runaway Indians. On July 26, 1843, M. G. Vallejo wrote to Sutter: "Since the frequent desertions of the Indians of this district to yours are a fatal and all-powerful example for others, and inasmuch as this office has definite information that several deserters are at present in hiding in your settlement with stolen horses and goods, I have ordered Lieutenant-Colonel Victor Prudon to set out to capture them. He will act under the instructions you have on the subject. I strongly recommend to you for the future not to continue protecting fugitives of any kind."[71] Governor Juan Bautista Alvarado, however, concluded that Sutter's activities might serve Mexican ends. If all the trails were guarded, he reasoned, thus preventing the horse thieves from robbing the settlements, then perhaps Sutter could persuade them to settle at New Helvetia.[72]

Shortly after establishing his rancho, Sutter created an Indian military force; his infantry eventually expanded to one hundred men, his cavalry to fifty. Two white men commanded the infantry, but a literate neophyte, Homobono, served as ensign.[73] He was a member of the group of neophytes residing on the Cosumnes.[74] Armed Indians led by one who could read and write shocked the Californios who visited the fort.[75] When not on duty the soldiers worked around the fort to help pay for their uniforms and food.[76] Sutter also maintained a personal bodyguard comprised of twelve to fifteen Indians, who assembled every Sunday morning to drill. Their uniforms consisted of blue pantaloons, white cotton shirts, and red handkerchiefs tied around their heads. An Indian sergeant commanded the unit.[77]

Sutter had to maintain a strong military force because hostile Indians resided in the vicinity of New Helvetia. Traveling south from the fort in mid-1844, Overton Johnson and William Winter entered dangerous territory: "We proceeded down the Sacramento, passed around the head of the Bay, and came to the St. Wakine [San Joaquin], River, thirty miles above its mouth.... This part of the country is inhabited, by a very troublesome tribe of Indians, called the Horse Thieves, and contains no white settlement.... They have long been hostile to the Spaniards, and a short time previous, had killed a white man; and it was therefore necessary for us to be very cautious, while we were passing through their country." The two men may have skirted the territory of the Muqueleme (Miwok): "They have their Villages in the small valleys, nooks, deep in the mountains; where they keep their women and children, and to which they fly, as soon as they have committed any depredation. Among these fastnesses, they enjoy their booty in quiet, the Spaniards not daring to follow them among the mountains.... Many of these Horse Thieves have been educated in the Catholic Missions."[78]

When Indians stole some of his horses in May 1844, John Marsh of Rancho Los Meganos suspected the Muqueleme. Sutter doubted they were responsible but informed Marsh he would look into the matter. He thought their reputation as horse thieves was exaggerated.[79] But an American who traveled from Sutter's Fort to the San Joaquin the following year may have referred to the Muqueleme when he noted in his journal that the Indians who resided on the river "hold indisputable possession of the country and steal & kill."[80]

In the fall of 1844 a party of Nez Perce, Cayuse, and Walla Walla Indians arrived from the Columbia River to trade. Sutter warmly received the thirty-six men and their wives and children. He knew some of them from his travels through their territories and gave them passports and permission to hunt within the limits of his jurisdiction. He advised them not to visit Mexican settlements. Near the fort these Indians acquired several horses and mules from stock raiders. A white man, Grover Cook, identified a mule as his and demanded it be returned. Elijah, son of the Walla Walla chief, Yellow Serpent, challenged Cook to take the mule if he dared, leveling his rifle at him as he spoke. According to Sutter, Ehijah was an arrogant young man who terrorized the older chiefs, including his father. While camped close to the fort, Elijah had killed a member of his own group and on the San Joaquin had attempted to murder another.[81]

Indian guard at Sutter's Fort, by Joseph Warren Revere, 1849. (Courtesy of the Bancroft Library, University of California, Berkeley.)

Sutter ordered the Indians to bring their animals to his corral, where those identified as stolen would be confiscated. The Indians refused to comply, stating that what they had acquired was theirs. A conference, attended by fifteen Indians and several whites, including Elijah and Cook, was held in Sutter's house. When Sutter left the house to attend to another matter, the two men argued violently. Cook shot and killed the Indian. The Indians quickly departed to the north, leaving behind the exchange items they had brought, the cattle Sutter had traded to them, and the stolen horses.[82] Upon retuning to the Columbia River, they recounted to the British at Fort Vancouver what had transpired in California, causing an employee of the Hudson's Bay Company to predict that they would return to Sutter's Fort the following summer "to rob, pillage and murder."[83]

Shortly, Sutter faced another crisis. As a Mexican citizen and governmental official, he could not remain unaffected by political intrigues. In late 1844, when General José Castro rebelled against the government, Sutter sided with Governor Manuel Micheltorena who instructed him to raise a military force.[84] Sutter enlisted about one hundred immigrants and between sixty and seventy Indians.[85] Joining Micheltorena near Monterey, Sutter marched to Los Angeles in early 1845. As events turned out, he joined the losing side. Most of his white soldiers defected, and he was taken into custody.[86] Sutter soon convinced his captors he had only followed orders and soon was reinstated as military commander of the northern frontier.[87]

While traveling homeward through the San Joaquin Valley, he and his companions confiscated stolen horses from a party of Indians.[88] In April he informed Thomas Larkin, U.S. consul to California, that during the journey he had given a good deal of thought to the horse thieves and concluded that if tens of thousands of dollars were spent and thousands of Indians killed, the problem still would remain. If, however, the Mexican government allowed immigrants to freely occupy land in the interior, the Indian raiders would be brought under control. Sutter claimed the immigrants were an industrious, peaceful people.[89] By this time, their numbers had swelled to nearly seven hundred.[90]

Several immigrants gained the trust of Pio Pico, the new governor of California. In February, for example, John Marsh and John Gantt signed a contract with Pico allowing them to organize an expedition against the Indian stock raiders. If the governor deemed the campaign successful, Marsh and Gantt would receive five hundred head of cattle and half of all the horses taken from the Indians. The remaining horses and other property confiscated would be divided among the men recruited for the campaign.[91] General Castro informed Gantt that the Tachi, Nutunutu, Telamni, Heuchi, and three other Yokuts groups were friendly. Hostile Indians resided to the north on the Tuolumne and Merced rivers.[92] Marsh and Gantt failed to enlist the necessary number of volunteers for such a dangerous mission.[93]

Another immigrant, William Gulnac, acquired in 1843 a land grant at Campo de Los Franceses near the juncture of the Stanislaus and San Joaquin rivers. His first attempt to occupy the area met with failure. Peter Lausen remembered passing "through the place called French Camp. William Gulnac was with me and we had our cattle together. ... He was looking for a place to settle. I would not stop there because the Indians were unruly.... Gulnac was also afraid to stop there and I took his cattle on with me to the Cosumnes."[94]

A short time later Gulnac's partner, Charles Weber, departed for Sutter's Fort, apparently to make contact with José Jesus, chief of the Siakumne (Yokuts).[95] As described by a contemporary, José Jesus was "six foot tall, straight as an arrow, majestic forehead and deep, penetrating look."[96] Educated at Mission Santa Clara where he had served as alcalde, he dressed in the attire of a ranchero—cotton shirt and pants, sash, serape, and sombrero. He abandoned the mission for life in the interior and may have succeeded Estanislao as leader of all the Indians on the Stanislaus River, although the Siakumne were under his immediate authority. His principal village, Chaspaiseme, was located about thirty miles up the

Stanislaus from its juncture with the San Joaquin. The influence of José Jesus extended from the Mokelumne River in the north to the Tuolumne in the south.[97]

At the meeting, Weber and José Jesus forged an alliance that lasted

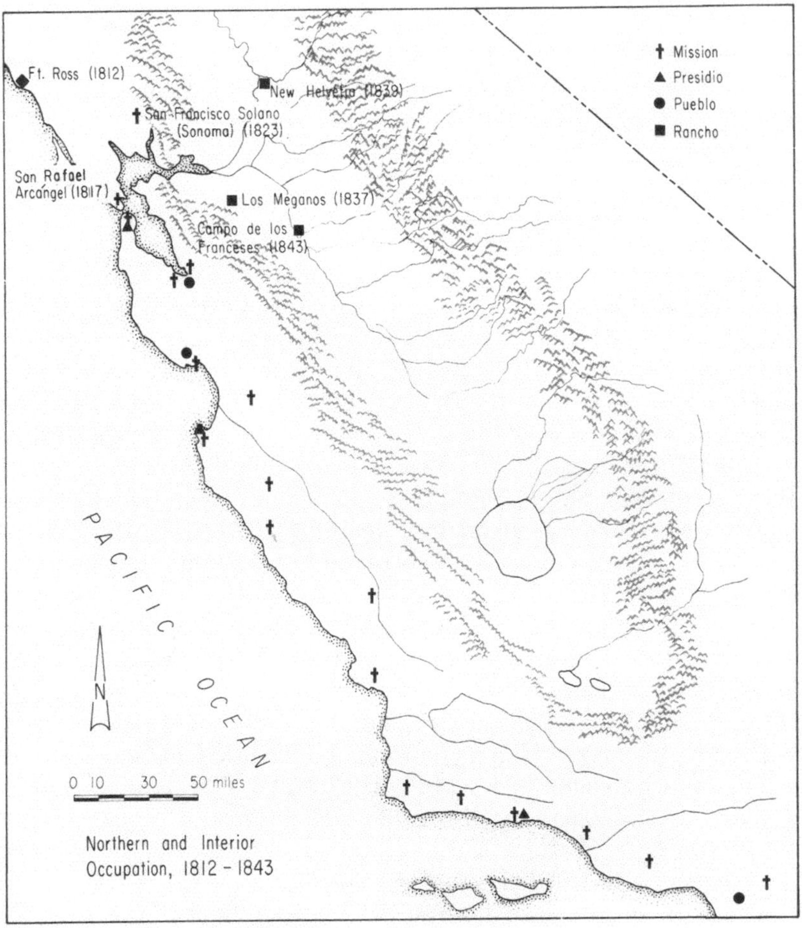

Northern and Interior Occupation, 1812 - 1843

for several years.[98] And with the friendship of the region's most powerful Indian guaranteed, Gulnac in August 1844 again attempted to establish a settlement at Campo de Los Franceses. He sent several persons, including a married couple with three daughters, to the rancho, but they soon fled because of smallpox. About two months later Thomas Lindsay returned to guard the stock. Locolumne (Yokuts) struck early the following year, killing Lindsay, setting fire to the buildings, and driving off the stock.[99] When Sutter located the Indians a few days after the attack, he must have been shocked at the ferocity of their response. The Locolumne killed his clerk, Juan Vaca, and wounded several of his men.[100] Thirty-six Locolumne may have died in the engagement.[101]

Because campaigns such as this were time-consuming and expensive, Sutter made a determined effort to solve his difficulties with local Indians. In June 1845 he wrote to Antonio Sunol: "I am negotiating a treaty with the principal leaders of the horse thieves, the object of which will be to put an end to their thefts, and have them come here in person. They send word that they would come if I pardoned them, which I have promised to do, and I expect them here in a short time. You may rest assured, sir, that my manner of treating with these Indians will result in much good to the country, and will be more efficacious than costly and pretentious campaigns that never meet with success."[102] Sutter's problems with Indians continued to mount, however. In July he received a letter from an American official in Oregon inquiring about the killing of Elijah. Upon retuning to the Columbia River, the Walla Walla told the official that they were willing to give up the horses not belonging to them on the condition that their property be returned and Grover Cook turned over to them or to the subagent.[103] Thomas Larkin wrote to the official, encouraging him to dissuade the Indians from returning to California. He feared the Indians would attack American settlers residing m the Sacramento Valley.[104]

The Mexican government became involved in the affair. In September the governor's secretary instructed the prefect of the district of Monterey to select a justice of the peace to investigate the killing and to bring those responsible to trial. The goods the Indians had left behind were to be secured and eventually returned to their owners. The justice could call upon the military for assistance. By this action the foreigners would learn that regardless of origin or position whoever "treads the Mexican soil" is "under the protection of our Laws."[105] Sutter, however, continued to defy Mexican law. On September 16, 1845 he tried for murder and executed Rufino, the leader of the neophytes residing on the Cosumnes.[106] Heleno took command of this group.[107] He maintained the economic relationship his people had established with Sutter.[108]

If the execution was intended to cow local Indians, it did not succeed. Stock raiders drove off some of Sutter's cattle in late December; the pursuit party recovered only part of the herd.[109] The setback may have prompted Sutter to meet with the two most powerful chiefs in the region—José Jesus and Polo, who was the leader of the Locolumne. Early in 1846 Sutter gave them gifts and issued them passports in Spanish and English. They, in turn, promised to assist him in campaigns against Indians continuing to steal stock, in particular the Muqueleme.[110] Thereafter, José Jesus and

Polo regularly visited New Helvetia, usually to deliver workers to Sutter.[111]

As Sutter's influence with local Indians grew, Mexican concerns increased. Sometime in May 1946 General José Castro encouraged the interior Indians to attack the immigrants. An American claimed the general had "made them promises of valuable presents if they would burn the crops and destroy the people."[112] Sutter was convinced that Castro had attempted "to revolutionize all the Indians against me."[113] He also suspected that a Muqueleme named Eusebio was in league with Castro. Apparently, the general addressed the Indian as "son" and "brother" and provided him with a gun.[114] The threat of attacks hindered Sutter's enterprise of providing Indian workers to various rancheros. He notified a friend in June that he could not send him workers because they feared to leave their families unprotected.[115]

In late May a party of Muqueleme made camp near New Helvetia. After meeting with local Indian leaders, who agreed not to interfere, the Muqueleme ran off a large herd of horses.[116] On June 1 Sutter wrote to M. G. Vallejo: "There has been another uprising among the Moquelumnes, and they have declared war against me. The roads are not safe for small parties from here to the pueblo of San José. In a few days I think of going out on a campaign, before they burn up our wheat, as some of the gentlemen at the pueblo of San José have advised them to do, and before Eusebio kills me with a firearm which he received at the pueblo from the said gentlemen."[117]

The campaign Sutter launched against the Muqueleme accomplished very little. One of the rafts capsized on the Mokelumne River; the whites lost ten rifles, six pistols, and a large supply of ammunition and clothing. An advance party located the Indians on the Calaveras River but suffered several casualties in the ensuing battle. When the remainder of Sutter's force arrived, the Indians retreated to the banks of the river, took cover among the dense brush, and continued the fight. Sutter claimed to have killed many Indians but acknowledged that "on account of having no more powder and balls, we found it very prudent to leave the Scene slowly, so that it appeared as [if] we wanted to Camp." Once out of sight of the Indians, the white men made a forced march back to New Helvetia.[118]

Sutter turned to Polo for help. He promised the Locolumne chief one hundred dollars in blankets, cotton twill, calico, and other items upon the delivery of Eusebio. In mid-June, Polo presented to Sutter the Indian's head.[119] Later, an American observed that "the gateway to the fort was ornamented with the scalp of an Indian, the long black hair hanging dejectedly down, as if mourning for the death of its late proprietor. I speak lightly of this scalp because it had been the property of an Indian who had been sent since my last visit—it was said by Castro—to burn the wheat crop of New Helvetica, and if possible to kill Captain Sutter himself. In endeavoring to put his nefarious purposes into practice he had met with his death, and his scalp was nailed to the outer-wall to deter others from engaging in similar undertakings."[120] But other Indians may have been hired to assassinate Sutter and to destroy his wheat fields.[121] The Indians of the Tulares would also pose a threat to American soldiers entering the valley.

CHAPTER VII

Americans Intervene

So frequent and devastating had Indian raids become by the middle of the 1840s that many rancheros no longer believed their government capable of solving the problem. At least this was the view held by Thomas Larkin, U.S. consul to California. He reported in July 1845 that the Californios refused to improve their lands, because "the Indians tame & wild steal several thousand head of Horses yearly." Without the requisite number of horses, cattle raising was unprofitable.[1] Early the following year Larkin complained that "the wild Indians are carrying off thousands of horses, and have shot with arrows, several people. Government appears to be doing nothing. If Mexico would command California as she ought to do, or let the people do it,... affairs would improve."[2] In April he claimed that "a considerable portion of the Californians are well aware, that their land and property would increase in value, by change of Flags! Some are quietly waiting the result.... The present deplorable state they are now in arising from the robbery of their Horses will hasten the result. They are convinced that a proper administration of affairs would put down the Indians."[3]

The following month the United States declared war on Mexico. In June, American settlers seized Sonoma, and in July, U.S. naval forces occupied Monterey and San Diego. Commodore Robert F. Stockton, commander of American military personnel in California, commissioned John Fremont a captain and placed him in command of the settlers. Eventually numbering over five hundred men, the California Battalion, in conjunction with U.S. Marines, occupied Los Angeles in August.[4]

By occupying the coastal zone, the American military assumed, inadvertently, the task of defending the pueblos, missions, and ranchos from Indian incursions. Always short of men, the military authorities called upon American setters and even Californios for assistance. Many Californios, however, had become resigned to losing stock and, according to Larkin, "seldom follow them to regain their property."[5] While the foreigner invariably pursues the Indians, asserted an anonymous writer, the Californio informs the local authorities and then "quietly submits to his loss.[6]

In late July, when Indians raided Mission Santa Clara, only two or three Californios joined the pursuit party.[7] Comprised mainly of Company A of the California Battalion, the party located Indian horse thieves in the Santa Cruz Mountains. The Indians escaped, but the soldiers recovered one hundred horses, which were returned to the owners. The editor of the *Californian*, the territory's first newspaper, predicted that the action "will go far to gain the confidence and respect of the Californians."[8] But he was not convinced the raiders had been properly chastised. The following week he argued that "the only effectual means of stopping their inroads upon the property of the country, will be to attack them in their villages, in the California Mountains."[9]

About the first of September a military force of some forty men moved against the stock raiders. Somewhere in the San Joaquin Valley, they killed and wounded several Indians and recovered one hundred horses. They remained in the field for two weeks, venturing farther into the interior than had previous American military units.[10] But no sooner had this command returned when Indians stole fifteen or twenty horses from ranchos in the vicinity of Mission San Carlos. The American military commander at Monterey provided horses for the six civilians who pursued the Indians. The *Californian* reported that the well-armed men expected to overtake the raiders before they reached the Tulares.[11]

Causing the American authorities considerable apprehension in early September 1846 was the rumor that one thousand Walla Walla were approaching New Helvetia, where they intended to take revenge for the killings of Yellow Serpent's son nearly two years before. Soldiers and volunteers quickly took up positions in strategic passes, as Californios and Americans braced for a major confrontation.[12] About fifty Indian soldiers and ten or twelve white men, under the command of Edward Kern, guarded Sutter's Fort.[13] On September 12 Lieutenant Joseph Warren Revere of the U.S. Navy and twenty-five men reinforced the local contingent.[14]

About fifty Walla Walla arrived at the fort. Yellow Serpent spoke with Revere:

> I have come from the forests of Oregon with no hostile intentions. You can see that I speak the truth, because I have brought with

> me only forty warriors, with their women and little children, and because I am here with few followers, and without arms. We have come to hunt the beasts of the field, and also to trade our horses for cattle; for my people require cattle, which are not so abundant in Oregon as in California. I have come, too, according to the custom of our tribes, to visit the grave of my poor son, Elijah, who was murdered by a white man.... When I came to California, I did not know that the Boston men had taken the country from the Spaniards. I am glad to hear it; for I have always been friendly to the Boston men, and have been kind to those who have passed through my territories. It must be plain to you that we did not set out on a hostile expedition against your countrymen.[15]

According to M. G. Vallejo the Walla Walla professed peaceful intentions only after observing American military power.[16]

Once that crisis was resolved, another developed. In September the Mexican inhabitants of Los Angeles, chafing under the arbitrary rule of their occupiers, rose in rebellion and drove the Americans from the pueblo.[17] The small U.S. contingent at Santa Bárbara abandoned its post a short time later.[18] Agustin Janssens recalled that the American garrison "crossed the mountains behind the mission to go down the Los Prietos Cañon."[19]

Mexican rebels and American soldiers badly needed horses. In October a party of one hundred Mexicans rounded up all the animals they could find, even old, sore-back, broken-down mares, near Mission San Carlos. They also took with them the Indian vaqueros in charge of the herds.[20] William Garner wrote in November that "the whole territory is now in a most pitiable state, both Americans and Californios having gathered into their possession all the horses they could find in the country. There is not a farm in the whole country at this present moment, that can boast of a horse or a saddle, unless they have secreted them in some place which has escaped the strictest searches of both parties."[21]

Entrusted with the task of crushing the uprising, John Fremont sought the assistance of immigrants and Indians.[22] John Sutter encouraged the Walla Walla to join the California Battalion and promised they would be paid for their services.[23] During a battle at Rancho Natividad, located a few miles northeast of Monterey, a contingent of thirty Mexican rebels attacked the Indians and a few Americans who had taken up positions in a grove of timber. As remembered by a participant in the fight, "the Walla Wallas were in their war dress and paint, which in itself was sufficient to strike terror to foes unused to such apparel; but when they jumped from behind the trees and scalped the one or two that they shot down, accompanied by their unearthly war-whoop, the Californians became utterly demoralized, and suddenly turned and never stopped running while in sight, not even to join their countrymen."[24]

Many years later, Sutter recalled that "the Walla Wallas brought back much spoils, trophies, clothing of the Mexicans they had killed."[25] After the battle Fremont instructed Edward Kern to tell Yellow Serpent, who remained at Sutter's Fort, that his men had fought bravely and that he would need them for another two months. Kern was to provide beef and flour to the families of the Walla Walla who served with the Americans.[26]

In mid-November a party of about twenty Americans departed Sutter's Fort for San José. Thirteen Indians, commanded by Antonio, joined them on the Mokelumne River and eighteen more, led by José Jesus, chief of the Siakumne (Yokuts), on the San Joaquin. The Indians were on foot and armed only with bows and arrows.[27] Subsequently, they received on loan thirty-two horses.[28] Under the command of José Jesus, they formed a separate company of the California Battalion.[29]

Before departing from Monterey for Los Angeles, Fremont left in the care of several friendly Californios over one hundred head of horses, including ninety with Francisco Pacheco. As reported by the *Californian*, "The Indians from the Tulares, who are always on the lookout, and besides, always get immediate information, when and where a quantity of horses may be found; could not resist the temptation, knowing as they do, that in this part of the country, at present, there is no force to follow them up, or otherwise injure them; accordingly in two or three days after Colonel Fremont had left these horses, and several others, which he had been kind enough to distribute amongst those individuals, who were most in need of them, they came down, and swept off every horse they could find, leaving the farmers entirely destitute of the means of carrying on their agricultural business."[30]

Had Fremont's battalion not been drawn south to quell the uprising in Los Angeles, reasoned William Garner, it would have put an end to Indian depredations.[31] The *Californian* drew the same conclusion.[32] But the Indian raiders may have inadvertently assisted the Americans. Although the Californios in the San Luís Obispo area supported the uprising, they feared to leave their ranchos. "The Indians might come to steal, burn, and commit such other deviltries as might occur to them," insisted Agustin Janssens.[33]

Los Angeles was retaken on January 10, 1847, and three days later the remaining Mexican forces surrendered to Fremont in the San Fernando Valley.[34] The coastal zone, from Sonoma in the north to San Diego in the south, came under the jurisdiction of an American military government. The military officials, however, had no governing experience and little precedent upon which to rule. Initially, the commander of U.S. forces served as governor. Appointed by the president and supported by the military, he possessed, at least in theory, enormous power and independence. But the laws and customs of war and orders from his superiors restricted his authority. Always short of financial support and military personnel and well aware that he would hold office only for a short time, the military governor of California ruled on an ad hoc basis.[35]

How to curtail the incursions of the Indian stock raiders became a major concern of the new government. In March 1847 Colonel Richard B. Mason wrote to General Stephen Watts Kearny, the military governor, claiming that there was no need to station troops at the pueblo of San José. They would be useless against the stock raiders who "come in small parties of two or three from different directions, meet at some preconcerted place & commence their operations, carrying off 200 or 300 head of stock." Instead, he recommended that detachments be stationed on the west bank of the San Joaquin River and at the passes through which the raiders must travel with the stolen stock. Mason suggested that the soldiers guarding the pass near Mission San Juan Bautista be augmented with about thirty mounted Californios who would serve for twelve months.[36]

Recently, Indians had raided ranchos in the area, not only stealing stock but also firing arrows at those who stood in their way. José Maria Sanchez, alcalde of San Juan Bautista, informed the governor about the attacks, pointing out that his people were without arms and ammunition and requesting that Kearny "put a remedy to the affair."[37] Kearny outlined his "remedy" in a letter to the Secretary of War: "I am of the opinion that much good might be done by making a few presents to them." He requested that medals, red flannels, colored handkerchiefs, tobacco, and a few colored blankets be shipped to him.[38]

Because of the incessant Indian raids most Americans and many Californios must have welcomed the one thousand soldiers who sailed into San Francisco Bay in March. Known as the New York Volunteers and commanded by Colonel Jonathan D. Stevenson, the unit arrived too late to participate in the war with Mexico. Subsequently, one of the companies was stationed at Sonoma, two at the Presidio of San Francisco, two at Monterey, three at Santa Bárbara, and two at Los Angeles.[39]

Stationing most of the companies at coastal localities made no sense to many residents, and in April the *California Star* lashed out at the government's policy: "Cannot the authorities do something for the protection of the frontier, and will they not do something? Will the government not listen to the complaints of the citizens; and will the large number of government troops now here, be kept idle along the coast, without any prospect of being either of territorial or national benefit, when the Indians are continually committing depredations along the whole line of the eastern frontier, and when they are penetrating the settlements to almost within sight of the Capital of the territory, plundering and killing the inhabitants."[40] A member of the New York Volunteers echoed this criticism: "The present disposition of the troops is of no real service to the country. They are stationed in comfortable and quiet quarters in towns where they are least wanted, and the thieving Indians are allowed to make nightly excursions into the settlements, and to infest the roads."[41]

As the stock raiders became more aggressive, the size of their raiding parties increased, sometimes numbering between one and two hundred men.[42] John Marsh believed the Indians had become more daring because the numbers of animals on the ranchos had decreased. Writing to the *Star* in early April under the nom de plume Agricola, Marsh recounted that during the past month the Indians had "shot and dangerously wounded four persons employed on the farm of Mr. Weber near the Pueblo of St. Joseph, and at the same time stole the horses of the farm, and those also from the farm of Capt. Fisher and Mr. Burnal in the same vicinity; in all above two hundred head. Within the last ten days, numerous parties of them have been committing depredations on many of the farms in the jurisdiction of the Contra Costa, and scarcely a night passes but we hear of their having stolen horses from some one."[43]

In another letter to the *Star*, Marsh predicted that if the raids were not curtailed the economic ramifications would be disastrous. He questioned whether the rancheros could honor their accounts to merchants "when the horse thieves are taking away the last of the miserable remnant of broken down horses, that the wars and revolutions have left behind." He acknowledged that "the people of San Francisco will take little or no interest in this subject, as they may think themselves and their property safe in their shops and on board their ships." But they will look in vain "for hides and tallow, or other produce of the country, if the farmers have no horses with which to manage their cattle."[44]

Marsh also reported that six white men from Los Angeles soon would take up residence with José Jesus and his ally, Felipe, Indians he considered to be horse thieves. Apparently, the Indians had invited the men to join them while serving together in the California Battalion. The whites possessed trade goods they intended to exchange for horses.[45] The editor of the *Star*, however, challenged Marsh's conclusions: "We feel entirely certain that those Indians who marched to the Pueblo de los Angeles in the battalion of Col. Fremont, have been connected in none of the thefts and outrages recently committed.... We have indubitable proof of this assertion, and therefore speak positively. They are entirely and wholly friendly to the Americans, and with proper treatment, will render most efficient service in ferreting out and bringing to punishment the wild, hostile, and thieving tribes which inhabit the western slope of the Sierra Nevada."[46]

Under increasing pressure to extend its authority to the interior, the military government attempted to regulate Indian activity through diplomatic means. In early April, upon the recommendation of Thomas

Larkin, Governor Kearny appointed John Sutter Indian subagent for the Indians residing near the Sacramento and San Joaquin rivers. Kearny instructed him to "explain to the Indians the change in the administration of public affairs in this Territory; that they must now look to the President of the United States as their great father; that he takes good care of his good children; that the officers now here are acting under his orders and instructions; that the Americans and Californians are now one people, and any offenses which they may commit against the latter will be punished in the same way as if committed against the former."[47] Sutter informed Kearny in mid-May that the Indians residing in the vicinity of his fort long ago had ceased raiding and had taken up farming. He predicted that shortly local Indians would harvest fine crops of corn, pumpkins, and melons. Some had planted wheat. Soon he would invite distant chiefs to visit his fort, where they would learn about the intentions of the new government. Sutter promised to punish those who failed to appear.[48]

On May 22 Cornelio and Carlos, chiefs of the Tauhalame (Yokuts), and the leaders of three other groups arrived at New Helvetia. Sutter gave them provisions and passports.[49] Cornelio and Carlos promised to cease stealing stock and trading with horse thieves. Aware that a military expedition soon was to enter the interior, Sutter cautioned the government against attacking the Tauhalame. He thought they would be useful in subduing the Chauchila and Pitkachi (Yokuts).[50] On May 27 he wrote to Kearny, recommending that force be used against these Indians.[51]

The previous month Kearny had made preparations to send a contingent of the New York Volunteers, under Captain Henry Naglee, into the interior to punish the stock raiders. He also sought to recruit thirty Californios for the campaign.[52] Kearny turned to M. G. Vallejo for help in this matter, and the prominent Californio recruited twelve men in Sonoma. At Santa Clara, Vallejo encouraged local Californios to join, but only ten volunteered. He informed Kearny that many could not participate because the Americans had not returned their weapons and because they had no horses.[53]

Naglee and sixteen men arrived at Mission San Juan Bautista on May 24, where they were joined by Lieutenant Philip Burton, and a few Californios.[54] Following the advice of John Sutter they entered Tauhulame territory and met Carlos, who escorted them south to the Merced. Captain Naglee sent Carlos, a lieutenant, and eight men to make contact with the Chauchila. When the party returned, the lieutenant accused Carlos of deliberately leading him in circles.[55]

Following the San Joaquin River upstream to the mountains, they contacted Tomquit, leader of the Pitkachi, and thirty of his followers. The Indians sought to trade horses and bows and arrows for what items the soldiers and volunteers possessed. When Tomquit offered Naglee three very fine animals, the captain, suspecting they had been stolen, declined. Offended by the refusal, the Indian was mollified somewhat when presented with a shirt and a pair of pantaloons. On June 18 the party headed back to Monterey. Although he gained some geographical knowledge and met a few Indians, Naglee accomplished very little. No Indians were punished; no animals were recovered.[56]

Shortly before Naglee returned to the coast, Yellow Serpent and several Walla Walla visited New Helvetia. They had yet to be paid for their services during the Mexican-American War and sought a meeting with John Frémont. Kearny, Frémont, and a large party were then passing through the area on their way to Washington, D.C. After visiting the camp of the Americans, the Walla Walla returned to Sutter's Fort, delivering to Edward Kern orders from Fremont to pay them in horses.[57] Evidently, they received about one hundred head.[58]

While Kearny and Frémont were in the interior, a rumor reached Monterey that they had lost horses to Indian raiders. The Californian regretted the loss but suggested that "it may be productive of much good; for if those two officers, both experienced in Indian character, with forty of the best mountaineers, could not prevent the Indians from stealing their horses, it is not to be expected that the Rancher's (sic) on a border of six hundred miles can protect their Ranches.... It is to be hoped, if Gen. Kearny had been robbed, that it will show the authorities the propriety of establishing military posts along the Tulare Valley in such a manner as to prevent this band of thieves from entering the settlements and carrying off such bands of horses as they have been in the habit of doing heretofore."[59]

Kearny's party, consisting of sixty-four persons, had lost no animals to Indians.[60] By commenting on the rumor perhaps the *Californian* sought to goad Colonel Richard B. Mason, the new military governor, into taking a more active role in curtailing Indian incursions.[61] In early June, William Dana pleaded with Mason to send troops to San Luís Obispo. Local citizens were helpless against Indian raiders, who were carrying off droves of horses. If the government failed to act promptly, Dana feared the rancheros would be forced to abandon their lands.[62]

A single company of the New York Volunteers was then stationed in the northern interior: one platoon at Sonoma, another at Sutter's Fort.[63] But the soldiers stationed at the fort failed in any appreciable way to reinforce Sutter's authority as Indian subagent. As two incidents clearly indicate, Sutter was virtually helpless in preventing disputes between Indians and whites. On July 10 two Californios entered a Yalesumne (Nisenan) village on Webber Creek, located about twenty miles northeast of the fort, appropriated a band of horses a military officer had left there, and whipped the headman, Shulule. Sutter issued orders for the arrest of the two men, but they were never apprehended.[64]

Shortly before this incident occurred, Antonio Maria Armijo, John

Eggar, and Robert Smith massacred thirteen Indians at a village located some sixty miles north of the fort; they also took thirty-seven captives.[65] As recounted by a resident of New Helvetia, the captives, mostly women and children, were "tied together and driven to the settlements. Young children who were unable to proceed were murdered on the road. In one instance an infant was taken from its mother, and killed in her presence, and that too in the most brutal manner."[66]

In a letter to the governor Sutter asked how he was to act in this case.[67] Mason replied on July 21: "I beg that you will use every exertion to cause the guilty persons to be arrested, for which purpose you will call on the military officer near you for all the assistance in his power to afford.... When arrested, I will organize a tribunal for their trial; and if sentence of death is passed upon them, will have it executed.... The Indians that have been captured you must at once seize, by any means in your power, and restore them to their people: tell them that these atrocious acts have been committed by lawless scoundrels,..and that the perpetrators of the outrages shall be made a public example of."[68] Mason also wrote to Lieutenant Charles Anderson, commander of the military force at New Helvetia, ordering him to give Sutter whatever assistance he needed in apprehending the murderers.[69]

Governor Mason appointed Sutter and M. G. Vallejo special judges to try, at or near New Helvetia, Armijo, Eggar, and Smith for the murder and enslavement of Indians.[70] Vallejo was subagent for the Indians residing north of San Francisco Bay.[71] Mason, however, moved the venue to Sonoma and appointed Lilburn W. Boggs to serve as judge.[72] Sutter failed to attend the trial, which was held in October. The accused were acquitted.[73]

Prior to the trial a military officer wrote to Sutter, further explaining the government's Indian policy: "Let them understand that while the government will punish them for their depredations, it will also protect them and their property from injury by the whites. Tell them that if any ill disposed person should do them injury they must complain of it to you, and not themselves attempt to inflict punishment, or to retaliate upon the offenders. The government will always be ready to do ample justice to the Indians, and will redress all their wrongs; but it cannot permit them to take this matter into their own hands."[74]

Sutter was encouraged to write frequently to the governor regarding "the best measures to be adopted for the government of the Indians and for the security of their quiet and happiness." Sutter was to collect information about the Indian societies within his district. Of particular interest to the authorities were means of subsistence, forms of government, and modes of warfare.[75] In December Sutter responded to the request, transmitting statistical information concerning Indians located east of the San Joaquin and Sacramento rivers. He calculated that in his jurisdiction resided 478 neophytes and 21,873 gentiles.[76]

The limited number of neophytes was reflected in the labor shortage then affecting New Helvetia. In September, Sutter complained to William Leidesdorff that he had work for two hundred Indians, but sometimes only twenty or twenty-five were available. The time had passed, he lamented, when he could depend on Indians.[77] Sutter later informed his friend that soon he would lose a large quantity of wheat.[78]

While Sutter lost workers, other rancheros lost stock. In late August Indians stole horses from the ranchos in the vicinity of San José. The following month a military officer informed the alcalde of the pueblo that "an expedition will start for the Tulares as soon as it can be fitted out, to look after these thieving Indians, and to adopt such measures as may check for a time their depredations."[79] Captain Henry Naglee of the New York Volunteers was given command of the expedition. He was to search to the very limits of the territory controlled by the stock raiders. Indians found with stolen horses were to be brought to the coast where they would be properly punished. His command was to travel light and, if necessary, remain in the field for fifty days.[80]

In a gorge in the Sierra Nevada, Naglee confronted Indians who denied participating in recent raids. They claimed another group was responsible. Located a few days later, its leaders also professed innocence. One of the soldiers recounted to William Redmond Ryan what transpired. Naglee told the chiefs that he did not believe them; they were all of the same colour, and, therefore, all thieves and murderers alike; and he should insist upon the culprits being given up. Again the chiefs remonstrated and protested against the injustice that had been done them; it was in vain: for the Captain commanded some of the men to take the chiefs into custody.... "Black Jack" [Naglee] pointed to a small space that had been recently cleared, and a firing-party took up its position there.... The two chiefs then folded their arms, and deliberately stalked to the place of execution—of murder, rather—exhibiting the greatest unconcern, whilst the few men of the tribe looked on in the same impassive manner. In less than another minute all was over, and the two chiefs lay stretched on the ground stone dead.[81]

Before his execution, one of the chiefs instructed his son, Chechee, to avenge his death.[82] And Indians harassed Naglee's command as it departed the area, firing volleys of arrows but causing no harm.[83] When the soldiers arrived at Monterey, Governor Mason placed Naglee under arrest for murdering Indians. He was released early the following year for military duty in Baja California.[84]

Naglee's expedition failed to deter the stock raiders. In December 1847 Locolumne (Yokuts) struck at ranchos in the Livermore Valley and in the Mount Diablo area.[85] John Marsh lost most of his animals.[86] A short time later Charles Weber received permission from the alcalde of San José to raise a party to punish the thieves.[87] Weber turned to his ally, José Jesus, for assistance, the Siakumne leader providing most of the two hundred men who formed the expedition. In February 1848 Weber and José Jesus located the raiders on the Calaveras River, killed a few, and rounded up the stolen horses.[88] The fight may have turned José Jesus and Polo, chief of the Locolumne, into bitter enemies. Polo insisted on stealing horses from the immigrants; José Jesus sought to remain at peace with them.[89]

In January 1848 Mexico ceded California (and the rest of the Southwest) to the United States, and the military authorities now had to protect American territory. Commanding badly undermanned and poorly equipped troops, they increasingly turned to their former enemies, the Californios, for assistance. In mid-February 1848, Colonel Jonathan Stevenson placed Andres Pico in charge of defending the ranchos between Los Angeles and Santa Bárbara. He ordered Pico to identify those men at each rancho capable of fighting Indians and to list the number of weapons they possessed. Those who refused to comply were to be fined ten to twenty-five dollars."[90]

This hastily formed alliance of rancheros and soldiers soon was tested. On the night of February 20, Indians struck at several ranchos in the Santa Bárbara area, including one only two miles from the military barracks. The following day ten soldiers and a few Californios, who received ammunition from the Americans, went in pursuit.[91] They recovered some thirty horses, and on a ridge in the nearby mountains discovered a few huts and a corral the Indians had constructed. The leader of the Californios considered it unwise to pursue the Indians farther, and they returned to Santa Bárbara.[92] While they were gone, another band of Indians attacked two parties of whites only a few miles from Santa Bárbara, wounding one or two persons.[93]

By supplying ammunition to the Californios the military authorities took considerable risk. Needing their support but fearing treachery, the Americans proceeded cautiously. In March 1848 the alcalde of San Luís Obispo, John Price, reported to Governor Mason that because they lacked ammunition local citizens were helpless against the Indians who recently had stolen stock from the area. Mason suggested that the alcalde organize a party of thirty men to move against the Indians on a moment's notice. He promised to deliver twenty-five or thirty pounds of powder and a proportionate quantity of lead. But he cautioned Price to ensure "that this ammunition is not applied to improper purposes; that it is taken care of, and only used for the service for which it is intended."[94]

In late February an Indian stock raider was captured near Santa Bárbara. Convinced that his life would be spared if he disclosed the whereabouts and strength of his band, he told Captain Francis J. Lippsitt, the local military commander, that three hundred to four hundred Indians resided on the margin of a small lake in the southern Tulare Valley. The corral they had built sometimes contained one thousand horses, but presently it held only two hundred. Some of the Indians were armed with rifles and pistols. Lippsitt identified the village as La Punta de la Laguna.[95]

Lippsitt and Pedro Carrillo, the alcalde of Santa Bárbara, attempted to form a joint command to attack the village. Lippsitt offered the alcalde ammunition to distribute to the Californios in exchange for the use of their horses. The Californios held two or three meetings, but those belonging to one faction refused to contribute their quota of men as long as Carrillo commanded the party. Lippsitt decided to send thirty soldiers against the Indians if the Californios provided horses and guides. The horses could not be obtained, and the mission was cancelled.[96]

In early April, Colonel Stevenson authorized Francisco Noriega of Santa Bárbara to raise a volunteer force for a campaign against the Indians.[97] But this may have been an unwise appointment, because Pedro Carrillo suspected Noriega of plotting to seize the American barracks. Supposedly, another party of Californios, organized in Los Angeles, was to join Noriega's group or attack the local military post or the one at San Diego.[98] Whether the Californios actually conspired against the Americans or whether Carrillo issued his accusations for personal or political purposes is not known. The plan to assemble a force of volunteers evidently was canceled.

Although the American military authorities attempted to recruit Californios in their campaigns against the Indian raiders, using friendly Indians for the same purpose was not considered. In late April 1848 José Jesus visited San José, seeking permission from Charles White, the alcalde, to attack some of his Indian neighbors who were constantly committing depredations. White told him the government would not sanction Indians waging war. If attacked José Jesus had the right to defend himself, but all prisoners had to be brought to San José.[99] White issued him passports so he and his delegation could travel unmolested throughout the district, a decision that angered local Californios.[100]

Once he returned to the interior José Jesus held two meetings with five or six Indian leaders and launched a campaign against an enemy group, probably the Muqueleme (Miwok). In July he informed White that he would arrive the following month with women and children captives. White reported this information to Governor Mason, suggesting the friendship of José Jesus "may be used to advantage."[101]

At this juncture Mason faced enormous problems. Gold had been discovered in January 1848, accelerating the occupation of California by Americans and others and intensifying the violence between Indians and whites. Because gold was found near New Helvetia but outside the boundaries of his grant, John Sutter immediately sought to acquire legal title from local Indians.[102] On February 4 Gesu and Pulpule (chiefs) and Colule and Sole (alcaldes) of the Yalesumne, leased to Sutter and his partner, James Marshall, a tract of land on Weber Creek near its entrance to the south branch of the American River. The lessees received the right to cut timber, erect a sawmill, cultivate the land, and open mines.[103]

In return Sutter and Marshall promised to construct two millstones to grind the Indians' grain. Every year on the first day of January, Sutter and Marshall would present to the chiefs clothing and tools worth $150. At the end of twenty years, the land would revert to the Indians, who would pay a reasonable sum for the stones and other improvements.[104] Sutter may have used his position as Indian subagent to convince the Yalesumne that all the provisions in the lease would be honored.[105] Apparently, the Indians agreed not to kill Sutter's horses, cattle, hogs, and sheep and not to burn the grass in the limits fixed by the lease.[106]

The lease was delivered to Governor Mason for approval. In an accompanying letter, Sutter claimed the Yalesumne would benefit greatly from the arrangement. They would be protected from their enemies to the north, furnished with food and clothing, and taught the "habits of industry." Moreover, by providing protection to immigrants, the settlement would advance the occupation of the foothills of the Sierra Nevada.[107] Mason voided the contract because the United States did not recognize the right of Indians to sell or lease the lands on which they resided. Mason informed Sutter that should the federal government extinguish title to Indian land, it would become part of the public domain. Private claims made at the present time would only complicate matters.[108]

Word of the gold discovery quickly spread. By the end of May half the eight hundred residents of San Francisco had departed for the gold mines; three-fourths had left by the middle of June.[109] Gold fever also spread to the military. By August twenty-six soldiers at Sonoma, twenty-four at San Francisco, and the same number at Monterey had deserted.[110] In November, Governor Mason wrote to the adjutant general of the United States, complaining that "so long as the gold mines continue to yield the great abundance of metal they now do, it will be impossible to keep soldiers in California, and it is of no use to send them here. Soldiers will not serve for seven and eight dollars per month when laborers and mechanics are getting from fifty to one hundred." Mason predicted that unless a civil government was organized at once "anarchy and confusion will arise, and murder, robbery, and all sorts of crime will be committed with impunity in the heterogeneous and mixed community that now fills California."[111]

Mason did not exaggerate the problem. Unruly individuals from several nations took up residence not just in the mines but also in the coastal towns, where they caused difficulties for the local authorities. In mid-March 1849 William Garner informed Mason that San Luís Obispo had become a "refuge for criminals and vagabonds of every description, there existing no person here in authority to restrain or arrest them."[112]

Indian stock raiders contributed to the chaos. Garner told Mason that "Indian horse thieves have been hovering about the farms and plundering almost daily for the last seventeen days." Local rancheros were virtually defenseless because they had no ammunition.[113] And when many of its residents fled to the mines, San Luis Obispo became especially vulnerable. According to General Bennett Riley, the new governor of California, Indians took advantage of the absence of male inhabitants to "become more daring in their incursions. Depredations are more frequent than formerly."[114]

William Garner was one of those who left San Luís Obispo defenseless. In April he led a party of fifty Californios to the Kings River where Indians reportedly had obtained large amounts of gold. For several days they camped on the south side of the river but found no evidence that local Indians possessed the metal. Garner and five men ventured upstream to a village but were driven off. A few days later he retuned with twenty men, but the Indians had burned their lodges and were nowhere to be seen.[115] The full contingent journeyed north, making camp on May 14 on the Fresno River in the territory of the Chauchila.[116] Garner wrote in his journal that "we have travelled about twenty miles today, the number of Indians around us have increased every hour for the last three days, and now number over a thousand—most of them have gold which is generally coarse, and to my enquires of them where they obtained it, they pointed to the Eastward. There is a great stir among the Indians, and their squaws and children have left. I have now the greatest fears for my safety."[117]

On the fifteenth, Garner led seven men to a village in the mountains, where he was greeted by an Indian, Ventura, who had been raised in Monterey. While engaging him in conversation Ventura shot and killed Garner; Indians also killed six of the seven Californios. The one who escaped rejoined his companions, and they fled to the coast.[118]

On May 4, 1849, shortly before the murders, Assistant Adjutant General Edward R. S. Canby sent Major Anthony S. Miller and a battalion of the Second Infantry to the main crossing of the San Joaquin River. Miller was to select a site where a fort would be constructed.[119] A few days later Canby issued further instructions: "Unauthorized interference with the Indians by the whites must, if possible, be prevented; and, on the other hand, the Indians will receive, through their agent, assurances of protection, if their conduct be such as to merit it; they will be advised to remain quiet in the pursuit of their ordinary occupations, and, when aggrieved, to make their complaints to the proper authorities; that any attempt to revenge themselves for fancied or real injuries will not be permitted, and that the offenders will in every instance be sought out and severely punished." If Indians committed crimes, Miller was to promptly arrest them, and if not promptly delivered he was to hold the entire group responsible for their conduct. Suspecting that the Indians most likely to cause trouble resided on the Merced, Canby instructed Miller to send detachments to the river for the purpose of "overawing these Indians, or punishing them for any outrages they may commit."[120]

In response to the deaths of Garner and his companions, Canby ordered Lieutenant Clarendon Wilson and a detachment of dragoons to the Kings River, where the murders were thought to have taken place. He was to apprehend those responsible or "seize the chief or head men of the tribe or rancheria to which they belonged." With his prisoners Wilson was to proceed to Major Miller's camp.[121] Once aware that no murders had been committed on the Kings River, Wilson journeyed northwards, passing through the territories of the Tachi, Nutunutu, and Wimilchi (Yokuts) and speaking with several of their leaders. In his report Wilson noted that the Indians "appear to be but little inclined to wander and have neither horses nor cattle at their Rancherias, but are said to have concealed in the Sierra Nevada large numbers of the former stolen from the settlements on the coast."[122]

At the encampment of Major Miller, Wilson learned that those responsible for the murders, the Chauchila, had withdrawn into the mountains. Wilson concluded that the Indians killed Garner and his men to deter others from entering an area rich in gold.[123] Governor Riley, however, theorized that Indians killed Garner "to revenge themselves for the aggressions committed by Americans upon the Indians of the Sacramento; indicating an evident understanding between different tribes speaking different languages, and separated by a distance of two hundred and fifty miles."[124]

Indian resistance already had begun in the gold-bearing regions. "The difficulties with the Indians are beginning to assume a more and more menacing character," exclaimed the *Alta California* in early May, "and sound policy would seem to dictate the propriety of sending bodies of troops into the disturbed districts.... This state of affairs is deeply to be regretted, and what is worse, it is believed generally, that it will to a great extent, prevent the successful working of the mines the present season."[125]

In early July 1849 Governor Riley led a few men into the interior, pausing for a time at Major Miller's camp on the San Joaquin River.[126] On the twenty-second he wrote to the assistant adjutant general of U.S. forces in California recommending that a military post be established on the Kings River. He was alarmed that the miners prospecting on the Merced, Stanislaus, and Tuolumne rivers were driving the Indians southwards to the headwaters of the San Joaquin and Kings rivers. The Indians residing on the rivers, "with the exception of two or three tribes, have given evidence of the most friendly disposition towards the Americans. The country bordering on these rivers is rich in minerals, and the population now in the southern mines is moving to the south, and the close contact that must result will inevitably lead to many aggressions committed by one party upon the other. It is important that our own citizens be protected against Indian hostilities; and the dictates of policy, as well as humanity, require that the Indians should be secured against the aggressions of the whites."[127]

Riley, in mid-October, wrote a long letter to the adjutant general of the U.S. Army, pointing out the legal difficulties he faced in California. The laws of the United States regulating intercourse with Indians implied an Indian territory over which Congress exercised exclusive control, but no such territory existed in California. He feared that once California achieved statehood, federal and state authorities would compete over Indian jurisdiction.[128]

Riley recommended "that the title of the Indians to the lands which they are in actual occupancy be immediately recognized by Congress and that measures be taken to remove them from the immediate vicinity of the White Settlements and to establish them in some suitable location to the east of the Sierra Nevada." If such a location could not be found, he suggested the area between Buena Vista and Tulare lakes and the Sierra Nevada be set aside for a reservation. A site on the Russian River north of San Francisco Bay also was recommended. Indians would be confined at these two locations "until sufficient time has elapsed to make some permanent arrangement."[129]

The governor concluded his letter with a plea that the Indians be treated with humanity to prevent further demoralization and that "provision should also be made for their support until they are so far civilized as to be able to support themselves wholly or in great part ... by the cultivations of the soil." Unless such efforts were undertaken immediately, Riley predicted that Indians soon would be surrounded by whites and would either starve to death or seize property. And "the commission of these depredations will be the pretense for the commencement of a war of extermination."[130]

In April 1850 Assistant Adjutant General Edward R. S. Canby ordered First Lieutenant George H. Derby of the Corps of Topographical Engineers to reconnoiter the Tulare Valley and select a spot for a military post on the east side of Lake Tulare, among the Nutunutu if possible. "The objectives to be attained in making this establishment," explained Canby, "will be the protection of the frontier east of San Luís Obispo from Indian incursions, and the control of the Indians inhabiting the borders of the lakes and slopes of the Sierra Nevada, east and north of those lakes." Derby was to report on the condition of the passes leading from the coast into the valley, to select a route by which supplies could be sent into the interior, and to report on the resources and geology of the country traversed. Difficulties with the Indians were not anticipated, but Derby was to maintain vigilance and never be "beyond the reach of assistance. You will see that the Indians whom you meet are treated kindly by your party, but you will not suffer them to remain in large parties about your camp."[131]

Departing from Monterey on April 10, Derby, eight soldiers of the engineers, and an Indian guide, escorted by a company of infantry commanded by Lieutenant Treadwell Moore, journeyed first to San Miguel and then to San Luís Obispo before entering the Tulare Valley. The expedition arrived at the southern end of Tulare Lake on May 4. Indians, led by a Spanish-speaking neophyte from Mission San Luís Obispo, ferried the soldiers across a slough on rafts made from tules. The headman possessed bits of paper on which were written statements of praise by Californios and Americans. Derby gave him a certificate stating that he had treated the soldiers with kindness.[132]

That night the soldiers camped at another village, where they exchanged dried bread for dried fish. The headman, a neophyte from Mission San Miguel, told Derby that his people formed part of the Tachi, which numbered eight hundred persons. They were peaceful and had never stolen or eaten horseflesh, he insisted. The soldiers continued to the east side of Tulare Lake, where they established a base camp. On May 7 Derby and his contingent left the infantry in camp and proceeded north to a village of the Telamni. Derby spotted several horses and skeletons of animals and warned the villagers that if they continued to steal from the whites they would be severely punished. In his report Derby admitted that he "made but little impression upon them, and I was unable to obtain from any of them the name of their captain, or the entire number of the tribe. After remaining about an hour at the rancheria we returned to camp, having asked two or three who spoke Spanish to accompany us, which invitation they declined. I suspected that nothing but our numbers and the well-armed condition of the party prevented our being treated with incivility." Derby turned back and arrived at the Kern River on the ninth. Three days later, he rejoined Lieutenant Moore.[133]

Informed by a white man traveling south that the Indians to the north posed no threat, Derby dispensed with the services of Moore, sending his detachment back to Monterey. Derby and his group headed north to the Four Creeks, where crossings would have been difficult without "the kind assistance of the neighboring Indians who flocked to meet us, and eagerly went to work carrying instruments and other property upon their heads, and swimming the animals and the little cart across without the slightest accident occurring." The Indians accompanied the soldiers "from creek to creek, assisting us cheerfully at each crossing, and in return for their kindness I gave them a portion of our provisions and some dirty shirts, stockings and worn-out boots which they prized as articles of exceeding luxury, and accepted with vast satisfaction." The Americans passed through the territories of two distinct societies. The Yokod, governed by Echa, occupied the southern creeks. The Gawia, commanded by Francisco, a neophyte from Mission San Luís Obispo, were located along the upper creeks. Among the four hundred residents of the two groups, Derby observed many neophytes from Missions San Juan Bautista, San Miguel Arcangel, and San Luís Obispo.[134]

On May 17 the soldiers arrived at the Kings River, Derby estimating that some three thousand Indians located in seventeen villages resided in the area. Those situated on the lower part of the river were "friendly and well disposed towards the whites; those high up among the hills are entirely ignorant, treacherous, and mischievous." Derby encountered two white men operating a ferry and from them learned that, five miles upstream two other white men were in the same business. Ferrymen provided an important service to immigrants heading for the gold fields.[135]

With permission from Chiefs Pasqual, Antonio, and Francisco, Oscar Field had founded the upstream ferry in December 1849 near a Choinimni village.[136] Although the Choinimni had used Field's horses without his permission and on one occasion attempted to ferry some Sonorans across the river in his boat, relations between the ferrymen and the Indians remained cordial until shortly before Derby's arrival.[137] On May 5, 1850 the Choinimni stole from Field gold dust, coin, treasury notes, two gold watches, flour, pork, sugar, dried apples, calicoes, and other items, in all worth seven thousand dollars.[138] A few days later, Chiefs Antonio and Francisco returned to Field some of the stolen articles.[139]

While Derby was exploring the surrounding area, Indians ordered the whites at the downstream ferry to vacate the area in four days. The ferrymen, however, were not alarmed, Derby wrote in his report, because "the knowledge that a body of troops were soon to be stationed in their neighborhood, had a very salutary restraining effect upon these Indians, who, I believe, would become exceeding troublesome if they had no dread of the consequences."[140]

On the nineteenth Derby followed the Kings River downstream into the territory of the Nutunutu, where he intended to establish a military post. Because the area consisted largely of tule marshland, he immediately abandoned the plan. But if the land did not impress him, the Indians did: "The No-tantoes are the finest looking Indians I have met with in the valley. All that came over to our encampment were large well-built athletic men, nearly six feet high.... Their captain was an old Indian named Antonio. He had certificates of recommendation from Colonel Mason and others, which, by his friendly appearance and offers of assistance to the extent of his abilities, appeared to be well merited. He stated the number of

No-tantoes at about three hundred."[141]

The following day the soldiers marched north. A week later they crossed the San Joaquin River, turned west across the northern edge of the lake, and headed south to a Tachi village situated on the western extremity of the lake.[142] The village, Walna, consisted of forty very large lodges built of tules, each capable of accommodating ten to fifteen persons. The chief of the Tachi, Quintin, a brawny man with five wives, lived in a lodge which could accommodate twenty persons.[143] Between 250 and 300 Tachi resided in the village. The few Indians who visited Derby's camp, two of whom spoke Spanish, were pleased with the treatment they received.[144]

Taking the route that brought them into the interior, the soldiers returned to Monterey on June 8. In his report Derby estimated the number of Indians in the Tulare Valley at about four thousand. "Those who have had an opportunity of becoming acquainted with the whites, are friendly and well-disposed; the others, although ignorant, mischievous and perhaps maliciously inclined, may easily be kept in subjection by a small force, and by kind treatment."[145]

Shortly after Derby's military reconnaissance, a group of civilians entered the valley. A member of the party noted that they were "treated with marked courtesy and civility" at the villages visited. Many of the Indians spoke fluent Spanish; some possessed fine horses and rode well. The Americans relied heavily on Indians in fording the numerous rivers, and "after these crossing operations were through with, they all formed in a circle, and each one was presented with a piece of cotton cloth and a handkerchief, and as much beef as he could eat, (which was not a small quantity.) At night they would favor us with a few of their songs while sitting around their fires, and occasionally a dance." At the Kings River the party encountered an American (probably Oscar Field) doing a brisk ferry business. He charged ten dollars for each wagon, one dollar for each individual, and one dollar for each animal ferried.[146]

Although the Indians had little to fear from miners and soldiers passing through, and a few ferrymen operating in their territories, they perceived as a distinct threat those whites intent on remaining permanently. Late in the fall of 1850, John Woods built a log house in the Four Creeks. A short time later several Mexican vaqueros, in the employ of two white men, built a corral on the north side of the Kaweah River to pen some twenty-five hundred head of cattle, it being too late in the season to drive them to the gold fields.[147] Early in January 1851 a large number of Indians, evidently Gawia led by their chief, Francisco, arrived at Woods' house in a friendly manner, as they had on previous occasions. Others took up positions in the nearby woods and near the corral. On a signal the Gawia attacked, killing Woods, five immigrants who were staying with him, and the vaqueros. Two white men escaped. The Indians plundered Woods' cabin, stripped the bodies of the dead, and departed with the cattle.[148] They may have killed as many as thirteen men in the attack.[149]

The same party proceeded to Rancho El Tejón, intending to drive off the cattle Dr. E. D. French was tending for José Antonio Aguirre and Ignacio del Valle.[150] French employed several Indians, raised crops, and had built an adobe house. Called the Old Adobe, it was located near the village of Tinliw, which was governed by Zapatero.[151] French and a party of forty immigrants encamped on the rancho drove off the attackers, but the Indians returned with reinforcements, totaling 150 fighting men. Again the whites forced them to retreat, inflicting as many as forty casualties. The immigrants departed a few days after the fight.[152] French abandoned the rancho about the same time.[153]

At least two white men offered explanations for the attacks. "The only reasons that can be assigned for them were a desire of plunder and a jealously of the whites settling upon their lands," noted one.[154] Benjamin Hayes suggested that the Indians intended to destroy the rancho on which French resided and thus close down the trail passing through their territories. "The friendly Indians in the vicinity…," he warned, "will be faithful if they see the Americans well-armed; otherwise prove treacherous."[155] The Tejoneños did not participate in the attack or the one in the Four Creeks.[156] But some of them, probably from the village of Tinliw, quickly occupied the lands vacated by French and planted corn and melons and fifteen acres of wheat.[157] Zapatero moved into the Old Adobe.[158]

In May 1851 the Tejoneños allowed Alonzo Ridley, Joel Brooks, and David McKenzie to settle in the area and plant crops.[159] Unsure of the ownership of the Mexican grant on which they squatted, they improved the land in no appreciable way.[160] Unknown to them and all the peoples of California, men with entirely different objectives soon would arrive.

PART II

Relocation

PART II begins with an overview of the formation of a new Indian policy, a policy well studied by historians resulting in a large body of secondary sources. The outlines of this policy as applied to California have also been examined, but those affected by it have not always received the attention they deserve. Without a corresponding examination of Indian response, Indian policy remains little more than legal history. Unlike the Spanish missionaries, foreign and Mexican rancheros, and American soldiers who entered the valley, those implementing Indian policy in California left an abundance of records that reveal their motives, doubts, and fears.

Even though the primary task of the ethnohistorian is to incorporate Indians into the historical narrative, this should not come at the expense of ignoring those who introduced programs designed to relocate, change, and assist Indians. Furthermore, those Indians adhering to the new programs deserve as much attention as do those resisting them. And those whites assisting Indians deserve as much space as do those exploiting or harming them.

Part II ends with an elaborate debate conducted by Americans on how best to manage the Indians on whose lands they had occupied. From their letters, speeches, and reports, little is learned about the Indians themselves but much information is gained about those seeking a solution to their "Indian problem."

CHAPTER VIII

Inventing a New Indian Policy

Between 1835 and 1842, the Seminole Indians of Florida violently resisted the efforts of the U.S. Army to remove them to lands west of the Mississippi River. By the time the conflict ended most of the Seminole, nearly three thousand persons, had been relocated, but the war cost the federal government $20 million and the lives of fifteen hundred soldiers.[1] With the end of Seminole resistance the goal of relocating eastern Indians to the west, suggested by Thomas Jefferson, proposed by James Monroe, and implemented by Andrew Jackson, largely had been achieved.[2] Some ninety thousand Indians had been persuaded, bribed, or coerced into signing treaties that extinguished titles to their eastern homelands in exchange for lands far to the west. Fewer than twenty- three thousand Indians remained in the east.[3]

Removed beyond all states and organized territories, the Indians nevertheless took up residence in land claimed by the United States in the Louisiana Purchase of 1803. Designated Indian Territory the area came under the jurisdiction of the Trade and Intercourse Act of 1834. The act prohibited unauthorized whites from entering Indian Territory and allowed for their expulsion by military force. Land could not be sold without permission from the Indian Office. Annuities promised in the removal treaties could be withheld if Indians stole property or committed depredations. In legal cases involving Indians and whites, American law superseded Indian law and custom.[4] Despite these restrictions the Indians generally were left alone to manage their internal and external affairs.[5]

With eastern Indians resettled on lands initially thought to be useless to whites, officials in the Indian Office probably concluded that Indian-white conflicts, which had raged for the previous 240 years, at last were over. Events unfolding in the 1840s, however, would change that perception. On the last day of 1845, Texas was admitted to the Union. The following year the dispute with Great Britain over Oregon Country was settled, giving the United States the territory south of the forty-ninth parallel. And in 1848, at the end of the Mexican-American War, Mexico ceded to the United States the vast territory of the Southwest. Between 1845 and 1848, the land claimed by the United States increased by 1,202,286 square miles.[6]

As a consequence of these momentous developments, officials in the Indian Office realized that the Indians residing in Indian Territory presented a barrier to whites seeking to move across the Great Plains to the newly acquired territories. Early in 1847 Commissioner of Indian Affairs William Medill considered moving some of the Indians out of the way of the emigrants' routes. If right-of-way were obtained, Medill reasoned, conflicts between Indians and emigrants would be prevented.[7] It was not long, however, before the idea of moving a few Indians out of the way became a policy of confining all Indians in out-of-the-way places.

In his annual report of 1848, Medill articulated what would become a new Indian policy:

> Indians should be resettled beyond the reach, for some years, of our white population; confining each within a small district of country that, as the game decreases and becomes scarce, the adults will gradually be compelled to resort to agriculture and other kinds of labor to obtain a subsistence, in which aid may be afforded and facilities furnished them out of the means obtained by the sale of their former possessions. To establish, at the same time, a judicious and well devised system of manual labor schools for the education of the youth of both sexes in letters—the males in practical agriculture and the various necessary and useful mechanics, and the females in the different branches of housewifery, including spinning and weaving; and these schools, like those already in successful operation, to be in charge of the excellent and active missionary societies of the different Christian denominations of the country, and to be conducted and the children taught by efficient, exemplary, and devoted men and women, selected with the approbation of the Department by those societies; so that a physical, intellectual, moral and religious education will be imparted together.[8]

Distinguishing the new policy of confinement from the earlier one of removal was the emphasis on controlling and changing Indians. No longer would Indians direct their own destinies Instead, they would be directed to the goals set by the Indian Office. Medill was convinced "that before many years, if we sacredly observe all our obligations towards them, they will have reached a point at which they will be able to compete with a white population."[9] The commissioner's conviction that Indians could be improved reflected the optimism of the 1840s, which saw a rise in concern for the blind, insane, poor, and delinquent.[10]

In his annual report of 1850 the new commissioner of Indian affairs, Luke Lea, elaborated on Medill's ideas: "In the application of this policy to our wilder tribes, it is indispensably necessary that they be placed in positions where they can be controlled and finally compelled by stem necessity to resort to agricultural labor or starve.... There should be assigned to each tribe, for a permanent home, a country adapted to agriculture, of limited extent and well-defined boundaries; within which all, with occasional exceptions, should be compelled constantly to remain until such time as their general improvement and good conduct may supersede the necessity of such restrictions."[11] Lea noted in his report of the following year that the Indian "possesses all the elements essential to his elevation; all the powers, instincts and sympathies which appertain to his white brother; and which only need the proper development and direction to enable him to tread with equal step and dignity the walks of civilized life."[12] Confinement, therefore, was a means to an end.

Secretary of the Interior A. H. H. Stuart, in his annual report to Congress of 1851, pointed out that the settlements springing up in the Far West "have given increased importance to our Indian relations, and may render a change in our whole policy in regard to them necessary." Before the war with Mexico, the expanding white population gradually had been pushing the Indians ever westward:

> But since the acquisition of California and Oregon, and the establishment of large settlements on the coast of the Pacific and in Utah, a new flow of while population is advancing upon them from the west. The pressure is, therefore, increasing upon them from both sides of the continent. On the north and south they are also hemmed in by civilized communities. They are thus encompassed by an unbroken chain of civilization; and the question forces itself upon the mind of the statesman and the philanthropist, what is to become of the aboriginal race? This question must now be fairly met. A temporizing system can no longer be pursued. The policy of removal, except under peculiar circumstances, must necessarily be abandoned; and the only alternatives left are, to civilize or exterminate them. We must adopt one or the other. A just, humane, and Christian people cannot long hesitate which to choose, and it only remains to decide upon the means necessary to be adopted to effect the contemplated revolution in the Indian

character and destiny. It is a great work, and will require time for its accomplishment; but it can, and I believe will, be achieved.[13]

The urgency expressed in Stuart's report was not exaggerated. The discovery of gold in California early in 1848 resulted in thousands of Americans and those of other nationalities intruding upon Indian lands in the inferior. "It was not only a new state and a new order of things in the moral but also in the physical world," wrote a firsthand observer, Samuel Ward, "for never, previously, had from fifty to one hundred thousand men assembled without a viceroy or an army, much less without government, as in California, to appropriate to themselves, by the democratic right of the strongest, the virgin treasures of the earth."[14]

Regarding the Indians of the state, Sylvester Woodbridge Jr., a clergyman, commented on their condition in a memorial he sent to President Zachary Taylor in January 1850. The Indians were being driven in large numbers from their usual haunts. Deprived of their traditional food sources and motivated by hunger, they were stealing horses and cattle from the American immigrants and were suffering indiscriminate retaliation in return. Woodbridge recommended that the Indians be collected on "ranches of their own, separate from the presence of the white community." Farmers and teachers would be placed in charge of the ranches, and missionary societies would be encouraged to assist in carrying out the project. There were several areas in California where the Indians could be relocated. Woodbridge did not wish to interfere with the operations of the Indian Office, but the urgency of the situation prompted him to appeal directly to the president.[15]

The Indian Office already had concluded that the California Indians deserved some attention. In mid-April 1849 William Medill appointed Adam Johnston subagent for the Indians residing on the Sacramento and San Joaquin rivers. He posted a bond of $2,000 and received an annual salary of $750.[16] A resident of Belmont County, Ohio, Johnston was an active member of the Whig party.[17] Trained in the law he had sought another federal position before being appointed Indian subagent.[18] In late 1848 he had asked to be appointed registrar in the land office in Milwaukee.[19]

Needless to say Johnston's knowledge of California Indians was nil, but so was Commissioner Medill's. "So little is known here of the condition and situation of the Indians in that region," admitted Medill in a letter to Johnston, "that no specific instructions relative to them can be given at present; and the department relies on you to furnish it with such statistical and other information as will give a just understanding of every particular relative to them." Johnston was to provide Medill with the names and locations of the Indian societies, the extent of the territory owned or claimed by each, and the Indians' "manners, habits, disposition, and feelings towards the United States and whites generally." Medill also wanted to know if the Trade and Intercourse Act of 1834 was applicable in California or "what modification, if any, will be required to produce the greatest degree of efficiency." Medill authorized Johnston to purchase horses for himself and the interpreter he would hire, but he was to "be as economical as possible, and confine yourself to such cases only as will effect some important object." Johnston was to report directly to Medill, "as it is extremely desirable that the department be kept well advised of the state of affairs in that region." Included with Medill's letter were copies of the 1834 Trade and Intercourse Act, the 1848 treaty with Mexico, and four reports written by individuals with California experience.[20]

Johnston arrived in California in November and in January 1850 informed the new commissioner of Indian affairs, Orlando Brown, that he would visit the interior when the rains had ceased. Regarding the Indians residing along the coast, he was unimpressed: "They are in general stupid, indolent, and ignorant, and in intellect far inferior to any of the tribes east of the Rocky mountains. This does not perhaps apply to the pure Indians inhabiting the more mountainous part of the country, but to those residing at or near to either a mission or a rancho."[21] In February, Johnston met with John Sutter, who earlier had accepted the Indian subagency for the Sacramento Valley offered to him by Brown. Johnston notified Brown that he was pleased with the appointment, because Sutter "is known to almost all the Indians of this country, and is, perhaps better calculated for success with them than most men."[22] At the end of May, however, Sutter informed Brown that age and business affairs had forced him to change his mind. He recommended that one subagent (namely Johnston) be appointed for both the Sacramento and San Joaquin valleys and paid a salary in line with the cost of living in California, that several interpreters be hired, and that money for contingency expenses be appropriated. The Indians were "scattered over a very wide extent of country, made up of many very small tribes, and treaties must be made with each of these, if treaties are made at all."[23]

Informed of Sutter's decision Johnston concluded that the Sacramento Valley deserved his immediate attention. On May 29 he met with Thomas J. Green, major general of the First Division of the California Militia. Green told him that after recently chastising hostile Indians on Bear River, he had negotiated a treaty with them.[24] The treaty had been conducted, "in the absence of higher authority" and "on behalf of the people of California and the Government of the United States," with the Indians under the control of three chiefs. In the seven articles of the treaty, the Indians agreed to live in peace and friendship with the Americans, to turn over to the proper authorities Indians who committed crimes against whites, and to carry no arms while visiting white settlements. The Americans promised to punish citizens or foreigners committing crimes against the Indians, to allow the Indians free access to the gold mines, and to return the Indian prisoners taken in the recent battle. Within six months the United States supposedly would "confirm, amend, or annul" the treaty. If confirmed each group represented in the treaty would receive for ten years a semiannual cash annuity of one thousand dollars.[25]

Johnston rejected Green's request that he forward the treaty to the Indian Office. He notified Brown in July that "it would be miserable policy on the part of the government to adopt the treaty as it stands." He opposed the treaty because the incident leading to it was of minor importance, because the few chiefs who signed it did not represent adjacent societies, and because the semiannual annuity was unnecessarily expensive and would be of no use to the Indians. Nevertheless, Johnston thought that some kind of plan should be implemented to "ameliorate their present condition, and gradually bring them into civilization." He suggested that the Indian Office provide the Indians with clothes, blankets, and provisions, to be distributed on a semiannual basis at two or three depots. Johnston was certain that under his plan "it would require but little time to induce the entire tribes of the valley and mountains to abandon their present mode of living and adopt a civilized life."[26]

The editors of the *Sacramento Transcript* commented favorably on Johnston's plan: "He takes it for granted that the Indians are entitled to something for their lands; that their customs are so much broken up by the whites, that they cannot subsist as formerly, and unless something is done for them, they will be forced to steal from the whites, or starve, when another winter arrives. It will be useless to make periodical installments to them in money. They have no conception of its value. If any one of them happens to have any, no matter how much, he is sure to get rid of it all at the first store he finds. But at the depots established by Government, the Indians should be supplied once or twice a year with cheap clothing and small supplies of provisions. Their wants are very small, and it will not be expensive to meet them."[27]

In September, Johnston again wrote to Brown, stressing that the policy he had proposed "would not only be the most economical for the government, and vastly more beneficial to the Indians, than annuity in money, but must be by far the best means of reaching the wild mountain Indians and bringing them into a state of civilization." He described aspects of Indian culture and estimated the numbers of Indians comprising the societies he had visited. Concerning the Indians residing along the coast, his views had changed significantly He now understood that disease had taken a frightful toll and that white people had "trampled upon the graves of their forefathers." Near Mission Dolores an old Indian told him, that "my people were once around me like the sands of the shore—many, many. They have all passed away—they have died like the grass. They have gone to the mountains—I do not complain; the antelope falls with the arrow. I had a son—I loved him. When the pale-faces came, he went away; I know not where he is. I am a Christian Indian; I am all that is left of my people—I am alone." Because of the Indians "age, his earnestness, and decrepit condition," Johnston felt "the deepest sense of sympathy."[28]

John Fremont also was concerned about the Indians of California. Responding to a request from Orlando Brown to provide him with information about their situation, Fremont suggested that California be divided into three sections, each administered by an agent. The agents would be under the control of a superintendent, who would reside at Sacramento or at some other central point from which the agencies could be conveniently supplied. One agent would be stationed at the head of the lower Sacramento Valley and with the help of three subagents would administer to all the Indians of the valley. Those residing north of San Francisco Bay might be placed under a subagent residing at Sonoma. Another agent would take up residence at or near Kings River to deal with all the Indians in the San Joaquin Valley. He would be assisted by three subagents. The other agent would be stationed in Los Angeles where he and two subagents would have jurisdiction over all the Indians of Southern California. The superintendent should receive three thousand dollars, each agent two thousand dollars, and each subagent fifteen hundred dollars per annum. The "Indians are generally docile, in greater part already disposed by missionary teaching and their mode of subsistence, to agricultural labor. Simple farming materials, grain and other seeds, stock, horses & cattle, provisions, blankets and light ready-made clothing, would be among the presents most suitable to them at the present time." With his letter Fremont included a map identifying the areas where the agencies should be located.[29]

Frémont's involvement in California Indian affairs was just beginning. On September 11, 1850, two days after California achieved statehood, U.S. Senator John Frémont introduced a bill to preserve the peace among the Indians of California by extinguishing their territorial claims in the gold-bearing districts.[30] His bill called for the appointment of three commissioners to conduct treaties with those Indians having territorial claims and for the appropriation of one hundred thousand dollars to cover the cost of the negotiations. It was read twice and referred to the Committee on Indian Affairs.[31] On the fourteenth the committee reported the bill to the Senate with amendments. It now authorized the president to appoint not more than three agents for the Indians residing in the State of California. To enable the agents to conduct treaties, the sum of one hundred thousand dollars was to be appropriated.[32]

The Senate discussed the bill at length. Senator David Atchison, a member of the Committee on Indian Affairs, pointed out that the Senate knew neither the number of Indians residing in California "nor the kind of title by which they hold the lands." He called upon the two senators from California to inform their colleagues on these matters. With a volume of Spanish laws in one hand, Frémont addressed the Senate. In its territories, he claimed, Spain had respected the right of Indians to occupy land, even though "ultimate domination" remained with the crown. He cited royal decrees, orders, and laws from the sixteenth and seventeenth centuries, which recognized Indian rights to land and their right to alienate it. Because "Spanish law clearly and absolutely secured to Indians fixed rights of property in the lands they occupy,... some particular provision will be necessary in order to divest them of these rights. In California we are at this moment invading these rights. We hold there by the strong hand alone.... Our occupation is in conflict with theirs, and it is to render this occupation legal and equitable, and to preserve the peace, that I have introduced this bill." William Gwin, California's other senator, doubted that Mexican law recognized Indian rights to the land. He recommended that no laws be enacted until the agents had reported their findings.[33]

On September 16 the Senate passed the bill.[34] Sent to the House of Representatives it was referred to the Committee on Indian Affairs, which struck out the section appropriating one hundred thousand dollars. The House agreed to the amendment.[35] So did the Senate, and on September 28, 1850 the bill became law. It authorized the president "to appoint, with the advice and consent of the Senate, not more than three agents for the Indian tribes within the State of California. Such agents shall perform the duties now prescribed by law to Indian agents, and shall receive an annual compensation of three thousand dollars each."[36]

In the meantime, an Indian Appropriation Bill, which the House had passed on August 31, was referred by the Senate to its Committee on Finance.[37] The committee reported the bill to the Senate on September 24 with several amendments. The following day Senator Gwin offered another amendment that would appropriate one hundred thousand dollars to conduct treaties with California Indians. Gwin introduced the amendment because he feared that Frémont's bill, which originally had called for the same amount of money, would not reach the President before the Senate adjourned. The amendment was adopted.[38] The Senate sent the bill to the House, which disagreed with several of the amendments, including Gwin's. The House and Senate then formed a committee of conference to adjust the differences.[39] Ultimately, the House accepted Gwin's amendment, but only after reducing the sum to be appropriated from one hundred thousand to twenty-five thousand dollars. On September 30 President Millard Fillmore signed the legislation into law.[40]

Redick Mckee. (Courtesy of the Carnegie Library, Pittsburgh.)

Although the Indian Appropriation Bill authorized twenty-five thousand dollars to conduct treaties with the Indians of California, Frémont's bill, in its amended form, authorized agents, who lacked treaty-making authority, to proceed to California. Moreover, the twenty-five thousand dollars was to cover only treaty expenses. None of it was designated to pay the salaries and expenses of the agents.[41] To solve the problem, Acting Commissioner of Indian Affairs A. S. Loughery suggested to Secretary of the Interior A. H. H. Stuart that the agents be given authority to negotiate with California Indians so their expenses and salaries could be drawn from the appropriation. Stuart agreed with the plan but ordered Loughery to suspend the appointments as agents already made to three

O.M Wozencraft. (Courtesy of William B. Secrest, Fresno, California.)

individuals and to designate them instead as commissioners with treaty-making authority. Consequently, the three men selected to go to California received the right to negotiate treaties only because of a mix-up in how to finance their mission.[42]

On October 10 Loughery notified George Barbour, O. M. Wozencraft, and Redick McKee that they had been appointed agents for the Indians of California.[43] Five days later he informed them they had been reappointed as commissioners.[44] Born in Kentucky in 1807 and trained in the law, Barbour served in the U.S. House of Representatives from 1837 to 1848 and in the Kentucky State Senate from 1848 to 1850. Wozencraft was born in Ohio in 1814 but practiced medicine in Louisiana before moving to California in 1849. Plying his profession among the miners, Wozencraft made many friends, and he served as the delegate from Sonoma at California's constitutional convention.[45] McKee, born in Pennsylvania in 1800 into a very religious household, became a Virginia businessman who bought and sold real estate and manufacturing and wholesaling companies. He also was active in the state's Whig party.[46] Like Adam Johnston, McKee eagerly sought to join the federal government. In March 1849 he asked to be appointed U.S. consul in Liverpool or any other commercial port.[47] In September 1850, he sought the office of U.S. marshal in California.[48]

Loughery informed the commissioners that once they reached California they would receive eight dollars per day in salary plus traveling expenses. They could hire a secretary at not more than five dollars per day plus traveling expenses but for no longer than was absolutely necessary. Obviously they would need interpreters, but only the "smallest number, for the shortest periods, and for the lowest compensation." Loughery admitted that the "precautions of economy are made solely with reference to the small amount of the appropriation, when compared with the great object to be attained." Loughery designated to McKee the responsibility of distributing the twenty-five thousand dollars. The commissioners were to keep journals of their daily activities and "report fully to this office everything that occurs in your operations." Upon the completion of their duties, they were to send to the Indian Office a full report and copies of the treaties.[49]

To guide them in performing their duties, they were to consult a manual entitled Laws, Regulations, Etc.., of the Indian Bureau, 1850.[50] Compiled by Charles E. Mix, the chief clerk in the Indian Office, the manual comprised the rules and regulations the employees were to follow. All active agents and officers received copies.[51] The manual, however, dealt with the post-treaty duties of agents rather than with the pre-treaty procedures of commissioners. At the end of October 1850 McKee requested from Commissioner Luke Lea a copy of the Digest of the Laws of the United States, a volume of Indian treaties, or "any other books you may find there calculated to throw light upon our contemplated duties in California."[52] The following month Lea sent him a volume of Indian treaties published in 1837.[53]

Upon arriving in California, the commissioners were to contact Subagent Adam Johnston, from whom they would receive valuable information. Johnston, in the meantime, would be instructed to assist them in any way he could. The commissioners were to obtain information regarding the Indians' "manners, habits, customs, and extent of civilization." They were to "conciliate the good feelings of the Indians, and to get them to ratify those feelings by entering into written treaties, binding on them, towards the government and each other."[54]

Before sailing for California, McKee purchased in New York items he thought the California Indians would find useful: blankets, red flannel shirts, sashes, calicoes, and shawls. Provisions for the Indians would be purchased in California, but paying for them already was a concern. He informed Lea that once the costs of traveling and shipping had been paid, he would have about $10,000 for operating expenses. Because the cost of living in California was two or three times greater than that in the east, he would need an additional $100,000 or $150,000.[55]

So vague were his instructions and so limited was his knowledge of the new Indian policy that McKee, as indicated in a letter to Lea, departed for the West Coast intent on *relocating* rather than *confining* the Indians of California: "Whether there is any district of country in California or Utah, or Oregon, to which these tribes can be removed out of the way of the whites; or, if there is, whether they can be induced to remove from the graves of their fathers, is of course unknown to me. Our attention will, at an early day after our arrival, be turned to this subject; and it seems to me to be a vital question, involving, if not the destruction and extermination of the Indians, at least the peace of that frontier. The commissioners regret that their instructions from the government at Washington, on these and other questions likely to arise and demand their immediate attention, are so meager and indefinite, and throw upon them necessarily so much responsibility. In the absence of direct and positive instruction, or even counsel and advice, we must do the best we can."[56] Their best would soon be tested in the region the miners called the Southern Mines.

CHAPTER IX

Conflict in the Southern Mines

According to their oral traditions, the Ahwahneechee once occupied a valley called Ahwahnee. When disease, perhaps carried by neophytes from the coast, decimated the Ahwahneechee, the survivors abandoned their homeland. Some of the refugees settled at Mono Lake on the east side of the Sierra Nevada, where an Ahwahneechee man married a Paiute woman. They named their son Tenaya. Tenaya's mother tongue, therefore, was Paiute, and the Mono Lake Paiutes always considered him one of theirs. Upon visiting Ahwahnee, Tenaya reclaimed the valley as a birthright.[1] Because the settlement took place in recent times, it represents the last movement of Paiute peoples to the western slope of the Sierra Nevada.

Although Tenaya established a Paiute "colony" in Ahwahnee, from it emerged a composite society consisting largely of Paiutes from the Mono Lake area and Miwoks from the Tuolumne River region.[2] Tenaya also welcomed disaffected Yokuts from as far south as the Kings River.[3] According to Lafayette Bunnell, who interviewed the chief in 1851, Tenaya, "by his cunning and sagacity in managing the deserters from other tribes, who had sought his protection, maintained a reputation as a chief whose leadership was never disputed by his followers, and who was the envy of the leaders of other tribes." Some of the "deserters" were neophytes from the coastal missions. Probably from them he learned the crude Spanish he occasionally spoke.[4]

The language they spoke clearly reflected their disparate origins. Their dialect "was a composite of that of almost every tribe around them," wrote Bunnell, "and even words of Spanish derivation were discovered in their conversations." Apparently, other Indians designated those residing in Ahwahnee as the "Yosemite," a term signifying a full-grown grizzly bear. Tenaya gladly accepted the appellation, because bears frequented Ahwahnee, because the Yosemite were adept in killing them, and because those bestowing the name feared Tenaya's band. Under the leadership of Tenaya, the Yosemite became one of the most feared Indian societies in the interior. From their well-protected valley stronghold, they launched raids on Indian villages and Mexican ranchos, mainly to obtain horses and mules. The animals were used primarily as a source of food rather than as a means of transportation.[5]

As recounted by Bunnell, a religious leader "assured Ten-ie-ya that while he retained possession of Ah-wah-ne his band would increase in numbers and become powerful. That if he befriended those who sought his protection, no other tribe would come to the valley to make war upon him, or attempt to drive him from it, and if he obeyed his counsels he would put a spell upon it that would hold it sacred for him and his people alone; none other would ever dare to make it their home. He then cautioned the young chief against the horsemen of the lowlands..., and declared that, should they enter Ah-wah-ne, his tribe would soon be scattered and destroyed, or his people be taken captive, and he himself be the last chief in Ah-wah-ne."[6]

Horsemen from the lowlands soon arrived. Perhaps as early as June 1849, James Savage established a trading post on the Merced River about fifteen miles from the entrance to the Yosemite Valley.[7] In October, William Abrams and a companion departed from the post on a bear hunt, got lost, and apparently entered the valley.[8] The same month Daniel Woods began mining the Merced below the entrance. The Indians, he noted, were "openly friendly, but their friendship is not to be trusted. They have acquired a growing distrust of the emigrant miners.... Even when they come into our camps with presents or to trade, their conduct says plainly, 'We bide our time!' It may be delayed, but the time will come when they will seek revenge; and woe be to those who are among these wild mountain fastnesses when that fearful time comes!"[9]

That "fearful time" came in early 1850 when Yosemite Indians attacked the trading post run by James Savage. Although he and his men repulsed the raiders, Savage relocated to the Mariposa River near the mining camp of Agua Fria. He also established a branch station on the Fresno. At both locations Savage exchanged merchandise for gold with both Indians and whites.[10] When Savage began placer mining on Rattlesnake Creek near the Tuolumne River, however, relations between Indians and whites again deteriorated. In June a Texan named Rose and an Indian leader, Lutario, argued and then fought. Rose killed the chief with his knife but died immediately when Indians riddled him with arrows. An

Indian also fired several arrows at Savage, who defended himself with a double-barreled shotgun. Five Indians may have died in the fight. Because the whites thought Lutario's people included some eight hundred fighting men, they quickly withdrew from the area.[11]

At the time of the fight James Savage was well known to Indians and whites alike. Born in Indiana in 1823, he spent most of his youth in Illinois.[12] While still a boy he went to live with the Fox and Sac Indians, remaining with them until the Black Hawk War broke out in 1832. He married in 1845, but his wife died the following year during the trek to California.[13] Arriving in California just in time to participate in the war against Mexico, Savage joined the California Battalion led by John Frémont. Patriotism, however, was hardly his motive for serving. A friend, Joseph Downey, remarked that Savage, "like most of the emigrants, being short of the needful, jumped at the chance of enlistment in the Battalion."[14] Apparently he did not take well to military life. "One of the worst of the malcontents" was William Swasey's assessment of him.[15]

Short of stature and weighing less than 140 pounds, Savage was a muscular man. His light brown hair he tied in the back or let hang down in ringlets.[16] James O'Meara described a face "of striking mold and expression, with broad forehead of fair front, strongly formed, projecting eyebrows, deep-set, large eyes of deep blue, tinged with gray, which changed in hue and luster with the humor of the man—ordinarily as placid as the motionless surface of the mountain lake, but in moments of passion, as flashing and penetrating as the fiery beams of the torrid sun; bold and high cheek-bones, large and finely shaped nose, a strong, firm mouth, with lips thin and denoting great decision, a well-rounded and prominent chin, and heavy, powerful jaws—all betokening the indomitable will of this master of his kind; and his complexion was of hearty bronze which robust health and constant exposure to the elements impart in the course of time."[17] "Physically, he was an Apollo," exclaimed Benjamin Harris.[18] To Samuel Ward, "in stature, air, and features, he bore a marked resemblance to the effigies I have seen of Peter the Great."[19]

Among his peers Savage gained a larger-than-life reputation. To Downey, "a more rollicking, devil-may-care, fun loving, mirth-provoking disposition was never placed in the body of any man."[20] Conversationally, he was "a polished, entertaining gentleman," recalled a more restrained Harris.[21] "No dog can follow a trail like he can," claimed T. G. Palmer. "No horse endure half so much. He sleeps but little, can go days without food, and can run a hundred miles in a day and night over the mountains and then sit and laugh for hours over a camp-fire as fresh and lively as if he had been taking a little walk for exercise."[22] A newspaper editor insisted that Savage "never heard of the word fear, can track an Indian or deer from sunrise till sunrise again, over the mountains, rivers, and valleys, and run either the one or the other down, before he gives out."[23] Ward thought that Savage's "habits and nature were externally consonant with his name. He excelled the Indians in every athletic exercise and skillful accomplishment, and was the equal in his powers of abstinence and endurance, being competent to subsist upon roots and seeds and to perform those long dog trot journeys on foot for which that race is celebrated."[24]

Renowned for his considerable linguistic skills, Savage arrived in California speaking English, German, French, and Spanish.[25] Soon he mastered the languages of the Yokuts-speaking Heuchi, Chukchansi, Chauchila, and Pohonichi and the Miwok-speaking Nukchu. He also learned the secret "language" the prominent members of those societies spoke among themselves. Keeping the knowledge to himself, he was able to obtain, surreptitiously, important information.[26]

After the California Battalion disbanded, Savage worked for a time at Sutter's Fort. With John Marshall, he dug the millrace on the American River where gold was discovered. He also served as a handyman, hauling wood, herding cattle, and probably as a translator.[27] From the local Nisenan Indians, he obtained some gold.[28] But soon he headed south and established his mining operations in the Southern Mines, the region between the Mokelumne River in the north and the San Joaquin River in the south.[29] Cultivating the friendship of prominent Indian leaders such as José Jesus of the Siakumne, he fought with them against their enemies.[30] Apparently, he supported the Muqueleme in their conflicts with the Siyante.[31]

For political reasons Savage married into several Indian societies. "Savage is a blasphemir fellow who has five squaws for wives for which he takes his authority from the Scriptures," noted a miner in October 1849.[32] When Robert Brownlee first saw him, he was traveling with three young women, "one after the other a little distance apart, and he an equal distance in advance of the oldest of the three, who was about sixteen years of age. The other two being about twelve or fourteen as near as I could judge." Brownlee recalled the time when Savage and his wives visited his store: "It was mid-day and my place empty, so they remained for several hours, he buying largely of clothing for himself and squaws. I had on hand a great many bolls of prints, some good, others not so much so, also some red blankets which took their eyes. All they fancied he bought for them; his bill I think was $75." Later, on a visit to Savage's post Brownlee had to share a huge bed, framed by logs, with Savage and three women. Brownlee watched as Savage "turned in among them, all seemingly happy"[33]

In exchange for blankets, old military coats, colored handkerchiefs, and provisions, Indians provided Savage with gold.[34] Brownlee recalled that Savage charged the Indians a pound of gold for a pound of sugar.[35] On one occasion, an Indian acquired a box of raisins for gold dust of equal weight. Harris estimated that Savage's profits often amounted to ten or twenty thousand dollars per day.[36] In 1850, G.D.W. Robinson saw a pork barrel full of gold dust in Savage's tent, guarded only by Indians.[37] "Today," recalled Harris, "he would hazard at a game hundreds or thousands, tomorrow would find him penniless but soon to be replenished by the rich earnings contributed by his red mining subjects."[38]

Promising the Indians camped near his Fresno post that he would return with blankets they badly needed, late in 1850 Savage journeyed to San Francisco with, according to Harris, fifty thousand dollars in gold dust. He lost the entire amount while gambling at monte.[39] Two of his wives and José Juarez, a highly respected chief of the Chauchila, accompanied him to San Francisco. Savage thought José Juarez would be so impressed with the numbers of whites in the city that fighting them would be out of the question. After drinking too much, however, José Juarez became verbally abusive and disclosed that soon the Indians would launch a war against the miners. Savage struck the chief, knocking him off his feet. José Juarez remained silent for the remainder of the trip."[40]

Back at his Mariposa post Savage learned that a large number of Indians had gathered near his Fresno station. He departed at once for the trouble spot, where he found chiefs Panwatchee, a Nukchu, and Bautista, a Poioyanti, nominally friendly. Savage had taken two wives from those groups. Also present were Chauchila chiefs José Juarez and José Rey and Tomquit of the Pitkachi. Savage warned the Indians that a war with the Americans, who were "more numerous than wasps and ants," would lead to their extermination. For support Savage turned to the Indian who had accompanied him to San Francisco.[41]

José Juarez, however, took the opportunity to openly challenge Savage:

> Our brother has told his Indian relatives much that is truth; we have seen many people; the white men are very numerous; but the white men we saw on our visit are of many tribes; they are not like the tribe that dig gold in the mountains.... Those white tribes will not come to the mountains. They will not help the gold diggers if the Indians make war against them. If the gold diggers go to the white tribes in the big village they give their gold for strong water and games; when they have no more gold the white tribes drive the gold diggers back to the mountains with clubs.... The white tribes will not go to war with the Indians in the mountains. They cannot bring their big ships and big guns to us; we have no cause to fear them. They will not injure us.[42]

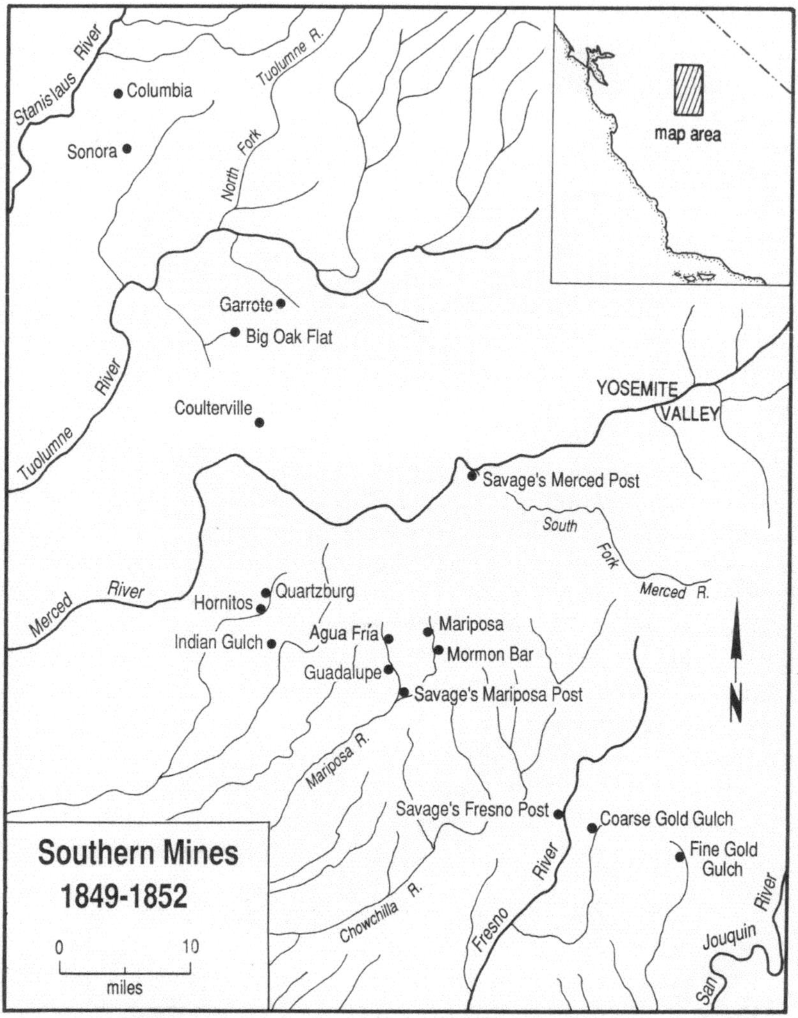

He encouraged the assembled Indians to commence immediately a war against the whites. The land belonged to the Indians, who, if united, could drive the gold diggers from the mountains. Savage responded by claiming that the whites were "all brothers, all of one tribe," and would come in great numbers to fight the Indians. José Juarez said that "if the other white tribes should come to their help, we will go to the mountains; if they follow after us, they cannot find us; none of them will come back; we will kill them with arrows and rocks." José Rey also encouraged the Indians to wage war against the miners: "My people are now ready to begin a war against the white gold diggers. If all the tribes will be as one tribe, and join with us, we will drive all the white men from our mountains. If all the tribes will go together, the white men will run from us, and leave their property behind them. The tribes who join with my people will be the first to secure the property of the gold diggers." Thoroughly outmaneuvered at the council, Savage withdrew to warn the miners about the Indians' intentions.[43]

On November 21 Subagent Adam Johnston left San Francisco for Savage's Mariposa post with presents he had purchased from an eighteen-hundred-dollar draft on the Department of the Interior. He arrived on December 1 and a few days later departed for the Fresno station where he spoke with several chiefs and headmen of the Chauchila. A chief asked: "Why do the Americans come here? They are good and brave, but they come upon the land of my people. What do they intend to do? I want to know, and must know, right now." The chief told Johnston that Savage was allowed to remain in his territory because "he made us many presents.... If you will make us presents, too, you may remain in our country awhile." Johnston explained the purpose of his mission and distributed the presents he had brought. The Indians assured him they would not harm the Americans, but they did not speak for other groups. Johnston also spoke with the leaders of surrounding villages, all of whom professed great friendship for the Americans. But he suspected there was "a general understanding among the various tribes that they should commence a predatory war, at an appointed time, all along the valley of the San Joaquin, if not along the entire base of the Sierra Nevada, from the northern to the southern boundary of the State."[44]

On December 17 Indians residing in the vicinity of Savage's Mariposa post departed for the interior. Savage and a few men followed them to an encampment some thirty miles away, abandoned except for two young boys and a dead woman. Savage located the Indians on a nearby mountain and from a distance spoke with their leader, Bautista.[45] Also known as Chechee, Bautista had been attached to one of the missions and after secularization had lived for a time in Monterey.[46] He stood five feet six inches tall and was of stout proportions."[47] A white man described him as "a fine looking fellow, and intelligent."[48] When he departed for the interior is not known, but Bautista probably assumed control over the Miwok-speaking Potoyani in 1847 after soldiers under the command of Captain Henry Naglee executed his father and a companion by firing squad. Before the execution, his father ordered Bautista to avenge his murder.[49]

Savage told Bautista that he and his people should return to their villages. With a little labor they could procure sufficient gold to purchase food and supplies. Bautista thought that a difficult way to earn a living, especially when the Indians could supply their wants by robbing the whites. They would kill all whites entering their country.[50] Bautista invited Savage to join him and the other Indians in fighting the whites. If Savage remained neutral, he would not be harmed; if he joined the whites he would be killed.[51] Bautista told Savage that the Indians had united and declared war on the whites. They had raided his post on the Fresno and killed three of his men.[52]

Apparently, Bautista had lured Savage away from his Mariposa post so Indians could attack the one on the Fresno. On December 17 Chauchila, Chukchansi, and Pohonichi raided the Fresno station, stealing money, horses, mules, oxen, tents, furniture, and other items, a loss Savage calculated at nearly twenty-five thousand dollars.[53] The raiders also killed three white men and wounded another. Taking a chief prisoner and keeping a gun to his head, the wounded man crossed the Fresno River and bolted. He ambushed the five Indians who gave chase, wounding two or three. Thirty miles from the station he stumbled upon some white men.[54]

The day after the attack on the Fresno station, four or five Indians, apparently emissaries from Bautista visited the Indians living near the mining camp of Washington City on the San Joaquin River, urging them to murder the miners. The local Indians refused and informed the whites of the situation. The emissaries fled with four or five of the miners' animals.[55]

"The Attack," by Charles Nahl. *Hutchings' California Magizine,* 1859. Courtesy of the Bancroft Library, University of California, Berkeley.

Upon receiving news of the attack, James Burney, sheriff of Mariposa County, called a meeting of miners to raise a company that would proceed to the mining camps south of Agua Fria. Forty-seven men volunteered and under the command of Savage departed immediately. The sheriff and a small party intended to visit the mining camps on the San Joaquin River to see, in Burney's words, "whether this was a general outbreak of Indians or only a matter between Savage and his Indians." Their departure, however, was delayed until a pack train arrived at Agua Fria with mules they needed.[56] Burney reached Washington City on the night of December 22, expecting to find the miners dead. One frankly admitted that they had survived only because the local Indians remained friendly.[57]

Burney and three men visited a village of the Pitkachi, located five or six miles distant. Initially, the chief, Tomquit, refused to speak with Burney, but he finally granted him an interview. What the chief said is not known, but when Burney returned to camp he advised the miners to leave immediately. An individual named Alsbury, who ran a ferry on the San Joaquin, persuaded the miners to remain, claiming the Indians were no threat. Burney and his party returned to Agua Fria by way of the ferry run by Wiley Cassidy. Cassidy, too, refused to leave.[58] A newspaper article published some years later described Cassidy as "one of those foolhardy, swaggering, thoughtless fellows, a very Georgia Major, who declared that he did not fear any Indian in the world and apprehended no trouble from them."[59]

On Christmas morning over one hundred Indians attacked Alsbury's ferry, killing one and wounding three of the ten white men present. The whites retreated upstream some three miles, recruited twelve or fifteen miners, and returned to the ferry, only to find it plundered and Alsbury's horses and cattle missing. The miners and ferrymen built fortifications and waited for the Indians to attack. C. D. Gibbes was confident they could defend themselves, but all work was suspended. "We number now 25 fighting men, but want arms and ammunition," he wrote to the *Stockton Times*. "I hope our friends will get Gen. Smith to send out some troops here. There are a number of emigrants coming on this route, and will be very much exposed."[60]

The attack never materialized, but on the night of January 3, 1851 Indians drove off a large number of mules from a miner's camp on the Tuolumne. The same night Indians stole animals from a ferryboat operator five miles downstream. The party that went in pursuit recovered the animals and killed an Indian in the encounter. A few days later Indians killed two white men and drove off several others from their camp on Maxwell's Creek. The miners retook the camp, killing one Indian.[61] A week later Indians attacked five men near the mining town of Sonora, wounding all seriously. The whites who gave chase killed and scalped twenty Indians.

A resident of Sonora wondered why "the Indians have not attempted to fire the town at night. It might be done with the greatest of ease and impunity, for there is never any guard; policemen, watchmen or sentinels are not known here, and the town within a few days journey of a dozen, probably a score of Indian Rancherias full of our mortal enemies."[62]

Several parties of Indians also attacked the mining camps on the headwaters of the Stanislaus, Moquelumne, and Calaveras, driving off large numbers of mules and horses. The miners were thrown into a state of panic. Long accustomed to losing animals to the Indians, never before had they lost so many at one time. Immediately, miners and sixty Indians, led by the Siakumne chief José Jesus, set out for the north fork of the Stanislaus to chastise the stock raiders. They located five hundred Indians with several hundred head of cattle on a table mountain three hundred feet in height. The settlement, moreover, was only one of several stretching in a north-south direction in a region whites had yet to explore. Considering the Indians' position impregnable, the miners and their Indian allies retreated. When José Jesus and his followers suddenly disappeared, some of the whites suspected they had joined the hostile Indians. The suspicion proved to be unfounded.[63]

Despite recent Indian attacks in the Southern Mines, a prominent San Francisco newspaper, the *Daily Alta California*, saw no reason for alarm. "Every little while war panics break out in new places," it editorialized on January 1, 1851. As soon as one is ended, "another terrific cry is raised through one of the Stockton papers and echoed here, in which one would be left to suppose that a perfectly annihilating war had broken out among the poor starving Indians of the southern mines." The newspaper blamed the hysteria on "the exaggerations of rumor" and on the "medium through which it is published."[64] A week later, the *Alta* reiterated its position: "It is extremely doubtful, indeed, if any intention exists on the part of any of the tribes to levy war upon the whites, further than a temporary feeling of anger for real or imagined injuries.... At any rate the entire extent of troubles there is within the confines of one small section, and the miners generally, except in that particular locality, know nothing and care nothing about all this bubble-blown exaggeration of a trifle. There are no troubles on the Merced, the Tuolumne, or the Stanislaus. Persons wishing to go to any of the placers on these rivers or their tributaries, need not be prevented by the very foolish reports which occasionally come teeming through upriver papers."[65]

Upriver papers, however, had no doubt that the Indians had combined to drive the whites from the mines. On January 25 the *Stockton Times* claimed "that with few exceptions the whole of the Indian tribes from the Cosumnes to the King's river are in a state of insurrection."[66] The same day the *Stockton Journal* warned its readers that the "frontier is in imminent danger from Indian attack, and subject to Indian incursions. Mules, horses, and cattle, are daily and nightly being stolen by Indians, and driven off in large droves. Indian murders are being daily committed upon the defenseless, isolated miners."[67] Early in February the *Times* maintained, "that the Indians, fearful of annihilation by the whites, have formed an extensive combination for the purpose of carrying on an exterminating war."[68] At mid month C. D. Gibbes predicted in a letter to the *Times* that there "is going to be a general Indian war from one end of the state to the other, and has been planned for months."[69]

In early January, Indians stole seventy-two mules and horses from the ranch of William J. Howard, located a few miles west of Agua Fria. Howard and a party of twenty followed the Indians' trail to Mormon Bar.[70] There they met James Burney, James Savage, seventy-two white men, and one Indian who had left Agua Fria on January 7 on a campaign against the Indians. Joining forces, they followed the trail of the stolen animals into the mountains.[71] Howard recalled years later that "we received orders to carry in addition to our regular arms, stout heavy sticks about eighteen inches long, with which to playfully tap the women and children over the heads if they refused to surrender."[72] About fifty miles from Agua Fria, they heard singing coming from a mountain village. Leaving behind their provisions under a guard of sixteen men, the rest of the party ascended the mountain at night to within two hundred yards of the village. Savage crept to the edge of the village, where he overheard a conversation in which his name frequently was mentioned.[73]

Situated on the top of a mountain of almost perpendicular walls, the village, about four acres in extent, was one of the largest the Americans had yet seen.[74] Its sixty or seventy lodges and large American tent housed between three hundred and four hundred fighting men. From the lodges hung large quantities of jerked mule meal; from the trees, baskets full of acorn meal.[75] Although a Heuchi village, 150 Chauchila, and a few Chukchansi were present. Expecting to find only Heuchi, the Americans intended to surround the village and take all the residents prisoner. The presence of so many Chauchila was unsettling.[76]

Discovered by an Indian at daybreak the Americans rushed the village, driving the Indians from the premises. Shortly, however, a rifle shot brought down one of the volunteers. "This was a surprise that almost whipped us," recalled T. G. Palmer, "for not knowing that the Indians had fire-arms, we were only expecting arrows."[77] The Indians counterattacked, forcing the whites to withdraw into some timber. With the eight or ten rifles and pistols they possessed, the Indians killed two Americans and shot off the nose of another. Their arrows injured several more.[78]

Several Indian women fought alongside the men. Using her foot to hold the bow, an injured woman put three arrows into the arm of a volunteer.[79] After an hour and a half of exchanging fire, the Americans again rushed the village, driving the Indians into surrounding cover and setting fire to the lodges.[80] From the screeching he heard, a participant in the fight inferred that many women and children burned to death.[81] The injured woman who wounded the American perished in the flames. Nearly thirty Indians died in combat.[82]

During the fight it became apparent to the volunteers that the Indians' main target was James Savage. As recounted by Palmer: "The whole body of Indians seemed bent on killing Mr. Savage, partly because he would not be their chief and lead them against the whites, and partly because he was, they knew, our greatest dependence as guide, and their particular dread. To kill him, many of them sacrificed their own lives. They would come one at a time and, standing in open ground, send arrows at him until shot down; and one old chief who used to cook for Savage, would ask him after every shot where he had hit him. They would talk to him to find out where he was, and as soon as he would answer, the balls and arrows would fly thick around his head: but he escaped unhurt; but as he said, worse frightened than he ever was before. He did not fancy such partiality."[83] Evidently, Bautista was the chief who had cooked for Savage. At one moment, his enemy only a short distance away, Bautista took careful aim with his rifle. His miss may have convinced him that Savage possessed special protective powers.[84]

As the Americans withdrew down the mountain, conveying their wounded and dead in litters, the Indians kept up a continuous but ineffective fire.[85] Two Indians waited in ambush to kill Savage, but their shots also missed. When a chief (probably Bautista) called to Savage about the number of men he had lost, Savage replied that none of his men, only a few strangers, had been hurt. The chief mockingly apologized for not making a better fight of it, explaining that three hundred of his men were then fighting the Americans on the Mariposa.[86]

Bunnell thought the engagement "was not a very satisfactory one to the whites. The necessity of a more efficient organization was shown. The Indians had here taken all the advantage of position and successfully repulsed the attack of the whites, who withdrew, and allowed the former to continue their course."[87] Bunnell did not participate in the fight, but William J. Howard did and admitted that the Americans "had come off second best."[88]

At the camp on the Fresno where they had left their provisions, the Americans built a log fort, buried the dead, and tended to the wounded. Most of the company soon departed to procure supplies, but thirty-six men remained at the fort. A short time later they confiscated nearly fifty horses from Indians who were driving them toward the village the whites had razed. Evidently, the Indians were unaware of the recent fight.[89]

James Savage proceeded to the Tuolumne and Stanislaus Rivers to enlist the support of Cornelius of the Tuolumne and José Jesus of the Siakumne, chiefs who had remained friendly to the whites. Savage sought to enlist five hundred men, divide them into two companies, and simultaneously attack the Indians residing on the San Joaquin and Mariposa rivers.[90] Successful in recruiting only two hundred men, Savage departed Agua Fria in mid-January on yet another campaign against the hostile Indians.[91] On this one, however, he concealed his identity by wearing a tattered coat, corduroy pants, tarpaulin hat, horsehair beard, and buffalo hair mustache.[92]

With seventy men Savage trekked ahead of the rest of the party, which was commanded by James Burney. The two companies were to rendezvous at Fine Gold Gulch, but after waiting one day Savage pushed on.[93] Burney and his men proceeded to the San Joaquin where they heard about an Indian attack in the Four Creeks. Continuing southwards they encountered two badly wounded while men who had survived the attack. At Four Creeks they buried the nine persons (five Americans and four Californios) Indians had killed. Burney destroyed the provisions at two abandoned encampments before returning to Agua Fria in early February.[94]

When Savage and his men arrived at the log fort on the Fresno, they learned that the thirty-six men who had remained there from the previous campaign had gone to the north fork of the San Joaquin River. They caught up with them at that spot. At a nearby village resided elements of the Chauchila, Chukchansi, Gawia, Nukchu, Potoyanti, Pohonichi, and Yosemite. Numbering some five hundred fighting men, they were led by Chauchila chiefs José Rey and José Juarez. As recalled by Bunnell, some of the Indians sneaked up to the Americans' compound and, protected by rocks and trees, "defiantly taunted the whites with cowardice and their late defeat. They boasted of their robberies and murders, and called upon Savage to come out where he could be killed. In every possible manner they expressed their contempt." Throughout the night "their derisive shouts and menaces in broken Spanish and *native American*, made incessant vigilance of the whole camp a necessity."[95]

At daybreak, shortly after the Indians had withdrawn, the Americans stormed the village. Because Savage was a special target of the Indians, he and his men brought up the rear. Surprising the Indians the Americans killed twenty-three and burned their village to the ground. Under cover of the smoke, most of the Indians escaped, including a wounded José Rey. Only one American was seriously injured.[96]

Although the Americans clearly won that fight, Indians struck at the mining camps the volunteers left undefended. Writing to the *Pacific News* on January 26, a miner recounted his experiences at Quartzburg: "For the last half hour our quiet village has been the scene of commotion and terror. We were first assailed by a shower of arrows in one of our tents. All were sound asleep. The arrows did not take effect… It would seem that the Indians are taking advantage of the absence of many of our men, on the present expedition…. They swept mules and horses for five or six miles around this evening…. There must have been a large body of Indians to have induced them to be so daring to have covered so much ground in so short a time…. Our people are being cut off by piecemeal. Some are flying to the lower country, or to he places of greater safety. Our ladies are terror-stricken."[97]

Early in February, Indians attacked ten men prospecting on the north fork of the Tuolumne River, wounding five. The party formed in the mining camp of Garrote pursued the Indians to their village and destroyed large quantities of acorns, dried horsemeat, and blankets. Back at their base camp, however, the whites discovered that Indians had driven off the two guards and absconded with fifty blankets superior in quality to those they had destroyed.[98] About the same time Indians entered the mining camp at Mariposa, stealing mules, several tents, and gunpowder.[99] They killed a lone prospector somewhere between the Mariposa and Merced rivers.[100] And they attacked two miners prospecting between the middle and south forks of the Stanislaus, killing one and wounding the other. Several men from the town of Columbia pursued the Indians to their village, where they killed a woman and several men and destroyed the lodges and a large supply of provisions.[101]

Mariposa in the 1850s. Courtesy of the Yosemite Museum Library, Yosemite National Park, California.

In late February ten or fifteen Indians killed and mutilated Wiley Cassidy a few miles from the ferry he ran on the San Joaquin River. Unable to locate him and fearful an attack was imminent, his partner and several employees fled the area. On the road to Stockton, they found two abandoned wagons and a dead man, whom they promptly buried.[102] He had died from gunshot wounds and belonged to a party of eight that Indians, probably Chauchila, recently had attacked.[103] On March 1, Indians also attacked twelve men between Greaser Gulch and Burns' Diggings, wounding three.[104] Two days later they killed four near Fine Gold Gulch. Regarding the latter attack, whites recovered eleven of the twelve oxen the Indians had stolen.[105] A resident of the interior reported on March 6 that the towns of Agua Fria, Mariposa, and Burns' Diggings were "left almost entirely to the mercy of the Indians since the volunteers have been in the field, and scarcely a night passes, but more or less property in goods or stock is stolen by them. Their object, at present, upon these places, seems to be plunder."[106]

In mid-March the *Alta* reversed its position regarding the situation in the Southern Mines: "Mariposa county has been for a long lime stagnant in business matters in consequence of the Indian depredations and the subsequent condition of affairs. Not only have the miners suffered, and in many cases to the entire ruin of their prospects and hopes. The ranches of the settlers have been broken up, nearly all the horses, mules, and stock generally, stolen and driven into the mountains, and the dwellings of the settlers deserted."[107] John Marvin, a witness to many of the events, estimated that between December 1850 and April 1851, Indians stole at least eighty thousand dollars' worth of stock in Mariposa County.[108] But a contemporary calculated that from the Four Creeks alone Indians stole five thousand head of cattle and that the total loss from Indian attacks exceeded half a million dollars.[109] Because of this loss, however, the State of California initiated its own Indian policy.

CHAPTER X

State Interposition

Because of incessant Indian attacks in the Southern Mines, local citizens increasingly looked to the state government for assistance. On January 13, 1851 two county officials penned a letter to Governor Peter Burnett: "Property is unsafe, and life is insecure, in Mariposa county; and if this state of affairs shall be permitted to continue for many weeks, this portion of our beloved State will soon become depopulated." They pleaded with the governor to submit to the legislature a special message on their behalf. Seventy-one residents of Mariposa County signed the document.[1] The same day James Burney, sheriff of Mariposa County, also wrote to Burnett. He recounted the recent campaign against the hostile Indians and sought authorization to keep active the company of men he had raised. The Indians could be defeated in a short time, but if not "commissioned to do so, and furnished with some arms and provisions, or the means to buy them and pay for the services of the men, my company must be disbanded, as they are not able to lose so much time without any compensation."[2]

On the eighteenth John McDougal, who had replaced Burnett as governor, submitted to the senate all the correspondence and other documents relating to Indian disturbances in Northern California, along the Colorado River, and in Mariposa County. In an accompanying letter he asserted that "the exposed situation of the interior frontier; the open declaration of hostilities on the part of some of the tribes; and, in short, the actual existence of an Indian War within our borders, seem not only to warrant, but imperatively require that the Legislature adopt some measures which shall afford, at least, the means of protection to those of our citizens exposed to the hostilities of the Indians." The governor mentioned that he had ordered the sheriff of Mariposa County to form a militia of one hundred men.[3] Subsequently, the number allowed was increased to two hundred.[4]

Regarding the specific situation in Mariposa County, two days later McDougal sent a special message and relevant documents to the legislature. From the federal government "no present aid need be expected at all commensurate with the emergency. We must, therefore, rely upon ourselves for protection, and take such steps for this purpose as circumstances warrant, trusting that the General Government will ultimately afford us surer means of more effectually punishing aggressors than are now at our command." Those citizens residing "where these disturbances occur are generally engaged in mining operations, and can illy [sic] afford to abandon their business at any season but especially at this, and gratuitously devote their time, as well as their private means, to the defense of the State." McDougal asked that action be taken to reimburse citizens for expenses incurred while fighting Indians and to protect the citizens in the interior, "until the General Government shall have adopted such measures as shall obviate the necessity of State interposition."[5]

In the senate the message and documents were referred to the Committee on Indian Affairs with instructions to report immediately. A bill entitled "An Act for the Protection of the Citizens of Mariposa County against the Indians," introduced by a senator from that county, was referred to the same committee. The bill allowed the volunteers to remain in service until the end of hostilities and authorized the comptroller to issue his warrant upon the treasurer for a payment of ten dollars per diem to the officers and men.[6] On the night of January 21, with Governor McDougal present, the senate debated and passed the bill.[7]

In the assembly the majority of the Committee on Indian Affairs recommended in favor of the senate bill. The minority report, prepared by D. P. Baldwin, however, stated that those residing in the disturbed districts were "bold and fearless, as well as numerous and well armed, and are capable of protecting themselves against the aggressions of the Indians of California, who are a weak, cowardly, and imbecile race, and only one in ten possessing or understanding the use of fire-arms." By calling out the militia the governor had done all that was necessary. Furthermore, California was not obligated "to assume all expenses of hostilities occurring upon her frontier, and if she pursues that policy it will involve her in a labyrinth of debt, from which she will never be able to extricate herself." By a margin of one, the assembly voted to indefinitely postpone the bill.[8] Apparently, the assemblymen thought excessive the ten dollars per diem the bill appropriated for each volunteer.[9]

The postponement of the bill prompted a correspondent for the

Daily Alta California to write: "The appeal which the Executive has made upon the Legislature for aid in this alarming exigency has therefore been denied by the economists because the war cannot be carried on without an expenditure of money!"[10] In a letter to the *Pacific News* a resident of the interior expressed disbelief that "the people of San Francisco remain so quiescent and inactive, when the commercial prosperity of their city and all their industrial avocations ... are in such peril." He predicted that unless the state and federal governments offered "immediate, prompt and effective protection," the interior would be abandoned. "Cannot something be done to save our state from this impending ruin?"[11]

Appropriating the necessary funds to fight the Indians, however, was no easy task. On January 24 an assembly bill to finance the suppression of hostilities in Mariposa County was defeated by a small majority because it made provisions for the defense of the citizens of only one county. Other counties also were in need of assistance. The subject was then referred to the Committee on Indian Affairs with instructions to report a bill for the protection of all citizens in the interior.[12] The following day the chairman of the committee called upon lawmakers to "provide some immediate measures for the protection of the lives and property of her citizens from Indian depredations. These hostilities are confined to no particular locality, but, from well authenticated intelligence, we believe exist along a great portion of our frontiers, and greatly impede, if they do not effectually prevent, mining operations in our richest mining districts." The bill accompanying the chairman's report provided for the suppression of Indian hostilities. With the rules suspended, it was read twice and referred to the Committee on Ways and Means.[13] On January 27 the chairman of that committee reported to the assembly a bill authorizing the treasurer of the state to negotiate a war loan upon the credit of the state. Again under a suspension of the rules, the bill was read two times and ordered printed.[14]

About the same time the senate instructed its Finance Committee to report a bill authorizing a war loan of three hundred thousand dollars.[15] The editors of the *Alta*, however, questioned the need to appropriate any money at all. They suspected "that these hostilities are seized upon as a pretext for issuing $300,000 State script, with an avidity which shows plainly that the object is not so much, on the part of some, a defense of the miners as a fleecing of the people." Furthermore, they doubted the wisdom of the state intruding into federal affairs: "This whole matter belongs to the United States Government. She has troops enough and money enough on this coast to make the war, carry it on, and pay its expenses. She has as fine a set of officers here as can be produced anywhere, and a little skirmishing would be to them pastime. Let the State authorities, therefore, attend to their own legitimate business, plunge the State no further in debt, and leave to Uncle Sam and his servants to conduct this matter, which belong exclusively to them."[16]

Unpersuaded, on January 28 the Finance Committee reported a bill to the senate calling for the creation of a war loan. The report accompanying the bill stated that without "an efficient United States force, to suppress the numerous Indian outbreaks upon our extended frontier, it became necessary for the Governor to order out a military force. In doing which, a necessary debt has been incurred, for which our State is legally and morally responsible."[17] The editors of the *San José Daily Argus* suggested that the war loan should be based on terms comparable to those practiced in other states. Capitalists would shun a loan of a few years' duration but would be attracted to one that ran ten or twenty years. And "a liberal price must be paid, or the loan will not obtain a bidder. If business profits, and the high price of labor at present prevailing are to continue in the State, money cannot be had for less than two per cent a month."[18]

The same day the Finance Committee reported its bill, Governor McDougal wrote to General Persifer F. Smith, commander of the Pacific division, requesting arms and ammunition for the militia. He also wanted to know if the general would commit troops to the campaign soon to be launched against the hostile Indians.[19] Smith, in a letter to the adjutant general of the army, challenged the wisdom of committing troops and supplying arms to the volunteers. The weapons would be "sold to the storekeepers in the mines and will be purchased by the Indians for gold, which they bring from the mountains." Smith had "no hope that peace will be maintained, for certain persons have determined that there shall be a war, and there is not sufficient military force and no judicial authority to restrain them."[20]

~

In late January, Governor McDougal dispatched his aide, J. Neely Johnson, to Mariposa County to organize the militia. He instructed Johnson to "let the Indians be conciliated. An Indian war is at all times to be deprecated, but especially so by us now, in the infancy of our career as a state, and especially before the General Government has provided us with the necessary means of protection and defense. We are in no condition to be harassed by expensive and protracted disturbances." Johnson could increase the number of men to be mustered into service but no more than was absolutely necessary He was "to practice the most rigid economy consistent with the interest to be subserved."[21]

At Agua Fria, Johnson found two hundred men, many of them Texans and veterans of the Mexican-American War, eager to fight Indians.[22] Most of those who had served in the recent campaign with James Savage and

James Burney volunteered for the militia, but competition was stiff for the limited number of openings.[23] Those selected were to be mustered in on February 10, but the event was delayed because arms and ammunition had yet to arrive. Further problems developed when Indians, probably Yosemite, stole fifty animals from the volunteers. Because they had yet to be organized, no one ordered the posting of a guard.[24] At the inception of the battalion, only about twenty volunteers had mounts.[25]

Addressing the volunteers Johnson raised the issue of responsibility: "While I do not hesitate to denounce the Indians for the murders and robberies committed by them, we should not forget that there may perhaps be circumstances which, if taken into consideration, might to some extent excuse their hostility to the whites. They probably feel that they themselves are the aggrieved party, looking upon us as trespassers upon their territory, invaders of their country, and seeking to dispossess them of their homes. It may be, they class us with the Spanish invaders of Mexico and California, whose cruelties in civilizing and Christianizing them are still traditionally fresh in their memories." Johnson expected the volunteers to "observe mercy where severity is not justly demanded."[26]

Johnson organized the men into three companies, each led by a captain. John Kuykendall commanded Company A; John Bowling, Company B; and William Dill, Company C. The companies totaled seventy, seventy-two, and fifty-five men and officers respectively.[27] Because of his knowledge of Indian languages and territories and because of his courage and sagacity, Savage was elected major and commander of the battalion.[28] James Burney did not campaign for the position because he noted years later, Savage wanted it so badly that "some foul means would be used to get me out of the way."[29] Subsequently, the legislature appointed Burney the battalion's paymaster.[30]

Johnson designated John Marvin as temporary commissary and quartermaster, authorizing him to purchase food, clothing, and transportation for the battalion. Arms and ammunition would come from the state arsenal and, if necessary, from individuals willing to sell. The cost of supplies issued to each volunteer was to be deducted from his pay. Johnson instructed Marvin to establish at Cassidy's Crossing on the San Joaquin River a depot from which supplies would be sent to the companies.[31] Supplies also were provided by Robert Brownlee and his partner, who served as sutlers to the battalion. They sold provisions, clothing, and utensils to the volunteers on credit.[32]

Apprehensive that the Mariposa Battalion, as it was called, might engage in premature military action, Johnson told Savage that "a defensive policy should be pursued by us. There is a seeming propriety under the circumstances in which we are situated, of strictly conforming to this request, so that in the event of the failing of their mission, no proper censure can attach to the conduct of the state authorities." He ordered Savage to station one company on the Little Mariposa, another on the Fresno (fifteen and twenty-five miles, respectively, from Agua Fria), and the third at Cassidy's Crossing on the San Joaquin. Savage was to confer with the commissioners as they negotiated with the Indians, and if they agreed, "that a peace cannot be effected without further bloodshed, you will then in the absence of further instructions be left to act in accordance with your own judgment and discretion guided by the one great ruling object, to effect a peace at the earliest possible moment."[33] Savage wrote to the governor about the policy he had been instructed to follow. He would adhere to the orders, but "in my humble opinion, it will be useless to hold forth, the olive branch, to those wild men of the Sierras, until they are made sensible of their inferiority in every particular."[34]

The battalion organized, Johnson departed for San José to encourage the legislature to appropriate the necessary funds to support it.[35] On February 15, three days before he arrived, the bill reported by the Finance Committee to the senate on January 28 had become law. It authorized the treasurer to negotiate a loan upon the faith and credit of the state to defray expenses incurred in suppressing Indian hostilities. The loan would not exceed five hundred thousand dollars and would be funded by issuing bonds payable in ten years or at any period after five years "at the pleasure of the State." The bonds would not exceed twelve percent per annum paid annually or semiannually. No bond would sell for less than one thousand dollars.[36]

The *California State Journal* wondered why capitalists would invest in such a loan where elsewhere they could secure six percent interest per month backed by good securities. The newspaper also pointed out that the majority of claims probably would not average over two hundred dollars. Thus, when a volunteer presented his claim, the paymaster "will tender him one of the $1000 bonds, on condition that the balance be paid in cash; and if the soldier is either too poor to afford it, or unwilling to thus invest his scanty earnings, he will be compelled to abandon his claims, or place himself at the mercy of speculators." Moreover, the law did not prohibit the paymaster or his agents from speculating in the bonds.[37] Evidently, the newspaper's concerns were well founded, because the state treasurer failed to obtain the loan.[38]

Quartermaster John Marvin had no choice but to operate on the assumption that state funds soon would be available for him to purchase supplies for the battalion. At Agua Fria he found the volunteers sorely lacking in clothing, camp equipment, rations, arms, and ammunition.[39] Most of the local residents were reluctant to sell their weapons, especially pistols. Marvin hired a blacksmith to work on the few guns purchased, noting sarcastically that once repaired "most of them would stand cocked, and could be fired without quite as much danger to the shooter as the person or thing shot at."[40]

In early March, Marvin visited the mining towns of Mariposa, Agua Fria, Burns' Diggings, and Indian Gulch, where he purchased on credit of the state supplies from some of the local merchants. In Stockton and Empire City he bought, also on the credit of the state, clothing and camp equipment, and in San Francisco he obtained ammunition and one hundred arms from the state arsenal. He sent the old flintlock muskets to Stockton. Because Savage had requested rifles with percussion locks, Marvin journeyed to U.S. army headquarters at Benicia, where he was told that no such arms were in stock.[41]

On the eleventh Marvin warned the governor that unless "immediate steps be taken by the State, to raise funds to meet past bills and current expenses, the battalion will, of necessity, have to be disbanded for want of requisite subsistence."[42] Recalling the events a year later, Marvin wrote: "The volunteers were discontented and believed that the Legislature were more intent on promoting their private schemes than in protecting the residents of a defenseless frontier."[43]

Governor McDougal sent a message to the assembly on March 15, urging it to pass a law relevant to the present emergency. Aware that the legislators were reluctant to unnecessarily spend taxpayers' moneys, the governor emphasized that the federal government, "under the political compact of the confederation of the States, is bound to protect them from invasion, insurrection, or rebellion, and Congress has always shown a liberal disposition in the payment of all expenses incurred by any of the States in putting down Indian disturbances, and I have no doubt but that Congress will promptly assume all the expenses attendant upon the expeditions that have heretofore or may hereafter be called into the service of the State."[44]

That day the senate, under suspension of rules, passed a bill authorizing the governor to call out troops to defend the interior and to provide for their pay. The bill went to the assembly the same day and quickly passed.[45] On March 17 the governor signed the bill into law. It authorized him to call into service as many as five hundred volunteers. Each volunteer was entitled to a per diem ranging from four dollars for a private to ten dollars for a major. Volunteers providing their own mounts would receive an extra dollar per day. They would be paid in warrants issued by the comptroller but not until the accounts and vouchers of each claimant had been approved by a board of examiners. The warrants were to be paid out of the war loan fund. For remuneration James Burney, the battalion's paymaster, was to receive three percent of the award.[46]

Which government, state or federal, ultimately would pay for the campaign was an issue yet to be resolved. On March 1, 1851 McDougal wrote to President Millard Fillmore, pointing out that the rapid settlement of California "has brought into close and sudden contact two races of entirely opposite pursuits and character." He claimed that one hundred thousand Indians were under arms: "Rendered bold by impunity and encouraged by success, they are now everywhere rising in arms, and every day brings the report of some new outbreak. There is no alternative but to coerce submission, and in my efforts to accomplish this, I confidently ask the aid and support of the general Government." The governor had no need for regular soldiers, who would be "unfit for a desultory Indian war, to be carried on among the fastness of our mountains." Rather, he called upon the president to convey upon him the authority to call out and organize the proper number of men who would be "equipped, provisioned and paid by the general Government." McDougal admitted that his request was unusual, "but you will remember that we occupy an extraordinary situation."[47]

Responding for the President, Secretary of War C. M. Conrad, explained that his department had information suggesting that Indian attacks in California had been provoked by whites. Moreover, the treaties soon to be conducted would establish boundaries separating Indians from whites and the "hostility which your Excellency considers as the necessary consequence of the two races being 'brought into sudden and close contact' would be avoided." Regarding the governor's request for authority to call out and organize troops, Conrad noted that the president only could call a state's militia into the service of the United Slates, in which the militiamen would be subject to the articles of war and would receive the pay of regular soldiers. Conrad also pointed out that

> Experience has shown that volunteers are everywhere more expensive than regular troops, and there is reason to believe that the difference between them would be greater in California than elsewhere. Your Excellency is silent on this subject, but this department has learned from other sources entitled to credit, that the pay stipulated to be paid, both to the officers and men belonging to certain volunteer companies in California recently raised, by what authority I am not prepared to say, is exorbitant and beyond any thing ever known in this country. For these reasons the Executive would not feel justified in authorizing the calling out of the militia in the mode recommended by your Excellency. There are other objections to the plan. Is there not some reason to fear, if that plan were adopted, that in a population like that of California, where there are so many ardent young men, the love of adventure with some and high pay with others, would operate as inducement to perpetual collisions with the Indians?[48]

A collision already had taken place. On March 1 Savage sent Captain John Kuykendall and his company to Cassidy's Crossing on the San Joaquin River with orders not to undertake military operations against the hostile Indians. Even if attacked Kuykendall was to "act on the defensive principles of warfare."[49] But when Indians stole seven mules from his command, Kuykendall took offensive action. He and forty men attacked a village thirty or forty miles from their camp. They killed ten Indians, wounded several others, and destroyed stores of jerked beef and large quantities of acorns. Powerless against the Americans the Indians called for a conference. Kuykendall allowed them to remove their dead, provided they moved to Cassidy's Crossing. The leaders agreed and promised to bring in between two and six hundred followers.[50] Subsequently, Savage ordered Kuykendall to send them and all other Indians contacted to the Fresno River, where they would meet with the Indian commissioners.[51] But not all Indians agreed to negotiate and those that did often drove hard bargains.

CHAPTER XI

Negotiations Begin

Indian Commissioners O. M. Wozencraft and Redick McKee arrived in San Francisco on December 27 and 29 respectively, and George Barbour on January 8, 1851.[1] At mid-month they departed for the capitol, San José, to consult with the governor and members of the legislature. From San José, Wozencraft journeyed to Benicia to meet with General Persifer F. Smith.[2] Smith provided the commissioners with a military escort. Commanded by Captain E. D. Keyes, the escort consisted of 101 soldiers and ten officers. Three wagons, each drawn by six mules, and 150 pack mules carried provisions, ammunition, and presents for the Indians.[3]

Assistant Adjutant General Edward R. S. Canby ordered Keyes to select a site on the Kings River or another place deemed appropriate for a military post. There he was to deposit all his stores and baggage, and from there he was to accompany the commissioners to their treaty-making destinations. To receive fresh supplies he was to keep the quartermaster at Benicia appraised of his movements. As long as the commissioners anticipated a peaceful end to the difficulties, he was to conform to their wishes. If, however, the commissioners concluded that war was inevitable, Keyes was to operate on his own initiative and subdue the hostile Indians. Canby warned him not to act in conjunction with other bodies of men, an obvious reference to the Mariposa Battalion.[4]

Barbour and McKee joined Wozencraft in Benicia and with the military escort sailed by steamer for Stockton, arriving on February 8.[5] While McKee supervised the unloading, Wozencraft and Barbour, accompanied by John Marvin and J. Neely Johnson, proceeded to the ferry run by John and Lewis Dent and James Vantine on the Stanislaus River. There the commissioners explained their mission to three hundred or four hundred Indians. A few days later José Jesus, chief of the Siakumne, and some of his followers arrived and agreed to meet the commissioners in a few months to conduct a treaty.[6] As recalled by Barbour, the Indians were "much pleased with the terms proposed, and particularly with the idea of an education that would enable them to read and write." They would not, however, provide the commissioners with runners to send to the hostile Indians, because "they had for many years been at war with those tribes, and dare not now venture among them." They recommended that the commissioners contact a small band of Indians on the Tuolumne River who "held a doubtful position between the whites and hostile Indians—friendly to both parties, but trusted by neither."[7]

On the Tuolumne the commissioners met Cornelius, chief of the Tuolumne, and Cypriano, chief of the Awal and a notorious stock raider.[8] Cypriano agreed to travel to the headwaters of the Mariposa, Merced, and Tuolumne rivers and inform Indian leaders, many of them hostile to the Americans, that the commissioners expected to meet with them on February 24 on the Tuolumne, about forty-five miles upstream from its junction with the San Joaquin River.[9]

On February 14 Wozencraft, Barbour, and twelve Indians joined McKee on the San Joaquin, near Graysonville, where McKee and the military escort had established a camp a few days before. The local Indians, led by Manuel, were neophytes from Mission Santa Clara and professed friendship to the Americans. Manuel wore a scarlet jacket with gilt wings on the shoulders, apparently a Mexican military uniform. The commissioners furnished him and his followers with three days' worth of rations, which they immediately consumed. The following morning the military escort held a dress parade for the edification of the Indians or "to give them an idea of the prowess and strength of our arms," as a civilian observer put it. Manuel was impressed with the ceremony.[10]

The closer the commissioners came to conducting a treaty, the more concerns they had. On February 17, in a letter to Commissioner of Indian Affairs Luke Lea, they raised several issues. Were they to recognize Indian usufructuary rights? Were they to establish, at suitable points, military posts for the protection of both Indians and whites? And "to what extent (if any) do our powers as commissioners authorize the appointing of suitable persons to trade with, superintend, and manage the various tribes, in our absence, with whom we may have made treaties?" Not expecting a reply before negotiations began, the commissioners answered their own queries. They would, "under the instructions heretofore given us, and in compliance with the demands of humanity, as we conceive, act affirmatively on all those questions until otherwise directed."[11]

The commissioners and the military escort departed for the Tuolumne on February 18 and the following day met James Savage and his staff. Savage thought the Awai chief, Cypriano, would bring in the hostile chiefs but doubted they would adhere to any treaty.[12] He favored launching as soon as the snow melted a vigorous campaign against them. If Captain Keyes would station his troops at four crucial points, Savage would prosecute the war in one month. To Savage's regret, however, the commissioners sought to reconcile the hostile Indians by presenting them with gifts.[13]

Cornelius and twenty of his followers visited the Americans on the February 23, the soldiers providing them with provisions. Cornelius and another Indian dined with the commissioners and, according to an observer, "handled the knife and fork very cleverly and to very good purpose." Shortly, three more Indians arrived, informing the commissioners that Cypriano was en route but giving no information about the hostile chiefs. Some of the whites thought the Indians had come to spy and doubted Cypriano would show up.[14] Cypriano arrived on the twenty-fifth with two of the hostile chiefs and messages from three or four other leaders explaining why they could not attend. Barbour and Wozencraft thought the excuses rather feeble. The commissioners explained to the chiefs "that it was the wish of the government that they should live on terms of friendship with the whites; that protection would be extended to them upon the condition that they would cease their depredations upon the persons and property of the whites, and of each other; that if they would act honestly and use industry, lands should be set apart for them, seeds to plant and implements to work with furnished them, schools established for them, and capable persons appointed to teach them how to cultivate their lands." Continuation of their depredations, however, would result in the "destruction, and even the entire annihilation of their whole tribe." The Indians listened with great interest. When pressed to encourage other hostile chiefs to meet with the commissioners, they agreed only after consulting with Cornelius. The Indians were to assemble on the Little Mariposa River on March 9.[15]

As the Americans were breaking camp, an Indian runner informed the commissioners that two of the hostile chiefs, Hawhaw of the Apalache and Numasecano of the Apangasi, soon would arrive. Cornelius, Cypriano, and the other leaders agreed to apprise them of the commissioners' demands. Two more chiefs and their followers visited the commissioners at their new camp on the Merced River. They, too, were instructed to assemble on March 9 on the Little Mariposa.[16]

The commissioners were now confident that they would treat with six groups, including the Yosemite. They had little hope the Pohonichi, Chukchansi, Pitkachi, Dalinchi, Heuchi, and Chauchila would attend the council. Of all the Indians, they most feared the Chauchila, believing them responsible for many of the recent killings and robberies.[17] In early March, only a few miles away from the commissioners' camp on the

Merced, the Chauchila attacked a party of seven white men, killing one with gunfire. After launching about one hundred arrows, the Indians fled with some of the miners' stock.[18]

On March 8 the commissioners established Camp Frémont on the Little Mariposa. The council was to begin the following day, but only one small band of Coconoon, under the leadership of Nuella, had arrived. Nuella told the commissioners that other Indians were on their way. And a few days later, chiefs Trypoxi of the Siyante and Bautista of the Potoyanti arrived with some of their followers.[19] The appearance of Bautista, the chief who had planned the attack on Savage's Fresno post, must have startled the commissioners. Bautista, however, convinced the Americans that José Rey had forced him to join the hostile Indians. When José Rey was wounded in combat, Bautista look the opportunity to assert his independence and seek peace with the Americans.[20]

Negotiations opened on March 15 between the commissioners and representatives of the Siyante, Potoyanti, and Coconoon.[21] Present were about 140 Indians, but additional parties arrived as the talks proceeded. The commissioners informed the Indians that the federal government intended to relocate them to the Merced River in the valley, where they would be instructed in stock raising and agriculture. When told of the extent of territory they would receive, the Indian leaders asked for, but did not receive, more land.[22] They discussed the proposals among themselves, and when the meeting reconvened informed the commissioners that they accepted all the terms except relocation to the valley. The commissioners explained that if the Indians remained in the mountains, conflicts between them and miners would continue and they would be forced to steal stock from the ranchers to sustain themselves. Again they discussed the proposal among themselves, finally agreeing to relocate.[23]

The following day Wozencraft, Barbour, and two chiefs (probably Bautista and Trypoxi) rode to the Merced to select the lands on which the Indians would be resettled. Apparently, the chiefs found the area satisfactory.[24] Captain Keyes thought otherwise. "The land is generally poor & not much of it is fit for tillage," he wrote to the acting assistant adjutant general. "It contains no building timber & the amount of wood for fuel is scant. The whole interior portion being bare of trees." For these reasons, Keyes found the area unsuitable for a military post. If, however, Wozencraft expanded the reservation to the Stanislaus River, as he intended to do, a military post might be established there.[25]

When informed that some Indians who had promised to attend the council were on the Tuolumne, Wozencraft departed to meet with them. They had not made contact because they feared retribution for not arriving on March 9. Wozencraft convinced them they would not be harmed if they came in. A few days later, members of the Apangasi, Apalache, and

Awal arrived at Camp Fremont.[26]

On March 19, 1851 Indians representing six societies agreed to the terms of the treaty and placed themselves under the "jurisdiction, control and authority of the government of the United States." Thus, they pledged "to refrain in future from the commission of any act of hostility or aggression towards the government of the United States, or any of the citizens thereof, and to live on terms of peace and friendship, not only with the citizens of the United Slates, but with all Indian tribes." The Indians also agreed to "severally relinquish, and forever quit claim to the government of the United States" all title or claim to any lands within the boundaries of California or the United States. In exchange they were to receive a tract between the Merced and Tuolumne Rivers, about the extent of four townships of land, which "shall be forever set apart and held for the occupancy of said tribes of Indians." The Indians received free access to all the land between the two rivers extending to the Sierra Nevada for the purpose of hunting and collecting, but were prohibited from residing there permanently.[27]

The United States reserved the right to establish a military post and to erect the necessary buildings for an agent, military officers, and other individuals who would reside with the Indians. The government would provide the Indians with one hundred steers and one hundred sacks or barrels of flour in 1851 and again in 1852. Furthermore, the Indians would be furnished ten brood mares and one stallion, twenty-five cows and a bull, ten plows, ten sets of harness, one hundred axes, one hundred hatchets, one hundred hoes, ten picks, a year's supply of seeds, eight hundred pounds of iron, two hundred pounds of steel, two hundred pairs of two-and-a-half-point blankets, two flannel shirts and two pairs of coarse pants for each man and boy, one linsey gown for each woman and girl, two thousand yards of brown sheeting, two thousand yards of calico, thread, needles, buttons, scissors, and other items. The United States further agreed to furnish the Indians with experts, including a farmer, blacksmith, and wagon maker or carpenter, to assist them in learning new skills. They would work with the Indians for a period of five years and as long thereafter as the President deemed advisable. A school superintendent and as many teachers as needed also would be assigned to the Indians.[28]

The Indians agreed not to retaliate against citizens of the United States who caused them harm but to seek redress from the civil authorities. They pledged to deliver to the proper authorities members of their own societies who committed crimes against Americans. The treaty concluded by stating that the articles would be "binding on the contracting parties when ratified and confirmed by the President and Senate of the United States of America."[29]

The three commissioners signed the treaty. John McKee (brother of

Redick and secretary), Subagent Adam Johnston, Captain Keyes and five of his officers, an interpreter, and two other white men signed as witnesses. Although thirty-nine Indians put their marks on the treaty, six signed as chiefs: Bautista of the Poloyanti, Trypoxi of the Siyante, Numasecano of the Apangasi, Hawhaw of the Apalache, Nuella (Mendo) of the Coconoon, and Cypriano of the Awal.[30] A copy of the treaty was entrusted to Cypnano.[31] Another copy was sent to Commissioner of Indian Affairs Luke Lea, who was "highly gratified with the results."[32]

For the commissioners, writing a treaty was a new experience. Apparently Barbour drafted the treaty, because McKee noted in a letter to Lea that it was "not exactly, either in its diction, direct provisions, or restrictions, such as I could have wished; but as it met the approbation of the author, and of Dr. Wozencraft, I yielded my assent, intending to try my hand at treaty writing upon the next occasion or opportunity."[33]

Guiding the commissioners on procedural matters was a manual called Laws, Regulations, Etc., of the Indian Bureau, 1850, with which McKee had been provided.[34] The manual consisted of the Trade and Intercourse Act of 1834 and other acts and regulations mainly dealing with eastern Indians. Nevertheless, from it the commissioners learned that they had the authority to set the time and place for negotiations; to employ commissaries, interpreters, and messengers; to determine the quantity of provisions and presents to be purchased; and to ensure that the rules of the intercourse law were followed. The secretary they hired was to keep full records of the negotiating proceedings, to record the speeches of the commissioners and the Indians, to keep files on all claims presented by whites and Indians, to record all accounts of the commissioners, and to prepare abstracts, accounts current, and vouchers for transmission to the Indian Office.[35]

Furthermore, the manual specifically stated that agents and subagents had the authority to manage relations between Indians and whites in their respective jurisdictions. They were to reside at and keep their agencies near or within the territories of the peoples in their charge. Agents could nominate to the Indian Office suitable persons as teachers, blacksmiths, farmers, and mechanics. The agents were to prepare and transmit annual statements indicating the quantity of agricultural implements or other equipment delivered to the Indians, the number and size of farms established, the kind and amount of crops planted, and the number of Indians instructed in agricultural or mechanical arts. At least once a year the agents were to visit the schools in their agencies and inspect the buildings, accounts, and clothing and food of the children. Reports of their inspections would include the number of teachers, the curriculum offered, and the capabilities and progress of the Indian pupils.[36]

The commissioners also drew upon a volume of treaties Lea had sent

McKee in November 1850.[37] Originally published in 1825, *Treaties between the United States of America and the Several Indian Tribes, from 1778 to 1837* had been updated to include many of the treaties negotiated during the removal period. The treaty Barbour composed clearly was a composite of those published in the volume. In wording and content, the articles in his treaty mirror those found in the earlier ones, although the numbers of animals, sacks of flour, agriculture implements, and tools and amounts of clothing and cloth promised the Indians differed significantly.[38] Notably absent from Barbour's treaty, however, was any mention of cash annuities, a common feature of most of the treaties in the volume.

By settling aside land for exclusive Indian occupancy and by promising the Indian residents food, animals, equipment, clothing, and technical and educational assistance, the commissioners, on their own initiative, introduced the reservation system to California. In less than three months, they had concluded that the Indians should not or could not be removed from the state. Henceforth, they would be relocated to lands within its borders.

How to get the Indians to comply with the treaty was the next hurdle faced by the commissioners. The key to success, they figured, was Bautista. At the conclusion of the conference, Wozencraft and four white men took him to Stockton. On the way they stopped for drinks at every tent selling liquor. At a stage play in Stockton, Bautista excused himself at least three times to visit the bar.[39] Nevertheless, he was impressed with what he saw, the plot being explained to him in Spanish by a white man.[40] A few days later Wozencraft and Bautista boarded a steamer for San Francisco. As recalled by Wozencraft the Indian "did not believe all that he had heard. He had been told there was a big tribe of whites, called the San Francisco tribe, and he wanted to see for himself." Now a celebrity Bautista was wined and dined and saw much of the city.[41]

The *Daily Alta California*, however, greeted his visit with ridicule: We had the distinguished honor of a street interview, an introduction, a shake of the hand, with Bautista, the Indian Chief, who has accompanied Dr. Wozencraft to this city to form an opinion of the whites. He was dressed in some old second edition of a soldier's pants and roundabout, with a wreath of dirty blue calico twisted about his head like a turban.... It is not known whether Bautista considered himself in ball dress, court dress, or dishabille; he seemed perfectly satisfied with his rig, and doubtless plumed himself upon the imagined impression he was mak[ing] upon the white people who have shown such an anxiety to secure the Indians' friendship. We have nothing to say against amicable relations with the Indians, on the contrary, have ever considered that policy the only true one. But it will not take many interviews with the leaders of these acorn-eaters to cure the most romantic of all previous ideas of "lords of the forest," "nature's noblemen," and similar appellations which have been applied to the Indian. We have fallen a great way from the ideal of our boyhood to the real of yesterday, from our imagined King Phillip [sic] to the personal Bautista.[42]

On their return journey Bautista asked Wozencraft how old was San Francisco: "I told him three years. He said, 'My people had better make peace. In three times three, it will be all over my country.' "[43] Back in the interior the two men learned that the Chauchila had spread a rumor among many Indian groups that Bautista had been taken to San Francisco and killed and that all the Indians who had come in to treat had been murdered by the Americans. The Yosemite, who had arrived within twelve miles of the meeting ground, became so alarmed they returned to their valley stronghold.[44] Seeking only to be left along, the Yosemite and other Indians defied those intent on dominating them.

CHAPTER XII

Yosemite and Chauchila Defiance

On the evening of March 19, 1851, the day the treaty was concluded, James Savage and two companies of the Mariposa Battalion moved to the South Fork of the Merced River to within seven miles of a Nukchu village. The Nukchu had failed to attend the council. On the morning of the twenty-third, Savage sent a Chauchila married to a Nukchu woman to inform the residents that they were surrounded and would be killed if they resisted. When their chief, Panwatchee, realized that Savage was with the Americans, he agreed to talk.[1] Evidently, some of the Nukchu, under the command of Chowchitiy, a brother of Panwatchee, had worked for Savage, and Savage had taken Eekeno, a Nukchu, as one of his several wives.[2]

Savage told Panwatchee that three commissioners had been sent to the Indians to give them presents and to teach them how to till the soil and live like the whites. The Indians were to come out of the mountains and reside on the plains. If the Indians refused the whites would kill all of them. Panwatchee replied that he had heard the same thing at different times but had not believed it. Because Savage had told him he now believed it and would go with him to the valley.[3] After collecting their portable belongings, the Indians, supposedly as a gesture of good will, set fire to their village.[4]

Panwatchee alerted Savage to a small band of Pohonichi camped up the Merced. Savage dispatched an Indian runner to them, and gradually and cautiously they straggled into the Americans' camp.[5] He also ordered

Panwatchee and Chowchitly to send runners into the Yosemite Valley to instruct Chief Tenaya to bring in his people.[6] Panwatchee, who doubted the Yosemite would comply, must have been surprised when a short time later Tenaya arrived at the camp. Fed and treated kindly he met with Savage who told him that if he made a treaty with the commissioners the fighting would end.[7]

As recorded by Lafayette Bunnell, Tenaya, after inquiring into the purpose of relocating all the Indians to the San Joaquin Valley, stated: "My people do not want anything from the 'Great Father' you tell me about. The Great Spirit is our father, and he has always supplied us with all we need. We do not want anything from white men. Our women are able to do our work. Go, then; let us remain in the mountains where we were born; where the ashes of our fathers have been given to the winds." In Tenaya's language, Savage asked several questions: "If you and your people have all you desire, why do you steal our horses and mules? Why do you rob the miners' camps? Why do you murder the white men, and plunder and burn their houses?" Tenaya remained silent for some time before responding: "My young men have sometimes taken horses and mules from the whites. It was wrong for them to do so. It is not wrong to take the property of enemies, who have wronged my people. My young men believed the white gold-diggers were our enemies; we now know they are not, and we will be glad to live in peace with them. We will stay here and be friends. My people do not want to go to the plains. The tribes who go there are some of them very bad. They will make war on my people. We cannot live on the plains with them. Here we can defend ourselves against them." Savage, however, insisted that the Yosemite conduct a treaty with the commissioners: "If they do not, your young men will again steal our horses, your people will again kill and plunder the whites. It was your people who robbed my stores, burned my houses, and murdered my men. If they do not make a treaty, your whole tribe will be destroyed, not one of them will be left alive." Tenaya told Savage that it was "useless to talk to you about who destroyed your property and killed your people. If the Chow-chillas do not boast of it, they are cowards, for they led us on.[8]

Finally, Tenaya promised to bring in his people and with Savage's permission departed. He returned the following day, informing the Americans that his people soon would arrive to conduct a treaty with the commissioners. Two days later, when the Indians had failed to appear, the Americans made preparations to enter the Yosemite Valley. The steep hillsides and deep snow, Tenaya argued, would hinder their progress, and his village lay deep in the valley.[9] Not deterred on March 25, 1851 Savage, Tenaya and two companies of the Mariposa Battalion, departed for the valley.[10]

Halfway to the entrance, some fifteen miles from camp, the battalion

Yosemite Lodge, probably by A.W. Chase. From Stephen Powers, *Tribes of California.* (Courtesy of the Bancroft Library, University of California, Berkeley.)

entered the Yosemite Valley.[14] Near the foot of the peak later named El Capitan they found a recently abandoned village. They also uncovered a large cache of acorns and other provisions. Savage sent a detachment to reconnoiter some of the open land, while the main column proceeded up the valley towards smoke billowing from, it was discovered, an abandoned encampment. Another village was located near the southwest base of a mountain to be called Half Dome, but it too was deserted. Scouting parties scoured the area but found only an old woman. When Savage asked where the Indians were, she curtly replied: "You can hunt for them if you want to see them!"[15] The Americans provided the woman with firewood and food and allowed her to remain in the valley.[16]

Other unoccupied villages contained the bones of horses and mules and miners' tools and other American manufactured items. One of the volunteers recovered a bridle and part of a reata that had been attached to a mule Indians had stolen while he and the other members of the battalion were camped near Agua Fria. Baskets, robes made of rabbit and squirrel skins, musical instruments, bone tools, obsidian, and salt also were found. Stores of food included acorns, piñon nuts, grass seeds, wild oats, dried worms, scorched grasshoppers, and the dried larvae of insects. Convinced that a scorched-earth policy would drive the Indians to the San Joaquin Valley, Savage burned all the artifacts, food, and clothing.[17]

Their work completed, Savage and his party rejoined the battalion at its camp on the Merced, where the Yosemite, Nukchu, and Pohonichi were being held. On March 29 the two companies and the Indian prisoners departed for the commissioners' camp on the Fresno River.[18] Captain William Dill's company moved out first and upon reaching the river encountered one hundred Indians, who voluntarily surrendered. Dill took them to the commissioners' camp. Captain John Bowling's company, Savage, and the other Indians followed. A few miles from their destination, they encamped, and the following day most of the volunteers, including Savage, departed for the Fresno. Left behind to guard the Indians were Bowling and nine men. More men were not deemed necessary, noted Bunnell, because the Indians "all appeared contented and satisfied, almost joyous, as we neared their destination on the Fresno. The truth is, we regarded hostilities, so far as these Indians were concerned, as ended. We had voted the peace policy a veritable success."[19] The "vote," however, was premature, because four Chauchila runners entered the camp at night and convinced the prisoners that the Indians already in custody had been harmed. About 250 escaped.[20]

Bautista, whose Potoyanti had gathered in the vicinity of the commissioners' camp to attend the forthcoming council, volunteered to bring in the runaways. He was to assure the Indians that if they returned they would be protected from the Chauchila. A few days later, Bautista arrived with about one hundred of the runaways, and most of the others came in a short time later.[21] But a snowstorm prevented Bautista from overtaking Tenaya and his followers, who returned to the Yosemite Valley. For his service the commissioners presented Bautista with two blankets, a pair of pantaloons, a flannel shirt, and a handkerchief.[22]

The commissioners understood that the Chauchila were the key to peace and decided to delay the negotiations until they arrived. On April 7, Indian runners told Savage that the Chauchila were coming in to effect a treaty. Two days later a few Chauchila women arrived, informing the Americans that others were on their way. On the twelfth a Chauchila emissary explained that the delay was a result of the severe illness and expected death of their chief, José Rey. He had been badly wounded in the engagement with Savage and his men in January. The Chauchila would arrive after the proper funeral rites had been conducted. O. M. Wozencraft told the emissary that his people should proceed to the recently established camp on the San Joaquin River. Already at Camp Barbour were two or three hundred Indians.[23]

As the commissioners prepared to treat with the Indians, the Mariposa Battalion departed on what was to be a major campaign against the Chauchila. Because "the meddlesome interference of these Indians prevented other bands from coming in," wrote Bunnell, "it was necessary, if a peace policy was to be maintained with other tribes, that this one be made to feel the power they were opposing."[24] A comrade anticipated stiff resistance from the Chauchila, because "they have refused all overtures of peace and have committed the most daring robberies and unprovoked murders in the neighborhood of fine and coarse Gold Gulches."[25]

One hundred men under the command of James Savage headed for the north fork of the San Joaquin River by way of Coarse Gold Gulch and the headwaters of the Fresno. They intended to sweep the area clean of Indians.[26] As soon as the battalion approached their territory, the Chauchila sent word to Savage: "Come on, we are ready for you." Savage soon realized that not until the mud dried and the rain and snow ceased could a successful attack be launched.[27] While the command was camped near Coarse Gold Gulch, a small party of whites, guided by a neophyte called Sandino, arrived with a letter from the commissioners requesting that Savage return to their camp. Turning over the command to John Bowling and issuing last-minute instructions, Savage departed for Camp Barbour.[28]

Bowling led the companies to the north fork of the San Joaquin, where they camped on April 24. The next morning a scouting party discovered the tracks of many Indians. The Americans followed the tracks upriver and up a mountain to a recently deserted village consisting of about 150 lodges and containing a large supply of acorns. The Indians had abandoned most of their provisions and some clothing.[29] The Americans also discovered the remains of an individual recently cremated. Arrows, a metal mirror, beads, and a knife were found with the body. Recognizing the knife, Sandino exclaimed: "José Rey, ah! he is dead!" He told Bunnell that a chief's property was easily recognizable and that the Indians had known for a long time that he would die. Sandino was certain that a large number of Indians had attended the funeral ceremony and that only a great chief would have drawn so many mourners.[30]

After destroying the village, Bowling and his men followed the Indians' trail to another vacated village of about the same size and with the same quantity of provisions. There they camped on the night of April 27. The next morning, the two companies separated, each following a different trail and each discovering a recently abandoned village. In his report to Savage, Bowling noted "that there are more Indians in this section of country than any one had supposed." Concluding that further pursuit would be fruitless and running low on provisions, Bowling turned back.[31]

As the companies moved downstream, Indians appeared on the opposite bank, yelling insults. Bowling sent an unarmed volunteer to the water's edge to speak with them. The Indians released a volley of arrows at him. The Americans returned fire, hitting four Indians. "The following morning," wrote Bowling in his report, "we made tracks for headquarters." Without twenty-five days' rations, "it would be labor lost, and money foolishly expended by this State, to send men into that portion of the country."[32] The companies arrived at Camp Barbour on May 1.[33]

Bunnell admitted that victory had eluded them: "We had expected that this tribe would resist our invasion of their territory and show fight. In this we had been disappointed. The self-confident and experienced mountain men, and the ex-rangers from the Texan plains, felt annoyed that these Indians had escaped when almost within range of our rifles. Our feelings—as a military organization—were irritated by the successful manner in which they had eluded our pursuit, and thrown us from their trail. *We had been outwitted by these ignorant Indians*; but as individuals, no one seemed inclined to acknowledge it; our lack of success was attributed to the restraints imposed on the free movements of our organization by orders of the commissioners."[34]

While the two companies under Bowling operated on the upper waters of the San Joaquin, John Kuykendall and his company marched to the Kings River, attacked a village, and captured several Indians. Most of the residents, however, fled toward the headwaters of the Kaweah. The Americans gave chase on foot, and on a ridge they spotted Indians who defiantly turned their backs to the Americans in what Kuykendall called "a very peculiar manner." The Indians then moved into country too rugged to be followed. Upon returning to the village they had attacked, the Americans discovered that in their absence Indians had carried away their dead. Kuykendall decided to end the campaign, because horsemen could not operate effectively in the mountains. Dismounted, his men were useless.[35]

With the return of Kuykendall's company, the Mariposa Battalion was reunited, and Savage decided on a two-pronged operation. He ordered Bowling and thirty-five men to march against the Yosemite: "You will, if possible, surprise them and whip them well. But in the event you cannot surprise them you will make use of any means in your power to induce them to come down and treat."[36] The other company, led by Savage, was to invade the region south of the Yosemite Valley, an area occupied by the Monos. Savage departed on May 4, locating and destroying a large cache of acorns on the seventh. Later, from a mountaintop Savage, three volunteers, and two Indian scouts spotted campfires far in the distance.[37]

Traversing extremely rugged country and discovering Indian trails but no Indians, Savage concluded that they had passed over the Sierras. On their way down to the valley, the volunteers encountered a party of male Indians on the opposite bank of the San Joaquin River. Savage sent Arosio, one of his Indian scouts, to make contact. Disdaining an invitation to hold a conference, the Indians told Arosio they were heading east. Savage and his command returned to their base camp on May 17. Although he had little to show for his efforts, Savage believed he had forced nearly all the Monos to retreat east across the mountains.[38]

By this time, Bowling's command had entered the Yosemite Valley. On My 10, at the upper end of the valley, the Americans captured five Indians.[39] Three were the sons of Tenaya.[40] Bowling told the Indians that if the Yosemite would accompany him to the San Joaquin Valley and negotiate a treaty with the Indian commissioners they would not be harmed. One of Tenaya's sons convinced Bowling that if he and a companion were released, he would bring in his father and all the Yosemite by noon the next day. Bowling agreed but kept three Indians as hostages.[41]

When the two Indians failed to return Bowling sent Sandino and other Indian scouts to contact Tenaya. A short time later Sandino reported that the chief had no desire to come in. He would make peace with the whites if allowed to remain in his own territory, but he would not relocate to the valley. His people would remain in the mountains or join the Paiute. Bowling immediately dispatched some of his men and Sandino to bring in the chief, alive if possible.[42]

While the party was searching for Tenaya, one of the Indian hostages escaped. The Americans promptly lashed the other two to an oak tree. Their guards, apparently seeking to endear themselves to their officers, allowed the Indians to untie themselves and shot and killed one as they dashed for freedom. The act, although condemned by most members of the battalion, went unpunished. The man killed was Tenaya's youngest son.[43]

The party sent to bring in Tenaya found a recently deserted village at the head of a small valley. The volunteers and Indian scouts pursued the Indians up the side of a mountain only to be met with a shower of huge rocks. Several were knocked down and one was seriously injured. From behind boulders the volunteers fired at the Indians, killing one and forcing the others to retreat.[44] On their way back to camp, two of the volunteers, carrying the injured man, encountered Lafayette Bunnell, Tenaya's other

Lafayette H. Bunnell. (Courtesy of the Yosemite Museum Library, Yosemite National Park, California.)

son, and another Indian. Under orders from Bowling, Bunnell and the Indians had set off to find Tenaya's hiding place. Had the injured man and Bunnell not intervened, the volunteers would have murdered the two Indians on the spot.[45]

Eventually captured and brought into camp, Tenaya saw the body of his son. As recounted by Bunnell, the chief "halted for a moment, without visible emotion, except a slight quivering of his lips. As he raised his head, the index to his feelings was exhibited in the glaring expression of deadly hate with which he gazed at Captain Boling [sic], and cast his eyes over the camp as if in search of the remains of the other son." Bowling expressed his regrets over the killing and allowed the chief to take the body up a canyon to dispose of it in the tradition of the Yosemite.[46]

For several days Tenaya remained silent, and when the opportunity was right he dashed for the Merced River. Caught just before plunging in and brought before Captain Bowling, Tenaya warned his captor "when I am dead I will call to my people to come to you,.. to avenge the death of their chief and his son. Yes, sir, American, my spirit will make trouble for you and your people, as you have caused trouble to me and my people.

With the wizards, I will follow the white men and make them fear me.... You may kill me, sir captain, but you shall not live in peace. I will follow in your footsteps, I will not leave my home, but be with the spirits among the rocks, the water-falls, in the rivers and in the winds; wheresoever you go I will be with you. You will not see me, but you will fear the spirit of the old chief, and grow cold."[47]

Apparently, only Lafayette Bunnell gained the trust of Tenaya, the chief providing him with the Indian names of many of the valley's geographical features. Allowed a certain amount of freedom of movement during his interviews with Bunnell, Tenaya bided his time. Again he ran for the river. Caught a second time, he was tied by a rope to a tree. He could move only as far as his tether would allow.[48]

In mid-May, Bowling sent a few of his men to the Fresno to procure supplies.[49] In a letter to James Savage, he recounted some of the events that had transpired and requested ten or twelve Nukchu scouts. With them he would capture the Yosemite women and children and thereby force the men to surrender. Bowling also intended to use Tenaya "to the best advantage in pursuing his people."[50] While the command waited for supplies, Bowling led some thirty men, including Tenaya and Sandino, up a ravine later known as Indian Canyon. Sandino served as guide and as translator for Tenaya. Upon reaching the third table-top in the canyon, most of the party rested, while Bunnell, nine whites, and the two Indians pushed on.[51]

Their progress, however, was hindered by the delaying tactics of his Indian guides. "Ten-ie-ya complained of fatigue," wrote Bunnell, "and Sandino reminded me that I was traveling very fast. My reply to both cut short all attempts to lessen our speed; and when either were disposed to lag in their gait, I would cry out the Indian word,' We-teach,' meaning hurry up, with such emphasis as to put new life into their movements." When Bunnell discovered a new trail, "Ten-ie-ya once more found voice in an attempt to dissuade me from this purpose, saying that the trail led into the mountains where it was very cold, and where, without warm clothing at night, we would freeze. He was entirely too earnest, in view of his previous taciturnity; and I told him so." Convinced that he had found the trail to where the Yosemites were hiding, Bunnell returned to camp. He told Bowling that Sandino stood in fear of Tenaya and "as a guide, no dependence could be placed upon him."[52]

The party Bowling sent to the Fresno to procure supplies returned on the twentieth with twelve Nukchu scouts.[53] Tenaya failed to convince their leader, Chowchitty, that the Yosemite had joined the Paiutes on the eastern side of the Sierra. Chowchitty assumed they were hiding in some rocky canyon either in the valley or near the Tuolumne River. Accepting Chowchitty's advice that they pursue the Yosemite on foot, Bowling and his men departed from their base camp with three days' rations. They proceeded up a canyon to above a body of water later known as Mirror Lake, where they discovered Indian tracks. They followed the trail to an area covered with snow from five to ten feet deep, but there the tracks ended. Chowchitty, however, pushed on, pointing out small pieces of granite, which he claimed had been displaced by Tenaya's scouts. Bowling, failing to discern any Indian signs, questioned Chowchitty about leaving the main trail. "The hiding-place of the Yosemities is not far off," he replied. "If they had crossed mountains their scouts would not be so careful to hide their trail. They would… hide their tracks when they were again far from the valley and near their rancheria."[54] Chowchitty led the Americans to the head of a canyon, where a trail crossed into the upper valley of the Tuolumne. Chowchitty told Bunnell that, "if we don't find them at the lake, we will soon know if they have crossed the mountains." Shortly, Chowchitty pointed to a dim circle of blue smoke under the lee of a large peak. As Bunnell lowered his "line of vision to the base of the cliff, to trace the source of the smoke, there appeared the Indian village, resting in fancied security, upon the border of a most beautiful little lake, seemingly not more than a half mile away. To the lake I afterwards gave the name of Ten-ie-ya."[55]

Discovered by a Yosemite, the Americans and Nukchus had no choice but to storm the village. The Yosemite had no time to resist or escape and surrendered without a fight. The half-starved captain of the village told Bowling that the thirty-five Indians present were all that remained of the Yosemite. The rest had returned to the groups from which they had originated. When asked if he and his followers would relocate to the San Joaquin Valley, he replied: "Where can we now go that the Americans will not follow us? … Where can we make our homes, that you will not find us?"[56] It was Chowchitty and his scouts, not the Americans, who located the Yosemite. Without their assistance, acknowledged Bunnell, "we probably would have gone back without seeing an Indian."[57] The Americans put the men but not the women and children under guard and escorted them back to camp. To facilitate the return journey to the San Joaquin Valley, Bowling divided equally the burdens to be carried by Yosemite men and women, but this interference in their division of labor brought protests from members of both genders.[58]

At the Fresno River, Bowling informed Commissioner George Barbour that the Nukchu scouts had "performed important service voluntarily and cheerfully, making themselves generally useful, particularly in catching the scattered Indians after surprising a rancheria. Of the Yosemities, few, if any, are now left in the mountains." The Indians had "been taught the double lesson, that the white man would not give up the chase without the game; and at the same time, if they would come down from the mountains and behave themselves, they would be kindly treated."[59] The Americans turned the Indian prisoners over to the commissioner who commended them for their success.[60] Rounding up Indians was one thing, but convincing them to relocate to reservations was quite another.

CHAPTER XIII

Negotiations Conclude

While the Mariposa Battalion was in the field, the Indian commissioners, accompanied by the military escort, moved from Camp McLean on the Fresno to the San Joaquin River, where they established Camp Barbour on April 14, 1851. There they met some five hundred Indians.[1] Tomquit led the Pitkachi but spoke for the Gashowu, Dumna, Dalinchi, and Posgisa. Pasqual governed the Wechihit but negotiated for the Aiticha, Choinimni, Chukamina, Nutunutu, and Wimilchi. Naiyakqua ruled the Heuchi but represented the Chukchansi, Chauchila, Pohonichi, and Nukchu.[2] On April 16, with Lieutenant John Hamilton serving as interpreter, Redick McKee opened the conference:

> We are happy to meet so many Indians in council to-day, evincing a desire to live on terms of peace and friendship with your white brethren, under the protection of the Great Father at Washington.... The President has sent a few presents of blankets, shawls, &c., as a token of his good-will towards you, which we will give you after a treaty has been made. The President has discovered, by experience in taking care of your many red brethren over the big mountains, that the Indian must have a home he can call his own; and the product of his labor should be his—not similar to the old missions in this country, where the labor of the Indian made the white man rich.... To accomplish this the President will give you a district of country bordering on the rivers you already know, where you may settle yourselves and families out of the mountains, and will furnish you with farming implements, stock, &c., that you may draw

your subsistence from the soil, and thus prevent the necessity for your stealing cattle and other property for a subsistence, as you do while you make the mountains your home. Also, when you are thus entitled, the President can protect you both from bad whites and bad Indians.... We wish you to take a little time to talk this matter over among yourselves; and when you meet us again come prepared to speak out your views plainly and fearlessly. In your deliberation you must consider that we are seeking your good, and have no other object in view; that the President will give you a farmer to teach you to farm, a blacksmith and a carpenter to work for you, and teachers to instruct yourselves and children; also stock, ploughs, some clothes, &c. If you take advantage of these things you will become a better people—your children learn to read and write, and the next generation may, perhaps, possess the knowledge of the whites; and, lastly, while you are making this change of living, he will give you some beeves and flour to assist in your support. Think of these things, and at 5 o'clock this afternoon meet us again and let us hear your reply.[3]

When the meeting reconvened at the designated time, O. M. Wozencraft, doubting the few Chauchila present were representational, called upon Poholeel, the leader of the Chauchila delegation, to address the issue. Yes, the Indian replied, he and his seventeen followers represented all the Chauchila. More were not in attendance because they were caring for their wounded chief, José Rey. Regarding the Monos allied with the Chauchilas, Poholeel claimed he lacked the authority to bring them in. Many of the Monos had fled into the mountains and refused to negotiate. Wozencraft remained dubious about Poholeel's status, but James Savage identified the Indian as the brother of José Rey and first in line to inherit the chieftainship. George Barbour and McKee overruled Wozencraft and recognized the authority of Poholeel to negotiate for the Chauchila.[4]

On April 28 the commissioners, with the assistance of James Savage and Lorenzo Vinsonhaler, delineated the territorial limits of the reservation and determined the amount of provisions and the kind of assistance to be provided. The commissioners then described to the Indians the area to which they must relocate, noting that they would have the right to collect wild foods beyond the reservation's boundaries. They promised the Indians 500 head of cattle, 260 sacks of flour, 3,000 pounds of iron, 500 pounds of steel, seeds, clothing, and other items each year during 1851 and 1852. Although some of the items would not be delivered until sanctioned by the President, others would be forthcoming. That day the commissioners contracted with Pablo de la Toba to deliver eighty head of cattle to what would be called the Fresno Reservation. Forty head also were to be supplied to the Merced Reservation where Adam Johnston would distribute them. Once the animals arrived Redick McKee would pay the supplier approximately five hundred dollars in cash, or what amounted to forty dollars per head.[5]

The following day, after the commissioners had explained in detail the provisions of each article in the treaty, the chiefs put their marks next to their names. As in the first treaty the Indians transferred title of their lands to the United States and permitted the army to construct a military post on the reservation. On behalf of all the Indians present, the commissioners presented to Naiyakqua a copy of the treaty.[6] They also delegated to Naiyakqua authority over the Yosemite once they relocated to the reservation. The Monos would be confined there as well. The three commissioners signed the treaty, as did nine witnesses: secretary John McKee, Subagent Adam Johnston, another civilian, and Captain E. D. Keyes and four of his officers. Lieutenant John Hamilton signed as interpreter.[7]

Of all the Indians present at the meeting, Pasqual most impressed Keyes. Many years later, he recalled that the Indian "had uncommon intelligence, and could speak Spanish, which he had learned at a mission where he was born, and from which he had fled to the mountains many years before. He wished to know all about San Francisco and the white people who were flocking to it." To Keyes, Pasqual proved "the unity of the human family." In a ceremony performed by the Indians, however, Pasqual also proved his Indianness: "His incantations in a war-dance surpassed anything of the kind I ever saw before or since. He was naked from the waist upwards, and the position of his body and arms, and the expression of his face in some of his attitudes, might have served as a mode for a statue of Moloch."[8]

The second treaty with the Indians of California concluded, the commissioners decided to separate, each to negotiate in different sections of the state. On May 1 they drew lots to determine their areas of operation. Redick McKee got the northern section, from the Oregon boarder south to the headwaters of the Sacramento River; O. M. Wozencraft received the middle district, from the headwaters of the Sacramento south to where the San Joaquin River flows in a westerly direction; and George Barbour drew the southern section, which extended from the San Joaquin south to the Mexican border.[9]

Before departing to their respective districts, they drafted a letter to Commissioner of Indian Affairs Luke Lea, informing him of the negotiations and describing the location of the Fresno Reservation. They estimated that it could support five or ten times the seven hundred Indians then in residence; between two and three thousand persons eventually would make it their home. The commissioners claimed they had "broken the confidence of the hostile tribes in their ability to contend with the whites, and we trust will end the war and bring about a general pacification of this whole frontier." The land set aside for exclusive Indian occupancy, although "liberal in extent," was unlikely "to be ever coveted by the whites." It had no agricultural value, "and so far as we can ascertain, not more than one Mexican grant, and that of very doubtful authenticity, covers any part of it." The Indians were "generally a hale, healthy, good-looking people, not inferior to their red brethren in the southwestern States." Many were neophytes who already had "some knowledge of letters, of stock-raising, and agriculture. We think they will therefore make rapid improvement when schools, &c., shall be established among them."[10]

They admitted issuing generous provisions of beef to the Indians, but "we have to do the best we can, fully satisfied that our policy is correct, and that it is in the end cheaper to feed the whole flock for a year than fight them for a week." They concluded their letter by explaining why they had divided the state into three districts and how they intended to proceed. Their object was "to expedite and finish these settlements and negotiations at the earliest practicable day, and thus economize both time and expense. We are now largely indebted for flour and cattle, and await the arrival of the mail with anxiety. If further remittances do not reach us soon, our operations must necessarily be suspended."[11]

McKee turned over to Barbour what remained of the goods purchased for the Indians and, in the company of John McKee and Wozencraft, departed for San Francisco. Arriving in early May, he learned that Congress had reduced the appropriation the Indian Office had requested for the continuation of negotiations from $75,000 to $25,000. McKee notified Lea that the original $25,000 granted by Congress had been spent. If the Indians again took up arms, he warned, it would result from the meager sum appropriated by Congress.[12]

McKee also wrote to Barbour. He calculated that the recent appropriation would cover expenses only for the two reservations thus far established. But peace "depends upon our ability to keep the Indians in good humor by liberal appropriations for their subsistence.... How this is to be done by means of a pitiful grant of $25,000 is beyond my arithmetic." Indians who sign treaties in the future would have to be satisfied with the provisions the commissioners had on hand and with the promise that beef and flour would be delivered sometime in the future. McKee was thankful that the most hostile and destitute Indians had been dealt with first and was hopeful that those still to be contacted would not object too strongly to a delay in receiving their provisions. He reminded Barbour that in November 1850 he had informed Commissioner Lea that to properly perform their duties they needed an appropriation of $100,000 or $150,000.[13]

McKee wrote to Wozencraft the same day, suggesting that it would be "inexpedient either to incur any large personal responsibility, or, by our action, implicate the Indian department, until the ways and means are provided by Congress."[14] Immediately, Wozencraft sent a letter to Commissioner Lea. Because the land set aside for the Indians was largely unsuitable for agriculture, the Indians should be provided not only with beef cattle but with brood stock as well. Providing the animals, of course, would cost money, "and it is a subject of surprise and regret that the appropriation for our use has been cut down so small." Wozencraft, however, would continue making contracts with individuals to supply the Indians with cattle. He pointed out that while the commissioners had operated conjointly McKee had served as disbursing officer and had made contracts and purchases without his knowledge and participation. Now that the commissioners operated separately, he intended to make his own contracts and disbursements for which he alone would be responsible.[15]

Commissioner Barbour, Captain Keyes, and the military escort, in the meantime, proceeded to the Kings River, where on May 5 they established Camp Belt. During the next few days, leaders representing ten Yokuts societies, including the Gawia, Telamni, and Tachi, and two Mono groups arrived.[16] Also in attendance were elements of the Nutunutu and Wimilchi, Indians represented at the previous conference under the general authority of Pasqual. Nine leaders spoke for the Nutunutu and Wimilchi.[17] Barbour informed Lea that the assembled Indians "have all been hostile, and a majority of depredations upon the lives and property of the 'whites' in this part of the State have been committed by these tribes; they are more athletic and warlike than any Indians I have seen in the State, and more intelligent."[18] Most likely Barbour was aware that only a few months before, several whites had lost their lives in the Four Creeks. On January 4, 1851 Gawia Indians, under the command of Francisco, had killed John Woods, his employee, and several immigrants and Californios.[19] They partially destroyed the bridges Thomas Paine had constructed in the area as well.[20]

With considerable apprehension, therefore, Barbour opened negotiations on May 12 with twelve chiefs, including Manuel of the Nutunutu, Francisco of the Gawia, and Quintin of the Tachi. He told them that "the President of the United States desired to see all of his people at peace with one another, that he desired to make his Red people as well as his white ones, happy." Far to the east, Indians like themselves had "been at war with the whites, but the whites had whipped them in many battles, killing a great many of their Chiefs and Warriors." Eventually, those Indians had made peace and now "all live like brothers." The President "had a great many warriors, and could send an Army strong enough to destroy all the Indians in California, but he did not desire to do so, and would rather be friendly with them, and assist them to live, and get Rich, and be happy, like the Indians beyond the Mountains."[21]

After consulting among themselves the chiefs, through their spokesman, Manuel, admitted that some of their men had fought the whites but insisted that most never had harmed an American. They were willing to negotiate and would not deceive the commissioner. That evening Barbour explained the articles of the treaty.[22] In most respects they mirrored those in the other two treaties. Six hundred head of beef cattle were to be delivered to them each year during 1851 and 1852.[23]

All the chiefs except Francisco of the Gawia agreed to the provisions of the treaty. He objected to giving up part of the Four Creeks, which was rich in game and fish and contained the ashes of his father. Barbour told Francisco that if his people did not vacate the area they would be destroyed by the whites, "who were much exasperated against them, for the many cruel murders they had committed." The other chiefs persuaded Francisco to relinquish his claim to the Four Creeks, and the following day forty Indians signed the treaty, thus creating the Kings River Reservation. Barbour gave a copy of the treaty to Manuel.[24] Barbour signed for the United States, and three army officers and two civilians witnessed the proceedings.[25] On May 14 Barbour distributed presents to the Indians, most departing for their respective villages the next day.[26] He sent a copy of the treaty to Commissioner Lea and noted in an accompanying letter that he had "succeeded in getting them to remove from the best portion of that country, and to settle upon lands not so good," He insisted, however, that for all practical purposes the lands would suit the needs of the Indians.[27]

By the middle of May 1851 the Indian commissioners had conducted three treaties and were well on their way to fulfilling the general goals of the United States. The specific features of the goals, however, took shape in the field and were determined to some degree by the ideas and actions of Captain E. D. Keyes. The orders he received to found a military post near each of the reservations had arrived too late to establish one at the Merced Reservation.[28] But he recommended to his superiors that a company of mounted men be stationed near the Fresno Reservation. The local Indians, he maintained, had yet to establish an allegiance to the United States.[29] Before receiving a reply and after consulting with Barbour, on May 21 Keyes sent two companies of infantry under Lieutenant Treadwell Moore to the Fresno Reservation to establish a military post.[30]

In a note to Keyes, Barbour emphasized, "that it is absolutely necessary to have a body of troops stationed at some convenient point within the territory set apart for the occupancy of the Indians that have been treated with." There were "vicious and unprincipled white men in the country who are ever ready and willing to take advantage of circumstances; and by vending ardent spirits, and otherwise imposing upon the Indians, would very soon force them to violate any treaty that may have been entered

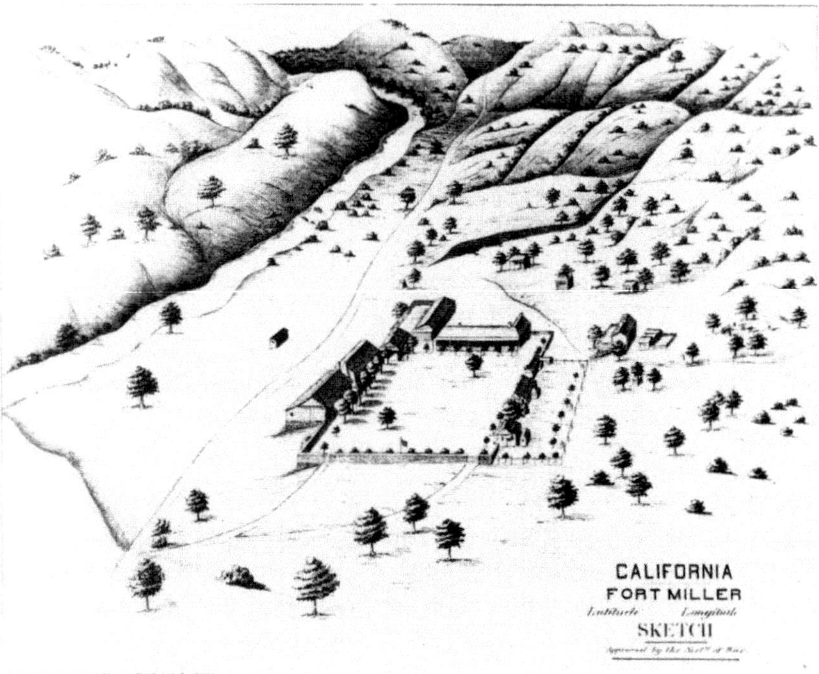

Fort Miller, Redrawn from a Sketch by Private C. F. Otto Skobel. (Courtesy of the National Archives, Washington, D.C.)

into by them. Such characters can only be overawed and prevented from committing such outrages by the presence of a force sufficient at all times to arrest them, and bring them to justice."[31] Keyes concurred. Writing to his superiors, he elaborated on what he perceived to be the military's role: "Until the Indians become habituated to their reservations and throughout impressed with the provisions of the treaties, there will be danger of misunderstanding; and a small active force on the reserves might probably prevent great subsequent evils."[32]

On May 26 Lieutenant Moore founded Fort Miller on the San Joaquin River, not far from where the Indian commissioners had conducted the second treaty.[33] Many years later, at about the age of one hundred, Pahmit, a Dumna Yokuts, told a white man that the soldiers recruited him and other Indians in the construction of Fort Miller. The Indians did most of the work. Sometimes they were whipped, and two or three died from the beatings.[34]

Two days after the founding of Fort Miller, O. M. Wozencraft, having returned to the interior after a visit to San Francisco, conducted treaty with several Yokuts and Miwok societies at the ferry run by John and Lewis Dent and James Vantine on the Stanislaus River. The treaty stipulated that four hundred head of beef cattle, two hundred goats, and two hundred sacks of flour would be delivered during 1851 and 1852. Goods and services similar to those promised in the other treaties also would be supplied. But the treaty stated that only those persons in the employ or service of the United States could use the ferries free of toll. For the benefit of the Indians, all the ferries on the Slanislaus Reservation, located between the Tuolumne and Slanislaus Rivers, were to be placed under the authority of the yet-to-be-appointed agent.[35] Wozencraft informed Lea that he had secured for the Indians the right of crossing the rivers bounding the reservation, and he recommended that the Indian Office "adopt measures at an early day to secure to them a full and exclusive right to ferries now established, as well as to those that may hereafter be established, within the limits of the reservations."[36] Wozencraft may have added that provision to the treaty because he realized the reservation lacked sufficient tillable soil to support the Indians.[37]

An additional article in the treaty stipulated that because "of the uniform friendly, honest and meritorious deportment of Captain Cornelius towards the American citizens, it is agreed and stipulated that the tract of land on which he now resides is hereby set apart for the sole use and occupancy of himself and his people...; and in further consideration of his appreciation of our republican form of government, we hereby present him with an American flag, it being the first request made by him to us." Cornelius signed for the Tuolumne, Packno for the Kotuplana. Leaders of four other groups also put their marks on the treaty. Wozencraft signed for the United Slates. The Dent brothers, Subagent Adam Johnston, and two other Americans witnessed the proceedings.[38] Noticeably absent from the meeting was the Siakumne chief, José Jesus. In February he had accepted the commissioners' invitation to conduct a treaty.[39] Sometime between February and late May he was murdered by a white man.[40] Yomillo signed in his place.[41]

On May 29, two days after Wozencraft concluded his treaty on the San Joaquin, George Barbour opened negotiations with the leaders of five Yokuts and two Mono societies at Camp Keyes on the Kaweah River.[42] Still in the territory of the stock raiders, Barbour dreaded the consequences if they became hostile. To his relief all the leaders except one were willing to negotiate. Only Pedro, a chief of a branch of the Koyeti, whom Barbour described as "a cunning, shrewd, and vicious Indian," was reluctant to leave his homeland for a reservation. But "after much 'talk' and counseling together, he finally agreed to the terms proposed."[43]

The treaty, concluded the following day, created the Kaweah and San Joaquin Reservations on two tracts of land separated by the reservations established on April 29 and May 13.[44] Barbour informed Lea that the

Indians had given up part of the Four Creeks, some of the best lands in California. The area they received, although inferior, "has a sufficiency of good soil, water, &c., to answer all their purposes for all time to come."[45] As in the other treaties, the Indians were promised a variety of goods and services, including two hundred head of beef cattle for 1851 and the same number for the following year.[46] After signing the treaty, the chiefs entrusted Pedro with their copy.[47] Barbour signed for the United Slates; five other Americans, including John Frémont, witnessed the proceedings.[48] Frémont had met Barbour on May 21. After a visit to his Mariposa ranch, he rejoined the commissioner in time to witness the conference at Camp Keyes.[49]

Barbour departed on May 30 and the following day reached the Tule River, where he learned that Juan, chief of the Chunut, with whom he had yet to treat, would contact him the next day. Juan failed to appear, and the Americans continued their march southwards. On June 2 an Indian runner informed Barbour that Juan and his party had arrived at the commissioner's previous camp. Having followed the Americans from the Kings River, the Indians were exhausted, and Barbour sent them some animals to butcher. That afternoon the Americans arrived at Paint Creek, established Camp Burton, and made preparations to meet with the local Indians the following day.[50]

Fourteen leaders, representing four Yokuts societies—Chunut, Wowol, Koyeti, and Yauelmani—agreed to the terms of the treaty. The Tulare Lake Reservation was situated on lands the Chunut and Wowol already occupied, the area between Tulare and Buena Vista Lakes. The Tule River Reservation extended from the Tule River south to Paint Creek and was located on lands the Koyeti and Yauelmani long ago had settled. The provisions and services promised in the treaty included two hundred head of beef cattle per year for the next two years.[51] Barbour was greatly impressed with the Indians, especially the Chunut and Wowol. "They seem to possess more courage, magnanimity, and intelligence, coupled with superior physical powers, than any Indians either in the San Joaquin or Tulare valley," he noted in a letter to Lea.[52] Barbour left a copy of the treaty with Juan, chief of the Chunut.[53]

Barbour and eight other Americans, including John Frémont, signed the treaty.[54] Immediately following the ceremony, Frémont departed for Los Angeles to purchase a herd of cattle he intended to sell to the Indian Office.[55] On June 4 Barbour and his military escort also headed south.[56] Shortly before Barbour arrived at the Tejón Pass, a party of Californios, probably searching for stolen stock, fought with Indians in the area. Apparently both sides lost a few lives. Although Barbour encountered terribly suspicious Indians, he soon convinced them of his peaceful intentions.[57]

On June 7, 1851 Barbour, Captain E. D. Keyes, and a military escort established Camp Persifer F. Smith at the Old Adobe, the house built by Dr. E. D. French.[58] "There are a good many Indians in this Vicinity," Barbour wrote in his journal, "and are a fine looking Race."[59] Captain Keyes remarked that among the several hundred Indians assembled, many were "good- looking," particularly the two daughters of a chief, whom he admired for their "graceful shapes and the unrivaled beauty of their teeth."[60]

Negotiations opened on June 10. Twelve leaders, representing nearly six hundred Indians speaking several languages and residing in eleven villages or village clusters, participated in the council. Chief Vicente and his brother, Chico, represented the Tejoneños. Urbano spoke for the village of Holoclame on the Kern River. Antonio negotiated for the Chumash village of Mat'apxwelxwel, located at the mouth of the Cañada de las Uvas. Felipe represented the Chumash village of Tecuya, situated a short distance to the west of Mat'apxwelxwel. Rafael was the spokesman for the predominately Chumash residents of Kashtiq, located at the top of the Cañada de las Uvas.[61] Apparently a Tataviam who had served as alcalde at Mission San Fernando, Rafael had gained valuable leadership experience before becoming the village captain.[62] José Maria negotiated for the Emigdiano Chumash who resided on the western side of the valley.[63]

The Yokuts also were well represented. Raymundo, born about 1804, negotiated for the Hometwoli, located near Kern Lake.[64] Baptized at Mission Santa Inéz, Raymundo, while still a young man, led a party of neophytes from the mission to the Cuyama Valley. Although unoccupied at the time, the valley was considered too close to the mission, so the neophytes continued on to the Tulare Valley.[65] Raymundo, however, remained a Christian.[66] Regarding the other Yokuts groups, Apolonia negotiated for the Tulamni, located near Buena Vista Lake, Francisco for the Paleuyami village of Huylmiu, José for the Chunut in the Four Creeks, and Emeterio for the Yauelmani village of Tsineuhiu on the lower Keen River.[67] Born at the village of Tubampet on Buena Vista Lake in 1799, Emeterio received baptism at Mission San Fernando in 1804.[68]

As in the other treaties, for receiving a variety of goods, animals and services the Indians "acknowledged themselves to be under the exclusive jurisdiction, control, and management of the government of the United States, and undertake and promise on their part, to live on terms of peace and friendship with the government of the United States and the citizens thereof, with each other, and with all Indian tribes at peace with the United States." The Indians and the United States agreed not to retaliate for wrongs committed by the other party, but to seek redress of their grievances from the proper civil authorities. The Indians accepted the right of the United States to erect on the reservation military posts and houses for officers, agents, and others employed in its service. In exchange for receiving the reservation, the Indian signatories quit-claimed to the United States all lands to which they had "any claim or title whatsoever."[69]

Witnessing the proceedings were four soldiers and two civilians. Barbour signed as the official representative of the United States. Twenty-nine Indians signed the treaty, including the six leaders of the Tejoneños: Chief Vicente and captains Chico, José Antonio, Martin, Francisco, and probably Zapatero, who signed as Pablo.[70] All the signatories agreed that Emeterio of the village of Tsineuhiu should receive the Indians' copy of the treaty. Barbour distributed presents to the leaders; a beef was butchered, and the Indians celebrated throughout the night."[71]

On June 11, the day after the treaty was conducted, George Barbour and his military escort departed for Los Angeles, camping some four miles from the pueblo on the sixteenth.[72] There he learned that the appointments of Redick McKee, O. M. Wozencraft, and himself as commissioners had been rescinded by an act of Congress. Because the act authorized agents, not commissioners, to negotiate treaties with Indians, the three men had been reappointed agents and were to continue operating on the instructions received as commissioners.[73]

Barbour notified Captain Keyes on the seventeenth that regrettably his services no longer were needed. Keyes had high praise for his friend: "During nearly five months that we have been associated together in the public service, I have not failed to observe the stem integrity of your conduct, and the entire forgetfulness of self which has characterized your course. You have labored to prevent war with the Indians with an intelligence and zeal which merit the approval of the country, and the remembrance of which must afford satisfaction to the succeeding years of your life."[74]

Barbour's pubic service was not yet over. While in Los Angeles he sent messages to Indian groups in the interior of Southern California to meet him on a fixed day. Before the meeting occurred, however, he heard that Indians in the Tulare Valley, with whom he recently had treated, were on the verge of war.[75] Assuming that all the Indians in Southern California remained friendly to the Americans, Barbour, in the company of ten men, left Los Angeles on June 30 for the Tejón Pass, where he met with the Indians who had signed the treaty at Camp Persifer F. Smith. He exhorted them to keep the peace, to observe strictly the promises they made in the treaty, and to rely on the United States for protection and justice. He gave them presents, and they pledged to abide by the treaty.[76]

Instead of returning to Los Angeles, Barbour headed north, holding meetings with many of the Indian leaders with whom he recently had negotiated. He found miners prospecting on the Fresno Reservation, noting in his journal that "unless the whites carry out in good faith their part, there is no telling how long the Treaties will be observed by the Indians." Barbour informed the miners of the terms of the treaty and persuaded some of them to leave.[77] He returned to San Francisco at the end of July, having been in the field for six months.[78]

On July 28 he wrote a long letter to Commissioner Lea, recounting his recent activities in the San Joaquin Valley. He acknowledged that some Indians were suspicious of American intentions, but "if the whites will not molest them, and the government will in good faith carry out the treaties that have been made with them, they will in good faith comply with the stipulation on their part." With proper attention, "In a very few years they will be greatly in advance of the Indians of the Atlantic slope in wealth, civilization and intelligence."[79]

In mid-August, Barbour again departed for the interior. Indians on the Fresno Reservation complained about intrusive miners. Again he warned the whites about provoking the Indians, but only a few ceased mining.[80] When he got word that Indians in Southern California were extremely upset at not receiving treaties, he decided to return to San Francisco, sail to San Pedro near Los Angeles, and journey inland to open negotiations.[81] While in Stockton he received a letter from the Indian Office informing him that when the money recently appropriated by Congress had been spent, he and his colleagues were to cease negotiations and assume the usual duties of agents. Back in San Francisco in early September, Barbour got another letter, this one from the acting commissioner of Indian affairs. It included an excerpt from a letter the commissioner had sent to Redick McKee ordering the agents to provide no beef or other provisions to Indians who might sign treaties in the future.[82]

Previously, Barbour had issued a license to Andrew Lane and James Noe to trade with the Indians on the Tejón and Tulare Lake Reservations. Lane and Noe had posted a five-thousand dollar bond with Barbour. On October 1 he granted George Stealey a license to trade with the Indians on the San Joaquin Reservation. Stealey also posted a bond for five thousand dollars. As it turned out those were the last official acts of George Barbour. His operating funds exhausted, he canceled his trip to Southern California and booked passage on a steamer to the East Coast. Barbour sailed from San Francisco on October 4.[83]

In Washington, D.C. Barbour recommended to Commissioner Lea that two agents or subagents be permanently assigned to California, one for the San Joaquin Valley and the other for Southern California. The agents would be subordinate to a superintendent of Indian affairs for the Pacific region, who would issue instructions from a central location. A military force of seventy mounted men would be assigned to each region. The soldiers would keep the Indians in line and prevent unprincipled white men from doing them harm.[84] On February 2, 1852 Barbour submitted his resignation as Indian agent to President Millard Fillmore.[85]

The departure of Barbour placed additional burdens on O. M.

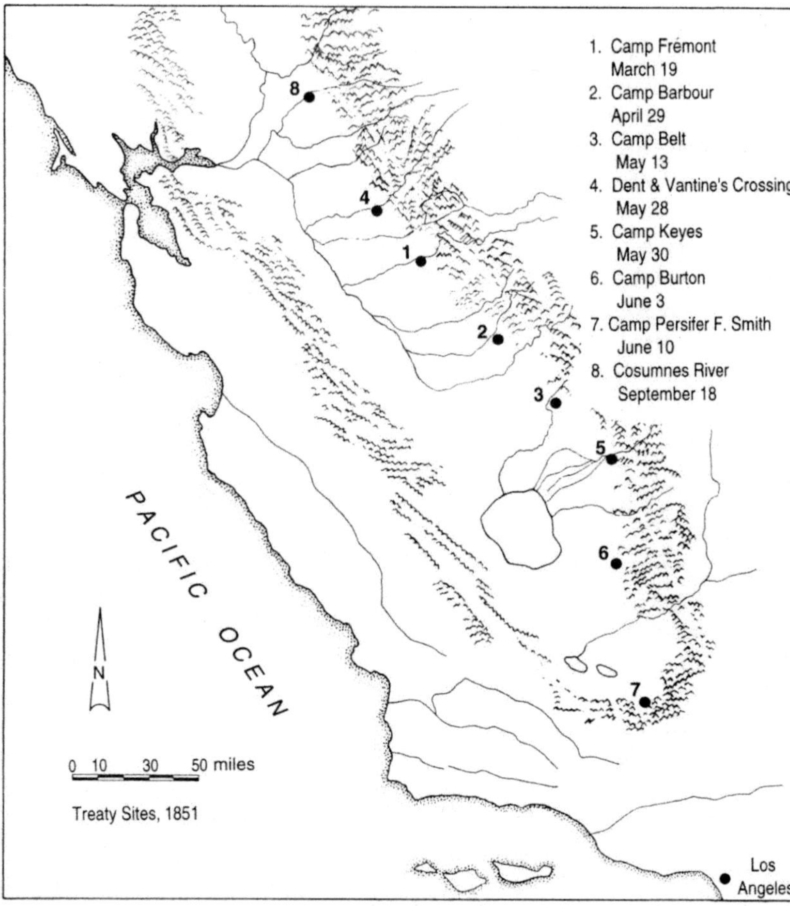

Treaty Sites, 1851

Wozencraft. At the Cosumnes River on September 18, Wozencraft conduced a treaty with three Nisenan societies and the Miwok-speaking Locolumne. Along with the standard provisions, he promised the Indians five hundred head of cattle per year for two years. Seven Indians and three white men signed the treaty.[86] But absent from the meeting was the Locolumne leader, Polo, notorious stock raider and antagonist of the Americans. He was murdered on the Mokelumne River by an ex-army officer before the council convened.[87] Poltok signed in his place.[88] Shortly after the conclusion of the treaty, Wozencraft issued to Havel Belcher a license to trade with the Indians on the Cosumnes Reservation. Belcher posted a bond for five thousand dollars.[89]

In Southern California in January 1852, Wozencraft conducted two treaties with the Indians Barbour had promised to treat with. Negotiations, however, were not undertaken until an uprising had been crushed. Antonio Garra, a Cupeño and neophyte from Mission San Luís Rey, had attempted to drive the Americans from Southern California by unifying all the Indian peoples from the Tulare Valley to the Mexican border.[90] In late 1851 he or another chief sent runners to the Indians in the valley, seeking their support. They refused to join, however, because recently they had negotiated a treaty with the Americans and intended to abide by it.[91] At the height of the crisis Zapatero journeyed to Los Angeles to inform the authorities that the Tejoneños had no hostile intentions. He presented to the authorities a certificate from George Barbour stating that he was a good Indian who had befriended white people.[92] In a letter to Commissioner Lea, Wozencraft claimed that by negotiating with the Indians in the Tulare Valley "a very formidable combination had been prevented."[93]

Despite the difficulties encountered with independent-minded Indians, the three Indian agents, in conjunction or separately, conducted between March 19, 1851 and January 7, 1852 eighteen treaties with what were perceived to be 139 Indian societies residing between the Oregon and Mexican borders. They set aside for Indian occupancy 11,700 square miles.[94] But managing Indians spread over such a vast area would prove to be difficult at best.

CHAPTER XIV

Administering to the Indians

On March 20, 1851, the day following the conclusion of the first treaty at Camp Frémont, Adam Johnston, Redick McKee, and a small military contingent escorted the Indians to the Merced Reservation.[1] A month later the agents notified Commissioner of Indian Affairs Luke Lea that the reservation contained between six hundred and seven hundred Indians, and when the Monos came in the number would increase to one thousand or twelve hundred. They estimated that between two thousand and three thousand Indians might eventually be relocated to the reservation.[2] Placed in charge of the reservation, Subagent Adam Johnston made it his headquarters.[3]

Problems with local whites soon developed. Before the reservation was established, Isaac Marks and Samuel Stone had erected three tents, built a corral, planted two gardens, and established a ferry landing on the north side of the Merced River.[4] One of the tents, which served as a store and tavern, was located only a hundred yards from an Indian village. In late March or early April a young white man got drunk at the tavern, staggered to the village, and demanded a woman for the night. The Indians rejected his demand, and when he attempted to take a woman by force, they promptly seized and bound him. He managed to free himself and took refuge in the tavern, which the Indians quickly surrounded. Adam Johnston persuaded the Indians to disperse.[5]

The following morning Johnston brought the white man before the assembled Indians where several accused him of attempted rape. As Johnston recalled the accused "protested that he 'was 'only looking for a mule,' when the Indians jumped upon and tied him. Being a white man, he elicited the sympathy of several others around, who occasionally let slip half-suppressed oaths at the Indians. Having no power at hand to adjust the matter properly, I told the Indians that the man was drunk, and did not know what he was doing." Although Johnston defused the situation by ordering the offender off the reservation, he realized that the incident was the beginning of "numerous difficulties that will naturally occur, under existing circumstances, here."[6]

In June, Johnston extinguished the claims of Marks and Stone to all their property, including tents and boats. He took the action, he explained to Lea, because the men ran a tavern and trading house and would "do mischief with the Indians in my absence." The financial disposition of the matter he left to the Indian Office.[7] Redick McKee thought the twelve-thousand-dollar claim Marks and Stone presented to the Indian Office three or four times the value of the confiscated property. He told Marks that the transaction was unauthorized and that the Indian Office probably would refuse payment. The difficulty had come about, he informed Lea, because there was no one person in charge of Indian affairs. There must be "a head, here on the ground, clothed with power to appoint, suspend, or depose agents and sub-agents; make all contracts for supplies or for carrying out treaty stipulations, conclude new treaties." In short, the head should have unlimited power."[8]

Adam Johnston continued to operate independently of McKee and the other agents. On June 10 he granted George Bell a license to trade with the Indians on the Merced Reservation. Attached to the license was a one thousand dollar annual fee.[9] Bell promised to establish a trading post, raise between six and eight thousand dollars in capital, and hire his brother, Upton, as clerk.[10] Johnston notified Lea that Bell had resided in California for several years "and is well known to the community as an energetic business man. His experience in the country and his business habits render him peculiarly fit for the position of trader in a community like that of California."[11] Between September 24 and October 24, Bell delivered to the reservation 12,100 pounds of beef at fourteen cents per pound and 3,450 pounds of flour at sixteen cents per pound. Johnston issued him a voucher for $2,246 to be paid out of the next appropriation approved by Congress.[12]

Bell hired Samuel Ward to run his store.[13] Born into a wealthy and distinguished New York family, educated in mathematics and languages at Columbia College and at Tubingen in Europe, and once married to Emily Astor, daughter of William B. Astor, the richest man in America, Samuel Ward knew nothing but privilege. After Emily died he remarried and fathered two sons, but the union did not last. By the end of the 1840s Ward saw no reason to remain in New York.[14] In February 1849 he and his cousin sailed for California, disembarking at San Francisco in June.

With a friend who had preceded them to California, they went into the merchandising business. Ward also speculated in city lands and with another partner started a mercantile and auction house. Before long he and his partners had amassed a small fortune. But after a visit to New York, Ward returned to California in 1851 to find his business affairs in a sorry state. When a fire swept through the city in May, destroying much of his remaining wealth, Ward decided to try his luck in the interior.[15]

In August he and two companions sailed to Stockton, their destination the Southern Mines. South of Stockton they stopped at the ferry run by George Belt.[16] Writing a decade later for a New York magazine called *Porter's Spirit of the Times*, Ward described the scene: "A tent, surrounded by a group of Indians, on a high bluff overlooking the river, and on the other side a narrow plain growing rapidly into hilly ground, brought us to a halt, and we learned that this was our crossing-place. Within the tent there was a small store, at the counter of which Indians were bartering gold dust, from quills and leather bags, for articles of necessity or luxury."[17]

The Indian miners fascinated Ward: "Generally the members of a wigwam kept together in their own watery pew, the father scooping into his *batea* the invisible mud and sand of the river bed, and the mother bearing it to the shore to perform those skillful gyratory manipulations by which the water is made to carry away from the shaken and rotated pan the earthy matter until after perhaps a hundred dippings and five times as many revolutions there remain at the bottom of the pan the yellow spangles surrendered by the incongruous mass and now glittering upon an enamel of black sand." The yield averaged between two and eight dollars per family.[18] Indians exchanged the gold at Belt's store for meat, flour, raisins, and brown sugar.[19]

Ward and his companions pushed on, visiting the mining camps of Quartzburg and Mariposa. Upon returning to the ferry they learned that the reservation Indians had taken from a pocket in the bend of the Merced several thousand dollars' worth of gold and with their recently acquired wealth had cleaned out Belt's store. To prevent the Indians from taking their trade elsewhere, Ward convinced Belt to sacrifice his small herd of cattle by selling the meat to the Indians at a bargain price. Belt, Ward, and his companions then hurried to Stockton to resupply the store.[20]

Henry Drought, one of Ward's companions, invested in Belt's company, and Ward, after a visit to San Francisco, accepted Belt's offer of employment.[21] He began work on September 10, 1851.[22] His duties, he recalled years later, were a "general superintendence of the purchases of cattle and flour, a fatherly care of the Indians.... and keeping Drought who lived in San Francisco advised of what was going on at the ferry."[23]

By the time Ward undertook his duties, two Indian settlements had emerged on the reservation. On the south side of the Tuolumne River

"An Indian woman panning out gold." Probably by Charles Nahl. *Hutchings' California Magizine*, 1859. (Courtesy of the Bancroft Library, University of California, Berkeley.)

resided the Coconoon, Awal, Apangasi, and Apalache.[24] At his store William J. Howard provided them with beef and flour. Because they often sought his advice regarding internal disputes and problems with whites, Howard exerted considerable authority over the Indians.[25] On the south side of the Merced, and thus technically outside the reservation, resided the Siyante and Potoyanti.[26]

The leaders of the two groups could not have differed more. As described by Ward, Bautista, chief of the Potoyanti, former resident of a Spanish mission, and onetime enemy of the Americans, displayed a Hispanic cultural heritage: "With a passion for cards, a greater belief in the efficacy of a fleet horse, fine saddle, gaudy sarape, and a tall glazed sombrero with a silver band than of prayers to the saints or the Virgin, he had acquired great skill in the use of the lasso, having been the vaquero or cattle catcher of the pious institution to which he was attached. His manners were polished, and he wore a civilized air over the quiet dignity of the savage; his face was handsome, the expression of the mouth good-natured, but he had the fugacious eye of a London 'cracksman' surveying a crowd, or a gentleman on a Mississippi steamer playing poker 'with the advantages.' His form was athletic, with indications of better feeding, as well as breeding, than the rest of his tribe." Ward, however, was more impressed with the leader of the Siyante:

> The chief of the other tribe, old Trypoxi, was a being of a higher order, though unadorned by those social and Christian graces which stamped his compeer a *caballero*. He was more dusky in hue (the other being of a bright and florid copper color) and spare of flesh, with a meekness and humility of manner which almost deepened into chronic melancholy. No episode of Mission flesh pots and scarlet kerchief had interrupted with enervating influences the sad monotony of his life struggle to keep together the small remnant of his once powerful tribe. The advent of the whites, and the comforts which they bartered for gold, had passed over his existence like sunshine over the sorrows it cannot dispel. I became subsequently greatly attached to this rare representative of savage self respect, honesty, and sensitive good faith; nor do I remember a more striking proof that the great Creator has planted all the elements of moral grandeur in the natural and unredeemed man. The intercourse between the two chiefs was as friendly and unassuming as that of the police captains of two contiguous districts in a well regulated city.[27]

A month after Ward assumed his duties, James Savage, John Marvin, and a few other white men visited the reservation. The Indians, particularly the women and children, were fascinated by Savage, who spoke to them in their own language. As recalled by Ward, "his remarks were listened to with breathless interest, and at times elicited explosive delight." Savage's visit convinced Ward that the Indians were "alive to other and deeper emotions than the superficial enjoyments of clothing and finery and the internal felicity of gratified appetites. The first step to their confidence was a knowledge of their language." Ward quickly formed plans "to approach, if not to rival, the white Savage in this particular influence over the red."[28]

The day after Savage and his party departed, Ward began his linguistic journey by inviting Bautista to a breakfast of bologna sausage. Ward also provided his guest with cigarettes and wine and got him to repeat the Potoyanti numerals. Teacher and student then moved on to the human family, anatomy, "the wants of man," the cardinal points, and the measure of time. A few days later Ward tested his vocabulary on the residents of the village. The Indians appreciated his efforts, "and often when I was stalled for a word half a score would crowd around with eager good nature to help me out of the mire. In my walks, the urchins would follow me and impress upon my attention the names of flowers, pebbles, grasses, squirrels, birds, etc., that we encountered."[29]

Although Ward learned the language of the Potoyanti to gain their affection, he also considered learning and thereby preserving the languages of other Indians, of those who "seemed already reduced to the limits of their own graveyards."[30] Writing to his sister, Julia, a few months after arriving on the reservation, Ward mentioned that he had mastered the language of the Potoyanti and was studying that of the Cheneche. The Miwok language of the Potoyanti he found "musical," but the Yokuts language of the Cheneche he thought "harsh, nasal, barbarous. I have made a grammar of the former and a vocabulary. The latter can never be pronounced from any written characters that I am acquainted with." Ward bragged that he was "a favorite with the Indians. I have great influence over the tribe.... The Chief tells me that if I could lay aside my anti-polygamic ideas and marry into the tribe they would make me an *Oyani*."[31]

It was not long before Ward's relationship with Bautista "softened from polite reserve into growing cordiality." So close had they become that the Indian could play a joke on the white man. When Ward returned from a trip to Quartzburg, Bautista invited him to dinner. As recounted by Ward, "The meal was fat and tender, but sweet! Nevertheless it was more palatable than fried bacon, which would otherwise have been my supper, and imparted a relish to the musty ship-biscuit to which our rations were reduced. When I had finished supping, the chief burst into an uncontrollable and undignified fit of laughter. While drying his tears, he replied to my puzzled look by exclaiming that I had been eating horse! It appeared that on some occasion I had expressed repugnance for that Scythian diet, and great was his glee at my unconsciousness of the trick. Their hunters, after an absence of some days, had returned from the Tulare with severalloads of meat, to the infinite delight of the tribe. My prejudice having thus been overcome, I invited him to repeat the joke as often as he should feel in the humor."[32]

Parties of Indians often journeyed to the floor of the San Joaquin Valley to capture wild horses, selling them to whites for ten to twenty dollars per head. For an additional fee of about two dollars an Indian vaquero would break each horse sold. On one occasion a white man who worked at the ferry hired a vaquero to break a roan mare. After the vaquero was thrown for the third lime, Ward jokingly "reproached Bau-tis-ta with this ignominious defeat of the rough rider of his tribe, and invited him to take the animal in hand himself. He declined undergoing the shock for any sum short of a doubloon." Bautista sent for his half brother, Sacate, who recently had lost some of his horses while gambling on the Fresno. Ward offered Sacate two silver dollars to break the animal. Although successful, Sacate "suggested an extra gratuity, alleging that every muscle in his body was still aching from the intense struggle."[33]

When circumstances warranted it, Ward could be firm with the Indians under his management. In late 1851, when a white man established a store and ferry upstream, Ward warned the chiefs and captains that anyone found selling gold or buying goods at the other post would force him to cease supplying beef and flour to all the Indians on the reservation. Ward was then distributing four beeves and eight sacks of flour a week to the Indians. Few if any Indians traded with Ward's competitor, and not many whites used his ferry.[34]

Keeping unauthorized and unwanted whites off the Stanislaus Reservation was a problem Adam Johnston also faced. On May 29, 1851 he posted a notice stating that the land was for the exclusive occupancy of the Indians and that no person would be permitted to trade with the Indians without a license. Anyone found illegally trading with the Indians would forfeit all the merchandise found in his possession and would be liable to a fine of five hundred dollars. The same fine would apply to anyone selling liquor or wine on the reservation.[35]

To those individuals he considered honest and responsible, Johnston issued trading licenses. In late May, John and Lewis Dent and James Vantine, who ran a ferry on the Stanislaus River, applied for a license to trade with the Indians on the reservation. They promised to pay a one-thousand-dollar annual license fee, to post a bond for five thousand dollars, to provide ten thousand dollars in capital investment, and to hire a clerk.[36] Johnston accepted their application and instructed them to furnish as much flour as their judgment dictated and four to five hundred pounds of beef per day to the Indians. The amount of provisions would be increased should more Indians be relocated to the reservation. They were to charge the Indian Office for their expenses and send Johnston a bill at the end of each thirty-day period.[37] Immediately, Dent and Vantine delivered $3,284.85 worth of beef and flour to the Indians on the Stanislaus Reservation.[38]

In a letter to Lea, Johnston admitted issuing licenses before receiving authorization. Had he not acted when he did, petty traffickers would have made "the most of the Indians while they could. By placing an authorized trader immediately among them, other traders were prevented from locating upon their reservations."[39] Acting Commissioner of Indian Affairs Charles Mix approved the licenses but not the fees. "In this particular," he informed Johnston, "you have fallen into error."[40]

Johnston continued to act on his own initiative. On June 1, Dr. W. M. Ryer warned him that if unchecked the contagious diseases then infecting the Indians would spread to the white population "and be attended with ruinous consequences to all those who would be living east of the coast range of mountains."[41] A short time later Johnston instructed Ryer to vaccinate the Indians residing between the Stanislaus and Kaweah Rivers. In lieu of a salary Ryer would receive two dollars per individual he vaccinated. He was to furnish his own transportation and medical supplies.[42]

Ryer found syphilis to be the most serious disease on the Stanislaus Reservation. Against it he had no remedy, but against smallpox he vaccinated 440 Indians, noting in a letter to Johnston that they "understand fully the object of the vaccination, and appreciate the interest taken in their welfare by the agents of the government."[43] They understood, Ryer believed, because some of them had been vaccinated while residing in the Spanish missions.[44] Johnston informed Lea that he had "seen them gather around Dr. Ryer in crowds, holding out their arms, eager to be vaccinated."[45] By the end of September, Ryer had vaccinated 5,230 Indians residing between the Stanislaus and Kaweah Rivers. He billed the Indian Office $13,401.[46]

Johnston explained to Lea that he had hired Ryer before seeking authorization because of "the necessity for immediate action." Vaccination would cost the government a small sum compared to the great good that would result. If his actions did "not meet the approbation of the department, I hope to be so informed immediately."[47] The acting commissioner of Indian affairs notified Johnston that his motives were "duly appreciated by this office." Because no money was available to pay for the vaccination, "the department will recommend the subject to the favorable consideration of Congress."[48]

With the health of the Indians in Ryer's hands, Johnston concentrated on the acquisition of food. Many Indians had relocated to the reservations only with the provisions they could carry with them. Some had arrived with nothing to eat because the Mariposa Battalion had destroyed the food they had prepared and stored. Moreover, the reservations lacked many of the wild plants and animals the Indians relied on for subsistence. Providing the four thousand Indians residing on the five reservations (Merced, Stanislaus, Fresno, San Joaquin, and Kaweah) under his jurisdiction with beef was the most difficult task faced by Johnston. Some of the chiefs told him they were without food and would either die of hunger or return to the mountains. In late June, Johnston informed Lea that in the absence of authority and in the best interests of the government he had furnished greater supplies of beef to the Indians than was stipulated in the treaties.[49]

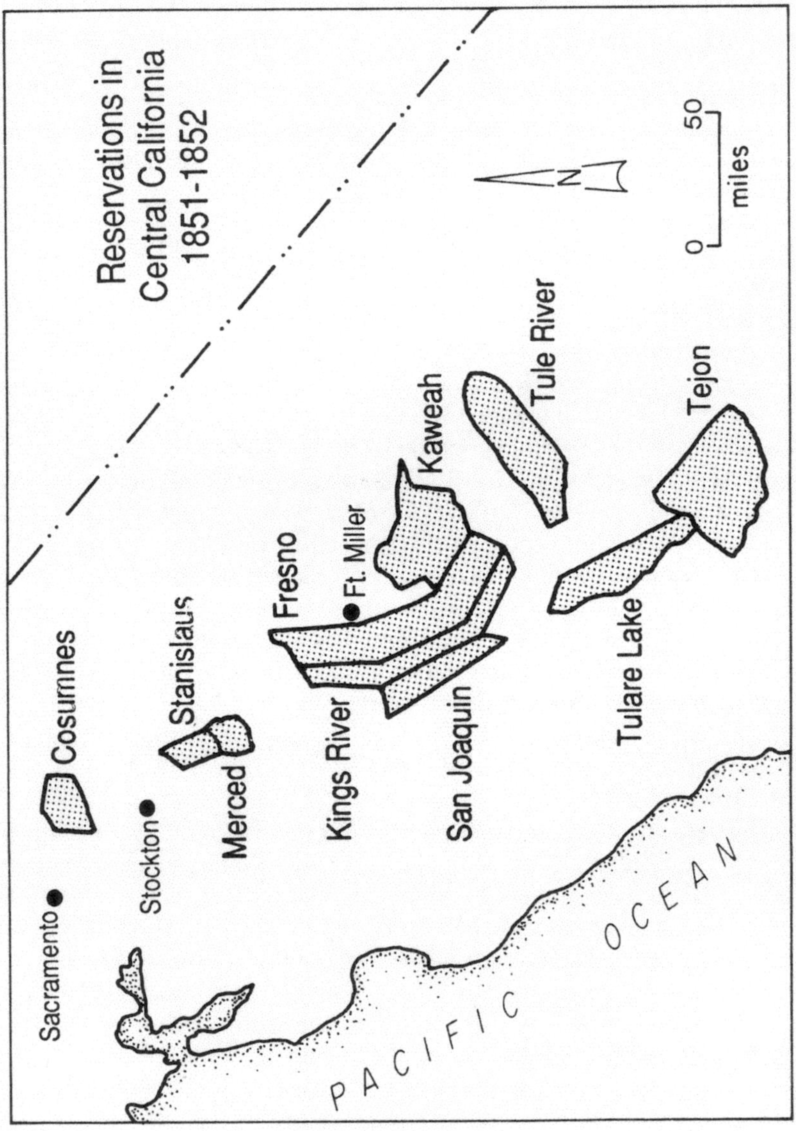
Reservations in
Central California
1851-1852
N
0
50
miles
Sacramento
Stockton
Cosumnes
Stanislaus
Merced
Fresno
Ft. Miller
Kings River
San Joaquin
Kaweah
Tule River
Tulare Lake
Tejon
PACIFIC OCEAN

A contract with the government to provide the reservations with beef was a prize eagerly sought by several ranchers, including John Frémont. On May 12, 1851, Frémont wrote to O. M. Wozencraft, proposing to furnish, between June 30 of that year and June 30, 1853, all the "beef cattle, brood-mares, and brood-cows" the Indians in Wozencraft's district would need. He would provide beef cattle on the hoof at fifteen cents per pound and the mares and cows at seventy-five dollars each.[50] Wozencraft notified Frémont that once the treaties were ratified, he would seek from the Indian Office approval of his proposal.[51]

In late May, Frémont called on Redick McKee in San Francisco, inquiring if he could make a contract with Adam Johnston or George Barbour to supply the Indians with cattle. McKee told him that neither one could make such a contract, especially Johnston, who had no authority to implicate the government in financial matters. Because Barbour had the authority to make treaties, he could purchase provisions for the Indians during negotiations, but he could not make contracts to procure daily supplies. Unauthorized contracts would be repudiated by the Indian Office, at least until the treaties were ratified by Congress. McKee warned Frémont that if he contracted with Barbour or anyone else, he did so at his own risk. Frémont said he would take the risk if the price was right.[52]

From his ranch on the Little Mariposa River, Frémont wrote to Barbour, offering to sell him beef cattle, mares, and cows at the same prices he had quoted to Wozencraft.[53] A short time later, he joined Barbour and witnessed the treaties conducted at Camp Keyes on May 30 and Camp Burton on June 3.[54] Barbour told Frémont that a conditional beef contract would be appropriate, but it would have to be approved by the Indian Office. Payment would be delayed until Congress appropriated the necessary money. Frémont accepted the conditions.[55] He was to confer with Adam Johnston regarding the number of animals to be delivered to the reservations.[56] In Los Angeles, Frémont obtained from several rancheros on personal notes three thousand head of cattle (bulls, steers, cows, two-year-olds, and yearlings) at $12.00 and $12.50 per head. Virtually worthless in the Southern California market, they would have cost between $6.00 and $7.00 if paid for in cash.[57] Frémont hired Alexis Godey, by coincidence then in Los Angeles on business, to drive the herd north. A Creole from Missouri, he had been a member of Frémont's expedition to California in 1844.[58]

Barbour caught up with Frémont in Los Angeles in the middle of June, and after tending to some business, he and ten men, including his secretary and interpreter, returned to the Tulare Valley.[59] They arrived on July 6 at the Tejón Reservation, where Barbour told the Indian leaders that a herd of cattle soon would pass through their lands and that a few head would be left with them. On the seventh he wrote to Frémont, instructing him to deliver ten or fifteen animals to the Tejoneños.[60] A week later he told

Frémont to deliver five bullocks to the Indians on the Kaweah Reservation.[61]

On July 20, from Mission San Fernando where the animals had been collected, Godey and a few vaqueros began the long drive to the north.[62] Frémont and Lorenzo Vinsonhaler remained with the herd only for a short time before pushing on ahead.[63] While the herd was slowly moving up the San Joaquin Valley, Frémont again met with Barbour. To purchase more cattle, Frémont persuaded the agent to draw on the secretary of the interior three drafts of two thousand, three thousand, and five thousand dollars. Because he lacked the authority to implicate the U.S. government in financial matters, Barbour initially objected to the request. But Frémont convinced him that only with the drafts would friends be willing to assist him in providing cattle to the Indians.[64] With the drafts, Frémont bought from American ranchers between seventyfive and eighty head of cattle at fifty dollars per animal and delivered them to some of the disaffected Indians.[65]

Although Barbour had instructed him to leave a few head with some of the Indians, Godey, according to Frémont, delivered 270 animals to six reservations: Tejón (80), Tulare Lake (50), Kaweah (36), Kings River (34), San Joaquin (34), and Fresno (34).[66] Frémont also claimed that 281 animals were butchered for the Indians: 44 at Tejón, 5 at Tulare Lake, 60 at Kaweah, 42 at Kings River, 26 at San Joaquin, and 104 at Fresno.[67] Thus, 551 head of cattle supposedly were delivered to the reservations.

In late August the vaqueros brought the herd to a halt on the San Joaquin River a few miles from Fort Miller.[68] Present were John Frémont and several of his friends and associates, including James Savage, Lorenzo Vinsonhaler, and Edward F. Beale. George Barbour and Adam Johnston also were there. Despite the loss of four-hundred head of cattle and forty to fifty horses on the drive, and the cost of paying some of the vaqueros as much as ten dollars per day, Frémont's profit was considerable.[69] For the 1,900 head he turned over to Barbour, Frémont received a draft for $142,500 on the secretary of the interior. The cattle thus sold for seventy-five dollars per head.[70] That day Barbour also issued Frémont a draft of $20,250 for the 270 animals delivered on the hoof to the six reservations. They too sold for seventy-five dollars per head. And for providing the same reservations with 140,500 pounds of butchered beef, Frémont received several more drafts totaling $21,075.[71]

Barbour turned over the herd of nineteen hundred to Adam Johnston to distribute to the Indians residing south of the Chowchilla River.[72] Johnston, in turn, assigned the animals to James Savage, who herded them to the Fresno Reservation. Most of the cattle Savage delivered to the other reservations were butchered on arrival.[73] In June, Johnston had instructed all licensed traders to provide the Indians with beef by the pound rather than cattle on the hoof. When delivered live to the Indians, the animals often escaped.[74] According to a newspaper correspondent, between August and December 1,180 head of cattle were delivered to the Indians residing on the Kings River and on the Four Creeks.[75]

Because he was continually traveling, Adam Johnston was unable to oversee the distribution of beef and cattle.[76] Keeping unauthorized whites off the reservations was his greatest concern. In late July about twenty Indians left the area near the Tuolumne River, the dividing line between the Stanislaus and Merced Reservations, because of the hostility of local whites.[77] For the same reason, Indians at some of the other reservations also fled into the foothills of the Sierra Nevada.[78] Johnston thought that a show of military force would convince unauthorized whites to vacate the reservations. On August 4 he asked General E. A. Hitchcock to place under his command a small contingent of soldiers.[79] Hitchcock, however, could not provide soldiers without permission from the President, which, he estimated, would take over two months. By that time the crisis would be over.[80]

Hitchcock informed the governor that he had received Johnston's request for soldiers. If the situation warranted immediate action, he, with the governor's approval, would remove the whites from the reservations before receiving permission from Washington.[81] The governor, however, was not about to become embroiled in such a politically delicate matter. His secretary of state notified the general that enforcing the provisions in the treaties "or preventing their infraction, belongs exclusively to the General Government,...without reference to, or regard for the approval of State authorities." The secretary warned the general that if he drove the whites from the reservations without special orders from the President, "the whole responsibility must rest with you."[82]

Hitchcock did not act but Johnston did. In August he enlisted the aid of Lieutenant Treadwell Moore, commander of Fort Miller, in removing miners from one of the reservations, probably the Fresno.[83] The miners left without incident but not without bad feelings.[84] "This would have been the result in every reservation within the valley of the San Joaquin," Johnston maintained in a letter to Lea, "could I have made the same demonstration with a few United States troops." Moreover, had he been granted either civil or military power "to carry out what had been promised the Indians, and to enforce the 'laws and regulations of the Indian bureau,' I perhaps should not have done some things in the manner I did."[85]

To convince whites to leave the reservations, Johnston sometimes made promises that far exceeded his authority. In October, for example, he appointed two men to serve as arbitrators in determining the value of improvements made by George Keeler and L. D. Chapman on the Stanislaus Reservation. Keeler and Chapman had opened a tavern and planted crops on the Stanislaus River before the reservation was created. The arbitrators estimated the two-and-a-half story frame house, a warehouse, two small buildings, and a corral were worth $21,000.[86]

Contingent upon the U.S. government accepting the terms of the settlement, Johnston promised the two men they would be compensated on March 1, 1852.[87] The day after the agreement was made, Johnston informed Keeler and Chapman that because their ferryboat landing was located on the south side of the Stanislaus River, it fell within the boundaries of the reservation, which extended to the middle of the river. They were to keep accurate receipts of tolls charged and turn over half their profits to federal authorities for the use and benefit of the Indians.[88]

Because of Johnston's personal attention, Indians on the Stanislaus and Merced Reservations received their provisions on a more regular basis than did those residing on reservations to the south. In late October, Pasqual, chief of the Indians on the Kings River Reservation, convened a council in the Four Creeks to discuss the situation. The Indians were concerned that those on the two northern reservations were receiving preferential treatment. The discontented Indians, reported the *Daily Alta California*, "are now left to the alternative of starving or violating the treaty."[89] The following month another San Francisco newspaper noted that "rumors of dissatisfaction among the Indians situated on the Four Creeks, have reached our ears, and the possibility of an outbreak had been openly discussed. The principal difficulty has been, that the supplies promised them have not been forthcoming."[90]

To head off a crisis, Johnston hastened to San Francisco in November to obtain beef and provisions for the discontented Indians. He met with O. M. Wozencraft who told him that no food could be procured. Wozencraft accused Johnston of interfering in his and George Barbour's districts and informed him that henceforth he, Wozencraft, would serve as agent in Johnston's area. In a letter to A. H. H. Stuart, secretary of the interior, Johnston claimed that "the Indians under my charge are the only ones in California who have received personal attention.... They are certainly under better control and in much better condition than in any other agency within the bounds of the State." Johnston concluded by criticizing Wozencraft. Instead of tending to the needs of those in his district, he "resides in this city, two hundred miles from any considerable number of Indians."[91]

Disregarding Wozencraft's claim that food could not be procured, Johnston found a few individuals willing to make deliveries on his word that the federal government would make good their claims.[92] John Frémont, for example, agreed to supply one thousand half sacks of flour and twelve hundred head of cattle. He charged the government thirty dollars per half sack and seventy-five dollars per animal.[93] In payment for the flour and cattle Johnston presented to Frémont's financial agent, George Wright, drafts totaling $121,500. Although he lacked authorization to make such contracts, Johnston was confident the government would honor them.[94] On November 11, 1851 he gave Frémont a receipt stating that the cattle and flour had been delivered to Frémont's ranch.[95] At that time, however, no delivery had taken place. Subsequently, James Savage obtained some of the cattle.[96]

Evidently, Wozencraft refused to assist Johnston in procuring cattle for the Indians because he intended to undertake the task himself. In December he contracted with Samuel Hensley to provide the Indians in the San Joaquin Valley with cattle. Frémont complained about the competition in a letter to George Wright, noting that "Wozencraft behaves badly." He hoped that Wright would be able to nullify Hensley's contract.[97] On February 11, 1852, however, Wozencraft awarded Hensley a draft of $142,500 on the secretary of the interior for supposedly providing the Indians with 1,900 head.[98] Hensley delivered only 1,285 animals to Wozencraft, who, in turn, assigned the herd to James Savage.[99]

In late December 1851, General Hitchcock informed the secretary of the interior about the irregularities in the delivery of cattle to the Indians, claiming that certain parties "share in the profits who would not dare be known in the transaction." Hitchcock suggested that a superintendent "of known ability and integrity and very large powers" be assigned to California. Something must be done immediately, or "the Indian Bureau in this country will be disgraced, the government deeply compromised, and the Indians probably more dissatisfied than if they had been let alone."[100]

That the Indians were being improperly served also was the thrust of Johnston's letter to Commissioner Lea in January 1852. Johnston estimated that the Indian population on the Stanislaus, Merced, Fresno, and Kings River Reservations numbered 4,450 persons. Except in limited areas none of the reservations was suitable for agriculture. He recommended that Indians on those reservations be relocated beyond the mining regions to the area around Tulare Lake, which contained fertile lands. Too many reservations had been created in California, making "it impossible for the agent, or other official, to give them his personal attention, which I look upon as all-imponant in their management."[101]

Johnston also recommended that a superintendent of Indian affairs for California and Oregon be stationed in San Francisco or some other central point. He should receive a salary of not less than $2,500 per year and be assisted by a clerk employed at $1,200. Because there was little difference in the duties and responsibilities of subagents and agents, Johnston thought that eight subagents should reside among the Indians and report quarterly to the superintendent and yearly to the Indian Office. They deserved a salary of $1,200 per annum. Six of them should reside on the west side of the Sierra Nevada, including one at Fort Miller and one near the Tejón Pass. In a thinly disguised reference to Wozencraft, Johnston emphasized that no agent "sent here by the government should consider his work so far accomplished, by rapidly passing over the country, and perhaps concluding a few treaties with the Indians, as to enable him to return to San Francisco for the balance of the year." Anticipating the problems that would ensue if traders were not properly supervised, Johnston recommended that subagents be given the authority to issue licenses. No license should be granted for longer than a year, and because "great profits are realized by Indian traders, they should pay to the agent or subagent granting the license a reasonable sum for such privilege, to be appropriated and expended for the use and benefit of the Indians."[102]

Furthermore, the unique situation in California warranted changes in the Trade and Intercourse Act of 1834. The superintendent and subagents should have more authority and independence than those operating to the east of California. Without seeking permission from the President, the superintendent should, if necessary, employ military force to ensure the implementation of Indian policy. "In a region like California," Johnston noted, "filled up with persons from every country and every clime, who, from the nature of their pursuits, are daily brought in contact, and not infrequently in conflict, with the Indians, the agent or other official should not only be a person of courage and energy, but should be clothed with such facilities as would enable him to act with promptitude and power. The most stringent laws can be of but little force unless they can be promptly administered."[103]

At the time he wrote the letter, Johnston was unaware that on January 9 Lea had terminated his services as subagent and had instructed him to turn over to Wozencraft all public property and receipts in his possession.[104] In early March 1852 Johnston notified Lea that he would render as soon as possible his accounts to the Indian Office and would send him word lists of several Indian languages.[105]

The reservations Johnston took the greatest interest in continued to function after his dismissal. From April through August 1852, Dent and Vantine delivered 52,000 pounds of beef and 15,700 pounds of flour to the Indians on the Stanislaus Reservation.[106] From the latter part of 1851 well into 1852, George Belt and Company made five deliveries of beef worth $10,715.19 to the Merced Reservation.[107]

Samuel Ward continued to manage the Merced Reservation, but not without difficulties. In March 1852 Ward took Sacate, the Indian bronco rider, to Stockton and then by steamer to San Francisco, where the Indian disappeared. Before returning to the reservation, Ward posted placards around the city, offering one hundred dollars' reward to the person who found the Indian and reported the disappearance to the police.[108] He even placed a notice in the lost-and-found section of the *Alta*.[109]

When informed about the incident, Bautista exhibited little concern. He figured Sacate would find his own way back to the reservation. Other Indians suspected that Ward had harmed Sacate, and Bautisia felt it necessary to assign him a bodyguard. For what purpose was he being guarded, puzzled Ward: "Were they precautions against my escape? or were they anticipatory of some peril to me?" On the third evening after his return, Ward heard wailing from the village. Convinced Sacate was dead, the Indians had begun their mourning ceremony. Ward summoned Bautista who explained that he had grown hoarse attempting to convince the mourners their grief had no basis. Let them "cry it out" was his advice to Ward.[110] Ward insisted, however, on going to the village "to reason or reproach the mourners into tranquilly." And with Bautista at his side, he entered the village "to face the music." Waving his hand to command silence, Ward "upbraided them with their little faith in me, who had been their father and benefactor for so many months—who had never broken a promise, nor deceived them in the faintest assurance." Then Bautista addressed the crowd, insisting that they were fools "to lament one whom I, his brother, and all the rest of his family, feel sure is alive and safe, and will return." The mourners, however, remained skeptical: "We are few upon earth, and soon shall be none; our brother is not here, and we weep; if he returns, we shall rejoice."[111]

Feliz was one of the mourners. Apparently, he had once governed the Potoyanti, but he had relinquished his office when Bautista rejoined his people.[112] Feliz had signed the treaty of March 19, 1851 as Bautista's subordinate.[113] As noted by Ward, "Feliz had not been a consistent dweller at the rancheria, though his handsome wife never attended him upon his frequent excursions, now after mustangs, now after antelopes, and sometimes after the accumulations of the Indians on the Fresno. He was a restless, uncontrollable spirit, insensible to the amenities of life, unless in view of some material result."[114]

The day after Ward visited the Indian village, Feliz, drunk and armed with a pistol, rode up to his house, spewing "a torrent of invectives and menaces." Ward demanded an explanation. Feliz, who had raised Sacate, exclaimed: "I came back last night to my people, and found my brother Sacate was gone. Our women mourned him for dead; you took him away, and have either slain or sold him. Life for life, and I want yours." Feliz then fired at Ward. Had another Indian not grabbed his arm, Feliz might

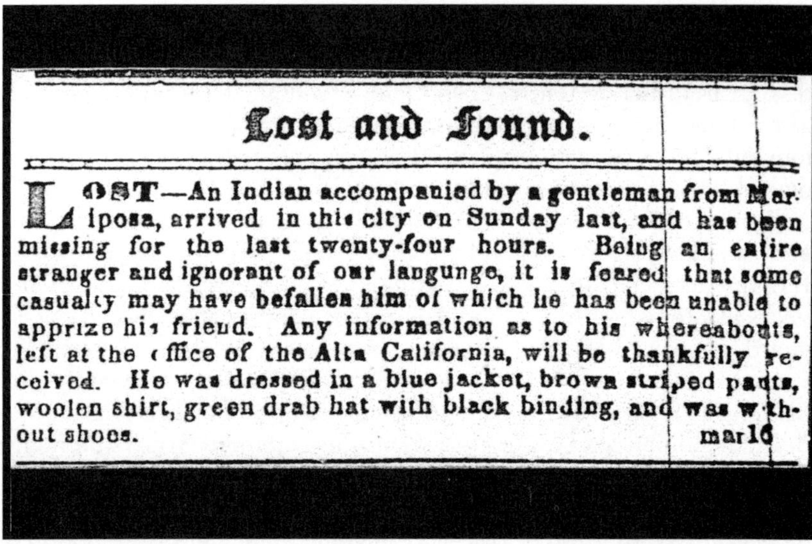

Lost and Found.

LOST—An Indian accompanied by a gentleman from Mariposa, arrived in this city on Sunday last, and has been missing for the last twenty-four hours. Being an entire stranger and ignorant of our language, it is feared that some casualty may have befallen him of which he has been unable to apprize his friend. Any information as to his whereabouts, left at the office of the Alta California, will be thankfully received. He was dressed in a blue jacket, brown striped pants, woolen shirt, green drab hat with black binding, and was without shoes. mar16

Samuel Ward's notice for Sacate. (*San Francisco Daily Alta California*, March 16, 1852.)

have hit his target. Leveling his gun at Feliz, Ward told the Indian that he deserved to die for attempting to kill "the benefactor of your tribe. If the white men up the river knew this, they would make bloody work with you all. I neither sold nor killed your brother Sacate; he ran away from me and will return; if not, others have detained him and he alone is to blame. You are drunk and crazy, and I spare you for the sake of your tribe." Ward placed Feliz under arrest, notifying the Indians that he would pass sentence the following day.[115]

That evening, while discussing with Ward the fate of Feliz, Bautista and Trypoxi recognized the distinctive howl of Sacate. Ward learned from Bautista that "for the purpose of recognition at a distance in the dark, every one of his tribe adopted, from childhood a distinctive cry or scream; that the sound we had just heard was Sacate's howl, passed on, as it were, by telegraph, perhaps two or more miles from camp." Arriving half an hour later, Sacate told Ward he had been afraid to take the steamer back to Stockton. He also explained to the quickly assembled Indians that he had left his white friend on his own accord and had not been mistreated. Sacate then recounted his recent adventures. During the journey from San Francisco to the Pacheco Pass via San José, he stole eight horses. At the pass he exchanged horses with a Mexican horse thief, ending up with six animals, a saddle, bridle, and spurs. Ward found the episode amusing and decided it was in his best interests to overlook Sacate's dubious activities.[116]

The following day, in the presence of Bautista, Trypoxi, and other

Indians, Ward banished Feliz from the Merced Reservation with the penalty of being hanged or shot if found within a ten-mile radius of the village. Ward instructed the two chiefs to inform Feliz of his decision. Later, Feliz, mounted on a horse, his wife and child on a mule, departed. "When I saw the outlines of the sad couple on the horizon," Ward recalled, "above the hill over which the path led to Major Savage's camp, I felt sincere sadness at having been compelled to inflict even so moderate a penalty upon so humble an enemy; but I steeled my heart with the reflection that, according to the criminal law of civilized society, I had but condemned the individual to suffer for the good of the many." Feliz's suffering, however, was short-lived. William J. Howard hired him to provide his store with fresh meat.[117]

Ward was equally firm with whites who disrupted the social order. In the spring of 1852, when the salmon failed to appear on time, Bautista and Trypoxi sent a party downstream to determine the cause. A short time later they informed Ward that some miners had constructed a dam across the Merced and warned him that preventing an attack on the intruders would be difficult. Ward proceeded to the area and told the whites that if they did not open the dam for about two weeks to allow the salmon to pass, "your work will disappear some dark night, like a spider's web beneath the foot of a mule." They opened the dam, and the "monarch of the water," as the Poloyanti called the salmon, again became a source of food. The catch, however, was limited, causing the Indians to spend a week fishing below the dam. They returned, Ward recalled, "with several quintals of dried fish, which, so far as I could judge, was very impartially distributed among the people of the *rancheria.*"[118]

Increasingly, Indians had to rely on wild foods for subsistence. The women who went on food-collecting excursions sometimes remained away for several days. According to Ward they had become the principal providers of food on the reservation. Their poverty also was evident. "The only external emblems of mourning," Ward observed at a cremation ceremony, "were the poor women's blackened faces, and it was heart-melting to realize the indigence of a race too poor to indicate their bereavements by the slightest change of dress.... I did not fully comprehend until I assisted at this mortuary ceremony that a pocket handkerchief would hold the worldly chattels of any women of the tribe. Perhaps their hopeless and lonely wretchedness enhanced a sorrow which I never saw more sincere beneath the most lugubrious weeds of civilization."[119]

That the Indians seldom complained about their circumstances touched Ward deeply: "In fact, with the exception of Feliz, and on a subsequent occasion, Bau-tis-ta, I do not remember an inconsistent Indian in the whole tribe. The scale of their joys was confined to the restricted gamut of gradations between famine and repletion. For the females, during the brief years of their unemployed gaiety and girlhood, an occasional plagiary, in silk or cotton, from the rainbow; for the men, a horse and saddle, *sombrero* and *calzoneros* [sic] constituted, next to plenteous food, the sum of their felicity."[120]

Ward chose not to explain why he labeled Bautista an "inconsistent Indian," but probably he had in mind the Indian's actions on May 19, 1852. During a feast Bautista got drunk and stabbed his young wife to death. She was cremated the following day with her personal belongings, including some recently obtained gold dust.[121] Indians from the immediate area and from the Tuolumne River gathered to discuss the incident, but Bautista's power and influence were so great that he remained immune from both Indian and American law.[122] No one interfered with him when he visited Stockton in June.[123]

In the fall, a few months after the incident, Samuel Ward departed for San Francisco, never to return.[124] About the same time, William J. Howard ceased trading with the Indians residing at the northern end of the reservation. Deprived of beef and flour, many of the Indians dispersed.[125] The California state census of 1852 reported that only 280 Indians resided on the Merced Reservation. At the ferry run by Dent and Vantine, headquarters of the Stanislaus Reservation, the census taker counted 275 Indians. Most, he noted, had "removed to the mountains."[126] A stricter management of another reservation would result in a longer but more violent history.

CHAPTER XV

James Savage and the Fresno Reservation

In May 1851 James Savage and his partner, Lorenzo Vinsonhaler applied to Subagent Adam Johnston for a license to trade with the Indians residing between the Chowchilla and Kaweah Rivers. They posted a bond of four thousand dollars and promised to employ M. B. Lewis and William Randolph as clerks.[1] On June 20 Adam Johnston granted the two men the license and instructed them to locate their trading house on the Fresno Reservation near the main Indian village. If another post were opened they were to inform Johnston in writing about the number of persons employed and the amount of capital invested. The traders would be held to strict accountability for any breach of the act regulating trade and intercourse with Indians.[2]

Some of the goods Savage sold at his store he acquired at public sales.[3] In May he bought sixteen pairs of cotton trousers, six woolen shirts, two Panama hats, handkerchiefs, pipes, tobacco, brandy, whiskey, molasses, cooking utensils, and several bottles of castor oil from the sutler of the Mariposa Battalion.[4] Savage also obtained guns. The adjutant general of the state militia ordered that thirty guns and the appropriate quantity of ammunition be delivered to John Frémont for the use of the residents of Mariposa County in emergencies.[5] Because Frémont was absent during the time of delivery, John Marvin, the battalion's quartermaster, deposited twenty muskets and one thousand cartridges with Savage. The remainder were sent to William J. Howard on the Merced Reservation.[6]

In late June, Savage and Marvin traveled to Buckeye Creek, a few miles from Agua Fria, to participate in the official disbanding of the Mariposa Battalion. Most of the volunteers were present, as were Robert Brownlee, the battalion's sutler, and James Burney, its paymaster. Burney had been paying the volunteers in state warrants since March 17, and apparently most of the accounts were settled at the gathering. The men used the warrants to pay off their debts to Brownlee. They also spent them in his makeshift store, eating-house, bowling alley, and card parlor.[7]

Marvin, on July 1, disposed at public sale the property belonging to the commissary and quartermaster. The volunteers could deduct the cost of items purchased from the money owed them by the state. They bought horses, mules, clothing, and other items. That evening the volunteers dined on roast beef, bread, cheese, walnuts, whiskey, and wine provided by Brownlee. The sutler, however, billed Savage fifty dollars for the feast. After dinner Savage, in a brief statement, thanked the men for their service. Marvin, in a much longer delivery, recounted some of the amusing incidents he had experienced as a member of the Mariposa Battalion.[8]

Savage purchased on July 9 two wagons and harnesses and thirteen horses and mules, apparently from the battalion.[9] Two days later, while in Stockton, he formed a partnership with Marvin, who bought an undivided half of the property. Savage agreed to pay Marvin half of all profits resulting from the service of two mule teams and single animals the two men jointly owned. Savage also authorized Marvin to buy general bills of merchandize for his trading post, promising to pay him ten percent on all the bills. On July 11, Marvin agreed to ship from Stockton to the Fresno Reservation 6,374 pounds of flour, and molasses, sugar, coffee, picks, shovels, whiskey, wine, and other items.[10]

Savage constructed a few temporary buildings, later called Fort Bishop, near the main Indian village. He also built a house especially for the five or six Indian females who lived with him. Ranging in age from ten to twenty-two years, they wore short-sleeve, white chemise blouses and either red or blue skirls. Robert Eccleston, who visited the reservation in July, found the women "not unhandsome;" they were clean and sewed neatly.[11]

To purchase items at Savage's post many reservation Indians took up mining, For one dollar in gold, an Indian could buy "pantaloons, or something of equivalent value," noted Eccleston.[12] By early September, Indians had extracted nearly ten thousand dollars in gold from the San Joaquin River but had been driven from the richest holes by American and foreign miners.[13] Late in the month several Indians under Tomquit became ill, and three or four died from working in the icy waters.[14] Apparently the Indians suffered from influenza, which also struck Savage and some of his white workers.[15]

As his administrative duties increased Savage sought to legitimize his

"Indians Panning Gold." Unsigned. Henry I. Simpson, *Three Weeks in the Gold Mines*. (Courtesy of the Bancroft Library, University of California, Berkeley.)

position. In October, Marvin recommended to U.S. Senator William Gwin that Savage be appointed subagent for the region between the Mokelumne River and Tejón Pass. Marvin claimed that Savage, through his influence with the Indians, was largely responsible for many of the treaties being successfully concluded.[16] Another individual told Gwin that the appointment of Savage as agent "would be a popular one, with all persons who are interested in that portion of the country, where the Indians reside."[17] Although no appointment ever came through, Savage acted as if he were an agent, and several of his friends and associates assumed he was.[18]

While on a visit to San Francisco in early November, Savage and Vinsonhaler informed the *Daily Herald* that many reservation Indians possessed rifles and pistols, which they handled with considerable proficiency. They had obtained the weapons from illegal traders. Because of the presence of unauthorized whites on the reservations, the Indians had an excuse to break the treaties they had signed with the Indian agents. Unless the rations promised in the treaties were forthcoming, ten thousand Indians would rise in rebellion and flee to the mountains where they would be impossible to dislodge.[19]

Savage's fears proved to be well founded, because during his absence Indians from the south contacted those on the Fresno Reservation and encouraged them to rebel. Although three of Savage's wives fled most of the Indians remained. When he learned of the visit, Savage told a merchant in Stockton that "Indian affairs look rather dark at the present time; what will be the result time will only determine."[20] Savage's wives returned a short time later, but the Indians in the area remained discontented because the rations promised in the treaties were not being delivered on a regular basis.[21] Writing from Fort Miller on December 18, an individual claimed that for two months the Indians had not received beef or rations, except those provided by the commander of the fort, and that during the past four months they had not seen an agent. Unless supplied with rations for the winter, "it is hardly expected they will remain on the reserve."[22]

The reservation Indians never had completely abandoned their traditional hunting, gathering, and fishing activities, but the miners had disrupted the natural food supply.[23] Competition for what remained sometimes led to difficulties. In late November, Tomquit and some of his followers encountered Pasqual and some of his on the San Joaquin River. Independently, the two groups had gone there to fish for salmon.[24] The reason for the argument that broke out between the women of the two groups is not known, but it may have been over rights to a decreasing resource.[25]

Appropriating the white man's food was another but risky option open to the reservation Indians. In January 1852 an Indian stole a miner's provisions. Arrested by the commanding officer at Fort Miller, he was tied to a tree and flogged until he revealed the location of the goods.[26] Hunger may have been the reason Indians killed a horse belonging to John Bowling in February. To ensure that those responsible were turned over to him, Savage arrested three Indian leaders, including Panwatchee of the Nukchu. Anticipating a violent Indian response, Savage sent word to miners in the immediate area to hasten to Fort Bishop. Poholeel of the Chauchila and another chief also assembled their fighting men at the post. As the Indians, bows and arrows drawn, were about to attack Savage intervened, explaining to Poholeel that once those responsible for the killing of the horse were brought in the leaders would be released. Two days later the Indians turned over three boys to Savage. It was decided that two of the boys should be whipped in the presence of the whites who had gathered at the post. An Indian carried out the punishment. The third boy, thought to be the instigator in the killing, was to be turned over to the civil authorities in Mariposa. But they refused to have anything to do with the matter, and apparently the boy was released unpunished.[27]

When Savage visited Stockton in January 1852 to procure seeds, he already had under cultivation nearly two hundred acres of barley.[28] The following month he sowed 350 acres in grains and 150 in corn, beans, peas, potatoes, squashes, pumpkins, tomatoes, beets, onions, carrots, parsnips, cabbages, and radishes. The produce was to be sold to miners and supplied to the Indians on the reservation. Indians also raised their own crops. In late February a visitor reported that every adult male with a family "has a patch of his own." Provided by Savage with seeds and farming equipment the Indians were "usefully engaged for the present, and their hopes excited for the future."[29] By the end of March Savage also had furnished the Indians with $4,278 worth of flour.[30] Apparently, he never charged the Indians for flour; he sold them only items not provided by the government.[31]

Savage also distributed government beef to the Indians, although the amount and regularity of the deliveries varied greatly. In May, Alexis Godey arrived at John Frémont's ranch on the Little Mariposa River with 2,400 head of cattle he had driven from north of San Francisco Bay. Frémont's financial agent, George Wright, had persuaded Felix Agenti to accept from Subagent Adam Johnston drafts for forty-nine thousand dollars on the secretary of the interior. Shortly after Godey arrived Savage appeared. Claiming to be an Indian agent and in possession of receipts for the cattle, he took charge of the herd. Godey initially refused to turn over the animals but relented when Savage, insisting that the cattle belonged to the Indians, threatened to take them by force. Savage and eight or ten Indian vaqueros drove the better part of the herd to the Fresno Reservation.[32] Also in May, Savage took control of another herd, this one purchased by Agent O. M. Wozencraft from Samuel Henley also on a draft on the secretary of the interior. Most of the 1,285 head were delivered to the Merced, Fresno, San Joaquin, Kings River, and Kaweah Reservations where they were butchered for the Indians.[33]

Savage devoted most of his time administering to the Indians on the Fresno Reservation. In late April he established a farm for them on the San Joaquin River below Fort Miller. In four and one-half days about twenty-five Indians dug an irrigation ditch five feet deep, four in width, that ran some four hundred yards parallel to the river. Brush fences at both ends enclosed the land. In the ten or twelve acres, the Indians planted potatoes, melons, pumpkins, beans, and other vegetables. "The Indians appeared to labor with uncommon spirit and cheerfulness," wrote a visitor. "In the operation of ditching, each man was tasked, which appeared to stimulate their ambition to excel."[34] Another visitor remarked that the quantity of work Savage had induced from the Indians "has astonished every body. Indeed, we all blush for our idle habits, compared to his energy, and what he has accomplished with his Indians."[35] Still another admitted that never had he witnessed a comparable number of whites undertake "so formidable a work." Never had he seen "ground in better order preparatory to receiving the various seeds." The Indians "look on the farm as their hope for the future, and are planting themselves in its immediate vicinity, in order to watch over, irrigate and cultivate it, as the season advances."[36]

In May, Savage recruited Indians from five groups to harvest between 200 and 250 acres of his own crop of barley.[37] It was "as fine barley as ever grew," exclaimed an observer.[38] For their labor Savage gave the Indian workers the gleanings of the harvest.[39] He sold the crop at Stockton prices to the army at Fort Miller.[40] By July, Savage had planted sixty acres of wheat, twenty-five of corn, and twenty of potatoes.[41]

That Savage was successful both as a reservation administrator and enterprising businessman impressed visitors to the reservation. "If he makes himself rich," reasoned one, "such a result is the desire of every man or woman who comes to California; and furthermore, if he civilizes the savage, and prevents mischief whilst he is doing it, what tongue so morbid but would yield him praise."[42] Those sentiments were echoed by another admirer: "The Major is doing much to civilize the Indians, and receives only half the credit he merits. —Why? Because he is judicious enough to reap some benefits himself, and will, no doubt, realize a handsome fortune in a few years."[43] If construction activity was any indication of his wealth, Savage already had made his fortune. It was reported in May that he was "ornamenting the plain with a stately pile of adobes, in the shape of a very capacious dwelling house, store, public house, and corral three hundred feet square. The house will be two stories high, surmounted by an observatory." [44]

Economic success was based on political control. "The Indians all love him, to all appearance," wrote an observer, "and still he manages them in such a manner that they also fear him as much."[45] Another while man noted that "Major Savage appears as their great benefactor or chief, each obeying his commands with promptness, and at the same time with apparent affection and respect."[46] In a letter to Commissioner of Indian Affairs Luke Lea, Adam Johnston doubted "the capacity of any other man in California than Savage to manage them so satisfactorily as he seems to have done thus far. His personal influence with them is of immense advantage in my intercourse with them, and he attends personally to their wants."[47] Only Savage, claimed a friend, kept the Indians from rebelling at not receiving the provisions and services promised in the treaties. "I believe that they would not be quiet one week," he told the editors of the *San Joaquin Republican*, "was it not for the influence of Major Savage, and though many might smile at such an idea, they would smile on the other side, were his influence and aids removed suddenly; he feeds multitudes of them, some of them work for him, but where one reimburses him, five do not."[48]

According to the editors of the *Stockton Journal*, Savage "possessed a greater influence over them than any native-born ruler ever possessed. Towards him the Indians acknowledged a reverence which partook of the supernatural; and at the same time they bowed to him as a sagacious man, whose counsel, if followed, was likely to result in much good to themselves."[49] Not in his entire life had Lorenzo Vinsonhaler observed anyone, Indian or white, as influential with Indians as was Savage. He "seldom if ever used even so much as a cross word to one of them, except for some misdemeanor." If the medicine Savage administered to them failed to cure their illness, "they thought it was because he wanted to punish them for something they had done." Vinsonhaler concluded that Savage's ability to control the Indians on the Fresno Reservation stemmed from the supernatural powers they believed he possessed. The belief had originated during the recent conflict when every attempt to kill him had failed. Only by killing Savage and thereby destroying his protective powers could they have defeated the Mariposa Battalion. Once confined to the reservation, the Indians deferred to Savage because he possessed stronger power than they.[50]

With power came responsibilities and obligations. In August, when their crops were sufficiently advanced, Indians, young and old, feasted on melons the size of a fist and on the corn as soon as it formed. Several Indians died every day for at least ten days until Dr. Lewis Leach, assisted by Savage and other whites, provided them with some kind of medicine, perhaps castor oil. The malady was restricted to the Fresno Reservation.[51]

Savage took considerable interest in the Indians' educational welfare. The *Los Angeles Star* reported in May that an adobe schoolhouse was under construction and that an experienced teacher had been hired. Apparently Savage also sought to improve the spiritual lives of his Indian wards. According to the *Star*, he had taught some of them to sing sacred songs and intended to take several to a camp meeting in Mariposa.[52] In mid-July a visitor to the reservation reported that "Savage has his Indian family now under training, and will shortly have an Indian school of fifty or sixty of both sexes opened, under the care of competent teachers." He was impressed with the Indian students, because they demonstrated "great teachability and fondness for their books.'" They sang for him several "hymn tunes by note, some with and some without accompaniment. Their voices are very soft and melodious, and time exact. They also sang several Indian tunes and songs, but they were much less grateful to the ear." He predicted that the reservation would become "the nucleus of domestication and evangelization of the Indian tribes of this valley."[53]

Not all the Indian residents were content with life on the Fresno Reservation. The Yosemites, frequently taunted for their downfall by the other Indians and largely ignored by Savage, hated their new home. Tenaya complained of the heat in the San Joaquin Valley and the rations he was forced to eat. He preferred acorns. Shortly after his confinement in late May 1851, Tenaya was allowed to return for a short visit to the Yosemite Valley.[54] The purpose of the visit may have been to dispose of his son's remains. Soon after his departure, the rest of the Yosemites left without permission. Tenaya's granddaughter, Maria Lebrado, remained on the Fresno Reservation for twelve days: "After that I went farther and farther for acorns. Finally I ran away from camp along with the other Indians and came back to Yosemite Valley."[55] When the Yosemites failed to return, no attempt was made to bring them back.[56]

For about ten months the Yosemites remained undisturbed. But in late April 1852, eight miners departed from Coarse Gold Gulch to the south fork of the Merced River. Close to the entrance of Yosemite, the men debated the wisdom of entering the valley. Three convinced the others that the Indians posed no threat, and the party continued its course. A base camp was established on the east side of the Merced. Of the five men who went prospecting and hunting, the Yosemites killed two and forced the third into hiding. The two who survived the attack joined the three who had remained in camp, and together they found protection on a shelf on the side of a mountain. In the distance they saw Tenaya and 150 Indians.[57]

To dislodge the miners Indians rolled rocks down the side of the mountain. "Fully believing ourselves doomed men," recalled Stephen Grover, "we never relaxed our vigilance, but with the two rifles we still kept them at bay, determined to sell our lives as dearly as possible." The attack ceased when a chief nearest the miners suddenly fell, apparently shot accidentally by another Indian. Under cover of darkness, the five men escaped, arriving at Coarse Gold Gulch a week later. The miner who survived the first attack also returned safely.[58] Those whites at Coarse Gold Gulch who vowed vengeance did not have long to wait. As recounted by Grover, an Indian was spotted on a mountain trail, "gaily dressed in war paint and feathers, evidently a spy on our track, and not three hours behind us. A party of miners watched him as he passed the settlement. E. Whitney Grover, my brother, and a German cautiously followed him. The haughty Red Man was made to bite the dust before many minutes had passed."[59] On June 2 thirty-five miners departed for the valley to bury the dead and, if possible, to chastise the Yosemites. A five-day march brought them to the scene of the attack.[60] As nearby Indians taunted them with threats, the whites buried the two men. After the Indians crossed the Merced River, which was especially high that year, the miners, unwilling to give chase, returned to Coarse Gold Gulch.[61]

Upon receiving word of the attack Lieutenant Treadwell Moore, commander at Fort Miller, notified his superiors that he intended to punish the Indians who had killed the miners and return the Yosemites to the Fresno Reservation.[62] On June 15 Moore, another officer, and thirty-two infantrymen departed for the Yosemite Valley.[63] A sergeant and four privates remained barricaded in the fort.[64] Joining the hunt, James Savage, Joel Brooks, and one hundred Indian allies left the Fresno Reservation on June 18. The second or third day out, Brooks, a notorious Indian hater, shot and killed one of the Indian guides. Savage and his men followed a trail toward the headwaters of the San Joaquin but turned back when their provisions ran out.[65]

Moore established a base camp on the Merced River below the entrance to the valley on June 20. Scouting parties scoured the area, and on July 1, Lieutenant Nathaniel McLean and ten men entered the valley and destroyed a large cache of acorns. On the fourth, however, the Yosemites put two arrows into a sentry; he died a short time later. Moore and twelve men departed the base camp on the first, followed the trail Savage had discovered, and crossed a main ridge of the Sierra Nevada. On the afternoon of the fourth, the soldiers surprised an Indian village capturing six men and fifteen women and children. The soldiers found clothing belonging to the dead miners.[66] A gold watch also was recovered.[67] One of the prisoners acknowledged they had witnessed the attack but denied participating in it.[68] The miners had been killed, the Indians told Moore, to prevent white men from coming into their territory. The land belonged to them, and no white man had the right to enter without their consent. Moore maintained that they had no claim to the land because they had signed a treaty of peace with the agents and had agreed to relocate to the reservation provided for them. The Indians corrected the officer by pointing out that Tenaya never had signed a treaty and that the other chiefs lacked the authority to dispose of the Yosemite homeland.[69]

To intimidate the Indians into providing more information, Moore arrested their leader and threatened to hang him. The Indian, however, managed to free himself and easily outran the sergeant who gave chase.[70] Perhaps in outrage over losing the prisoner, Lieutenant Moore pronounced the five adult males guilty of murder and on July 5 executed them by firing squad.[71] When Tenaya heard about the executions, evidently observed by one of his scouts, he led his people east across the Sierra Nevada to the Paiutes at Mono Lake. Lafayette Bunnell was not disappointed to learn that Tenaya "was too much for Lieutenant Moore, as he had been for Major Savage and Captain Boling [sic]. Lieutenant Moore did not overtake the Indians he was pursuing, neither was he able to get any information from the Paiutes, whom he encountered, while east of the Sierras. Lieutenant Moore crossed the Sierras over the Mono trail that leads by the Soda Springs through the Mono Pass. He made some fair discoveries of gold and gold-bearing quartz, obsidian and other minerals, while exploring the region north and south of Bloody Canon and of Mono Lake. Finding no traces whatever of the cunning chief, he retuned to the Soda Springs, and from there took his homeward journey to Fort Miller by way of the old trail that passed to the south of the Yosemite."[72]

To James Savage, Tenaya had ceased to be a problem in May 1851, after he left the Fresno Reservation. Indians in the San Joaquin Valley, not the Yosemite Valley, occupied his attention. In August he sought to employ Bunnell and locate him at a trading post on or near the Tejón Reservation. A post in the vicinity of the Tejón Pass, he reasoned, would control the trade destined to spring up on both sides of the Tehachapi Mountains. Large profits were to be made. Bunnell, detecting a conspiracy to defraud the Indians and the federal government, turned down the offer.[73]

In late 1851 or early 1852 Savage also made plans to develop the Four Creeks, an area described "as one of the best farming districts in Southern California, and the garden of the Tulare Valley." Savage intended to supply and send several families to the area. Those interested were to write to him at Fort Bishop, and evidently he received several inquiries.[74] To persuade the Indians residing in the Four Creeks to relocate probably was Savage's motive for inviting them in late May to a feast at Fort Bishop.[75] Two or three thousand Yokuts attended, including members of the Chauchila, Pohonichi, Chukchansi, Nukchu, Heuchi, Piikachi, Dalinchi Dumna,

Gashowu, Nutunutu, Wimilchi, Tachi, and Choinimni.[76] Most likely under the prompting of Savage, the Indians created an intertribal organization and elected Pasqual of the Wechihit and Tomquit of the Pitkachi as coleaders. Savage hoped that future dealings with the Indians would be conducted through the two men. Over the course of a week, he delivered to the Indians one hundred head of cattle to butcher. One night during the festivities uninvited Indians crept into the camp and stole many of the visitors' horses.[77] Although Savage failed to persuade the Indians to vacate the Four Creeks, he may have convinced them to allow a few whites to settle in the area. A short time after the feast, eight white men established a farming communally in the area.[78] Several were ex-volunleers of John Kuykendall's company of the Mariposa Battalion.[79]

In April the state legislature had selected Savage, John Bowling, M. B. Lewis, and H. W. McMullen to serve as a board of commissioners to designate precincts for elections to be held in July in the new county of Tulare. Carved from Mariposa County, Tulare County encompassed the Four Creeks.[80] The Kings River Reservation was also located in Tulare County, and there was bad blood between Savage and the traders residing on the reservation. They resented Savage because the local Indians often took their trade to him.[81] On June 17 Savage presented a written statement of support to Watoka, chief of the Choinimni, who resided on the Kings River Reservation. Signed by Savage the statement proclaimed that Watoka "has treated with the commissioners for land which he now occupies, which said land, he, the said Watoka, is resolved to hold and occupy with his people, apart and alone, entirely free from white men and their settlements. He, the said Watoka, desires me to say that no molestation or hindrance will be given to white men travelling through his country, but that he is determined to prohibit and prevent all encroachments on his people's land."[82] To get the traders off the reservation probably was Savage's reason for issuing a proclamation on behalf of Watoka. Savage also attempted to enlist Joel Brooks in his scheme, but Brooks refused the offer and immediately left Savage's employ.[83]

Watoka and some sixty followers, armed with bows and arrows, arrived on July 1 at the store and ferry run by William Campbell, B. F. Edmonds, and John Poole on the Kings River. Through an interpreter Watoka told Edmonds that when Savage first arrived among the Indians he offered them blankets and camisas, but Edmonds and the other traders had given them nothing, Watoka handed Edmonds the proclamation and ordered the Americans off the reservation. The Indians then departed. Leaving a small party to guard the store, Campbell and Edmonds hurried to Fine Gold Gulch and Coarse Gold Gulch, where they recruited about twenty-five men, including Joel Brooks. Commanded by Walter Harvey, the party arrived at the reservation in two groups. Leaving a dozen men to guard the store, Harvey led the others to Watoka's village, located a few miles upstream. They took up positions on opposite sides of the village.[84]

The three men who entered the village persuaded Watoka to meet with Harvey under a nearby oak tree. Unable to convince most of his subordinates to accompany him, Watoka attended the meeting with only two Indians, one serving as interpreter. When the Americans attempted to take them prisoner, they bolted for the village. On the run one of the Indians attempted to snatch a gun from a white man. From cover near the village, the Indians fired volleys of arrows at the Americans and received rifle and pistol shots in return. Watoka and the others withdrew to the village but abandoned it a short time later. Apparently, nine Indians died in the fight.[85] Of the ten seriously wounded two later died.[86] Fearing that Pasqual, head chief of all the Indians residing on the Kings River Reservation, would take revenge for the attack, the Americans hurried back to the ferry where they met several white men from Mariposa who had come to vote in the Tulare County elections.[87]

At least one white man considered the attack foolhardy. Writing to the *Daily Alta California* he suggested that if the whites had calmly investigated the matter, "there is no doubt but the whole affair might have been settled to the satisfaction of all parties; for I believe it to be the desire of the Indians to preserve the treaty. But instead of making any inquiries regarding the threat, the whole party rode into the rancheria, and after a few words had passed, the import of which I did not understand, they commenced firing."[88] Another American concluded that the attack, whether justified or not, cowed the Indians of the Tulare Valley. They "are now quiet in this quarter and are disposed to live and be on terms of friendship and peace."[89] In a statement published in the *San Joaquin Republican*, Walter Harvey placed all the blame on the Indians and left it "to the public to determine how far the party under my command have transcended the rules of propriety; conscious myself of having done no wrong, I do not feel the tongue of slander."[90]

At the time of the attack Pasqual and a large number of his followers had just finished a month's work for Savage on the Fresno Reservation.[91] When informed of the incident, Pasqual pulled down the American flag he flew above his lodge.[92] He feared the old and young people left behind may have been harmed.[93] Only through the intercession of Savage, who promised to bring the perpetrators to justice, did Pasqual agree to keep the peace.[94] Pasqual, however, asked Savage some difficult questions: "What shall we do? We try to live on the lands the commissioners gave us, in friendly relations with the white man, but they kill our women and our children, and, if we flee to the mountains, then they hunt us and kill us, and we have no peace on the lands the commissioners gave us, or in the mountains. Where shall we go and what shall we do? When the commissioners gave us the U.S. flag, and our papers, they told us that it would protect us, but now the flag is all stained with our blood, and our papers are all bloody, and who shall wash it off? We are poor and weak—the whites are rich and strong, and we pray for mercy."[95]

A visitor to Fort Miller reported on July 4 that the local Indians "have been holding council with each other all day; in fact they do not look like the same Indians. They are sulky, distant, and do not leave their camp."[96] A chief told the assistant surgeon at the fort that he would attempt to keep his people on the reservation. But the surgeon feared a general uprising was imminent and that the chief would support it.[97]

Encouraged by the soldiers to consult with the Indians residing on or near the Kings River Reservation, Savage, in the course of three days, visited between twelve and fifteen villages. A witness to one of the meetings wrote that "never was an audience at Divine service, more strict, and orderly, more attentive and quiet, than those Indians, in listening to his message to them. All of them expressed to Maj. Savage a desire to live amicably with the whites, and in good faith with their treaty obligations." They also wanted to be protected, as the agents had promised, from whites encroaching on their lands.[98] "Near by to where I am writing," noted an observer at the meeting at Four Creeks, "under the shade of a stately oak, Maj. Savage and Pasquale are having a 'talk,' with about one hundred of the Kah-we-ah tribe who have come in from their rancheria for that purpose. The lithograph of Old Penn in council, with the Indians of his day and time, is a striking illustration of the gathering."[99] The observer's romanticism aside, the Indians remained discontented and displayed a distinct hostility to whites passing through their territories.[100]

The attack by Harvey revived fears among the whites in San Francisco that the Indians were on the verge of war. The *Daily Herald* warned its readers that "the consequences would be terrible, and it would be the work of years to restore peace." Comparisons were made with the recent Seminole conflict: "The Florida war is fresh in the recollections of the public. Every one knows how tedious it was, the great sacrifice of life that it caused, and the large amount of money that was expended during its continuance. Similar results would follow an Indian war in California"[101] The *Alta* also was concerned: "We are informed that threats and intimations have been made by the Indians of gathering the warriors of formidable tribes, whose territory lies beyond the mountains, and with allied forces to overpower the whites and drive them from their valley. It is said that between the Indians of the Upper San Joaquin country and the tribes inhabiting the eastern slope of the Sierra Nevada, and along its base, a covenant exists of which the Tulare Indians in time of war can avail themselves, to bring into the field against their enemie thousands of savage and desperate allies, brave and well skilled in Indian warfare, and invincible in a mountainous region."[102]

Because most of the soldiers stationed at Fort Miller had departed to chastise the Yosemite, the whites in the area were apprehensive.[103] Thus, in early July the commanding general of the Pacific Division dispatched a company of infantry to the fort.[104] The head of the company and new commander of the fort, Major George W. Patten, reported to his superiors that the Indians demanded the arrest of those responsible for the recent slaughter on the Kings River Reservation. If immediate action were not taken "a general war with the whole of the tribes is inevitable." A strong display of troops where the Indians planned to hold a grand council would "save both blood and treasure."[105]

O. M. Wozencraft wrote to Governor John Bigler about the attack on Watoka's village. He emphasized the importance of maintaining the rule of law to prevent the occurrence of similar incidents and asked the governor to write to him in San Francisco. Evidently he received no reply.[106] The U.S. distinct attorney told Wozencraft that he knew of no federal law that would apply to the attack, the United States having no jurisdiction in cases where a life was taken. Although Wozencraft intended to issue warrants against those responsible for the attack, once informed that Walter Harvey had been elected judge of recently created Tulare County he realized that prosecution would be in vain.[107] Wozencraft, however, intended to meet with the disaffected Indians at the council they planned to hold in the Four Creeks in mid-August. The *Alta* praised his decision but doubted his presence would be of much help: "We look upon this as the most difficult undertaking he has had to encounter. It has been an easy matter heretofore to secure the fidelity of the Indian, but when he sees that there is no confidence to be placed in the white man, the establishment of peaceful relations becomes a difficult matter."[108]

On August 15 a detachment of artillery and ninety dragoons, led by Patten, departed for the Four Creeks. Convinced that his life would be in danger once he crossed the Kings River, Savage intended to join the soldiers before they reached the river. Patten, however, arrived at the crossing before Savage and spoke with Walter Harvey about the attack on the village. He did not question Harvey's motives but thought the attack an error in judgment. Harvey told Patten that Savage had made certain statements he found offensive. Shortly, Patten departed to select a campsite.[109]

Savage, in the company of John Marvin, arrived at the crossing on August 16 and immediately got into an argument with Harvey over the attack on Watoka's village. Savage told Harvey that the U.S. Army probably would investigate the matter and advised him to surrender. Apparently, Harvey agreed to do so. There the matter might have ended had Savage not accused Harvey of slandering him. Harvey had told mutual acquaintances that he thought O. M. Wozencraft was a gentleman and honest in his dealings with the Indians but that Savage was not. Savage asked Harvey to retract his charge that he was no gentleman. Harvey refused. In the fight that followed, twice Savage knocked Harvey down. Twice John Marvin and some other men separated the two. When Savage struck again his pistol dropped from his belt and was picked up by Marvin. Harvey then drew his gun and shot Savage three or four times, killing him instantly.[110]

Appraised by Marvin of the particulars of the incident, Patten confronted the difficult task of convincing the Indians that the killing of Savage, their friend, by Harvey, their enemy, was more accidental than intentional. Once the Indians had assembled Patten told them about the tragedy and expressed his deep sorrow over the event. He asked the chiefs to send runners to neighboring villages to inform them that the death of Savage was as unanticipated as it was disastrous. They complied and agreed to accompany him to the Four Creeks.[111]

The meeting got off to a poor start. Patten had promised the Indians beef and beans, but those in charge of the food supplies had turned back when they heard of Savage's death. Patten was forced to distribute army provisions to the Indians. Disappointed at not receiving the promised food many Indians retuned to their villages, leaving their chiefs to represent them.[112] Several of the fifteen chiefs attending the council brought with them their copies of the treaties they had negotiated with the Indian agents.[113]

Ill health prevented Wozencraft from attending the council, so Patten acted as chief representative of the federal government. He told the Indians that the United States would protect them as long as they committed no acts of aggression. All their complaints must be brought to the attention of the commanding officer at Fort Miller. Several chiefs accepted his assurances and promised to keep the peace. As a gesture of good will Francisco of the Gawia, a chief the whites held in fear, presented his daughter of twelve or thirteen years as hostage. Later, the girl was turned over to Tomquit of the Pitkachi.[114]

During the discussions Watoka remained silent until told that the killing would be the subject of an official inquiry. He sought permission to relocate his village to the one governed by Pasqual. "This permission of course was granted," Patten wrote in his report, "and the flag of Pas-qual, protecting the inmates of two contiguous Rancheries [sic], is once more given to the wind under the firm belief that the grand chief at Washington is disposed to do the red man justice, and that they who represent the United States authority in California are not false hearted."[115] To impress the Indians of the might of the U. S. Army, Patten conducted military exercises. The dragoons charged, the infantry fired in rapid order, and the howitzers thundered twice.[116]

The editors of the *Stockton Journal* concluded "that the council was a failure—that the feast was a failure—that justice to them will be a failure—that they do not expect protection from the lawless men who infest the borders of civilization—and that all peaceful arrangements will be a total failure.... All the rights of the Indians have been trampled on, their peace disturbed, and defenseless women and children ruthlessly cut down, without cause or provocation. Such are the inducements to war; and if we judge them by the rule of savage nations we may expect a long and disastrous border struggle."[117]

To calm the fears of the whites at Woodville, as the Four Creeks settlement became known, Patten temporarily stationed the dragoons in the area, but a permanent military presence he thought unnecessary.[118] He was concerned, however, about Governor John Bigler's prediction that the treaties creating the reservations would not be ratified by the U.S. Senate. In a letter to Patten, the governor advised him to inform the Indians of the situation. Patten refused to comply because the information might ignite an Indian war. If the treaties were not ratified, he warned his superiors, the efforts of the Indian agents would be "a mere farce, which requires but the lifting of the curtain to turn into a grand tragedy."[119] To prevent such a tragedy twenty-five citizens of Woodville petitioned General E. A. Hitchcock to establish a permanent military post in the area. They emphasized that the local Indians were upset at not receiving the provisions and items promised in their treaty. Whites were "thrown into daily contact with these Indians and liable at any time to fall into petty quarrels with them which without a day's notice might result in general hostilities." Because of their numerical superiority the Indians easily could wipe out the settlement. The petitioners were disturbed "that the friendly professions of the Indians when in the presence of a display of military force should have any weight in forming the opinion of men who have perhaps our fate in their hands."[120]

The settlers had reason to be fearful because the person exerting the most influence over the Indians was dead. Brought in a coffin to the Fresno Reservation, the body of James Savage was viewed one last time by those who regarded him as chief. As recalled by Lorenzo Vinsonhaler, "After taking a look at the corpse, they walked off saying *nothing would ever go right with them again.*"[121] A witness to the Indians' mourning ceremony wrote: "The night he was buried, the Indians built large fires, around which they danced, singing the while the mournful death chant, until the hills around rung with the sound. I have never seen such profound manifestations of grief. The young men, as they whirled wildly and distractedly around in the dance, shouted the name of their 'father,' that was gone; while the Squaws sat rocking their bodies to and fro, chanting their mournful dirges." The Indians told the writer "that their 'father' was gone and they would not live with the whites any longer."[122] A short time later, two

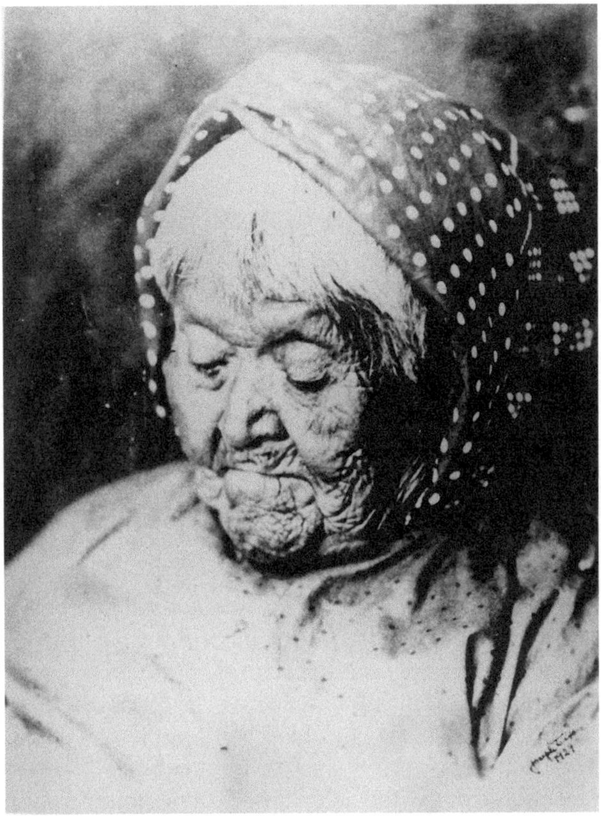

Maria Lebrado, 1928. Courtesy of the Yosemite Museum Library, Yosemite National Park, California.

groups departed the reservation.[123]

California's newspapers widely commented on the life and death of James Savage.[124] The editors of the *Alta* wrote: "Major Savage, in the exercise of his official duties, doubtless made many enemies among our countrymen; but he also had warm and numerous friends. In his death our State has lost an old and respected citizen, the while residents of the San Joaquin valley an able exponent of their true rights and demands among the Indians, and the Indians themselves probably their best and most influential friend."[125] How the Indians viewed Savage, however, was better summed up by Maria Lebrado: "All Yosemite Indians hated Savage although some of the Indians of the foothills and the San Joaquin Valley near Fresno liked him."[126] To most white residents of California, however, more pressing issues than the death of one of their own were being deliberated throughout the state.

CHAPTER XVI

Public Debate

As the reservations were being founded, a public debate regarding the divestment of the Indian estate and the destiny of the Indian residents was being conduced through newspapers in editorials and letters to editors and in the state legislature. It began on January 14, 1851, when the three Indian commissioners published in the *Daily Alta California* a proclamation announcing they had come to negotiate treaties of peace and friendship with the Indians and calling upon those in the "disturbed districts to adopt and pursue towards the Indians a course of conduct marked by mildness, moderation and forbearance." Miners and others were to remain on the defensive until the agents had time to investigate and if possible redress the grievances of the Indians. Because "there is now no farther west, to which they can be removed, the General Government and the people of California appear to have left but one alternative in relation to these remnants of once numerous and powerful tribes, viz: *extermination* or *domestication*. As the latter includes all proper measures for their protection and gradual improvement, and secures to the people of the state an element greatly needed in the development of its resources, viz: cheap labor—it is the one which we deem the part of wisdom to adopt, and, if possible, consummate."[1]

The proclamation further stated that the United States, "as a Christian and civilized nation," had an obligation to stop the shedding of blood. If "depredations are committed by the Indians, upon either the persons or property of the whites, and if you will apprize us of the facts, we will use all proper exertion to bring the offenders to justice, by the military force of the United Slates, or otherwise." If whites should kill Indians "without the authority of law, we request that in like manner, information may be sent to us. The shooting in cold blood, of a white man by an Indian, is murder punishable by death. So likewise if an Indian be killed by a white man, the crime is the same, the punishment should be the same, and the safety and security of every community demands that equal and exact justice be meted out to all alike." The agents encouraged miners and traders to explain the proclamation to those chiefs and captains they might encounter.[2]

In their next issue the editors of the *Alta* expressed hope that the proclamation "may have weight with the public, and induce that forbearance and moderation which the importance of the matter demands." Rhetorically, they asked if annihilation were humane and Christian: "We answer it is not.... Our agents are already upon the mission. Let all good citizens give a helping hand." An Indian war was to be avoided at all cost, because the "calamity would not alone be one to the Indian. It will cost the lives of many valuable citizens." Moreover, even if the Indians were totally destroyed, it "would be a result over which the philanthropist, the Christian, and every true hearted man would mourn as the last great sin of national injustice, violence and oppression."[3]

A San Francisco newspaper located far from where Indians resided and secure in its liberal readership, the *Alta* could assume a high moral tone and stake out a position of objective moderation. Newspapers located in the interior more accurately reflected the attitudes of the miners. The *Stockton Journal* of January 25, for example, published a scathing and sarcastic editorial regarding the requests of the commissioners: "The miners on the frontier have read the peace proclamation of the Indian Commissioners, and have taken to themselves great comfort and strong assurance of no further Indian aggression, knowing well how potent are such paper bullets.... One more such proclamation, promptly issued, and generally published in the California press, so as to be read by all the aborigines of the country, would doubtless speedily put an end to further Indian massacre and aggression.... Thanks to the Board of Indian Commissioners and their potent proclamation!—and thanks to the scrupulous and precise neutrality of our army, in peaceful contentment at Benicia! We can assure the merchants of San Francisco that a good time is coming to them in the early spring. Let them only be patient! What gold the Indians don't get, they shall have."[4]

Writing to the *Stockton Times* in mid-February, C. D. Gibbes challenged the notion that those in the interior should remain on the defensive until negotiations were concluded: "Make a treaty with them before they are punished? No, sir-never! The people on the frontier are all opposed to it.... It. is very well for those at a distance and in a safe place, to talk in this way; but let them come and live on the frontier in small parties, as we are obliged to do that are out there; let them see their friends go out in the morning, well and strong, and before night be brutally murdered—stuck full of arrows—some others skinned and their ears cut off;—let them see the wounded brought in day after day, and hear their groans as they lie on their beds for weeks! ... Now is the best time we will ever have to subdue them...; it has to be done, and has been the case ever since America was first settled, and the sooner done the better for them, and us, too."[5]

Thomas Paine held a similar view. He wrote to the *Times* early in March, claiming the course "adopted by the Commissioners in relation to the Indian difficulties is extremely impolitic; and it is not difficult to foresee the result. The Indian tribes may accept their presents, and pretend to be reconciled, but the whole affair will be proved to be a delusion. Unless they are first chastised, and made to ask for quarters, any treaty will prove a mere hoax or trap, for all who confide in Indian promises; and if the snow leave the hills before they are forced to terms, I predict there will be another Florida war," an obvious reference to the stiff resistance recently offered by the Seminole Indians.[6]

The *Alta*, however, thought the Indians would adhere to the stipulations in the treaties as rigidly "as one set of men can maintain good faith with another. They are not lacking in sense, and are perfectly aware of the necessity they are under of living upon amicable terms with the whites."[7] In May the newspaper evaluated Indian policy in California also by drawing historical comparisons:

> The experience of years, the cost of many millions of dollars expended in wars, the beneficent and economical advantages resulting from a peace policy, have taught the Government at home and should teach all the lovers of their country that the principle upon which William Penn acted, so far as it may be carried into effect at the present time, is the only true policy to be pursued towards the aborigines of the country. And especially is this true respecting the Indians of California. They have been very much under estimated. They are as brave as the Indians to the east of the Rocky Mountains, and only need the experience in war and arms which those tribes possess, to make them personally and in bands, as formidable as any other Indians with which our country has had to deal....
>
> The treaties contracted with them as yet cost the United States Government less each than any treaty among the eastern tribes. This policy should be continued, not only for the sake of economy, but also for the love of humanity towards both races. This is the only policy, which will stand the test of time and receive the approval of posterity.... The nation has been taught by the Florida war, its

cost of life and treasure, how much trouble a few Indians may give.[8]

The following month the *Alta* reminded its readers that Indian affairs was a federal, not a state, responsibility: "The only policy which will stand the test of history and experience, which will secure quiet on our borders and leave the mines and agricultural valleys to the quiet possession and development of our people, is to allow the United States Government to conduct the whole affair and pay the bill.... All the authority of the State, through its officers and people, should be exerted to sustain the action of the Federal Government through its commissioners. That power was slow in moving, but its policy towards the Indians, when once commenced, is wise and just, and through it alone can we hope for peace and quiet."[9] A few weeks later, however, the newspaper was not so hopeful: "Treaties may be formed, and compacts made between our agents and the wild tribes, but the same obstacles which were presented to the early pioneers of the western wilds of the Mississippi, in the settlement of the country, will be found to maintain in our uncultivated or mountain districts, viz: Indian depredations and cruelties."[10]

To many whites the treaties reserved for the Indians valuable lands. On July 26, for example, the *Alta* published excerpts from a letter written by an individual who asserted that from the Stanislaus River to the end of the Tulare Valley every acre of land either rich in minerals or suitable for agriculture had been ceded by the agents to the Indians. The region contained "rich and exhaustless mines of gold and silver. It is, besides, in an agricultural point of view, the garden of California, and no where else in California can agriculture be so well rewarded. The soil of the San Joaquin valley, now in possession of the Indians, is exceedingly well adapted to the growth of rice, cotton, and tobacco." Because of the region's natural wealth, "the miners will utterly disregard any article or stipulation of any treaty made or said to be made by the Commissioners with the Indians."[11]

In the same issue the editors of the *Alta* challenged the notion that all valuable land in the San Joaquin Valley had been reserved exclusively for Indian occupancy, pointing out that the Indians had received only enough land for subsistence purposes. That reservations were established on good lands "does not give the covetous any right to bring complaints against the action of the Commissioners." In the past it had been the policy of the United States to place Indians on lands "beyond the bounds of civilization," but geography prevented such a policy working in California. Therefore, "the reservations must be made where the Indians at present exist."[12] Two days later Redick McKee called ridiculous the reports "about our having allotted to the Indians, all the good mining and agriculture lands." Some people, "with a far greater show of benevolence, complain of our having made their reservations to [sic] small, and given them, for the relinquishment of their rights to the whole, too little compensation."[13]

A member of George Barbour's escort, in a letter to the *Alta*, also rejected the claim that the reservations were located on lands rich in minerals and nutrients. Parts of the San Joaquin Valley were the most desolate "it has ever been my lot to pass over. It is true that in the spring any part of California looks beautiful, but I will ever remember the suffering sustained by man and beast, in traveling from the Tejón Pass to the Merced River, in the middle of July." Moreover, never had he heard anyone discuss the possibility of cultivating cotton or rice. There was good land on the Kaweah and Tule Rivers, but the Indians retained only a portion of it. If the rivers could be managed, a large agricultural community might take hold. The mineral wealth of the southern valley, however, was highly exaggerated. Gold in small quantities remained in the Merced, Fresno, and San Joaquin Rivers, but none was to be found in the Kaweah, Kern, and Tule. The writer thought absurd the claim that the Indian agents had assigned lands to the Indians: "He says the *Commission* ceded away, I say the *Indians* ceded away. This is no verbal quibble, but the fact. The Indians were in possession of the territory by birthright; they had driven off some, and were sorely harassing others of these miners, who now so patriotically declare that they will abide by 'no stipulation made or said to be made' by the Commission."[14]

The editors of the *Placer Times & Transcript* insisted that "the most valuable mining lands in California cannot be conveyed to the Indians in large quantities, without creating in the end the most serious results. Miners will encroach upon those lands sooner or later, for the gold which they contain. Besides, we do not believe it to be right for the General Government to send agents to the State, to set aside what little valuable land now remains uncovered by the immense claims under shadow of title from Mexico." They accused the agents of "forming plans which, if consummated, will transfer to the Indians fully one-half of all the arable or mineral lands in California, which belong to the General Government. They have divided the State into three districts, and each Commissioner, ambitious of making the greatest possible number of treaties, feels himself fully authorized to cover the State with Indian reservations."[15]

In a long letter to the *Alta*, George Barbour entered the debate. He provided the newspaper with a description of the boundaries of the reservations he had established "for the purpose of disabusing the public mind in relation to the supposed extent and great mineral and agricultural wealth of those districts, and to relieve myself and colleagues from the odium that has been attempted to be brought upon us, by those who are either ignorant of the facts themselves or willfully misrepresented them." Barbour claimed he had removed Indians from those areas where mining was profitable and farming possible: "In carrying out this object, information was sought from those citizens and miners, who from their experience and knowledge of the country, were supposed to be best qualified to advise. And with those who have a knowledge of the facts, I venture nothing when I assert, that within the boundaries of the Indian Reserves herewith given, at the time of making said treaties there were not twenty miners and settlers, all told, included."[16]

The following day, September 10, the *Alta* praised the work of Barbour and the other commissioners and reiterated that, "conciliation is the only policy which, with any justice, can be adopted." The Indians must be relocated to where they can support themselves and receive assistance. "To do that, and to separate them from the interests of the whites, has been, and is the policy of the Government."[17] When attacked by the *Times & Transcript* for praising the work of Barbour and the other agents, however, the editors of the *Alta* insisted they never had favored the policy pursued by the government: "We simply stated what course was determined upon by the three gentlemen composing the commission, and endorsed the action of Col. Barbour."[18] On September 20 they accused the *Times & Transcript* of insinuating "that we have some personal ends to answer in sustaining the Commissioners or approving the reservations they have made" and challenged it to prove the reservations contained gold. Relocating the Indians to lands no white man coveted would be an impossibility. The Indians were "expected to cultivate the lands: would the *Times* have them placed upon a barren rock?" Until persuaded they had erred, the editors would continue to favor the ratification of the treaties.[19]

The *Times & Transcript* quickly responded: "We have made no reflections upon the editors of the *Alta California* or the U.S. Indian Commissioners—this is entirely imaginary with them. But we have commented somewhat freely upon the subject which we believe is destined to create a vast amount of trouble in California." The commissioners may have had the best of intentions, but they created serious problems: "There are men who hover about the Indians in California, … who intend to make themselves rich out of these reservations. It is to this class that we charge corruption." The editorial concluded by sharply criticizing the *Alta*: "It is not always consistent, neither is it always right. Its leading editorials are oftentimes weak and vacillating. Today it gives place to articles like the one quoted, in relation to the Indian reservations, to-morrow it goes diametrically opposite."[20]

The Alta struck back:

> The *Times*, after showing evidently to its entire satisfaction that it has never made an allegation against the Commissioners, goes on to say that, "There are men who hover about the Indians in California, ...

> who intend to make themselves rich out of these reservations. It is to this class that we charge corruption." And thus they abandon the whole line of their argument. They are unceasing in their assaults upon the Indian Commissioners, and when the matter comes to be probed, they tacitly exonerate the Commissioners from all blame, and charge it upon these "men who hover about the Indians in California." If the editor had gone a little farther in his researches, he would have found that it was these "men who hover about the Indians in California," who have produced the horrors of our Indian wars, and who have made it necessary that reservations should be made, and Commissioners sent among the savages to bring them back to peace and friendship.[21]

Early in October, General E. A. Hitchcock, commander of the pacific division, became embroiled in the debate when he submitted a long letter to the *Alta*. How well the Indian agents had discharged their duties, he did not "pretend to know, but until the contrary be shown I am bound to suppose they have acted with judgment, and certainly they have had no design of disregarding the true interests of the State. It is alleged that they have reserved to the Indians lands containing gold; but perhaps it is not too much to say that this must have been the case if any reservation whatever had been made.... Therefore this complaint comes to nothing, except on the assumption that the Commissioners were bound to remove the Indians altogether from California, which I think no one is so insane as to suppose was their duty."[22]

A few days later the *Alta* presented a similar position. At one time the federal government had sought to "remove the red man as far as possible from the white," but given California's "peculiar physical conformation" that policy no longer was feasible. "They cannot cross the Sierra," it noted, "unless you would doom them to the certain terrors of famine upon the arid deserts of the Great Basin; they cannot be driven into Oregon, because Oregon already contains too many for her own peace, happiness and security; nor could you urge them 'farther west,' unless you sought at once plunge them into the waves of the mighty Pacific." The remaining option "was to assign them reservations within the State, and thus secure them from intrusion and the whites from danger."[23]

Early in 1852 the state legislature took up the issue of the reservations and the treaties creating them. On January 16 the senate formed a Special Committee to Inquire into the Treaties made by the United States Commissioners with the Indians of California. The committee was to investigate the condition and location of the reservations and the character and mood of the Indian residents. Most importantly, it was to assess the effect confirmation of the treaties would have on the future prosperity of California.[24] On January 19 the president of the senate announced that Senators M. M. Wambough, J. J. Warner, J. H. Ralston, B. Frank Keene, and James Miller would comprise the committee. During the same session, Senator James Estill submitted a resolution to allow Redick McKee use of the senate chamber to present the views of the United States. The senate agreed to the resolution.[25]

McKee addressed the governor, legislators, and other interested officials on January 24. In some detail he explained the nature of his mission and his treaty-making activities in Northern California. He and his colleagues had arrived in California with no definite instructions but had quickly determined that the policy of removal was inapplicable in California. Instead, they had decided to colonize Indians on several distinct tracts of lands, each separated or surrounded by the white population. By separating Indians from Indians, any future combination would be prevented. By separating Indians from whites, mutual security would be achieved.[26]

McKee maintained that once the Indians adopted the food, clothing, and working habits of whites they would support themselves. In their improved condition, they would provide whites with vital labor for their mines and farms. Thus, it would be in their best interests to adopt a conciliatory course towards the Indians. Once the federal government provided the Indians with the assistance promised in the treaties, no further hostilities need be anticipated. The four or five teachers assigned to each reservation would instill in the Indians the habits of peace and industry. Regarding the claim that too much land had been set aside for Indian occupancy, McKee calculated that if California were divided into 1,000 squares, the white population would receive 990 and the Indian population 10.[27]

On the evening of January 30, O. M. Wozencraft also addressed the state's legislators. "In what way and in what manner," he rhetorically asked, "did our forefathers succeed best in passing through the trying period of their Indian troubles? Was it by waging a war of extermination? or was it by pursuing a firm, uniform, kind, just and conciliatory policy with those Indians? I am sure there can be but one answer to this query, by those who are at all familiar with our infantile history; and that is—The humane policy has been most expeditious as well as the cheapest." Wars of extermination had succeeded but constituted "one of the darkest pages of our history." Removal policy, moreover, "ever will prove fruitful of mischief. It but gives a respite, a temporary calm—soon to give birth to the full grown storm, which too frequently terminates in a deluge of blood."[28]

Wozencraft continued with a discourse on the goals and achievements of the Indian commissioners. He also addressed the issue that valuable land had been set aside for the Indians: "I would ask, what particular objections are there to the Indians having lands sufficient for their support? Would their producing impoverish us? ... Look abroad over the country, and satisfy yourselves in relation to this matter. I think that you will then admit that we will not be seriously impoverished by their making enough to support themselves." Wozencraft concluded his speech by asking if "any one would sustain a loss or otherwise be harmed by the ratification of those treaties? If there is, I have not been able to see it; on the contrary, I can see that we, the citizens of California, will be the recipients of a great benefit."[29]

Present at the address was recently elected U.S. Senator John B. Weller, who, according to Wozencraft, asked questions as if he were a member of a tribunal investigating an officer under charge. Weller accused Wozencraft and his colleagues of negotiating with irresponsible Indian leaders who would not adhere to the stipulations in the treaties. Wozencraft's retort was that Indian depredations had ceased once the Indians signed the treaties, even though the promises made to them had not been kept. To that point Weller had no response.[30] The editors of the *Stockton Journal* predicted that Weller would be quickly put in his place if he debated the issue with Sam Houston in the Senate: "It is more than probable our Senator had enough on this subject from Dr. Woozencraft [sic], and that forever hereafter, he will hold his peace."[31]

The same day Wozencraft delivered his speech, John Bigler, recently elected governor of California, sent a special message to the legislature. He discussed a variety of issues confronting the state, including Indian affairs. From statistics provided by the comptroller, he claimed that, as of December 31, 1851, the debt derived from fighting Indians consisted of $212,000 in war bonds and interest incurred and $233,375.79 in war loan warrants. The costs of Indian expeditions in the extreme north and south of the state had yet to be tallied, but the comptroller estimated they would total about $1,000,000. Accordingly, the state owed $1,445,375.79 in war debts. Confident that the federal government would cover the bill, Bigler pointed out that in the 1840s the United States had reimbursed the states of Georgia, Alabama, and Louisiana for expenses incurred while fighting Indians. Bigler, however, was concerned about the activities of the commissioners. He had been "credibly informed" that large tracts of land, "rich in minerals and valuable for agricultural purposes," had been set aside as reservations. By "settling in the very heart of our State, vast tribes of savages with exclusive landed privileges," collisions between Indians and whites were inevitable. Bigler urged the lawmakers to do all in their power to insure that the U.S. Senate rejected the treaties when submitted for ratification.[32]

In a letter to the *Alta*, McKee, writing under the nom de plume "Shasta," suggested that it was a manifestation of the governor's "ignorance" or "willful perversion" to recommend that the legislature oppose the ratification of the treaties based "purely upon the strength of his ex parte assertion that he has been 'credibly informed.'" That the governor's recommendation was made at the same time he called upon Congress to assume the state's war debt baffled McKee. Without the efforts of the commissioners, the debt "would by this time have been eight or ten instead of two millions of dollars!" Without ratification, he reasoned, "Indian depredations, wars, war loans, depreciated warrants, increased taxation, or utter ruin and bankruptcy" would follow. McKee concluded with a plea for fairness:

> What matters it then to the great state of California, whether the Indians, *till lately the owners of the whole*, shall have in their reservations a few acres more or less?
>
> Apart from the chance of making political capital, I think, Messrs Editors, you will agree with me, that it is a matter of very little consequence, at least at present, and will remain so while nineteen-twentieth of the lands in the State are lying idle, unoccupied, and to agriculture useless. Some of our *very wise aspirants for office*, I understand, are afraid that we shall not have land enough—that our laboring population will he redundant and that all the Indians should forthwith be removed without the limits of the State, and settled on the arid plains of Utah. Let me tell you, gentlemen, the Indians of California can never be removed into another State or Territory remote from the sea coast. You have but one choice—KILL, MURDER, EXTERMINATE, or DOMESTICATE and IMPROVE THEM.[33]

The editors of the *San José Weekly Visitor* thought McKee's ideas worthy of consideration. If Congress concluded that the agents had not exceeded "a just construction of their powers," had reserved no more land than was necessary, and had established the reservations in areas relatively free of precious minerals, they would support ratification of the treaties. Admitting their view was an unpopular one, they favored ratification because a "shifting, sliding policy pursued with Indians, is and always has been attended with the worst consequences to our Government and people." Furthermore, "the proposed alternative, a violent and immediate removal will entail upon our people and State a long disastrous Indian war, and its unavoidable concomitant, a mammoth State debt."[34]

Governor Bigler's statistics regarding the war debt came under close scrutiny. A select committee reported to the senate on February 12 that the war debt amounted to $795,135.87, of which $233,375.79 resulted from the Mariposa War. The senate adopted a resolution calling upon the comptroller to explain how he calculated the much higher numbers presented by the governor.[35] In a letter to the senate, the comptroller stated that the amount of the debt was only an approximation and had been derived from information obtained from those connected with expeditions against the Indians.[36] Upon receiving the letter the senate passed another resolution. It acknowledged that the governor, by presenting the figures, had fulfilled his constitutional duties and was not responsible for any errors contained in the message. The creation of the select committee to ascertain the indebtedness of the state "was intended in no manner to reflect upon His Excellency Governor Bigler."[37]

The press was not so kind. Although rejecting the rumor that the governor and the comptroller had inflated the figures of both the civil and war debts to depreciate the state's credit so accomplices could purchase securities at low rates, the editors of the *Alta* argued that there was "little excuse or palliation for the wrong done to the community through such gross carelessness and unpardonable inaccuracy. The public are in the habit of relying upon official statements; and when officers become so unmindful of the great interests committed to their keeping as to make 'rough guesses' at matters which so intimately and deeply affect the State in its most vital part, they are in danger of securing the execrations of the body politic."[38]

To several legislators the body politic was shrinking in size. On February 11 four of the five senators appointed to the Special Committee to Inquire into the Treaties made by the United States Commissioners with the Indians of California submitted their majority report to the senate. They claimed that the commissioner had assigned valuable mineral, grazing, and agricultural lands to the Indians, who were "incapable, by habit or taste, of appreciating its value." Because California "should be wholly occupied by a homogeneous population, all contributing, by their character and occupation, to its strength and independence," the "wild" and "hostile" Indians residing in the interior should be removed beyond the limits of the state "with all practicable dispatch." To support their position they pointed to Andrew Jackson's removal policy, in which tens of thousands of Creek, Cherokee, Chickasaw, Seminole, and other Indians had been relocated from the states in which they had lived to lands west of the Mississippi River. If the removal of eastern Indians had resulted in "the happiest results both to the red man and to the white," why was that policy not applied in California?[39]

The committee recommended the adoption of five resolutions: that the policy pursued by the federal government towards the Indians in California was wrong and should be rejected; that California's senators should be instructed to oppose confirmation of all treaties that granted

Indians exclusive rights to public lands in California; that the policy long pursued by the federal government of removing Indians beyond the jurisdiction of the states was conceived in wisdom, dictated by humanity, and productive to tranquility; that California's senators and representatives in Washington be instructed to use their best efforts to ensure that the federal government implemented the removal policy in California; and that the governor present to each senator and representative a copy of the report and resolutions.[40]

The state senate debated the merits of the report and resolutions. Senator James Estill cautioned against action that might jeopardize California's relationship with the federal government. Once the commissioners began their work, conflicts with the Indians and the attending expenditures had ceased. The situation in California precluded removing the Indians beyond the borders of the state. Senator R. T. Sprague, however, defended the report because it called upon the United States to act precisely as it had done in the past; that is, to continue the policy of removal. The agents' policy, he reminded his colleagues, differed sharply from that previously implemented by the federal government. Their own judgments had dictated their activities in California. Sprague challenged Estill to prove that during the past twenty years the United States had granted reservations to Indians within the limits of an organized state. Sprague also questioned McKee's claim that the land set aside for reservations was virtually useless for agricultural purposes. He was convinced that the reservations, in nearly every case, contained the finest valleys in the state.[41]

J. J. Warner, a member of the special committee, moved that the resolutions be laid on the table until he could prepare a minority report that argued against the position taken by the majority. Senator Thomas B. Van Buren agreed to the motion but sought, in the meantime, the publication and circulation of the majority report. Estill opposed the printing of the majority report because it defamed the reputations of the Indian agents. Publication of the report, he argued, might also damage relations with the federal government. Soon the state would seek compensation for expenditures incurred while fighting Indians, so nothing should be undertaken that might jeopardize the relationship. But Senator Van Buren insisted that passage of the resolutions would not damage relations with the federal government and again called for their publication.[42]

Van Buren took the opportunity to ask what was "the effect of the policy pursued by the Indian commissioners, as far as we are enabled to learn it? In no instance, within my knowledge, have they effected good, while everywhere has evil followed in their footsteps. The treaties, so called, which they have formed with the wild Indians of the Sierra Nevada, are but ropes of sand, which the first breath of discontent will scatter to the winds." According to Van Buren's view of history, Indians in great numbers had lived and worked for many years with the old settlers of California and were "comfortable, contented, peaceable and happy" until the commissioners "induced them to flee to the mountains." To the senator "these transactions approximate too nearly the operations of those abolition gentry who induce desertion and flight by the slaves of the south, in my opinion, to meet the approval of the citizens of our state."[43]

The senator also was concerned about the citizens in his district (which included the Stanislaus Reservation) "who have in good faith settled there upon lands belonging to the United States, and who, since the visit of the commissioners, have been ordered to abandon their possessions." If the Indians were allowed to occupy "these fertile lands," it would cost millions to purchase them in twenty years. Regarding expenses already incurred, between five hundred thousand and seven hundred thousand dollars had been spent on beef, but who "has received the benefit of this item?" The Indians got beef, but "in many instances they have learned to believe themselves of vast importance, and entitled henceforth to the same magnanimous treatment." The main beneficiaries were the beef contractors, many of whom had become rich.[44]

Employing inflammatory language, Senator M. M. Wambough sharply criticized the commissioners for introducing in California a policy significantly different from that practiced in the East. After "praising" Wambough for his "temperate and statesmanlike demeanor," Estill made several points. Only by promising the Indians reservations near where they resided were the agents able to conduct the treaties and thus end the violence. The reservations divided the Indians like squares on a checkerboard, thus prohibiting future combinations from forming. Should it be necessary to remove them to some remote area sometime in the near future, that easily could be accomplished because they had placed themselves under the control of the Indian agents. The Wyandot, Piankashaw, and other Indians, he noted, had been removed from their first reservations to those across the Mississippi River. Estill concluded by chiding his fellow senators for their avarice: "If the Indian gets on a rock, they think it may be *gold-bearing quartz*. If on a hill, it may be *excellent dry diggings*. If on a plain, it is excellent *for gardening*. If up a tree, I presume the gentleman from Yolo [Wambough] might want it for *timber*."[45]

McKee thought the resolutions of the Special Committee to Inquire into the Treaties "evinced not only a lamentable ignorance of the rules of English grammar, but of the history of the policy and negotiations to which they refer." Regarding Senator Van Buren's position that the commissioners had induced the Indians to flee to the mountains, he was even more critical. First of all, the Indians had fled to the mountains weeks before the commissioners arrived; second, the commissioners had induced them to come down and make peace with the whites. As to the claim that five hundred thousand to seven hundred thousand dollars had been spent for beef, McKee estimated that the cost was less than sixty thousand dollars. The profits, moreover, went to Van Buren's personal and political friend, John Frémont.[46]

On February 13 Senator Warner issued the minority report. He considered it impracticable to remove the Indians from California: "We cannot suppose that the General Government will remove them to Oregon, to Utah, New Mexico, or to the Indian territory east of the Rocky Mountains. And where else will you locate them? On the desert and sterile regions east of the Sierra Nevada, that they may die of starvation? or if, perchance, a few survive, that they may become the Arabs of America? Better, far better, drive them at once into the ocean or bury them in the land of their birth." Keeping them within the state, however, would benefit members of both races. On sufficient portions of land the Indians "would be ennobled, and escape that certain destruction which awaits them on every other side. Here philanthropy and charity, hand in hand, might find a field in which to labor. From them, the farmer, grazier and owner of vineyards, might derive their accustomed and needed laborers." Was the land "not broad enough for them and us? or that while our doors are open to the stranger from the uttermost parts of the earth, we have not spare room for the residence of the once sole inhabitants of our magnificent empire? Shall future generations seek in vain for one remaining descendant of the sons of the forest? Has the love of gold blotted from our minds all feelings of compassion or justice?" If Congress failed to ratify the treaties, the Indians would consider it a breach of faith and would be reluctant to enter into any future agreement. "Can it be expected," queried Warner, "that they will place any reliance on any Government Agent who may be sent to negotiate for their removal"[47]

A heated and sometimes vituperative debate followed the reading of the report. Senator Frank Soule was elated that one legislator dared to side with the oppressed against the oppressor. He saw the Indians as an unfortunate people whose few privileges and rights should be respected. He encouraged the senate to adopt liberal and enlightened legislation regarding their welfare. Senator Van Buren, however, refused to believe that Indians and whites could live on adjacent lands. He preferred to leave the Indians alone rather than resettle them on productive lands. Van Buren wondered how Warner, whose ranch had recently been burned down by Indians, could profess sympathy for such people. Senator Henry E. Robinson considered the Indians more sinned against than sinning and supported Warner's report because it left to Congress the discretion to do what it thought was in the public good. Warner then addressed the senate at some length, defending the principles set forth in his report and charging Van Buren with corrupt, ungentlemanly, and outrageous motives. Senator Estill supported Warner. To explain the impracticality of removing Indians from California, he claimed that it had cost the federal government thirty-six million dollars to remove the Seminoles from Florida. The Indians of California must be either killed or given land on which to live. The cost of killing them would be prohibitive. Van Buren called Warner's remarks unjust, ungenerous, and untrue. He questioned Warner's motives by asking him if his ranch in San Diego County was located on one of the reservations. Warner replied that it was.[48]

The senate postponed voting on the majority and minority reports, probably because it was presented with an alternative proposal.[49] The day before Warner voiced his opinions, Senator A. Anderson delivered to the senate a report intended as a memorial from the people of California to the Congress of the United States. The memorial dealt mainly with the disposal of public lands but also addressed the Indian question: "We profess to be neither behind the age in that philanthropy which embraces the happiness of the greatest number and the highest welfare of mankind; nor, we hope, deficient in the just sympathies which we should cherish for the aboriginal man of America. While we feel it to be a high duty of the Christian to preserve and protect him, and, as fast as practicable, to win his descendants from his savage ways, we are unwilling to see him placed in a false position as to himself, or as to us, by new relations, fashioned for him rather by mistake than by his actual condition." In place of reservations, a string of "missions" would serve the Indians. There, annuities would be distributed and parcels of land assigned. Indians would be provided with stock of every description and guaranteed the same grazing privileges as those granted to whites. Indians residing at the posts would come under the authority of one agent and two subagents. Those residing on private lands and in the employ of whites would be encouraged to remain, because already they were "in the best school of civilization." By substituting his plan for the one proposed by the agents, Anderson guaranteed that less acreage and fewer agents would be needed.[50]

Following the reading of the memorial to the senate, Anderson submitted several resolutions: that California's senators and representatives attain an amendment to all the treaties, striking out the provisions that granted permanent occupation to the Indians and substituting the system proposed in the memorial; that they introduce a bill requiring the agents to modify the existing treaties with the Indians to conform to the amendment; that they vote against the ratification of the treaties unless the amendment was passed; and that they procure remuneration for those citizens who lost property when the reservations were established.[51] On March 18 the senate, by a vote of nineteen to four, approved the memorial and the resolutions.[52]

To investigate the feasibility of the reservations, the state assembly also formed a special committee. Chaired by Thomas H. Coats and called the Committee on Indian Reservations, on February 16 it issued a report claiming that ratification of the treaties would deprive the state of taxable property, which would result in higher taxes for other areas. Supposedly twenty thousand American citizens were living on lands designed for the Indians—lands valued at one hundred million dollars. Indians and whites could not live in proximity of one another without the former becoming extinct. For their own preservation, therefore, the Indians "should be removed to regions abounding in game and fish, and which presents all the natural facilities for obtaining their subsistence to which, from time immemorial, they have been familiarly accustomed."[53]

The report accused the Indian agents of wrongdoing. Persons in their employ, it charged, had acquired at extremely reduced prices the claims of miners who were forced to vacate the reservations. The report also accused the agents of issuing beef and other contracts not to the lowest bidder but to those intending to cheat the government out of enormous sums of money. Four resolutions were recommended: that California's senators and representatives in Washington use all proper means to prevent the ratification of the treaties; that they convince their colleagues in Congress that the people of California would suffer great evils if the reservations were established; that they urge the authorities in Washington to conduct an inquiry into the official conduct of the commissioners; and that the governor transmit a copy of the resolutions to the president of the United States and to each California senator and representative in Congress.[54]

McKee called the report "a tissue of false and slanderous declamation from beginning to end. Upon four-fifths of the reservations made by the Commissioners no white family or individual resided at the time they were made, and on all the others there could not have been, including Mexicans, Chilians [sic] and Chinese, certainly over 200 whites—Mr. Coats says 20,000! As to the value of improvement included in the reservations, all is guess work. Mr. Coats guesses 100 millions of dollars—I guess ten, or at most twenty thousand dollars!" That some men connected with the agents' expeditions "may have bought claims and remained behind to work or improve them, is probable enough, but that the Commissioners have any such interest, or were in their negotiations influenced by any such considerations, is wholly untrue and slanderous."[55]

On March 4 McKee wrote to William H. Lyons, chairman of the Committee on Indian Affairs, requesting that the report either be recommitted or a special committee convened to investigate it. If such a committee were formed, "composed of gentlemen wholly disinterested in pecuniary results, I flatter myself that I can with little difficulty satisfy them and the majority of the Assembly that the report of the Committee on Indian Reservations, presented by Mr. Coates [sic], is a very unsafe foundation upon which to base grave legislative proceedings."[56]

That day the assembly resolved itself into a committee of the whole and debated the report and the resolutions. Lyons told the legislators that McKee sought to have the report recommitted. Coats defended the accuracy of the report but was willing to refer it back. The people he represented were deeply concerned and wanted the matter promptly settled. Other assemblymen emphasized that their constituents opposed the reservations. S. A. Merritt, for example, noted that five of the reservations were located in his district and were universally condemned. Lyons, who represented a district where a reservation was situated, stated he would be derelict in his responsibilities to his constituents if he failed to support the report and the resolutions.[57]

The issue of fraud also was debated. Coats argued that none of the resolutions charged the commissioners with fraud, only inferred that fraud had been committed. Assemblyman Parrish noted that the resolutions merely called upon members of Congress to investigate the matter; if the commissioners had acted honorably, they had nothing to fear. Ellis thought fraud had been committed but was unprepared to say by whom. Henry A. Crabb found no evidence of fraud and recommended that the assembly proceed with delicacy and circumspection. James W. Coffroth accused the commissioners of favoritism; they allowed certain parties to trade with the Indians but prohibited others from entering the reservations. The debate ended with a motion that the Committee on Indian Reservations report back the following week.[58]

Receiving permission to address the committee, McKee informed the press that he would state the facts "*not to clear myself of charges of fraud or peculation for I throw all that sort of thing back in the faces of the insinuators, with the utmost disdain and defiance*—but to show that the whole system of opposition to the policy of the United States Agents in this Indian business, grows out of either the most wretched partisan feelings—a desire to make political capital at the expense of the people of California; or extreme and most reprehensible *ignorance of the whole subject*."[59] On March 20 the *Daily Union* announced that the assembly's Committee on Indian Reservations would hold a public meeting that evening. The paper encouraged all governmental officials to "arrange their business as to be present. The subject is one of vital interest to the State and to the whole country."[60]

McKee began by referring to the address he had made in the senate chamber in the latter part of January. Convinced the matter had been put to rest, he was shocked that "my remarks on that occasion were scarcely published, before the most absurd, ungenerous, unfounded attacks upon both our policy and proceedings, in the shape of formal reports from committees, and speeches in both Houses, made their appearance in the public prints." To prevent the legislature from undertaking unwise action, he was compelled to speak to it once again.[61]

Following a long overview of the activities and objectives of the Indian commissioners, he explained why so many reservations had been established. He and his colleagues had discovered that the best "policy was not to congregate the mountain and warlike tribes, with those of the plains, upon one or two large districts, but to separate and divide them upon several small reservations, fifty or sixty miles apart, with room for white settlements between them, and thus guard against future combinations." He had sought the advice of white citizens in the interior regarding the location of the reservations, and several times "the lines, or boundaries, have been altered to suit the views of citizens, or to remove the Indians further from the mining country. The only objections I ever heard against any of our early treaties, were, that we assigned for the Indians, too poor, or too little land."[62]

The agent called upon the legislators to give his policy "at least a candid trial and examination before it is condemned, disavowed, and repudiated." He warned the legislators that "if the promises we have made to the Indian tribes in California, in the name of the Government and people of the United States, shall from any cause whatever fail to be made good, carried out fairly and to the letter, you need never again attempt to secure their confidence.... I shall blush for my country and my color, if our solemn assurances are not made good."[63]

Those opposing the reservations actually hindered white settlement, because "Indian title has first to be extinguished, purchased by treaty and payment made, or agreed on, before the domain passes fully even to the Government. Till then, the lands are not liable to be squatted on or improved." To emphasize his point McKee called upon the clerk to read from one of the treaties articles three and four, which stated that the signatories had relinquished and forever quitclaimed to the United States their lands in California. McKee reminded his audience that the public domain belonged to the United States and that the California legislature could not interfere with its disposal. The federal government also maintained exclusive jurisdiction over Indian peoples. Yet, he noted, there were individuals who insisted that California should control both. By deliberately obstructing the fulfillment of the promises to the Indians, they were leading the state into another Indian war.[64]

In some detail McKee explained how the Indians would benefit from residing on the reservations. The United States would provide them with animals and equipment. White men with families would live with the Indians and teach them how to farm, build houses, and blacksmith. Indian children would be taught how to read and write the English language and how to make clothes and perform housework. Upon each reservation, or in every district, an agent would reside. He would attend to all their complaints and see that justice equally was applied to Indians and whites. Merchants or traders would be licensed to trade with the Indians but would be strictly prohibited from selling or giving them alcohol. On some of the reservations, at intervals of fifty or one hundred miles, the government would establish small military posts that would protect both whites and Indians. The officers assigned to the posts would befriend the Indians; physicians would tend to their medical needs.[65]

Because the reservations would bring economic benefits to many whites, especially cattlemen, traders, and governmental employees, McKee could "conceive of nothing more injurious, fatal, suicidal, to the best interests of California, than this apparently indiscriminate organized opposition to the proposed arrangements of the U.S. Government." McKee concluded his address by challenging the data and interpretations presented in the reports prepared by the special committees of the senate and assembly.[66]

On March 22 Coats reported back to the assembly the report and resolutions the Committee on Indian Reservations had issued on February 16. Coats notified the assembly that the committee members, after listening to McKee's exposition of Indian policy, nevertheless remained "confirmed in the opinion expressed in their former report that the reservations of land which have been made within the limits of this State, would, if confirmed, prove most ruinous to the best interests of both the Indian and white population." The committee recommended adoption of the four resolutions presented in the report. In the debate that followed an assemblyman moved to recommit the resolutions to the committee with instructions to strike out the third resolution because it slandered the commissioners. His motion was not agreed to. The resolutions were read a third time, and the assembly voted thirty-five to six in their favor.[67]

Writing to McKee on April 15, Governor Bigler claimed that he had "assurances of the united opposition of our delegation in Congress to the ratification of the treaties, and that their rejection by the United States Senate may be regarded as beyond a doubt."[68] But McKee refused to believe the Senate would reject the treaties. Some of the treaties might have to be modified, he told the governor, but surely California's delegation to Congress would not "open up again former causes of disquietude and warfare, at least without proposing some other, and manifestly better policy." Even if California's senators voted against ratification, "in a full Senate, there might be sixty equally honorable members of a different opinion." McKee hoped the issue would be resolved "with calmness and wisdom in entire disregard of all mere local, or party influences or prejudices."[69]

McKee also hoped to be appointed superintendent of Indian affairs of California, an office Congress created on March 3, 1852.[70] Later that month twenty individuals petitioned President Millard Fillmore to consider McKee for the office. To them "his integrity, industry, business habits and qualifications, together with his knowledge of Indian Affairs, his conciliatory manners, and the success of his negotiations and treaties with many of the native Tribes, demonstrate his peculiar fitness of the Office."[71] On April 3 McKee wrote to the president, noting that shortly the petition would arrive and that several individuals, including Captain E. D. Keyes, had written to the secretary of the interior on his behalf. Included with his letter was a copy of his address to the assembly's Committee on Indian Reservations.[72] McKee, however, could not possibly have foreseen that political considerations in Washington D.C. would trump his practical experiences in California.

PART III

Subjugation

PART III begins with a short biography of the individual instrumental in consolidating Indian policy in California. His life is well known, but the abundance of data regarding the reservation he created has attracted few historians. The data reveal the structure of that reservation and the ways the Indian residents adjusted to it. As any ethnohistorian will attest, one must know the intruder to know the Indian, but one must also know the intruder's institutions to know the Indian's roles in them.

The subjugation of the Indians, however, did not result solely from the imposition of foreign institutions. In fact, most Indians never resided on the reservation or its satellites called farms. Many competed with white settlers for the same lands, and the competition was not always as uneven as it might seem. Only by recognizing that for a time some Indians remained members of independent societies can their role in the region's history be appreciated. In the long run, however, Indians were finally subjugated not by government policies buy by the inundation of white settlers. Ironically, many individuals survived by working for the people responsible for their condition.

Part III concludes with an examination of the two major institutions—one private, the other governmental—remaining in the San Joaquin Valley, where a few hundred Indians lived and worked. By describing how one led to a dead end for the residents while the other contributed to the preservation of their culture, some resolution is brought to the history of the interior zone.

CHAPTER XVII

A Superintendent for California

Not far from Washington, D.C., at Bloomingdale, Virginia, Edward F. Beale entered the world on February 3, 1822 as one of its privileged members. His Scotch-Irish forbearers had settled in the West Indies before moving to Virginia in the 1660s. His father, George M. Beale, Jr., chose a naval career, serving with distinction in the War of 1812. In 1819 he married Emily Truxtun, also from a prominent naval family. Thomas Truxtun, her father, had served in the navy during the American Revolution and commanded the Constellation during the undeclared naval war with France of 1798-1800.[1]

George Beale instilled in Edward and his older brother, Truxtun, a love of sports and the importance of education. As a youngster Edward excelled at hunting, fishing, riding, and swimming. He also loved to fight. On one occasion, none other than President Andrew Jackson broke up a fight between Edward and another boy. When Edward explained that the altercation was about the president, whom he was defending, Jackson told the young man to visit him at the White House if ever in need of assistance.[2]

An indifferent student at the lower levels, Beale excelled in his studies at Georgetown College (an academy) where he and his brother were enrolled in 1832. At the Jesuit-run institution, which accepted non-Catholics, Edward studied Latin, the classical writers, mathematics, and modern languages. Because of the unexpected death of her husband in April 1835, Mrs. Beale was forced to withdraw her sons from the college. A short time later she and Edward called upon President Jackson. Seeking a commission in the navy for her son she recounted the contributions to the service made by her father and husband, and Edward reminded the president of his pledge to him. Jackson recommended to the secretary of the navy that Edward receive a commission as acting midshipman, which was granted on December 15, 1836.[3]

Immediately upon boarding the frigate Independence, Beale, defending his honor against the midshipmen who ridiculed his home-made uniform, got into a fight. He won the fight and respect of his shipmates. From May 1837 to April 1840 Beale served in the Gulf of Finland and off the coast of Brazil, followed by eight months aboard the Levant in the West Indies. After six months at the Naval Asylum (college) in Philadelphia, he passed his officer's examinations in June 1842. He then spent the next two years at sea.[4]

A handsome young man Beale came of age in Brazilian ports, where he found women and alcohol readily available. On the surface he appeared to be well adjusted, but in fact was a contradictory, quixotic individual subject to mood swings, often induced by too much liquor that sometimes took him to the depths of melancholia. Regarding one of his adventures in Brazil, Beale wrote in his diary that he had "visited the haunts of the low and the guilty and mingled for a brief season with the profligate, the criminal, and the base."[5] Beale also developed a cynicism about personal relations. "Love is the fickliest of the things in life," he wrote, and one should never confide "in any man, much less *woman*." Nor should one let "any being control you through your dependence on him for a portion of your happiness."[6]

During his years at sea Beale grew intellectually, reading the Koran, Keats, Shelley, and Wordsworth, but he remained more a man of action than a serious thinker. When the Mexican-American War broke out in 1846, that side of his character was immediately demonstrated. At the time he was serving aboard the *Congress*, commanded by Commodore Robert F. Stockton. In early October the *Congress* sailed into San Francisco Bay, and Beale led a party in small boats across the bay to Sonoma to make contact with John Frémont who was then encouraging American settlers to rebel against the Mexican government. He informed him about the Californios driving American forces out of Los Angeles. Frémont and approximately 120 settlers boarded the *Sterling*, a merchant ship, another 40 boarded the *Congress*, and the ships set sail for San Diego. From there the settlers were to proceed overland to Los Angeles. The ships, however, got separated in bad weather, and the *Sterling* put in at Monterey. The *Congress* continued on to San Diego where Stockton prepared his men and the settlers to march north to Los Angeles. He placed Beale in charge of obtaining horses, mules, and cattle. Beale and his men rounded up some animals in the interior but had to fight off some Californios who attacked them with lances. Later, an American died of his wounds.[7]

Midshippman Beale. (From Historical Collection, Title Insurance and Trust Company, San Diego, Cal. Courtesy of the author.)

In December, before departing for the north, Stockton sent Captain Archibald Gillespie, Beale, and 40 men to meet General Stephen Watts Kearny and 350 dragoons encamped several miles east of San Diego. They had arrived in California from Santa Fe, New Mexico. Against Beale's advice, Kearny attacked Mexican forces at San Pasqual. The Californios, superbly mounted and armed with lances, thoroughly mauled the Americans, killing nineteen, wounding an equal number, and surrounding the rest of the command. Negotiating in Spanish with Andres Pico, the Mexican commander, Beale arranged an exchange of prisoners, one being Alexis Godey who had slipped through Mexican lines to inform Stockton in San Diego about the situation only to be captured on his way back to Kearny. Unable to move and not knowing what Stockton was intending, Kearny sent Beale, Kit Carson, and an Indian through the Mexican lines. Each took a different route, the Indian arriving first. The relief force Stockton sent to the besieged soldiers escorted them safely to San Diego.[8]

At this juncture Beale became embroiled in a controversy regarding who would govern California. Over the strong objections of General Kearny, who claimed to be the legitimate head of the military government then being established, Stockton appointed Frémont military governor. Stockton, however, acted prematurely, because President James Polk already had appointed Kearny governor. To get his side of the controversy to the government, Stockton sent Beale to Washington, D.C. Arriving in May, Beale delivered Stockton's letters to the secretary of the interior, who forwarded them to the President. Beale intended to recuperate at his estate in Bloomingdale, Virginia, but Polk ordered him back to California. One hundred miles west of Fort Leavenworth, Kansas, Beale collapsed from exhaustion and returned to Washington. After testifying to no avail on behalf of John Frémont at his court-martial, Beale sailed for Mexico. By the time his ship arrived in Mazatlan in May 1848, the war between the two nations had ended. Beale grew bored with garrison duty and took to drinking heavily. On one occasion he attended a military parade drunk and improperly dressed.[9]

In July 1848, when Beale learned that gold had been discovered on the American River in Alta California, he persuaded Commodore Thomas Catesby Jones to allow him to take to Washington, D.C. a small quantity of gold and dispatches about the discovery. At considerable personal risk, he crossed Mexico to Vera Cruz, where he caught a ship to Mobile, Alabama. Arriving at the capital on September 14, he informed President Polk of the discovery and became something of a celebrity for his daring exploits.[10]

At the beginning of April of the following year, Beale was back in San Francisco, having crossed the Great Plains in the dead of winter. In less than two weeks, he sailed for the East Coast with dispatches and an eight-pound lump of gold. In New York in late May, he visited the Wall Street offices of William H. Aspinwall, president of the Pacific Mail Steamship Company. With Aspinwall by his side, Beale informed a crowd of brokers, merchants, and speculators about the wealth of California. On display was the lump of gold, worth more than two thousand dollars.[11]

Beale returned to California in mid-1849, only to sail from San Francisco in November, again with dispatches from Commodore Jones, arriving in New York on December 7. Ordered back to California by the navy in late April, Beale also embarked as an employee of Aspinwall and Robert Stockton. They had hired him to oversee the shipping of their quartz-mining equipment and to manage their mining operations in the gold fields. Beale left behind Mary Edwards, whom he had married the previous year, and their baby daughter, but he was not without company on the voyage. He sailed with Harry Edwards, his brother-in-law, Gwin Harris Heap, a cousin, and William Carey Jones, Frémont's brother-in-law. Upon arriving in California Beale oversaw the delivery of the mining machinery to Frémont's ranch on the Little Mariposa River. Frémont had leased the rights to quartz gold to Aspinwall and Stockton.[12]

Determined to make California his new home, Beale sought employment with the federal government. John Frémont wrote letters to the secretary of state and to President Zachary Taylor, recommending that Beale be appointed United States marshal for California. Senator Thomas Hart Benton, Frémont's father-in-law, also supported the appointment. Perhaps because of the sudden death of the president in July, Beale was bypassed. Fremont and Benton, however, wrote to the recently appointed secretary of state, again recommending that Beale be considered for marshal. No action was taken on the request. Beale returned to the East where he received his commission as a lieutenant in the navy. Immediately, he took a year's furlough to devote all his time to the affairs of Aspinwall and Stockton.[13]

Beale arrived in San Francisco in February 1851, intent on salvaging the mining operations of his employers. He sold the mining equipment and invested the returns in a freighting business, which for a time dominated the transportation of goods and equipment from San Francisco to the Northern Mines. Not satisfied at remaining an employee, Beale sought but failed to win a nomination for Congress at the Democratic Convention held in Benicia in May.[14] Nevertheless, by this time Beale had acquired powerful friends in the federal government.

William Gwin, senator from California, was one of those friends. In November 1851 he introduced "A Bill to Provide for the Appointment of a Superintendent of Indian Affairs in California." The superintendent would reside in the state and would be given the same powers and responsibilities as those held by the superintendent of Indian affairs stationed at St. Louis, Missouri. He would have "the power also of exercising administrative examination over all claims and accounts, and vouchers for disbursements, connected with Indian Affairs in the said State of California." Furthermore, the superintendent could "suspend any agent for the Indians in California for causes which he may deem sufficient, and of supplying his place by the temporary appointment of another until the President shall confirm or remove such suspension."[15] Gwin and Congressmen Joseph W. McCorkle and Edward Marshall wrote to President Millard Fillmore, recommending Beale for the superintendency. Beale was "fully identified with the early history of our State, & has served it faithfully & to the great advantage of the country. His thorough knowledge of the whole state & of Indian character seems to point him out as fully & particularly adapted for this office."[16]

Except for removing the section giving the superintendent the authority to suspend any agent from duty for causes he deemed appropriate, Congress, on March 3, 1852, passed Gwin's bill intact. The superintendent was to receive a salary not in excess of $4,000 per annum and the clerk he hired not more than $2,500.[17] The following day President Fillmore nominated Beale superintendent of Indian affairs in California.[18] On the eleventh, the secretary of the interior sent Beale's commission to the commissioner of Indian affairs, who was to deliver it to Beale with the necessary instructions.[19] Beale's financial dealings, party affiliation, and dubious qualifications caused many to question the nomination. Rumors also spread that Beale was a drunkard. James Crane apparently told the president that Beale, while in Sacramento, was in the habit of getting drunk and running around the town naked. Had the rumors proved true the president was prepared to rescind the appointment. But Crane's credibility was destroyed when it was learned that he had spread a malicious rumor about an official in the Department of State. Confronting Crane on March 9 at Brown's Hotel on Pennsylvania Avenue, Beale kicked and cuffed him and drove him from the premises.[20]

Surviving that controversy Beale soon faced another. In 1851 he had entered into an informal, or "silent," partnership with John Frémont and was present when Frémont received drafts from Indian Agent George Barbour for delivering cattle to the Indians who had signed the treaties.[21] Evidently, Frémont promised Beale twenty-five percent of the settlement when the drafts were honored.[22] Concerned that their association might prove embarrassing, Frémont wrote to Beale shortly after the nomination, authorizing him to say "upon all fitting occasions" that the beef contracts were made by him alone and emphasizing that "you are not and never were a partner of mine in any transaction or party to any contract in which I am or have been engaged." Beale was "at liberty to make what use of the letter you please."[23]

Because he intended to investigate the accounts of the Indian agents, especially those concerned with supplying beef to the Indians, Beale asked Commissioner of Indian Affairs Luke Lea to appoint someone from California to assist him in the matter: "My reason for this is, that among the contractors for those supplies, and consequently interested in the payment of the drafts, is my intimate friend and companion Col. J. C. Frémont. The investigation of any pecuniary matter in which he is interested would be exceedingly delicate, unpleasant, and embarrassing to me; and while I believe the strictest scrutiny possible into this affair will result beneficially to Col. Frémont, I would nevertheless prefer that it should be made by some other person than myself."[24]

In New York a correspondent for the *Sacramento Daily Union*, an admitted critic of Beale, concluded that the rumors about his business connections with Frémont were unfounded. With Beale's permission he included in his dispatch the letter Frémont had written to Beale in early March, stating that he alone had been responsible for the beef contracts. The Union published the dispatch and Frémont's letter on May 1.[25] So did the *Stockton Journal* the following month.[26]

News of the superintendency had reached California in April. At midmonth the editors of the *Union* published a letter, written in March by their correspondent in Washington, D.C., announcing the creation of the office and predicting that either Pearson B. Reading or George B. Tingley would be appointed superintendent.[27] On the sixteenth, the editors acknowledged they had received a letter from New York, dated March 9, informing them of Beale's appointment. But they refused to believe the report, because Beale was one of the most uncompromising and "illiberal" Democrats in California, and "we can scarcely suppose that he has been so specially favored by our Whig President."[28]

An individual calling himself "Amicus" also discounted the rumors. Would not the president, he queried in a letter to a San Francisco newspaper, be "likely to look at the eminent services rendered by at least one of the present Indian Agents, and promote him to the office? Is it not the general opinion of our people, of all political parties, that Colonel McKee's acquaintance with Indian matters in California is superior to that of any other man in the State, and his ability and integrity unquestioned? Why, then, should this vastly important business be entrusted to inexperienced hands? I understand the strongest letters have been prepared and sent forward, by many of the political men of both parties and a long list of our first merchants and banking houses, urging the appointment of Col. McKee. For one I hope they will not arrive too late."[29]

Writing to the *Union*, an individual suggested that Beale had "spent only so much of his life in California as was made necessary by the orders in obedience to which lie his professional duty and his means of support." Moreover, he remained in line for a naval promotion, and "with an indefinite leave of absence in one pocket, and an Indian commission in the other, goes on a pleasure tour through California, at a salary of $4,000 per annum. The whole thing appears to me too barefaced a swindle for excuse or apology. For one, I should button up my pocket in the presence of a man whose moral perceptions would permit him to accept an appointment under such circumstances."[30]

Surely, wrote the editors of the *Union*, in California there were citizens "matured by age and experience, who were probably much more competent to discharge the duties of such an office, who were permanently identified with our State, who have for a long time had houses and families amongst us demanding their support and protection, and who were presented to the administration not as quasi Whigs, but as the active, generous, and faithful supporters of the party." He questioned whether a naval officer possessed the "practical knowledge which is so essential to the general management of affairs upon terra firma."[31]

While citizens in California debated his appointment, Beale, still in Washington, prepared to undertake his duties. On May 10, 1852 Commissioner Lea instructed him to examine the eighteen treaties (seven in the San Joaquin Valley) recently conducted by Indian agents, "particularly as to the expediency of ratifying or rejecting them."[32] Beale replied the following day. The issue was "whether the Indians are to have any lands set apart for them; and if so, whether those selected for them may be justly considered as suitable and appropriate? … It is evident, that if allowed to roam at pleasure, their early extinction is inevitable; and I am slow to believe that the government, recognizing as it does their possessory right to all the soil inhabited by them, would deny them the occupancy of a small portion of the vast country from which such extraordinary benefits are in progress of receipt."[33]

Provisions in the treaties Beale found objectionable were the supplying of agricultural implements and the founding of schools. Unaware of the economic and cultural changes many Indians had undergone, Beale insisted they were not yet "disposed, nor can they be induced at the present time, to engage in agricultural pursuits." The implements provided to them soon would fall into the hands of whites. Schools also were unnecessary, the Indians' "present state of civilization and advancement being such as to preclude the possibility of their appreciating the benefits to be derived from such instruction."[34]

Nevertheless, rejecting the treaties "would be unwise and injudicious," even though it might be necessary to do so in the future. "To reject them outright, without an effort to retain their confidence and friendship, ... would undoubtedly involve the State in a long and bloody war, disastrous and ruinous to her mining and commercial interests, and affecting, more or less the prosperity of our whole country." Although he lacked statistical evidence, Beale claimed that exports of gold had dropped by millions during the recent conflict with the Indians in the Southern Mines. "If this was the result of a war with very few tribes, what may be considered as the effect of a war with the entire Indian population of California?"[35]

Lea transmitted the treaties to Secretary of the Interior Alexander H. H. Stuart on May 13. The following day Lea wrote to the secretary, concurring with Beale "that a rejection of the treaties without the adoption

Table 2. Superintendency Expenses

Item	*Amount*
Salary of superintendent	$4,000
Salary of clerk	2,500
Office rent, stationary, fuel, lights, and postage	7,500
Messengers	2,500
Interpreters	3,000
Contingent expenses, including traveling expenses of agents	12,500
Presents and provisions for Indians visiting the superintendency	3,000
Traveling expenses of superintendent, including the purchase of animals and camp equipment	5,000
Furniture for office	1,000
Iron safe for office	1,000
Flags for Indians	500
Total	42,500

Source: Adapted from Edward F. Beale to Luke Lea, Washington D.C., July 14, 1852, Office of Indian Affairs, Special Files, File 159.

of precautionary measures guarding against a general outbreak on the part of the Indians would be hazardous and unwise." Some of the stipulations in the treaties were new, the most important being the "entire relinquishment of title by some of the tribes, and their permanent settlement within the limits of the State on lands not previously owned by them." Another unique aspect of the treaties was the absence of annuity stipulations, a system Lea considered "fraught with evil" and impossible to end once begun. To assist the secretary in determining whether the public interest would be "promoted or impaired" by the ratification of the treaties, Lea included with his letter the one Beale had written to him on May 11.[36]

On May 22 Stuart sent the treaties, relevant documents, and a letter to President Fillmore, noting the strong opposition to ratification in California. Unable to form an opinion regarding the merits of the treaties, he nevertheless recommended they be sent to the Senate, "to be disposed of in such way as that body in its wisdom shall direct."[37] The president submitted the treaties and documents on June 1, 1852.[38] Meeting in secret session on the eighth, the Senate rejected each treaty. Of the thirty-seven members in attendance, all, including William Gwin of California, voted against ratification. California's other senator, John B. Weller, apparently was not present.[39]

Ratification of the treaties would have given Beale a strong legal foundation upon which to implement the policy created by the Indian agents.

Now he had to devise some way to subjugate the Indians of California without the use of treaties. In mid-July he submitted to Commissioner Lea his estimate of expenses for the first year of his superintendency, which included $3,500 for provisions, presents, and flags for the Indians. Beale explained to Lea that provisions and presents were necessary if the Indians were to remain peaceful after learning the treaties had been rejected. The flags were "intended for distribution to the Captains & headmen of the tribes. It is believed no present will sooner touch the vanity of these rude chiefs than the custody of that emblem which they have been taught by our troops to respect & which they themselves regard as 'big medicine.'"[40]

As Beale prepared to depart for California, Secretary Stuart wrote to the attorney general, seeking his opinion whether the law creating the superintendency in California allowed Beale to investigate the beef contracts undertaken by John Frémont. The attorney general replied that Beale had such a right but could investigate only when asked to do so by the government or by Frémont.[41] Stuart met with the president and removed his concerns that Beale would be prejudicial in examining the claims of those who had dealt with the Indians. On July 26 Stuart wrote to Commissioner Lea, instructing him to inform Beale that he was to depart without delay "to the scene of his duties."[42]

Beale sailed from New York in early August 1852.[43] The *Daily Alta California* greeted his arrival in San Francisco on September 5 by noting that he had performed "good and efficient service here" and was "ready to assume the arduous and important duties of that office."[44] One of his "duties" was to assert his authority over Indian Agents Redick McKee and O. M. Wozencraft, both of whom had sought the office of superintendent."[45]

Wozencraft wrote to Beale shortly after his arrival. Reviewing the history of Indian-white relations in his district and highlighting his achievements, he was pleased to report "that there has been no serious infraction of treaty stipulations by any of the numerous tribes with whom I have treated." He had negotiated with nearly one hundred groups, many of them hostile to the whites, and had saved "life and treasure, as well as alleviating the wants and suffering of a race who have just claims on our sympathy." Moreover, he was delighted that "your views are measurably in accordance with the policy which we have deemed just and expedient in conducting our negotiations" and was convinced "that time will demonstrate to the world the entire practicability of a system which in some respects is novel."[46]

When the two met on September 14, Wozencraft turned over to Beale duplicates of all his accounts.[47] The superintendent then subjected the agent to an interrogatory regarding his role in various beef contracts.

Wozencraft admitted he had issued drafts on government cattle before the animals were delivered; that he had ordered fifteen hundred head of cattle delivered to the Indians residing between the Fresno River and the Four Creeks but had never been in the area and did not know the number of Indians residing there; that the only proof the cattle had been delivered was the word of the traders; that in some cases those who contracted for the cattle were the same persons who traded with the Indians; that verbal contracts had been made with James Savage, Lorenzo Vinsonhaler, and another trader; and that he had seen traders butchering cattle on some of the reservations but was unsure they were government animals.[48]

Beale also interviewed Joel Brooks about his involvement with James Savage in the distribution of cattle. Brooks claimed that shortly before Savage's death, he had taken receipts for double the number of cattle delivered to the Indians on the San Joaquin and Kings Rivers and had provided the Indians on the Fresno River with one-third fewer head than the receipts indicated. He insisted that Savage had issued to him a written order to deliver 78 head of cattle to Alexis Godey to be sold to miners and later had received a similar order to turn over another 450 head to Godey, who was to sell as many as possible and keep the rest. Another 800 animals had been herded to Savage's farm on the San Joaquin, but only a few reached the Indians.[49] Brooks was known in California as a scoundrel and a liar, but apparently Beale failed to question his veracity.

In a letter of September 30 to Commissioner Lea, Beale articulated the dilemma he faced regarding the cattle contracted by the Indian agents: "Now if I send and collect them, there will be altogether nearly a thousand head of cattle for which drafts on the government have been given, or liabilities contracted; but as the department does not recognize the transactions of these gentlemen [the Indian agents], and has protested the drafts, if I take the cattle I place the government under some additional obligation to pay the contractors, and may, by that means, put myself in the same position as those gentlemen now are. On the other hand, if I do not collect them, and the government should at any subsequent period conclude to pay these drafts, it will be the loser to the amount of this one thousand head of cattle, which in the mean time will have passed entirely out of the reach of the agents of the department."[50]

Also on the thirtieth Wozencraft informed Commissioner Lea that he intended to resign his commission, in part because "the superintendent of Indian affairs has expressed his disapprobation of my official acts." If the date of his resignation were delayed until the beginning of the new year, he would have time to arrange his affairs so they could be examined by the Indian Office and the Senate. He hoped to be in Washington, D.C. by December 1.[51] In transit, however, was a letter Lea had written in early September, notifying him that upon its receipt his commission was terminated. He was to transfer to Beale all public property in his possession.[52]

On October 1 Beale ordered Wozencraft to make a list of government properties for which he had contracted.[53] Late the following month, Wozencraft transferred to Beale 744 head of cattle, 21 horses, and a saddle and bridle. Another 212 head of cattle, managed by Lorenzo Vinsonhaler on the Fresno Reservation, were turned over as well.[54]

Although Beale easily had outmaneuvered Wozencraft, he faced a formidable intellect and determined opponent in Redick McKee. Expecting to be appointed superintendent McKee was stunned when informed of Beale's selection. In a letter to Commissioner Lea, written in mid-April 1852, McKee sought to have his and Beale's responsibilities clearly defined. The appointment of Beale was "wholly unexpected by the people here of either party" he noted.[55] In a follow-up letter he emphasized that Beale's "selection for that important and responsible post appears to meet the universal disapproval of not only the State Central Committee, but of all other influential whigs in the country." Be that as it may McKee pledged to "forgo all personal feelings and considerations, and render him all the information and assistance in my power. My chief anxiety is for the adoption and consummation of a system which may elevate and improve the naturally docile, and amiable, though much-abused natives of this country."[56]

Beale notified McKee on October 8 that he had placed in his account $500 for expenditures and $750 for his salary for the first quarter of the fiscal year. McKee was to proceed immediately to Nevada City (approximately fifty miles northeast of Sacramento), where his agency was to be located until a more suitable place, nearer the center of the Indian population, was determined. His district extended from the Feather River to the Tuolumne.[57] Later in the month McKee took up residence in Nevada City.[58] Upon returning from a trip to the Yuba River in November, he was shocked to learn that Beale had refused to transfer to him operating funds and had ordered him never to leave Nevada City, except in emergencies, without his permission.[59]

McKee decided to fight back. In a long letter to Beale, he emphasized, that "there exists a wide discrepancy between our understanding of our respective privileges, duties, and responsibilities as agents of the federal government, which should be explained and reconciled if possible." With his appointment came traveling expenses and a per diem. Beale's authority as superintendent did not abrogate the authority conferred upon the Indian agents. An important authority, exclusive to the Indian agents, was negotiating treaties. The Indian *agents were "agents for the whole State at large*, unless formal districts have been established (unknown to me) by the late Congress, or some recent authority from the Department of the Interior. If in this I am not mistaken, you will appreciate the surprise with which I read your peremptory order *not to travel in the region among the tribes, or even to leave the city, without first asking your consent!* In my judgment a restriction of this kind, even were you fully authorized to issue the order, would be highly impolitic." If peace with the Indians were to be kept, the agents must visit the disaffected groups to explain why promises had not been fulfilled.[60]

In conclusion McKee claimed "the right of knowing that 'orders' are issued by competent legal authority, and do not contravene *other* orders previously issued by the head of the department." He was convinced, moreover, that "The powers of a superintendent to control and direct the official conduct of an agent or sub-agent located among a particular tribe, with limited and specified duties, on the Atlantic side of the continent, are clearly laid down and *essential to his office*, but wholly inapplicable, as I conceive, to the service on this coast, where there are as yet no subagents, and the three principal agents *appointed for the whole State clothed with the powers of commissioners or ambassadors*. Until this whole matter can be reviewed and a new system agreed on and sent down from the authorities at Washington, we must get along in this State, I suppose, on the principle of comity, accommodation, and the exercise of our best judgments and exertions for the public good."[61]

Lacking the authority to do so, Beale suspended McKee as Indian agent, turning the case over to the commissioner of Indian affairs. He informed McKee that he found extraordinary his claim to possess authority "extending even to the making of treaties with Indians, without advice or instruction from this office." Given the burdens of his office he had "no time for extensive discussion upon that and other, only less important, claims set up by you."[62] But Beale found the time to extensively discuss the issues in a letter to Commissioner Lea. He insisted that public opinion was critical of the actions of the Indian agents, but he hesitated in replacing McKee because of the agent's close relationship with Secretary of the Interior Stuart. If an agent "takes it upon himself to disobey my orders, the department should sustain me by his removal." Beale was troubled, moreover, by McKee's claim that the authority to negotiate treaties remained with the agents. If such were the case how was he to develop a new Indian policy? Beale also challenged McKee's notion that he had the right to know if the orders issued to him came from a competent legal authority. It would be impossible to "administer the duties of my office properly if my subordinates are allowed the right to question the legality of my orders." To support his decision to suspend McKee, he referred to McKee's insistence that the three agents had been appointed to the whole state and had been clothed in the powers of commissioners or ambassadors. Upon arriving in California, Beale had not recognized

McKee as an ambassador. He saw him only as "an Indian agent, subject to my orders." Beale concluded his letter by proclaiming that there could be no friendly understanding between McKee and himself.[63]

Lea replied in January 1853, pointing out that the general rule required all agents, even those in California, to obey all instructions issued by their respective superintendents. Furthermore, there was "nothing in the instructions heretofore given to agent McKee, in any capacity, that impairs or interferes with your authority to superintend and control his official conduct." Not prepared to replace McKee, Lea directed Beale to reassign him to duty and to give him a copy of his letter.[64] Reassignment proved to be unnecessary, however, because in March McKee was officially relieved of his duties.[65] The founding of permanent reservations in California would result from the efforts of others.

CHAPTER XVIII

Formulating Plans

In mid-September 1852, a few days after arriving in San Francisco, Beale wrote to General E. A. Hitchcock, commander of the pacific division of the United States Army, requesting information that would help him in executing his duties as superintendent. Hitchcock promised to furnish him with all information at his disposal.[1] On October 29 Beale informed Commissioner of Indian Affairs Luke Lea that he had greatly benefited from Hitchcock's knowledge of Indian affairs. In that letter, Beale presented his plan in outline:

> In the first place, I propose a system of "military posts" to be established on reservations, for the convenience and protection of the Indians; these reservations to be regarded as military reservations or government reservations. The Indians to be invited to assemble within these reserves.
>
> A system of discipline and instruction to be adopted by the agent who is to live at the post.
>
> Each reservation to contain a military establishment, the number of troops being in proportion to the population of the tribes there assembled.
>
> The expenses of the troops to be borne by the surplus produce of Indian labor. The reservations to be made with a view to a change in location, when increase of white population may make it necessary.
>
> A change of present Indian laws to be made, so as to suit the condition of this State and the proposed policy.[2]

Included with his letter was a note from Hitchcock in which the general hinted at his role in formulating policy: "The plan for the protection of the Indians in California, sketched by the superintendent of Indian affairs above, has been the subject of some conversation between that functionary and myself, and I am decidedly of the opinion, so far as Mr. Beale has developed his plan, that it is better than any hitherto proposed, and well calculated to meet the actual condition of things in this country. It is, perhaps, the only one calculated to prevent the extermination of the Indians, and I therefore entirely concur in it, and would recommend its adoption."[3]

Hitchcock also supported Beale in a letter to the secretary of war: "By the plan proposed, a small portion of land is to be set apart within which there is to be a military post, and some provision made for the subsistence of the Indians, to be supplied as far as possible from their labor. Within this reserve the Indians are to be protected, but not beyond it." The superintendent should be given considerable latitude in implementing the plan, and he and the military commander should work in concert. As long as he retained his command, Hitchcock hoped that Beale remained superintendent.[4]

Apparently, Beale spoke with the editors of the *San Francisco Daily Herald* or provided them with a copy of his letter to Lea, because on December 1, they recommended in similar language a similar plan:

> Let the United States Government establish a system of Military Posts on Reservations from the Public Lands. These should be regarded as Military or Government Reservations—for thus only can the whites be prevented from intruding. The Indians should be invited to assemble within these Reserves, and the Agent at each post should bring them under a system of discipline and instruction.
>
> Each Reservation should contain a garrison, the number of troops being proportioned to the Indian population around. The expenses of the troops may be borne by the surplus produce of Indian labor. To dissatisfaction on the part of the whites, the Military Reservation might be made with a view to a change of location, in case the increase of whites should make it necessary.[5]

Three days later the editors of the *Democratic State Journal*, a Sacramento newspaper, responded to the plan the *Herald* supported, questioning its wisdom and noting its similarity to that introduced by the Indian agents: "Upon the same principles that we have hitherto opposed Indian Reservations heretofore made within the border of our State, to the detriment of our highest interest, shall we still oppose any system contemplating similar practical results.... The wants and interests of our State demand—the great requirements of the commercial world

B. D. Wilson. (From Historical Collection, Title Insurance and Trust Company, San Diego, Cal. Courtesy of the author.)

asks, that every foot of California soil so pregnant in marvelous results be left untrammeled to Anglosaxon enterprise." The editors called for the removal of the Indians beyond the Sierra Nevada, "where Military Officers in Military reservations might exercise their talents of subjecting the savage and the wilderness to their fullest extent." The editors concluded with a warning: "If the government will not remove the Indians our own citizens will do the work for themselves. It is folly then to reason otherwise. California enterprise is not be stayed by the ideal picture of digger hunting grounds, or utopian schemes of Indian amelioration."[6]

In January 1853 Beale provided the editors of the *San Joaquin Republican* with an outline of his plan which they published on the twenty-second, noting that "it is exactly suited to the emergency of the case."[7] A few days later the editors of the *Democratic State Journal* printed the plan as it appeared in the *Republican* and reiterated their position: "That a few Digger Indians, having no capacity or ambition beyond filling their stomachs when nature suggests its propriety, should be interposed as a barrier to the development of some of the finest portions of our State, not only mineral but agricultural, was too great an absurdity to be tolerated for a moment." Again they called for the removal of the Indians across the Sierra Nevada, where the federal government would "feed them from the public crib."[8]

Beale intended to administer to the Indians within the state, not expel them beyond it, but clearly he needed help. He persuaded B. D. Wilson, a resident of Los Angeles County, to serve as agent of the Indians of California. President Millard Fillmore made the appointment on September 1, 1852.[9] Wilson replaced O. M. Wozencraft who was dismissed the same month.[10] Beale told Lea that Wilson was "a gentleman of high standing, and perhaps better acquainted and of more influence with our southern tribes than any other resident of this State."[11] The editors of the *Los Angeles Star* thought the appointment "a good and proper one. Mr. Wilson is thoroughly acquainted with the Indian character, and has visited most, if not all, the tribes within one hundred miles of this point. In occasions of difficulty between themselves, he is always looked to as a mediator, and scarcely a week passes that does not bring some of the chiefs to his residence, invoking his aid and protection. Mr. Wilson accepts the office as much from a desire to secure peace and justice to the Indians, as from a disposition to render to the government of the United States whatsoever service may be in his power." Immediately after receiving his appointment, Wilson was visited by two chiefs from the Four Creeks. They came to protest the kidnapping of several of their children by settlers. Wilson promised to look into the matter and correct the situation, but apparently he took no action.[12]

When they met in San Francisco in early November, Beale sought from Wilson his opinions regarding the presents purchased for the Indians in New York.[13] Costing $15,600 and consisting of small white, black, and red porcelain beads, assorted large glass beads, turkey red prints, gray-colored shawls, clothes, and calicoes, they had been shipped from New York in September.[14] Not reluctant to speak his mind, Wilson told Beale that "the greatest part of the goods are entirely useless" and not worth the cost of distribution. "What our Indians want is something to eat. Clothing, with Indians of this country, is a secondary matter; but food they must have, if we expect to keep them from committing depredations upon our settlements."[15]

Beale and Wilson exchanged notes on November 22. Beale wanted to know which part of the state was in most need of protection and what means could be employed to shield the Los Angeles district from Indian incursions.[16] Wilson replied that the Indians of Southern California were friendly and easily managed, and those on the Colorado River were peaceful, although sometimes they annoyed immigrants passing through their territories. But the Indians occupying the Four Creeks were another matter. They occupied a central position in the state and exercised great influence over groups living in proximity to white settlements.[17]

That day Beale passed on to Commissioner Lea information and opinions probably originating with Wilson: "Los Angeles county is the cattle market of the State. If an Indian war were to cut off our communication with that single county (which could be easily done, as the cattle are driven directly through the Indian country) for one week, beef would rise to fifty cents a pound in the market of San Francisco, and in six months there would be scarcely any at twice that price." The Indians of Los Angeles County would not ignite the war, because many of them were "Christians" who worked on the ranchos and thus were dependent on the whites. Rather, it would be started by those "who owe no such allegiance, and whose only source of food for years, during the winter season, has been robbed from the fertile vegas of Los Angeles.... It is these tribes from whom we are to expect trouble, and against whose depredations we must guard." Through the Tejón Pass, rancheros drove their cattle to northern markets and Indian stock-raiders descended on the ranchos. The pass was the key to Los Angeles.[18]

Beale continued with a discourse on the benefits to be received from Indian labor once reservations were established. Of the approximately ninety thousand Indians residing in California, he estimated that one in five males, some eighteen thousand, were able and willing to work. To be safe in his calculations, he lowered the number to ten thousand. If the Indian farm laborer received fifty cents per day, the annual cost of employing Indians would be $1,700,000 (actually $1,825,000), but the value of the products produced by the Indians would be double the cost of the labor. And even if the labor costs resulted in no pecuniary advantage, the plan was valid because it kept Indians employed and therefore peaceful.[19] His policy, he insisted, resembled that introduced by the Spanish:

> To those who would oppose the argument of want of intelligence and ability of the Indians for useful labor, I would direct their attention to every great national work of Spanish enterprise, on the whole continent of America. Not a city, a cathedral, or a fortification, but furnishes a proof that Indian labor, directed by white intelligence, may be made as effective as that of any other purely laboring class.

> Let us take, as an exemplification of this assertion, the stately missions raised by Indian labor, which at one time flourished in every part of California, the ruins of which to this day astonish those who have visited them. I could draw a picture of the condition of those flourishing colonies, as they existed at that day, which has no parallel in the early settlement of any country on the face of the earth. That narrative would need no embellishment, or exaggeration, and history substantiated by living witnesses, would sustain its truth. Every useful mechanic art, all necessary knowledge of agricultural pursuits, was here taught under a system of discipline at once mild, firm, and paternal. It is this system modified, and adapted to the present time, which I propose for your consideration; nor can I conceive of any other which would preserve this unfortunate people from total extinction, and our government from everlasting disgrace.[20]

To achieve a modified version of the Spanish mission system, Beale asked B. D. Wilson, probably at the November meeting, to prepare a report on how to subjugate the Indians of California.[21] Wilson turned over the task to Benjamin Hayes, a judge of the southern district of California, which included Los Angeles and San Diego Counties. An avid collector of government and private documents, newspaper articles, and whatever else he could lay his hands on, many of which dealt with Indian matters, Hayes would eventually compile over one hundred scrapbooks. He also interviewed many prominent figures of Southern California and recorded his thoughts and experiences in several diaries.[22]

Hayes was well aware that three Indian agents had negotiated eighteen treaties and had established reservations from the Oregon to the Mexican borders. Because at least one of the treaties had been published in the California press, he probably knew that artisans and teachers were to be assigned to the reservations to assist the Indians in acquiring new skills and that soldiers were to be stationed on the reservations to protect and control the Indians. He was familiar with the controversy the reservations had generated and obviously knew that the treaty system had failed to take hold in California.[23] In his diary of January 1, 1853, Hayes wrote that he had "finished the map to accompany the report of Indian Agent (Benj. B. Wilson).... This Report is of date December 26, 1852, prepared by me, at his instance, from information derived from Don Juan Bandini, Hon. J. J. Warner, and Hugo Reid, Esq. One copy for the Superintendent, Lt. E. Beale; with the other, Mr. Wilson goes to the Legislature, now in session, to obtain their co-operation in his plans for the Old Mission Indians."[24]

Hayes organized his sixty-nine-page report, "The Indians of Southern California," into two roughly equal parts. The first part summarized the ethnographic and historical backgrounds of the Indians of Southern

California, in particular the Cahuilla, Luiseño, and Kumeyaay (then called Diegueños). To Hayes, Southern California extended north to the Four Creeks where Indians he called the Tulareños resided. Most of the peoples described in the first section either had been attached to the missions or had been influenced to one degree or another by the Spanish presence along the coast.[25]

In the second section Hayes called for the establishment of an Indian territory in the interior of California, extending from the Mexican border some 360 miles north to the Four Creeks. He recommended that "this Territory be subdivided into the requisite number of Indian Reserves, distinguished by the names of the nations; the lands to be reserved from sale or private entry, or occupation by others than the Indians, until Congress shall otherwise order, with their consent." Furthermore, the federal government should exercise its power "with a firmer hand than it has ever been, and in the full spirit of 'the greatest amount of good to the largest number.'"[26] Unlike the Indian agents and Superintendent Beale, who advocated stationing troops on or near the reservations, Hayes thought that military posts should be situated where they could protect rancheros from Indian incursions. As a resident of Southern California, Hayes was well aware that Indians had stolen thousands of horses and cattle from the region's ranchos during the 1840s and early 1850s. Only when it was absolutely necessary to enforce laws in extreme cases should troops be posted among the Indians.[27]

Although a Catholic, Hayes advocated that religious instruction be introduced under "the different Christian denominations, showing equal favor to all." As promised in the treaties negotiated by the Indian agents, carpenters, blacksmiths, and other experts should be attached to the reservations, but they "should be men of families; this ought to be almost a *sine qua non*." As had the Indian agents, Hayes advocated the founding of schools on the reservations: "If I do not completely mistake the character of these Indians, they will yield themselves to instruction more readily than almost any other tribe in the Union." Schools should be limited to secular subjects, and parents punished if their children failed to attend. Boys would attain practical skills in the fields and workshops. From the Indian women, girls would learn "plain needlework, washing and ironing, and a various household knowledge."[28]

Neither the Indian agents nor Beale had considered whether the Indians would be bound by law to the reservations. But Hayes was adamant that they remain in their respective territories and leave only with permission from the subagents "upon reasons fixed by law, or in cases of necessity." Hayes also took into consideration the needs of local whites: "Some of these Indians would, probably, still wish to bind themselves as servants in families, as before; they ought to be permitted to leave the Territory for

Bejamin Hayes. (From Historical Collection, Title Insurance and Trust Company, San Diego, Cal. Courtesy of the author.)

this purpose." With the approval of the subagents, some Indians would be assigned to whites on contracts not to exceed one year.[29]

While the Indian agents and Superintendent Beale offered only generalities for subjugating the Indians, Hayes presented a concrete plan. On each reservation the majority of the Indians would reside in one principal village or town. Most of the land would be held in common and cultivated by all except those assigned other tasks. Most of the crops produced by the Indians would be held in a common stock and distributed in daily or in triweekly rations. Indians would work six hours per day, six days per week. Division of labor would be decided by each subagent. Indians already growing crops might be allowed to retain their own tracts of land, and in the course of time, individual land concessions might be made to those who had succeeded in their agricultural and stock-raising endeavors. But at the incipiency of his plan, Hayes insisted that "two rules—common-stock and compulsory labor—are absolutely indispensable."[30]

The Indians would be provided with "a plain and simple code of laws and 'ordinances' adapted to their genius and pursuits, to be changed according to the state of their progress.... They have a very correct notion of right and wrong; value life and property; are familiar with the idea of 'alcalde' (Magistrate); like speedy accusation and trial; are used to obedience." Their political leaders would punish on the spot those convicted of stealing or trespass. The jury system would not be introduced, and reservation officials would handle murder cases. The agents and subagents would have the authority, in some cases, to punish summarily, but in order to prevent the abuse of the power, they would be required to report all such cases, under oath, to the proper authorities.[31]

Hayes also called for the modification of the Indians' political system, insisting that the office of chief be abolished: "The desire of power and place may be as well gratified by the substitution of other analogous offers of more civilized life, such as justices of the peace and sheriff. These appointments should emanate from the superintendent or agent, and depend upon good behavior. They are accustomed to this mode of filling even the office of chief, and sometimes pride themselves on it." Although the Indians could master self-government in a short period, "the elective franchise" should not yet be imposed. "But, let them be governed with the least possible violence to their personal independence and freedom; and so that, in all measures, they may be able to discover the strict justice of the government."[32]

On January 14, 1853 Hayes wrote to Senator David R. Atchison of Missouri, hinting that he was the author of the report and praising Wilson at the same time: "Let me beg you to notice the Report of the Indian agent for this District, Benjamin D. Wilson, Esq. I am acquainted, of my own knowledge, with nearly all the facts stated by him concerning the character of these Indians, the country they live in, their troubles for the last three years and the causes of them. I have travelled over a great part of their country and camped in it. My opportunities have been various and constant for observing them. And I have given no little attention to the subject—more I suspect, than any other resident here, unless I except Mr. Wilson." Congress, Hayes insisted, should publish the report and circulate it in California and elsewhere.[33]

The *Los Angeles Star* summarized "The Indians of Southern California" and encouraged its adoption by the federal government: "The report contains a vast fund of information, and the publication of it will be an important addition to the cause of science. The views of Mr. Wilson touching the management of the Indians become important at this time, when the whole course of Legislation seems tending towards the extermination of the Indian race. If the government of the U. States desires the preservation of the Indians, some system must be adopted similar to that proposed by Mr. Wilson."[34] The *San Francisco Daily Herald* reprinted the *Star's* summary and praised the report.[35]

In early December 1852 Beale departed San Francisco for Los Angeles where, presumably, he was to pick up the report. Along the way, he intended to hold conferences with as many groups as possible.[36] Evidently, a council was to be held at Tejón, because Indians residing south of the Tehachapi Mountains sent a large delegation to the area in early January 1853.[37] From Los Angeles, Beale was to proceed to the Colorado River to meet with the Indians there.[38]

Upon arriving at the Fresno River, Beale discovered that many villages on its lower reaches had been vacated. Convinced the Indians had retreated into the foothills of the Sierra Nevada, from where they would launch raids on white settlements, Beale contacted the Heuchi chief, Naiyakqua.[39] At the treaty conducted by the Indian agents on April 39, 1851, creating the Fresno Reservation, Naiyakqua had spoken for his own people and for the Chuchansi, Chauchila, Pononichi, and Nukchu.[40] Beale persuaded the chief to send runners to the disaffected Indians to meet with him in council.[41]

Once assembled Beale told the Indians he would make no promises he could not keep. If they would return to their villages and work to support themselves, the government would provide them with assistance. But those who continued to steal from the whites would be severely punished. The Indians' promise to keep the peace prompted an observer to write that the local whites "who much feared another such outbreak as we experienced two years since, are now relieved, and all can sleep at night without dread of being awakened by an Indians yell and a tent full of arrows."[42]

Beale distributed to the Indians a variety of items, including forty-five flannel shirts, fifty calico shirts, forty-five pantaloons, seventeen pairs of boots, fifty blankets, and vests, handkerchiefs, sashes, serapes, and hats. For $2,564.50, Beale purchased all the items at a store run by Lewis Leach and Lorenzo Vinsonhaler.[43] This provided Beale and five companions with provisions, Vinsonhaler billed the government $1,140, or $60 per diem for nineteen days.[44] The two men had started the business when the Fresno Reservation was first established. Later Samuel Bishop bought into the outfit, and the three men purchased the land on which the store was located for $1,800 or $2,000. Although it was called Leach and Company, Vinsonhaler was the major investor.[45]

Before departing Beale, apparently on the spur of the moment, decided to create a reservation, choosing a tract of land lying between the Fresno and San Joaquin Rivers some thirty miles downstream from Fort Miller. Twenty-five thousand Indians, he calculated, could be assembled on the property, which was forty miles in length and fourteen in width. He told Commissioner of Indian Affairs Luke Lea that the land between the two rivers was unfit for cultivation and thus would not attract settlers seeking preemption claims. Miners would not be drawn to the limited gold deposits upstream, and no more than twenty-five whites were in the area. On the bottomlands of the two rivers, the Indians would support themselves by their own labor, and after one crop had been raised he would "leave them under the charge of intelligent men, to complete what I have commenced."[46] In a follow-up letter Beale stated that the reservation should be founded exclusive of the claim of Vinsonhaler, the only person owning property within the proposed boundaries.[47]

Instead of continuing south Beale returned to San Francisco, and on January 15, 1853, sailed for the East Coast.[48] Beale's failure to visit Los Angeles troubled the editors of the *Star*. The report prepared by Benjamin Hayes "should be acted upon at the present session of Congress, and therefore Mr. Beale's absence is the more to be regretted; as he was to have taken it to Washington, and from his acquaintance with the subject, would have been enabled to give such explanation of the necessity of some change in our Indian system, as would have ensured for the report of the favorable action of Congress."[49] Beale, however, was familiar with its contents. On one occasion, apparently irked over the publicity the report had received, he remarked that "Mr. Wilson's policy, is nothing more than a repetition of that told him by me... on his visit to me in November."[50]

In late February 1853 Beale submitted his own report to Commissioner of Indian Affairs Luke Lea.[51] On March 3 Lea sent it to Secretary of the Interior Alexander H. H. Stuart, who forwarded it to William King Sebastian, chairman of the Senate Committee of Indian Affairs.[52] Comprising mainly letters by civilians, state officials, military officers, and the Indian agents, interspersed with comments by Beale, the report focused on the supposed improprieties of the Indian agents regarding the distribution of beef to the Indians.[53]

Included in the report was the interrogatory Beale had conducted with O. M. Wozencraft in September 1852, in which the agent admitted having no evidence the cattle he purchased with government drafts had been delivered to the Indians. Also in the report was the testimony Joel Brooks had given Beale the same month. Brooks had insisted that only a small portion of the nineteen hundred head of cattle John Frémont delivered to George Barbour in August 1851 had been distributed to the Indians in the San Joaquin Valley. Accepting Brooks' statement at face value, Beale claimed in his report that the greater part of the herd had fallen into the hands of James Savage. He accused Barbour of committing no crime but implied that the agent had failed to oversee the distribution of the cattle properly. Beale also criticized Redick McKee. Two letters written by a military officer, questioning the way contractors estimated the weight of the cattle delivered to Indians in McKee's district in northern California, were included in the report. According to the officer on one occasion contractors claimed delivery when none had taken place.[54]

To expose the massacres and kidnapping of Indians by Californios in Northern California, Beale included some of his own correspondence and that of local residents. He also included letters Wozencraft had written to Governor John Bigler on July 13,1852, and to Beale on September 9, 1852, criticizing the attack by whites on a Choinimni village on the former Kings River Reservation. Beale, however, took the opportunity to accuse Wozencraft of negligence, if not collusion, in the attack. Supposedly, it had been plotted for weeks, so Wozencraft had ample time to prevent its occurrence. Beale labeled the attack a "massacre of defenseless women and children."[55]

Beale saved his recommendations for the last page of the report. Congress should appropriate five hundred thousand dollars for the immediate subsistence and support of the Indians; military reserves should be created where the Indians would support themselves by their own labor and where a few soldiers would be stationed; whites employed by the Indian Office should reside on the reserves or among the Indians; the three Indian agencies should be abolished and six subagents should be appointed who would reside on the reserves and discharge various duties, such as assisting the Indians in the cultivation of their lands.[56]

On March 3, 1853 Senator Sebastian offered an amendment to the annual Indian appropriation bill. The amendment authorized the president to create five military reservations from the public domain in the state of California or in the territories of Utah and New Mexico. The $250,000 to be appropriated would cover the cost of subsisting the Indians and removing them to the reservations.[57] In the debate that followed Senator Sebastian asserted that Beale had, "after a complete investigation of the subject, made a report, which for comprehensiveness of plan, for clearness of conception, and for its practical adaption to the institutions of the country, I think stands unequaled but by few documents of the kind." Beale's plan was "the only one that is practicable for what prevails there. It is certain that if the present order of things long remains, the Indian population will starve out and die under the cruelty to which they are subjected." The entire Indian population could be congregated in small districts, which would not interfere with white settlements.[58]

Once that amendment was agreed to, the Senate debated the issue of size. Senator Sebastian proposed that each reservation be limited to twenty-five thousand acres, about equal to a township of land. California Senator John B. Weller argued that if five reservations of that size were created in California, too much land would be withheld from the citizens of the state.[59] Weller's argument was rejected and the amendment passed. The House of Representatives concurred with the Senate, and the president signed the bill into law.[60]

Secretary of the Interior Robert McClelland informed Beale in April that the $250,000 was to be used exclusively for the relocation and subsistence of the Indians. Beale would draw funds from the federal collector of customs for the port of San Francisco but was to make no single draft over twenty thousand dollars. Detailed accounts of his expenditures, not to exceed the sum appropriated by Congress, were to be sent quarterly to the Department of the Interior. The cost of founding military reservations would be defrayed from another fund. Beale was to select sites for the reservations in conjunction with the military commander in California or such officer the commander assigned for that purpose. And "in all other matters connected with the execution of this 'plan,' you will, as far as may be practicable, act in concert with the commanding officer of that military department." Beale was to lose no time after his arrival in California in notifying the agents that their agencies had been abolished and in obtaining from them all public property and money.[61]

In California editors and others discussed Beale's report. On April 22 the *San Francisco Placer Times and Transcript* published a letter from an individual possessing a copy. He quoted the testimony of Joel Brooks in the report and referred to the interrogatory Beale had conducted with Wozencraft. The author concluded that the conduct of the Indian agents appeared "to be the most villainous scheme of plunder that ever defiled the pages of administrative history in our country."[62] The same day the *San Francisco Daily Herald* published without comment part of the report, including the interrogatory.[63] And from April 23 to May 7, the San Joaquin Republican printed the entire report. The editors began the series by claiming that it "will be read with avidity by the victims of the late commissioners. No comment is necessary, other than that the thanks of the people of California are due to Lieut. Beale for his masterly expose."[64]

Beale's "masterly expose" offended Wozencraft, who on April 29 wrote to the *Times and Transcript*. While in Washington, D.C., he had demanded an investigation into his official acts and had been assured by the president and the secretary of the interior that no charges of fraud would be brought against him, although they disapproved of his spending practices. Wozencraft was particularly upset that the interrogatory had been published. He assumed it would have been presented in an investigating tribunal, when he could have defended himself. Wozencraft concluded his letter by emphasizing that he had been "more sinned against than sinning, and all I now ask is a suspension of prejudicial opinion until such time, when it may be proper that the facts and truth may be known."[65]

The claim that helpless Indians had been massacred also offended many settlers and miners in the Southern Mines. "The charges against the people of Mariposa by the Superintendent of Indian Affairs were absurd and grossly insulting to their intelligence," wrote Luis Bunnell. "There had been no assault upon the Indians, except that at King's River, led by the hangers-on at one of his own agencies."[66] On October 25 the residents of Mariposa and its vicinity held a meeting and issued several resolutions challenging Beale's report. Among other things, they asserted that Beale and those who provided him with "information in reference to the massacre of defenseless women and children...have done great injustice to the American citizens who reside in this section of the State." They also pointed out that the plan submitted by Beale differed "but slightly from the reservation system adopted by the former Commissioners, which was so fully denounced and condemned by the Legislature and the people of this State." The Indians should be removed beyond the limits of California to lands not inhabited by American citizens. Furthermore, the federal government had "no right to select the territory of a sovereign State to establish reservations for the Indians, nor for any other purpose, without the consent of the State." Copies of the resolutions were to be sent to the state legislature, California's senators and representatives in Congress, the secretary of war, and the president. The *Times and Transcript* published the resolutions on November 17.[67]

Two days later it expressed incredulity that the president had sanctioned the establishment of five reservations in California or in the territories of Utah and New Mexico: "How in view of the established policy of the Government, such a provision should have become a law, except by mistake or inadvertence, we can not conceive. It is subversive, so far as it relates to California, of every thing that has hitherto been done by the General Government and directly an infringement of the rights of our State." The Indians should be removed to the eastern slope of the Sierra Nevada, which, they insisted, had a climate as genial and a soil as productive as that found on the west side. They fervently hoped that Beale, "to avoid all difficulties," would establish reservations there.[68] That hope was dashed with the creation of a reservation within the State of California.

CHAPTER XIX

Founding a Reservation

Early in 1853 Congress considered constructing a transcontinental railroad and debated the best route it should take. Senator Thomas Hart Benton proposed to Secretary of War Jefferson Davis that Edward F. Beale and John Frémont lead an expedition across the Rocky Mountains to ascertain whether the railroad should follow the central route to the Pacific Coast. On the way Beale would examine sites for reservations in the territories of New Mexico and Utah and in the state of California. Frémont declined to join the expedition, but Beale agreed to the plan, which was to be privately financed.[1]

Aware that Beale was considering the offer, Secretary of the Interior Robert McClelland ordered him on April 13 to "repair to California without delay, and by the most expeditious route." In other words, he was to sail to the West Coast. The secretary insisted that "the execution of the plan adopted in relation to the Indians in California, their security, subsistence, and protection should constitute your sole object, and no other subject must be permitted to engage your time or attention."[2] Ignoring the secretary's orders Beale departed from Westport, Missouri on May 10.[3]

The superintendent's arrival was eagerly anticipated in California. In late May, Frederick Kerlin, Beale's clerk, informed Indian Agent B. D. Wilson that Beale would arrive in California by the Old Spanish Trail and would follow Walker's Pass over the Sierra Nevada. Because Beale would be anxious to consult with him regarding the founding of reservations in Southern California, Kerlin suggested that Wilson meet him at the pass or follow the trail east until he did.[4] Apparently, Wilson saw no reason, or could not find the time, to undertake the task.

Because the founding of reservations in California would be of great interest to the army, General E. A. Hitchcock, commander of the pacific division, ordered First Lieutenant Nathaniel H. McLean to Walker's Pass to apprise Beale of the army's role.[5] On June 15 McLean and twelve men departed Fort Miller for the Kern River where a note was left for Beale with local Indians. McLean also dispatched an Indian to Tejón with another message for Beale. He reached the head of Walker's Pass on the twenty-sixth. A few days later, McLean departed for Tejón. When Beale failed to appear there, he returned to Fort Miller.[6]

McLean considered Tejón an ideal location for a reservation. If it was not covered by a claim, he wrote in his report, "I am sure there is no place in the State better calculated for the reservation.... The valley is free from underbrush, perfectly healthy, and but few mosquitoes at any time of the year." A military post could be supplied by way of Los Angeles and its port of San Pedro. Timber was available, and the soil would make good adobe bricks.[7]

The key to founding a reservation at Tejón were the Tejoneños, who sought to remain on good terms with the Americans. In June 1852 Zapetero and other Tejoneños captured a party of Sonorans with stock they had stolen from a rancho in the Los Angeles area. Apparently, the Tejoneños returned the animals to their owner but released the Sonorans, one of whom may have been the notorious bandit Joaquin Murrieta. Later they delivered to the justice of the peace of Los Angeles three horses and some clothing of the women members of the gang.[8]

When it suited their own ends, however, the Tejoneños were not reluctant to challenge the authority of local officials. On May 9, 1852, a party of one hundred Tejoneños and other interior Indians arrived at Mission San Buenaventura to settle a dispute between the local Indians and the Californios who managed the mission. The mission's Indians had complained that the officials provided them with liquor and abused them.[9] Among the visiting party were two Indians who two weeks before had escaped from jail in Santa Bárbara while awaiting trial for murdering a peddler. Many of the Indians were mounted on horses the whites recognized as stolen and some possessed firearms.[10] Vicente, chief of the Tejoneños, and Emeterio, leader of the village of Tsineuhiu, both signatories of the treaty with George Barbour, commanded the party.[11] When word reached Santa Bárbara that Indians supposedly had captured two Americans, a party of eighteen white men quickly formed and proceeded to the mission. Determining that the visiting Indians had neither prisoners nor hostile intentions, they returned to Santa Bárbara.[12]

On their return journey the Indians robbed two travelers of their horses, saddles, and bridles. Overtaken by twenty-five whites led by John Powers, who recently had lost horses and who convinced them that 150 more men were on their way, the Indians turned over three horses.[13] Emeterio also turned over the two Indians who had broken out of jail. They wanted to die, he explained to Americans, or they would not have committed the crimes.[14] Taken to Santa Bárbara and put on trial, they confessed to murdering the peddler and commanding a band of horse thieves. They were hanged on May 11.[15]

Once back in the Tulare Valley, Emeterio convened a council and advised the assembled leaders to abide by the advice of George Barbour, act only on the defensive, and not offend the whites. In early June, Vicente journeyed to Los Angeles to explain to local officials the affair at San Buenaventura. Denying the Indians held hostile intentions, he insisted they had greatly pleased the settlers by willingly surrendering those accused of murder.[16]

Perhaps to keep the Tejoneños contented and thus "loyal," B. D. Wilson in early 1853 contracted with T. S. Hereford in Los Angeles to provide the Indians with supplies. Between February 23 and April 2 Hereford delivered $362.32 worth of blankets, hoes, shovels, axes, butcher knives, harnesses, flour, and sugar to the Tejoneños. One delivery went directly to Chief Vicente. By early June, Samuel Arbuckle had delivered additional goods worth $276.75.[17]

For providing the Tejoneños with material items, perhaps Wilson expected their assistance in dealing with Paiute stock raiders. From their homelands at Walker Lake and in the Owens Valley, the Paiutes proceeded south along the east side of the Sierra Nevada, entering the Tulare Valley by way of Walker's Pass. Continuing southwards, they crossed the Tejón Pass and headed for the ranchos in the San Fernando Valley and the Los Angeles region. Those residing near Walker Lake were the most active, carrying off droves of animals from Southern Califomia.[18] The editors of the *Los Angeles Star* noted in early 1853 that the Paiutes were "expert thieves, and are under no control of our government."[19]

In Los Angeles in April a delegation of Tejoneños told Wilson that they were friendly with the Paiutes residing in the Owens Valley. Wilson instructed the delegation to visit them and report back to him on their condition. On May 2 a Tejoneño informed Wilson that the raiders were part of a group comprising some fifty fighting men, from which two "renegade" Indians (probably neophytes) commanded two bands, each numbering about seven or eight men. Alternating each month the bands stole animals mainly to eat but also to trade to Indians living north of Owens Lake and to American immigrants for blankets and other items. According to the Tejoneño, the leaders of the Paiutes opposed the actions of the stock raiders and would gladly turn them over to the Americans for punishment. The Tejoneños intended to send a large party to Owens Lake to capture the thieves, but they would willingly join a party of Americans with the same goal.[20] In late July, Chief Vicente guided a party of white men up the east side of the Sierra Nevada, apparently to chastise the stock raiders. But the Paiutes convinced the whites to turn back and except for the intervention of Vicente would have killed them.[21]

A short time later an incident occurred that strained relations between Americans and the Tejoneños. From the Kern River, six or seven miners left those they had been traveling with and headed south, intent on stealing horses from the Tejoneños. Once he realized a raid was pending, Joel Brooks, who had guided the miners to the Kern, raced back to the Tejón to warn the Indians. Arriving before the party of whites, he sent runners to all the villages. The Indians were to arm themselves and herd their horses to Vicente's village of Mumumpea. In the skirmish that took place, the whites fired a few harmless shots at the Indians and made off with one horse. The Tejoneños told Brooks that had the whites stolen their horses or shot one of their people, they would have killed him and other whites. In a letter to the *San Francisco Daily Alta California*, Brooks recounted the events and suggested that relations between Tejoneños and Americans had been seriously harmed: "I do not believe that there is an American in California who has passed through this valley, in want of provisions, but what they have accommodated them with the best they had; and are ever ready to furnish them guides, and every other information as to roads, &c., that they might need. And they think it is a poor return for all their kindness to attempt to steal from and murder them."[22]

Relations between Indians and whites fared better on the "reservation" Beale had founded on the San Joaquin River in December 1852. To supervise the agricultural operations of the San Joaquin Farm, as it became known, Beale had employed Samuel Bishop at $240 per month.[23] Because Bishop had only a limited investment in Leach and Company that ran a local store, Beale apparently saw no conflict of interest. He also saw the store as the logical place to buy items for the Indians. Purchasing goods from Stockton would have entailed time and heavy expenses.[24] Beale also had hired Harry Edwards, his brother-in-law, as special agent to manage the farm. Edwards furnished the farm with plows and other farming implements and persuaded the Indians in the surrounding area to settle there. Dividing his workforce by age, Edwards got the young men between the ages of twelve and twenty to perform most of the manual labor, and in three weeks they had plowed about 350 acres for wheat. The older men dug a ditch four feet wide, four feet deep, and two miles in length to protect the field from domestic and wild animals. After sowing the wheat, the Indians planted potatoes and then prepared another field of 250 acres for corn, pumpkins, and melons. It too was enclosed by a ditch.[25]

The Indian workers also constructed a branding corral one hundred yards in diameter and 'dug a ditch seven feet wide by six deep around it. Eight miles down river, they built two enclosures for threshing grain and a corral to pen the cattle at night. By the time those projects were completed, the wheat, corn, potatoes, and other vegetables were up. Damaged by insects, though, the wheat field produced only 250 bushels.[26] The poor harvest might have discouraged Indians from relocating to the farm. According to a military officer, the Indians were well aware of the infertility of the soil and the lack of timber for housing and fuel. They wanted farms established in their own territories.[27]

When their labor was no longer needed, Edwards allowed the Indians, with the exception of the plowmen who remained to keep the farm operational, to pan for gold on the Fresno River. The gold, he assumed, would be exchanged for the clothing at the store owned by Leach and Company.[28] The company benefited from the farm in other ways. By the end of March 1853, it had provided the farm with $1,837 worth of food, including 5,000 pounds of barley, 2,000 of flour, 200 of beans, 200 of sugar, 190 of pork, 85 of coffee, 40 of salt, and 40 of dried fruit. For Indians holding a conference on the farm in June, the company provided fifty shirts, forty-nine pants, fifteen hats, twenty yards of calico, and twenty pounds of tobacco, for a cost of $279.60.[29]

On March 1 Charles F. Janis had delivered four hundred head of cattle to the farm and billed the government $28,00.[30] But the number of cattle butchered for the Indians steadily declined during much of 1853, as did the number of Indians associated with the farm. Never an official governmental entity, the farm was abandoned in October.[31]

Shortly before the closure Beale arrived in California. Instead of entering the Tulare Valley by Walker's Pass, he chose the southern route, arriving in Los Angeles on August 22.[32] Immediately, he wrote a long letter to Commissioner of Indian Affairs George W. Manypenny, emphasizing his concerns that a recent act of Congress abolishing the three Indian agencies in California had failed to establish new ones. Without the assistance of subordinate officers, he could not "carry into execution an almost entire change in the hereditary mode of life of one hundred thousand persons, scattered over a distance of seven hundred miles, and living, for the most part, in mountains difficult of access." Moreover, he was unsure he possessed the authority to hire blacksmiths, farmers, carpenters, and other workers, because the law stipulated that the money appropriated was only for the subsistence and removal of the Indians. He feared that "the construction put upon 'subsistence' might be such as to make me pecuniarily accountable for moneys disbursed in paying their wages." It would be impossible to keep his accounts "with the precision and regularity of other superintendents, who have certain fixed routines of duty." Beale intended to be "continually in the field, forever actively and actually employed, to the almost entire exclusion of office business,

Table 3. Beef Distribution on the San Joaquin Farm, 1853

Month	*Indians*	*Cattle butchered*
Feburary	700	125
March	650	113
April	400	70
May	350	60
June	200	32
July	60	20
August	45	15
September	40	15

Source: Adapted from Frederick Kerlin to Thomas Henley, An approximate statement showing issues of Provisions to Indians on the San Joaquin Reserve, U.S. Congress, Senate, Records of the Senate.

unless I neglect that for which I am sent here-the establishment of a new order of things." If allowed five years without interference and provided with proper assistants, he guaranteed success.[33]

Beale informed Wilson his agency no longer existed but hired him as an assistant.[34] At the end of August, Beale, Wilson, and eight men departed Los Angeles for Tejón.[35] Arriving on September 2 they found the Tejoneños quietly engaged in farming but anxious to know the intentions of the Americans.[36] Beale dispatched India runners to villages between Tejón and the Four Creeks, announcing that a council was to be held at the Tejón Pass, where he would explain his plan. On September 12 he spoke to over one thousand Indians, including the Tejoneños, Wilson translating his speech into Spanish.[37] Beale told the Indians that if they would relocate to the reservations he intended to establish, the government would protect them from whites and provide them with seeds and provisions. He pointed out to those who had come from beyond the area the differences between themselves and the Tejoneños, who had taken up farming.[38]

If they lived among the white population, continued Beale, they could never rise to an equal station, but among themselves they would improve their condition significantly. On the reservations they would live in peace and happiness, and their children would become prepared for the future. Following the recommendations set forth in "The Indians of Southern California" (a copy perhaps provided by Wilson), Beale explained that for the time being the products of their labor would be held in a common stock and all labor performed would be based on the physical capability of each worker. The Indians would farm on plots of land assigned to each family, but they could continue to hunt and fish. As further suggested in the report, the Indians would be allowed to develop their own system of rewards and punishments. Beale promised the Indians he would never personally benefit from their labor. And Wilson assured them that even though the government had failed them before, Beale's promises would be honored.[39] Only when convinced that the reservation would be located somewhere in the vicinity of where the conference was being held were Indians residing beyond Tejón receptive to Beale's plan.[40]

In the area at the time of the meeting was a contingent of fifty soldiers, led by three officers, surveying the valley for a possible railroad route. Beale presented the officers with a questionnaire regarding where they thought a reservation and military post should be established. Responding in detail the officers noted that whites had appropriated most of the land between the Sacramento and San Joaquin rivers. Along the Kings River and in the Four Creeks, tracts remained unoccupied although the best spots had been taken. But the area south of the Four Creeks was free of settlers and miners. The officers were certain that the Indians would be more willing to concentrate in the southern Tulare Valley than in any other area. There, at much less expense than elsewhere, they could be collected, fed, and protected. A military post would serve the interests of both whites and Indians and should be established in the Tejón Pass.[41]

Their work completed Beale and Wilson departed for the Four Creeks to hold another council, but Beale decided to press on to San Francisco, arriving on September 21.[42] The following day, a San Francisco newspaper informed its readers that Beale had selected a site for two reservations near the Tejón Pass: "It possesses many advantages for subsisting the Indians—is far removed from the whites, and admirably suited for a military post, which the law requires shall be established on each reservation to protect the whites from the attacks of the Indians, and the Indians from the encroachments of the whites. The post can be so located also, as to cut off the marauding parties of savages who have been accustomed to run off large numbers of horses and cattle from Los Angeles through the Tejón and Walker's Passes."[43]

Beale notified Manypenny at the end of September that based on the recommendations of the surveyors and B. D. Wilson, "late Indian agent, on whose experience I placed great reliance," he had selected a site in the Tulare Valley on which to found one of the reservations. The land, although covered by a Mexican grant, was free from whites. Because it was impossible to find land unclaimed by rancheros or by those holding preemption rights, he would "leave it to Congress to purchase the land should the title prove good." Beale sought the authority to purchase land held under Mexican grants and requested an additional five hundred thousand dollars to carry out his plans.[44]

Convinced that a reservation at Tejón could accommodate Indians from throughout the state, Beale appointed rancher Simon P. Storms special agent in late September and instructed him to arrange a council with Nisenan Indians in Grass Valley, located fifty miles northeast of Sacramento. Storms provided the Indians with eight hundred pounds of beef, one thousand pounds of flour, fifty pounds of sugar, and other items, costing $342.90. Presents for the Indians, consisting of ten blankets, ten pairs of shoes, two shirts, and a cotton handkerchief, cost an additional $107.22.[45]

With Storms serving as translator, the meeting began on October 5, Beale told the Indians that if they relocated to Tejón, they would be protected from the whites. If they remained where they were, their lands would be lost to an expanding American population. The most powerful chief at the meeting, Weimah of the Daspah, professed a willingness to move.[46] Weimah had signed the treaty Indian Agent O. M. Wozencraft had conducted with the local Indians in July 1851.[47] Other leaders, however, objected to leaving their homelands for an unknown area. How could they persuade their peoples to believe in the word of the government after the treaty signed in 1851 had been rejected? Apparently, Beale had no answer to the question, but he convinced them to send a delegation to Tejón to inspect the area.[48]

Fearful they might lose valuable and cheap labor, settlers told the Indians that they were being sent south to be killed.[49] Their ploy failed, and a few days after the conclusion of the conference nine Indians, escorted by Nathaniel Blackstone, departed for Tejón.[50] At Sacramento they caught a boat to San Francisco, where they boarded a ship for San Pedro. As reported by the *Alta*, the Indians "will remain upon the reserve a short time, travel over a considerable portion of it, and then come back to report to their tribes. If their report be favorable, it is probable that all the tribes will move down to the reservation this spring."[51]

Upon arriving in Southern California, Blackstone turned the Indians over to B. D. Wilson, who immediately assigned them to a supply train heading for Tejón.[52] Blackstone billed the government for $1,483.32.[53] Storms' salary for forty-five days' work amounted to $183.42.[54] When informed that relocating five hundred Nisenans to Tejón would cost $15,050, Beale developed second thoughts.[55] Writing to Commissioner Manypenny

Table 4. Projected Expenses at Tejón

Budget item	*Cost*
One thousand head of cattle	$65,000
Agricultural implements, provisions, and clothing	10,000
Freight	10,000
Mules and horses	20,000
Wages of laborers, mechanics, and other workers	10,000
Removal of Indians to the reservation and incidental expenses	10,000
Total	$125,000

Source: Adapted from Edward F. Beale to George W. Manypenny, San Francisco, October 10, 1853, U.S. Congress, House, 32d Cong., 1st sess, 474-75.

on October 10, he emphasized that "any removal on a large scale during this season would be unwise and impolitic. The appropriation would be exhausted in the removal of a comparative small number of Indians, leaving nothing for the support of those already on the reservation."[56]

He informed Manypenny that he had drawn $125,000 (far more than the $20,000 allowed for one withdrawal) from the collector of customs for the port of San Francisco. Beale explained that the large sum was necessary to support some ten thousand Indians residing between the San Joaquin River and the Tejón Pass on the two reservations of twenty-five thousand acres each he intended to establish. The remainder of the appropriation would be used to found other reservations.[57] Beale also wrote to California's congressional leaders, pointing out the difficulties he faced in finding suitable and unclaimed lands for reservations and indicating that he might have to purchase lands for the Indians, subject to the approval of Congress.[58] Senator John B. Weller's response was to the point. If Beale found unoccupied land, claimed under a Mexican grant, that was sufficient for a reservation, he should take it: "If the grant is in the end sustained by the courts, the government, having taken private property for public use, will have to make compensation therefore." But Weller was steadfastly opposed to creating large reservations. None should be larger than eight thousand acres.[59]

Troubled by how Beale intended to spend the appropriation and by his request for authority to purchase land, Manypenny, on November

18, ordered him to follow strictly the directions set forth by the act of March 3, 1853—namely, that the appropriation of $250,000 was to be used exclusively for the relocation and subsistence of the Indians and that incidental expenses, such as founding reservations, were to be defrayed from the other fund appropriated by the same act. Manypenny emphasized that he could not alter the way Congress intended the appropriations to be spent. If Beale failed to locate sufficient land in the public domain unoccupied by whites, he should "postpone for the present all action touching the practical operations of the 'plan,' and await further legislation on the part of Congress. Under no circumstance can the department sanction the purchase of any lands or claims laid thereto for the purposes indicated."[60]

The land on which Beale intended to create a reservation was not in the public domain. It was covered by a Mexican grant, claimed Ignacio del Valle and José Antonio Aguirre. In November del Valle notified Beale that he and Aguirre had "vested and equitable title to twenty two Mexican leagues" in the area. He was "disposed to offer no unreasonable or unjust obstacle to the Indian policy of the Government" and was "ready to receive any fair proposition on its behalf for the acquisition of his rights in the Tejón."[61] Beale replied to del Valle in late December. If his claim to the land were approved by a federal land commission, Beale would abandon the reservation. If his title were not confirmed, the reservation would remain. He closed his short letter by promising that in the meantime he would "do the land no injury."[62] The land was improved and the reservation successfully launched.

CHAPTER XX

Auspicious Beginning

On November 4, 1853 Edward F. Beale arrived at Tejón from Los Angeles and established his headquarters near the village of Tinliw, governed by Zapatero, and occupied the Old Adobe, the house Dr. E. D. French had built in the area. Following Beale to Tejón were ten wagons loaded with farming equipment. A supply train consisting of twenty white men riding and driving fiftythree horses and mules, along with the delegation of Nisenan Indians from Grass Valley, reached Tejón on the seventh.[1]

Immediately, Beale purchased work animals and equipment. The price of stock varied with the season, costing more in the winter months, when animals often were lost crossing swollen rivers and boggy plains.[2] On November 10, Beale bought five yoke of oxen for $1,250 and a wagon for $250.[3] On the twentieth, he purchased six mules for $1,096.[4] In late November or early December, he acquired seventy more mules and wagons and harnesses for $25,080. Because Indians were to drive the mule teams, Beale thought it necessary to obtain the highest quality and most thoroughly trained animals. Mules not properly broken would initially have cost less, but by smashing wagons and running off, they would have cost more in the long run.[5]

Brood animals also were expensive. Before arriving at Tejón, Beale had instructed B. D. Wilson to provide the reservation with cattle. Wilson told Beale in early November that he had contracted with W. T. B. Sanford to deliver 500 head of beef cattle, at $60 per head, noting that it was the best arrangement he could make.[6] In December, Sanford drove to the reservation 521 head of large beef cattle, earning $31,260.[7] A short time later he sold 44 ewes with lambs to Beale for $440.[8] The same month Beale purchased from Francisco Maria Felís 500 milch and breeding cows, 500 yearlings and calves, and 499 head of beef cattle for $64,935.[9]

In October, Wilson had made arrangements with businessmen Andrew Sublette and James Thompson to provide wheat at 22¢ per pound. The grain could have been purchased in southern California at 6¢ to 7¢ per pound, but Wilson expected the cost to increase and was certain that supply would not match demand. He explained to Beale that the price asked by Sublette and Thompson was high, because they had to purchase the grain from northern growers and ship it to San Pedro. Still, Wilson thought it reasonable and asked whether one hundred thousand pounds would be excessive.[10] Beale agreed that the amount was about right. The grain was for the Tejoneños and Indians from the Four Creeks.[11]

From December 1853 through April 1854, Sublette and Thompson delivered 102,700 pounds of wheat to the reservation at 22¢ per pound.[12] A mill Beale purchased in San Francisco for $1500 ground the wheat into flour.[13] Sublette and Thompson also supplied 100,000 pounds of barley at 20¢ per pound and 9,109 pounds of barley at 5¢ per pound, grossing $43,049.45.[14] During the same period, the clerk at Tejón designated for planting 75,000 pounds of wheat and 30,000 pounds of barley. In addition, 27,700 pounds of wheat were distributed to the Indians for food, and 82,629 pounds of barley were fed to the mules.[15]

Although Beale intended to sell surplus products on the open market, as of late November 1853, the reservation was not yet self-sufficient. Concerned about immigrants pausing on the reservation to buy food and equipment, he placed a notice in the *Los Angeles Star* announcing that henceforth no supplies could be purchased at the reservation. Provisions produced at Tejón were for government use and not for the traveling public.[16] Beale could prohibit the selling of goods to immigrants, but he could not prevent them from driving large herds of cattle through Tejón Pass or the Cañada de las Uvas and the western part of the reservation. Some of the immigrants settled on the Kings and Tule Rivers, others in the Four Creeks.[17]

Beale told Commissioner of Indian Affairs George W. Manypenny in December that the plan he had submitted to the last session of Congress was now in "full and successful operation" and that the reservation would soon be paying for itself. He estimated that the wheat fields would produce 35 bushels to the acre; thus, the 2,500 acres to be put under cultivation would yield 87,500 bushels. From 1 bushel, 50 pounds of coarse or superfine flour would result. If the 4,375,000 pounds of flour were sold at 10¢ per pound, the reservation would turn a profit of $43,750 from its first crop. But that was only the beginning. During the following year, he would increase his acreage tenfold and plant tobacco, sugarcane, rice, corn, and all kinds of

NOTICE

To Travellers and Emigrants.

THE supplies at this Post being the property of the General Government, it will be impossible for me to sell or any way dispose of them.

This notice is intended to guard emigrants and others travelling in this valley, to purchase their provisions &c. before leaving Los Angeles or the Four Creeks.

E. F. BEALE.
Sup't Indian Affairs.

Tejon Military Reserve, Nov. 25. 1853.

Los Angeles Star, December 3, 1853.

vegetables. The surplus products would be sold on the open market, "and the proceeds invested in such other matters, as the Indians may require, and which cannot as yet be supplied by their own labor." Beale admitted that he might be accused of proceeding "on a visionary basis" but was convinced that the "facts will speak for themselves, and I trust to them to do me justice." That he might be prevented from completing his program also was a concern: "Jealously, envy, and the detraction, is the fate of any one who attempts an innovation, on any old established custom, and I am not vain enough to suppose that I may escape this inevitable fate. I hope therefore the Department, at least, will sustain me in my acts for the short period I propose to retain this office."[18]

As called for in "The Indians of Southern California," the report written by Benjamin Hayes, Beale formed a governing council over which he would preside. Comprised of six Indian leaders and himself, it met on the first of each month to dispose of surplus produce, discuss the welfare of the Indian residents, punish law-breakers, and settle disputes.[19] "Their quarrels are adjusted by their chiefs, who appear alone to be responsible to Lieut. Beale," reported a newspaper in January 1854. "Surely such a system of government will be productive of much good."[20] Evidently, the leaders of the Tejoneños initially formed the council: Chief Vicente and captains Chico, Zapatero, José Antonio, Martin, and Francisco. Each council member was responsible for providing a quota of laborers for such tasks as threshing wheat, hauling grain, and manufacturing adobes.[21]

Visiting the reservation in February, Captain P. Edward Connor was impressed with the Indians he saw plowing, sowing, digging ditches, and serving as vaqueros. He observed "a very ingenious fellow learning the blacksmith trade, and another the carpenter['']s. In fact it is most astonishing with what facility and readiness they perform the duties assigned them. They have already planted several acres of Potatoes, and are to plant more, also several acres of corn, and the various vegetables in their proper season."[22]

Beale told Manypenny the same month that he had divided the workers into different parties: "Those who plough and harrow, seventy-five in number, go to the field, after harnessing, in regular order; those who ditch have their work laid out—each one so much, according to the nature of the soil; and so on through every department of work which happens at the time to be necessary." That he had punished only "a few lazy ones with proper but not severe correction" was proof that discipline was maintained by "moral force." And such force would have failed "but for the confidence they feel in what I have told them, that all this work is to benefit themselves, and not the government." The Indian workers had completed an irrigation canal six feet wide by eight in depth, connecting two streams and running nine miles. The canal surrounded the common grain field. Two thousand acres of wheat were up, and five hundred acres of barley were being planted.[23]

The Indians, however, perceived the growing of common and private crops differently. In the immediate vicinity of each village, the Indians grew grains and vegetables. In the aggregate they totaled 80 acres of wheat and 175 of corn. A crew from the common labor pool plowed the fields, but the Indians at each village tended and harvested the crops. "These fields were evidently viewed by the Indians with peculiar and special gratification," noted an army officer, "as they seemed, unable fully to realize that the common fields, so large were they, could be intended for their use and advantage."[24]

Work of a more domestic nature was undertaken by women, girls, the elderly, and in one case the handicapped. In February, Beale sent Manypenny a pair of garters made from a worsted saddle girth by a boy who was lame: "They were intended as a present to myself, and to be used to tie the leather leggings necessary here to protect the limbs in riding through a thorny undergrowth in hunting game. Much as I value them, I cheerfully resign the gift to you, as a proof of what they are capable."[25] Captain Connor noted that while the old people did the household work, the girls and young women were employed making garments for themselves and the men: "My attention was yesterday called... to a woman making a shirt, and although the style of cutting may not be as fashionable as some our Stockton dames could execute, still I will defy any of them to beat the sewing."[26]

To keep the Indian workers in line, Beale hired Samuel Bishop at $250 per month as overseer of the reservation. Beale employed several other men as well, and apparently the salary of an employee was determined

Samuel Bishop. (Courtesy of Kern County Museum. Used by permission.)

by his skills, ethnicity, or connections. Tomás Enriques (shepherd and vaquero) and José Soto (vaquero) earned thirty-five dollars and fifty dollars per month, respectively, whereas White Elliotte (teamster), Robert Wilson (cattle majordomo), and Adam Bower (cook) each took home seventy-five. Jesús Gorrdoyo, who was in charge of the vineyard and the orchard, consisting of orange, peach, apple, apricot, pear, and pomegranate trees, earned fifty-five dollars per month, but Alexander Jackson (assistant farmer) received one hundred. Alexander Clapp (blacksmith) and Samuel Dummer (clerk) each got $125. Others were paid on a per diem basis.[27]

In October 1852 Beale had hired his old friend Alexis Godey as interpreter at three thousand dollars per year.[28] On one occasion Beale acknowledged Godey's indispensability: "His wonderful knowledge of the country, and great influence with the tribes of the mountains enabled me

Alexis Godey. (Courtesy of Kern County Museum. Used by permission.)

through him to preserve peace in the Joaquin Valley, and it was also by communication kept up with him that I was constantly appraised of every important occurrence among the tribes in that portion of the State." To keep him in his employ, Beale granted Godey special trading privileges.[29]

Reversing policy in February 1854, Beale allowed Godey to plant crops to sell to immigrants passing through the area.[30] In the western part of the reservation, in an area called La Pastoria, Godey and Samuel Bishop initially sowed forty or fifty acres of barley.[31] In need of workers to tend to their private crops, the two men might have encouraged Indians to found the village of Chipowhi in the area. Estanislao, a Serrano from Puninga in the Antelope Valley, governed the village with the assistance of Clemente, a Tataviam from Lake Elizabeth. Both men had been baptized at Mission San Fernando. Most of those residing at Chipowhi were of

Tataviam ancestry.[32]

The residents of Chipowhi planted and harvested the crops of Godey and Bishop and transported them in government wagons. Godey and Bishop returned one-third of their profits to the reservation as compensation for using Indians and government property. Two-thirds of the profits they kept for themselves. On one occasion Bishop provided the small detachment of dragoons bivouacked on the reservation with four thousand pounds of government barley. He did not charge the army, because he lacked the authority to sell government supplies. But he replaced the government barley with "his" crop once it was harvested, and billed the army for the sale. One-third of those profits also were returned to the reservation.[33]

The land on which both whites and Indians grew their crops was covered by a grant not yet to be confirmed by a federal land commission. Beale understood that before the federal government could purchase the land, it had to be surveyed. Thus, he contacted the United States surveyor general, and on February 1, 1854 Deputy Surveyor H. Storrs Washburn and four assistants arrived at the reservation. Beale told Washburn to mark out four reservations, each comprising twenty-five thousand acres, and to include within the one hundred thousand acres all the streams, springs, and as much of the best land as possible.[34]

On the twelfth, however, Beale instructed Washburn to reduce the land surveyed to fifty thousand acres, as long as it included the Tejón Pass, La Pastoria, Cañada de las Uvas, and the site of the agency buildings. But if these areas could not be included in the survey, he was to expand the area to seventy-five thousand acres. Washburn and his team surveyed a tract of land comprising 49,928 acres.[35] Because it consisted of nearly fifty thousand acres, twice the size Congress allotted for a single reservation, Beale intended to divide it into two contiguous administrative units.[36]

Bishop informed Washburn on February 22 that Beale also wanted a twenty-fivethousand-acre reservation surveyed at San Emigdio, which also was covered by a land grant. After reconnoitering the area, Bishop concluded it was not suitable for a reservation, and Washburn and his team departed on March 1 for the Kern River to lay out a township. But Beale insisted that the area be surveyed, and once his work on the Kem was finished, Washburn returned and laid out another reservation.[37] Labeled the Santa Remelia (San Emigdio) Military Reserve, it was situated on land, according to Washburn, not very fertile but unsurpassed for stock raising.[38] Unlike the Sebastian Military Reserve (the official name of the Tejón Reservation), it remained only lines drawn on a map.

Staking out land and calling it a reservation was one thing; convincing Indians to reside on it was quite another. Initially, Beale experienced some difficulty in keeping Indians at Tejón. In November 1853, for example, twenty Indians from the Fresno River came in but fled a month later with eight horses belonging to the Tejoneños. Also, a small group from the Four Creeks stayed only a short time.[39] Despite a few setbacks Beale told Manypenny in December "that the force of example which this place will afford, will cause many to remove of their own accord, and in this case at least, one volunteer would be worth a dozen of those removed by compulsion."[40] Having been deceived by whites in the past, some Indians played a waiting game. It was reported in early January 1854 that certain chiefs of "mountain tribes" observed with intense curiosity what was transpiring on the reservation, but remained dubious they would receive provisions there because of past treatment by white men.[41] Others were reluctant to come in because they were certain the area soon would be occupied by whites.[42]

Sometime in late 1853 or early 1854, Juan Viejo, a Chunut chief who resided at Tulare Lake, sent his brother, Calistro, to the reservation, where he planted twenty-five acres in corn and ten in melons and vegetables.[43] Juan Viejo and fifty of his followers visited the reservation in February, remaining a fortnight. "I came here to laugh, at your work," he told Beale, "and to take back some of my people who were with you. I go away with peace in my heart; and if not another Indian of the valley comes, I will make my home with you. In two months I shall return with my people."[44] Juan Viejo and Calistro had signed the treaty at Camp Burton with George Barbour on June 3, 1851.[45] Barbour had entrusted Juan Viejo with the Indians' copy of the treaty.[46] Beale predicted that Juan Viejo would bring five thousand Indians to the reservation.[47] As of early May, however, he had yet to relocate.[48] And when his group finally moved to the reservation, it consisted of only twenty-four Chunut men and their families.[49] Evidently, Juan Viejo and his followers settled at the village of Laikiw.[50]

Raymundo, a Hometwoli Yokuts and neophyte from Mission Santa Bárbara, also settled at Laikiw. Sometime after signing the treaty with Barbour at Tejón Pass on June 10, 1851, Raymundo moved from Kern Lake to the village.[51] In February 1854 Beale sent Raymundo and another Indian, Jesús José, to San Francisco, apparently to witness firsthand the might of the Americans. Accompanied by an interpreter, they sailed from Los Angeles with $375 in traveling expenses.[52]

Indians from the headwaters of the Kern River led by Andres, those from the Sierra Nevada commanded by José, and those from the mountains under Felipe relocated to Mumumpea. Pressured by a settler who claimed they stole his cattle, other Indians from the Kern River, under the leadership of Urbano, moved to the village of Hoshtsiw.[53] As leader of the village of Holoclame, Urbano had signed the treaty with Barbour at Tejón on June 10, 1851. Emeterio, from the village of Tsineuhiu, had signed the same treaty.[54] Apparently, Emeterio settled at Tsuitsan, as did Joaquin and Juan Chico from the Tule River. Indians from the Four Creeks, led by Pedro,

Table 5. Village Leaders at Tejón, 1854

ORIGINAL VILLAGE		INCOMING INDIANS	
Name	*Captains*	*Leader*	*Home area*
Chipowhi	Estanislao	Clemente	Lake Elizabeth
Hoshtsiw	José Antonio	Urbano	Kern River
Laikiw	Martín	Juan Viejo	Tulare Lake
		Raymundo	Kern River
Mat'apxwelxwel	Antonio	José María	San Emigdio
Mumumpea	Chico and	José	Sierra Nevada
	Chief Vincente	Andrés	Kern River
		Felipe	mountains
Tinliw	Zapatero	Pedro	Four Creeks
		Chico	Tule River
		José María	Tule River
Tsuitsau	Francisco	Emeterio	Kern River
		Joaquin, Juan Chico	Tule River

Source: Adapted from "Superintendent Beale—The Tejon Reservation," *Los Angeles Star,* June 17, 1854.

and two groups from the Tule River, one governed by José Maria and the other by Chico, relocated to Tinliw. And Indians from San Emigdio, governed by José Maria, settled at Mat'apxwelxwel, situated at the extreme western end of the reservation.[55]

The arrival of Indians from all over the Tulare Valley forced Chief Vicente and the captains of the Tejoneños to incorporate into their villages individuals from diverse groups, and apparently the incorporation went smoothly. In mid-1854 Captain Connor observed Indians arriving daily in small parties: "A more happy set of beings it has never been my lot to see, and although each tribe speaks a different dialect, such a thing as a fight or quarrel has never happened among them." Upon arrival, Bishop immediately assigned them to work details.[56]

Assisting Indians in relocating to the reservation took time and money.

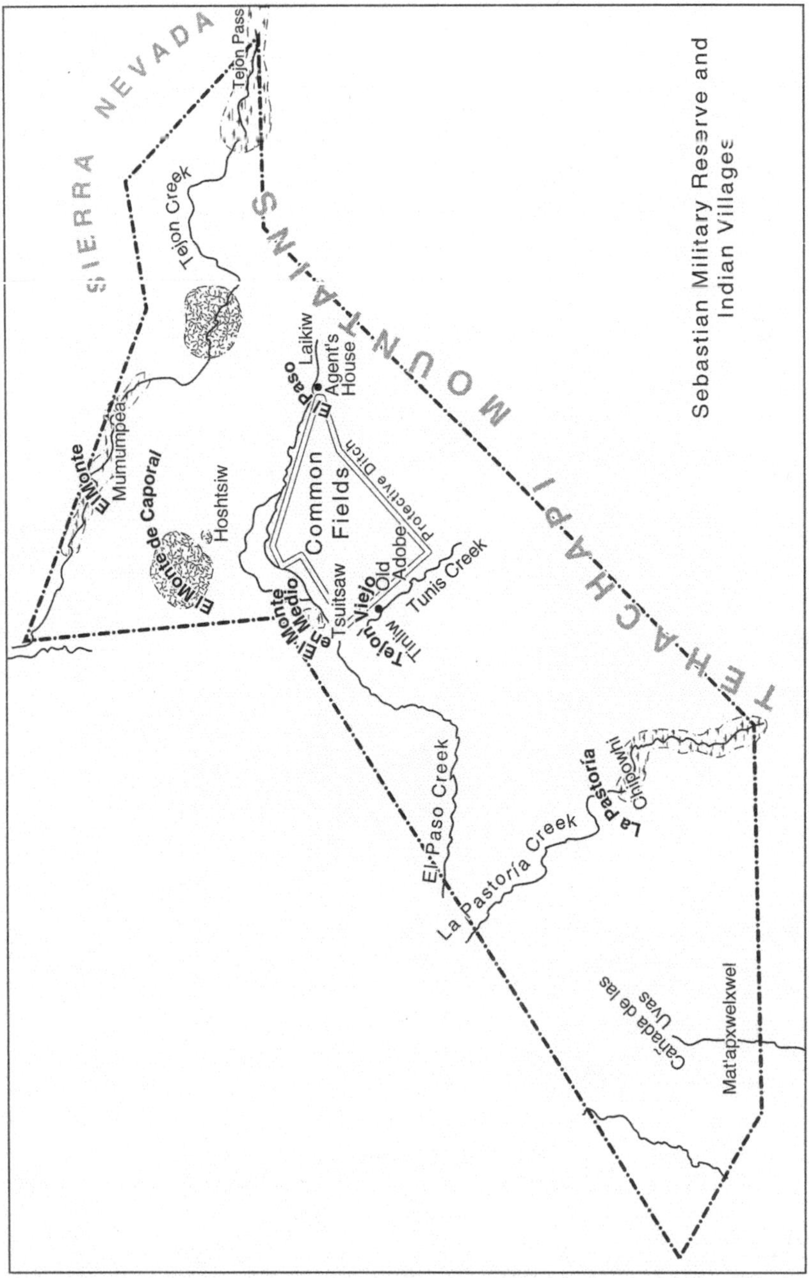
Sebastian Military Reserve and
Indian Villages
SIERRA NEVADA
TEHACHAPI MOUNTAINS
Tejon Pass
Tejon Creek
El Monte
Mumumpea
El Monte de Caporal
Hoshtsiw
El Paso
Laikiw
Agent's House
Common Fields
Protective Ditch
Old Adobe
Tunis Creek
El Monte Medio
Tsuitsaw
Tejon Viejo
Tinliw
El Paso Creek
La Pastoría Creek
La Pastoría
Chipowhi
Cañada de las Uvas
Mat'apxwelxwel

Table 6. Village Crop Acreage at Tejón, 1854

	CROP			
Village	*Corn*	*Wheat*	*Garden*[a]	*Total*
Chipowhi	10	6	5	21
Hoshtsiw	30	20	10	60
Laikiw	25	0	10	35
Mat'apxwelxwel	20	10	8	38
Mumumpea	30	20	25	75
Tinliw	45	20	20	85
Tsuitsau	50	15	10	75

[a] Includes melons, beans, other vegetables, and the like.
Source: Adapted from "Superintendent Beale—The Tejon Reservation," *Los Angeles Star,* June 17, 1854.

Beale sent his employees and Indian teamsters on long journeys over difficult terrain to bring Indians to Tejón.[57] And Beale often hired individuals on an ad hoc basis to round up Indians. In February he paid José Soto $150 for bringing Indians to the reservation and tending cattle for their subsistence.[58] Gabriel Allen received eighteen dollars for six days' work in March for removing thirty-two Indians from Tulare Lake.[59] In June, John Browman got forty-five dollars also for bringing in Indians from the lake.[60] For escorting Juan Viejo's people to the reservation during May and June, N. M. Dubois received $150.00.[61]

Occasionally, Beale placed conditions on Indians seeking to settle on the reservation. In late April, Paiutes from the eastern side of the Sierra Nevada stole six mules from the reservation. The party that went in pursuit traversed some three hundred miles of desert before turning back.[62] When a deputation of twelve Paiutes from Owens Valley arrived in mid-June in a starving condition seeking permission to bring their people to the reservation, Beale told them that once the mules were returned they would be welcomed and given land, provisions, and clothing. Five men departed, promising to return with their people and, if alive, the mules. According to Vicente the Paiutes stole horses and mules only to keep from starving. From firsthand experience he knew that the lake where they lived contained sodium and thus no fish. Vicente found nauseating the worms

Mountains near the Entrance of the Cañada de las Uvas. (From Williamson, Explorations and Surveys.)

on which they relied. [63]

By June the permanent residents of the reservation had cut a road, "equal to any in the country," seven miles into Tejón Canyon, noted a visitor. "All the lumber used upon the Reservation has been got out and sawed here by the Indians. And Indian boys, unaccompanied, have hauled all the lumber; driving six and eight mule teams without accident, and fully justifying every confidence that has been reposed in them." At the time of his visit, the labor force numbered approximately four hundred men, women, and boys and included delegations from the Sacramento, San Joaquin, and Fresno Rivers. Indian boys from the Four Creeks were especially "industrious and intelligent, and emulous of doing a great deal for their people."[64] The following month Captain Connor wrote: "Matters go on handsomely at the Indian Reservation. The harvest is all gathered, and the threshing machine is doing its work of separation. It is, indeed, a most lovely and interesting sight to observe parties of Indians in their various occupations, working with the utmost cheerfulness and alacrity; some driving four & six mule teams, some feeding the threshing machine, and others attending the large crops of corn, potatoes and water-melons."[65]

Table 7. Beef Distribution at Tejón, 1853–1854

Month	*Cattle butchered*
September	9
October	0
November	76
December	76
January	160
Feburary	130
March	113
April	120
May	118
June	130
July	110
August	22

Source: Adapted from Edward F. Beale, An approximate statement, showing the issue of provisions to Indians on the Tejon Military Reserve in Edward F. Beale to George W. Manypenny, Washington, D.C., December 14, 1854, U.S. Congress, Senate, Records of the Senate.

Indian labor was not limited to reservation projects. Indians spent considerable time cultivating their own crops. As of mid-June 1854 they had approximately four hundred acres under cultivation.[66] Of all the villages on the reservation, Mat'apxwelxwel was the most economically independent. Isolated at the western point of the reservation, it relied less on government assistance than did the other villages. Its residents subsisted on the wild plant and animal life that flourished in the Tehachapi Mountains and on the products of their gardens.[67] For many of them, knowledge of farming had been acquired at Missions San Fernando, San Buenaventura, and Santa Inés.[68]

Beef was the main food distributed to the Indians. Costing $60 per head during the winter months, it was cheaper to purchase cattle to butcher than to buy grain at 30¢ to 75¢ per pound.[69] How many Indians happened to be on the reservation on a given day determined the number of cattle butchered. A tally was conducted at the end of each month.[70]

Construction projects continued. In April or May, at El Paso near the village of Laikiw, Indians began work on a large adobe house for Beale and his family.[71] Mrs. Beale joined her husband in June and apparently was pleased with the recently completed accommodations. To celebrate the occasion, on the night of June 23, Indians performed a dance in front of the house.[72]

Colonel Joseph K. F. Mansfield, who was on an inspection tour of western forts, arrived in June. He inspected a squad of soldiers from Fort Miller bivouacked near Laikiw. Commanded by Lieutenant Thomas F. Castor, the squad, from Company A, First Dragoons, consisted of ten privates and a corporal, all of whom were armed with swords and muskets. According to Mansfield, the men maintained good discipline and kept their horses and equipment in good order.[73] It was to this squad that Bishop and Godey provided the barley they grew at La Pastoría.

In his report of July 1 to General John Wool, commander of the pacific division, Mansfield recommended that one company of dragoons be permanently stationed on the reservation, mainly to protect the rancheros of Los Angeles, Santa Bárbara, and San Luís Obispo from Indian stock raiders. He considered the Tejón Pass the best spot for the post: "It is beautifully located among large oak trees near the mountains and with abundant water, wood, and grazing near." Until a post was established, the squad of dragoons should remain on the reservation.[74]

By this time Wool had ordered Major James L. Donaldson, the assistant quartermaster, to the reservation to construct quarters for one company of dragoons and one of infantry. The post was to be established near the Tejón Pass, at a spot selected by Beale and approved by Captain Thomas Jordan, commander of Fort Miller.[75] Donaldson, however, concluded that the fort should be situated some twenty miles to the west, in the Cañada de las Uvas. There, he reasoned, the soldiers would check Indian outbreaks on the reservation and prevent collisions between Indians and immigrants. Water, pasture, and building materials were available, and the area was closer to the harbors of Santa Bárbara or San Pedro, from where supplies would come.[76]

Inadvertently, Major Donaldson located Fort Tejón outside the reservation. At the end of July 1854, Congress had reduced the number of authorized reservations from five to three and reduced the acreage per reservation from twenty-five thousand to ten thousand- sand acres.[77] The reservation's contracted boundaries excluded the Cañada de las Uvas.[78] The fort, moreover, like the reservation, was located on a Mexican grant.[79] Despite its promising beginnings, the experiment in assisting and controlling Indians could not remain immune from both state and national politics.

CHAPTER XXI

Politics and Policies

Less than a year after founding the Tejón Reservation, Edward F. Beale was coming under considerable criticism for the means he employed in its creation. In June 1854 the editors of the *Los Angeles Star* noted that

> Beale was a man of untiring energy, and is entirely and unselfishly devoted to the work. Let him have a fair trial, and he will make the miserable wild Indians of California the happiest people in the State. He is a young man, and, of course, is ambitious; but his ambition lies in a road which few have the capacity or taste to travel; and therefore, though he may be closely watched, there are none who ought to envy him his success. In the revolutions of party and the desire to reward favorites, he may be displaced. For the good cause in which he is engaged, and for the sake of degraded humanity, we hope the day of his displacement is far off. But should the evil time come, when his office shall descend into the vortex of politics, we trust the Government will insist that his successor be fitted for the post; that he reside upon the Reservations and follow out the system already so auspiciously commenced, and which is admirably suited to the character and associations of the California Indians.[1]

Beale's office already had descended into "the vortex of politics." President Franklin Pierce had dismissed Beale on May 31, 1854, ostensibly because he had been instructed to take the quickest route to California but had traveled overland to explore a route for a transcontinental railway;

because he had been ordered to make withdrawals of only $20,000 at a time from the $250,000 appropriation but had withdrawn half the amount three days after making the deposit; because he had reported infrequently to the Indian Office; and because he had submitted accounts that were confusing and extravagant.[2]

Beale's achievements, however, generated considerable discussion. In July 1854 the editors of the *San Francisco Daily California Chronicle* noted that the experiment begun by Edward F. Beale had "proved a most successful one. It may not have been an original idea, but at any rate, as a practical attempt to render the wild Indians independent and self-sustaining men and communities, living in harmony and comfort, with the necessities of civilized life, produced by their own labor, it was a new thing in the United States."[3] Two months later the editors of the *Mariposa Chronicle* spoke highly of Beale's management of the Indians at Tejón but noted that the Indian agents had laid the groundwork of the reservation system. They had "set the ball in motion" and "were the first in the field." Beale had done wonders, "and we would be the last to detract from his well-earned reputation. But he would not claim any, due fairly to another."[4]

On January 22, 1855, Special Treasury Agent J. Ross Browne issued a report regarding Beale's activities and finances. He criticized him on several specific points but concluded by speculating on larger issues:

> What results Mr. Beale might have produced at the Tejón had he remained in office a sufficient length of time to have carried his plan fully into execution, it would be very difficult to say. It is scarcely fair to judge adversely of a system of operations, commenced under many difficulties, and barely under way, when placed under the control of a new Superintendent whose views and interests may be entirely different.
>
> If the system of reservations therefore has not produced such striking results as might be expected, from the large sums of money expended, it arises from other causes than the natural obstacles encountered with the attempt to civilize a barbarous race. I do not think there is any reason to despair of its ultimate success. The Indians of California are generally intelligent and tractable. They readily learn the uses of agricultural implements and are docile and easily managed when well treated. I know of no better way to benefit them than by a faithful administration of the system which has been adopted.[5]

The editors of the *San Francisco Daily Alta California*, however, insisted that the federal government had spent large sums of money on a system "founded in error." Like many Americans in California, they thought the reservation was based on the Spanish mission but found "it difficult to believe that in the twenty-one establishments which once existed in California there was anything like the happiness and contentment which we find pictured in the books of some travelers." Just as the Spanish mission system had failed to elevate the Indians to a "state of civilization," so had the reservation system, "and sorry indeed are we to confess it. There is not a right-thinking man in California who does not desire to see the condition of the Indian ameliorated. Philanthropy had been continually at work, but Destiny is ever thwarting its labors.... Year by year the Indians are dwindling away, and a few generations more and they will live only in history."[6]

Responding to the editorial in a letter to the *Alta*, recently appointed Superintendent of Indian Affairs Thomas Henley acknowledged that the reservation system had not produced the desired results: "I admit the difficulties attending any system for ameliorating the condition of the Indians. I know that the expenditure of millions heretofore appropriated to that purpose, has resulted in accomplishing comparatively very little, and it may perhaps be considered safe to predict a failure in all future efforts. But I entertain the belief that when you have made yourselves acquainted with the policy now in operation you will be of a different opinion."[7] In the same issue the editors advocated a return to the old system of removing Indians "beyond the confines of civilization." There they would be "to some extent exempt from those influences which so quickly debase them." For the Indians this would be "a great blessing," because they find no happiness "amid the crowded thoroughfares of civilization.... It matters not where they live, so that it be in a healthful climate, and where they can roam over uninhabited fields, and through dense forests."[8]

The editors of the *San Francisco Golden Era* took issue with those advocating removal. In September 1856 they recommended that the reservation system be extended to all the Indians of California, especially to those in the northern part of the state: "The reservation and domestication system is undoubtedly the best, if not the only plan for the government of the Indian. The Cherokees, Choctaws, and other tribes, have thoroughly tested its practicability, and its efficiency is no longer a matter of speculation. The two reservations in this State are also proofs of its excellence." Six more reservations should be established, and all the Indians in the state collected upon them. "Five thousand in one community will be more easily managed than ten or twenty thousand. After the first or second year, they need be no expense to the Government; they can be made self-supporting. Why, then, should this matter not be attended to, since economy as well as humanity recommend it?"[9]

Expanding the reservation system meant the further involvement of the military, but the duties and responsibilities of the army in implementing Indian policy remained ill defined. In October 1856 Major General John Wool pointed out to Senator John B. Weller some of the problems the military faced. Until the state of California ceded specific land to the United States for reservations, the army could not even prohibit a white man from taking Indian women or children from a reservation. "In such cases the civil law of the State would be invoked to prevent the evil, and not the military. The same remarks are equally applicable to Indians, who are alike punishable for offenses committed under the laws of the State. California is in no respect considered an Indian country, and therefore the military have no control over whites or Indians, excepting on where jurisdiction is ceded to the United States for such purposes."[10]

Wool expressed similar concerns early the following year in a letter to Senators William Gwin and David C. Broderick. Regarding the stationing of troops on the recently created Nome Lackee Reservation in northern California, Wool wrote: "It has not been surveyed, metes and bounds given, number of acres mentioned, nor the jurisdiction of the State ceded to the United States. Without these prerequisites, with my approval, as required by the Secretary of the Interior, it can no more be considered a military reservation for the protection of Indians than the city of Benicia."[11] To Captain Thomas Jefferson Cram, the system of confining Indians to reservations within a state was "under all circumstance, the most humane, economical, and practicable that can be adopted." But he too blamed the Indian Office for not surveying the reservations: "It is too commonly the case that the reservation is but a mere paper reservation; no survey having been made, no bounds or monuments set to mark its existence, or to show where jurisdiction begins or ends."[12]

The selection of Thomas Henley as superintendent of Indian affairs in California generated some controversy, but it lacked the furor that had accompanied Beale's appointment. According to the *San José Semi-Weekly Tribune*, Henley, postmaster of San Francisco, was "by nature and education far better fitted for making stump-speeches than for acquiring influence over savages."[13] But the *Star* insisted that Henley lacked "none of the energy that characterizes, Lieut Beale. As a gentleman and consistent Democrat, we have reasons to congratulate the administration in its happy selection to fill so important an office. As the administration saw fit to make a change in this office, we feel confident it could not have chosen a man better qualified."[14] The change, however, troubled those managing the *Daily California Chronicle*, a San Francisco newspaper. Because of the "lamentable fickleness" of the government, the confidence of the Indians had been lost: "Where they expected permanency of a system and of friends, they are destined to find, probably, neither. Change, of all things should have been avoided. The continuance of a good and successful policy ought never to have been left to the chances of revolution. And we fear that the action of the Government will prove a death blow to the whole experiment."[15]

Regarding the importance and purpose of the Sebastian Military Reserve and Fort Tejón, individuals also expressed strong opinions, opinions based on personal loyalties, political affiliations, military objectives, and especially economic considerations. The businessmen of Los Angeles, for example, expected the reservation and fort to be highly profitable outlets for their products. In August 1854 several merchants donated nearly $2,900 to build a wagon road over the San Fernando Hill, the only real obstacle blocking the pueblo from the fort, the reservation, and the Tulare Valley. To the editors of the *Southern Californian*, the development of the valley and the prosperity of Los Angeles were linked: "A large portion of the Tulare Valley is of the finest quality of agricultural land, lying unoccupied, with every facility of water and timber for farming purposes, which is inviting occupants.... As soon as they begin to raise a surplus of produce, they will seek a market for it. If Los Angeles provides proper facilities, we will command the trade of this region."[16]

The newspaper reported in mid-November that the road was nearly completed but the donations had fallen short by about one thousand dollars. Because the road was "destined to be the great thoroughfare" linking the north and south, it was the duty of all those "whose interests are identified with this country" to help make up the deficiency.[17] By late December the road had been completed and was ready for travelers.[18] To tap into the lucrative market, in January 1855 local freighters Phineas Banning and David Alexander placed an advertisement in the *Alta*, offering their services from San Pedro (the port of Los Angeles) to the Tulare Valley.[19]

Many of the merchants and cattlemen of Southern California failed to benefit from the new policy introduced by Henley. During Beale's brief tenure as superintendent, they had received top priority in supplying the reservation with provisions, equipment, and stock. But Henley cut costs at Tejón and bought goods and supplies from San Francisco merchants who shipped them to San Pedro. On June 20, 1855 the editors of the *Southern Californian* complained bitterly that their region had not benefited economically from the reservation: "The sugar, the tea, the coffee, the molasses, the beads, the tin pans, the cotton cloth, the matches, the Jews-Harps, indeed everything merchantable, is purchased above and brought down here in small parcels."[20]

More serious difficulties also lay ahead, warned the editors. The men Beale employed to manage the reservation brought prosperity and contentment to the Indians, "at the same time securing to whites an immunity from thefts and robberies which stem necessity had ever prompted this 'scattered remnant' to commit." Because Indians supposedly were fleeing the reservation, soon there would be "a renewal of those scenes of violence and robbery, from the presence of which, we have for the last year or two been secured. Indeed such a disposition is already manifested and word has gone out from some who were formerly at the Reserve, that necessity would prompt them to resume their old habits. Should this be the case, where would the blame rest!"[21]

To many rancheros in Southern California, the blame would rest squarely with those who located Fort Tejón in the Cañada de las Uvas. J. Ross Browne, special treasury agent, who arrived at the fort in October 1854, also questioned the decision: "Should the station remain in its present position it will probably be necessary to have a small detachment ordered to the reservation for the protection of the whites, in case of any sudden out-break among the Indians. The distance from the Fort to the Superintendent's Quarters on the reservation is twenty miles. I do not think the removal of the Military Station from the vicinity of Tejón Pass, was judicious in the first place." As Browne saw the situation nothing prevented Indians from the eastern slope of the Sierra Nevada from crossing Walker's and Tejón passes to commit "serious depredations upon stock and other public property."[22] Captain E. D. Townsend, visiting Fort Tejón in October, noted in his journal that of the two sites suitable for a military post, the one near the Tejón Pass should have been selected.[23] According to the *Los Angeles Star*, however, Fort Tejón was ideally situated for "keeping at bay the hostile and intrusive hordes of the interior."[24] The *Southern Californian* agreed. Locating the fort in the Cañada de las Uvas was the right decision, because it "completely controls the great thoroughfares through which hostile Indians make their incursions into our valleys, for the purposes of robbery and spoils."[25]

Regarding the purpose and worth of the Tejón Reservation, however, the editors of the two newspapers sharply disagreed. Those managing the *Southern Californian* insisted that it was founded to protect the whites from the stock-raiding Indians, to accommodate the Indians who lived in and near Los Angeles, and "to elevate if possible the character of this unfortunate race." As of June 1855 none of those objectives had been achieved. "On the contrary, facts compel us to believe that such results have been and are considered of secondary importance, and that the aim and great object has been to evade as far as possible any outlay of time, trouble and money, —except possible for individual interests."[26] The editors of the *Star* countered by suggesting that the criticism emanated from those who had failed to obtain from Superintendent Henley beef, grain, or other contracts.[27]

FOR KERN RIVER GOLD MINES VIA SAN PEDRO.

The subscribers beg leave to inform the public that they have completed the necessary arrangements for running a LINE OF STAGES and a TRAIN OF WAGONS and PACK MULES from this point to the KERN RIVER GOLD MINES, stopping at Los Angeles, San Fernando Mission, Lake Elizabeth, Fort Tejon, Gody & Bishop's Rancho, and the Indian Reservation.

Goods will be receipted for in San Pedro and delivered at any of the above points or at White River.

ALEXANDER & BANNING.

San Pedro, January, 1855. j23-is

"For Kern River Gold Mines via San Pedro." (*San Francisco Daily Alta California*, January 23, 1855.)

Included in the same edition was a report Henley had sent to the commissioner of Indian affairs in April, in which he claimed that fifteen hundred acres of wheat and barley had been sown on the reservation. Supposedly, he had arranged for Indians to plant at their villages gardens, cornfields, melons, and pumpkins. From the common field wheat had been harvested and was in storage. The Indians had moved into adobe houses they had begun building in the fall, and the women manufactured clothing at little expense except for the wholesale cost of the cloth. Henley emphasized that he provided no clothing except shirts to the men who refused to labor.[28]

Samuel Bishop, Beale's close friend, challenged Henley's claims point by point in a letter to the *Southern Californian*. Eighty acres, not fifteen hundred, had been planted since Henley became superintendent, and the Indians had sown their gardens and cornfields during the previous administration. Wheat was in storage, but it too was produced during Beale's tenure. Only Raymundo and Zapatero had built adobe houses, and only their families were living in them. Henley's claim that the Indian women made clothing at little expense was correct, but they had to purchase the material. Moreover, if Henley gave shirts to men who did not work, then the distribution must have been considerable, because on a given day not more than ten or twelve Indians labored. Bishop ended his letter by claiming objectivity: "I am neither a 'disappointed beef, flour, or grain speculator,' but quietly pursing my business as farmer, directly within view of the Reserve."[29] Bishop failed to mention that he was pursuing his business at La Pastoría on the reservation.

Articles critical of the reservation published by the *Southern Californian* had made no impression in the state, Henley stressed in a letter to the commissioner of Indian affairs: "They were not copied by any other paper. The Editors were never at the Reserve and have no personal knowledge on the subject. I am fully advised as to their sources of information. It came from the late employees of Mr. Beale who sought employment from me and failed to get it; and the publication was instigated by parties who had solicited and failed to get beef contracts." Before the criticism began, claimed Henley, individuals had warned him that articles "very severe upon me" would be published if the contracts were not forthcoming. "My reply was that I would need but few cattle and those I did want would certainly not be purchased of those parties."[30]

That the *Southern Californian* had a political motive for attacking Henley was the position taken by John Grice, a reservation employee. He told the commissioner of Indian affairs that commercial interests had targeted Henley: "The merchants and speculators of Los Angeles find a great deal of fault with him because he does not pay them a hundred percent more for their goods than he can buy the same article for in San Francisco."[31] Walter Harvey said essentially the same thing in a letter to a military officer: "The Merchants of this place (Los Angeles) are of the impression that the Government established the Sebastian Reservation for the benefit of this portion of the State and that Col. Henley should purchase all the goods that are consumed at the Reservation from there, and not go to the San Francisco Market." Moreover, the reduction in the number of beef contracts issued since Beale's dismissal greatly upset the speculators. As Harvey saw it, Henley was criticized because he was "too economical in his expenditures.... It is prejudice that has caused all the reports that have been put into circulation injurious to the Sebastian Reservation."[32]

The relentless criticism of the reservation issued by the *Southern Californian* might have contributed to rumors spreading in Los Angeles in September 1855 that Henley intended to close Tejón. In response the editors of the *Star* emphasized that the reservation was "eminently beneficial" to the citizens of the state, a large majority being opposed to its removal. Included in the edition was an announcement of a meeting to be held at the courthouse on Thursday, September 20, to discuss the situation.[33] After the meeting the editors of the *Southern Californian* pretended not to know how many citizens were in attendance but insisted that few would be alarmed if the reservation were removed: "What is there to remove that should create any uneasiness? is it a few broken-down and dilapidated wagons, with a few old cart wheels and bits of odd harnesses?... Can it be the few bushels of grain that have withstood and survived the attacks of man and beast?... Is there anything frightful in the emancipation of the two or three old mules from their daily duties at the grist mill?... It cannot be that the fear of the $100 yearly disbursed here for odd pounds of sugar, isolated bars of soap, stray pints of molases [sic], discordant Jews Harps, and '*yaller*' cotton handkerchiefs is considered of vital importance to the business of the South!"[34]

Although Edward F. Beale's views are not recorded, most certainly he favored the continuation of the reservation, because he and his former employers continued to raise animals on it. Moreover, while in Washington, D.C. in 1855, Beale informed B. D. Wilson that upon returning to California he sought "to purchase some good Rancho, at a cheap rate, and go into stock raising."[35] What he had in mind was a rancho located south east of the Tejón Reservation in the Antelope Valley, a high desert ecosystem spanning 2,200 square miles and home of the Pronghorn Antelope and the Joshua Tree, a species of the yucca.[36] Passing through the area a few years later, an individual recorded his impressions:

> The valley appeared to have an average width of about five miles, and to be thirty or forty miles long, bounded by bare mountains colored with beautiful tints of yellow, brown, purple and blue, according to their distance and relation to the sun and shade.
>
> The low land was spotted with green grass-like vegetation, and on the other side of the valley, and in front of us we saw great masses of trees, with dark green foliage, resembling that of the oak in color.... But as we advanced and came near to the trees our opinion changed. They were not the cheerful and useful trees of a rich soil, but the growth of the desert. They were the Yucca, a species of palm, an endogenous tree, which, like the onion, grows at the heart and does not increase in size.... The trunk of the Yucca is rarely over ten feet high, with a crooked, twigless trunk, and leaves like bayonets, growing in thick clusters out of the body of the tree.[37]

Obviously, Beale saw more in the land than twigless Yucca. And in August 1855 he acquired Rancho La Liebre in the name of his wife from William C. Walker, who five days earlier had bought it from José Maria Flores. Apparently, Flores sold the property because the U.S. Board of Land Commissioners had failed to confirm his claim to the title. Beale paid $1,500 for the property.[38] Sometime before the purchase, Beale's brother-in-law, Harry Edwards, had received permission from Flores to pasture animals on the rancho. And in September Samuel Bishop herded several thousand head of stock, half of them owned by Beale, onto La Liebre.[39]

"I bought this forty thousand acre tract," Beale told a journalist some years later, "and started to raise cattle. In those days my nearest neighbors were at Visalia on one side and at Los Angeles on the other."[40] Beale, however, failed to acknowledge his Indian neighbors. His ranch house was located on the northern boundary of the Tatavian, close to the village of hwi'tahovea. East of La Liebre were the villages of pavuhavea, kwarung, tsivung, and pu'ning. Many of the residents probably were neophytes from Mission San Fernando and thus skilled in a variety of crafts.[41]

In October 1855 a military party heading to Fort Tejón paused near Elizabeth Lake, in the Antelope Valley, where it encountered some Californios herding several hundred head of cattle. A civilian member of the party noted that they were taking the cattle "to the upper country to sell."[42] Continuing westward for about ten miles, the party arrived at "Irish" John's, property claimed by an individual from Vermont. As described by an officer, "There is some good land on his claim, and his spring yields water enough to irrigate all he will desire to cultivate. John is a man of taste and varied genius. He now inhabits a tent, but has the walls of an adobe house finished. His spring is enclosed with a willow hedge, and there is quite a little pond formed artificially, from which he draws water for his own use and that of the many travellers entertained by him."[43]

The same month the *Los Angeles Star* reported that cattle were grazing on La Liebre.[44] Juan Coluco, a Tejoneño, claimed that Beale had sent them to the rancho from the reservation while superintendent. They were herded by José Soto, commonly known as José Chihuahua, a "short-statured Chihuahua Indian, very dark."[45] Beale had hired Soto in 1854 to relocate Indians to the reservation and to manage cattle for their subsistence.[46] The 1860 census identified José Soto, age 23, as an overseer, probably of La Liebre. Five Indians worked for him.[47]

Regarding the Tejón Reservation, some of the prominent citizens of Los Angeles County, including B. D. Wilson, now a state senator, were truly concerned about the possibility of its closure and on October 6 drafted a petition to Henley. By protecting rancheros from Indian depredations and by teaching Indians "peaceful habits," the reservation had materially benefited Los Angeles County. Had the reservation not been established, the county would have lost one hundred thousand dollars worth of horses and cattle to Indian stock raiders: "When it is considered that nearly one third of the whole Indian population of the State of California is in the neighborhood and to the south of the Tejón it would seem that a due regard for the interests of Southern California, as well as an appreciation of the obligations of humanity itself, would not only prevent the removal of the Reserve, but would require its being placed on a more substantial, permanent & extensive foundation."[48]

Two days later seven citizens of Santa Bárbara County, five of whom were Californios, also petitioned Henley, claiming that the peace of the southern counties depended on the continuation of the reservation. They encouraged him to put Tejón on a permanent basis. If the Indians understood that the reservation was not a temporary repose but their permanent home, "we have no doubt but that even more direct benefit would result to them, and to us." The petitioners "respectfully join in the protest of our fellow citizens of Los Angeles County, and would earnestly press upon the Government, the policy of fostering and protecting, even to a much greater extent than heretofore, so important a Reserve as the one at the Tejón."[49]

According to the editors of the *Star*, three months after Tejón's founding Indian attacks in the southern five counties had ceased: "The Mission of San Fernando whose owners suffered in the four years previous to the establishment of Reserve, a loss of between four or five thousand head of horses, now brand in security their yet numerous stock. The Ranchos of San Francisco and Capuntos, from which had been driven all their horses to pasture in the vicinity of this city, pastured last spring upwards of seven hundred horses, while San Cayetano, Tin and La Liebre formerly without a single horse or beef now have their thousand head upon their thousand hills." Moreover, "the hardy settler, who penetrating through the gorges of the Cañon de las Uvas and descending into the fertile plains of the Mohave, scattered his flocks far and wide, while the beautiful Tehatchapy[sic] has commenced to assume the appearance of a thriving settlement. Where in 1854 there was not five Americans, over one hundred Americans last month exercised their elective franchise as freemen by voting."[50]

The editors of the *Southern Californian* saw things quite differently: "Magnificent pictures are drawn of the wonderful progress that has been made; of the multiplied herds of stock that are already thronging the thousand hills, where a few months since all was desertion and desolation; of the broad vallies teeming with population; of wide thoroughfares opened; of desert places being made to blossom like the rose; of peace and prosperity and progress and improvement throughout the entire region round about; and all directly resulting from the fact that there exists at the Tejon an Establishment known as the Sebastian Indian Reservation." The editors admitted they could not identify the reasons for the cessation of Indian raids but doubted the reservation was a factor. Were the twelve or fifteen whites on the reservation so powerful they could control thousands of Indians? Settlements had taken hold in the Four Creeks, in the Tehachapi

Mountains, and elsewhere not because of the reservation but because of Forts Tejón and Miller.[51]

Quickly responding, the *Star* pointed out that the editors of the *Southern Californian* admitted they did not know why the Indians had been restrained from committing depredations. The answer, however, was simple. A few months after the establishment of the reservation and the fort, "the wholesale Indian robberies, with which this section of California had been afflicted for many years, entirely ceased."[52] In early November the editors of the acknowledged the right of their rival to criticize the management of Tejón but could not comprehend its call for removal. Removal would place in jeopardy "the immense herds of cattle in this county, worth about two millions of dollars, would expose our frontier ranchos and settlements to destruction, that would depreciate our real estate and light the torch of a fierce Indian war." The prosperity of the southern counties, "as far as our Indian policy can affect it, is connected with preservation of the Reserve system, and the continuance of the Sebastian Reserve where it now is; and we cannot believe that any personal feeling or local influence can induce the Government to put in peril so much real prosperity and material progress, as is exhibited by the Southern counties, for the purpose of hazarding new experiments."[53]

The ongoing debate between the two newspapers regarding the merits of the fort and reservation concluded in November 1855, when the *Southern Californian* suspended publication because of financial embarrassments.[54] Now the *Star* could voice its opinions unchallenged. Moreover, it found an ally in the *Santa Barbara Gazette*, whose editors on November 15 argued that the strategic location of the reservation prevented hostile Indians from raiding the coastal ranchos:

> If for some incomprehensional purpose, it should be the policy of the Administration to check our prosperity, to break up our ranchos, to expose the lives of our frontier settlers, then let them remove the Reservation, and thus, by breaking the most solemn pledges given to the Indians that it was to be permanently established for their benefit, destroy their confidence in the Government, and give to their discontent a substantial evidence of its justice, in order that they may recommence their work of robbery and murder.
>
> There may exist among us some difference of opinion about the present good or bad management of this Reserve, but we have yet to learn that there is a single resident of this county that does not regard the preservation of this Reserve, in its present location, and the Indian policy that dictated its establishment, as not only important, but essential, to our peace and prosperity.[55]

A week later the editors of the *Star* supported the *Gazette's* position. Not only were the citizens of Los Angeles County "deeply impressed with the necessity of adhering to the present policy, and of maintaining the Sebastian Reservation in its present location,—not only are they prepared to characterize any abandonment of either as an aggression upon their rights, for which, to the extent of their ability, a rigid responsibility will be exacted, but the people of Santa Barbara county express in emphatic terms similar opinions and sentiments."[56]

B. D. Wilson notified United States Senator John B. Weller about concerns in Southern California over the possible removal of Tejón. Weller assured him in mid-January 1856 that his committee on Indian affairs had no intention of recommending the reservation be abandoned. Tejón had successfully concentrated Indians at one area and had brought peace and security to the citizens of the region. Because of the importance of that reservation to the protection of the citizens of Los Angeles, San Bernardino, and San Diego Counties, he could never consent to its removal.[57]

On March 20 the state legislators passed concurrent resolutions in support of the Tejón Reservation. The resolutions called on California's senators and representatives in Congress to introduce legislation to prevent the removal of the reservation and to pressure the executive department for the same end. The governor of California was to transmit copies of the resolution to congressional representatives and to the secretary of the interior.[58]

At the end of May, Senator Weller and Representative P. T. Herbert sent the resolutions to Secretary of the Interior Robert McClelland. In an accompanying letter, they noted that the private claim to the land on which the reservation was located had been confirmed by a federal land commission. The congressmen encouraged the secretary to find the means of obtaining title to the land, emphasizing that California was vitally interested in the preservation of the reservation at its present local. Removal, many in the state believed, would precipitate an Indian war as expensive as that raging in the Oregon and Washington Territories.[59]

Treasury Agent J. Ross Browne was interested less in the politics of removal than in the corruption of those implementing policy. Individuals, not the system, he contended, had failed the Indians. In 1857 he reported on the condition of the reservations in California. The limited success of the system should not be attributed "to any want of capacity for civilization" on the part of the Indians "but to the notorious fact that Agents, Contractors and others have derived the chief benefits resulting from the appropriations made by Congress." The reservations might still serve the interests of some Indians, but "sanguine hopes" as well as a "wholesale condemnation of the system" were to be avoided. As Browne saw it "any mode of relief which could be devised by human ingenuity would be subject to abuse."[60]

Early the following year Browne offered a radical and long-range plan. Because of their resistance to change, little, if any, improvement could be expected from adult Indians. So long as the association between younger Indians and adults continued, no permanent change would be achieved. Reports by agents claiming the Indians were changing were "colored by a natural desire to promote the continuance of the system, and probably a laudable hope that it will eventually result successfully." To correct the situation the government should establish school farms for all Indian children between five and fourteen years of age. By purchased or coercion the government should take the children from their parents and place them in the farms. There they would be taught "the rudiments of an English education, the arts of husbandry and mechanics; giving each male child a knowledge of some useful trade, and fitting each female for housework and domestic duties of various kinds." Occasionally, parents would be allowed to visit their children "so as to satisfy them that the children are kindly and beneficially treated; but to prohibit any prolonged intercourse, from which the children could derive an attachment to Indian habits, or a desire to acquire the vices of Indian life." Finally, at age eighteen or twenty the Indians would be apprenticed to whites as workers or servants for terms not exceeding three or four years.[61] Browne's proposal anticipated the Indian boarding-school program introduced to California and other areas of the West a few decades later.

Cognizant that his plan might be considered a new type of slavery, Browne explained that it was "no more slavery than to force the Indians away from their own country, and gather them upon a Reservation against their will, where they are kept in subjection by a military force." He also was aware that the reservation system could not be abolished overnight. In ten years, once the older generation had passed away, "under the plan proposed, there will be a new and more enlightened generation, to succeed them, who from their education and associations, will be amply competent to take care of themselves and earn their own subsistence."[62]

The same time Browne was formulating his ideas, Superintendent of Indian Affairs Thomas Henley was coming under considerable criticism. The editors of the *San Francisco Daily Morning Call* sarcastically suggested that Henley's tenure as superintendent had proved to be eminently "successful," but whether this was because the Indians had no newspapers in which to present their position, they were unable to say: "True it is, that once in a while we hear of their miserable conditions, but that is only through the columns of some village newspaper, whose editor is not supposed to know anything about Indians affairs, that branch of knowledge being reserved exclusively for the Superintendent." Annually, the government "pays for blankets, shoes and clothing sufficient for more than double the entire number of Indians in the State, yet throughout the year the large portion of them are but little better clad than were our first parents during their sojourn in the Garden of Eden." The editors guaranteed that a thorough examination of Henley's affairs "would reveal venality and corruption to an extent rarely known in any branch of the public service. At each session of Congress large appropriations are made, intended for the benefit of the Indians, but a strict scrutiny will show that but a fractional proportion of the whole amount ever reaches the object designed."[63]

Because of the mismanagement of Indian affairs in California, the federal government again called on Browne to investigate the situation. Also assigned to the case was Godard Bailey, special agent of the Department of the Interior. The two men, in the company of Thomas Henley, visited the Nome Lackee, Nome Cult, and Mendocino Reservations in Northern California in August 1858.[64] Browne's report focused on the purchases Henley had made from merchants in San Francisco. Although several testified they had sold the superintendent goods of the highest quality at the lowest rates, Browne discovered that prices stated by two companies did not always correspond to the vouchers issued by Henley. In some cases, he found it impossible to distinguish between Henley's private and public purchases. "The fact cannot be disguised," wrote Browne, "that the decay of the Indian race in California... has been accelerated by the incompetency and neglect of public officers." Browne completed his report on September 4.[65]

Bailey issued his report to Commissioner of Indian Affairs Charles E. Mix in November 1858, concluding that the system was more flawed than the individuals managing it. He was not prepared to say that the plan introduced by Beale "could not, under certain conditions, be successfully applied in practice, but it must be admitted that the experiment has so far proved a lamentable failure." The reservations were "government alms-houses, where an inconsiderable number of Indians are insufficiently fed and scantily clothed, at an expense wholly disproportioned to the benefit conferred. There is nothing in the system, as now practiced, looking to the permanent improvement of the Indian, or tending in any way to his social, intellectual or moral elevation."[66]

After reviewing the condition of the reservations in northern California, Bailey discussed the nature of the system itself. He questioned whether the reservation "civilized" the Indian:

> By the term civilization, then, as applied to the Indian, I understand not the mere teaching him to ape the dress and habits of the white

> man, or even the instructing him in the rudiments of mechanical and agricultural knowledge, but the planting in his mind the germ of some idea which shall be self-developing, and which in its development shall lift him out of the slough where he now wallows. It implies the teaching him, practically, the "immense superiority of a fixed over a roving life," and the dignity of labor, and this not so much by ministering to his physical appetites as a reward for labor done, as by enabling him to apprehend how labor, properly applied, will procure for him the objects of his desire. It might, perhaps, more briefly express the idea by saying he must be taught to use his reason for his own improvement. The system does not civilize the Indian in this sense; scarcely, indeed, in any sense. Some few of them, it is true, are taught to plough, to sow, to reap, to handle an axe, and the like, but they are not taught the use of this knowledge. They learn the thing but not the reason of it, and therefore it makes no permanent impression and leads to nothing.[67]

Beale's plan was flawed, continued Bailey, because it was "not in the nature of things that one should work for another as he would for himself; and it was not to be expected that a salaried superior of a farm should manage it as profitable as the owner of it." According to Bailey's view of history, in the Spanish missions Indian labor produced surpluses belonging to the institutions and thus to the laborers themselves. Reciprocity, therefore, had been the key to success. Dubious that the federal government could ever establish a similar kind of reciprocity, he nevertheless opposed abandoning the reservation system, "chiefly because of the difficulty of devising a substitute."[68]

To Bailey the Indians of California fell into three categories, each one deserving unique treatment. Because the Indians residing in the Coast Range north and east of Mendocino in Northern California supposedly would be secure for years before "the wave of civilization" swept over their domain, they should be left alone. Because many of those residing at Owens Lake, Tejón, and south of the Tehachapi Mountains in Southern California cultivated the soil, the government should secure to them the lands they then occupied. Visiting agents would provide them with seeds, agricultural equipment, and some clothing, but the assistance should be limited to supplying deficiencies; otherwise, they would lose all self-reliance. Because the Indians residing in the Sacramento and San Joaquin Valleys occupied lands coveted or claimed by whites they should be removed to a reservation and put to work.[69]

Until such reforms were introduced, the present system should continue but with modifications: "The labor should be performed exclusively by the Indians, and no more white men should be employed than are necessary to instruct and control them; no white person should be permitted to come upon the reserve, and the Indians should never be permitted to leave it; such of the Indians as desire it should have assigned them a small field, the product of which should be their own; and lastly they should be kept constantly occupied."[70]

Commissioner of Indian Affairs Charles E. Mix passed on some of Bailey's recommendations to Secretary of the Interior Jacob Thompson, including the need to reduce the number of whites employed on the reservations. No more reservations should be established than absolutely necessary, but if new ones were founded, they should be situated where the Indians would be temporarily isolated from whites. Expanding on Bailey's view that the Indians should be given plots of land to raise their own crops, Mix called for a program anticipating the General Allotment Act of 1887, which dissolved the common lands on many reservations into individual allotments. A year after a reservation was founded, he wrote, "the lands should be divided and assigned to the Indians in severalty, every one being required to remain on his own tract and to cultivate it, no persons being employed for them except the requisite mechanics to keep their tools and implements in repair, and such as may be necessary, for a time, to teach them how to conduct their agricultural operations and to take care of their stock. They should also have the advantage of well conducted manual labor schools for the education of their youth in letters, habits of industry, and a knowledge of agriculture and the simpler mechanic arts." Mix also recommended that an apprenticeship system be established for Indian orphans and other children of both sexes. For some years they would be placed in homes of "humane persons," provided state laws authorized such activity, where they would be taught trades and occupations.[71] Secretary Thompson, in turn, passed on some of Mix's recommendations to the president, in particular those calling for the reduction in the number of whites working on the reservations and the assigning of allotments to individuals and families.[72]

The reports by Bailey, Mix, and Thompson did not go unchallenged in California. On January 13, 1859 the editors of the *San Francisco Weekly National* wrote that Godard Bailey, "under the imposing garb of special agent.... fires a shot in the shape of an annihilatory report. This is followed up by Mr. Mix, Indian Commissioner, who endorses Baily's [sic] views. Next the Secretary of the Interior, in his last annual communication to the President, declares the whole arrangement wrong and signifies his determination of carry out a radical and entire change of policy." The editors quoted the parts of the secretary's report calling for a reduction in the number of white employees on the reservations and for the assignment to each Indian family of a plot of land. If there were too many white employees, they should be dismissed, but to employ only Indians was at present impracticable: "The California Indian is perhaps the most inferior of all the North American races. Reared in our salubrious climate—procuring abundant food in the shape of acorns, roots, game and fish, without labor—inured, in fact, to no hardship—he has become a weak, degenerate creature, both physically and mentally. He is a child in moral restrain and mental capacity, with the animal passions, propensities and appetites of the man. He, therefore, needs a master, and one too who can compel him to obey. Leave it all optional with him, and he will labor not, neither will he spin. There must be employed a sufficient white force to work in the fields with them, and if necessary inflict occasional chastisement." The editors went on to claim that allotting land to families would not work because the Indians were gregarious: "These allotments would soon be left to neglect and ruin. The Secretary's plan, therefore, if attempted to be put into immediate practice, would be a virtual abandonment of the Reservation system and a dispersion of the Indians among our people to butcher and be butchered." The present system, therefore, should continue "until some one competent can make a thorough investigation of the whole matter, and give the details of a better plan."[73]

A better plan had been put forward by the first Indian agents, claimed O. M. Wozencraft in January 1859. Had the eighteen treaties been ratified, he asserted in a letter to the *Weekly National*, "there probably would have been less contention and trouble, for the Reservation labor system which we proposed, and wished to adopt, was one of economy—one by which the Indians should be taught and made to support themselves." The plan of the agents limited expenditures for seeds, implements, and stock and limited the number of persons assigned to the reservations. It was not "too late to recur to first principles, and adopt the neglected work of the Commissioners, by which a just and economical administration of affairs may be carried out."[74]

Others clung to the notion that a version of the old removal policy could be introduced to California. Transporting the Indians to Indian Territory would be impractical, but there were lands much closer where they could be relocated. On January 25, 1859 the editors of the *San Francisco Daily Herald* declared the reservation system a costly failure. As long as Indians remained in the vicinity of whites or in areas that whites were likely to penetrate, hostilities would continue. Thus, the United States should purchase Baja California from Mexico, a land supposedly of mild climate, fertile valleys, and abundant game: "The different sea ports of Lower California could be made available as military posts, and for the purpose of carrying on a trade with the Indians; but no white resident whatever should be allowed to possess any land beyond a stated distance from such towns. The whole interior of the country should be exclusively dedicated to the Indians, and all outside interference strictly prohibited, except through the regularly constituted authorities appointed by Government. The nature of the Government ought to approach as near the patriarchal as possible, and it should be administered by proper agents, supported and backed by military power." Admitting that their plan was "open to many objections," the editors offered it "in its crude shape to invite a close analysis of its merits, and a free public discussion of its expediency."[75]

A few months later, the *San Diego Herald* continued the discussion by referring to the policy of removal introduced in the 1830s by President Andrew Jackson. Because of the incessant wars occurring between Indians still remaining within the limits of the United States and whites, he "recommended to Congress the removal of the Indians to the Territory set apart for their future home West of the Mississippi. This policy was dictated on the ground that it would be a saving to the nation, promotive of peace in the white settlements, and be more conducive to the safety and better security of the Indian race from the depredations of lawless white men.... The policy pursued on the Atlantic side should find equal favor on the Pacific. Lower California should be purchased and set apart as an Indian Reservation or Territorial Government, if that would answer best, for the numerous Indian tribes who now inhabit large districts of the country in this State, Oregon and Washington Territory." Supposedly, the federal government could acquire Baja California without difficulty and at a very low price.[76] Although the federal government would not purchase land outside the United States for Indian use, it continued to set aside land inside California supposedly for exclusive Indian occupancy.

CHAPTER XXII

The Indian Farms

In September 1854, a year after the abandonment of the Indian farm Edward F. Beale had founded on the San Joaquin River, Superintendent of Indian Affairs Thomas Henley established a more permanent one in the same area. Henley leased at one thousand dollars per year land on the Fresno River owned by Lorenzo Vinsonhaler.[1] The editors of the *Mariposa Chronicle* had no doubt that the farm would induce many Indians "to adopt some of the habits of civilization and eventually end in their permanent removal to the Tejon Reservation, beyond the influence of the white population, the better portion of whom desire their removal to some place where they may live by themselves, undisturbed by the vices of a class found in every country, who pander to the corruptions of the Indians for their own base and selfish purposes."[2]

On the five hundred acres of enclosed land on the Fresno Farm, as the property was known, Henley thought grain could be grown at less cost than if purchased, and because Indians would perform all the labor expenses would be insignificant.[3] At $150 per month Henley hired D. A. Enyart as special Indian agent and placed him in charge of the farm. He also employed a farmer, a cook, three farmhands, and, at one hundred dollars per month, Lorenzo Vinsonhaler as assistant overseer. Vinsonhaler thus received both rent and a salary.[4] He was also part owner of the store where goods were purchased for the Indians.[5]

Enyart visited Fort Miller in October, encouraging Lieutenant Lucien Loeser, the fort's commander, to induce the Pitkachi residing in the area to remove to the farm. Loeser could not act without orders from his superiors, and the Indians he spoke with, then engaged in salmon fishing and mining, exhibited no interest in relocating. The water at the farm, they told the Lieutenant, was stagnant and contained no fish. The area was generally unhealthy, many Indians having died there.[6] A river in name only, the Fresno flowed over a sandy bed, usually ankle deep, for only two or three months of the year.[7]

Nevertheless, Enyart still hoped the Pitkachi, led by Tomquit and numbering some 250 persons, would relocate. Convinced that the farm could carry a population of two thousand, he intended to bring in one thousand Indians residing on the Stanislaus, Tuolumne, and Merced rivers. By early November 440 Indians had moved onto the farm. The Chauchila under Naiyakqua and Poholeel numbered only 30 persons, but the Chukchansi totaled 220, the Pohonichi 90, and Potoyanti 100. Because food was in short supply, Enyart encouraged the Indians to collect what few acorns were still available and to hunt, fish, and mine.[8]

Upon returning from San Francisco in late January 1855, Enyart issued twenty sacks of wheat to the Indians. He also gave the women calico, needles, and thread and the boys and men each a shirt.[9] At the time the Indians had nearly completed the fence around the wheat and barley fields and had constructed a large stable and two outbuildings. Three hundred acres of wheat and 350 of barley had been sown, and vegetables had been planted in the rich bottomlands. Growing in the garden were turnips, cabbage, lettuce, potatoes, onions, and peas. Enyart told Henley that he intended to assign a plot of land to each of the four groups and provide them with vegetable seeds. He would manage with only a few white workers, "as the Indians take pride in being allowed to do any work by themselves."[10]

At the end of January, when the winter rains failed to commence, a group of Indians began a rainmaking ceremony. "I hope it may have the desired effect," Enyart told Henley. "They are confident they can make it rain."[11] On February 1 it rained from 10 a.m. to the evening but then abruptly stopped. The rainmakers blamed the phenomenon on a shaman working against them. They remained, however, fully confident in their power to make it rain. On the twenty-eighth, the heavens opened up.[12]

In mid-April Henley reported to Commissioner of Indian Affairs George W. Manypenny that the four hundred Indians on the farm were "in a good condition and are very well contented" and that the five hundred acres of wheat and barley under cultivation looked "more flourishing" than the crops at Tejón. In preparation for their removal to a more suitable location, he intended to relocate several thousand Indians living in a one-hundred-mile radius to the farm. The policy designed to provide food and clothing only to those who worked had "induced the chief of this tribe to solicit labor for all his people that they might be clothed and fed alike."[13]

With sickles and scythes, in mid-May one hundred Indians labored in the fields. By the time the upper field of barley was harvested, the lower field was expected to be ripe, and when that field was harvested, the wheat would be ready. For sustenance the Indian workers relied on horsemeat. The Indian hunter hired by Enyart killed three wild horses on the sixteenth and was expected to provide fresh meat for the Indian workers throughout the harvest.[14]

An incident at the end of the month severely strained relations between the Indian workers and white employees. George Williams, the head farmer, had on several occasions roughed up some of the Indians for refusing to work or for disobeying orders, and the Indians had decided to resist, even kill him, if he attempted to punish them again. Prepared for such a possibility several Indians showed up for work armed with clubs. When Williams seized an Indian boy who had disobeyed an order and attempted to take him into his house to inflict some kind of punishment, twenty Indians rushed the white man, beating him severely over the head and shoulders with their clubs. Williams fought back with a club he wrestled from one of them and ran for his life. Dashing around a corner of his house, he encountered an Indian armed with a rifle. He wrenched the weapon from the Indian, initially wielding it as a club against his pursuers. When about to be overpowered he fired, killing an Indian.[15]

Williams fled to Fort Miller where he informed Lieutenant Loeser and Enyart of the situation. Immediately, Loeser sent Lieutenant Romeyn Ayers and a detachment of dragoons to the farm. The soldiers and Enyart arrived at five o'clock in the evening and learned that thirty Indians armed with bows and arrows had visited the farm searching for Williams. When informed that he had fled to Fort Miller, they returned to the villages. Lorenzo Vinsonhaler visited one of the villages, but the only leader to speak to him ordered him to leave. He complied. Enyart and the fort's surgeon also visited the village and persuaded some fifteen leaders to accompany them to the farm for a meeting. Halfway to their destination, however, an Indian called Ghalvo broke and ran. The other leaders also fled. Enyart fired two shots in the air, and when the Indians refused to halt, he fired a third into the leg of an Indian and took him prisoner. The white men captured three other Indians.[16]

Lieutenant Ayres and his detachment followed the San Joaquin River some eight miles upstream only to realize that the Indians had entered the Sierra Nevada. Had they not stolen six horses on their flight, Ayers would have called off the search, convinced that the Indians would return on their own. Unwilling, however, to let Indians abscond with horses belonging to whites, Ayres, supported by more men from Fort Miller and with fifteen days' rations and accompanied by Enyart, pursued the Indians for some twenty miles. Realizing that further flight was fruitless, the Indians sent word that they would come in, and all but a small party led by Ghalvo returned to the farm with the stolen horses. Still intent upon apprehending Ghalvo, the main body of the command went in one direction. Ayers, two soldiers, and Enyart searched another area and unexpectedly came upon the Indians, capturing all except Ghalvo, who might have been wounded from the three shots fired at him. Unsuccessful in their day-long search for him, the whites returned to Fort Miller.[17] In a letter to the San Joaquin Republican, Enyart described the recent events and claimed the disturbance was "the best thing that ever happened to the place. The Indians now know that if they commit depredations they will be pursued and punished. We have more at work now than usual, and they work much better."[18]

By this time Indians were hard at work on another farm. Early in April 1855 Superintendent Henley, on his way north from the Tejón Reservation, had paused on the Kings River. Settlers sought the removal of the local Indians, and the Indians sought protection from the settlers. Henley took immediate steps to assert governmental authority. "Preparatory therefore to bringing them under subjection," he noted in a letter to Commissioner Manypenny, "I have sent up from the Tejon a team of mules, a wagon loaded with flour, plows etc. and have directed an agent to plant at one of the Rancherias a field of corn—say fifty or one hundred acres."[19] William Campbell, received $125 per month to manage the Indians residing along the river.[20] Henley may not have known that Campbell had operated a store and ferry on the former Kings River Reservation. When ordered off the reservation by Chief Watoka in July 1852, Campbell recruited miners to attack the chief's village. They killed at least eleven Indians. The leader of the miners, Walter Harvey, later killed James Savage in an argument over the attack.

Campbell's jurisdiction became known as the Kings River Farm, and shortly after undertaking his new responsibilities, Campbell took Pasqual, who was chief of the Wechihit and the most prominent leader residing along the Kings River, and fifteen chiefs of groups residing between the river and Tejón to the reservation to meet Henley. By the time the delegation arrived, however, Henley had departed. The Indians were disappointed at not meeting the superintendent.[21]

In mid-April the Indians associated with the farm planted one hundred acres in corn, pumpkins, melons, and vegetables. A short time later, they enclosed two hundred acres with a fence and dug an irrigation ditch. The initial success of the farm attracted Indians from the mountains, but Campbell rejected their request to relocate. He would accept only as many Indians as the crops would support. Campbell notified Henley in July that the crops were doing reasonably well, considering the want of water. The Indians had gleaned twenty thousand pounds of wheat, evidently from the common fields, and Campbell expected them to obtain thirty thousand more. Because the Indians under his jurisdiction residing downstream at Tulare Lake lacked food, Campbell furnished them with six thousand pounds of wheat. In about six weeks, when the acorns would be ready to harvest, he expected their condition to improve. Campbell also told Henley that lands occupied by setters residing on the big bend of the Kings River could be easily purchased and turned into a reservation.[22]

The following month Henley sent D. A. Enyart, to the Kings River to search for locations for a reservation. Enyart was concerned about the whites occupying lands below and above the Kings River Farm. Some of the lands, he told Henley, would have to be purchased. He favored the area occupied by a Mr. Lirey, who resided about five miles above the farm at the foot of the Sierra Nevada. The settlers he talked with favored the northern location, because in the event of a disturbance, the Indians could easily disperse into the mountains and not pass through and possibly plunder white settlements. Lirey possessed over nine hundred acres, two hundred of which were under cultivation. The fields, claimed Enyart, would produce more grain than would the five hundred acres at the Fresno Farm. Because Lirey would sell if offered about two thousand dollars, Enyart recommended to Henley that the land be purchased immediately and turned into a reservation. He estimated that most of the one thousand to fifteen hundred Indians residing along the river would relocate. He predicted that some of the Monos living far upriver in the mountains would also move to the farm.[23]

Enyart's efforts were for naught, and in October Henley replaced him with M. B. Lewis as special agent of the Fresno Farm. Shortly, Lewis persuaded the Indians residing on the Merced, Chowchilla, Fresno, and San Joaquin rivers to assemble at the farm for a council. At the meeting, the Indian leaders agreed to accept the authority of Lewis and to leave as permanent residents of the farm three hundred of their followers. Consisting of Chukchansi, Chauchila, Huechi, and the remnants of other groups, they were to perform all the labor required for the common good.[24] By mid-December over sixteen thousand pounds of flour of good quality had been produced at the mill that was located near Vinsonhaler's premises. The wheat was hauled in wagons to the mill; the flour returned the same way. The Indians also had planted 150 acres of wheat, 3 in turnips and 2 in beets, cabbage, radishes, and other vegetables. "All is peace and quietness with the Indians," Lewis told Henley, but he did not know how to deal with those congregating at the farm. Claiming to have labored there the past season, they demanded a share of the harvest.[25]

Recently, several Indians had returned from the Tejón Reservation with two of the four or more horses they had stolen from some of the Indians residing there. Samuel Bishop sent a message to Lewis, requesting that he arrest the horse thieves and turn them over to the civil authorities or send them, under military escort, to the reservation. Because either course would entail time, trouble, expense, and perhaps disrupt the operations of the farm, Lewis refused. Besides, he told Henley, the horses probably had been stolen from Indians who obtained them in the same way. But Lewis intended to "give the boys a severe reprimand, and put them to hard and constant labor."[26] A few weeks later Indians from the farm, while hunting wild horses, killed and butchered two horses belonging to two white men. The owners presented to Lewis claims of sixty and seventy dollars.[27] Lewis forwarded the claims to Thomas Henley and recommended that they be honored.[28]

By mid-January 1856, the plowing and sowing of the barley field had been completed and the wheat had come up, but the vegetables had failed because of freezing weather.[29] In mid-March the wheat and barley were growing well enough for Lewis to expect a fair crop.[30] But the first planting of turnips failed in April for want of moisture although the second and third sowings showed promise. Squirrels had harmed the corn, but most of the vegetables were doing well.[31] To irrigate the crops Indians began constructing a dam on, and an irrigation ditch from, the Fresno River.[32] Although completed by the beginning May, the ditch failed to carry enough water to sufficiency irrigate the wheat and barley, which Lewis anticipated would be short and thus tedious to harvest.[33] Still, he reported in mid-month that the irrigation ditch "affords a beautiful small stream of water, and enables me to irrigate the potatoe patch thoroughly, and I am now in hopes of fair crop of potatoes."[34] Because the ground was dotted with gopher and squirrel holes, breaks in the ditch occurred almost daily. Lewis thought the ground moisture in the forty acres of bottomland along the Fresno River would be sufficient to support the barley the Indians had planted there. Before realizing his mistake and cutting another ditch to the field, the barley had perished.[35]

Despite the difficulties of growing crops on the Fresno Farm, Lewis, in his report to Henley of July 22, 1856, calculated that over one thousand Indians "live on, visit, and recognize this place as their home and headquarters."[36] At the end of September 1,980 Indians were associated with the Fresno and Kings River farms, the two farms of the Fresno Indian Agency. Included were the 325 Indians residing along the upper Kings River, consisting of the Choinimni under Watoka and the Wechihit under Pasqual; the 300 Indians living along the lower Kings River and Tulare Lake; and the 225 Gawia in the Four Creeks.[37] Providing so many Indians with provisions was, according to Henley, beyond the financial means of the federal government. Consequently, he instructed Lewis to encourage the Indians under the jurisdiction of the agency to maintain their traditional modes of subsistence and recommended that white men accompany and assist them. Lewis also was to provide the Indians with horses and wagons.[38] A banner year for acorns, the Chauchila gathered large quantities on the Frenso River above Coarse Gold Gulch, as did the Mono farther upriver. The Choinimni harvested a large quantity on Watoka Creek, above the Kings River Farm. To the south along the Tule River, Indians also found acorns in abundance.[39]

In his annual report to the commissioner of Indian affairs of September 1856, Henley commented on the Indian Farms: "Owing to the difficulty of procuring a suitable location for a reservation in the central portion of the State, no permanent selection has yet been made; but in order to provide for the Indians according to the intentions of the government, land has been rented at Fresno and King's rivers, and the Indians collected and subsisted at these points in the same manner as upon permanent reservations." Henley was confident "that, by industry, energy, and judicious management, we shall be enabled to provide for them in such a way as to prevent starvation, and preserve the peace of the country."[40]

To flush out a variety of animals, including fowl, Indians had long practiced the art of burning, especially during the dry season. In fact, the whites called the area from the Four Creeks to the Kings River the "burnt district" because much of it was covered in potash.[41] On threat of severe punishment, settlers prohibited the Indians from setting fires. When, in July 1856 along the Kings River, three Indians defied the order, whites killed one and forced his companions to flee. M. B. Lewis commented on the act: "The justification of this unexpected and rash treatment towards these Indians for the exercise of a privilege which they have been allowed from their infancy, it is rather hard to explain to them."[42]

Other sources of food were still available. In August three Indians cut loose three horses tied near the house of Elisha Paterson, who resided on the river, one firing on the settler when he went to investigate. As Patterson retreated to his house, the Indians fled but with only one horse. William Campbell, agent of the Kings River Farm, assumed that the Choinimni, led by Watoka, who resided upstream from the farm, were responsible for the theft. He gave the Indians four days to deliver the horse and thieves to him. When the time had expired, he placed Watoka, thirty-six of his fighting men, and two other chiefs under arrest and put another chief, Pasco, in charge of them. Campbell threatened to hang them if the horse and thieves were not delivered.[43]

The night before their supposed execution, Watoka and the other chiefs escaped, taking with them some of Campbell's wheat, barley, and other property. Joined by men from other villages, Watoka and his followers retreated into the mountains. When twenty settlers located the Indians,

Table 8. Indians Associated with the Fresno Farm, 1856

Group	*Location*	*Number*
Chauchila	Fresno River	125
Cheneche (joined with some Chukchansi)	Fresno River	80
Chuckchansi	Fresno River	275
Mono	San Joaquin River (headwaters)	250
Nukchu (and remnant	Chowchilla (headwaters)	75
of the Yosemite)	Fresno River	
Pitkachi	San Joaquin River (Fort Miller)	100
Pohonichi	Fresno River	100
Potoyanti	Merced River	100
Tauhalame	Tuolumne River	100
Total		1,205

Source: Adapted from M. B. Lewis to Thomas Henley, Fresno Indian Farm, July 22, 1856, *Annual Report of the Commissioner of Indian Affairs for the Year 1856,* 252–54.

they were met with volleys of arrows. The whites charged the Indians on foot, driving them into a rocky area and killing five. One white man was wounded. The Americans confiscated six horses belonging to the Indians and all the wheat they had taken.[44] The settlers scoured the area for Indians and on August 13 burned all the property found at an abandoned village located twelve miles south of Fort Miller. Alerted to the pending attack, the Indians had fled to the fort for protection before the whites arrived.[45] Later the son of a Mono chief delivered Patterson's horse to Campbell, explaining that it had been stolen by Indians from the other side of the Sierra Nevada. Although Watoka was "entirely exculpated," noted Campbell in a letter to Henley, the whites refused to return the horses they had taken from the Indians.[46]

In late August or early September, Campbell found the Indians in the mountains in a destitute condition. Watoka was willing to return but feared the settlers would annihilate his people. A short time later he arrived on the San Joaquin River near Fort Miller, seeking peace with the whites. Preferring to live near the Kings River where acorns were plentiful, he would nevertheless relocate to wherever the government wanted.[47] Late in October Watoka and his people returned to their villages near the river.[48]

As whites occupied lands downstream at Tulare Lake, the Tachi and

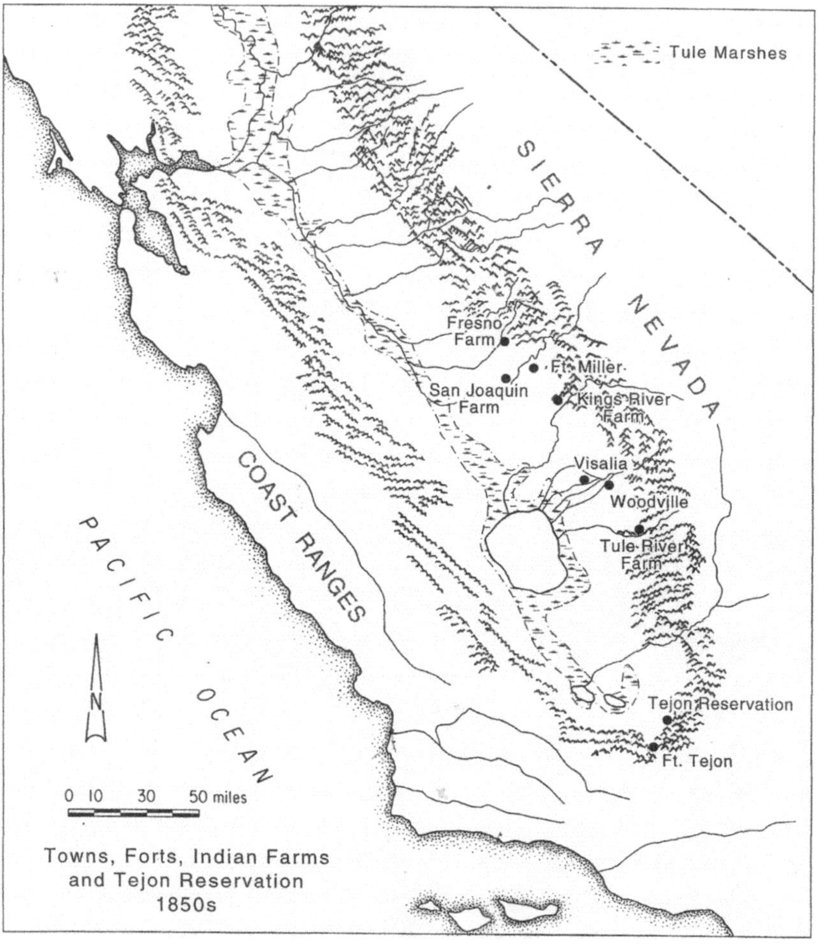

Nutunutu stole their stock, especially hogs and cattle.[49] In October 1857 thirty-five settlers sent a petition to M. B. Lewis, suggesting that the Tachi and Nutunutu be relocated. Because most of the area had been purchased, they saw no reason for leaving Indians "on lands devoted to grazing and farming." They understood that as their stock increased the Indians' food supply decreased, but warned that unless the Indians were removed "it will become necessary for the people to act and protect their property as best they can."[50] Lewis sent the petition and a letter to Henley.[51] The superintendent, in turn, told Lewis that he wanted to assure the whites that it was his "desire to rid them of this population as soon as possible," but Lewis was to remove the Indians to the Fresno Farm only when they could be provided with food.[52] Henley forwarded the petition to the commissioner of Indian affairs and in an accompanying letter emphasized that the money he had requested for the following fiscal year must be appropriated if he were to remove the Indians from the lower Kings River. Henley recommended that they be taken to San Francisco and sent by ship to the Mendocino Reservation in northern California.[53] No action was taken on his request.

The Fresno Farm was hardly in a condition to accommodate additional residents. By mid-1857 one hundred of the two hundred acres planted in wheat had failed, and the remainder promised only about five bushels per acre. Of the two hundred acres planted in barley, seventy had been cut for hay, ten had failed, and the rest suggested a yield of about eight bushels per acres. The garden consisted of two acres in potatoes, two in corn, one in onions, two in cabbages, and three in beans, peas, and melons, but the yield was uncertain. Four white men resided on the farm: Lewis, a carpenter, a farmer, and a herdsman.[54]

The remnants of only three groups permanently lived on the farm: the Chauchila, Chukchansi, and the Heuchi. A few Pohonichi also were in residence, but most of them were located at the headwaters of the Fresno. Lewis told Henley in August that the Indians had "conducted themselves in a peaceable and becoming manner towards both employees and citizens. They have also made fair progress in learning the use of all kinds of agricultural implements, and have acquired quite a knowledge of that kind of agricultural pursuits best calculated to enable them to sustain themselves in case they should hereafter be thrown on their own resources." Those not residing permanently on the farm worked for the settlers and "have cheerfully followed the good example set by those on the farm." He knew of no thefts committed by Indians during the year.[55]

In November, Lieutenant LaRhett L. Livingston asked Lewis to relocate to the Fresno Farm the Indians residing near Fort Miller. Only a few Indians would require total support, but all needed to "be removed from causes that are now fast destroying them." Livingston was certain that Henley, if notified of the situation, would honor his request.[56] Lewis told Livingston that he had no objection to bringing the Indians to the farm but questioned whether it would improve their condition. Provisions could be provided only to those who were sick or unable to work. The Indians already on the farm comprised a full workforce.[57] When thirty-one Monos arrived from the mountains early in January 1858, seeking blankets and clothing, Lewis gave only a few items to their chief who was ill.[58]

Bad weather further weakened the Indians' economic condition. Between December 1, 1857 and March 24, 1858, only two showers of note occurred. By the end of April, only the irrigated field suggested a satisfactory crop of wheat. Little hope was held for the upper un-irrigated field, located near the Fresno River. The barley sown at a low elevation failed to reach sufficient heights to cut even for hay although that planted at a higher level showed promise.[59] Emphasizing the positive in an August letter to Henley, Lewis claimed that the farm had produced sufficient food to see the Indians through the fall and winter seasons.[60] But the following month he encouraged all the Indians on the farm to gather acorns and promised assistance in transporting the harvest.[61] In his annual report of September 1858, Superintendent Henley noted that the crops at the Fresno Farm were "ordinary" and that the Indians "will be as usual compelled to rely to a considerable extent on wild foods for their subsistence."[62]

Special Treasury Agent J. Ross Browne arrived at the farm the following month. The government spent twenty or twenty-five thousand dollars per annum to maintain the Fresno Farm, he reported to the commissioner of Indian affairs, but for the past four years, it brought no benefit to the Indians. At the Kings River Farm, Browne saw no evidence that it served the Indians in any appreciable way. He observed only twenty Indians, most having departed for the mountains to gather wild foods. He learned, moreover, that Indians from the farm had recently harvested the fields of the settlers, receiving the gleanings as payment. They stored the grain in their villages, only to have it confiscated by the whites who put it in their public storehouse.[63] More than likely, the confiscation was in retribution for losing stock. In a letter to the *San Joaquin Republican* written on November 12, 1858, a settler acknowledged the Indians' dilemma but warned that the whites were prepared to take matters into their own hands: "The large number of stock in this country consumes every acorn almost as soon as it falls and keeps the grass eaten down so as to prevent its going to seed. You know the Indians main dependence is upon acorns and grass seed. Those gone, what is he to live on? What more natural that they should go to work on our own hogs or cattle, as these take from them their subsistence and afford a pleasant substitute. This may suit the Indians, but it does not suit the owners of the stock, and one thing is certain, that if the proper Indian authorities do not attend to their removal, the citizens will have to do it."[64]

No longer protected or restrained by the soldiers at Fort Miller, which in June had been largely abandoned, the settlers decided to do just that.[65] Evidently, they acted on the belief that Henley no longer sought to concentrate Indians on reservations but to scatter them in small bands over the landscape to fend for themselves.[66] In mid-November settlers rounded up some two hundred Indians, nearly all the Nutunutu and Wimilchi and about half of the Tachi and Wowol, most of whom were women, children, and invalids. Seventy Tachi and Wowol men eluded capture by fleeing into the tule swamps. The prisoners were taken to the farm of L. A. Whitmore.[67]

Gregorio, the Tachi chief, informed Lewis about the situation.[68] Lewis was convinced that only through the intervention of Gregorio had the Indians refrained from attacking the settlers.[69] In a letter to Whitmore, delivered by Gregorio, Lewis explained that he could not adequately provide for the Indians if brought to the Fresno Farm and pleaded with him to treat them "with humanity and moderation. It would seem a human calamity for those people to be forced to leave their homes and winter supplies at this time, where they have abundance of the natural products of the soil." Lewis concluded by thanking Whitmore for any assistance he might give.[70]

On November 13 a party of settlers delivered the Indians to Lewis at the Fresno Farm.[71] An individual recounted the event:

> [w]e beheld an approaching mass of humanity, very suggestive of Huns, Goths and Vandals, on a plundering excursion; but which, on nearer approach, took more the form of Falstaff's heroes, or an assemblage of malicious Georgians, at a general muster. Conjecture was rife until arriving in front of the Agency, the procession halted, and the enigma solved. A party of seven rather formidable looking Americans, were conducting an involuntary immigration of over two hundred Indians—men, women, and children, of all ages, sizes and conditions, whom they had quietly captured without bloodshed or other violence—from their homes, and hunting grounds in the vicinity of Tulare lake to this Agency....
>
> The poor creatures were really in a pitiable plight. Nearly destitute, and many of them invalids. They will be provided for, but as a people, their doom is fixed, their destiny is certainly evil.[72]

In a letter to Lewis the "formidable looking Americans" warned of further action. The Tachi, Nutunutu, and Wilmilchi had been rounded up because they killed hogs and cattle and stole provisions. Indians and a "stock growing people" could not inhabit the same country. No violence was employed in capturing them, but that was "the last time their peaceable removal will be attempted." Those who remained in the area, including the thirty neophytes who were "daring and expert marauders," had been told that they too must leave. They would be "summarily treated should they not peaceably retire."[73]

In early December, Lewis took the two hundred recently relocated Indians to the upper Kings River, where they were released to fend for themselves. Furious that Indians from downstream had been dumped in their midst and fearful they would target the four to five thousand head of cattle grazing in the area, local settlers gathered at the spot where the

Indians had been delivered and prohibited them from dispersing into the mountains. The settlers also quickly rounded up the nearby Choinimni led by Watoka and few Wechihit led by Pasqual and brought them to where the other Indians were being held.[74]

Confronting the settlers a short time later, Lewis admitted that releasing the "Lake Indians" in their midst was a mistake but refused to take charge of the Choinimni and Wechihit. The settlers insisted that the Choinimni had killed their cattle with impunity and must be relocated. Lewis offered to move the Lake Indians immediately and the others by February 1 the following year. Removing them sooner was impossible, Lewis explained, because he could not provide them food. When the settlers persisted in their demands, Lewis promised to relocate the Lake Indians to the Kings River Farm. That too was rejected, and Lewis agreed to move them across the San Joaquin River. The settlers promised to transport at their own expense those who remained and on December 20 herded 110 Indians, the sick and feeble on wagons, to the Fresno Farm, where they were turned over to Lewis' subordinates.[75] Most were Choinimni.[76]

On December 19 Lewis departed for the lower Kings River. At Whitmore's farm, the two teamsters he had sent to the area had collected all the Indians in the neighborhood except for seventeen Tachi. Many Tachi had perished from hunger and cold, and those who remained preferred to die at the lake rather than relocate. Santiago, a Nutunutu chief, long a resident on the lake near the mouth of the Kings River, also chose to stay. Ill but assisted by his family and four or five friends, Santiago remained in his sweat lodge. Lewis took the Indians, numbering some three hundred, to the south bank of the San Joaquin River, opposite the spot where the old San Joaquin Farm had been located.[77]

During November and December 1858, between five and six hundred Indians had been uprooted from their villages.[78] Unable to maintain their unity of purpose, though, the settlers made no effort to prevent some of them from returning to their homes.[79] Watoka and 190 followers returned to Watoka Creek at its juncture with the Kings River about twelve miles above the Kings River Farm. Pasqual and seventy-five persons resettled on the farm.[80] Indians on the Tejon Reservation would also find themselves subjected to an inconsistent Indian policy.

CHAPTER XXIII

Cross Purposes

In July 1854, when informed about the dismissal of Edward F. Beale as superintendent of Indian affairs, Indians on the Tejón Reservation suspended work to gather in groups to discuss the situation. They could not understand why the man who had brought them together and provided them with seeds had been taken from them and a man with no interest in their welfare sent in his place. Some advocated abandoning the reservation for their homelands; others argued that remaining at Tejón was in their best interests.[1] Frederick Kerlin, Beale's former clerk, told B. D. Wilson in midmonth that the Indians were "very much displeased at the idea of Mr. Beale leaving them, and I think they will give 'Uncle Sam' a great deal of trouble if some steps are not taken with them."[2]

A few parties left for the mountains to gather wild plants and apparently returned a short time later.[3] But on July 14 one hundred Indians departed for Owens Lake on the east side of the Sierra Nevada.[4] Overseer Samuel Bishop and eight men caught up with them. Beale had fulfilled his promises, the Indians told Bishop, but now they did not know what was going to happen to them. The new man might be a good man, but they did not know him. Prepared to fight to remain at large, the Indians forced Bishop to return to the reservation empty-handed. Subsequently, other Indians left the reservation, taking with them large quantities of wheat, which they cached in the mountains.[5] The delegation of Nisenan Indians from Grass Valley departed for their homeland.[6]

Recently appointed Superintendent of Indian Affairs Thomas Henley probably was unaware of the situation on the reservation until late July, when he called on Beale in Los Angeles. As soon as possible, Beale promised to turn over all government books, money, and property. Once Henley had posted a bond and took the oath of office, he, Beale, and, Frederick Kerlin departed for the reservation to meet with the Indians.[7] Before the council began the Indians objected to Beale's interpreters, a white man and an Indian, apparently Alexis Godey and Raymundo. They approved of Henley's choice, Alonzo Ridley, who had resided with them before the founding of the reservation. Beale addressed the Indians, reminding them that their lives had been improved on the reservation and wishing them continued advancement. Henley was a good man, and they would like him. At the conclusion of the talk, the Indians shook Beale's hand.[8]

Henley then spoke to the Indians. For good conduct they would be rewarded; for breaking the law they would be punished. By continual industry they would procure the things they needed and thus enjoy happiness and contentment. He promised never to lie to them and expected the same courtesy in return. In two months he would return from the north with the supplies they needed; while he was gone they were to obey the white men left in charge. The leaders praised his speech and promised to obey his directions.[9] But they demanded that Samuel Bishop and Godey be removed.[10] When Henley met with the leaders again that evening, he promised to replace the two men. The leaders insisted on retaining political authority over their followers but agreed to provide laborers for reservation projects.[11]

An accounting of the property at Tejón, conducted in August 1854, indicated that the new superintendent took charge of an institution of considerable public wealth. In addition to the 1,172 domestic animals, government property included fruit trees and vines; barley, wheat, corn, and pumpkins in storage; houses for employees; and an assortment of practical items such as anvils, bedsteads, lamp wicks, nails, and wash basins.[12] But many of the articles, noted Rasey Biven, a friend of Henley's, were missing: "*A large lot of barley has been sold and delivered from the reserve. Goods belonging to the reserve have been sent away to private places.*"[13] Failing to mention the missing items in their deposition before a notary public in Los Angeles, a panel of citizens, including B. D. Wilson, Alexis Godey, and Samuel Bishop, calculated the wealth of the reservation at $981,818.[14]

Over four hundred head of cattle of dubious ownership also grazed on the reservation. They were remnants of three herds: the one John Frémont delivered to Indian Agent George Barbour in June 1852; the one Indian Agent O. M. Wozencraft transferred to Beale in November 1852; and the one Harry Edwards delivered to the San Joaquin Farm in January 1853.[15] Initially, the herds had been collected on the farm and managed by Lorenzo Vinsonhaler.[16] Beale offered to turn the cattle over to Henley, but fearing a legal entanglement he refused.[17] Nevertheless, Henley was convinced that the animals belonged to the government.[18]

Table 9. Government Stock at Tejón, 1854

Animal	*Number*
Cows	490
Yearlings and calves	350
Mules	121
Beef cattle	100
Lambs	36
Horses	34
Ewes	32
Oxen	9

Source: Adapted from Invoice of Public Property, Tejón Reservation, August 7, 1854, Office of Indian Affairs, Letters Received, 1824–81, roll 33.

Beale requested from Henley permission to keep privately owned stock on the reservation. Grazing at La Pastoría were 800 sheep and 750 goats, evidently property shared by Beale and Samuel Dummer. One or two hundred hogs belonged to Beale, and Harry Edwards owned forty-five mules and eight horses.[19] Not wanting to be discourteous to Beale and understanding the hardship removing the stock would entail, Henley granted his request. Godey and Bishop remained at La Pastoría in charge of the stock.[20] Although unwilling to take action against Beale and his friends because they were private citizens, Henley fired Dummer, a government employee, for raising stock on the reservation.[21] Regarding the practice of allowing whites to graze their animals on government property, Rasey Biven noted that the Indians "say that they have been treated as they were in the old Spanish missions. Then they were made to believe that all was common property and for their benefit, as in this instance.... It has caused great discontent among them, and of course their confidence is shaken, when they perceive that, at least one half of

Tejón Pass from the Indian Reservation. (Land case map D-1366. Courtesy of the Bancroft Library, Berkeley, Cal.)

property considered as their own, belongs to private individuals, and that their time and labor has gone to benefit others than themselves."[22]

Surplus grain planted and harvested by the Indians and some of the animals they tended were also sold for profit. In July or August 1854 Henley sold to the quartermaster at Fort Tejón twenty thousand pounds of barley at 13¢ per pound and ten mules at $200.00 per head. He also intended to supply the post with flour and fresh beef at prices yet to be determined. Henley acknowledged in a letter to Commissioner of Indian Affairs George W. Manypenny that "abuses might grow out of the practice of allowing the Superintendent to dispose of the public property at private sale," but he considered it in the best interests of the government to do so.[23] In a follow-up letter he pointed out that once the quartermaster was able to procure supplies at Los Angeles, no further sales, unless advised otherwise, would be made to the fort. But purchasing the surplus barley and flour produced at the reservation, he added, would cost the army considerably less than buying the same amount from merchants in Los Angeles and transporting it to the fort.[24]

Convinced that the affairs of the reservation were in good order, on August 11 Henley departed for San Francisco by way of the San Joaquin Valley. On his journey he visited many of the Indians residing between Tejón and the Fresno River and reported his findings in a letter to Manypenny. The fifty Indians residing on Posa Creek and the one hundred on the Kern

River could be relocated to Tejón at any time. The three hundred on the Tule River were in good condition, but they should be removed because whites were settling there. The Gawia and Wimilchi, occupying the Four Creeks and numbering five hundred, also should be removed because they interfered "with the progressive settlements of the country." Many of the one thousand Tachi, Nutunutu, Chukamina, and Telamni living along the Kings River worked for whites. Because settlers needed their labor, Henley opposed removal. The five groups located along the San Joaquin River, including the Gashowu, Pitkachi, and Huechi, numbered four hundred and were too demoralized and diseased to be removed. They required immediate attention and assistance. The five hundred Chukchansi, Chauchila, Nukchu, Pohonichi, and another group residing along the Fresno River could easily be moved to Tejón.[25]

Upon arriving in San Francisco, Henley notified Manypenny that many of the Indians encountered spoke Spanish and had resided in the missions, where they learned to cultivate crops and construct buildings of impressive size. He also pointed out that John Sutter had built a fort in the northern San Joaquin Valley and made good use of Indian labor. "The Indians in the southern and central portions of the State are willing to labor," he wrote, "and many are anxious to avail themselves of the privilege of settling upon the reservations." There they would receive food and clothing "to supply their immediate wants," but Henley opposed issuing provisions and clothing to Indians at their present locations, because it would make them indolent. He concluded his report by acknowledging that subjugating the Indians, "according to the plan now in progress, is a task which will require time, energetic and assiduous industry, and prudent and judicious management; without which, more than partial success need not be anticipated."[26]

Henley told Beale in mid-September that he had "entire confidence in the practicability of the plan of subsisting the Indians, in California, on your reservations, by the proceeds of their own labor…. Your selection of a reservation at the Tejon, I regard as the very best that could have been made in the State. The progress which has already been made there I consider the best evidence of the success of the plan."[27] Henley also wrote to Samuel Bishop, noting that he had received his letter of resignation of September 20. Ever the gentleman Henley praised Bishop for his "honesty and integrity" but accepted his resignation because he had been instructed to reduce the number of individuals employed on the reservation.[28] Bishop and Godey, however, remained on the payroll until the end of September.[29] Shortly after Henley dispensed with their services, they put in a crop at La Pastoría, but most of it perished because of lack of rain.[30]

In San Francisco in October, Henley met J. Ross Browne, a special treasury agent sent to California to investigate the accounts of Beale. Henley and Browne examined Beale's receipts and vouchers and in a letter to Manypenny emphasized that Beale had "afforded us every facility necessary for a complete and satisfactory examination of his accounts, and expressed his readiness to remain here, should we desire his presence."[31] When Beale sailed for the East Coast on October 16, the *San Francisco Daily Herald* reported that Henley and Browne had found his accounts to be in order: "Mr. Beale goes to Washington with such proofs of the fidelity of his stewardship as will exact from the Government an acknowledgment that he was removed without cause. That business accomplished, he returns immediately to California, which is now forever hereafter his home."[32]

On October 18 Henley and Browne sailed to San Pedro and continued on to Tejón. Browne spoke with Bishop and Godey about the four hundred head of cattle of questionable ownership located on the reservation. Browne suggested that they transfer the herd to the government and thus relieve themselves and Beale of any liability. Bishop refused to turn over the animals without Beale's permission. After consulting with Browne, Henley proposed holding the animals in trust until Beale released them to the government. Because it would violate his agreement with Beale, Bishop refused, but he offered to give a reasonable security for their safekeeping until ownership was determined. Neither Browne nor Henley had the authority to take securities, so the offer was rejected. Browne told Bishop that legal proceedings would be taken to ensure that the animals remained on the reservation. There would be no need to pursue that course, retorted Bishop, because he had no intention of removing the animals. When Browne suggested to Henley that he take legal action to secure the stock, the superintendent said he would refer the matter to the Indian Office.[33]

Browne also instructed Bishop and Godey not to increase the number of privately owned animals grazing and the amount of private crops growing at La Pastoría. They were to vacate the reservation as soon as it was convenient. Bishop and Godey agreed to leave but not until the spring, when they could make the proper arrangements. In his report to Commissioner Manypenny, Browne explained that "this notification was not given in an unfriendly spirit, or from any want of confidence in the propriety of their future conduct towards the Indians, under the new Superintendent; but because it appeared to me improper that any white persons but those in public employ, or any property but such as belonged to the government should be on the reservation."[34]

Practical considerations also shaped Browne's views. Privately owned animals should not be pastured on the reservation, because as they increased in numbers, it would be difficult to distinguish them from public stock. Told that all the property on the reservation was for their benefit, the Indians might not understand why any of it should be sold, killed, or removed for the benefit of others. The more time employees spent managing private stock, the less time they spent working for the government. No matter how "small these private interests might be in the beginning, it would be difficult to determine the extent to which the practice might be carried,

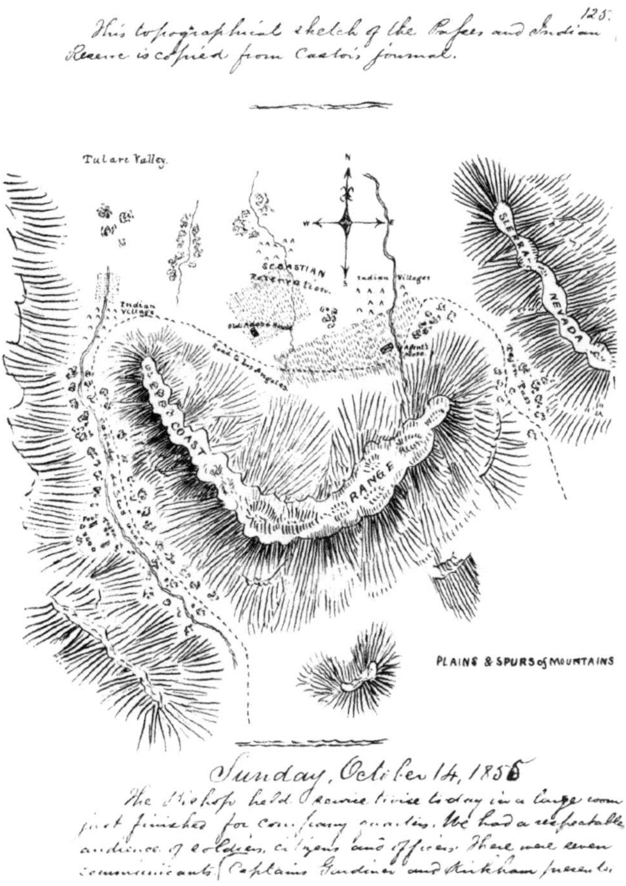

Topographical Sketch of the Passes and Indian Reserve. (This item is reproduced by permission of the Huntington Library, San Marino, California.)

should it once be established; and that it was better for the public interests that no privilege of the kind should be permitted."[35]

After a brief stay on the reservation, Browne departed for Los Angeles where, apparently, he called on B. D. Wilson.[36] Beale had informed Wilson that Browne would be contacting him: "I beg you will render him every assistance in your power, and endeavor to make his visit to your city agreeable." Because Browne would require information on a variety of subjects, Wilson should "afford him all that he requires."[37] In his report to Manypenny of January 22, 1855, Browne absolved Beale of any wrongdoing. But he was troubled that Beale had created two reservations in the Tejón area: "This was evidently in conflict with the intention of the law which was to distribute these reservations over different parts of the country, so as to afford as much benefit as possible to the different tribes inhabiting localities remote from each other." Concentrating and managing so many Indians in one location would be expensive and difficult.[38]

Beale wrote to Wilson the same month, complaining that the Indian Office could not admit it had wronged him, even though his accounts were found to be in order. For some unknown reason he blamed Browne and Henley for his problems. They were "just about a match for each other, and my feelings of contempt for both are equal."[39] A short time later, Frederick Kerlin told Wilson that "all our accounts have passed, and all the attempts to injure Mr. Beale's reputation have been unable to justify any of the slanderous assertions put forward."[40]

Well aware that Beale had been removed, in part, because he invested too much money in one reservation, Henley intended to cut costs whenever possible. When he took charge of the Tejón Reservation, the policy was to butcher for the Indian and white residents twenty-one beeves per week. Henley immediately reduced the distributions to one beef per day and later to one every other day, providing just enough meat to support the employees and the Indians who labored. The meat was given to the village captains to distribute, a move which caused some dissatisfaction among the Indians.[41] By January 1855 he had increased the allotment back to one beef per day. But he had "succeeded better than I expected in stopping the allowance of beef to the Indians who do not labor," he explained to Manypenny. "I am confident to the correctness of this policy and shall rigidly pursue it as far as it can possibly be done."[42]

At the end of 1854, 970 acres were under cultivation: 20 in corn, 202 in barley, and 748 in wheat.[43] As soon as the rains, which were late, commenced, the Indians intended to plow and sow an additional five hundred acres in wheat. Henley thought the crops would be sufficient to support all those relocating to the reservation the following year.[44] Henley visited the reservation again in late March or early April 1855, informing Manypenny that the recent rains had produced healthy crops. A small mill driven by mules produced chopped wheat which made a "very good and substantial food," with which the Indians were "very well satisfied." Soon the Indians would break new ground for next year's crops, which could be sown anytime during the fall to be ready for the winter rains.[45] By mid-May, however, even though it had rained from time to time on all the lands adjoining the reservation, all but two hundred acres of the wheat had been ruined for lack of water.[46]

The following month Henley sent Vicente, chief of the Tejoneños, to San Francisco. At sea he was forced to sleep on deck, on land in the yard or outbuilding of his host, George Henley, the superintendent's son. Instead of meeting with representatives of the government, as promised, he was largely ignored and subsisted on the bag of piñon nuts he brought with him. Upon disembarking at San Pedro in mid-July, Vicente recounted his trip to the editors of the *Southern Californian*, who noted that he was "deeply chagrined" at the treatment received.[47]

Shortly after Vicente returned to Tejón, Henley assigned a new subagent to the reservation. Previously, he had replaced William Lauius, the first subagent with John Jones of Los Angeles, perhaps because Lauius had illegally sold a government blanket to an Indian woman named Louisa.[48] On July 1 he replaced Jones with Alonzo Ridley.[49] The *Los Angeles Star* praised the latest appointment, claiming that it "gives great satisfaction to the Indians, and also to the men that are employed there.... The utmost order and economy is exercised by the new agent, which is truly gratifying to those who feel a sympathy for the poor Indian and are anxious that he should receive that attention which was intended, when the Reserve was established."[50]

Ridley managed the reservation's business affairs and its personnel. W. Martin, clerk and commissary, controlled all goods and rations; George Henley, miller, distributed allotments of flour, grain, and meat; Charles Weicks managed the Indians in the fields; F. E. Warren and A. Frier, teamsters, ran the reaping and threshing machines and hauled the grain to storage; John Grice, millwright, oversaw all the carpentry and assisted the blacksmith, John Loham, in repairing wagons and tools; and Robert Wilson, majordomo, managed all the animals. Other employees included James McKenzie, miller, Charles Chade, harness maker, John Gotea, gardener, and David McKenzie and Page Tucker, overseers of Indian labor.[51]

Henley instructed Ridley to divide the Indian labor force into three divisions and to build an adobe house immediately for the Indian leader of each division. Ridley put Zapatero in charge of the first division. His workers were to run six plows, cultivate the barley fields, the new wheat field below his village of Tinliw, and the old wheat field. Raymundo got the second division. His men, with five plows, were to cultivate the upper half of the old field. Vicente and Chico received the third division. Their workers were to cultivate the fields at Chico's village of Mumumpea and those near the Tejón Pass.[52]

The work report for September 24 through October 1, 1855 reflected the division of labor. On the twenty-fourth, Weicks and ten Indians worked on an adobe house in Vicente's third division. Frier and eight Indians had gone to one of the nearby lakes to gather tules for roofing. Page Tucker and five Indians worked on a house in the first division. The following day eight Indians continued to construct the house in the third division, while eight women picked grapes to make vinegar. On the twenty-sixth Warren and two Indians left in a wagon for the woods to cut poles for roof beams. Weicks and nine Indians put up a partition wall in the house in the third division. Tucker and seven Indians continued work on the house in the first division. September 27 was much the same. Indians put in place the poles to support the eaves of the house in the third division. Frier and twelve Indians, men and women, departed in two wagons for the lake to cut more tules. Warren and the two Indians returned from the woods with poles. Tucker and eight Indians continued building the house in the third division. The next day Weicks and nine Indians worked on houses, as did Tucker and his crew of nine. On the twenty-ninth Frier and the Indians returned from the lake with two loads of tules. Eight Indians labored on the house in the first division. Work was suspended the following day, Sunday.[53]

On certain occasions Indians suspended work on their own. In December 1854, for example, Vicente hosted a mourning ceremony at Mumumpea in El Monte. The clerk keeping the labor report noted that it prevented "our getting a full supply of hands." The feast ended on December 12, and he and three or four Indians sought permission to go hunting and fishing. Permission was not granted, because they had promised several times to return to work once the feast ended.[54] On October 7 the following year, a mourning ceremony began at Pedro's village in Tejón Viejo. During the next ten days, remarked Ridley, "we shall not expect them to work much."[55]

As many as a thousand Indians, many from the mountains, participated in that event. "At the commencement of the feast," wrote E. D. Townsend, "some of the poles we had seen at the burial ground are moved to the camp; long white streamers are tied to them, and they are planted in the ground. At the foot of them some of the trinkets belonging to those who have died during the year, are buried. Early every morning a wailing is commenced; after this follows breakfast of dog, meat, or what they choose." Games were played throughout the day, but in the evening the wailing began again. After the buried items were dug up and burned, some of the men and women performed a dance. "The dance is kept up all night.... The monument poles are then carried back and replaced over the graves.... No tribe can dance until its trinkets have been burned."[56]

Later that evening Indians ignited a bonfire in front of Zapatero's house in the village of Tinliw, and eight men and two women began to dance. They were accompanied by five or six old women "chanting a low mourning strain, and beating time with some reeds split at the ends, and the men joining in a chorus. They sat in this way about half an hour, and then got up and danced in a circle, chanting in a louder voice, for about ten minutes." During this time, they recounted "the deeds and characters of their deceased friends, and they sometimes become much excited and cry bitterly. This wail being over, the whole party went round in the front of the house and ranged themselves in two lines, the dancers fronting us, and the singers sitting on the opposite side of the fire and fronting them." The women began to chant, "shaking their reeds in time, and the dancers taking up the chorus, began to jump up and down, stamping first with one foot and then with the other." The dancers were "painted with white daubs along the ribs and over the shoulders, and the two medicine men had black paint on their faces which made them look like some ugly animal. After all had danced in a row for a few minutes one medicine man commenced a pantomime representation of a warrior in battle. He pursued and fled, and finally received his death wound, and falling on his knees, bowed to the ground. Then, springing up, he suddenly commenced a brief, quick chorus, in which they all joined." Thus, the first scene of the act ended. By yelling or laughing the bystanders offered "a kind of applause." After a short rest the dancers began again and performed throughout the night."[57]

Townsend also observed activities and objects of a much more recent origin. At the ceremony, six Indians played musical instruments of both Spanish and traditional origin. Three played the flute, one the violin, one the triangle, and one the drum. He found their Mexican airs sweet, their Spanish airs pretty. And while the Indian women played a traditional gambling game of tossing sticks upon sticks, the men played cards, the stakes being strings of shells.[58]

Participation in ceremonies and feasts served to integrate disparate Indians residing throughout the reservation and beyond its boundaries. Whites who worked on or resided near the reservation were much less unified. Those hired by Henley, such as Alonzo Ridley, supported him. Bishop and Godey, who remained on the reservation at La Pastoría, supported Beale, as did those employees Beale had hired.[59] Also in Beale's camp was Lieutenant Colonel Benjamin L. Beall, commander of Fort Tejón. From the time of Beale's dismissal, Beall became a severe critic of Henley and the reservation. In October 1854 Beall informed the editors of the *Los Angeles Star* that the reservation was in a sad condition, that the man in charge had no control over liquor being supplied to the Indians, and that supplies and grain were being wasted.[60] The editors printed the account but retracted it a week later, explaining that the information had been "founded on rumor, and put into circulation by sundry persons that have been discharged at the reservation. It was no doubt a malicious attempt to cast reflection upon Col. Henley, and it is with pleasure we make the correction."[61]

The following month Colonel Beall directly intervened in the affairs of the reservation. Sometime in November, W. Redman, a former employee at Tejón, killed an Indian on the Kern River. The reservation Indians threatened to kill a white man if Redman were not delivered to them. Once Redman presented himself to Beall at Fort Tejón, the colonel sent a detachment of soldiers to the reservation. Beall instructed the lieutenant in command to inform the Indians that if they killed a white man, ten Indians would be executed. While the lieutenant was conveying the message, a white man and an Indian leader from the Kern River explained, apparently to the Indians' satisfaction, that Redman had acted in self-defense. Colonel Beall turned Redman over to the civil authorities in Los Angeles.[62] The *Southern Californian* reported on December 7 "that the Indians, since the arrest of Redmon [sic], are satisfied that the laws shall take their course, and have gone to work as if nothing unusual had happened. They have confidence in our laws and are willing to abide by them."[63]

At the end of May 1855, Henley informed Manypenny that the colonel "takes every opportunity to disparage the system, and throw obstacles in the way of its success. This course has been pursued, with such obstinate perseverance, that I have determined, on my next visit, there, if it is not changed, to ask for a change of officers, at that Post, and, I do not hesitate, now, to say, that in conducting the new Reserves I would prefer to have no soldiers, at all, and take the risk and danger, of holding the Indians in subjection with my own employees, than to encounter the opposition I meet with, from the Officers at Ft. Tejón."[64] Henley must have been further upset when informed in late June that Edward F. Beale, a friend of Beall's, had visited Samuel Bishop at his adobe in La Pastoría.[65]

Tensions increased in early August when General John Wool, commander of the pacific division, ordered Colonel Beall to report on the condition of the reservation. Beall met Samuel Bishop and Raymundo at the mouth of the Cañada de las Uvas and proceeded to Bishop's adobe. Bishop sent for Robert Wilson and the Indian vaqueros. They were to tell no one of their destination and were to arrive in the middle of the night. From them the colonel obtained information regarding the number of Indians in residence, the quantity of grain produced, and the size of the herds. The following day Beall called on Ridley, informing him of his intention to inspect the reservation. Because Ridley recognized only the authority of the superintendent of Indian affairs, he offered Beall no more privileges than those granted any visitor. Beall departed without visiting the Indian villages, the fields, the gardens, the mill, and the granary, the latter only two hundred yards from Ridley's quarters.[66]

When informed that Colonel Beall had secretly visited Bishop and had prepared a report of his "inspection," Henley quickly dispatched a letter to General Wool: "Was there any necessity for applying in the night to a mere vaquero, a man of course without character, and a recently chastised Indian, for information that could have been obtained in open daylight & by open & direct means?" The chastised Indian was Raymundo; recently, Ridley or one of his assistants had punished him for disobeying orders.[67]

Henley told Manypenny in October that Colonel Beall was "hostile to the Reservation System and has done every thing in his power to produce unfavorable impressions in regard to the Tejón ever since his arrival there as commander of the post."[68] The following month John Grice, the millwright, informed Manypenny that Henley was attempting "to elevate the mental and moral condition of the Red man here; but everything is thrown in his way by some of the friends of Lieut Beale that they think will retard the prosperity of the place. The Indians are conciled to the reverse of what Colonel Henley tells them. They are told, so they say, not to obey Col. Henley nor his Sub Agent. They are told not to work, that the government is bound to support them. They are told to do as they please, the soldiers shall not be used against them. They are told this so they say by Col. Beall … and Alax. Godey."[69] A few months later Henley, in a letter to the governor of California, was just as explicit: "From the time of Mr. Beale retiring from office to the present moment, several of his late employees have lounged about in the vicinity of the Tejon Reservation using most untiring efforts to disaffect the minds of the Indians, and induce them to leave the Reserve, and abandon the protection of the Government."[70]

By this time the legal status of Rancho El Tejón, the land grant on which the reservation was located, was resolved. In May a federal land commission had confirmed José Antonio Aguirre and Ignacio del Valle as the rightful owners of the rancho but also acknowledged that a reservation was located on part of the land. The rights of the Indians living on the land would be determined at another tribunal.[71] Henley informed Manypenny about the decision, questioning whether it would be best to purchase title or relocate elsewhere.[72]

Early in 1856 Henley wrote to J. Lancaster Brent, the legal representative of Aguirre and del Valle, inquiring whether the owners would sell to the United States the twenty-five thousand acres on which the reservation was

Table 10. Indian Workforce at Tejón, 1856

	MALE		FEMALE	
Captains	*Herding*	*Agriculture*	*Domestic*	*Agriculture*
Vincente (chief)	4	20	5	17
Antonio	4	20	15	16
Chico	4	10	10	12
Emeterio	3	27	12	25
Estanislao	1	19	8	10
Felipe	6	26	5	14
José Antonio	2	18	7	6
Pacifico	10	26	14	11
Zapatero	6	30	12	19
Total	48	210	96	142

Source: Adapted from J. R. Vineyard to Thomas Henley, Sebastian Military Reserve, July [?], 1856, *Annual Report of the Commissioner of Indian Affairs for the Year 1856,* 248.

located. Brent informed Henley that the owners would sell their entire rancho at $1.25 per acre. But they would not sell only that portion on which the reservation was situated, because it contained the most fertile soil and had the best access to water.[73] Informed about the title and the offer to sell, Commissioner Manypenny wrote to the secretary of the interior, recommending that the attorney general examine the case; if the title proved to be valid, the government should purchase the entire tract."[74]

No action was taken on his request, and Henley continued to operate the reservation on private land. In mid-1856 he replaced Alonzo Ridley with J. R. Vineyard as subagent.[75] Vineyard, often acting on his own initiative, made a determined effort to improve the condition of the Indians. He estimated that four-fifths of the Indians were syphilitic and soon convinced some of them to undergo treatment with Dr. R. Y. Hayes, the physician he had hired. Only gradually did they overcome their distrust of the white man's medicines.[76] But many of the Indians wanted to learn to read and write, and Vineyard suggested to the superintendent that "competent missionaries or teachers" be sent to the reservation.[77]

As of July 1856, 693 Indians resided on the reservation: 256 male and 191 female adults, 133 male and 113 female children. They were governed by 10 captains, each of whom provided a specific number of workers for reservation projects. Those engaged in agriculture tended to a vineyard, 600 fruit trees, and 475 acres of wheat, 200 of barley, 156 of corn, 21 of melons, 6 of potatoes, 4-5 of beans, 2 of peas, and 1.5 of onions, peanuts, tomatoes, and cabbage.[78]

Regarding the Indian leaders, Chief Vicente and captains Chico, Zapatero, and José Antonio were original Tejoneños. The others had moved onto the reservation after its founding. Emeterio, Pacifico, and Estanislao were Yokuts; Antonio, Felipe, and Pedro were Chumash. Except for Pacifico and Estanislao, all had signed the treaty with Indian Agent George Barbour in June 1851.[79]

Vineyard called Henley's attention to the treaty, which supposedly had secured for them a reservation in exchange for relinquishing all claims to their homelands. He recommended that Henley purchase the land on which the reservation was located: "You will see, from the reading of the treaty, that the Indians have a right to expect it. This step would give a permanency to the institution, and warrant certain necessary permanent improvements." Should the same "liberal policy" hitherto followed be continued, the reservation soon would become practically self-sufficient.[80]

Henley ignored Vineyard's request that the "liberal policy" be continued. Ever conscious of cost he instructed him to send those Indians who could be trusted into the mountains to collect wild foods. "In this way," he wrote, "a large quantity of food can be procured, and brought in, which will be a great relief in decreasing the issue of food, produced on the farm."[81] During the second half of August, several parties entered the mountains to gather piñon nuts and other wild foods.[82] They returned a month later with a large supply of nuts.[83]

Most of the able-bodied remained to work on reservation projects. In September and October, Indians constructed four adobe houses: one with three rooms for Pedro and José; one with three rooms for Urbano and Pasqual, one with two rooms for Corporal, and another with four rooms for Vicente and Chico.[84] In his annual report Henley noted that on the reservation were eight adobe structures. The six houses occupied by Indian leaders measured twenty by forty feet, the one occupied by Vineyard was twenty by sixty feet, and the two-story storehouse measured twenty-five by one hundred feet.[85] An earthquake struck the area on January 9, 1857, collapsing one house and damaging the others.[86]

Six hundred acres of wheat and 115 of barley had been planted in the common fields, but on January 30 the rains ceased.[87] Three hundred and fifty acres of wheat were ruined, and as of June the balance was expected to yield only about three bushels per acre. Seventy acres of barley also had failed, and there was little hope that the remainder of the crop would produce over five bushels per acre. In better condition were the four acres of potatoes and six of corn. And the garden, occupying sixteen acres, was

Table 11. Village Crop Acreage at Tejón, 1857

Captains	*Acres under cultivation*
Vincente (chief)	6 corn, pumpkins, barley, melons
Calistro and Mateo	4 corn, melons
Chico	2 melons, corn, 1 peas
Estanislao	4 wheat, corn, pumpkins, melons
José Antonio	5 corn, wheat, melons
José Dios	15 wheat, corn, melons, beans, pumpkins
José María	1.5 wheat, melons
Pacifico	9 corn, wheat, melons
Pedro	5 barley, 6 corn, pumpkins, melons
Pedro	12 corn, pumpkins, melons
Raymundo	4 barley, 2 wheat, 1 melons, corn
Zapatero	8 wheat, barley, 3.5 melons, corn

Source: Adapted from Thomas Madden to Thomas Henley, Office of Tejon Agency, June 25, 1857, Office of Indian Affairs, Letters Received, 1824–81, roll 35.

expected to produce about ten bushels of onions. Already fifteen bushels of peas had been gathered. The vineyard suggested a small yield, but the peach, pear, apricot, pomegranate, and fig trees showed promise. An employee lamented that "this has been the most disastrous season for crops since the Reservation has been established."[88]

Although the drought was in its third year in the Tulare Valley, as of June 1857 the Indians had, by careful management, kept their own small fields productive. The Indian farmers, however, were not immune from nature. Most of the 140 bushels of wheat Chico recently had harvested was damaged by smut. And Pacifico and Antonio, both residing at Mat'apxwelxwel, lost crops to grasshoppers.[89]

Because the common fields failed to produce sufficient amounts of food, Henley, as he had a year before, told Vineyard to encourage the Indians to collect as much wild food as possible:

> Mules and teams should be furnished to pack & haul them from the mountains, and white men should be sent with the Indians to superintend the collecting and transporting them to the quarters. Every facility should be afforded for the saving of this article of food, as it seems to be almost your only alternative from starvation; for it must be borne in mind that there is no appropriation which can be used to any extent for the purchase of provisions on Reservations already established, and if that were even the case it would be impossible to buy provisions for the Tejon as there is no grain in that region of the state for sale, and the transportation from these places too expensive.
>
> There seems therefore to be no alternative but to subsist the Indians upon the natural resources of the Country upon which they have lived before the assistance of the government had been extended to them.[90]

Provided with animals, axes, knives, clothing, blankets, and ammunition, in late September several parties departed for the mountains to gather piñon nuts and other wild foods. The following month another party set off for Kern and Buena Vista Lakes to fish and hunt waterfowl.[91]

A shortage of food was not the only problem facing the reservation. The granary and some chimneys had been damaged by a recent earthquake, and the goat barn, located near Vicente's village of Mumumpea, needed a new roof. Many of the wagons were old and dilapidated. The threshing machine, deemed beyond repair by the blacksmith, had broken down before the recent harvest, so the grain had to be trampled. The twenty-four horses belonging to the reservation had been overworked, and several were no longer fit for service. The thirty-three mules were in better condition but were thin, there being insufficient grain to feed them.[92]

Farming operations were further damaged by immigrants passing through the reservation. Parts of the reservation had been rendered useless to agriculture because of the numerous herds of cattle, horses, and sheep driven through the Cañada de las Uvas and Tejón Pass.[93] Vineyard, in a letter to Henley, noted that the passes "constitute the means of communication between all the country south and east of this and the Tulare and Sacramento valleys, thereby bringing the Indians in frequent contact with a set of men whose character, calling and disposition, render them the least desirable of all others."[94] Apparently to trade with the immigrants and drovers, Joseph Rice had established a post in one of the public buildings on the reservation, but in July Vineyard ordered him to move beyond its boundaries. Rice reestablished his trading post a quarter of a mile from the granary on El Paso Creek, which flowed past the agent's house.[95]

Confined to a reservation that increasingly benefited whites more than themselves may have been the reason that a large number of Indians, in mid-February 1858, refused to work or obey the orders of Vineyard and the other employees. Some of the Indians possessed weapons and demonstrated considerable hostility. Shortly, twenty-five dragoons from Fort Tejón arrived and encircled the striking Indians. "On seeing this display," reported the *Los Angeles Star*, "not liking the looks of carbines, sabers and pistols, the Indians backed down, laid down their arms, and the ringleaders were taken out and received from twenty to one hundred lashes, according to quality, and were then let off on promise of good behavior."[96]

The unsettled condition of the reservation may have caused John Temple, whose wife had become a part owner of Rancho El Tejón, to write to Commissioner of Indian Affairs Charles E. Mix, offering to sell that portion of the grant where the reservation was situated.[97] Evidently, he received no reply because in March 1858 J. Lancaster Brent, representative of the owners, told Mix that they were prepared to sell to the United States at $1.25 per acre the land on which the reservation was located.[98] Apparently, he too received no reply.

In August, Vineyard sent a mixed message to the commissioner of Indian affairs. The 650 Indians residing on the reservation, he insisted, were happy and contented. Nearly every adult male owned at least one horse, and several families had "milch cows, poultry, and other things that tend to make a good living and a comfortable home." The health of the Indians was generally good, "most of the suffering arising from improper associations and excesses." They continued to gather acorns, piñon nuts, seeds, and roots to supplement their diet. To the parties gathering wild foods, he provided tools and animals. The Indian women now made their own clothes, so he no longer provided them with ready-made attire.[99]

Nevertheless, the future of the reservation was in jeopardy. In a field located about a mile from the one which had produced smut-infested crops in previous years, Vineyard had planted wheat seeds of the finest quality, but the harvest was limited because of the drought. The failure of the common crops over the past few years convinced him that "it is impracticable, if not impossible, to raise good crops of wheat and corn on this reserve, except in very wet and favorable seasons, a thing which has not occurred since 1853.... In justice to the Indians I deem it my duty to suggest, for the consideration of the department, the propriety of selecting a more suitable point for agricultural purposes, to which these Indians could be removed."[100]

The condition of the reservation was reflected in an inventory compiled in mid-June 1859. Stock consisted of fifteen horses, thirty-one mules, seven oxen, and fifty fowls. Crops on hand totaled 9,200 pounds of barley and 12,000 pounds of wheat. Horse collars, harnesses, and bridles were labeled as "much worn." Of the fifteen houses (fourteen constructed of adobe), only the frame house was listed to be in good order.[101]

Social disorder accompanied economic decline. The same month, an Indian named Tomás threatened his wife and daughter for assisting in the grain harvest. Placed under arrest he was released on the promise of good behavior. Tomás, however, killed both wife and daughter with a butcher knife. He wounded another Indian before being overpowered and locked up. When friends of the murdered women assembled and threatened to kill the prisoner, employees on the reservation sent an urgent message to Fort Tejón. A detachment of dragoon arrived and defused the situation. But a little past midnight, a large body of Indians assembled outside the house where Tomás was being held. Convinced by the guards that any attempt to seize the prisoner would be strongly resisted, they dispersed. With Tomás in their custody, the soldiers departed the following day for Fort Tejón, where their prisoner was delivered to the civil authorities.[102] The physician stationed at the reservation told Judge Benjamin Hayes that the Indians were afraid of Tomás and desired his death. In Los Angeles, Hayes convicted Tomás of murder and sentenced him to die on September 27. Tomás escaped, only to be caught and brought before a jury of twelve men to determine his sanity. Found sane he was executed early the following year.[103]

Apparently, alcohol played no role in the affair, but drunkenness had become a problem at Tejón. From grog shops located near Fort Tejón, liquor was smuggled onto the reservation by, in the words of Vineyard, "a disreputable class of Mexicans and Americans." Most of the insubordination and difficulties he faced resulted from drunkenness.[104] And any attempt to discipline the offenders, he feared, would result in retaliation. Owing to the reduction in the number of employees working at Tejón, in August he asked the commissioner of Indian affairs to station a detachment of troops on the reservation. They should be located near the agency buildings "to protect our lives and public property from destruction in case of an outbreak among the Indians."[105]

Vineyard also requested that Tejón be resurveyed; pointing out that it had never been surveyed since being reduced from fifty thousand to twenty-five thousand acres. Once a survey was accomplished, he could remove the squatters who were "encroaching more and more upon what has heretofore been considered, by all the property of the Indians." Unless checked, the encroachments would "weaken the faith of the Indians in the ability of the government to protect them, and their confidence in the officers of the department whose duty it is to control them and guard their interests." Vineyard closed his report by admitting that he knew neither the proper course to pursue nor the extent of his authority.[106] Ignoring the increasingly discontented Indians living beyond the reservation would produce even more problems for the agents.

CHAPTER XXIV

Resistance and Retaliation in the Tulare Valley

Although the Indians residing on Tejón Reservation received special, if often contradictory, governmental attention, most of those who called the Tulare Valley their home had to fend for themselves. In 1852 approximately eight thousand Indians resided in the valley.[1] Those in the Four Creeks, an area rich in fish, acorns, and deer, totaled twelve hundred.[2] Divided into twelve distinct Yokuts societies, they included the Tachi, Nutunutu, Wimilchi, and Gawia.[3] Francisco of the Gawia, the most powerful chief in the area, had brought remnants of the Yokod, Telamni, Wukchamni, and Choinok under his rule.[4] The Gawia had killed John Woods and several other white men when they attempted to settle in the area in late 1850.[5] According to an army officer, the followers of Francisco were "generally the worst Indians I know anything of, the Indian difficulties in all that section of the State having originated with them."[6] In mid-1852 eight white men successfully planted an agricultural colony in the Four Creeks.[7] One of the men recalled that the Indians they encountered possessed axes and knives belonging to Woods and the other settlers the Indian had killed.[8] A year later a thriving American community had taken hold. Fifty whites resided at Woodville, another seventy-five at nearby Visalia.[9]

Late in 1853, when Indians killed an ox owned by a white man, Lieutenant John Nugen led a detachment of soldiers from Fort Miller to the area and attacked a village near Woodville, killing an Indian.[10] Nugen noted in his report that ever since the difficulty over the ox, Indians had been on most friendly terms with the settlers. Indian leaders promised to prevent their followers from stealing from or molesting in any way the settlers. Nugen had no reason to believe the Indians would not keep their word, because "the chastisement they have received, will effectively serve, as a check on their conduct, for a long time to come."[11] Major Henry W. Wessells reported early in 1854 that the Indians, "docile and tractable," were living "on amicable terms" with their white neighbors.[12]

By mid-1855 those terms no longer existed. Indian cattle stealing had begun, and in May the settlers demanded that the local Indians turn over to them four well-known stock thieves. When the Indians failed to comply, the settlers promptly took Francisco prisoner and threatened to hang him if the thieves were not delivered within five days. Francisco's supporters complied. The whites hanged two Indians and shot and killed another as he attempted to escape. Because he chose to be shot rather than hanged, the fourth Indian was released, his courage impressing his would-be executioners.[13] Late in the year Captain E. D. Townsend visited the area, noting in his diary that the settlers "will not allow the Indians to violate the law prohibiting to them the use of fire-arms and liquors, and there seems to be no sign of animosity between the two races. Occasionally an Indian is detected stealing some trifle, when he is whipped, generally taking his punishment quietly. When a mountain Indian comes down to steal cattle, he is shot."[14]

Although successful in controlling the Indians in their midst, the settlers thought that Superintendent of Indian Affairs Thomas Henley was neglecting them. In August 1855 thirty-five whites petitioned Henley to establish an Indian subagency in the area. The neglect, they reasoned, operated "against the peace and quiet of present settlers" and hindered the development of the region. They recommended that one of their own, Samuel Jennings be appointed agent.[15] The following month Henley chose Jennings as special agent for the Four Creeks. Instead of fostering immigration, however, Jennings was to resolve Indian-white disputes and protect "Indians from the imposition and abuse by evil disposed white persons." He was to settle inter-Indian conflicts as well.[16]

Jennings soon had a crisis on his hands. Sometime in late 1855 or early 1856, someone murdered an Indian boy in the vicinity of Woodville. The local authorities arrested, tried, and acquitted a young white man, age eighteen. Not satisfied, the Indians demanded that the accused be punished, but apparently the whites took no further action. The Indians, noted Jennings in a letter to Henley, "desire to know whether and when anything is to be done for them. They are unwilling to leave the valley, and wish the friendship and good treatment of the Americans."[17]

South of the Four Creeks on the Kern River, tensions between Indians and settlers also increased. In February and March 1855 miners swarmed over the Kern River, where gold had been discovered supposedly in large and rich deposits. Newspapers in Stockton and Los Angeles, towns seeking to trade with those seeking instant wealth, published letters attesting to a bonanza. As it turned out the deposits were limited and quickly claimed by those first on the scene. Most of the five thousand who mined the river departed after a short stay.[18] But some of those who remained founded the town of Keysville, located at the base of the Greenhorn Mountains and a few miles southwest of the junction of the north and south forks of the Kern River.[19]

So many people moving so quickly into so limited an area alarmed the local Indians. To prevent hostilities from breaking out, in early 1856 Henley appointed Thomas Maltby special agent for the area.[20] In particular he was responsible for the Indians led by Urbano, who had resided for a time at Hoshtsiw on the Tejón Reservation.[21] Numbering about 250 they lived in a village on the south fork of the Kern a few miles above its junction with the north fork. Maltby provided the Indians with oxen and tools from the Tejón Reservation; they planted several acres of potatoes and corn and started a garden. Maltby considered Urbano "a very good sensible man, possessed of complete control over his own tribe and also able to exert a considerable influence over the wild Indians inhabiting the country east of the Sierra Nevadas."[22]

Urbano's influence did not extend to a party of Paiutes, who in mid-1856 camped some twenty miles upstream from his village after returning from a stock-raiding expedition to the Los Angeles region. The Paiutes insisted that Urbano join them in a campaign against the whites and promised to return in ten days to kill all the whites in the area and all the Indians who cooperated with them. Urbano appealed to Maltby for protection but was told to remain at his present location. Although none of his people was injured when attacked by a party of Indians (most likely the Paiutes), Urbano took his people four miles upstream to a ravine where they built fortifications. The move aroused the suspicion of the whites in the area. Those in Keysville demanded that the Indians move closer to them where they could be watched and provided with provisions. Refusing to move to the town, they nevertheless agreed to relocate to Maltby's farm. But they feared to leave their new camp to hunt and gather, convinced that local whites had hostile intentions.[23]

The Indians remained there for ten weeks, during which time Maltby provided them with provisions at considerable cost to himself. He encouraged them to return to the Tejón Reservation, where they would be protected and fed. They refused because Indians on the reservation had stolen their horses and killed members of their group. They preferred to die where they were, rather than live at Tejón. In mid-july they returned to their home village and planted thirty acres of potatoes, beans, wheat, and corn. But the winter was extremely dry, and unable to irrigate their fields they lost their entire crop. The expanding white population, moreover, had driven off most of the wild game on which they relied. Of the wild plant life they regularly harvested, only acorns remained in abundance.[24]

Indians residing along Tule River experienced similar pressures. In April 1856 a white man accused local Indians of stealing animals in his charge. The only "proof of a theft came a short time later, when an Indian from the Tejón area offered to sell the meat of a recently butchered calf at a feast held by the Indians in the Yokohl Valley.[25] Rumor quickly increased the number of animals stolen to five hundred.[26] W. G. Poindexter, sheriff of Tulare County, formed a company of nearly sixty men.[27] Thirty-three members of the Tulare Mounted Riflemen, as they called themselves, located the Indians supposedly responsible for the theft on the north fork of the Tule River at a spot later called Battle Mountain. The Indians had built breastworks of rocks and brush at the entrance to a valley and the shower of arrows they poured on the Riflemen forced them to retreat from the area.[28] Upon returning to Visalia, they expelled all the peaceable Indians who had entered the town for protection.[29]

Once they heard about the fight, a party of whites not associated with the Riflemen attacked a small village located some twenty miles to the south on White River, killing five or six Indians and forcing the others to disperse.[30] Some of those assaulted were under the command of Pacifico and Henriel, Indians from the Tejón Reservation who were visiting the village.[31] Evidently, Pacifico, who lost a brother in the attack, blamed some of the reservation Indians for stealing the cattle of the whites and thus inviting the retaliation. The reservation Indians feared they would be harmed both by Pacifico's people and by those whites who blamed them for the thefts. Subagent J. R. Vineyard sought assistance from Fort Tejón, and a detachment of soldiers arrived on April 29. Finding no evidence that an attack was imminent, the soldiers returned to their barracks the following day.[32] Shortly, Pacifico and Henriel returned to the reservation and participated in the harvest. Vineyard told Henley that he anticipated "no further difficulties in this section of the country, unless the white people come and attack the Indians on the Reservation, as I am told they have threatened to do, alleging that the Indians, here, had stolen their stock."[33]

According to a newspaper correspondent, Indians from the reservation stole stock because the government failed to provide for their wants: "Heretofore the thieves, when pursued have taken refuge upon the Reservation, and when the offenders have been demanded, the reply has been that this is their home, and they have a right to be here, and must not be molested. The principal offenders have hitherto been the Tejon Indians, and their depredations have so exasperated the people of Tulare county that you must not be surprised to hear of a complete cleaning out of the Reservation, Fort and all."[34]

That did not occur, but some of the settlers in the Four Creeks advocated an all-out war against the Indians they blamed for stealing cattle. At a meeting convened in late April or early May, those seeking a peaceful solution to the difficulties greatly outnumbered those calling for war, but the so-called war party prevailed.[35] Dr. Samuel Charles George, representing the Tulare Mounted Riflemen, hurried to Stockton and on to San Francisco, where Governor J. Neely Johnson was staying. Johnson gave him the authority to raise two companies of men in addition to the men already in the field.[36] Johnston persuaded General John Wool, commander of the pacific division, to supply the volunteers with arms and ammunition, all of which were to be deducted from the quota of arms the federal government owed the State of California. Wool provided sixty rifles, five thousand cartridges, and some equipment.[37] Johnson told George that furnishing the arms did not confer the authority to embroil the state in another expensive Indian war: "In fact, it is hoped that the protection and defense of the citizens of that part of the State will be speedily, if it has not already been obtained, without further hostile demonstrations against the Indians.[38]

Apparently, the arms and ammunition had not arrived by May 7 when another "hostile demonstration" against the Indians occurred. The Tulare Mounted Riflemen, now numbering about eighty men, again attacked the Indians' stronghold. A participant in the attack wrote that they found the Indians "entrenched behind a brush breastwork that was thrown up across the mouth of the canon.... The Americans went up close, but could only see an Indian now and then in the brush, and would fire. The Indians would return the fire by a volley of arrows." Unable to dislodge them without losing many of their men, the Riflemen retired and sent a dispatch to Fort Miller for assistance.[39]

Convinced that the Indians had combined and posed a deadly threat, many whites feared the worst. In a letter to the sheriff of Los Angeles County, miners on the Kern River insisted they were "in the midst of an Indian war." Indians had come from different "quarters and threatened to annihilate all the whites both in the Tulare valley and these mountains."[40] The editors of the *San Joaquin Republican* identified Francisco, the Gawia chief, as the leader of the hostile Indians. Supposedly, he had enlisted to his cause most of the Indians from the Fresno River to the Tejón Pass, as well as the Paiutes on the east side of the Sierra Nevada: "There seems to be a preconcerted movement among the Indians of the south to wage a war of extermination against the whites, and if this emeute is not speedily crushed, many lives will be lost."[41] The editors of the *Sacramento Daily Union* expressed similar concerns. Informed by Dr. George that from the San Joaquin River to the Tejón Pass one thousand Indians were under arms, the editors predicted that the war "will cost much time and a large outlay of money and loss of life."[42]

Whites exaggerated the threat. Most Indians sought to live in peace with their white neighbors. The Tachi, for example, residing on the shores of Tulare Lake, had sufficient game, acorns, and fish on which to subsist and thus had no reason to fight the Americans. Their chief, Gregorio, who had traveled to the East with John Frémont, had mastered English, and had signed the treaty with George Barbour at Camp Belt in May 1851, told a white man in late April or early May that he would gladly relinquish every bow, arrow, knife, hatchet, and other deadly weapon his people possessed and go anywhere the Americans wanted."[43] Sheriff Poindexter, however, feared that Gregorio and other Indians residing on Tulare Lake would join those supposedly in rebellion.[44]

Special Agent Thomas Maltby in early May appealed to Lieutenant Colonel Benjamin L. Beall, commander of Fort Tejón, for support, claiming that eight hundred Indians had assembled on the Kern and soon would strike at the settlements in the valley.[45] On the fifth Beall ordered Lieutenant Ben Allston and Company A of the First Dragoons to the scene of the hostilities. Allston was to inquire into the difficulties between Indians and whites and, if necessary, provide protection to settlers and miners in the region. The company departed with thirty days' rations.[46]

Allston and Maltby met on the Kern River, the agent encouraging the soldiers to pursue some Indians who recently had stolen stock from the coast. Allston refused because his horses were unsuitable for a mountain campaign. He continued on to the Tule River.[47] Already bivouacked on the river was a detachment of infantry from Fort Miller, commanded by Lieutenant LaRhett L. Livingston.[48] In mid-May, Livingston's contingent, supported by the 150 volunteers, proceeded to the Indians' stronghold.[49] Evidently, most of the additional civilians came from the San Joaquin River, probably from Millerton.[50] Participants in the fight, John Barker and W. R. Bower wrote years later that as they approached the fortifications, the Indians "climbed their breast works, and reviled and defied us in the vilest and filthiest manner in Spanish expletive."[51]

Before Livingston's artillery piece was put in place, the Indians fired on the soldiers. The soldiers and a few of the volunteers attacked and drove the Indians from their stronghold. Some escaped to the Tejón Pass, where they reported that forty of their friends and relatives had been killed. Upon entering the redoubt, however, the whites found only eight bodies.[52] They also found, recalled Barker and Bower, "a great quantity of dried beef..., stores of pine nuts, arrows, grass-seed, and grasshopper cheese. There was the plunder they had stolen..., and such a store of Indian baskets as would today delight the heart of a connoisseur, all of which were condemned to the flames."[53]

The volunteers from the San Joaquin River were not impressed with the Tulare Mounted Riflemen, christening them the "Petticoat Rangers" because of the blouse of canvas padded with cotton some wore for protection.[54] "The 'Petticoat Rangers' were upon the field, but effected nothing," wrote the *Stockton Argus*, "as their padded garments only served the purpose of sleeping accommodations."[55] Recounting the events years later, a participant wrote that the "armor was so cumbersome that if a man stumbled he could not get to his feet again unassisted." The riflemen were "a rank failure and the show a dozen of them made in those suits was enough to make a horse laugh."[56]

More serious assessments of the conflict also were offered. Writing to Henley on May 25, Joseph Daniels, a settler on the Kern, insisted that there was no combination among the Indians to attack the settlements: "They are in no condition for a war, having no rifles or firearms, in fact no rifles were fired by the Indians during the three fights with our people."[57] Writing the same day to the *San Joaquin Republican*, an individual insisted that the war "was a cowardly farce, the threatening legions of Indians turning out to be about one hundred, seeking refuge in a brush from the rowdies, who, on the least occasion, delight in the sport of shooting them.... The herds of cattle said to have been stampeded, have turned out to be a single calf, taken to supply the deficiency of meat during an Indian feast. Retaliation of a brutal character, for this trifling offense, created all the disturbance."[58]

Although some Americans claimed that the recent battle had ended the conflict, a correspondent for the *Stockton Argus* thought otherwise: "As for the Indian war having come to a close..., simply on account of the Indians having been defeated in one instance, is absurd and false. The truth of the case is this: they have but commenced their depredations, and have now much in the favor to do a great amount of damage to the settlers. A few nights since a body of them came within half a mile of a company of dragoons, stationed for the protection of settlers and property, and burned a dwelling house."[59] Near Woodville they destroyed structures and stole animals. The sawmill and one hundred feet of lumber they set ablaze amounted to $15,000. Then seven houses they burned down were valued at $3,500. They also absconded with seven horses worth one hundred dollars per animal, and from seventy-five to one hundred head of cattle, valued at fifty dollars each.[60]

By this time Governor Johnson had commissioned Edward F. Beale, the former superintendent of Indian affairs, a brigadier general in the state militia and conferred upon him the authority to make war or conduct a treaty of peace with the hostile Indians.[61] General Wool authorized Beale to draw troops from Forts Miller and Tejón to carry out his mission.[62] And true to his nature, Beale undertook his new task with single-minded determination. He and his aide-de-camp arrived on the Kings River on June 5 where they met William Campbell, manager of the Kings River Farm.[63] On the first Campbell had contacted some of the hostile Indians and persuaded them to hold a council with him in a few days.[64] Beale insisted on attending, but Campbell resented the interference and argued against Beale's intention to take soldiers to the meeting. The Indians, he feared, might interpret their presence as a hostile act.[65] Beale, however, took charge and sent Campbell with five bullocks to the Indians with instructions that they select a spot to hold a council. Beale then proceeded to Visalia to meet with the settlers, many of whom were convinced that only the severest punishment would deter the Indians from further raids. But Beale was pleased to find that some of the most respected citizens were willing to consider his plan to persuade the Indians to cease hostilities. Several agreed to accompany him to the meeting with the Indians. He also enlisted the services of Lieutenant Allston's dragoons and Lieutenant Livingston's infantry.[66]

Campbell informed Beale that the Indians had selected a site for the council. On June 9 Beale, the prominent citizens of Visalia and Woodville, and 30 infantry and 40 dragoons met with 160 or 170 Indians, representing twelve groups, including the Gawia, Mono, Telamni, Tachi, Yokod, Wolasi, Chukamina, and Nutunutu. Though an Indian interpreter Beale told the Indians that the purpose of his visit was to make peace, but if they refused to relocate to areas deemed best for them, he would chastise them severely. He ordered those living on the Kings River to proceed to the Kings River Farm. Those residing south of the river, including those in the Four Creeks, were to go to the Yokohl Valley on the Tule River, where they would remain until Superintendent Henley found them a permanent home. Those located on Tulare Lake were to return to their homelands. Convinced they would follow his instructions, Beale distributed to the Indians twenty-five hundred pounds of beef, two thousand pounds of flour, six bolts of cotton cloth, six bolts of calico, thirty-six colored shirts, fifty-nine spools of colored thread, and other items.[67] Because the Indians residing on or near the Tule River failed to attend the council, Beale sent them a message to meet him in the Kaweah Valley, approximately ten miles from Woodville. Beale and an escort of dragoons arrived on June 14. Present were about three hundred Indians, comprising elements of five groups, including a branch of the Gawia that had failed to attend the first council. Prepared to make peace they agreed to remain at their present camp until the arrival of Henley. Asked by Beale why they had burned down the sawmill, they said they had been at war with the whites and sought to inflict as much damage as possible.[68]

For peace to be maintained, Beale, in his report to Governor Johnson, recommended that the superintendent provide the Indians with food and that twenty-five dragoons continually patrol the area.[69] Beale instructed Samuel Jennings, special agent for the Four Creeks, to purchase at least ten thousand dollars' worth of beef, flour, and other items for the Indians represented at the councils. But William Campbell advised Jennings to be cautious and economical and not run the Indian Office into debt.[70] Jennings took some of the Gawia to the Kings River Farm, where they were reluctantly accepted by Campbell.[71] Subagent M. B. Lewis favored uniting the Gawia living in the mountains with those relocated to the farm, but he disagreed with Beale's policy of sending those Indians quietly supporting themselves in their villages to the farm. What were the Indians to do, he pondered in a letter to Henley, when "instructed by Mr. Jennings, Lieut. Beale, the war party, the peace party, Mr. Campbell, and others." The Indians, he insisted, "know no other head quarters but the Adobe [Fresno Farm], and no other counsel but myself."[72]

That Beale, his predecessor, had held councils with Indians under his jurisdiction troubled Henley. Beale, of all people, he stressed in a letter to Governor Johnson, should have known that promising Indians assistance which could not be guaranteed was fraught with danger: "I have great fears that his operations in that quarter will give me infinite trouble."[73] Henley also wrote to Beale, requesting that he be provided with copies of the treaties and a statement of the promises made to the Indians. He acknowledged that Beale's authority had not emanated from the Indian Office but pointed out that he was responsible for the implementation of the treaties.[74] Apparently, Beale failed to act on the request.

In late June the *Los Angeles Star* explained to its readers that the treaty, although only temporary, was the best arrangement that could be made under the circumstances. But it was "absolutely necessary that the attention of the Agent [Superintendent Henley] be given to this matter immediately—if not, a war will break out, disastrous to all parties. The Indians are peaceable, but are starving. The game has left its usual range—the streams are dried up, and they can get no fish; and to add to their misfortunes, the white people burned up their acorns which they had stored up for their future sustenance. In such a state affairs, we cannot blame the poor Indian for stealing a horse and a mule for food."[75] Revisiting the story two months later, the newspaper noted that the arrangements made by Beale had "failed, owing to the fact, that no notice was taken of the proceeding by the Indian agent, who alone could give force and effect to the treaty. The consequence is, the Indians are again wandering over the country in search of food, and it is not to be expected that they will endure the pangs of starvation, when they see cattle grazing on the hills."[76]

To the editors of the *San Joaquin Republican*, the difficulties resulted from earlier events: "This discontentment seems to have originated in the following manner: In 1851, a commission composed of Col. McKee, Col. Barber [sic] and Dr. Wozencraft, assigned a district of country, extending from the Chowchilla to the Ka-wee-ah, or Four Creeks, a distance of some seventy five by thirty or forty miles, to the use of these Indians forever, and made a treaty to that effect.... Recently that region of country, including the part reserved to the Indians by the commission, has been pronounced open to the settlement of the whites, who in anticipation of such an event, had already to a considerable extent occupied it. This created distrust in the minds of the Indians, particularly as no other provision had been made for them." The editors concluded by predicting that the winter season soon would force the Indians out of the mountains and into the valleys where they would collide with the settlers.[77]

Concerned that the Indians along the Tule River had lost faith in the government, Alonzo Ridley, subagent at the Tejón Reservation notified Superintendent Thomas Henley in September that he had persuaded some of them to meet with him at a designated spot on the river where they would begin laying in a supply of acorns. Although they were to support themselves, he promised them 1,000 pounds of flour and the same amount ofwheat.[78] A short time later Ridley relocated to the reservation Indians (probably Koyeti and Yaudanchi) from the Tule River. The lands vacated he claimed as a site for an Indian farm. During the following six or eight months, the land remained unoccupied, but Ridley prohibited whites from settling in the area. A few reservation employees and some equipment were sent to the area, and a large adobe house was constructed.[79]

At the end of September 1856 Thomas Madden, and evidently a silent partner, sought title to the vacated land on the Tule River by applying for school land warrants.[80] Shortly, he took possession of 1,280 acres, which he immediately leased to the government. Thereafter, along with two townships of less productive government land, the tract became known as both the Madden Farm and the Tule River Farm.[81] In September 1857 about 100 of Indians removed from the river returned to work on farm. Provided with a wagon, four mules, and tools, they immediately began digging an irrigation canal.[82]

In mid-1858 Indian agent J. R. Vineyard placed an employee of the Tejón Reservation in charge of the two hundred Indians on the farm and furnished them with the necessary implements for cultivating a small crop. The Indians were to build a suitable house for the individual managing the farm.[83] The location of the farm, however, clashed with the claims of settlers. According to H. A. Bostwick, he and three other individuals had in 1857 commenced improvements on the Tule River, evidently based on the rights of preemption, until informed that Madden had obtained school warrants for the land. Bostwick was convinced that Madden had his warrants antedated in the Land Office in San Francisco in order to secure the land. Henry G. Sears claimed that Ridley had ordered him and his partner not to settle on the river because the land was to be set aside for an Indian reservation. They ignored the order, convinced that Ridley had no right to hold public lands that were open to settlement. J. S. Clapp, once employed at Tejón as a blacksmith, also claimed land on the river, and he too was told that it had been secured by school land warrants. The land would either be sold to the government or retained for private benefit.[84]

Treasury Agent J. Ross Browne voiced concerns over private citizens purchasing land they thought that the U.S. government would purchase. Once such a policy became established there could be "no limit to speculations upon the public Treasury." Any person controlling the transfer and disbursement of public money could settle upon and improve public lands on the anticipation that the government might purchase it. "But suppose Government does not deem it expedient to pursue that course, who will pay back the money expended?"[85] The government, however, did not purchase the land from its owner, Thomas Madden, but leased it instead. In September 1859, James McDuffie, the recently appointed superintendent of Indian affairs for California noted that, "A small farm at Tule river had been established.... On it some corn has been raised this season, and considerable improvement made. The number of Indians collected here is about three hundred, and this number can be increased. It has always been the home of a very considerable tribe, who are contented to remain; but the country is rapidly being settled, and public sentiment is against them doing so."[86]

The *Visalia Weekly Delta* reported in April the following year that the affairs of the farm, "under the management of Mr. M. Tucker are in an most prosperous condition. About 225 acres of grain now in, looks remarkably fine; the rains this season having been sufficient to nature crops without irrigation. In addition to this he will have about 150 acres more planted this season, which will produce ample for the Indians in and around this farm. If all other agents do as well, there will not be much need of Indian war appropriations, in the future, to pay for mercilessly butchering Indian women and children, because their warriors pilfer to obtain sustenance of life, in a land once their own."[87]

In 1860 the state was divided into two superintendencies. John P. H. Wentworth who received the Southern District reported in 1861 that the farm contained a few acres of good land cultivated by the Indians. Adjacent to the foothills of the Sierra Nevada made it an ideal place for Indian occupancy. He recommended to his superiors that the land be purchased from Madden and that Indians scattered throughout the region be relocated to it. Because the farm was near the foothills, the Indians had relative easy access to wild animal and plant life.[88] In May 1862 some of them departed the farm for the foothills in search for food. They told a white man that if food were provided on the farm, then all the Indians in the region would be on it by Sunday night. They even suggested that the agent register them and conduct a roll call every morning. They were anxious to remain on the farm but would not stay and starve. The white man secured for them a few beeves and some flour from local settlers.[89] Of the four white men employed on the farm in 1862, J. S. Clapp, who once had sought land on the river, was one of them.[90]

That year Wentworth informed the commissioner of Indian affairs that he had rented the farm for the current year but recommended its abandonment and removing the Indians to Tejón.[91] But Wentworth changed his mind the following year. Deciding to continue renting the farm for two more years, he told the commissioner that the land was well suited for the needs of the Indians. Moreover, "Mr. Madden, the proprietor, gives the use of a very fine vineyard and also a fine orchard of fruit trees. These the Indians prize very highly, and during the fruit season afford the a great means of subsistence." Although drought had ruined the grain crop, mainly of 250 acres of wheat, the Indians were preparing to plant grain and vegetables for the wet season. Nevertheless, the rational for maintaining the farm was not because of its productivity but because "there is no place aside from this farm, within my district to which these Indians could be removed for the present."[92]

Writing to The *Visalia Delta* in May 1864, an individual estimated the expenses accrued at the farm beginning in late 1861. He admitted having no vouchers or books, relying instead on the information provided by the farm's employees. Because the expenses added up to $5,310 and because the farm produced 1000 sacks of grain worth $1,750, the cost to the government came to $3,560. He calculated that these expenses were much the same for the years 1862 and 1863. But if the costs of the agent and clerks traveling to and from San Francisco were added, the government spent $10,000 more than what the farm produced over the three years. The writer questioned whether the government was getting its money's worth in renting land from Madden. Although two hundred acres had been fenced and ditches dug, "Why the agent did not make these improvements on Government land is best known to himself. There is plenty of Government land within five miles. If these improvements and rent of farm for three years had been expended on Government land the Indians would to-day have homes of their own and be able to support themselves."[93]

In fact, some improvements had been made on government land that was unofficially part of the Tule River Farm. To the west of Madden's property, Indians had fenced and cultivated crops of wheat and barley. But on January 9, 1864, John D. Taylor, an employee on the farm, claimed the land as a homestead. Later in the year the superintendent of Indian affairs ordered Taylor off the land and even requested military assistance in removing him. The army refused because the land had not been officially set aside as a reservation. Taylor remained on the land.[94]

George J. Hoffman, special agent assigned to the farm, reported in July 1864 that the recent harvest had produced 70,000 pounds barley and 200,000 pounds of wheat. These crops and those of beans and potatoes, he claimed, would be ample enough to feed the local Indians and those who might be sent to the farm.[95] The Indians remaining in the Southern Mines, however, had no official place to where they could relocate.

CHAPTER XXV

Defiance and Degradation in the Southern Mines

As in the Tulare Valley, most of the Indians residing in the area the whites called the Southern Mines also remained outside of governmental control, but they faced much greater and more ruthless population of intruders than did those to the south. Bounded by the Mokelumne River in the north and the San Joaquin River in the south, the Southern Mines, recalled a miner, contained a diverse population: "There were many villages peopled nearly altogether by Mexicans, others by Frenchmen; in some places there were parties of two or three hundred Chilians [sic] forming a community of their own. The Chinese camps were very numerous; and besides all such distinct colonies of foreigners, every town of the southern mines contained a very large foreign population. The Americans, however, were of course greatly the majority."[1]

According to the California state census of 1852, the population of Tuolumne and Mariposa Counties, which roughly corresponded to the Southern Mines, consisted of American citizens (whites), "Negroes," "Mulattos," and foreigners and totaled 30,173. Those Indians thought no longer to belong to particular groups were classified as "domesticated Indians" and numbered 5,123. Those still belonging to functioning societies were identified by the rivers on which they resided. "San Joaquin Indians" consisted of five groups, numbering 3,107, of whom 1,605 were males, including 1,000 fighting men. The "Fresno Indians" also consisted of five groups, numbering 1,337, of whom 718 were males, including 500 fighting men. Three groups of "Merced Indians" numbered 280, of whom 151 were males, including 75 fighting men. The population of the so-called river Indians thus totaled 4,724.[2]

Only for Mariposa County did the census taker include the number of fighting men, probably because it was in the Southern Mines, in 1850 and 1851, that Chiefs José Juarez, José Rey, Bautista, and others offered a concerted, if short-lived, resistance, which was crushed only after the intervention of the state government. Although defeated in most of the military engagements, few Indians had actually surrendered, and many had negotiated with Indian Agents George Barbour, Redick McKee, and O. M. Wozencraft from positions of strength.[3]

When the goods and services promised in the treaties ceased after their rejection by the United States Senate, Indians, as individuals and as members of small raiding parties, again stole animals, property, and provisions from the different immigrant groups occupying their territories. In late 1852 and early 1853, for example, Indians, probably Yosemite and Chauchila, raided the mining camps on the Mariposa and Chowchilla rivers, absconding with large numbers of horses and mules. Five or six Americans followed the trail of a well-shod horse to a village of about one hundred Indians. Dismounting, they entered the village, intending to speak with the Indians, but Jesse Starkie, a former member of the Mariposa Battalion, perceiving some kind of belligerent activity on the part of the Indians, panicked and shot and killed a prominent individual. In the fight that followed the Indians riddled Starkie with arrows and wounded another white man in the hand. Fearing the Indians would cut them off from their horses, the whites quickly retreated. A day or two later, they returned to the village, now vacated, where they found the mutilated body of Starkie. Twenty-five men, including Alexis Godey, followed the Indians to another village about five miles distant. They attacked at daybreak, killing ten or twelve Indians and forcing the rest to flee. The Indians superficially wounded only one of the whites but nearly killed Godey.[4]

The attack caused an American to ask: "Why is it that our government does not do something to prevent the recurrence of these things? These Indians think the government of the United States has not acted in good faith with them, in not carrying out the stipulations of the treaty, and they complain that the Americans have cut off their supply of fish, destroyed their acorn trees, and have killed or driven away the deer from their hunting grounds, and that they are in a state bordering on actual starvation."[5] Frederick Kerlin, Edward F. Beale's former clerk, insisted that "the whites have been entirely in the wrong, and the men who went and attacked the Indians can be placed under no other category, than that of murderers."[6]

During two weeks in April 1853, nearly every night Indians stole animals from miners residing in the vicinity of Agua Fria. A few of the animals drifted back, some with arrows in them, others with their hamstrings cut. A resident acknowledged that the Indians "seemingly steal them to eat, and not to speculate on, as is supposed by some of our citizens." Whites chased the Indians into the mountains; deep snow forced the pursuers to turn back.[7]

In the northern sector of the Southern Mines, Indian raiders also were active. During the last months of 1852, Indians, probably a composite group of Miwok-speakers and mission refugees, residing at the juncture of the Mokelumne River and Dry Creek, stole stock and robbed ranches. The seventy-five fighting men possessed firearms and were good marksmen. In late January 1853 they stole a rifle, pistol, blankets, and provisions from Charles Drew and J. W. Bragg who had settled in the area.[8] The men discovered their property at a nearby village. They asked the Indians to return the goods, but a chief put a gun to Drew's head and threatened to shoot if they did not leave. They complied.[9]

Drew returned with sixteen men and again informed the Indians they came not to fight but to recover the stolen items. As the Indians slowly emerged from their lodges, one of them fired his rifle at a white man but missed. The Americans returned fire, killing two or three Indians. They also seized the chief who previously had threatened Drew and lashed him to a tree. After an exchange of fire, the whites began to withdraw but not before murdering the chief. A man named Gardiner dashed into the village, set a couple of lodges on fire, and rejoined his comrades unscathed. The Indians followed the retreating whites, keeping up a steady fire but inflicting no harm.[10]

The thirty to forty men who arrived at the village a few days later chased the five or six Indians present to Dry Creek. On an island in midstream the Indians had fortified themselves with breastworks of brushwood and had taken or destroyed all the boats along the river. Words were exchanged, the Indians informing the whites that their chief had stolen the goods from Drew and challenging them to come and take him. The Americans opened fire; the Indians returned fire their bullets forcing the whites to take shelter. As reported in the *Sacramento Daily Union*, the whites withdrew, "leaving the Indians masters of the field."[11]

Although the Americans thought they had their enemy trapped, a party of Indians crossed to the mainland and plundered a farmhouse. The editors of the *Union* commented on the Indians' audacity: "Success seemed to delight and embolden them very much, and should they be suffered to remain in their present fortified position, it is believed that their robberies and murders will become common throughout the neighborhood.... The rascals have exhibited a courage which will secure their inevitable destruction; and although many may desire this result, the brave man will both pity and admire their fate, after the assumption of so bold a defiance in a populous country, where every man who is not a fellow Indian, is a foe."[12]

In April, Indians stole several animals, including horses intended for a stage line, from whites on the Tuolumne River and drove off some fifty animals from those residing in the vicinities of Coulterville and Big Oak Flat. A party of Americans, supplied with provisions for a two-week campaign, went in pursuit. The editors of a San Francisco newspaper wished them success, "as nothing but a salutary chastisement will teach those rascals a lesson.[13] The following month other "rascals" stole horses and mules from prospectors up the Tuolumne at Cherokee Diggings. The whites giving chase found an Indian village of several hundred residents too strong to be attacked. "The Indians are in large force in the mountains," reported the *San Joaquin Republican*, "and their constant depredations upon the whites will, we fear, result in their extermination or expulsion from this section of country."[14] Late in May or early in June, Indians stole horses from whites residing east of Sonora. Miners Clark, Tuttle, and Duffield lost valuable stock. The latter organized a company of several men, followed the Indians for two days and three nights but failed to overtake them.[15]

In the mountains twenty miles from Sonora, Indians in early July broke into the cabin of two teamsters, who were away at the time, and departed with some blankets. The teamsters arrived the following day, intending to haul a load of ice to Sonora. Fearful that their mules might be the Indians' next targets, they locked one team in a stable, the other in their cabin. The following day about one mile from the cabin, Indians ambushed the teamsters. A rifle shot to the head and several arrows into his body killed one man instantly. The other took an arrow in the chest but managed to escape and find shelter with some whites three miles distant. The Indians were unable to release three mules hitched to the wagon, and five of the seven they absconded with managed to escape. That night, however, they stole a mule, a horse, a colt, and a saddle from a Mr. Knight, who resided eight miles above the teamsters' cabin. The day after the raid, while on his way to Sonora, Knight came across five mules and his saddle.[16]

On July 10 miners held a meeting to organize a company that would launch a campaign against the Indians residing between the Stanislaus and Tuolumne Rivers. "A strong feeling of exasperation is abroad, and the force now organizing against them will deal severely with them," reported a resident of Sonora.[17] One of the companies sent to "deal severely" with the raiders returned a week later with nothing to show for its efforts.[18]

The other ventured to the north fork of the Merced, but it too failed to locate those responsible for the attacks.[19]

Indians continued to raid in and about the town of Mariposa. "The Indians are becoming very troublesome here, stealing and killing animals every night," reported a miner on August 1. "A few nights since, they made a descent upon Lyons' gulch and drove off every animal owned there; they also served the miners on Buckeye in the same manner last Monday evening. Two days ago they entered the corral of Messrs. Green & White, at the Saw Mill, on Sherlock's creek, and after shooting an arrow into the shoulders of one fine mule decamped with three others—two of which, however, returned next day."[20] The residents of Mariposa met to discuss steps to punish the Indians. They agreed to solicit money to defray the expenses of those who joined a company that would move against the stock raiders. In a letter to the *San Joaquin Republican*, a miner blamed the depredations on the Yosemites, who "heretofore refused to treat with the Indian Agents. They have a large Rancheria, on the head-waters of the Mercede River. They are a wily tribe and somewhat noted for bravery and daring."[21]

In the summer of 1853 the Yosemites suffered a serious defeat, not by whites but by Indians. As recounted by Luis Bunnell, a member of the Mariposa Battalion which had captured the Yosemite in 1851, a party of Paiutes from Mono Lake, situated on the east side of the Sierra Nevada, crossed the mountains and attacked the Yosemites in their valley homeland, killing Chief Tenaya and many of his men and capturing most of the women and children. The Paiutes attacked because the Yosemite had stolen some of their horses while residing with them at Mono Lake. Shortly after the attack a few Yosemites, some wounded and all frightened, sought from miners on the South Fork of the Merced food and protection from their Indian enemies. Bunnell, who had become a trader on the river, invited them to his post, from which they could fish, collect acorns, and mine. With tools provided by Bunnell, they mined the north fork for a time, but when one of them died from some kind of injury, they departed for the Hetch Hetchy Valley. From these Indians, Bunnell learned the particulars of Tenaya's death.[22]

Late in the fall three Yosemites visited Bunnell's post, informing him that they were encamped on the Tuolumne and had come to the Merced to fish. Bunnell gave them some provisions, and they departed a few nights later. Missing was one of his best mules. Bunnell followed its tracks, concluding, "that it had been stolen by Indians, and my suspicions were that my Yosemite friends were the culprits. I made every effort to recover the animal, but without success."[23]

When Bunnell returned to the post sometime in the winter of 1853-54, he found it plundered and his two employees, Robert Sevil and Robert

Smith, missing. Their bodies were discovered a short time later. John Bowling, sheriff of Mariposa County and former commander of Company B of the Mariposa Battalion, blamed the murders on the Yosemites and recommended that Bunnell lead a posse to chastise them. Bunnell and another man searched along the Tuolumne divide but found no Indians. Apparently those who killed the two men had gone to the upper Tuolumne River and joined the remnant of the Tauhalame, a group once under the control of Tenaya. Later, while visiting the Fresno Farm, Bunnell learned from the local Indians that the Yosemites had killed the two men and had robbed the post mainly to obtain clothing and blankets. Indians from the farm offered to join the whites in an expedition against the offenders because they were "bad Indians." No expedition was formed, and those responsible for the killings were never apprehended.[24]

The remnant of the Yosemite, along with other dislocated Indians, evidently reoccupied the Yosemite Valley, because in July 1854 Indians from the valley robbed a follower of Cypriano, chief of the Awal.[25] In March 1851 Cypriano had signed the first treaty conducted by the Indians agents.[26] Described by an acquaintance as "a tall, majestic-looking Indian," he spoke "the Spanish language fluently, and by the by, is quite an intelligent fellow."[27] When the robbery occurred Cypriano and his people were mining at the juncture of the north and south forks of the Merced River. The chief led a large party into the valley, plundering and destroying a recently abandoned village.[28]

In September, Cypriano told the miners residing on the south fork of the Merced that the Yosemites had killed three women and two children belonging to his group. He offered to supply the whites with provisions if they would support him in a campaign against them. The miners sought assistance from the residents of Mariposa, who sent a company to the river. Those leading the company, however, quickly realized that Cypriano sought to embroil the miners in his conflict with the Yosemites so he could take over their fishing grounds. They informed the miners about the deception and reprimanded the Indians for their duplicity.[29]

Perhaps in response to the affair, Cypriano sought to contact the whites residing near Mariposa. Because of their reputation as stock raiders, his people were prohibited from collecting acorns in the vicinity of the town, forcing them to live with the Monos during the winter months. According to Jean-Nicolas Perlot, a Belgian miner, Cypriano told a gathering of miners that he had been accused of crimes committed by another group and that he and his people held no hostile feelings toward the whites. All they wanted was to collect acorns on the big flats surrounding Mariposa. Let his women gather seeds, and Indians and whites would be friends. Perlot was impressed with the speech, but Cypriano was momentarily speechless when the Belgian asked him to display his copy of the treaty conducted with the Indian agents. Unaware that Perlot knew about the document, Cypriano drew it, carefully rolled in oilcloth, from his quiver. Perlot encouraged him to show the treaty to the sheriff of Mariposa County. If Cypriano repeated to the sheriff what he had told him, his people would be allowed to gather acorns wherever they wanted.[30]

In a letter to the sheriff, Perlot emphasized that if treated fairly the Indians posed no danger to the whites. He asked him to lift the edict prohibiting the Indians from residing near Mariposa and offered practical reasons for doing so. If allowed to remain in the environs of Mariposa, they would lack nothing and would remain at peace. But should violence erupt they could be easily apprehended. The sheriff invited Cypriano to Mariposa. At the meeting the two men conversed in Spanish, and Cypriano agreed to everything asked of him. To distinguish the good Indians from the bad, Cypriano promised that his followers would be decently clad, each covered by a shirt which came down at least to the knees. The sheriff gave Cypriano a certificate permitting him to travel throughout Mariposa County.[31]

Contact with the Indians was the key to peace, insisted Perlot. He and other miners had worked with Indians during the summer, and "after having exchanged services and sometimes perhaps a few thumps, knowing them better, we judged them more favorably. They themselves seemed to have come to a better feeling with regard to us: it was from lack of understanding each other that we had exchanged tomahawk blows and gunshots. This habit of judging without knowing each other is, I think, most of the time, the source of wars which break out between peoples, whether they are savage or civilized."[32] Overlooked by Perlot, however, was the economic motive of the attacks. Although Indians occasionally killed miners and others in revenge, their primary goal in raiding farms, ranches, and towns was to obtain provisions, equipment, and animals.[33]

Indians preferred stealing domestic horses to hunting feral ones, but the latter, in times of emergencies, had been a reliable source of food.[34] By the early 1850s that source was drying up, as Indians found themselves in competition with American settlers and Mexican vaqueros. Subagent M. B. Lewis reported in November 1852 that thousands of wild horses occupying the area south of the mouth of the Merced were being "intruded upon by man, and afford employment for hundreds of Mexican horse catchers, who prefer that kind of occupation to that of digging for gold."[35] The *San Joaquin Republican* noted early the following year that recent inclement weather and floods had driven many horses to the area between the Merced and Mariposa Rivers "and the hunters with the lasso are taking them by the hundreds. At the present time the horses are easily caught. They are driven from the rolling country onto the plain, where they mire down and become easy prey."[36]

Because horses and mules transported most of the supplies to the mines, the Gold Rush created a market that had not existed before. As recalled by John Barker, parties of Mexicans, each numbering from ten to twenty men, entered "the valley at various points and prepared, in a systematic way, to capture the wild horses, and tame such of them as were suitable for the purpose and sell them to the packers and others who could use them."[37] Whites also found another use for the wild horses, a use Indians long had enjoyed. In early January 1853, a newspaper reported that "the people of the upper sections are now doing a thriving market trade in the flesh of such wild horses as can be captured and killed. The plan is to drive a herd of mustangs into the bogs, and when they are mired down so that all chance of locomotion is destroyed, then the settlers rush in and lasso such as are good for the farm, while the others are killed and consumed in the absence of veal and mutton chops.—Hundred of animals have been destroyed in this manner this winter, and the herds of wild horses that once roamed over the plains are now fast disappearing."[38]

To Americans progress was measured in the replacement of wild animals with domesticated stock. As Lewis noted large settlements were springing up in Mariposa County, and extensive preparations were being made for the cultivation of the soil and the breeding of stock: "Present appearances would indicate that ere long the sluggish elk, the deer, the antelope and coyote will soon have to abandon the original homes of their ancestors, and give place to the husbandman with his domesticated herds."[39]

The cattle, horses, and hogs of the "husbandman" consumed the seeds, berries, and acorns of the Indian. Regarding the situation near the Fresno Farm, Lewis wrote in mid-1856 that, "acorns, the most important and most available bread stuff, in the low hills and vicinity of the plains, where it is most plentiful and easiest obtained, are consumed by the hogs of the whites. True, as a general thing, there is plenty higher up in the mountains, but not so easily obtained and transported to desirable places for winter quarters; and there are, at this time, droves of hogs as high up the mountains as there is an acorn to be found at accessible points."[40]

Settlers also interfered with the Indians' fishing operations. In late 1856 whites built a dam on the Merced River, downstream from the Indians residing on the north and south forks. "Large quantities of salmon are annually killed by these Indians," reported the *Mariposa Gazette* in November, "and being prepared in their own manner, form the staple article of food during the winter. Fishing thus, being a failure, we may look out for some stealing, particularly if the season should be severe."[41]

Part and parcel with the replacement of wild animals with domestic stock was the replacement of hunter-gatherers with yeoman farmers. Between January 17 and May 29, 1852, James H. Carson provided the *San Joaquin Republican* with a series of articles clearly articulating the attitudes of many Americans. The interior, he wrote in one, was "the garden of California." It should be settled "with hardy farmers of our country. We can imagine their neat cottages peeping out from amidst fields of flowing grain. We can see the neat village with its church spires, marking the march of civilization—and hear the lowing herds that browse on the luxuriant grass around."[42] In another article he assessed in florid language the Indian modes of subsistence: "Variable, doubtful, wonderful, and unbelievable, are the ways in which the digger Indian supports life; he sows not, neither does he reap, but feeds upon grass and the roots of the earth, with the wild beasts; he knows no seed time nor harvest, but watches with a keen eye the growth of the grass and the fall of the acorn; he tilleth not the earth, nor buildeth stone-houses, nor granaries, nor lays up stores for the morrow, for fear they may spoil."[43]

As J. D. Borthwick saw it, the presence of Indians was "not compatible with that of a civilized community, and, as the country becomes more thickly settled, there will be no longer room for them. Their country can be made subservient to man, but as they themselves cannot be turned to account, they must move off, and make way for their betters." What he advocated, Borthwick admitted, "may not be very good morality, but it is the way of the world, and the aborigines of California are not likely to share a better fate than those of many another country."[44]

Morality was far from the mind of a man named Ogle in July 1853, when he wrote that the Indians "take up more room than the rest of the world can afford them! They are, in fact, the greatest land-monopolists in the universe, and the most worthless squabs at that: so the fine fellows must either go to work when the time comes, or else pull up stakes and put our [sic] for the Rocky Mountains, or for kingdomcome. The earth must be farmed, not foraged, by man; and the vagabonds that have neither forts nor fences, must give it up.... Progress required a fresh soil, a wide field and a clean sweep."[45]

About the same time, Cypriano presented an Indian perspective on land usage. Addressing a large gathering of Indians in Spanish, he proclaimed that "we are one of the most independent nations on earth; for while the Americans, and other nations, have to depend on the cultivation of the soil to keep the inner man alive, we can subsist sumptuously on acorns, pine nuts, wild clover, roots, herbs, etc. As the Americans call us 'the children of nature,' Nature in the most bounteous manner supplies us in the greatest abundance."[46]

Cypriano also predicted the revitalization of traditional Indian culture. Acknowledging that the Indians had learned much from the Americans, he was nevertheless pleased to announce "that the time is not far distant when the Americans will leave our favored land, and then, and not till then can our time-honored festivals be revived as in by gone days." To prepare for that time, he directly addressed the women in the audience: "My countrywomen, permit me to ask of you, with the kindness of a brother, to abstain from vice; for by so doing, your sojourn on earth will be extended to that period which our fore-parents attained; but should you step aside from the true paths of virtue, our nation would soon, yes very soon, dwindle down to a few emaciated beings. Be obedient to you husbands, shrink from no responsibility, and the Good Spirit will reward you in the happy and prosperous country."[47]

Clearly, Cypriano had in mind the women residing in and near the mining towns. Because white women shunned their domestic services, many turned to the one profession where they could earn money for food and clothing. As a consequence, the number of marriages between Indian men and women declined, prospective husbands not wanting women who had associated with white men. And those women who earned a living on their own in the mining camps found it difficult to return to the domestic existence demanded by Indian men. M. B. Lewis was convinced that Indian women, if given the chance, would prove to be intellectually and morally superior to Indian men, but "being looked on by the men in no other light than tools and servants, and treated as such, they have no chance for profitable employment of a praiseworthy character; … at the same time sought for by white men, and encouraged by those who ought to be their friends and protectors, they have been led astray at an early age, and soon thereafter become the sport and traffic of worthless Indian men. In one or two brief years they become diseased, and at the age of twenty wear the features of thirty-five to forty; outcasts among their own people; and, as a general thing, before they arrive at the age of thirty, die a shameful and miserable death."[48]

The Indians most exposed to the inundation of whites and thus the first to undergo steep population decline resided along the San Joaquin River, from its turn to the north to the delta. In January 1852 the *San Joaquin Republican* reported that recently ten Indian families had visited Charles Weber at his residence near the juncture of the Stanislaus and San Joaquin Rivers. The purpose of the visit was to exchange presents with Weber, a custom that had begun when he first settled in the area in the mid-1840s but which had been discontinued for the past three years. In what amounted to an obituary called "The Last of the Yachicumnes," the editors wrote that it was "known to our readers that this portion of the San Joaquin county was formerly occupied by a formidable tribe of Indians; and the places of their encampment are still visible in the neighborhood of the city. Soon after the white faces appeared on the river, their numbers were thinned, and the remainder of tribe removed to the wild country on the Coast Range."[49]

In August 1853 an army officer estimated that the population of the Indians residing on the Fresno and San Joaquin Rivers had, within the previous ten months, dropped by half, largely because of the disease which had "sown the seeds of their almost entire destruction."[50] Passing through the area a year later, Thomas Henley found the Indians on the San Joaquin in a most miserable and degraded condition. They reside, he told the commissioner of Indian affairs, "in the mining region, and from an exposure of some four years to its influences, they are reduced to a condition of utter destitution, and to confirmed habits of idleness and dissipation, readily yielding to vices the most degrading and revolting, resulting in disease, which is gradually reducing their numbers."[51]

Some of the most dissipated Indians resided up the San Joaquin in the vicinity of Fort Miller and the nearby town of Millerton. The assistant surgeon at the fort, William F. Edgar, summed up the deterioration the Indians had undergone:

> When I first came to Fort Miller in 51 the Indian Rancheria or village on the Military reserve was large and the Indians numerous and appeared healthy and happy, but a town soon sprang up in the vicinity of the post and as it and the White population increased the Indians and their village decreased rapidly. The facilities for obtaining their accustomed supplies of subsistence gradually decreased while those for obtaining bad whiskey… rapidly increased.… By 54 they began to show the effects of the evils to which they were subjected, a preference for which, it could be seen, was taking the place of that for labour and sobriety.…
>
> On my return to the post in May 57 I was somewhat surprised to find them or the remnant rather, of the original tribes still there—reduced probably to one fourth of their original number and these diseased, drunken, and almost worthless.[52]

Early in 1857 Lieutenant LaRhett L. Livingston reported to his superiors that the Indians residing in the vicinity of Fort Miller came into contact "with the worst class of whites to be found in any country. They have contracted diseases—to them the most fatal—and are constantly furnished by the whites with liquor so that every day an observer may see a dozen Indians reeling drunk." Although it was beyond his authority to prohibit the use of liquor, Livingston was continually on call to quell disturbances among whites and Indians.[53]

Upon returning to Fort Miller in 1858, Captain E. D. Keyes was unprepared for what he observed:

> It was on the very site of Fort Miller, in the same month of May seven years before, that I saw assembled above 1,200 aborigines, natives of the adjacent plains and mountains, many of whom had never seen a white man till they came to treat with us. I was then impressed with the appearance of several chiefs, and remember the general aspect of all. Especially was I struck with the activity of the young Indians of both sexes while they amused themselves with football and other rough sports. As all those Indians had been assigned to a reservation of which Fort Miller was a central point, I inquired for several individuals whom I remembered. I was told that they were nearly all dead, victims to drunkenness, and that of the whole number I then saw in such full activity not above fifty remained. I took pains to see the wretched survivors, and was shocked with the spectacle of degradation and self-abandonment they presented.[54]

Regarding the effects alcohol had on the Indians in the mining town of Columbia, in September 1858 the editors of the *Tuolumne Courier* wrote: "At midnight their savage howls may frequently be heard, as they return to their sleeping places, half crazy from the poisonous drink which they have imbibed from some of the low groceries about the outskirts of the town.... Why do not our citizens ask the Legislature to have them removed to one of the reservations, where they will be comfortable, and be afforded an opportunity of learning some of the Christian ways of civilized beings?"[55] The same month the editors of the *Sacramento Daily Union* also called for removal but for a different reason. Not only was disease "carrying the red man rapidly to his grave," it also demoralized whites by exposing them to "the most disgusting and revolting species of lechery which the most depraved and abandoned mind can possible conceive."[56]

Had they a public voice, the most recent immigrant group to intrude upon Indian territories, the Chinese, also would have advocated removal. Imitating the behavior lawless whites manifested toward the Chinese, Indians beat, robbed, extorted, and sometimes killed them.[57] The *San Francisco Herald* reported in early August 1853 that the "Indians entertain a remarkable antipathy to the whole Chinese race, and never lose an opportunity to manifest it. Unrestrained by white people, the poor ignorant celestials would be massacred by wholesale by those proud and merciless savages, who claim a great superiority over Asiatics. A fear of punishment restrains them from violence."[58] Early the following year an army officer stationed at Fort Miller noted the "unaccountable aversion, mutually existing between these Indians, and the Chinese emigrants, who in point of numbers, are becoming an important element in the population of this sparsely settled frontier. These latter regard the Indians with feelings of terror and abhorrence, with a vague notion that they are a species of cannibals, whilst the former view the strangers with the contempt due to an inferior being, ridicule their language, manners, and personal appearance, and impose upon them with impunity, when they can do so with safety to themselves."[59]

Although Indians' antipathy to the Chinese may have been primarily cultural, it also stemmed from economic competition. Writing in July 1856 M. B. Lewis pointed out that industrious Indians in the vicinity of the Fresno Farm once had found employment among the miners and farmers, but presently "the chances for mining are not encouraging, on account of the diggings in their vicinity being all taken up by whites and Chinamen, and when labor is required, the service of Chinamen is sought in preference to that of Indians."[60]

Forced to adapt economically, some Indians engaged in what might be called seasonal begging and scavenging, a subsistence strategy added to that of hunting and gathering.[61] A resident of Tuolumne County, bounded by the Stanislaus and Tuolumne Rivers, noted that Indians would camp on the outskirts of the mining camps "asking charity, picking up the old clothes, in the shape of shirts, hats, boots and shoes thrown away by the miners. They hang around slaughter pens and beg offal, and are often seen winding their way out of town with their baskets loaded with refuse of the butchers' shops." Late in the spring they would depart for the Sierra Nevada to gather wild foods, returning in the fall to escape the snow.[62]

Of all the practical items sought by the Indians, clothing may have been the most highly prized. According to J. D. Borthwick, Indians disposed of their money in two ways: playing monte with Mexicans and purchasing articles of clothing.[63] On one occasion Cypriano ordered all his followers to mine for gold so they could buy clothes. Scavenging, however, was the more common means of obtaining clothing. Jean-Nicolas Perlot noted that "the miners didn't throw away the least bit of worn-out clothing without its soon being gathered by an Indian who covered himself with it on the spot."[64] The end of the week, when miners often discarded old clothes and bought new ones, was the optimal time for obtaining these items.[65]

Indians dressed in discarded clothing amused and offended many whites. Friedrich Gerstaecker wrote that "equally funny and disfigured do they look, when they put on European clothes. They frequently have no idea for what purpose, and in what order they ought to be worn. First, a dress-coat, and then a waistcoat, then part of a shirt, or a waistcoat by itself, or a pair of trousers, or three and four pair of them, at the same time, they do not care; and they admire a uniform most, red, if possible, with gold or silver."[66] Borthwick thought the Indians "dressed in the most grotesque style.... One man wore a coat, another the remains of a shirt and one boot, while another was fully equipped in an old hat and a waistcoat:

but the most conspicuous and generally worn articles of costume were the coloured cotton handkerchiefs with which they bandaged up their heads."[67] According to Perlot the Indian who found the most clothing was "the most, if not the best, dressed. Some had shirt and trousers, or rather the remnants of what had been shirt or trousers; they were the best endowed. Others had nothing but a shirt, so much the better if it was long enough." If the trousers were too long, the owner split both legs from the crotch, so he could raise them to his arm pits or over his shoulders. The trousers thus covered his entire body, "save precisely that which civilized man wants especially to cover." Perlot also mentioned those who wore only overcoats, "whose skirts they fastened together in front, thus uncovering St. Peter to cover St. Paul. I saw one who had nothing but a vest, which he had taken the precaution, 'tis true, of buttoning from top to bottom; and another decked out solely in a dress-coat!"[68]

When it came to describing how Indian women dressed themselves in new materials, Perlot exhibited more sensitivity:

> The Indian woman, very often, clothed herself with what she found and, naturally, she could not find woman's clothing since civilization, in California, was still represented only by men, but, although having only the same rags to cover herself with as the Indian man, she knew how to make use of them with more ingenuity. The first dress that she imagined was extremely simple: it consisted of a piece of calico having in the middle of its length a tear through which she passed her head. This sort of chasuble covered her well enough in front and behind; it was drawn in at the waist by a belt ordinarily consisting of a simple rope or string. Not having been slow to learn about needle and thread, she began to sew the side of her chasuble; soon after, she added sleeves to it and the dress was complete.[69]

According to Gerstaecker, Indian women liked "to dress like European females, but as they never wash their dresses, they looked rather the worse for it after the first two or three days. They most frequently, though, when they want something beside their usual wide and long apron of dressed deer skins… throw a piece of calico around them, in the same way as the Spanish ladies use their mantilla."[70]

As noted in the *San Joaquin Republican*, the Indians could be terribly persistent:

> There are a great many Indian men and women loitering about Stockton, getting their living by begging and stealing, and there are

> but few articles that they will not take possession of if they can, by fair means or foul, even to a deceased dog. They have of late become an especial nuisance to families in retired parts of the city, the males of which are absent in the daytime about their occupation in town. The creatures are excessively insolent, and do not fail to remind the ladies of the houses which they visit that they are aware there are no men about, which announcement sometimes causes a little alarm, and articles are handed over to them which the proprietors would prefer withholding. The vagrants do not scruple to steal the ax, pot, or kettle, clothes from the line, or anything else which is not made fast or locked up. A good dog is invaluable in cases of such visits, and presence of a revolver is equally efficacious in hurrying the departure of the unwelcome intruders.[71]

In August 1858 other "unwelcome intruders" entered Stockton and set forth to beg and pilfer. "The dusky visitors," wrote the editors of the *San Joaquin Republican*, "also, are very apt to appropriate to their own use any little article that may be lying carelessly around. It is time they were walked off to their home, if they have one."[72] Consisting of some forty Paiutes from Carson Valley on the east side of the Sierra Nevada, they were in no hurry to walk off. They camped near the center street bridge under two large oaks, reported the *Republican* in mid-September, and "piled upon the branches and the trunk all manner of 'traps,' blankets, shocking bad hats and bonnets, skirts of more colors than Joseph's coat of old, rags, and babies in baskets." Some of the women were "comely," and several of the party, especially the younger ones, spoke excellent English.[73] The females, who comprised most of the party, spent part of each day at the levee, where the town garbage dump was located, eating whatever they could find.[74] Evidently, the Paiutes departed before the end of the month.[75]

By modifying the purpose of a traditional undertaking, some Indians employed another survival strategy. Dressed in what remained of their traditional regalia, Miwoks entered Sonora to dance for money. As recalled by one resident, "They wore high feather headdresses and had grotesque stripes painted on their chests, and would grunt and dance and whistle through long reeds until we threw down some dimes." Adorned with feathers, beads, shells, and body paint, Miwoks also danced in Jamestown and Columbia, also for money.[76]

As an economic strategy fostered by the dislocation that came with the miners' intrusion, scavenging, begging, stealing, and dancing produced some short-term benefits, but in the long run, there was little the Indians in the Southern Mines could do to check the rapid decline of their populations. In August 1859 M. B. Lewis enumerated only 1,501 individuals residing in the region.[77] This was a significant drop from the nearly ten thousand identified in the state census of 1852.[78] That a demographic collapse had taken place was better put metaphorically by the *Visalia Delta*: "Frosts of advancing civilization,… course and rude, sear them, and they drop off and go before the wind as leaves in autumn."[79] Although Indians residing in the Tulare Valley would be spared the same degree of population decline, they would soon lose the institutions designed to support and protect them.

CHAPTER XXVI

Closure

In mid-January 1859 M. B. Lewis informed Superintendent of Indian Affairs Thomas Henley that unless he was provided with operating funds, the Fresno Indian Agency would not last much longer. The patience of his creditors had run out. Grain produced on the Fresno and Kings River farms had been largely consumed, and the supply of acorns the Indians on the lower Kings River had gathered soon would be as well.[1] Early in April he again informed Henley about the seriousness of the situation. Most of the Fresno Farm Indians had departed for the mines in search of food and clothing. Only the sickly and inexperienced remained to cultivate the crops and maintain the property. He had no operating funds and knew of no person in the area who "would credit the Indian department with one dollar, unless I should make promises that I do not feel safe in doing."[2] The following month he told Henley that William Campbell, owner of the Kings River Farm, demanded payment and had threatened to confiscate the Indians' crops as security. An explanation as to when the Indian Office would meet its debts "would be thankfully received by me, and no doubt afford much relief to the minds of its anxious creditors."[3]

In one of his last reports to commissioner of Indian affairs, issued in late August 1859, Lewis identified the location, estimated the numbers, and assessed the physical condition of the Indians in his jurisdiction. He emphasized that the white man attached no more importance to his patent for land than the Indian "for his right to the land of his adoption or nativity." Of all the 2,436 Indians enumerated, only the Potoyanti and the Chauchila had permanently relocated, the former from the Merced

Table 12. Indians Associated with the Fresno Indian Agency, 1859

Group	*Location*	*Males*	*Females*	*Health*
Chauchila	Fresno Farm	45	40	Good
Choinimni, Aitcha Toichicha	Watoka Creek	150	140	Poor
Chukchansi	Coarse Gold Gulch Fresno Farm	115	125	Good
Gashowu	Dry Creek	40	48	Poor
Gawia	Four Creeks	60	50	Fair
Heuchi	Fresno Farm	8	18	—
Mono	Fine Gold Gultch	260	275	Good
Nukchu, Yosemite, other remnants	Chowchilla (north fork)	45	40	Poor
Nutunutu	Tulare Lake	100	90	Poor
Pitkakchi, Dalinchi	Millerton	80	70	Poor
Pohonichi	Fresno (headwaters)	55	50	Good
Potoyanti	Chowchilla	60	50	Fair
Tauhalame	Tuolumne	45	40	Poor
Telamni	Visalia	50	55	Fair
Wechihit	Kings River Farm	40	35	Poor
Wimilchi, Tachi, Wowol	Tulare Lake	80	85	Poor

Source: Adapted from M. B. Lewis to Alfred B. Greenwood, Fresno Indian Agency, August 30, 1859, Office of Indian Affairs, Letters Received, 1824–81, roll 37.

to the Chowchilla, the latter from the Chowchilla to the Fresno Farm.[4]

James McDuffie, Henley's replacement as superintendent, visited the Fresno Indian Farm in late July or early August.[5] He told the commissioner of Indian affairs that the continual drought and the resulting failure of the crops year after year had convinced him that the purpose and utility of the farm had long had passed. The improvements were of little value to the owner of the land and none to the government. Furthermore, the "scarcity of water renders every effort at farming on the part of Indians abortive, and irrigation is attended with great labor and expense."[6]

McDuffie found the Kings River Farm in better shape, although public property had not been well maintained. Eight hundred bushels of wheat, one thousand bushels of barley, and four or five tons of hay had been harvested. The grain was in storage and the hay secured in stacks. The soil was good, and the crops well watered from the Kings River. For their own use, the Indians had seeded two hundred acres, mostly in wheat and barley but some in corn. Although the farm possessed advantages, the rent paid to Campbell failed to justify its continued existence, and it was "too closely surrounded by settlers to answer the purposes of an Indian agency." McDuffie recommended that the Fresno, Kings River, and Tule River Farms, as well as the Tejón Reservation, be abolished. A subagent would periodically visit the Indians who remained in the vicinities of the abandoned institutions.[7]

In late October 1859 McDuffie and J. Ross Browne visited the Fresno and Kings River Farms. Writing to the commissioner of Indian affairs the following month, Browne noted that the Fresno Farm belonged to the heirs of the late Lorenzo Vinsonhaler, "and has been ditched and fenced at public expense, and a heavy rent paid for it since 1854." Having visited at the farm several times, he had always been informed by the subagent that the Indians were away in the hills collecting wild foods: "This was the case in May, in September, in October, and in November. The average number there may be fairly estimated at from twenty to thirty." Moreover, the Indians relocated there the previous winter had scattered over the San Joaquin Valley. The subagent had built himself a house, and his own farm was on an adjoining claim.[8] At the Kings River Farm, Browne observed good fences, barns, and houses the Indians had built for its owner, William Campbell. Never very impressed with the Fresno Farm and convinced the one on the Kings River served mainly the interests of its owner, Browne advised McDuffie to abolish both, discharge Campbell, and remove government property either to the Tejón Reservation or the Tule River Farm.[9]

A short time later McDuffie instructed Lewis to secure all the public property at the farms and discharge the employees. He explained his actions in a letter to the commissioner:

> The advantages gained heretofore by the cultivation of these farms has not been at all commensurate with the expenses incurred; the amount of money paid for their rent alone has been almost sufficient to cover the entire value of the crops raised upon them. Great neglect been shown by the sub-agents in charge, in guarding public property from decay. Most of the agricultural implements on hand are useless, from the want of proper care, the replacing of which would incur an expense the necessities of the department will not warrant....
>
> The number of Indians supported upon these farms does not,

> in my opinion, exceed fifty, for whom it is my intention to purchase the food necessary during the present winter, which will prove to be a more economical system than that of maintaining farms at exorbitant rents.[10]

Evidently, the rent paid to the owners of the Fresno Farm ceased at the end of 1859, and public property was transferred to the Kings River Farm.[11] But M. B. Lewis continued to purchase supplies for the Indians in his jurisdiction through June 1861.[12] In November rent to the owner of the Kings River Farm was discontinued.[13] Public property was sent to the Tule River Farm. To the editors of the *Visalia Delta*, the future of the Indians once associated with the Fresno Indian Agency was as bleak as their past: "That the Indians have been demoralized at great expense, other than improved in any particular, is a matter with which the people of this region are conversant. The new order of things—the new Reservations, or rather locations of these, may be an improvement. This remains to be seen. Our faith, however, is a very weak decoction of uncertainties."[14]

In his annual report for the year 1859, issued in December, the secretary of the interior emphatically stated that "the reservation system of California has proved a failure." To better manage Indian affairs in California, he recommended to the president that the superintendency, agencies, and subagencies be abolished and replaced by two districts, each managed by an agent with the authority to employ as many assistants as authorized by the Indian Office.[15] In June 1860 Congress divided California into two superintendencies, each to be administered by a superintending agent. John A. Dreibelbis got the northern district; James McDuffie the southern.[16] Shortly, Augustus D. Rightmire took over for McDuffie. It was not long before he too was replaced.[17]

As Indian policy changed so did military strategy. According to an editorial in a San Francisco newspaper published in January 1861, Fort Tejón offered no protection to white settlements, was located in a cold, bleak, inhospitable, and worthless area subjected to earthquakes, and cost the government about $55,000 per year to maintain. It should be abandoned and the troops relocated to Los Angeles.[18] The following month Samuel Bishop, Edward F. Beale, and eighty-six other persons sent a petition to General Albert S. Johnston, commander of the military department of the pacific. If the fort were abandoned, they warned, those who "made their homes in the wilderness will be left to the mercy of ruthless savages, and a beautiful district about to be reclaimed by civilization again abandoned to its original condition."[19] Many of those signing the petition most likely resided in or near the "town" of Tejón, which had sprung up near the post.[20] The seven merchants operating in the area and those running grog shops probably signed as well.[21]

In June the army transferred most of the troops to Camp Fitzgerald near Los Angeles. Left behind to guard government property were Lieutenant M. T. Carr and two enlisted men. Immediately, Indians in considerable numbers entered the grounds to gather up what items the soldiers had discarded, and Carr had some difficulty in persuading them to leave.[22] A few days later, two or three Indians who had had too much to drink attempted to lasso a white man in his buggy and later tried to break into a woman's house. She fired her pistol out a window and the Indians fled.[23] The incidents convinced Carr that an outbreak was imminent, and on June 21 he telegraphed Camp Fitzgerald, requesting reinforcements.[24] Major James H. Carleton quickly ordered a detachment of eleven dragoons to Fort Tejón.[25]

A month later Lieutenant B. F. Davis visited the fort to ascertain whether the Indians were hostile. Davis placed the blame for the disturbances squarely on the local whites. Nearly every family employed Indians as house servants or laborers, he wrote in his report, and thus it was "in their power to prevent all trouble in future by simply prohibiting the sale of liquor by any member of the community." The whites had "lived so long upon Government patronage that they now find it difficult to do without it, and they will use every means to have troops restationed at that place." The soldiers returned to Los Angeles by way of the Tejón Reservation, where they met the recently appointed supervisor, Theodore Boschulte, who confirmed Davis' position that the Indians posed no threat.[26] Superintending Agent John P. H. Wentworth, who had succeeded Augustus D. Rightmire, had hired Boschulte on June 5.[27]

The following month Wentworth informed Commissioner of Indian Affairs William P. Dole that the Tejón Reservation suffered from mismanagement, but with an investment of fifteen hundred to two thousand dollars to purchase animals and equipment it could be turned around and made self-sufficient. Because Wentworth needed to employ several white men during the planting and harvesting seasons, he was troubled by a law that limited an employee's salary to fifty dollars per month. To be competitive, the government should revise the law to reflect the economic conditions in California and pay workers seventy-five dollars per month.[28]

Writing again in October, Wentworth again claimed that the reservation could become self-sufficient, but the land on which it was situated should be purchased by the federal government. He encouraged Dole to make "some permanent arrangement for the continuance of this reservation, as at present great embarrassment is experienced from the want of federal jurisdiction." There was "no law defending agents and supervisors, in the performance of their duties, against the advancements and encroachments of a class of whites who are always inimical to their interests."[29]

When Wentworth visited Tejón in November, he found no grain,

Table 13. Tejoneño Population and Property, 1862

	PEOPLE			ANIMALS		
Leaders	*Men*	*Women*	*Children*	*Cows*	*Horses*	*Cultivation acreage*
Chico and Rafael	52	65	45	—	20	50
Raymundo	80	88	63	—	30	50
Vincente	36	40	20	22	33	33
Total	168	193	128	22	83	133

Source: Adapted from John H. Wentworth to William P. Dole, San Francisco, August 30, 1862, *Annual Report of the Commissioner of Indian Affairs for the Year 1862,* 325; and Boschulte, Statement of Farms, March 31, 1862.

agricultural implements, or materials of any kind. The buildings, moreover, were in a state of decay.[30] Boschulte told him that those in the previous administration had either neglected or willfully destroyed most of the crops on the reservation. The Indians, in want of provisions, were in a wretched and destitute condition. It would cost one thousand dollars to put the mill in order, and a jack, mares, cattle, and sheep were needed.[31] In Los Angeles, Wentworth purchased a few plows and ten thousand pounds of wheat seed and sent them to the reservation.[32] He intended to plant three hundred acres in grain.[33]

At the end of January 1862, the department of the interior summoned Wentworth to Washington, D.C., to confer about Indian matters.[34] Arriving about the middle of March, he notified commissioner Dole that the delay in receiving funds from the Indian Office had prevented him from issuing disbursements until very late in the rainy season. Heavy flooding had further hindered his efforts to supply the Indians, and thus his accounts for the third and fourth quarters of 1861 were delinquent. Because the floods had severely damaged the crops of those residing on the Tule River Farm, he would be compelled to purchase supplies for their subsistence. Thus, his estimated expenses for the first and second quarters of 1862 were larger than previously presented.[35]

In August, Wentworth again urged Dole to have the Tejón Reservation set aside by an act of Congress for the exclusive use of the Indians, "It is, I believe, claimed by private parties under a Spanish grant. I am of the opinion, however, that the United States have the best title to it." He suggested that the secretary of the interior instruct a United States district attorney in California to determine the title of the property, "as it is one of the best locations for an Indian reservation within the whole southern country."[36]

Wentworth observed 250 acres of wheat and barley growing in the common fields. The crops were in excellent shape, he told Dole, "the grain yielding extraordinarily even for California, averaging from thirty to forty bushels per acre." The buildings, however, were in need of repair,

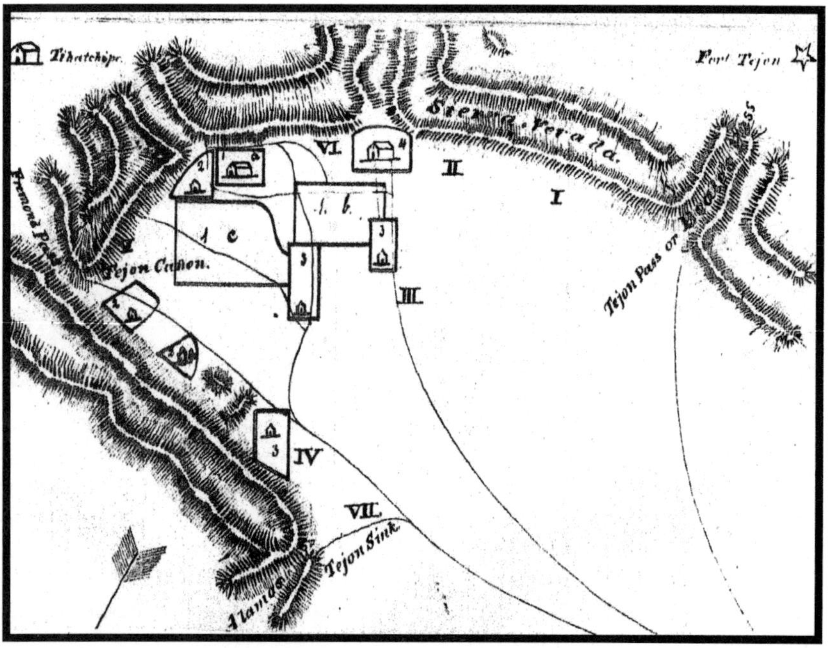

Statement of Farms and acres worked by Government for the Indians on Tejon Reservation, Theodore Boschulte Supervisor, March 31st 1862.

having been damaged by the rains of the past winter, and the wagons and agricultural implements were exposed to the elements. Relying on statistics compiled by Theodore Boschulte, Wentworth claimed that 1,370 Indians belonged to the reservation, although only 489, now coalesced into three groups, were in residence.[37]

Included in Wentworth's report to Dole was a map of the reservation Boschulte had prepared. Wentworth wanted the commissioner "to form a correct idea of the localities of the several tribes and their farms on this reservation, and also of the encroachments made by the white settlers in the vicinity. Of the urgent necessity existing for the immediate removal of the latter evil I need not dilate. Their presence corrupts the Indians, and makes them discontented under the most favorable treatment and circumstance, and their real object is to break up the reservation and 'squat' on the land."[38] The squatters' houses identified on the map belonged to, among others Beale, Bishop, and Alexis Godey.[39] Apparently, Godey resided primarily on Rancho San Emigdio and at Tejón.[40] While on the reservation, he served as Beale's agent, issuing notices in his name and herding his sheep.[41]

By mid-February 1863 the wheat and barley, planted in 450 acres, were up and according to a Los Angeles newspaper promised "a full yield the coming harvest."[42] A grain thresher, purchased in San Francisco and shipped to Los Angeles, arrived in May.[43] Two months later the Indians harvested 250 acres of crops in their own fields and 500 in the common fields. Because of grasshoppers and the lingering drought, however, only four thousand bushels of wheat, two thousand of barley, and thirty tons of hay survived. Most of the vegetables failed as well.[44]

Indians and whites residing on and near the reservation also had to contend with man-made problems. Inadvertently, they became embroiled in an Indian-white conflict raging on the eastern side of the Sierra Nevada. Paiutes from Owens River, fleeing the war, had crossed the mountains and settled on the south fork of the Kern River. From there some of them stole cattle and horses from local ranchers and may have killed a white man.[45] Pursuing the raiders, however, appealed to few. The theft of one thousand head of cattle during March 1863, prompted a resident of Keysville to write: "Strange to say, the prospect of overcoming the rude obstacles of mountain wastes, and deep and rapid streams, on weak horses, with poor rations, and the attendant glory of no pecuniary compensation, and to rush upon a wily, treacherous, and merciless, foe, ambuscaded in the ground of their own choosing, excited none of that fiery ardor and martial enthusiasm naturally to have been expected." The seventeen men who went in pursuit found the Indians' encampment high up the south fork of the Kern impenetrable: "Indications were seen all through the country they passed of large numbers of cattle having been butchered, without any attempt at concealment, but, on the contrary, most provoking and defiant efforts and ostentation. They were estimated to number about three hundred warriors, and seemed to be possessed of numerous horses." As of April 1, a large, better-equipped party, supported by contributions from local residents, was to leave in a few days.[46]

Also in early April the citizens petitioned Lieutenant Colonel William Jones, commander of Camp Babbitt near Visalia for protection.[47] Jones was an officer in the California Volunteers, a militia unit formed during the Civil War when regular troops were sent east.[48] Jones ordered Captain Moses A. McLaughlin to look into the situation on the Kern while on his way with two detachments to the Owens Valley.[49] While camped on the Kern, McLaughlin enlisted the services of José Chico, who spoke Spanish and some English.[50] In mid-1859 José Chico had led a detachment of troops from Fort Tejón to the Owens Valley, searching for Paiute stock raiders. In his report on that expedition, Captain J. W. Davidson noted that his guide had provided "essential service to me throughout the expedition, not only as being my only means of communication with the Indians, but from his knowledge of the country."[51] In mid-1862 José Chico also had served as interpreter for Lieutenant Colonel George S. Evans after

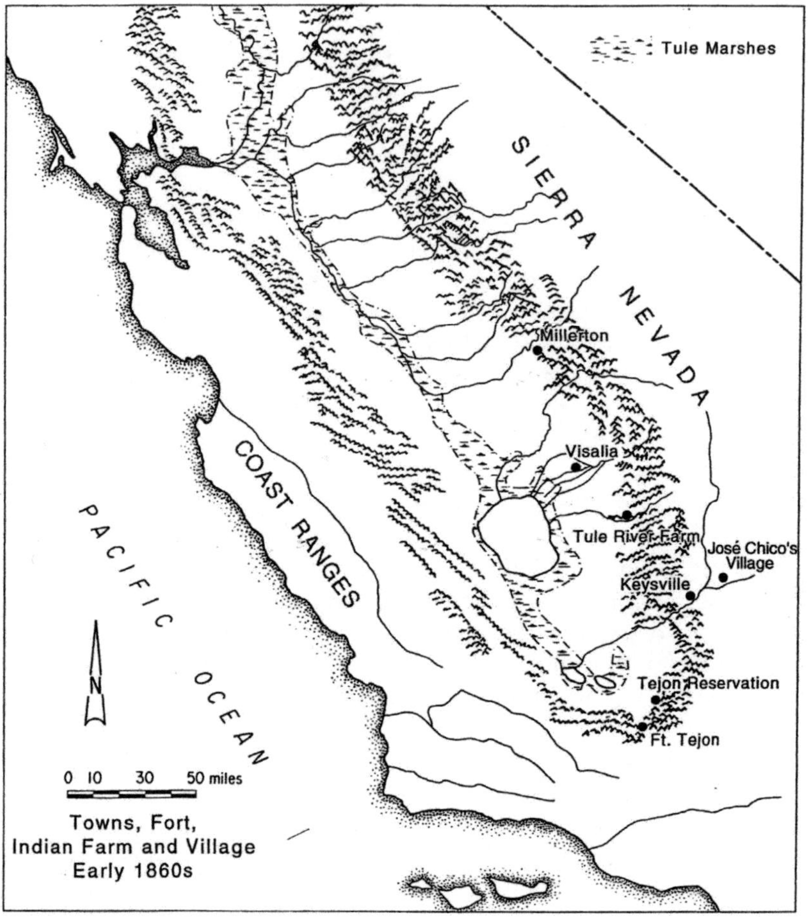

he established Camp Independence in the Owens Valley.[52]

An Owens River Paiute about thirty-five years old in 1863, José Chico had resided in the area since early youth, when his parents moved across the Sierra Nevada. Upon reaching adulthood, he married, fathered two children, and assumed leadership of his village.[53] At his village, located at the juncture of the two forks of the Kern, he pastured two horses and four cows, planted potatoes, corn, wheat, squash, and melon, selling some of the produce to miners.[54] Nanna Rankin, a resident of Keysville, recalled that "the chief of the Kern River Indians was a very fine man and a staunch friend to the whites. His family soon found out our house was a good place to come. They were always satisfied by the food and other gifts. They often visited us and named two young daughters after my sister and me."[55]

After José Chico refused to join the Paiutes in their war against the Americans, they stole and slaughtered one of his cows and forced him and his family to abandon their village and seek refuge in Keysville.[56] Some of his followers, however, sided with those waging the war.[57] Assured that his family would be fed and protected by a Mr. Harmon, José Chico agreed to lead Captain McLaughlin to the hostile Indians, well aware that once his service was completed, he and his family could no longer remain in the area.[58]

On April 19, 1863 McLaughlin, José Chico, Urbano, another Indian, and a detail of twenty men surrounded a village some ten miles upstream from Keysville on the right bank of the Kern. Surprised at daylight, the Indians surrendered without a fight. McLaughlin called upon José Chico and some settlers to identify all the men they considered to be peaceable residents. Those selected, along with old men, women, and children, were released. The adult males no one could vouch for were labeled stock thieves.[59] In his report McLaughlin coolly recounted that the Indians were "either shot or sabered. Their only chance for life being their fleetness, but none escaped, though many of them fought well with knives, sticks, stones, and clubs."[60] Many years later an Indian woman recalled that José Chico had saved her father's life by identifying him as a peaceable Indian.[61]

According to an observer the volunteers killed thirty-two Indians, the majority being "a part of those who have been engaged in stealing stock from this vicinity since the outbreak on Owens River; the balance were Kern River Indians, who were in the habit of disappearing whenever the Owens River Indians broke out, and were unable, on their return, to give any satisfactory account of themselves."[62] Claiming to regret inflicting such "extreme punishment," McLaughlin nevertheless thought that a few "such examples will soon crush the Indians and finish the war in this and adjacent valleys." And convinced that the Tejón Reservation sheltered Indians who had participated in the stock-raiding, McLaughlin threatened to do there what he had done on the Kern and thus leave the agents "very little to do, and save the Government some treasure."[63]

McLaughlin had nothing but praise for José Chico. In a letter to a friend, published on June 9 in the *Daily Alta California* under the heading "Reward for the Trustworthy," McLaughlin recounted the Indian's important services and recommended that he and his family, because they could not return to the Kern River, be provided with a partially stocked farm. Donations were to be sent to the *Alta*, which would forward them to the Wells Fargo Bank.[64]

On July 22, three months after the massacre on the Kern, the California Volunteers deposited at the Tejón Reservation some 850 Paiutes they had rounded up on the Owens River.[65] When Alexis Godey prohibited the

Paiutes from cutting brush to make shelters, Lieutenant Robert Daley of the Volunteers ordered him to cease interfering with the Indians. When Godey drove a herd of cattle among them, Daley forced him to remove the animals from the area.[66] Once informed about the incident, the editors of the *Alta* recommended that Lieutenant Daley be court-martialed for ordering the removal of the animals, because they grazed on private land owned by Edward F. Beale.[67]

Beale had long sought title to Rancho El Tejón.[68] And Beale never abandoned his house on the reservation.[69] On May 9, 1863 a federal land commission presented to José Antonio Aguirre and Ignacio del Valle title to the rancho.[70] Although he would not obtain title to the rancho for another year and a half, Beale somehow obtained the deed, which he showed to Wentworth.[71] In July, Wentworth notified Beale that his patent was "full and complete and I yield the possession of the property under that title without reserve and on the instant." Nevertheless, he told the commissioner of Indian affairs in September that he thought the "United States have the best title to it, and I would respectfully suggest that the Secretary of the Interior instruct the United States district attorney of the northern district to examine into the title of said property, as it is one of the most desirable locations for an Indian reservation within the whole southern country."[72]

When apprised that over eight hundred Paiutes had been resettled on "his" land, Beale became incensed. On July 24 he fired off an angry letter to Wentworth, claiming that the cattle supplied to the Indians had destroyed his orchard, vineyard, and garden. He demanded to know on what legal grounds was Wentworth going to "occupy for public purposes land which the courts have always decided to be private property, and which is protected by the sanctity of patent from the government."[73] Wentworth responded a few days later, pleading with Beale not to eject the Indians until arrangements could be made for them and promising he would seek from the Indian Office funds to compensate him for his losses. He also wanted to know at what rate Beale would rent his land to the government.[74] Beale replied the same day he received Wentworth's letter. Not wanting to sell or rent any portion of his land, he nevertheless understood the difficulty in removing the Indians. He would rent, therefore, twelve thousand acres at twelve thousand dollars per annum. Beale erroneously claimed the rate was less than what the government was paying for the Tule River Farm.[75]

On August 10 Wentworth informed Beale that he would forward his offer to the Indian Office.[76] Beale immediately responded, claiming that he had been misinterpreted. He did not want "to go before the public as desiring to rent to the government, as your letter, without explanation, might lead any one to believe. On the contrary, if I rent at all, it will be as a great favor, and one only reluctantly granted." But Beale adamantly refused to rent if the "hostile and vicious Indians" recently located there remained. He strongly urged Wentworth to remove them at once. Regarding the Tejoneños who had resided on the land before the reservation was established, he preferred that they too leave but would not demand it. Even though they had "occupied this place under the government protection for twelve years without paying rent at all," he would lease a portion of the land for their use.[77] Approximately three hundred Indians remained on the rancho, about the same number Beale found in the area when he created the Sebastian Military Reserve in 1853.[78]

Desperate for guidance, in early August Wentworth sent a telegram to Commissioner Dole, pointing out that Beale had offered to rent twelve thousand acres.[79] Receiving no answer, he wired again on September 12, seeking funds and noting that the Paiutes were "suffering for food."[80] Two days later he wrote to the commissioner: "It is of the utmost importance that the department instruct me how to act, immediately, as the time is very near, when our grain crops should be put in." Insufficient funds remained in the appropriation, ending June 30, 1864, to remove the Indians to the Tule River Farm.[81]

Before receiving a reply, in early October Wentworth sent the Paiutes to Fort Tejón.[82] But as many as 250 escaped before arriving at the post.[83] Wentworth promised the fort's commander he would supply the Indians with such provisions as his limited means would allow.[84] The fort supported the Indians for a short time, but at midmonth the assistant adjutant general ordered the commander to cease providing the Indians with provisions.[85] The Indians survived on the cattle they stole from Samuel Bishop, on the food they begged from the soldiers, and on acorns. By January 1864, however, the acorn supply was exhausted.[86] Many of the Paiutes drifted away from the fort.[87]

When Captain John C. Schmidt of the California Volunteers took command of Fort Tejón in January, 380 Paiutes (170 women, 120 men, and 90 children), were encamped a short distance from the post in a state of near-starvation. From José Chico, Schmidt learned that the Indians wanted to be sent to the Tule River Farm, where they could raise crops, which they could not do at the fort. Also in January a delegation of Indians from the reservation visited Schmidt, seeking permission to move to the farm. They sought relocation because Alexis Godey would not provide them with mules and plows with which to prepare the ground for planting. Consequently, the fields designated for wheat, barley, corn, and potatoes had yet to be sown. Schmidt lacked the authority to grant their request but recommended to the assistant adjutant general that the Paiutes and some two hundred other Indians residing on the reservation be sent to the farm. By consolidating the Indians in one area, the government would save considerable money. Schmidt also recommended that José Chico be retained by the government as interpreter at a salary of fifty dollars per month.[88]

A few months later José Chico dictated a letter to General George Wright, commander of the pacific division, about the condition of the Paiutes residing near the fort:

> While in charge of the soldiers they were well fed, but since they have been turned over to the agents here they have had very little to eat except acorns and such roots and game as they could procure themselves. Some of the children used to go about the fort and get what the soldiers had left when they were done eating, but now there is an order against it and a sentry posted to keep them away; and what is still worse, the acorns are all gone, and the game is very scarce and hard to get, and there is little else to eat than tule roots and a little clover, which you must know is very poor living. They have had no clothing except 100 very poor blankets and a little calico which was distributed soon after they were brought to the fort. They are nearly naked, and have had hard work to keep warm this cold Winter.... We are willing to work if we had anything to do, and need not be an expense to the Government. We do not want to go to war because we know that you have got more warriors than we have, and could easily beat us and drive us from our country, even if we were united, which we are not. I should not have troubled you with this letter, dear General, did I not think that the agents here had wronged us.... I do not think we get the provisions and clothing intended for us by our Great Father; the agents keep it from us and sell it to make themselves rich, while we and our children are very poor and hungry and naked.[89]

In May a visitor to a store near the fort claimed that the proprietor sold government goods and foods designated for the Indians. He observed beans, rice, knives, calico drillings, and blankets, all purchased from the reservation supervisor.[90] On one occasion, in a dispute over dividing up the profits, the proprietor challenged the supervisor to sue him if he wanted more money.[91] Alexis Godey was the supervisor. At the end of April, Wentworth had transferred Boschulte to the Colorado River District and placed Godey in charge of the reservation at a salary of eighteen hundred dollars per year.[92] Godey's tenure, however, was short lived.

On March 17, 1864, a bill to reorganize the Indian administration in California had become law. The law again placed California under one superintendency. It also stated that no more than four tracts of land in California "be retained by the United States for the purposes of Indian reservations."[93] At the time five tracts were in use: Smith River,

Round Valley, and Mendocino in Northern California, and Tule River and Tejón in the central portion of the state.[94] Austin Wiley, recently appointed superintendent, had no choice but to remove the Indians from Tejón. Already he had hired a temporary special agent and ordered him to relocate as many Indians as possible from the fort and reservation to the Tule River Farm.[95] Most of the Paiutes had departed by early July, when a military detachment escorted two hundred Indians from the two institutions to the farm.[96] In mid-September the California Volunteers stationed at Fort Tejón moved to quarters near Los Angeles, and the fort was abandoned.[97] Of all the federal institutions created to assist Indians, only Tule River Farm remained open, and it was owned by a white man.

CHAPTER XXVII

From Farm to Reservation

With the closure of the Tejón Reservation, the Tule River Farm remained the only governmental institution in Central California designed to assist and control Indians. As of September 1864 at least 800 Indians resided on the farm—350 Paiutes and 450 Yokuts and others. On 185 acres of common land, the Indians had raised 3,300 bushels of wheat, 1,000 of barley, 400 of potatoes, 900 of sweet potatoes, and 40 of beans. They had seventy-five acres under cultivation for themselves. On the farm were 129 horses (one hundred owned by Indians), 43 mules, 4 swine, but no chickens or cattle. They lived in lodges built of posts stuck in the ground and covered with split boards. Superintendent of Indian Affairs Austin Wiley reported that "The crops are excellent this season, much better than on any farm in that section of the country, owing principally to the fact that the crop was sowed early, and to the exertions of the agent in charge in carefully attending it. I am confident that there is no lacking of food at this point. The climate of Tule River valley is generally considered rather unhealthy, but the proximity of the agency to the mountains (to which the Indians frequently resort) obviates all that is detrimental in the climate."[1]

The *Visalia Weekly Delta* reported in early 1866 that the farm was progressing well: "Six hundred acres of land is now sown in grain, and a good substantial fence four miles in extent is completed. This also is no mean work for Indians, and only shows what they can do under prudent and skilful [sic.] management.[2] The new superintendent, Charles Maltby, however, noted setbacks. The eight hundred Indians were in good health and were "willing to labor." But of the 350 acres of wheat sown, 250 had failed because they were planted late and because a drought had hit the region. The forty acres of barley produced a harvest of only 3,500 pounds. Of the forty acres in corn, only a light crop was expected, but the thirty-five acres in sweet potatoes, beans, and pumpkins looked promising. On lands set aside for their own private use, the Indians produced 60,000 pounds of wheat and corn. Maltby thought the farm could be purchased at a price far lower than removing the Indians to a new location. Nevertheless, he had rented it for another eighteen months at one thousand dollars per year.[3] In mid-April 1866 the owner, Thomas Madden, notified Maltby that he would sell his land for ten dollars in gold coin per acre, "which is about what the place has cost me."[4] In his annual report to the commissioner of Indian affairs, Maltby highly recommended the land be purchased.[5] No action was taken on his request.

In July the *Visalia Weekly Delta* reported that it was "a pleasure to call attention to this subject, because, under its present arrangement, we can always speak well of one of those institutions which have so generally failed in their purpose. This Reserve has fed and covered for some six or eight hundred Indians during the season. A large amount of labor has been done in the way of permanent improvement." The Indians had harvested 600,000 pounds of wheat, 50,000 of barley, 10,000 pounds of rye, and 3,000 pounds of peas. In addition, a "generous supply" of corn, potatoes, pumpkins, melons and vegetables had been produced. "We don't think all the other Reservations on the coast have equaled this, and we attribute the success in large measure to the energy and good sense of Mr. G. J. Hoffman the resident Superintendent who has gone into the work heart and soul. Capt. Maltby, also deserves great credit for his discretion and his wisely liberal policy in regard to the establishment."[6]

Although the Indians were willing to work, Maltby reported in August that on rented land "their labor can only be effective so far as to provide for their subsistence." By this time they had constructed a five-mile irrigation ditch from the Tule River to the elevated portion of the farm and on to public lands connected to it.[7] Born on the farm about the time the ditch was constructed, José Vera heard stories about how the agent enlisted Chief José Chico in persuading the Indians to construct the ditch and how the women carried the dirt in their baskets.[8]

José Chico may be the same person who served as guide and translator for Captain Moses McLaughlin in his subduing and slaughtering of Paiutes on the Kern River in 1863. His allegiance to the whites forced him to abandon his home on the river, but he sought to ameliorate the condition of the Paiutes while they were confined at Fort Tejón. Being a Paiute he may have relocated with them to the Tule River Farm. When Steven Powers visited the farm in then early 1870s, he spoke with only one Indian—a Paiute named Chico—whom he described as presenting "the traditional physique of the Californian—very dark-skinned, pudgy in stature, large cheek-bones.... He was a singular Indian, a real philosopher; had traveled much over Southern California, Nevada, Utah and Arizona, broadening the range of his intellectual vision; spoke English and Spanish fluently, besides several Indian tongues." He recounted to Powell the creation legend of his people.[9]

Without José Chico's influence, however, it is unlikely the Indians would have built a twenty-five mile road to a pine forest where fencing and building materials could be obtained and a brush fence enclosing seven hundred acres of public land for pasture and cultivation. Constructed for their personal occupation were several adobe houses. Maltby was convinced that if the government could purchase the lands "which I have recommended in former communications to the department, their labors could be effective in permanent improvements, in the erection of buildings, fencing, and planting of orchards, vineyards, &c.... I am fully satisfied that, with the reservation permanently established on lands owned by the government, necessary buildings erected and improvements made, and proper and competent teachers employed, (a man and his wife would be desirable,) much good and lasting benefit to young Indians, both male and female, would be effected."[10]

George J. Hoffman, however, had little to say that was positive about his wards:

"Whether they are capable of any improvement, beyond being made useful as laborers, is extremely doubtful. Their character is the most despicable, and, I may safely say, in an experience of over four years I never saw among them an indication of a virtue."[11] Robert J. Stevens, special commissioner to investigate Indian affairs in California, mentioned the agent's views in a report to the commissioner of Indian affairs: "Mr. Hoffman informs me that he has been in charge of these Indians for five years; that he has but little faith in his ability to improve them; that he is heartily disgusted with the business under the disadvantages with which he has labored, and is anxious to be relieved. He has tendered his resignation some time since. His opinion of the Indian's capacity to improve is less hopeful than that of any man—having so intimate a knowledge of them—that I have met."[12]

Still, Stevens had much to say that was positive about the Indians: "They seem more cheerful, happy, and contented, and are, on the whole, rather better clad than any reservation Indians I have seen. There is a strong Mexican cast about them, and many of them converse only in the Spanish tongue. The lodges and utensils of the better ones are as good as any I have seen. Among them were two artisans, a spur-maker, and a saddle maker. Many of them had money. I was asked here for the first time by an Indian in good Spanish, to change a $20 gold piece." They frequently gambled, using "a pile of sticks, cards, and other games peculiar to themselves." At harvest time, many of them obtained employment with neighboring whites.[13]

In 1867 yet another superintendent, B. C. Whiting, reported that public lands north of the farm would be useless without the Madden property because it blocked access to the Tule River: "The two tracts combined would be amply sufficient for a permanent and desirable reservation, and its products would be abundant in the subsistence of the Indians now there, and as many more as could be ushered in from the bands of Indians scattered throughout that portion of the state." Whiting emphasized that "The Indians are very much attached to Tule river, and are always troubled when they hear any suggestion about the probability of removal. As of August 1867 they had produced 237,780 pounds of wheat, 38,400 of barley, 23,700 of rye, 6,000 of turnips, 1,000 of peas, and 50 tons of hay.[14]

Charles Maltby, the former superintendent, became the farm's agent in October 1867 and reported a year later that he had found the condition of the service at the agency very unsatisfactory. This was not so much owing to the management of the former agent as to the unwise policy of endeavoring to conduct and manage an Indian reservation on private lands rented from individuals from year to year. This policy prevents permanent improvements, retards progress in improving the condition of the Indians, and has the effect to keep them discontented and unwilling to engage in the various kinds of labor required to making even their necessary improvements wanted for present use. While they readily engage in labor necessary to cultivate the soil and provide for their subsistence, they are adverse to making any improvements, making the excuse that they have no surety that they will enjoy the benefits which would necessarily follow their labors.[15]

Nevertheless, the Indians had repaired the agent's adobe house and had constructed an adobe-stone storage facility and a granary. Most lived in adobe or frame houses, except for some of the Paiutes who preferred huts made of straw and grass for their winter quarters and brush dwellings during the summer months. The Paiutes were reluctant to till the ground. But some members of the different groups worked for the settlers, earning between fifty cents to a dollar a day in wages which they spent mostly on clothing and groceries but occasionally on liquor. The Indians on the farm worked "cheerfully and readily, stealing is rare among them, they are not vicious, and they seem to appreciate kindness and good treatment. No cases of insubordination or disposition to disobey the rules and regulations of the agency have been manifested, with the not very rare exception of drinking too much whiskey." In November 1867 the agent's wife started a school, attended by twenty-five scholars, but it was discontinued in May when she became ill. Maltby noted that, "The attendance of the

Indian girls was quite regular and their improvement encouraging and satisfactory." The school was to reopen in October.[16]

The health of the Indians had been good until July when ague affected large numbers. Measles spread in August. "The Indians are much alarmed," reported Maltby, "and being complicated with other diseases—many chronic cases—it is feared that many cases will prove fatal."[17] Whereas the Yokuts suffered only seven deaths, fifty-seven Paiutes died during August, September, and October, and fifty more fled the farm for the Owens Valley across the Sierra Nevada. When smallpox struck Visalia thirty miles distant in February 1869, the local whites feared that Indians passing through the town would become contaminated and spread the disease. To allay their fears and curtail the spread of the disease, agents had all the Indians on the farm—198 Yokuts and 107 Paiutes—vaccinated. Maltby reported in August that since the vaccination, the health of the Indians had been good, except for the frequent and chronic cases of syphilis. Twenty-two Indians had died; eleven births had taken place. In July 1869 thirty more Paitues left, reducing the number on or near the farm to seventy-five.[18]

Maltby alerted the commissioner of Indian affairs to the Indians "frequent use of whisky, to which many are addicted.... Until this evil is remedied and prevented, the labor and efforts of the agent for the improvement and elevation of the Indians under his charge will be retarded and ineffective." There was "sufficient labor on this reservation, which, if applied, in two years would put up good and substantial buildings and fences, and would return to the government value received, in improvements from all the supplies they receive, and all the expense they would be to then department." But he could not "go forward and make valuable and lasting improvements on land rented from year to year; and consequently the labor of the Indians is only periodically employed." Nevertheless, the Indians produced 256,477 pounds of wheat and barley, although grasshoppers destroyed their summer crops of potatoes, onions, beans, and cabbage.[19]

In 1869 a change of policy in the Indian Office resulted in army officers replacing civilian officials. Bvt. Major General J. B. McIntosh became superintendent, and on August 7, 1869, Lieutenant John H. Purcell replaced Maltby as agent. He counted 217 Indians on the farm and another 120 in the mountains hunting and collecting acorns. With an average labor force of twenty-five Indians per day, he put some to work manufacturing adobe bricks and laying stone foundations for the quarters for the employees. "Under the superintendence of the carpenter and blacksmith (employés) they have worked admirably," he reported.

Apparently, the school teacher, Maltby's wife, departed, with him, because Purcell noted that "A school-house and a teacher are very much needed, and several have asked me for then same. I find that some of them know the alphabet perfectly well." The Indians wanted to "remain here and are very much afraid of being moved away." Other Indians, especially members of the Gawia, Wukchamni, and Mono, preferred living away from the farm and working for the white settlers. And nearly all the Paiutes had departed for the Owens Valley. Purcell recommended that the farm be purchased.[20]

Superintendent McIntosh visited the farm in early November and was not impressed. In a letter to the commissioner of Indian affairs, he noted that most of the land cultivated on the farm belonged to Madden and that only 300 of the 1280 acres Madden had leased to the government were cultivated in any one year. McIntosh found the location of the farm "an unfortunate one," because it was only three miles from Porterville, where "the Indians get what liquor they want. It is also within three miles of the main road from Visalia to Havilah, and the consequence is, that there is a bad influence exerted over the Indians. For these and many other reasons I deem it advisable to break up this Reservation as soon as it can be done to advantage."[21]

To keep the twenty "working" Indians satisfied, the following year Purcell issued them one and a half pounds of beef per day along with three pounds at the end of each week which all 212 Indians received. He told McIntosh that to omit the working hands in the general issue "would cause quite a jealousy and a great deal of dissatisfaction." Should he make "a change in the issue now, the majority of them would leave and work for parties outside, from whom they receive per month from $25.00 to $30.00 and as for detaining them, not less than a Company of Soldiers could do it."[22]

In August 1870 Purcell noted that the Indian population—now 229—had changed little from the previous, year, but his opinions of them had changed significantly. The Indians "are all unwilling to do any work at the agency; it is only when compelled that they do anything at this place. I must say that I consider them a useless and worthless lot of vagabonds." Yet Purcell claimed to understand the reasons for their indifference to work. Although they were "naturally an indolent people," they found employment among the whites who had convinced them that at seventy-five cents to one dollar per day they were better off working for them. They believed the government would soon "send them adrift, and take away from them their 'Old Homes,' which they call this place." By making them dissatisfied, noted Purcell, "parties requiring their labor can obtain it without permission from the agent."[23]

Purcell honestly admitted that in his earlier report he had erred in recommending that the farm be purchased. He had not known "how injurious it was to have them in close proximity to any settlement. In view of these fact I would suggest that those who are not capable of taking care of themselves, which are very few, be placed on a reservation; those that are capable, allowed to go wheresoever they may choose." The only hope he exhibited was in the children, who were "very apt to learn." Mrs. Purcell had taught school from October 1869 to April 1870 when she quit owing to "household matters." The average daily attendance consisted of twenty scholars, of whom sixteen were taught spelling, reading, and figures, as well as "cleanliness and order, and how to cut and make their clothing." Purcell recommended that the school be continued, because it was "a great benefit to them."[24]

In late May, Superintendent McIntosh traveled to the farm to investigate charges issued by Dr. N. G. Turley that Purcell abused Indians. McIntosh, however, was troubled by the rumors that Turley might be "somewhat crazy" and that he sought to have Purcell dismissed to secure the position of physician on the farm.[25] McIntosh interviewed an employee of the farm who told him that on different occasions Purcell had severely punished four Indians. He kicked and struck Logan with his fist and then with a stick for "drunkenness and loud talking around the agency building." He struck Ben with a stick for riding without permission a mare belonging to the farm and making its mouth bleed. He slapped Tom with the flat part of his sword for being drunk, and he punished another Indian for an unknown cause. Moreover, other employees of the farm accused Purcell of striking his wife and on one occasion saw her running from her home "shrieking, and trying to get away from him."[26]

Aware that Purcell was being investigated, on June 2 seven citizens of Porterville came to his defense in a letter to the secretary of the interior, claiming that Turley was "an insane man and not accountable for his actions, particularly where he may be entrusted." They insisted that "the Indians have never behaved themselves as well as since taken charge of by Lieut Purcell."[27] Turley also wrote to the secretary, insisting that Purcell was "unfit for any post of trust or honor in the government." Regarding the claim that he was "laboring under mental aberration," he left "that matter for the judgment of your honor, at the distance of 3500 miles."[28]

In his report to the secretary McIntosh, believing those who testified against Purcell, recommended that he be relieved of his duties.[29] On August 14 1870 Purcell turned over the management of the farm to John W. Miller and was relieved of all duties pertaining to the Indian Office.[30] Miller reported in September that Purcell had resigned because "of sickness of himself and family."[31]

No matter the outcome of the investigation, Purcell soon would have been relieved of his duties anyway. In its session of 1869-70, Congress prohibited the employment of military officers in civilian offices, which resulted in C. B. Whiting replacing McIntosh as superintendent.[32] But before being relieved McIntosh purchased for the farm blankets, clothing, beef, dry goods, hardware, lumber, medicines and stores of coffee, tea, sugar, soap, and candles at a cost of over $12,000. Probably the result of Indian labor, an old building was repaired and three-room adobe house was built for the employees. Each room measured 12 by 16 feet. The cost of the improvements totaled $350. Many wagons, blacksmith and carpenter tools, and agricultural implements, however, were old and some were unserviceable.[33]

Most of the wheat crop planted in 1870 had been lost because the fences surrounding the fields has not been properly maintained and because the Indian boys guarding the fields failed to prevent stock from breaching them. The corn, potatoes, pumpkins, squash, beans, melons, and grapes were nearly destroyed by several hundred hogs belonging to white men living near the farm. Agent Miller, speculated that if "The Indian department had owned the Tule River Indian farm, instead of leasing it from Mr. Madden, then these fences and other improvements would probably have been of a more substantial character." Miller thought "the Government should provided them with a permanent home, and hold out inducements for civilization and the cultivation of peaceful arts. These Indians are intelligent enough to know whether they are at working for themselves and their posterity, or whether they are building fences and houses for Thomas P. Madden." At this time 450 Indians resided on the farm, but another 1,200, supposedly belonging to it, were scattered about in the Tulare Valley in Kern, Tulare, and Fresno counties.[34]

Although the federal census of 1870 put the total number of Indians in these counties at 2,883, more than likely the figure is an underestimation.[35] But whatever their number, the Indians were obviously aware that their populations were declining, that their home territories were shrinking, and that the wild plants and animals on which they once depended were fast disappearing. Thus in late August 1870, when Indians along the Fresno and Kings rivers moved into the foothills of the Sierra Nevada, some whites at Coarse Gold Gulch feared an uprising was immanent. But when contacted in September in the Crane Valley, the Indians declared they had no intention of rising. Stockmen may have spread the rumor to keep Indians out of the area.[36]

The Indians probably had moved inland in to engage in a mourning ceremony, which was usually held in September. Periodic activities, in particular mourning, jimsonweed, rattlesnake, and puberty ceremonies, brought together Indians from adjacent groups usually for six days. When the leaders of a particular group decided to hold a dance, messenger were sent to those groups they wanted to participate. The host group was expected to provide food for the guests. But the guests also brought food—ground squirrels, acorn meal, and other items—which they could exchange at the gathering. The messengers told the guests where to camp and provided them with wood and water and informed them when food would be distributed. The messengers would announce when the ceremony was to begin, and the host would address the assembled Indians, informing them why and for what purpose the ceremony was being held. He would usually conclude by telling them to have a good time.[37]

The same month the Indians moved to the headwaters of the Fresno and Kings rivers, Miller recorded the departure of many Indians from the Tule River Farm: "Most of the reservation Indians went, carrying their sick relatives on their backs, in baskets, and upon rude litters constructed of poles and wicker-work. Their superstition led them to suppose that their great medicine man could restore them to health, give elasticity to cripple limbs, restore sight to the blind, and youth to old age. This was but a periodical gathering of all the Indians in this portion of the State, yet it gave rise to serious apprehensions on the part of the white settlers. Many of them pretended to anticipate another Indian war, and reported the assembly of 3,000 Indians all around, and prepared for a attack on the whites." This rumor spread for a few days, "but it was soon ascertained that the Indians were peaceful, and were drawn together partly by superstition and partly from a desire to breath the healthful mountain air, and to gather roots, grasses, and nuts, which are not found in the valleys." Those attending the ceremony returned to the farm with about forty-four Indians. A portion of them had fled the farm a year ago, because of the change of officers and the outbreak of measles.[38]

Shortly after the Indians returned to the farm, an incident occurred that seriously disrupted Indian-white relations. J. C. Bonsall ran stock and raised grain and potatoes on the south side of the Tule River. He hired Indians from the farm to plant and harvest the potatoes, each to be paid one sack of the best potatoes and all of the small ones not sacked. But the Indians thought that each was to receive three sacks. After the harvest in December 1870, the Indians, convinced they had been cheated, returned to the farm where they told their version of the incident to friends and relatives. The next day, the three Indians left the reservation, began drinking heavily, and joined up with some others. At the Bonsall place they murdered his wife and her two children.[39]

The *Visalia Weekly Delta* reported the murders and noted that a company of whites was scouring the country for the responsible Indians. On December 6, however, the sheriff notified the citizens that a white man was under suspicion.[40] But an Indian woman told Miller that her husband, Tom, had admitted to the killing. Miller arrested Tom and another Indian and turned them over to a group of white men who promptly hanged them. When Bonsall arrived at the scene, he murdered a third Indian under arrest.[41]

Although a mouthpiece for the white population, the *Delta* did not hold back in its assessment of the tragedy: "These Indians had been drinking and whiskey may be regarded as the sold cause of the horrible affair. A sad commentary indeed upon the universal disregard of the law prohibiting the sale of liquor to Indians."[42] In a letter to the editor Miller warned that as long as the Indians can obtain liquor, "there will be murder and robbery." He urged him to reason "with the community in order to put a stop to such horrible cases as this late murder."[43] But Miller failed to explain why he turned over to civilians Indians under his jurisdiction.

He told the editor "that all Indians within sixty miles square of the Tule River Reservation, belong to that Reservation, by their right of their maintenance by the Government, and that they have no right to leave the Agency without permission from the Agent." Miller noted that "there are some unprincipled people who are constantly enticing them to various parts, to obtain their labor at a very small price; when their time of labor has expired, these Indians instead of being sent home, are allowed to wander off wherever their fancy takes them." It was his "humble opinion" that the editor "should take up the matter and inform your readers that there is a law to the effect, that, 'No person or persons have the right to hire any Indian for the purposes of labor, without the consent of the Agent.'"[44]

By this time, a rumor had spread among the white population that Miller was soon to be replaced by Charles Maltby, the former superintendent. In a petition to the commissioner of Indian affairs, several whites noted that they "had hardly yet recovered from the shock occasioned by the late most atrocious murders & are just beginning to feel some security for our families." Being "totally incompetent" to manage Indians, Maltby would "throw them again into the midst of the community & will be the means of the extermination of the Indians, for we are fully determined to put an end to such horrible crimes." Ignoring the fact that the murders had taken place while Miller was the agent, they remained "determined that no more murders shall be committed on our families & under Mr. Maltby's Agency we fear it."[45]

The petition resulted in no action being taken to retain Miller, and Indians, as the whites feared, continued to leave the farm for the mountains. Concerns that Indians would commit outrages and that whites would retaliate led to a U.S. army contingent arriving in February and remaining until July 1871. By then those fleeing to the mountains had returned.[46]

Adding to the volatility of the times was a spiritual movement then spreading throughout the interior. Many Indians were highly receptive to the message of the Ghost Dance that by 1870 had crossed the Sierra Nevada from then east and was diffusing throughout the San Joaquin Valley. By performing a proper ceremony their ancestors would return and initiate everlasting life. A Paiute spiritual leader greatly influenced Joijoi, a Paiute, residing on the north fork of the San Joaquin River. Joijoi conducted a ceremony in his home territory of Saganiu, attended by members of the Chukchansi, Kechayi, Gashown Dumna, Entimbich, and other Yokuts groups and the Mono. Followers of Joijoi, who were singers and dancers, spread the word south along the foothills of the Sierra Nevada to the Wowol Chunut, Telamni and Tachi peoples around Tulare Lake, including those residing on the Tule River Farm.[47]

The dance was held at the Wakashi village of Chitatu situated on a low crest at one end of Eshom Valley, a deep depression of about a mile in length that was isolated from white settlers. Four or five hundred Indians from various groups located between the Tule and Kings rivers set up separate camps and erected brush shelters. A Waksachi killed some of his steers and sold the meat to representatives of the various political leaders in attendance. Once this supply of food was exhausted, the visitors had to depend on game and acorn meal.[48]

Indians of both sexes from a variety of groups and in no particular order joined hands and circled to the left facing inward. Occasionally, the dancers would take three steps to the right and the three to the left and repeat the movement three times. The dancers kept time by thrusting their arms downward from shoulder level. From time to time, they rested and listened to then exhortations of prominent persons. Inside the circle of dancers sat the singers shaking elder wood clappers in time with their songs. The dancing continued until the participants became exhausted.[49]

In attendance at the dance in the Eshom Valley was Yoimut, a Chunut, who recalled that when she was about seventeen:

> Some Pah-ute Indian Doctors came from across the mountains to the east and talked to our doctors for a long time. They were worried because so many Indians had been dying. Our doctors so wanted to stop the dying because they had been blamed for lots of it. So they talked about it for a long time. The Pah-ute Indian Doctors said that if we held a big new kind of dance in Eshom Valley we could stop all the dying and could bring back all of our dead people….
>
> It was a nice place in Eshom Valley where the dance was held. The Indians used to go there to gather clover to eat. There was

> always a nice field of sweet clover there in the spring….
>
> The Eshom Valley dance was the biggest dance I ever saw. Indians came from everywhere, some from Tule river and Deer Creek, some from Lemoore and some from Kings river….
>
> The chiefs who had charge of the dance told us that we must not get angry or be mean to one another at the dance. We were to keep dancing all the time. Only the little children could sleep. If anyone did not dance he would be turned into a rotten log of wood.[50]

Also in attendance were a few white men. Tom Love brought a large supply of whiskey to the dance, but apparently sold only a small amount to a few women. Enos Barton was also there and late in his life wrote about his experience. Most of what he recorded differed little from that of Yoimut except for an event that suggested not all activity was spiritually based. Twenty or thirty mounted Indians with six shooters formed a straight line, with the leader a bit to the left of the rest. At his command the riders struck out across the valley as fast as their horses could run. At the end of the valley they pulled their horses to a quick stop and fired their guns into the foreground. They then wheeled around and raced to another spot and did the same thing. This was continued until they had emptied their guns.[51]

Before the dance was over, according to Yoimut, the Indians dispersed, having been told that white men were coming to kill them. Yoimut hid for a week before some whites informed her that she and the other Indians were in no danger.[52] Barton recalled that two white men found some of the Indians hiding in a small canyon leading to the Kings River and convinced them that no white men were coming to kill them.[53] Despite that ordeal Yoimut insisted that "We had a good time at Eshom Valley but we were sorry we did not see our dead people. Lots of our people had been dying and we wanted to see them."[54] Upon returning to the Tule River Farm, the Indians conducted their own dance that was attended by Indians from the Kaweah River and the Tejón area.[55]

Several months later, another dance was held at the village of Sulawllalhne, located on the Fish Rice ranch near Visalia. Apparently, Gawia and Wukchamni found employment on the ranch, and at one time at least sixty-five Indians resided there.[56] Yoimut's mother worked for Mrs. Rice, and when her husband died, she earned enough money to buy clothes to burn in his memory at a mourning ceremony."[57] That a Ghost Dance was held where a mourning ceremony) had taken place indicates the new was grafted on to the old. As at a mourning ceremony, the Indians danced for six days and nights but none of their ancestors appeared. Yoimut then realized that "the Indians from across the mountains had been fooling us. So we did not have any more of those Heut Hetwe dances to bring back the dead people."[58]

Although Charles Maltby, again agent of the farm, failed to mention the Ghost Dance in his report in September, he did note that 374 Indians were in residence, an increase of about 150 from the previous year. All were identified as Tules (Yokuts) and Tejoneños. "The condition of the Indians is materially improving," noted Maltby; "many of them becoming quite proficient in all kinds of farm work, and perform all labor required of them readily and cheerfully. They take an interest in cultivating lands on their own account; and this desire has been encouraged by the agent, the present season, by giving to each a piece of land for cultivation in corn and vegetables. Their work as been generally on their gardens performed efficiently and promptly." When not working on the farm, many found employment harvesting, herding, and shearing for the white settlers. Except for the white men and Mexicans who continued to sell liquor to the Indians, the agent detected no problems between the races.[59]

The Indians lived in eight adobe and fifteen frame houses. The forty acres they had planted in wheat had produced 516 bushels worth $1,295; thirty acres had been planted in corn and beans. The corn was estimated to produce 600 bushels worth $1,200. Forty-five tons of hay were worth $900. Add sweet potatoes, peas, beans, grapes, peaches, and watermelons and the value of food produced on the farm totaled $3,826. But most of the forty-eight government horses and mules were old and virtually useless, and the three wagons were unfit for service.[60]

Flora J. Saxe, the school teacher issued her report on June 30:

> For the first ten days in May there was an average attendance of 35 and 40 scholars; since that time the average has been about 25. As they have so little encouragement and influence from their parents, they do not attend so regularly as I could wish for their own advancement; but when they are in school they appear to take an interest in their studies and manifest a desire to learn. With two or three exceptions, they all had to begin with the alphabet. They have now all learned their letters, and about 12 or 14 are commencing to read. They also write words of four and five letters very correctly. Thus far I have been obliged to confide myself to reading and writing, but if they continue to progress as they have done, I shall commence other branches soon.
>
> I have found them very obedient and attentive, and I think they

> have done as well as the same number of white children placed in the same circumstance.
>
> I find they understand most of the English language, but the girls particularly are very backward about speaking it. But I hope time and patience will overcome this difficulty.[61]

The following year Maltby reported that classes had been held in the granary, but when it was needed for storage, school was discontinued. Maltby promised that a schoolhouse soon would be built. The number of Indians residing on the farm numbered 127 men, 140 women, and 107 children. All were Yokuts (now including a few Gawias) and Tejoneños. Intoxication was on the decline, many Indians having taken a temperance pledge. The Reverend J. Edwards, a Presbyterian from Visalia preached monthly at the farm, and a Sabbath School, regularly attended, was held weekly. Maltby mentioned that residing within seventy miles of the farm were about 1000 Indians over which he had "to some extent" supervision. All should be removed to the farm "to receive and enjoy the benefits to be derived from the President's Indian policy, a humane and Christian civilization."[62]

The amount of wheat harvested—2,355 bushels—had increased significantly over the year. And 1,350 bushels of barley had also been produced. The vineyard yielded 2,000 pounds of grapes; 1,800 pounds of figs had been picked, and the peaches harvested weighed five tons. Corn, beets, and potatoes were also grown. The Indians grew for their own consumption 433 bushels of wheat, 101 of barley, 160 of corn, 25 of sweet potatoes as well as large quantities of melons, squashes, beans, tomatoes, and onions.[63]

In late 1873, 374 individuals resided on the farm. According to Maltby, for the past year the Indians "have been well disposed, peaceable; and a marked improvement in their moral and domestic relations is gratifying to note." The school was in session for seven months, but lessons were discontinued because there was no schoolhouse. The sixty-two children in attendance "made excellent progress in their studies." Religious instructions were held every Sunday and the "Indians are quite regular in their attendance, and good results are observed in their daily deportment and their observance of the Sabbath."[64]

In economic matters, however, "good results" were lacking. No rain had fallen since February 24, resulting in a wheat harvest of only 815 bushels. The barley crop failed, a portion of it being cut for hay. Moreover, by September the water ditch company formed to supply water to that part of the farm situated on government lands cut off the flow. Consequently, no vegetables were grown.[65]

Supplies were still being provided to the Indians on the farm. A list of such, dated March 31, 1874, needed the certification of Chief José Chico, whose mark and that of three other Indians was witnessed by two white men. The items provided included four bedsteads, four tables, two doors, six brooms, five butcher knives, fifteen blankets, eight hats, fifteen spools of cotton, twenty-eight wool shirts, four shawls, thirty-seven pairs of men's shoes, ten pounds of apples, over eleven thousand pounds of fresh beef, and various pounds of bacon, beans, coffee, flour, oat meal, rice, sugar, salt, soap, soda, syrup and tea.[66]

By this time President Ulysses S. Grant had, by executive order on January 9, 1973, created the Tule River Reservation, located on pubic land up river to the east of the Madden Farm.[67] According to Maltby, the new location was situated away from "those disreputable persons who take every occasion clandestinely to furnish the Indians with whiskey." Then agent also claimed that the Indians "will take great pleasure and pride in planting their vineyards and orchards, in cultivating their gardens, and their moral improvement and physical and intellectual development will increase with their improvements made with the labor of their own hands." At the time of the agent's report, a survey had been completed and buildings were under construction. The agent claimed the land was arable and suitable for stock and sheep raising. As soon as the Indians were relocated, the farm would be closed and the lease ended. Maltby hoped that all of this would transpire by November 1.[68]

The seven Indian families and a white employee relocated to the reservation built nine houses, a barn, and a blacksmith shop. But work stopped for want of funds, and perhaps because a new agent had been assigned to the reservation. J. B. Vosburgh took charge in December 1873 and found that two-thirds of the 48,551 acres of the new reservation was useless, although 15,000 acres were suitable for sheep raising. Of the 200 acres of arable land, not a single acre had been enclosed. The crops of corn, wheat, barely and vegetables had produced only a light return. Concluding that the Madden Farm should not be vacated, Vosburgh moved the seven families back there in 1874.[69]

At the farm only about 250 of the 307 Indians were in residence at any one time. They were mainly Yokuts and Tejoneños but had, at least to Vosburgh, "so intermingled as to have lost all tribal identity." The Indians seeded two hundred acres of government land and eighty of their own, but the yield was only fair. Vosburgh reported in September that the Indians worked steadily at seeding and harvesting time, but spent considerable time working for whites or "rambling about without employment and out of the way of all restraining influences." His reference was to unprincipled white men and Mexicans who continued selling liquor with impunity to the Indians.[70]

A minister of the Methodist Episcopal Church held services on Sundays and Thursdays in the schoolhouse. As noted by Vosburgh, "The attendance of the Indians, consisting mostly of the youth, has been fair, sometimes all the room could contain. They have manifested a good degree of interest while being instructed in the Word of Life, and have readily learned to sing many of the songs selected from our Sabbath-school music. Could the young be kept aloof from the degrading influences of then older ones, there would be much to hope for in their future, for many of them are bright and intelligent and all of them well disposed."[71]

Those attending school numbered forty-five, but the average daily attendance was only twenty-three, most being between the ages of six and sixteen. About twelve could read the First Reader and were learning to write elegantly. All were being instructed in the first principles of arithmetic. Outside the classroom, the pupils continued to converse in their native languages or in Spanish and thus gained little practice in English. The solution to this problem, claimed Vosburgh, would be the founding of a boarding school where English would be used exclusively.[72]

As of September 1875, 276 Indians resided on the farm. There had been ten births, twenty-three deaths, and some had departed to live among Indians located outside the jurisdiction of what was now known as the Tule River Agency, with its headquarters in Porterville. Of the one thousand Indians belonging to the agency, most were situated along the Kings, Kaweah, and Kern rivers and near Visalia and at Fort Tejón. Vosburgh noted that "From what little I have been able to learn regarding them, though they do not accumulate any property of consequence, they are mostly all sufficiently industrious to gain a considerable living. I have heard no complaints against them during the year."[73]

Religious services were held twice a week, and about the same number as the year before attended school. But few remained past the age of fifteen, preferring to find work among then white settlers. As vaqueros and shepherds they could earn from thirty to thirty-five dollars per month. As day laborers their pay amounted to one dollar to one dollar and a half per day.[74]

Those who labored on the farm spent most of their energy on improving the track owned by Madden and the adjacent land. Even though the land was carefully prepared and the seeds planted earlier than in previous years, the drought prevented any grain from being harvested on lands not irrigated. The Indians, however, produced 150 bushels of grain, 20 tons of hay, and several wagon-loads of squashes and melons on the 100 acres, some of it irrigated, set aside for their personal use.[75]

Agent Vosburgh regretted to report an increase of drunkenness and a corresponding increase in crime. Five Indians and a Mexican had been murdered, all the deaths related to the consumption of whiskey. "In every instance there was no evidence other than Indian, and through every proper means was employed to convict the murderers and the whiskey-vendors through the courts, the evidence, being contradictory or insufficient, has defeated the object." At one time Vosburgh had opposed removing the Indians to the Tule River Reservation because it contained only 200 acres of barely arable land, but he had concluded that the reservation was preferable to the farm, because the value of the products produced would not match the rent which had risen to $1,920 per annum. He told the commissioner of Indian affairs that "Before removal can be effected, there must be built at least twenty-five more houses for Indian families, one or two more for agent and employés, one for a store-room, and one for school purposes." Five thousand dollars would cover the cost of the construction.[76]

In August 1876 only six Indian families resided on the reservation.[77] Between August and the end of the year, however, most of the Indians from the farm were relocated to their new home. And according to C. G. Belknap, yet another agent assigned to the farm, the majority of them were "well satisfied with the removal, and are laboring with commendable zeal in making permanent improvements and gathering around them the comforts of home."[78] Chief José Chico relocated with the others to the reservation.[79]

A few Indians remained on the Madden Farm, still hoping the government would purchase it for them. Evidently, white men had persuaded some to remain by promising that the government would do just that. The whites sought to maintain their illicit trade with them. Moreover, because stockmen wanted to continue using reservation land for summer pasture, they told the Indians it was useless.[80]

On two occasions Belknap sent men to the farm to convince those who remained to relocate. They refused. Belknap understood that it was "not strange, with all these influences, that a few families should hesitate to leave the place once promised them a home, and to which they have, by long residence, become so warmly attached. Their minds, however, are becoming gradually disabused, and all will, without doubt, move here before the coming winter."[81]

According to Belknap in late 1877 the population of the Tule River Reservation numbered 254 individuals, excluding the sixteen who had recently died and the thirty-nine who had left, "some on account of the transfer of the agency, and others from a desire to live in different parts of the country."[82] By August 1878 sixty-nine Indians had returned to the farm. They informed Belknap "that a man representing himself as the owner had given them permission to cultivate, free of rent, as much of

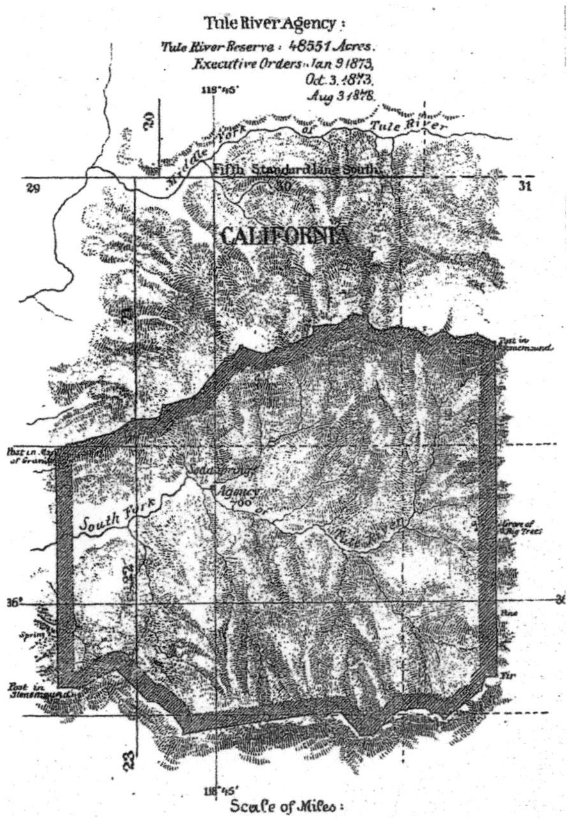

Tule River Agency, 1879.

it as they pleased, assuring them at the same time that the government would finally purchase it for them."[83] The farm was never purchased for the Indians. Because the Tejoneños lacked title to their land, they too would experience dislocation.

CHAPTER XXVIII

From Reservation to Rancho

In mid-1861, President Abraham Lincoln had nominated and the U. S. Senate had confirmed Edward F. Beale as Surveyor General of California, a federal office responsible for surveying public lands in the state.[1] Beale used his office to his advantage. Accompanying his annual report of 1861 was a map that identified Rancho La Liebre and Rancho El Tejón but not the Tejón Reservation. Because the map of lands surveyed in 1857 clearly identified the reservation, Beale had literally wiped it off the map.[2] In August 1862 he had Rancho la Liebre, his private estate, surveyed at government expense—$1,028 to be exact.[3]

A traveler pausing near Mud Springs in the Antelope Valley in mid-1862, inquired as to the ownership of the area. A Sonoran family responded with "the proverbial answer '*quien sabe*,' followed by the explanation, that it was now claimed by Lieutenant Beale, who had established a claim to it by some process to my informants unknown." The transaction brought out the irony in the traveler: "It is well, I said to myself, that this man of arms should have secured for himself a piece of land in these quiet and secluded valleys, in which, after the manner of Cincinnatus and Washington, he may retire when the active duties of life are over, and devote himself to the serene and peaceful pursuit of agriculture."[4]

The traveler continued westward for twenty miles to Beale's house on Rancho La Liebre:

> Here are enclosed and cultivated fields, with a spacious mansion, huge barns and every manner of outhouse that taste could suggest or convenience require. Here, too, are the remains of a government

General Edward Fitzgerald Beale
From a Woodcut

General Edward Fitzgerald Beale. (From Historical Collection, Title Insurance and Trust Company, San Diego, Cal. Courtesy of the author.)

saw mill, and divers other implements and appliance that seem to carry a sort of "odor of nationality" about them. Riding up and inquiring of a smart looking colored boy [probably José Soto], having the appearance of a majordomo, who was the owner of this goodly establishment, he informed me that it was the property of one Lieut. Beale, who owned the land as far around as we could see. Coming on to Fort Tejón, a distance of 20 miles, I made occasional inquires as to the proprietorship of the intervening country, and finding it mostly owned or claimed by Lieut. Beal[e] and his former

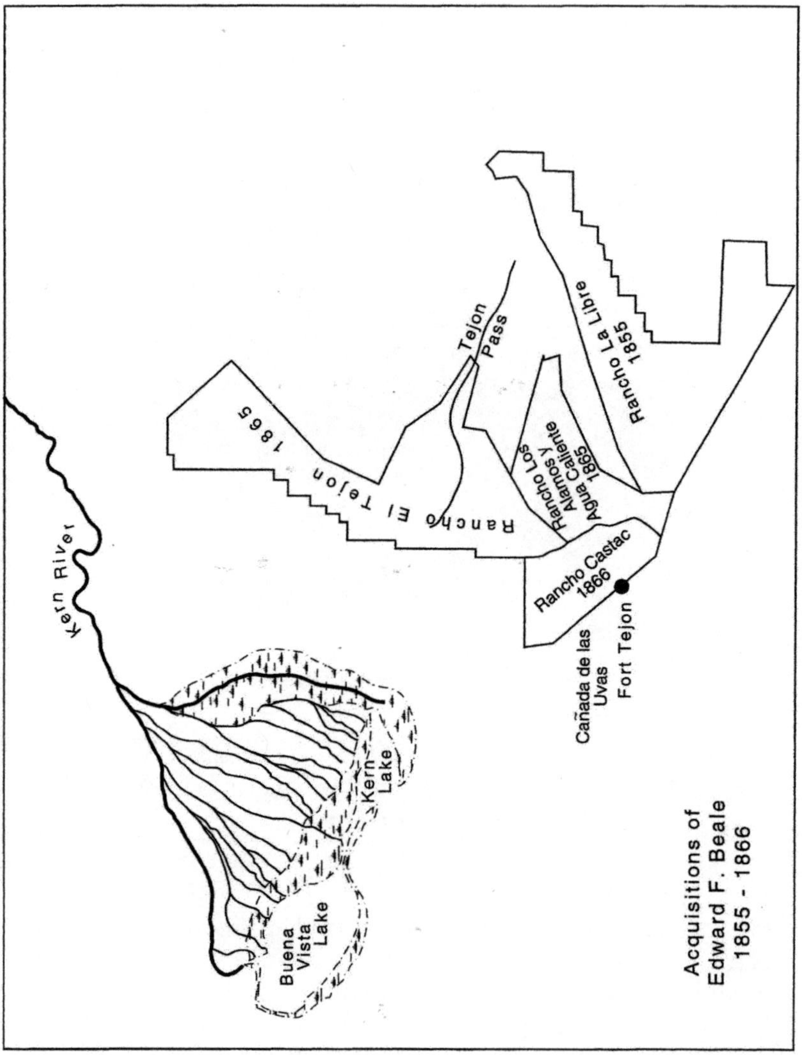
Acquisitions of
Edward F. Beale
1855 - 1866
Kern River
Buena
Vista
Lake
Kern
Lake
Tejon
Pass
Rancho El Tejon
1865
Rancho La Libre
1855
Rancho Los
Alamos y
Agua Caliente
1865
Rancho Castac
1866
Cañada de las
Uvas
Fort Tejon

partners, I ceased further inquiry.[5]

In December 1862 Beale acquired Willow Springs, located about twenty-five miles northeast of Beale's house. Possessing the best springs in the area allowed Beale to control all the intervening land.[6] The following year William H. Brewer passed through the area, noting that by owning La Liebre Beale had access to much more land. The rancho "controls nearly all the water and, consequently feed, for three times that amount, in fact for a hundred miles east. We had a letter from the owner to his Spanish *major-domo* (head man in charge), and we were hospitably entertained according to the Mexican fashion." Brewer called the majordomo "Chico," but perhaps he meant "Soto."[7]

As indicated in a letter Beale wrote to his wife in 1865, the primary function of the Rancho La Liebre was raising cattle: "On the first of May I rode from noon until six o'clock, forty-five miles. Then from that time until night worked anxiously and hard on the rodeo ground with from five to seven thousand head of cattle parting out five hundred for market. Unfortunately in putting them in the corral for the night they became alarmed and many escaped, which gave me all the next day to collect again, so that it was noon to-day before I could start Mr. Hudson on the road with them, and after seeing him ten miles on the way, rode back and threw myself perfectly exhausted on the bed, and went to sleep, and have just now awakened. An good bath has greatly refreshed me."[8] Also in May, Beale acquired Rancho Los Alamos y Agua Caliente.[9]

As Beale was becoming a true land baron, Samuel Bishop was becoming truly wealthy. In 1860 he purchased Ranch Castec (which had already changed hands several times) from Albert Packard for $9,000 in two promissory notes. Fort Tejón was located on the rancho.[10] When visited by William Brewer in 1863, the fort had been abandoned: "The buildings, some fifteen or twenty, are neatly arranged, all built of adobe, but many already falling to ruin. The old stables are crumbling, the corrals are down. After Uncle Sam had located here and had built buildings costing at least $60,000 to $80,000, spending here in all over half a million, of course it turned out that it is on a Spanish grant, and is private property."[11] In June 1866 Bishop sold the rancho to Robert S. Baker for $65,000.[12] Bishop died in Bakersfield on June 3, 1893.[13]

Alexis Godey failed to become wealthy but he fared well. In January 1862 he was appointed Indian agent for the Colorado District.[14] San Bernardino was the headquarters of the agency.[15] By the end of the year he was serving in the same capacity for the Owens Valley District.[16] His tenure as an Indian agent was short-lived, and in October 1863 he entered into a partnership with Beale, who spent most of his time in San Francisco. Godey's primary task was the buying and selling of sheep. In

January the following year, Beale terminated the partnership, because Godey had failed to account for money expended. They divided the sheep; Beale got 6,706, Godey 3,356.[17] Quite likely Godey herded the sheep forty-five miles west to the Cuyama Valley.[18] There he remained until the early 1870s when he relocated to Rancho San Emigido, where he served several owners probably as majordomo.[19]

Brewer described the rancho as "a large and valuable one, near the mouth of the canyon, commanding a lovely view of the plain of Buena Vista Lake, and of the coast ranges. Two large springs water the gardens—fruits and grapes grow to perfection." The main "house was surrounded by the houses and huts of his Indian and Mexican servants and vaqueros. The residence was of adobe, the floor of rough stones, the furniture rude."[20] A local newspaper reported in mid-1870 that Godey had, "by a well planned and most substantial piece of engineering, has diverted the waters of San Amedio [San Emigido] Creek to a commanding position on the edge of the foot hills for the purpose of irrigating a planting of shade trees.... A more delightful spot for a residence could not have been selected in the whole valley. The view is one which combines every element to please and interest. Immediately below is the thriving little village of San Amedio with its fertile fields and gardens. Lower still are the broad expanses of Kern and Buena Vista Lake."[21] In the early 1880s Godey moved to Bakersfield where he died in 1889.[22]

Of the three whitemen so instrumental in shaping the history of the southern Tulare Valley, Beale was by far the most successful. In October 1866 he bought the Rancho Castec from Robert S. Baker for $65,000, completing his land acquisitions.[23] The estates—Tejón, La Liebre, Los Alamos y Agua Caliente, and Castac—and contiguous land totaled 265,215 acres and became known simply as Rancho El Tejón.[24] In 1869 he purchased Rancho Emigido but disposed of the property two years later.[25]

By acquiring the land on which the Tejón Reservation was situated, he got not just property and animals but all the improvement made over the course of a decade— buildings, corrals, vineyards, irrigation ditches, fruit trees, and equipment. More importantly, with Tejón came a highly trained and efficient Indian work force, divided into three divisions and residing in nineteen adobe houses. As of early 1862, they had planted 120 acres in wheat, corn, peas, and melons in their own fields. And they tended to the same kinds of crops in the 250 acres of common fields. Because of this Indian work force and the several non-Indians then working on the reservation, the transition from reservation to rancho went smoothly. In fact, the reservation always resembled a Mexican rancho much more than a Spanish mission, the institution Beale claimed was his model.[26]

Some of Beale's contemporaries questioned the legality and morality of his transaction. William Brewer, for example, mentioned that Beale had purchased Rancho Tejón, "and now has it confirmed as a Spanish grant—a tract of twenty-two leagues or 87,750 acres, over 137 square miles!—that is the way to get land."[27] Writing to the *Visalia Delta* in late May 1864, an individual noted that Beale "came here a poor Lieutenant of the Navy, and is now said to be the proprietor of over 250,000 acres of land, and many thousand head of cattle, horses and mules, many of the latter are said to still carry the brand of the Government.... A stranger would almost conclude, judging by the Government Agents, that there were no honest men in the country."[28]

The following month Superintendent Austin Wiley told the commissioner of Indian affairs that it was regrettable the

> government could not have held possession of the Tejón ranches for reservation purposes. It was originally the peaceable abode of many Indians, and having been taken possession of by the department for a reservation, and having an immense amount of government money expended upon it in that capacity, it is certainly a hardship, not to use a harsher term, that the Indians should be driven from it to seek new abodes upon rented farms contiguous to white settlements, and their fine pasture lands and fields given over to the herds and laborers of him who expended the government money in improving the lands for the ostensible benefit of the Indians. I refer to E. F. Beale, who holds possession the entire ranch under government patent. There is some little government property on the ranch yet, which Mr. Beale is modest enough to admit belongs to the Indian department.[29]

The editors of the *Los Angeles Tri-Weekly News* clearly had Beale in mind when in July 1864 they wrote that "the reservations have been stolen and patented to those who were among the first Superintendents—those who were first to cry aloud for bread for 'the poor Indians,' and never have been found 'guilty' of furnishing them any at all.... Large numbers of them have been brought away from their mountain homes and placed upon a tract of land termed a 'reservation,' to find that their stay was to be short, but richly 'spiced' with pangs of hunger; to leave it followed by the accusations that they had killed thousands of head of stock belonging to the present legitimate owner—by fraud—of the tract of land formerly known as the Tejón Reservation."[30]

Beale and Robert S. Baker formed an informal partnership that focused initially on sheep raising. In 1866-67, 900 American, 5,000 Mexican, and 8,000 mixed sheep browsed on the rancho. The total number rose to 19,983 the following year.[31] During the winter of 1867-68, however, a serious drought began to take its toll on the sheep, and Beale and Barker lost over $20,000 in livestock.[32] But recovery was rapid, and the rancho possessed 37,000 sheep in 1871.[33] And the following year the rancho produced 175,000 pounds of wool. Beale and Baker usually sold the wool locally, but seeking a higher return they shipped the entire amount to Boston. A warehouse fire, however, destroyed the wool, and the company it was ensured with failed. Beale and Baker lost $50,000.[34]

What effect the loss had on the Indian workers is not known, but not all were satisfied with their situation. Yoimut, a Chunut, recalled that "My stepfather worked on the Tejón Ranch for a while, but none of us like it there. The Indians there did not speak our language.... The white people at Tejón Ranch wanted the Indians to go to Tule River. Some went before we did." Eventually, Yoimut and her family moved to the Tule River Farm. "There were lots of our people there. We liked it there and stayed for about two years."[35]

Relocation, however, was not always voluntary. According to Ricardo Francisco, a Tejoneño, Beale allowed the Indians to live where they wanted, but later, "the *mayordomos* of the ranch, always acting for the owners, succeeded in moving all the Indians up to Posun Tiliw, the present rancheria. This was helped by some of the Indians of the lower rancherias going to the [Ghost] dance at Kolopow... and not returning."[36] Mary Austin , who began visiting the rancho in the late 1880s, referred to the dance and expulsion in her book, *The Flock*. It occurred at shearing time when "there came out of Inyo a Medicine Man who gathered the remnant of the tribe to him at Whisky Flat. He was credited with an unfailing meal-sack and promised healing to the sick, the maimed, and the blind.... Whispers of it ran with the click of the shears in the sheds. Question grew into conviction and conviction to a frenzy, man after man they dropped their shears with unclipped merinos, and for this defection, a serious hindrance when no workers were not to be had for sixty miles, they were never taken back into employment."[37]

Juan Coluco recalled that the Mono

> and other tribes were about to hold a big dance at Kolpopow, near Glennville, Kern County, for the purpose of bringing back the dead people. It was in midsummer, a good time for holding a fiesta. We were urged strongly to attend the order to see the dead. Many of the Indians started. My wife wanted to go. I did not want her to. She went and I never saw her again. She died at the Porterville [Tule River] Reservation. After the Indians left to attend the fiesta, the only family left at Tinliw was that of José.... And at Hoshtsiw were left only our family and that of Estanislao.... Mr. Hill [the superintendent] came down and ordered José and the others at Tinliw to move up to the 'Canyon,' meaning Posun Tinliw. He told

> them that they were scaring the cattle and that be did not want them at Tinliw. José and then others moved and the houses at Tinliw were torn down and the place was added to the cattle range.[38]

Coluco insisted that

> Hill and later J. J. López were not contented even now that all the Indians were herded together at Posun Tinliw and after they had razed all the houses of their former villages elsewhere on the ranch. They told us that we could not raise cattle and must have only a few horses. Our fields were small but they begrudged us even these. They were clearly uneasy about having us on the ranch. They wanted us off the ranch but did not know how to accomplish it without making great publicity. They did not want to see us make any improvements on our land.... The conditions were so unpleasant for the Indians that many left to find homes at Bakersfield, Tehachapi, Kern River Tule River, or elsewhere. When my friend, Guadalupe Isidro, returned to the Tejón after the dance at Kolpopow, it was made so unpleasant for him there that he returned to the Tule River.[39]

Born at Tinliw of Tejoneño parents but baptized by a visiting priest, Guadalupe Isidro remembered returning to Tejón after attending the dance at Glennville. He remained only six or seven months because "The Indians had been huddled together at Posun Tinliw in the Cañada as one rounds up cattle. There were no Indians the living anywhere else on the ranch. The management of the ranch did not welcome newcomers and did not allow the Indians already there to take up more land. The people were very poor."[40]

Juan Dionisio lived at the Tejón until the dance at Kopoplow. "I went with my Indian friends to attend the dance. They said that we would see the dead and that Indians would regain possession of the country. The dance at Kolpopow lasted a week and the grub was scant.... I went with them to Porterville, and moved from there to the Tule River Indian Reservation. Knowing that the Indians at the Tejón were not free to raise cattle or to have liberal holdings of land, I did not return to the Tejón. It was the policy of the owners of the Tejón ranch to move all the Indians from the downstream rancherias to Posun Tiniw. Our houses at the downstream rancherias were knocked down, our orchards cut down, and our farms were turned into cattle range or else cultivated by the owners."[41]

About the time of the Ghost Dance, José Jesús Lopez, a Mexican-

American from Los Angeles, arrived at the southern end of the San Joaquin Valley with a flock of sheep. Beale purchased his sheep and hired him as manager of sheep operations on Rancho El Tejón.[42] As pointed out by a traveler, however, sheep suffered from the heat on the "hot, arid plains of the San Joaquin…. Instead of comfortably lying down and ruminating, as they do in colder climates, they huddle together in small bands, each sheep trying to obtain shelter from the scorching sun by putting its head under the belly of its neighbor."[43] Because La Liebre was located at a much higher elevation than the other estates that made up Rancho El Tejón, López introduced sheep there once the cattle had been sold. He established the sheep camps and directed the use of the range.[44]

Charles Nordhoff visited the rancho 1872 and was fascinated with its workings. An easterner Nordhoff noted that "What we call at home a flock is in California called a band of sheep. These bands consists usually of from 1300 to 2000 sheep, and each band is in then charge of a shepherd." The shepherd slept in a hut in the mountains on a *tepestra*, a platform twelve feet high to protect him from grizzly bears. "Of course the shepherds have to be supplied with food. They usually receive a week's rations at once and cook for themselves. At the Tejón there are two supply stations; and every morning donkeys and mules were sent out with food to some distant shepherds."[45]

A general superintendent manage the rancho, with the help of an accountant and a store keeper. Several mayordomos were each in charge of the several bands of sheep. Assisting them were the ration masters who counted the sheep and delivered the rations. According to Nordhoff the ration masters were "to see that the shepherds are competent; that new pasturage is ready when a band has heed for it; to see that the corrals are in good order; to provide extra hands at lambing-time; to examine the sheep to keep out the scab, which is almost the only disease they are subject to in this State; and to give out the rations for distribution." In addition to the shepherds, gardeners, servants, teamsters, ploughmen, and a blacksmith kept the rancho operational. Most were non-Indians.[46]

Indians monopolized the shearing, however. "There was never anything to equal the spring shearing at old Tejón;" wrote Mary Austin, "when there were eighty thousand head to be clipped, you can imagine it was a considerable affair. Seventy-five or eighty Indians bent their backs under the sheds for five or six weeks at a time…. All this finished with a fiesta lasting a week with prizes for races and cockfights, with monte and dancing, and, of course, always a priest at had to take his dole of the shearing wage and confess his people where the altar was set out with drawn-work altar-cloths and clusters of wild lilies in the ramada, that long two-walled house of wattled brush that served the Indian so well."[47]

Nearly all of the vaqueros at Rancho El Tejón were Indians, either

Indian Vaqueros in the San Joaquin Valley, n.d. C. C. Pierce Collection, Huntington Library.

full or part blood. "This crew was the most capable and dependable of any that ever worked under me," claimed Lopez. The vaqueros resided a mile and a half north of the ranch house. "The place was improved by General Beale for his cattle foreman.... The entire 300,000 acre range was supervised from this vaquero headquarters"[48] Because the Indian vaqueros were employed individually and occupied with their families a special place on rancho, evidently they were immune from the pressures to remove experienced by those Indians residing collectively in villages and on their own plots of land.[49]

Of all the vaqueros Juan was the best, recalled Lopez: "He was a fullblood local Indian. Juan could bring such cattle as ours out as quictly and with as little effort as some vaqueros can handle these present-day white faces [Herefords] in an open field." Pedro Cowaye, also an Indian, managed and trained horses. "I never saw a horse buck with Pedro. I understand that sometimes they did, but I never saw it. I have seen him work for four hours with an entirely unbroken horse and then get on it while it stood as quiet as an old plow animal. He would quiet them entirely and get their entire confidence before he got on them."[50]

Jo Mora described the training of a horses in more general terms:

> [O]rdinarily when a hacendando had a number of good colts he wanted broke, he would choose his favorite *amansador* [tamer] and have him move in for the job. He stayed there till all these prospects had been topped and ridden several times and could be turned over as gentle to those who from then on, would teach them to rein and educate them in the orthodox ways of a good cow pony. Their education might take six months to a year or more....
>
> After the *amansadores* turned their tractable colts over to those in to whose hands their further education was entrusted, the colts' real school days commenced. The trainer might change hackamores several times before he was finished, but a bit was never placed in the colt's mouth until he was a finished hackamore horse, with a perfect neck rein, who could back straight and fast. He had to know how to tuck his hind legs under him and come to a sliding stop.... Even when the trainer felt he had finished a hackamore colt, he would put a spade bit in his mouth without any reins and let him pack that around for weeks until he got the feel of it and it didn't bother or distract him in the slightest. Then the reins were attached to the bit, and for many more weeks the trainer handled him with the double rein. Little by little he used the neck rein, and all the other demands were gradually transferred from the mecate reins to those attached to the bit. Then came the day when the hackamore and mecate reins were discarded and the full-fledged finished, bitted horse was added to the caballada.[51]

Well-trained horses and highly skilled horsemen were crucial to the management of cattle. Nordhoff noted that the roundups—the rodeos—were held "in the San Joaquin Valley at stated places and preordained times; and one succeeds the other, going from south northwards, until at last all the cattle have been seen, and all the calves branded.... Sometimes 20,000 head of cattle are gather on the plain, and the working of 'parting out,' as it is called, and the branding, lasts for several days. A carefully defined set of laws regulated this work, and the law officers, called 'Judges of the Plains,' attend to settle disputes as to ownership and regulate the procedure. These officers appointed the times and places of rodeos, and attend at each."[52]

What Nordhoff observed had a long tradition:

> In the old times, when cattle had been gathered, and all was ready, the mayor-domo—an important person on all these estates—came to the proprietor with hat in hand, and formally announced that all was ready. The company, dressed in holiday attire got to horse and rode out to the plain, and at the word the work began.

> There were seen some really magnificent feats of horsemanship; each vaquero vied with the other in this display; and as the day grew, fresh horses were saddle, and no bull was so wild that he did not find his master.
>
> The state and ceremony have gone out; but the skillful riding still remains, as well as the feats with the lasso, which are really like jugglery or witchcraft. I have a hundred times watched the fling of the riata, and yet have never in a single instance been able to detect the precise moment of the capture.[53]

As explained by Arnold R. Rojas, who worked on the ranch at a much later time, Tejón was known from one end of the state to the other for its horses: "Our horses had to be good in those days. The Tejón had fifty thousand head of cattle; besides those which strayed onto the ranch from Walker's Basin, from the Miller and Lux and the Kern County Land Company ranches, and from ranches in the Tehachepi Mountains, the Coast Range, and the Sierra Nevada. Riders from three countries met at the Tejón rodeos."[54]

Rojas emphasized the importance of the Indian vaquero as a model for others:

> When a vaquero was especially skilled, and he was asked how he had reached such a degree of proficiency, his answer would be: "*Me crié entre los Indios.*" I was raised among the Indians. Or when some vaquero had performed his work with great skill, the other men would look at each other, smile approvingly, and say, '*Se crió entre los Indios pues!*' Well, he was brought up among the Indians.
>
> Contrary to a lot of false statements, a man took pride in calling himself 'Indio.' The Indian vaquero was highly respected for his skill and good qualities—that is, by those who knew him. And then proof is that very few of the men who have ridden on the Tejón stayed there any length of time without becoming 'Indios del Teión,' Tejón Indians, whatever their true race many have been.[55]

About 1874, Beale appointed an Indian from Sonora, Francisco (Chico) Acuña, superintendent of the rancho. As recalled by José Jesús López, Chico took a back seat to no one when it came to handling "men and stock and feed and water." Because Chico was trained in the vast desert country of Mexico, "the problems at El Tejón Ranchos were comparatively simple." Furthermore, "Chico was possessed of a most wonderful personal character. He was honest and truthful as it is possible for a human to be. General Beale realized that Chico was the most loyal friend he ever had. This I have heard the General say." Chico's influence over men was

Patio–Old Ranch House and Headquarters, circa 1890. Courtesy of the Tejón Ranch.

demonstrated one day when an Indian, Francisco, got drunk and abusive. "As Francisco came near, Chico began speaking. He addressed Francisco as though he were sober, and with all of the respect he would have shown General Beale. In a few seconds Francisco broke down into tears, turned and ran away."[56]

The store keeper was another person who exerted a certain amount of power. On most ranchos, a company store, or commissary, provided goods and food to the Indian and other workers. Rancho El Tejón was no different, except the store was located in a stone building the Indians had constructed in 1854. Fred Cury ran the store until replaced by Jimmie Rosemyre, nephew of former Subagent James Vineyard. There, Indians, travelers, and neighboring rancheros purchased beans, bacon, boots, clothing, and other items.[57] As on other ranchos, the Indians and other workers probably spent most of their salary at the commissary and some may have purchased items on credit and thus went into debt. If they also bought liquor, a common practice on many ranchos, López failed to mention it.[58]

As recalled by Beale's daughter-in-law, "close by the house stood the 'tienda' where a stock of a little of everything was kept for sale to the

Indians and vaqueros. On Saturday the outer patio was filled with them, come to buy their provisions or a new 'riata' or 'serape;' exchange the latest gossip and see the little world at the Casa. The Indian women and girls in their best clothes, conservatively riding sideway although on cross saddles, brought the house laundry, tamales, or a 'regalo' for me, 'la patrona.' They stayed about all day eating 'dulces,' watching and flirting with the vaqueros as they rode up."[59] According to Juan Coluco the vaqueros often had their way with the Indian girls.[60]

The rancho's recent history was everywhere to be seen, noted López: "The old hoes and picks and the scythe we found...were part of the equipment furnished the Indians by the government when first they placed the Indians there. I have heard this many times from the Indians themselves, and also from Alexis Godey, who first had charge of them and who knew their history very well. Tunas was the place were the Indians held all of their dances and where Godey used to dress and paint like an Indian and dance with them." Down the creek past the rancho house was a field of barley and the remains of the irrigation ditch Beale had built. "General Beale told me about this himself while we were on that ground. He told me of having a ditch made from Tunas Creek and irrigating some of the land with water which flowed out into the plains, even after I came to the Tejón."[61]

As the reservation became a rancho, Indian political leadership became less effective, although several Indian leaders were alive when López settled on the rancho. Vicente died shortly after his arrival, but his son, Santiago, and two grandsons lived northeast of the ranch house at El Monte.[62] In 1873 Vicente would have been seventy-five years of age.[63] Zapatero, as López remembered him, was "a man of fine character, truthful, honest, and honorable in every way. In fact, all of those chiefs were the finest characters you could meet. They had to be in order to hold their positions as chiefs. Zapatero did no work for the Tejón Ranch. He and his tribe supported themselves with the gardens and by a few cattle which General Beale allowed them to run on the near by plains." He "lived in a small Indian hut across the creek to the east, under a fine old oak tree which still stands. This was the place where we found the old hoes and garden tools which once had been issued to the Indians by the government agents when Alexis Godey and General Beale were in charge."[64] Zapatero would have been fifty-one years of age in 1873.[65]

Estanislao was alive but was no longer an active leader. Martín, now a cripple, lived with his two brothers a mile and a half east of the commissary. Joaquin occupied a track of land about four miles east of the ranch house granted him by Beale. He told López that he had signed the treaty of 1851 with the Indian commissioner. He was, as remembered by López, "a tall, straight, fine looking Indian. He never wore a hat, he wore his hair in a queue down his back, and always it was ornamented with beads and spangles. He was one of the finest horsemen I ever knew, both as a rider and a vaquero, and a breeder and trainer of fine saddle animals." He "had quite a few Indians under him, even in my time, and really was quite well-to-do." Joaquin died in the late 1880s and was buried in the Indian cemetery.[66]

Francisco was one of the five leaders who signed the 1851 treaty as a Tejoneño.[67] Under his leadership Indians resided at the Monte, northeast of the ranch house. López noted that Francisco had served as an alcalde at Mission San Fernando, "spoke good Spanish, could read both Spanish and Latin, and sang in the church choir." Beale had known Francisco since the Mexican-American War, and when Beale visited the rancho, "Francisco always came to the ranch head-quarters to see him. They would stand facing each other almost like soldiers, and talk together for as long as two hours." Francisco lived to an advanced age and was "one if the most universally respected persons ever to live at Rancho El Tejón."[68] He died in September 1891 and received an obituary in the *San Francisco Bulletin*.[69]

According to Mary Austin, scenes like these took place in an idyllic setting: "The ranch house sits by the water that comes down guardedly between tents and tents of wild vines. Below the house by the stream-side then Indian washer women paddle leisurely at the clothes and spread them bleaching in then sun. Silvering olives and mists of bare fig branches slope down to the blossomy swale; deep in the course between the long adobes, summer abodes, and yearly about the fences of the garden the pomegranates flame. The beginning of all these, and the oranges, Jimmy Rosemeyer brought up from Mission San Fernando, going down with two live deer in a wagon and returning with cuttings and rooted trees. Six miles up the canon are the adobe huts and the *ramadas*, the bits of fenced garden that make the Indian rancheria."[70]

The economic difficulties the rancho experienced in the late 1870s, however, stands in sharp contrast to Austin's romanticism. Although 1874 was a banner year for the production of wool—242,000 pounds valued at $70,000—sheep raising was on its last legs.[71] The extremely dry years of 1877 and 1878 and a drop in the demand for sheep convinced Beale and his mayordomo to switch to cattle. Grazing on the Rancho Tejón in 1879 were 68,000 sheep and 10,000 head of cattle. In May of that year, Beale sent López and 16,000 sheep from La Liebre to the Owens Valley where they were to be sold. Once there, Beale changed plans and ordered his drovers to take them across the Nevada Desert to near the Utah border. Another change in plans sent the animals to Green River, Wyoming. Along the way much of the band was lost, and Beale received only $5,000 for the effort.[72] López thought the removal of sheep from La Liebre was a mistake: "this was the first portion of El Tejón Ranchos to

Indian House at the Mouth of the Tejón Canyon, circa 1890. Courtesy of the Tejon Ranch.

be cleared of sheep and returned to cattle, for which the range was not so well adapted as it was for sheep."[73]

In 1880 the shift from sheep to cattle was well underway. The 11,000 head then grazing on the rancho Beale intended to expand to 25,000. In June vaqueros would drive the herds to summer pastures in the mountains. In October they would return them to winter pastures or to a spot on the northern edge of the rancho where they would be loaded on to cars of Southern Pacific Railroad for shipment to markets.[74] Obviously, the Indian and other vaqueros were kept busy during this seasonal enterprise, but apparently the village Indians gained nothing from it.

By 1883 the Indian population may have dropped by half, to 150.[75] Whether Beale, mainly attending to business and politics in San Francisco and later in the East, knew or cared about this decline is not known.[76] But on his occasional visits, he exhibited a sincere interest in the welfare of the Indians. "Beale was always kind to the Indians," insisted Juan Coluco. "It was the mayordomos who took actual charge or who succeeded Beale, that oppressed the Indians."[77] In the company of López, Beale would ride to their settlement and inquire into their welfare. "Any Indian on the ranch would have laid down his life for the General, and I mean this literally," claimed López. "'Don Heneral,' they called him. He had his Mayordomo distribute meat among them once a week. He hired every one of the who could work, and care for their families. He paid the funeral expenses of every Indian who died on the ranch."[78]

The funeral of José Acuña, on October 18, 1886, was the most elaborate to date. It was described by Beale in a letter to his wife:

> All work was suspended on the place. Half way from his house I met then procession, accompanied by Pogson and Godey. Then coffin was borne by the Vaqueros who relieved each other at intervals. In front was carried in the arms of one of our men his eldest child. All the Indians and men followed chanting in Spanish the burial service—the men one verse and the women another.
>
> I never heard any thing so solemn and sweet as this chant. When the body arrived at the house it was placed in then parlor, where it was permitted to all, Indians and white people, to come and look at him for then last time.
>
> The flower garden was full of roses and other beautiful flowers which soon filled the coffin. Here at intervals the funeral songs and hymns of the Catholic Church were sung as before—the women and men's voices in alternate verses.[79]

When Beale returned to Tejón in January 1889, he met Mary Austin, shortly to become a successful and famous author. Beale related to her his exploits and she explored the rancho, meeting shepherds and vaqueros and observing shearing and brandings. She noted in her autobiography that she saw "how the cattle bedded on the warm, last-lighted slopes, turning around before lying down as a dog does; how the coyotes hunted in relays; how the stallions managed their seraglios of brood mares, guarded and served them." Austin learned how the Indians lived "off a land upon which more sophisticated races would starve, and how the land itself instructed them." The whole basis of her social philosophy was altered "beyond the capacity of books to keep pace with it."[80]

What Austin missed or failed to address were the policies then being implemented regarding the Indian residents. In 1891, when Beale had the rancho appraised, cattle had replaced sheep as the dominant animal, 25,000 to 7,500. In addition, there were 350 mules. Two-hundred miles of fences had been built.[81] And overseeing the ranch at the time probably was Robert M. Pogson who evidently had succeeded Acuña as superintendent. Juan Coluco remembered an occasion when Pogson assembled the Indians to inform them that Beale wanted each to donate one dollar to help pay his taxes. About twenty Indians agreed to pay and put their crosses on a "contract" provided by the storekeeper, Jimmy Rosemyer. "I was the first put his cross," noted Coluco. "None of us knew how to write. All of us worked and lived on the ranch. At the end of the year Pogson docked the monthly pay checks of each of us $1.00. I have one or two of these

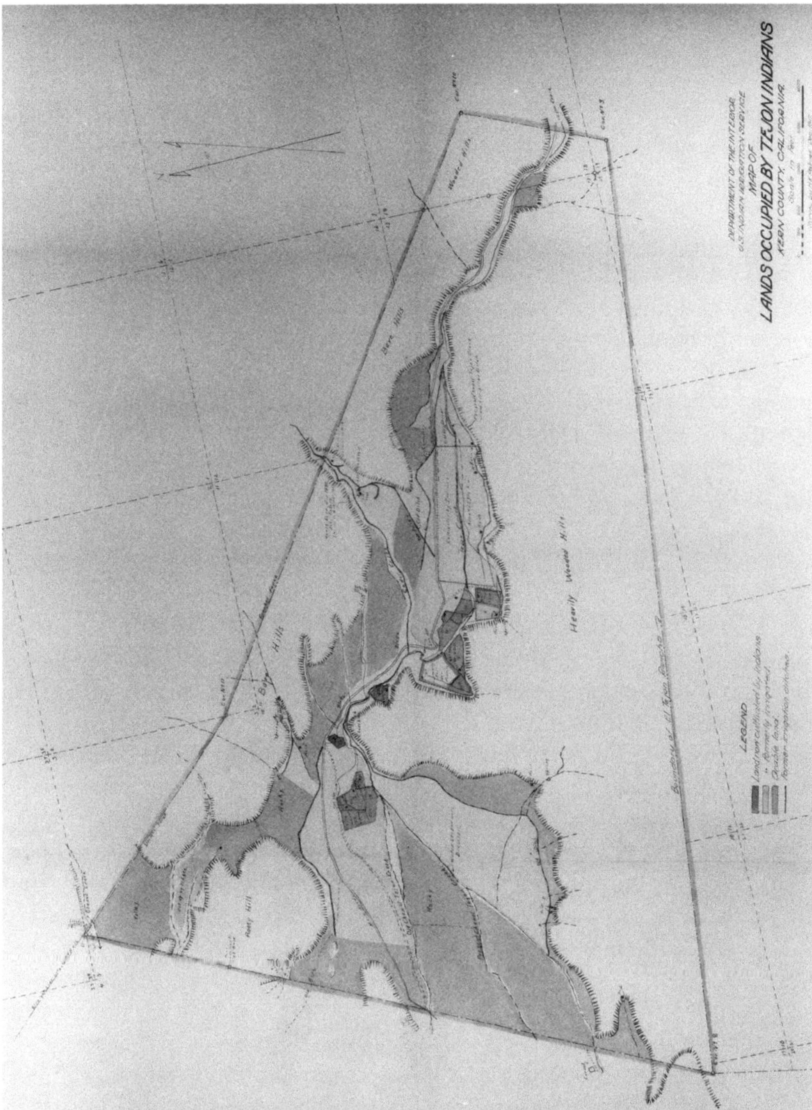
MAP OF
LANDS OCCUPIED BY TEJON INDIANS
KERN COUNTY, CALIFORNIA
Heavily Wooded Hills
LEGEND

receipts still in my possession."[82]

In 1892 Beale directed that upon his death Pogson be given full control over the rancho.[83] Beale died the following year, and Pogson and Beale's relatives continued the policy of evicting Indians. On December 7, 1899 Juan Coluco received a telegram stating that, "I hereby notify you that you must surrender your lease-hold on the Tejón ranch on January 1." It was signed by Truxton Beale, Edward's son. On December 26, Coluco received a notice terminating his tenancy. He was instructed to deliver possession of his property to Pogson on February 1, 1900. It was signed by Mary Beale, Edward's wife, and her attorney, D. P. Hatch.[84]

Convinced that the owners were bluffing, his friends advised Coluco to remain on his property at Posun Tinliw, which he did. But on April 15, 1901, while at Poso Creek shearing sheep, he received the following notice: "In the Superior Court of the County of Kern, State of California. Mary E. Beale, Plaintiff, v. Juan Coluco.... For the possession of certain premises and sum of $75.00 damages for the rents of said premises and the detention thereof and cost of the suit." Coluco left the ranch "and almost at once heard the news that my house and ranch had been destroyed, even the fruit trees having been cut down. I have since that time been living at Bakersfield and at the Tule River Indian Reservation."[85]

Rapid population decline continued, and when Truxton Beale sold the rancho to a syndicate in 1912, it had dropped significantly. As reported in 1915, eighty-one Tejon Indians remained: "The syndicate claiming title to the land occupied by the Indians prohibits them from pasturing cattle on the ranch lands, and the little band are permitted to keep very few horses, and now have only 15 head of all kinds of live stock."[86] Three years later, a surveyor of the ranch noted that many Tejonenos had relocated to Bakersfield, Lenoore, the Kings River Canyon, and the Tule River Reservation. He counted only sixty-five acres under cultivation and estimated the population at sixty, although forty more (evidently the vaqueros) may have lived near the ranch headquarters. He recounted the plight of Sebastiana Hignio who lived on Cedar Creek was forced to move to the upper settlement where she cultivated a few aces and started a small orchard. Shortly after she died in February 1917, her house was razed on the orders of J. J. Lopez. Her plot was leased to an Italian who diverted most of the water used by the Indians to his crops.[87]

This process continued until the few remaining Indians served more as symbols of a romantic, bygone era than as the descendants of those who introduced agriculture and stock raising to the Tulare Valley.[88]

CONCLUSION

Historical Reconsiderations

For about one hundred and thirty years, the Indians in the Tulares interacted with Spanish explorers and missionaries, neophyte auxiliaries and refugees, Mexican soldiers and rancheros, and American miners and settlers penetrating their territories. While undergoing considerable social and economic change, for about eighty years of that period they maintained their political independence and exhibited an aggressiveness that hindered foreign occupation and later damaged coastal settlements.

With a few exceptions, historians have overlooked these developments, largely because Indian activity in the interior does not fit neatly into conventional periodization.[1] Each period—the Spanish, the Mexican, and the American—is associated with an important turning point: the initiation of Spanish colonization in 1769, the achievement of Mexican independence in 1821, and the intrusion of American military forces in 1846. Historians have long acknowledged the presence of Indians in these periods but, until recently, mainly as members of institutions established by the intruders—as neophytes in the missions, as workers on the ranchos, and as residents of reservations. Indians thus appear in the historical literature mainly as a dominated, passive, and often tragically mistreated people. When applied to the coastal region after 1769 and to the interior after 1850, the image has some validity. But when applied to the interior before 1850, it badly distorts historical reality.

Considered to be of little historical importance until white settlement began with John Sutter, the San Joaquin Valley has been largely ignored, with some important expeditions, by historians of the first two periods.

As a consequence, they have overlooked important aspects of Spanish and Mexican colonialism and more importantly have failed to appreciate how Indian activity affected Hispanic institutions. The strategies interior Indians directed toward a mission or a rancho sometimes affected the institution more profoundly than did the managerial policies of the missionary or ranchero.

The history of Indian-white interaction in the interior to 1850 has been overshadowed by that of the coast, mainly because much more documentary evidence was produced by those who explored and settled there than those who penetrated the interior and because Indian-white interactions along the coast fit (although not perfectly) into conventional periodization. Consequently, the importance of Indians in shaping aspects of California history in the interior can best be appreciated when the ethnohistorian places the historical data in a spatial and temporal framework that accounts for the processes of interaction. Once San Joaquin Valley is conceived as a zone of interaction, the limitations of conventional periodization are, to a large degree, overcome. Events the interaction shaped, not familiar historical periods, determined the temporal framework.

Initially, the Indian history of the interior zone is characterized by a series of adaptations to changing circumstances. As long as Spaniards sought ethnographical and geographical knowledge, Indians demonstrated curiosity and friendship. When Spaniards and later Mexicans sought human beings, Indians exhibited fear and hostility. By withdrawing into tule swamps or mountain retreats, by refusing to turn over children and runaways, and by violently opposing the penetration of their territories, Indians during this phase implemented strategies of defensive resistance.

The resistance of Estanislao in 1829 exemplified the shift from amicable to inimical interaction. Although defeated militarily and reincorporated into Mission San José, Estanislao demonstrated to Mexican secular and religious authorities that discontented neophytes were prepared to fight to remain in the interior. Gone were the days when soldiers, civilians, and auxiliaries from the coast could penetrate the San Joaquin Valley with impunity. Further adaptation began the following year when trappers and traders began arriving on a regular basis. The New Mexicans provided interior Indians with opportunities and incentives that sent them to the coast on stock-raiding expeditions. Although Indian raiding had begun before 1830, it accelerated dramatically after this date. Indians increasingly implemented strategies of offensive resistance.[2]

Dovetailing with the arrival of trappers and traders was the breakup of the missions. As a watershed in the history of the coastal region, secularization is viewed mainly as the replacement of one Hispanic institution by another—the rancho for the mission. Californios, therefore, are perceived as the principal actors in the historical drama, and those most affected by secularization, the neophytes, are given no role to play. Many California historians regard the breakup of the missions as the coup de grace of the neophyte population. Driven from the missions by unscrupulous land grabbers, the Indians became a marginal and thus historically insignificant people within Mexican society.[3]

This interpretation calls for substantial modification. The neophytes who drifted into the pueblos such as Los Angeles often experienced social disintegration and population decline, but those who trekked into the interior to join existing societies successfully reordered their lives.[4] Secularization provided interior Indian societies with informed and skilled individuals, many of whom rose to positions of authority. Rebel neophytes conducted most of the raids to obtain stock.

That Indians raided the ranchos for animals has long been recognized, but the historical significance of this activity has been largely ignored. During the 1930s and 1940s, for example, the anthropologist Anna Gayton produced a large body of first-rate scholarship about the Yokuts and Mono but mentioned Indian raiding in her publications and research notes only on occasion. Concerned with reconstructing Yokuts society as it existed before white contact, she probably did not press her informants for this kind of information. And when a Chukchansi told her about raiding the ranchos, she noted in her journal that, "stealing horses sounds like lots of fun, to hear tell of it and see them look satisfied about the game."[5]

This view resembles that held by most anthropologists of the time. Regarding Indian warfare on the Great Plains, Robert Lowie insisted it was "an exciting pastime played according to established rules, the danger lending zest to the game."[6] More recent research has shown, however, that the acquisition of horses by trade and raid was a crucial activity in an extensive economic network that linked most Plains societies in ever-shifting relationships and which also connected them commercially to a succession of non-Indian nations.[7]

Long ago Sherburne F. Cook identified the aggressive behavior of interior California Indians but concluded the raids were conducted mainly to acquire food. Certainly, Indians stole stock for food, and this dietary adaptation was crucial to their survival. Many interior peoples shifted from subsisting primarily on vegetable foods to relying heavily on meat.[8] But Indians had no need to continually raid the ranchos for this food source, because the San Joaquin Valley teemed with wild horses and other large game.

The commercial motive explains to a large degree why Indians raided the ranchos on such a regular basis. To acquire the woolen goods the New Mexicans brought to California, Indians appropriated horses and mules from the Californios. Because it called for thorough planning and preparation, because it was largely undertaken by those who had acquired new skills and knowledge, and because it fulfilled commercial needs, the raid represents a "modern" economic enterprise. In this regard the stock raiders performed a function similar to that of Indian trappers and hunters in the fur and hide trades in other regions of North America.[9] As "middlemen" in a long-distance trade network, they transferred a valuable product from Californios to New Mexicans.

Throughout North America, trade either solidified or exacerbated relations between Indians and non-Indians. David Weber, for example, has shown that Americans undermined Indian- Mexican relations in the Southwest by trading illegally with a variety of groups during the 1830s and 1840s.[10] In California, however, most of the illegal trade with Indians was conducted not by Americans, but by New Mexicans. Americans never brought to California the quantity of trade goods that comprised the caravans from New Mexico. Moreover, because New Mexicans encouraged interior Indians to steal stock from the coast, they, not Americans, were largely responsible for undermining Indian-Californio relations. The irony here is that Mexicans from New Mexico damaged the economic foundations upon which Mexican society in California was constructed.

In the major study of the Old Spanish Trail, historians LeRoy and Ann Hafen claim that most of the animals illegally acquired were appropriated by traders and trappers. They acknowledge that Indians participated in the raids, but mainly in conjunction with New Mexicans and Americans.[11] Most of the stock, however, was obtained not by outsiders, whose raids were limited and sporadic, but by Indians, whose raids were extensive and systematic.[12]

Because the variety of trade goods exchanged between California and New Mexico was limited, historians have concluded that the Old Spanish Trail was of limited commercial importance. Certainly, when compared to the variety of goods hauled over the Santa Fe Trail, the items taken to and from California suggest economic insignificance.[13] Volume, however, may be as important as variety. How many animals were taken from California is not known, but the evidence suggests many thousands.[14]

As animals left the province, foreigners, such as John Sutter, entered it. The subject of several full-length biographies, Sutter has been depicted as the pioneer who came to control much of the interior of northern California. "With the help of friendly tribes of his neighborhood," wrote James Peter Zollinger, "Sutter gradually made subservient the other Indians of the Sacramento and of the lower San Joaquin Valley."[15] Richard Dillon asserted that "by the fall of 1845, even with the Walla Walla war scares, Sutter had the northern California Indian situation very much in hand."[16] Interpretations such as these stem from the failure to understand the complexities and difficulties that came with residing in a vast Indian territory. The time and energy Sutter spent cultivating the friendship of Indian leaders and pursuing those he sought to dominate indicate the precariousness of his existence.

Failure to realize how vulnerable most of the rancheros were to Indian raids has also led to a misunderstanding of Mexican society. Often romanticized by visitors, the Californios have been presented as a people living in isolated splendor.[17] This romantic view, however, clashes with that held by the rancheros themselves. In 1876, Juan Bautista Alvarado called for an understanding of the plight of the Californios. "It is all very well for those who came to Alta California when there were no more Indians to fight," he wrote in his memoirs, "to make fun of us who for so many years did nothing...(except) to fight day and night against our eternal enemies, the heathen barbarians." Fearful that this aspect of life in Mexican California would be forgotten, he hoped "there might be found in the archives the reports concerning the many, many battles which the troops and militiamen...sustained against the mountain Indians."[18]

About the same time, an American, Edward Kemble, voiced similar concerns. Regarding the stock raiders, he noted that their "fame and exploits are fast passing from the minds of California pioneers and are hardly known to later generations of Californians, having no special or appropriate mention in such modern books as I have seen of the country. They were the scourge of the eastern and middle portion of California in the period following the decadence of the missions and before the settlement of the Territory by Americans and other foreigners.... Those who arrived in California in 1845-46 heard much more of horse thief Indians than any other foe to civilization and settlement. They were much more dreaded when war broke out than the native Californians."[19]

Because historians only began to investigate the deleterious effects Indian raids had on Mexican society a century after he wrote, Kemble's concerns were well founded. Historical amnesia, it seems, can strike historians as well as the general public. But it can also be cured. In separate articles published in the 1970s, Sylvia Broadbent and Charles Hughes analyzed the ramifications of Indian raids near Monterey and San Diego respectively. My own research has continued the investigation of Indian raiding.[20]

Until recently historians have paid more attention to Mexicans and Mexican-Americans than Indians in California history, but they have tended to focus on developments transpiring after 1846. Leonard Pitt, for example, has investigated the dynamics of interethnic relations that evolved during the second half of the nineteenth century. By exposing the difficulties faced and analyzing the responses undertaken by Hispanics under American domination, Pitt has filled in important gaps in the historical record. His contribution to the historiography of California is not in question here. Questioned, rather, are his particular views regarding the rancho system as it supposedly existed at the time of the American takeover. To him, the rancho was a relatively stable, if hierarchical and inegalitarian, institution that provided its residents, Indian and Mexican with a semblance of social and economic security. "Owing to the happy combination of good climate, ample land, and cheap Indian labor" he wrote, "the rancho order worked smoothly."[21]

According to Pitt the social stability of the rancho was immediately shattered with the American occupation. Especially devastating to the rancheros was the Land Law of 1851, which forced them to prove title to their estates. The cost of traveling to San Francisco where the Board of Land Commissioners sat, hiring lawyers, producing documents, and locating witnesses forced many of them to sell sections of their lands or to go heavily into debt. Certainly, the law of 1851 and the exorbitant tax the state legislature placed on land contributed significantly to the demise of the rancho system.[22] But state and federal policies did not initiate the process of decline for many rancheros.

Nearly two decades of relentless Indian raiding preceded the American takeover, and by the time the Land Law was implemented, many, but certainly not all, the ranchos in and on the edge of the San Joaquin Valley were in a condition of economic stagnation if not ruin. The loss of large numbers of horses and mules deprived the rancheros of the means to effectively work their herds of cattle. This hampered their efforts to modernize their industry and thus to effectively compete with American farmers and ranchers.

It is apparent, therefore, that the rancho system did not always work smoothly and that the dramatic changes affecting the Hispanic residents of California did not begin with the American conquest. This is not to suggest, however, that without Indian raiding the rancheros somehow would have overcome the pressures that came with the American occupation. But with their estates intact, they would have been in a much better bargaining position to deal, at least initially, with the American intruders. And perhaps this would have cushioned to some degree the trauma of rapid change. The ramifications of Indian raiding thus extended far beyond the immediate economic losses suffered by the rancheros.

Consideration of Indian activity also generates a different perspective regarding the response of the Californios to the American military intrusion. The conventional interpretation holds that many Californios failed to take up arms or did so reluctantly because they were disillusioned with their leaders, whose perpetual bickering had led to numerous bloodless "revolutions" between 1824 and 1846.[23] During that period a dozen governors attempted to rule California. Certainly, political instability contributed to the discontent, but who occupied the governor's chair at a given moment was of less concern to the rancheros than the inability of any government to protect them from Indian raids.

Although operating independently of the Americans, the raiders inadvertently assisted them in their conquest of the coastal zone. For many Californios protecting their ranchos from Indian raiders took precedent over defending their territory against American invaders. Others concluded that only with a change of government would Indian raiding be brought to an end. Realizing the hopelessness of their situation, many Californios thus accepted, if not welcomed, the American takeover.

Trained to fight a conventional war and burdened with the responsibility of occupying the coastal towns, the American military failed to protect the rancheros from Indian raids. By sending a few expeditions into the interior and by appointing a few civilians to serve as Indian agents, the new government established the outlines of an Indian policy. But the soldiers lacked the means and numbers to defeat hostile Indians, and the agents lacked the support and authority to protect peaceful ones.

Consequently, when historians claim that the conquest of California was achieved by U.S. military forces in 1846, they overlook an important dimension in the region's history. What they mean to say is that the coastal zone, from San Diego to San Francisco, was brought under military rule that year. Interior Indians had yet to be conquered. And once conquered the federal government had no idea what to do with them.

The federal Indian agents arrived in California with the intention of making treaties of peace and friendship with the Indians, but their instructions said nothing about creating reservations. Redick McKee initially thought the Indians might be removed beyond the borders of the state. Unexpected, however, was the conflict in the Southern Mines. Although the whites inflicted heavy casualties on the hostile Indians, they failed to deter them from raiding mining towns, killing isolated miners and ferrymen, and stealing animals. The idea of removing large numbers of aggressive Indians to other areas was, therefore, quickly abandoned. Indian resistance influenced he agents' decision, to negotiate rather than to dictate, to relocate rather than to expel.

The activities of state officials also affected the agents. By authorizing the formation of the Mariposa Battalion and by appropriating the funds to support it, the state sought a stopgap military solution to "the Indian problem" in the Southern Mines. Only by asserting their authority over James Savage and the battalion were the agents able to implement their policy. And unlike state policy, which failed to take into consideration future relations with the Indians, the federal program, as improvised by the agents, sought to deliver to them long-range benefits.

Because state officials and militia deferred to federal agents and soldiers, the first treaty was successfully concluded. Although based on treaties conducted during the removal period, it confined the Indians to lands near where they then resided. In this regard the treaty and the policy which produced it broke tradition. The old policy uprooted Indians from their homelands within states and moved them across a distinct physical boundary, the Mississippi River, to a politically unorganized area—Indian Territory. The new policy designated lands to Indians within the politically organized unit where they resided—the State of California. In other words, the old policy removed Indians beyond; the new one relocated them within.

Put yet another way, the old policy created "overseas colonies" ruled "indirectly" by the Indian Office and resembles British policy of indirect rule in which some colonies were governed through indigenous rulers.[24] That Indian Territory was analogous to overseas possessions was recognized by the *Daily Alta California* in 1851: "It was fortunate that the eastern states had a kind of Van Dieman's land on the western side of the great river where they could transport these poor red children of the forest. It is not so, however, with California."[25] The new policy created "interior colonies" which had to be governed directly.

Convincing Indians to settle in the colonies presented problems. When the Yosemite failed to attend the conference in March 1851, the agents gave James Savage permission to bring them in. Whether this action was necessary at the time is questionable and suggests that the agents succumbed to pressure from those seeking conflict with the Indians. Consequently, the Yosemite had to abandon an area isolated from whites for lands directly in their midst. They were confined to the Fresno Reservation not to improve their condition but to punish them for their defiance. Always at the disposal of those shaping the new Indian policy was the use of force.

Coercion, however, was applied selectively. Against a small band easily targeted in a valley, it was successful. With larger and more powerful societies, persuasion was the best policy. Thus, when negotiating with Indians noted for their aggressiveness, the agents proceeded with caution. When some chiefs opposed moving to the reservations, the agents turned to the more accommodating leaders to persuade them to relocate. Furthermore, by signing the treaties, restraining their followers from attacking miners, and assisting the agents in rounding up those unwilling to relocate, several Indian leaders, for a variety of reasons and motives, helped to bring peace to the interior of Central California and thus actively participated in the founding of the reservation system.

Not all Indians had to relocate. Powerful groups in the Tulare Valley "obtained" lands they already occupied and remained for a time politically independent. The location of lands allocated to the Indians, therefore, depended as much on the size and power (or lack thereof) of Indian societies as on the actions and goals of the United States. Indians also influenced military policy. Because many Indian leaders signing the treaties governed societies that were militarily strong, George Barbour and Captain E. D. Keyes agreed that the army had an important role to play in implementing the new Indian policy. The founding of Fort Miller near the Fresno Reservation initiated in California what was later known as the military reservation system.

By the time he returned to the East Coast, Barbour realized that subagents, agents, and a superintendent should be permanently assigned to California. Redick McKee and Adam Johnston reached the same conclusion, probably because they envisioned roles for themselves in a new administration. Both demonstrated different but complementary abilities. McKee excelled in originating and eloquently defending policy. Johnston exhibited a talent for getting things done. He licensed traders, provided credit to beef contractors, hired a physician, and extinguished the claims of ferryboat operators and tavern keepers. Left to implement the policy the agents created, Johnston single-handedly got some of the reservations operational.

For enterprising individuals such as James Savage, the reservations provided opportunities for economic advancement. By managing much of the cattle purchased for the Indians and by trading with both Indians and whites, Savage turned the Fresno Reservation into his own economic preserve. He also brought the Indian residents under his political control, becoming, in effect, their surrogate chief. In exchange for obedience and labor, they received provisions and assistance. By establishing a self-sufficient and well-run institution, Savage, in his own peculiar and self-serving way, contributed to the founding of the reservation system in California.

Regarding the feasibility of the Fresno and the other reservations, a prolonged debate brought the issue before the English-speaking residents of California. In legislative speeches, public addresses, editorials, and letters to editors, the idea of congregating Indians on lands where they would be separated from the majority of Americans but controlled by a select group of them was examined in some depth. On the one hand the debate convinced many that the reservations were located on lands so extensive and valuable that the treaties creating them should be rejected and the Indians removed from the state. On the other hand, the debate convinced others that the reservations would serve the best interests of both races. On the reservations Indians would be protected and improved. From the reservations whites would draw Indians to work on their farms and ranches. This suggests economic exploitation, but it also implies that Indians deserved a place, albeit a lowly one, in America's recently acquired western "empire."

Although the founding of the reservation system throughout the West may be viewed as an act of American imperialism (that is, the confining and controlling of tens of thousands of indigenous peoples), in California it was an act of feeble imperialism. The four agents sent to California hardly represent a serious investment in the expansion of "imperial" authority. Taking advantage of a weak federal presence, the State of California, by opposing the ratification of the treaties and by forming its own plan for the management of the Indians, openly interfered with the implementation of federal Indian policy and defiantly challenged the authority of the United States. What took place in California, however, was not unique. In the British Empire, tension always existed between the Crown and colonial governments regarding the management of Asian and African peoples.[26]

In California many elected officials expressed little sympathy for the Indians. But the numerous letters written by private citizens and military personnel deploring the crimes committed against them indicate that feelings ran deeper than mere "pious handwringing," as claimed by the anthropologist Robert Heizer.[27] Historian Ray Raphael is correct in noting that "these good men, with no vested interest at stake, never congealed into an organized force acting in concert towards a common goal. There were no committees for the preservation of the Indians, no political lobbies of organized voters."[28] By implying there should have been committees and lobbies, however, Raphael ignored the political realities of mid-nineteenth-century California and imposed modern values on a historical situation. What he, Heizer, and others have failed to understand is that compassion for Indians is not limited to those looking back in anger but was present among many of those witnessing and even creating the events so deplored by later generations.

Concerning the goals and activities of the Indian agents, superficial evaluations also abound. Writing in 1925, William Henry Ellison asserted that "the judgment of history must be that the commissioners badly blundered."[29] In 1966 Kenneth Johnson acknowledged that the Indian agents were sincere and serious, but "certain aspects of the treaty making expedition seem now to have hints of the ridiculous."[30] As of 1972, Robert Heizer could not "imagine a more poorly conceived, more inaccurate, less informed, and less democratic process than the making of the 18 treaties in 1851-52 with the California Indians. It was a farce from beginning to end."[31]

Views such as these miss the obvious. The Indian agents did not fail in their mission. They negotiated in good faith, set aside over seven percent of the State of California for exclusive Indian occupancy, and vigorously defended their program in letters and public addresses. The U.S. Senate failed the Indians. By rejecting the treaties the senators succumbed to political pressures and abrogated their responsibilities to the Indian peoples of California. To reach their unanimous decision, they had to accept the verbal arguments presented by the California delegation and reject the written evidence provided by the commissioner of Indian affairs and superintendent of Indian affairs of California.

Later, the rejection of the treaties became the target of those intending to demonstrate how badly the Indians of California were treated. In 1975 Chad L. Hoopes insisted that the treaties were "marked secret and deliberately concealed from the public." Only after their "discovery" in 1904 could Indians and their white allies consult them and take action to correct the wrongs their rejection inflicted.[32] Evidently, Hoopes did not consult an article published in 1973 by Harry Kelsey that demolished the theory of secrecy.[33] Hoopes and others failed to recognize that the rejection of the treaties—not their "disappearance"—was the injustice committed against the Indians.

The rejection of the treaties forced Edward F. Beale to come up with a new plan. Although he had to operate without the legal basis the treaties, if ratified, would have given him, he was initially provided with considerable authority and financial support. Beale founded an experimental reservation in the Tejón area and thus became a major force in the development of the reservation system in California. Because of the initial success of the Tejón Reservation, however, historians have exaggerated his role in the national origins of the system. The idea of congregating Indians on lands near military posts they claim was Beale's. In 1928, for example, Charles Berdan Leonard wrote that Beale "finally hit upon his scheme for military reservations." Indians would be treated as wards of the nation and "live under the protection of a military post."[34] In 1960, Richard E. Crouter and Andrew F. Rolle also maintained that Beale "hit upon the idea of an experimental reservation, to offer agricultural work to about one thousand Indians. This self-supporting farming unit became so successful that Beale made plans to establish other small reservations.... Each reservation was to be garrisoned by a military post."[35] Regrettably, I wrote in 1975 that the military reservation system was "introduced by Edward Fitzgerald Beale."[36] Albert Hurtado noted in 1988 that "Beale set about creating a new design for federal Indian policy in California, proposing...a system of 'Military Posts' where Indian people would be 'invited to assemble.'"[37]

By the time Beale assumed his duties as superintendent, however, most of the elements of "his" military reservation plan had been widely disseminated in government reports, private and official correspondence, and newspaper articles. It is true that Beale established a "permanent" reservation at Tejón, whereas Barbour created only a temporary one in the same area. But the claim that Beale founded the system is valid only if the reservations established by the Indian agents are perceived not to have existed because the treaties creating them were rejected by the Senate. James Rawls, for example, concluded that because of the rejection, "the vast reservations proposed by Wozencraft, Barbour, and McKee were never created."[38] But at least two of the reservations, although managed by private citizens rather than by Indian agents, functioned for a time. The Merced Reservation operated for a year and a half. And the original Fresno Reservation evolved into the Fresno Farm.

Moreover, by claiming that the Sebastian Military Reserve served as a model for reservations founded throughout the West, historians writing about Indian policy in California have further enhanced Beale's reputation.[39] Not since the removal period of the 1830s had so many treaties been conducted as in the 1850s. Not all the treaties produced reservations. Some were designed to extinguish Indian lands; others were conducted to establish peace and friendship. But during that decade, dozens of temporary and permanent reservations took hold in California, Oregon, Washington, Texas, Utah, and New Mexico.[40] Because reservations sprang up simultaneously over a vast region during such a short period, it is difficult to accept the premise that Tejón served as their model.

Major James H. Carleton, who founded the Bosque Redondo Reservation in New Mexico in 1863, had been posted to Fort Tejón in July 1858.[41] And in a study of that reservation, a historian has claimed that Carleton sought to accomplish in New Mexico what Beale had achieved in California.[42] Perhaps in a general sense this is correct, but Carleton observed at Tejón a reservation in steep decline, hardly the model on which to found a similar institution. Indian agents stationed outside California may have read and been impressed with the initial reports issued by Beale and others. But it is unlikely that what transpired in faraway California would have been applicable to the unique situations they encountered.

Pride and personal dislike prevented Beale from acknowledging the contributions to Indian policy made by Redick McKee, George Barbour, and O. M. Wozencraft. In none of his correspondence does he credit them with making any contributions to the founding of the reservation system in California. And Beale readily appropriated as his own some of the innovations introduced by the agents, such as the stationing of troops on the reservations. Beale also claimed as his the ideas and recommendations Benjamin Hayes presented in his report, "The Indians of Southern California," such as compulsory labor, the distribution of food from a common stock, and the modification but not abandonment of Indian political organization. Beale made no mention of the report in his correspondence with the Indian Office or in his own report to Congress, which was long on criticism and short on specifics.

Beale also failed to acknowledge that the local Indians played a crucial role in the initial success of the reservation. How well a particular reservation functioned was determined by a variety of factors, including the socioeconomic orientation of the Indians confined and the degree and length of contact they had experienced. A hunting and gathering people confined shortly after first meeting whites would respond differently to subjugation than would a sedentary agricultural group long in contact with foreigners. At Tejón many of the less "acculturated" Indians found it difficult to understand and accept the regimentation and routines. Some eventually adjusted; others departed after a short stay. Because most of the Tejoneños had been associated with the Spanish missions, they had little difficulty, at least initially, in accepting the programs and goals Beale and others set for them.

The Tejoneños, not Beale, established farming and stock raising in the Tulare Valley. Instead of introducing agriculture to the Tejoneños, Beale furnished them with new implements and seeds. Instead of introducing irrigation, he got them to build a bigger irrigation system. Instead of introducing domesticated animals, he provided them with a greater variety of stock. In short, instead of bringing a hunting and gathering people to the reservation, Beale took the reservation to Indians who were on their way to becoming what whites thought Indians should become. The prior socioeconomic adaptations of the Tejoneños affected the structure and therefore the history of the reservation imposed upon them, and the initial success of the reservation must be attributed as much to them as to the policy introduced by Beale.

Beale claimed he had reintroduced a version of the Spanish mission, with its work routine and strict discipline, to the interior. Perhaps his teachers at Georgetown College, a Jesuit institution, had instilled in him the notion that the mission system had achieved remarkable results throughout the Spanish empire. To Beale the crumbling missions were a physical reminder of a period in California history characterized by Spanish dedication and Indian contentment. Evidently, the myth prevented him from seeing the irony in creating a new "mission" in the interior for Indians who had fled the old ones along the coast.

To Beale's credit he genuinely sought to create an ideal institution at Tejón, where under his careful guidance Indians would markedly improve their material lives. If he had conspired from the beginning, as some might suspect, to obtain the land on which the reservation was situated, he certainly would not have spent such vast sums of money on animals, equipment, and salaries. Nor would he have written such glowing reports about the progress the Indians were making under his tutelage. As much to advance his own career as to improve the condition of the Indians, Beale sought to create a model reservation for which he would take full credit. Once replaced as superintendent, however, Beale's ethnological idealism gave way to a cynical opportunism. His purchase of Rancho La Liebre might not have been part of a long-range plan to acquire Tejón, but it took place only a few months after his dismissal and certainly was his first step in becoming a true land baron.

Although it is impossible to determine conclusively if squatters Samuel Bishop and Alexis Godey conspired to undermine the reservation so it would fall into the hands of Beale, the evidence points in that direction. By turning parts of the reservation into their own private estates, they certainly undermined its legitimacy as a government institution. By utilizing Indian labor to grow commercial crops and manage private stock, they clearly violated the spirit, if not the law, of the reservation. Indians working for private individuals were Indians not working for the common good. The complaints issued by those being exploited indicate that they were well aware that a trust had been broken.

From the time of Beale's dismissal, factions emerged on the reservation, and because factionalism has long fascinated those studying reservations, it is difficult to imagine one without it. The Tejón Reservation was no exception, except that whites, not Indians, created the factions. Whereas the mourning ceremony and other celebrations served to integrate Indians from a variety of groups forced to live in a new social environment, whites residing on or near the reservation had no such integrative mechanism and divided into sides loyal to either the most recent or the former superintendent. Bishop and Godey, the key members of the pro-Beale faction, clashed with the faction comprised of employees hired by Thomas Henley. The degree to which Indians were drawn into the factionalism remains unclear, but Bishop was not fondly remembered by some of the Tejoneños interviewed by the anthropologist John P. Harrington early in the twentieth century. "Bishop was a coarse man, and a great swearer," recalled Eugenia Mendez.[43] Bishop would "threaten the Indians with a blacksnake whip when they would not work," remembered Juan Coluco.[44]

The summary punishment occasionally inflicted upon the Indians does not negate the fact that through its representatives—superintendents, agents, and employees—the federal government introduced at Tejón a benign form of subjection. Indians were encouraged, not coerced, to settle on the reservation; they were encouraged, not coerced, to learn new skills and values. Village headmen were pressured to provide quotas of labor, but the work routines were not excessively rigid. That Indians ceased work on their own to hold ceremonies indicates that they were not without options regarding how they spent their time.

The progress made during the first few years must have convinced Indians and whites alike that the experiment had a good chance of succeeding. Even those politicians who had opposed the ratification of the eighteen treaties creating the first reservations supported the continuation of Tejón. Had title to the land on which the reservation was situated been secured by the federal government, the superintendents could have made long-range plans for its continued development. Title would have allowed the agents to remove private individuals and their stock from the reservation, thus giving the Indians some assurance that the land on which they resided truly was theirs.

Permanence, of course, does not guarantee success. A permanent reservation can be as badly managed as a temporary one. Tejón was not so much mismanaged as managed under difficult circumstances. And to their credit Indian agents such as Alonzo Ridley and J. R. Vineyard kept the reservation operational, despite Superintendent Thomas Henley's cost-cutting policies. Whereas Beale had set out, perhaps naively, to create a modern institution, no matter what the cost, Henley sought to maintain the status quo at little cost. By encouraging Indians to hunt, gather, and fish to save reservation expenses, Henley emphasized the practical over the innovative. The message to Indians was that traditional modes of subsistence were equal to a modern farming existence. At the time perhaps they were, but a major goal of the reservation was to replace an economy based on the procurement of wild foods with one based on the production of domestic crops. In this regard the reservation never became a modern institution. Furthermore, Beale and his successors had to experiment with irrigation, a technique long used by Indians, Spaniards, and Mexicans in areas of the Southwest but not by Anglo-Americans to any significant degree. Tejón, therefore, was as much a pioneering Anglo economic institution as it was an experimental Indian reservation.[45] Its first crop being the exception, sufficient amounts of foods were never produced in the common fields, even with irrigation. During the drought that extended throughout much of the 1850s, the Indians' small-scale subsistence farming proved to be more successful than the whites' large-scale, "cash-crop" approach.

Unlike the reservation, with its large concentration of Indians, the Fresno Farm served more as the headquarters for a variety of groups than as a place of permanent residence. Nevertheless, both espoused the same goals: to subjugate, concentrate, and educate (in practical matters) the Indians within their jurisdictions. On both, agents and employees provided goods and services to a variety of Indians intending to give up a mobile for a sedentary existence. Each was protected by a nearby fort, and each was occupied, in part, by Indians who had adopted agriculture prior to its founding. Many of the advancements made by the Indians associated with the farm had been achieved under the tutelage of James Savage and Lorenzo Vinsonhaler two years before Beale arrived on the scene.

Even though two additional farms were founded, the subjection of most of the Indians in the San Joaquin Valley resulted more from the inundation of individuals than from the imposition of institutions. In the Southern Mines the intrusion of whites was so massive and swift that Indians had little time to adjust. By 1853 miners had extended their political will and economic institutions throughout the area. Other than raid the camps and towns for stock and provisions, the Indians could do little to reverse their declining populations, maintain their cultural values, and preserve the plants and animals upon which they depended. Thus, it is difficult to imagine how the social disintegration and individual degradation that followed the intrusion could have been checked without a massive federal presence in the form of soldiers and agents. Such an investment in money and men was, at the time, far beyond the will and reach of the federal government.

Because more stock raisers than miners settled in the Tulare Valley and because the occupation was less extensive and rapid than in the Southern Mines, the Indians there had more time to adjust. Initially, they maintained a vast numerical advantage over whites and were still able to engage in political, military, and diplomatic activities thought to be crucial to their wellbeing. The resistance offered by Indians in the Four Creeks is a case in point. Later, when agents failed to respond aggressively to the settlers who took the law figuratively into their own hands and Indians literally into custody, Indian restraint, not white power, prevented hostilities from erupting again. Although the Indian population declined as the white population increased, Indians survived the inundation.

During the process of subjugation Indian policy was openly and frequently discussed. Most of those who wrote the reports, editorials, and letters clearly identified its distinguishing characteristics and flaws. A few called for changes that clearly could not be implemented, such as removing the Indians from the state. Hindsight suggests that a policy applied often with tragic results in the East in the 1830s was inapplicable in the West in the 1850s, but removal was the only model the government had developed to separate Indians from whites. Thus, from their limited perspective, some whites advocated relocating Indians to the east side of the Sierra Nevada or even to Baja California.

Although that plan was never implemented, relocation was a fact of life for many Indians. Those settlers who rounded up Indians participated, illegally, in the removal process. And the plan adopted by Beale and followed by Henley was a kind of state version of national policy. Instead of removing Indians to a region beyond California, Beale sought to relocate them to a few isolated areas within it. Thus, Beale broke a precedent established by the Indian agents who preceded him. Whereas the agents had created numerous small reservations where, or close to where, the Indians then resided, Beale sought to establish a few large ones where all the Indians of the state would be concentrated. Interestingly, the reservation system that eventually took root in California, especially in Southern California, resembles more what the agents had in mind (small reservations scattered over a vast area) than what Beale had envisioned.

The vast majority of the Indians, labored not for themselves on a government reservation but for others on private farms and ranches. This was certainly the case of those Tejoneños who remained on Rancho el Tejón where they were subjected to the control of individuals whose primary task was managing animals rather than assisting peoples. Yet shortly after becoming a land baron, Edward F. Beale's reputation shifted from land-grabber to Indian benefactor. Those visiting the rancho observed Indians they thought had undergone significant change under Beale's direction. Charles Nordhoff, for example, first in an article for the *New York Tribune* and later in a chapter in *California: For Health, Pleasure, and Residence*, published in 1872, offered his views regarding the progress the Indians supposedly had made under Beale's management:

> Now these Indians came to the Tejon naked except a breech-clout, feeding miserably on grasshoppers, worms, and acorns; ignorant, savage nomads. They were first brought here when a part of this rancho was used by the Government as an Indian reservation. General Beale, the present owner of the Tejon, was then Superintendent of Indian Affairs in this State, and he has seen these people emerge from a condition of absolute barbarism and wretchedness into a degree of comfort and prosperity greater than that enjoyed by the majority of Irish peasants; they have abandoned their nomadic habits, have built neat and comfortable houses, and fenced in ground which they cultivate. Their women dress neatly, and understand how to cook food. The men earn money as sheep-shearers. In some places vineyards and fruit-trees have been brought by them to a bearing condition.
>
> In short, these human beings were savages, and are—well, they are as civilized as a good many who come in emigrant-ships from Europe to New York.
>
> And all of this has been accomplished under the careful and kindly management of the owner of Tejon Rancho.[46]

Writing in 1883, Wallace W. Elliott claimed that the Tejonenos still benefited greatly from residing on Beale's rancho:

> Some 150 remnants of the Indian tribes still live at the entrance of

> the Tejon Canon in cottages of adobe, covered with thatch. They have been taught a simple form of civilization. Their dwellings are well constructed, comfortable, and neatly and cleanly kept. They cultivate the ground to the extent of their wants, and have gardens and vineyards and free range for their ponies.
>
> They work mostly on General Beale's ranch, who pays them cash for their labor. They are faithful and trustworthy, and do their work just as they are told. A few have learned to read and write, and are generally inclined to save their earnings, but are inclined to games of chance.
>
> They profess the Catholic religion which seems to have peculiar adaptation to their wants. They have an humble place of worship at their principal settlement surmounted by a cross. One of the congregation often reads prayers, and supplied the place of a priest.
>
> Both men and women since the advent of civilization have adopted, as nearly as possible, the dress of the whites. The women wear the brightest colors of calicos, and sometimes are rich enough to own an old shawl.[47]

In an article published in Bakersfield's *Daily Californian* in 1904, John Barker also praised Beale for his efforts to wean the Indians "from their wild nomadic life, and teach them the arts of civilization, and how to plant and harvest crops of grain and vegetables, so as to give them flour for their bread instead of the astringent and insipid acorn." After the reservation closed, Beale "exercised a fatherly care over them, employing them in all the various labors involved in the conduct of the vast principality that constitutes the ranch and paying them liberally for their service." But he also noted that they "do not increase in numbers, nor can it be reasonably expected that any other fate awaits them than the general doom that seems to be the lot of the all whenever brought into contact with the superior race."[48]

Two years later Mary Austin published *The Flock*, noting that Beale was the kindly protector of the Indians. Once he became superintendent, Beale drew "to him in devotion its swarthy people, and the Reservation being finally removed to Tule River, there passed to him with the purchase of El Tejon, the wardship of some dozen of Indian families." Those who remained on his rancho received "certain rights of home-building, of commons and wage-working rights never abated nor forsworn during the lifetime of Edward Beale."[49] Beale's reputation got further boost in 1912 with the publication of *Edward Fitzgerald Beale: A Pioneer in the Path of Empire, 1822- 1901*. "To the end of his life," wrote Stephen Bonsal, "Beale was a generous and self-sacrificing friend of the Indians and to the end...the Indians were loyal to their protector."[50]

With local writers Elliott and Barker praising his accomplishments, and nationally known authors Nordhoff, Austin, and Bonsal singing his praise, no wonder Beale has emerged in the popular and historical literature as the person who, first as their superintendent and later as their patrón, introduced civilization and enlightenment to a savage, backward people.

Those Tejoneños who relocated to the Tule River Farm found some assistance and protection. The farm provided a temporary refuge for relatively few individuals, but it had a history nearly as long as Tejón's. Like the reservation, it operated on land owned by private individuals, thus preventing the Indian residents from developing a sense of ownership and a vision of a better economic future. Yet for nearly a decade Indians planted, harvested, and consumed crops and vegetables on the farm, and some children, unlike those at Tejón, received a rudimentary education. The farm, therefore, served to bridge the gap from the past to the future. Put another way, it linked the beginning and experimental phase of the reservation system to its modern and permanent phase. The relocation of the Indians from the farm to the Tule River Reservation corresponds with the founding of reservations in Southern California. And with the reservations already functioning in Northern California, the reservation system—initiated in 1850—finally took hold.

More so than in Northern and Southern California, the founding of foreign institutions in Central California resulted in the near total contraction of the Indians' land base. It began with the creation of a few ranchos and continued with founding of the first reservations, the Tejón Reservation, and the Indian farms. As they were disbanded, only the Tule River Reservation remained. The Indians of the Tulares did not disappear, but the contraction came at a great cost. Experiencing relocation and subjugation, they underwent cultural, economic, political, and demographic transformations of staggering proportions.

Indians of the Tulares

Adaptation, Relocation, and Subjugation in Central California

1771-1917

Dear Readers,

Pechanga established the Great Oak Press in order to provide an avenue by which Native voices and topics of significance and of importance to Native Americans could find their way into the contemporary discourse and become both a growing and permanent part of recorded knowledge.

As a publisher of scholarly and academic books, Pechanga's Great Oak Press is dedicated to working with the leading experts and also the up and coming experts in a wide range of fields, ranging from the arts to the sciences and from history to languages. Our focus, though broad in topics, is finely centered on publishing works of great importance that preserve and expand knowledge as well as encourage creative thought and intellectual exploration.

However, Great Oak Press is not focused solely on producing scholarly titles that only the academic and higher education community find accessible. Rather, Great Oak Press is committed to producing books of exceptional quality that literally begin with First Readers for children and will include works for the entire range that comprises the K-12 reading levels. After all, the health of society is directly related to its efforts at raising and educating its youth.

In this work, George Harwood Phillips, one of the first scholars of California Indian history to give both a voice and agency to California Indians, has assembled a remarkable study to continue in his tradition of exceptional works that shape an entire genre.

We thank you for your support.

Mark Macarro

Tribal Chairman of the Pechanga Band of Luiseño Indians

Indians of the Tulares

Adaptation, Relocation, and Subjugation in Central California

1771-1917

George Harwood Phillips

Combined into one volume, revised with additional chapters, *Indians and Intruders in Central California, 1769-1849*; *Indians and Indian Agents: The Origins of the Reservation System in California, 1849-1852*; and *"Bringing them Under Subjection:" California's Tejon Indian Reservation and Beyond, 1852-1864.*

A CIP catalog record for this book is available from the Library of Congress.

ISBN: 978-1-942279-05-1

Publisher: Great Oak Press, Pechanga, California

Printed in the United States of America

Contents

Preface

The three books that form this volume were written over the course of about fifteen years. Each book was designed to stand on its own, but each is set in the same region and each follows the previous one chronologically. Nevertheless, to establish cohesion and continuity, it was necessary to eliminate the background chapters in the second and third books and revise, condense, move, and combine others.

Some chapter titles have been changed as well. And because two original chapters have been added, the time frame has been extended. Therefore, even though the three parts in which the book is divided correspond to the three volumes on which it is based, it is far more than a sum of its original parts.

Reviews of the books upon which it is based were highly favorable, due in large part to those who assisted me in their preparation. Their support has been acknowledged in each volume and will not be repeated here. But those assisting me in the publication of this volume were Myra Masiel-Zamora, Thomas Maxwell-Long, and Lauren Kirschke Niezgodzki. Their support has been most valuable. Since the publication of the first volume, books and articles have been published that have been valuable in what rewriting has been necessary. Important works by James Sandos, Laurence H. Shoup and Randall T. Milliken, Gelya Frank and Carole Goldberg, Thomas Maxwell-Long, Glenn J. Farris, Rose Marie Beebe and Robert M. Senkewicz, and Donald Cutter have been consulted.

Notes

Introduction: Ethnohistorical Considerations

1. Evans-Pritchard, "Anthropology and History," 176.
2. Ibid., 190.
3. For reviews of this literature, consult *The Journal of African History*, a British journal founded in 1960.
4. See Schapera, "Should Anthropologists Be Historians?" 143-56.
5. Lewis, "Introduction," xiv.
6. Thomas, "History and Anthropology," 10.
7. Ibid., 17.
8. Fenton, "Ethnohistory and its Problems," 3.
9. Kroeber, *An Anthropologist Looks at History*, 183-84.
10. Anderson, "Anthropology and History," 6.
11. Levi-Strauss, "Introduction: History and Anthropology," 24-25.
12. Sahlins, "Other Times, Other Customs: The Anthropology of History," 534.
13. Kroeber, *An Anthropologist Looks at History*, 4.
14. Levi-Strauss, "Introduction: History and Anthropology," 18.
15. Evans-Pritchard, "Anthropology and History," 183.
16. *Ethnohistory*, an American journal, published its first issue in 1952.
17. Sturtevant, "Anthropology, History, and Ethnohistory," 1-51.
18. Dening, "Ethnohistory in Polynesia: The Value of Ethnohistorical Evidence," 23-25.
19. Wylie, "The Uses and Misuses of Ethnohistory," 707-709, 720.
20. Axtell, "Ethnohistory: A Historian's Viewpoint," 6-7.
21. Kretch III, "The State of Ethnohistory," 348, 365.

22. Myer and Klein, "Native American Studies and the End of Ethnohistory," 182-216. See also Klein, *Frontiers of Historical Imagination*, 183-212.
23. Dening, *Islands and Beaches*, 35.
24. McBryde, "Ethnohistory in an Australian Context: Independent Discipline or Convenient Data Quarry?" 147.
25. Sturtevant, "Anthropology, History, and Ethnohistory," 1.
26. Trigger, "Ethnohistory: Problems and Prospects," 9.
27. White, "Using the Past: History and Native American Studies," 224.
28. Cohn, "History and Anthropology: The State of Play," 199.
29. Trigger, *The Children of Aataentsic*, vol. l, 12.
30. "The Significance of the Frontier in American History" has been reprinted many times; See Taylor, ed., *The Turner Thesis Concerning the Role of the Frontier in American History.*
31. Jennings, "Growing Partnership: Historians, Anthropologists and American Indian History," 27.
32. Wells, "Frontier Systems as a Sociocultural Type," 6.
33. Forbes, "Frontiers in American History and the Role of the Frontier Historian," 207.
34. Thompson and Lamar, "Comparative Frontier History," 10.
35. Wyman and Kroeber, "Introduction," xiii.
36. Ortiz, "Indian/White Relations: A View from the Other Side of the Frontier," 9.
37. In my other studies of California Indians, I begin each book with a chapter on the indigenous populations in a particular geographical area prior to contact. Although I did not identify the areas as zones of interaction they nevertheless fit the definition presented. See *Chief and Challengers: Indian Resistance and Cooperation in Southern California, 1869-1906*, 12-26, and *Vineyards and Vaqueros: Indian Labor and the Economic Expansion of Southern California 1771-1877*, 37-56.
38. Many historians trained in conventional historical methodologies and lacking a background in anthropology begin their studies of Indigenous-intruder interaction with the activities of the intruders and later present a chapter about the culture of the indigenous peoples. This approach may not significantly diminish the quality of their work, but it inadvertently implies that the intruders are historically more important than the intruded upon.
39. Trigger, "Ethnohistory: Problems and Prospects," 9.
40. Ibid., 15.
41. Trigger, *The Children of Aataentsic*, vol. 1, 26.
42. Dening, *Islands and Beaches.*
43. Ibid.

PART I: ADAPTATION

Chapter I: Indian Occupation

1. Gayton and Newman, "Yokuts and Western Mono Myths," 28.
2. Preston, *Vanishing Landscapes*, 2.
3. Ibid., 2-3.
4. Gayton and Newman, "Yokuts," 28.
5. Chartkoff and Chartkoff, *The Archaeology of California*, 37 -38.
6. Ibid., 39-40.
7. Ibid., 68.
8. Gayton and Newman, "Yokuts," 28.
9. Chartkoff and Chartkoff, *The Archaeology of California*, 75.
10. Ibid., 117.
11. Ibid.
12. Ibid., 120.
13. Ibid., 168-69.
14. Ibid., 186-93.
15. Ibid., 120-21.
16. Shipley, "Native Languages of California," 81.
17. Heizer and Elsasser, *The Natural World of the California Indians,* 19.
18. Sutton, "Some Aspects of Kitanemuk Prehistory," 214-25.
19. Carson, *Recollections of the California Mines*, 110.
20. *San Francisco Picayune*, November 15, 1851.
21. Beals and Hester, Jr., "A New Ecological Typology of the California Indians," 82-83.
22. Baumhoff, "Ecological Determinants of Aboriginal California Populations," 162-65.
23. Wallace, "Southern Valley Yokuts," 450.
24. Baumhoff, "Ecological Determinants," 163-66.
25. Ibid., 166-67.
26. Heizer and Elsasser, *Natural World*, 93, 100.
27. Stewart, "The Yokut Indians of the Kaweah Region," 398.
28. *San Francisco Picayune*, November 15, 1851.
29. Stewart, "Yokut Indians," 393.
30. Martinez, *California in 1792*, 33-34.
31. Timbrook, "Virtuous Herbs: Plants in Chumash Medicine," 173.
32. Applegate, "The Datura Cult among the Chumash," 8-11. See also Hudson and Blackburn, "The Integration of Myth and Ritual in South-Central California, 225-50; and Timbrook, "Virtuous Herbs," 174-75.
33. Lewis, *Patterns of Indian Burning in California*; Timbrook, Johnson, and Earle, "Vegetation Burning by the Chumash," 163-86.
34. Martínez, *California in 1792*, 51.
35. Stewart, "Yokut Indians," 397.

36. Powers, *Tribes of California*, 370.
37. Garcés, *On the Trail of a Spanish Pioneer: The Diary and Itinerary of Francisco Garcés (missionary Priest) in His Travels through Sonora, Arizona, and California, 1775-1776*, vol. 1, 284.
38. Heizer and Elsasser, *Natural World*, 45.
39. Cook, *The Population of the California Indians, 1769-1970*, 43.
40. [Warner], "Reminiscences of Early Life in California."
41. Cook puts the figure at 83,820. See "The Aboriginal Population of the San Joaquin Valley, California," 70.
42. Goldschmidt, "Social Organization in Native California and the Origin of Clans," 444-56. This theory is supported by Baumhoff in "Ecological Determinants," 228. For another theoretical discussion of social organization, see Kunkel, "The Pomo Kin Group and the Political Unit in Aboriginal California," 7-18.
43. Baumhoff, "Ecological Determinants," 228-29.
44. Gifford, "Miwok Lineages and the Political Unit in Aboriginal California," 389-90.
45. Ibid., 390-91.
46. Bennyhoff, *Ethnogeography of the Plains Miwok*, 15.
47. Gayton, "Yokuts and Western Mono Social Organization," 423-25.
48. Ibid., 417-18. See also Powers, *Tribes of California*, 370-71.
49. Gayton, "Yokuts-Mono Chiefs and Shamans," 388-89.
50. Stewart, "Yokut Indians," 393.
51. Ripoll, "Statement to Daniel Hill," unidentified newspaper article in "Indians of Santa Barbara," See also Librado, *Breath of the Sun: Life in Early California as Told By a Chumash Indian, Fernando Librado to John P. Harrington*, 4.
52. Davis, *Trade Routes and Economic Exchange Among the Indians of Southern California*, 28.
53. Garcés, *On the Trail*, 278.
54. Davis, *Trade Routes*, 28.
55. Stewart, "Yokut Indians," 391.
56. Steward, "Ethnography of the Owens Valley Paiute," 257-58.
57. Stewart, "Yokut Indians," 389.
58. Davis, *Trade Routes*, 31-32.
59. Sample, "Trade and Trails in Aboriginal California," 4.
60. Martínez, *California in 1792*, 50.
61. James and Graziani, "California Indian Warfare." 95-97.
62. Bowers, "The Santa Barbara Indians," 1879.

Chapter II: Spaniards Enter the Valley

1. The most thorough account in one volume of the founding of Spanish institutions in California is Hackel, *Children of Coyote, Missionaries of Saint Francis: Indian-Spanish Relations in California, 1769-1850.*
2. The definitive, although biased, work on the missionsis Engelhardt, *Missions and Missionaries of California,* 4 vols., For an in-depth discussion of Franciscan ideology, see Gutierrez, *When Jesus Came, the Corn Mothers Went Away: Marriage, Power, and Sexuality in New Mexico, 1500-1846,* 66-94.
3. For a discussion of Spanish colonizing policy, see Garr, "Planning, Politics and Plunder: The Missions and Indian Pueblos of Hispanic California," 291-312. See also Guest, "Junípero Serra and His Approach to the Indians," 223-61.
4. See Bancroft and Engelhardt for the details of the founding of the missions and presidios.
5. Bolton, "In the South San Joaquin Ahead of Garcés," 211.
6. Fages, "Fages' Note to His Diary of 1772," in ibid., 218-19.
7. Crespi, "Diary Kept during the Exploration that was Made to the Harbor of Our Father San Francisco," 279-293.
8. Ibid., 293-95.
9. Ibid., 295-98.
10. Font, *Font's Complete Diary: A Chronicle of the Founding of San Francisco,* 365.
11. Ibid, 366-67.
12. Ibid., 367-68.
13. Ibid., 372.
14. Ibid., 376.
15. Ibid., 383-84.
16. Cutter, "Spanish Exploration of California's Central Valley," 23.
17. Ibid., 24-28.
18. Garcés, *On the Trail of a Spanish Pioneer,* 272-74.
19. Juan Bautista de Anza, "Anza's Diary," 1-3.
20. Bancroft, *History of California*, vol. 1, 269.
21. Garcés, *On the Trail of a Spanish Pioneer*, 302-303.
22. Ibid., 275-77.
23. Ibid., 277-78.
24. Ibid., 278-82.
25. Ibid., 283-87.
26. Ibid., 288.
27. Ibid., 292-95.
28. Ibid., 297-300.
29. Ibid, 302-30.
30. Felipe de Goycochea to Pedro Fages, Santa Barbara, December 14,

1790, in dossier regarding the killing of two soldiers by gentile Indians (1790 and 1791), trans. Maureen Campión de Necochea, Archivo General de la Nacion-Californias, vol. 46, Mexico City, transcript on file in U.S. Forest Service, Goleta, Calif.

31. Goycochea to Fages, Santa Barbara, September 2, 1790, in ibid.
32. Goycochea to Fages, December 14, 1790, in ibid.
33. Senior Auditor Gava to Gen. Pedro de Neva, Chihuahua, April 25, 1792, in ibid.
34. Goycochea to Fages, September 2, 1790, in ibid.
35. Ibid.
36. Ibid.
37. Gava to Neva, April 23, 1792, in ibid.
38. Goycochea to Fages, Santa Barbara, October 9, 1790, in ibid.
39. Goycochea to Fages, December 14, 1790, in ibid.
40. Jose Joaquin de Arrillaga to Gen. Pedro de Neva, Loreto, September 20, 1792, in ibid.
41. Marcos Briones to Hermenegildo Sal, San Luis Obispo, January 8, 1797, in Cook, trans. and ed., "Colonial Expeditions to the Interior of California," 241.
42. Briones to Sal, San Luis Obispo, February 8, 1797, in ibid.
43. Briones to Sal, San Luis Obispo, January 14, 1797, in ibid.
44. Briones to Sal, February 8, 1797, in ibid.
45. Cook, "The Aboriginal Population of Alameda and Contra Costa Counties, California," 142.
46. Ibid., 142-43.

Chapter III: Refuge

1. For a detailed account of the founding of these institutions, see Bancroft, *History of California*, Vol. 1, 1542-1800. See also Bowman, "The Resident Neophytes (Existentes) of the California Missions 1769-1834," 145-46. Indian population decline is discussed by Cook, "The Indian versus the Spanish Mission," in *The Conflict between the California Indian and White Civilization*, 3-34.
2. José de la Guerra to José Joaquín de Arrillaga, Monterey, January 29, 1804, in Cook, trans. and ed., "Colonial Expeditions into the Interior of California," 243.
3. Juan Martín to José Señan, San Miguel, April 26, 1815, in ibid., 243.
4. Engelhardt, *San Miguel*, 10.
5. Cutter, "Spanish Exploration of California's Central Valley," 88-89.
6. Ibid., 90-91.
7. Ibid., 91-92.
8. Jose Arguello to Governor Arrillaga San Francisco, June 25, 1805 in Cook, trans. and ed., "Colonial Expeditions into the Interior of

California" 244; Milliken, *Native Americans at Mission San Jose*, 43; Cutter, "Spanish Exploration of California's Central Valley," 93- 94.

9. Shoup and Milliken, *Inigo of Rancho Posolmi*, 52.
10. Milliken, *Native Americans at Mission San Jose*, 47.
11. José María de Zalvidea, Report, July 19 to August 14, 1806, in Cook, trans. and ed., "Colonial Expeditions into the Interior of California," 245.
12. Because horses had multiplied so rapidly in parts of the coastal zone, Spaniards may have killed some thirty thousand in 1812. See Cox, *The Columbia River*, 96n.
13. Zalvidea, Report, 245.
14. Ibid., 245-46.
15. Ibid., 246.
16. Ibid., 246-47.
17. Pedro Munoz, Diary, September 21 to November 2, 1806, in Cook, trans. and ed., "Colonial Expeditions into the Interior of California," 248.
18. Ibid.
19. Ibid., 248-49.
20. Ibid., 249-50.
21. Ibid., 250.
22. Ibid.
23. Ibid.
24. Ibid.
25. Ibid., 251.
26. Ibid.
27. Ibid., 252.
28. Ibid., 252-53.
29. Felipe Santiago García, Account of Moraga's 1807 Expedition, in ibid., 255.
30. José Palomares, Report on the Expedition to the Tulares, October 25 to November 4, 1808, in ibid., 256.
31. Ibid., 256-57.
32. Ibid., 256 57.
33. José Viader, Report, August 15-28, 1810, in ibid., 259.
34. José Viader, Report, October 19-27, 1810, in ibid., 259. For an account of Indian auxiliaries in the service of Spain in another area of the Southwest, see Jones, *Pueblo Warriors and Spanish Conquest*.
35. Viader, Report, October 19-27, 1810, in Cook, trans. and ed., "Colonial Expeditions into the Interior of California," 260.
36. Fr. Ramón Abella, Diary, October 15-31, 1811, in ibid., 260-65.
37. Ibid.
38. José Arguello to Gov. José Joaquín de Arrillaga, San Francisco,

October 31, 1813, in ibid., 265.

39. Ibid., 265-66.
40. Duran, "Expedition on the Sacramento and San Joaquin Rivers in 1817: Diary of Fray Narciso Duran," 343.
41. Ibid., 345-49.
42. Cutter, "Spanish Exploration of California's Central Valley," 205.
43. Ibid., 206.
44. Beattie, "California's Unbuilt Missions," 245-46.
45. Ibid., 246-27.
46. Juan Ortega, Diary, November 4-15, 1815, in Cook, trans. and ed., "Colonial Expeditions into the Interior of California," 267.
47. Ibid.
48. Ibid., 268.
49. José Dolores Pico, Diary, November 3 to December 3, 1815, in ibid., 268. Cook claims that Cheneche and Nupchenche, along with Tape and Malin, were distinct villages within a large Nopchinchi political unit. See Cook, "The Aboriginal Population of the San Joaquin Valley, California," 51-52.
50. Pico, Diary, in Cook, trans. and ed., "Colonial Expeditions into the Interior of California," 268-69.
51. Ibid., 269.
52. Ibid., 270-71.
53. Fr. Antonio Jaime to Gov. Pablo Vicente de Solá, La Soledad, March 30, 1816, in ibid., 273.
54. Fr. Luís Antonio Martínez to Fr. Vicente Francisco de Sarría, San Luis Obispo, May 29, 1816, in ibid., 271-72.
55. Fr. Mariano Payeras to Capt. José de la Guerra, La Purísíma, December 24, 1817, *Writings of Father Mariano Payeras*, trans. and ed., Donald Colgett Cutter, 141.
56. Fr. Mariano Payeras, List of Neophytes Who Have Fled Mission La Purísíma, 1818, in ibid.
57. Fr. Mariano Payeras to Capt. José de la Guerra, May 4, 1818, in ibid., Cutter, "Spanish Exploration of California's Central Valley," 149.
58. Fr. Juan Cabot to Capt. José de la Guerra, San Miguel, May 23, 1818, in Cook, trans. and ed., "Colonial Expeditions into the Interior of California," 280.
59. Thompson, *El Gran Capitan, José de la Guerra*, 55-56.
60. Fr. Mariano Payeras to Capt. José de la Guerra, La Purísíma, September 29, 1818, Cutter, ed., *Writings of Mariano Payeras*, 155.
61. Beattie, "California's Unbuilt Missions," 248-49. Also cited in Cutter, "Spanish Exploration of California's Central Valley," 245.
62. Fr. Mariano Payeras to Fr. Guardia Baldomero López, La Soledad,

July 4, 1819, in Cutter, ed., *Writings of Mariano Payeras*, 245.

63. Quoted in Richman, *California under Spain and Mexico, 1535-1847,* 227.
64. Fr. Mariano Payeras to Gov. Pablo Vicente de Solá, n.p., September 17, 1819, quoted in Engelhardt, *The Missions and Missionaries of California*, Vol. 3, 33-34.
65. Fr. Narciso Duran to Gov. Pablo Vicente de Solá, San José, June 2, 1819, in Sherburne F. Cook, ed., "Expeditions to the Interior of California: Central Valley," 166.
66. Fr. Narciso Duran to Gov. Pablo Vicente de Solà, San José, October 28, 1819, in ibid.
67. José Manía Estudillo, "Estudillo among the Yokuts: 1819," trans. and ed., Anna H. Gayton, in *Essays in Anthropology*, ed. Robert H. Lowie, 68-71.
68. Merriam, "California Mission Baptismal Records," 211.
69. Estudillo, "Estudillo among the Yokuts," 70-72.
70. Ibid., 72-76.
71. Ibid., 76-80.
72. Ibid., 81-85.
73. Mariano Payeras to the Reverend Father Apostolic Preachers and Ministers, La Purisima, June 2, 1820, in Cutter, ed., *Writings of Mariano Payeras*, 264.
74. Cutter, "Spanish Exploration of California's Central Valley," 254.

Chapter IV: Rebels, Trappers, Raiders, and Traders

1. Engelhardt, *The Missions and Missionaries of California*, vol. 3, 195-96. The causes of the uprising are discussed by Sandos, "'Levantamiento!' The 1824 Chumash Uprising Reconsidered," 109-33; and by Coombs, "With What God Will Provide: A Reexamination of the Chumash Revolt of 1824," 21-29.
2. Bancroft, *History of California*, vol. 2, 1801-1824, 529.
3. Ibid., 532. Two Californios claimed that José Pacomio masterminded the uprising and sought the elimination of all white men in California. See Juan Bautista Alvarado, *History of California*, vol. 2, 1824-1834, trans. Earl R. Hewitt, C-D 2, 42-52; and Mariano Guadalupe Vallejo, "Historical and Personal Memoirs Relating to Alta California," vol. 1, trans. Earl R. Hewitt, C-D 18, 276-91, both in Bancroft Library, Berkeley, Calif. Bancroft disputes these claims. See his *History of California*, vol. 2, 527n.
4. Engelhardt, *The Missions and Missionaries of California*, vol. 3, 196.
5. Fr. Antonio Ripoll, "Fray Antonio Ripoll's Description of the Chumash Revolt at Santa Barbara in 1824," 347-48. For an account of the alcaldes, see Hackel, "The Staff of Leadership: Indian Authority in

the Missions of Alta California," 347-76 and Phillips, "The Alcaldes: Indian Leadership in the Spanish Missions of California," 83-89.

6. Agustias de la Guerra Ord, *Occurrences in Hispanic California*, 9-10.
7. Ripoll, "Fray Antonio Ripoll," 350.
8. Ibid., 350-52.
9. Ibid., 352.
10. Johnson, "Indian History in the Santa Barbara Back Country," 10.
11. Fr. Juan Cabot to Gov. Luis Arguello, February 28, 1824, in Cook, trans. and ed., "Expeditions to the Interior of California," 152.
12. Ibid.
13. Engelhardt, *The Missions and Missionaries of California*, vol. 3, 203.
14. José Rafael Gonzales, "Experiencias de un Soldado de California," in Cook, trans. and ed., "Expeditions to the Interior of California," 157.
15. Interrogatorio, Santa Bárbara, June 1, 1824, in ibid., 153-54.
16. Ripoll, "Fray Antonio Ripoll," 349.
17. Interrogatorio, Santa Bárbara, June 1, 1824, in Cook, "Expeditions," 153-154.
18. Ripoll, "Fray Antonio Ripoll," 354.
19. Fr. Blas Ordaz to Gov. Luís Arguello, Mission Santa Inés, March 26, 1824, Doc. 2593, Archives of the Archdiocese of San Francisco, photostat copy on file at Mission Santa Barbara Archives, Santa Barbara, Calif.
20. Gov. Luís Arguello to Capt. José de la Guerra, Monterey, May 5, 1824, in Cook, "Expeditions," 152.
21. Fr. Luís Antonio Martinez to Gov. Luís Arguello, San Luís Obispo, April 30, 1824, Doc. 2609, Archives of the Archdiocese of San Francisco, photostat copy on file at Mission Santa Barbara Archives, Santa Barbara, Calif.
22. Leonard, *Narrative of the Adventures of Zenas Leonard*, 199-200.
23. Capt. Pablo de la Portilla, Report of the Expedition to the Tulares in Pursuit of the Rebel Mission Indians, Santa Bárbara, June 27, 1824, in Cook, trans. and ed. "Expeditions to the Interior of California," 155.
24. Ibid.
25. Gonzales, "Experiencias," in ibid., 157.
26. Portilla, Report, in ibid., 155.
27. Ibid., 155-56.
28. Ibid., 156.
29. Bancroft, *History of California*, vol. 2.
30. Pablo de la Portilla to Gov. Luís Arguello, Santa Bárbara, June 28, 1824, in Portilla, Report, 156.
31. Bancroft, *History of California*, vol. 2, 536-37, 537n. Between 1823 and

1825 the neophyte population of La Purísima declined from 722 to 532. Fugitivism may account for much of the loss. During the same period, Santa Bárbara and Santa Inés lost only 77 and 64 persons, respectively. See Bowman, 147.

32. Sgt. José Dolores Pico, Report, December 27, 1825, to January 31, 1826, in Cook, trans. and ed., "Expeditions to the Interior of California," 181.
33. Ibid., 181-82.
34. Ibid., 182.
35. Ibid.
36. Ibid., 183.
37. Ibid.
38. Ibid., 183-84.
39. Ibid., 184. Apparently Bubal had been moved from the west shore to Atwell's Island for security reasons. See Cook, "The Aboriginal Population of the San Joaquin Valley, California," 43-44.
40. Beechey, *Narrative of a Voyage*, vol. 2, 24-25.
41. Peard, *To the Pacific and Arctic*, 175.
42. Beechey, *Narrative of a Voyage*, vol. 2, 26-27.
43. Peard, *To the Pacific and Arctic*, 175.
44. Bancroft, History of California, vol. 3, 1825-1840, 156n.
45. Quoted in McCarthy, *The History of Mission San Jose California, 1797-1835,* 187.
46. Ibid., 187-88. See also Lieut. Ignacio Martínez to Gov. José Maria Echeandía, San José, May 21, 1827, Doc. 3047, Archives of the Archdiocese of San Francisco, photostat copy on file at Mission Santa Bárbara Archives, Santa Bárbara, Calif.
47. Smith, *The Southwest Expedition of Jedediah S. Smith*, 133-40.
48. Ibid., 146.
49. Ibid., 153-54.
50. Ibid., 156.
51. Morgan, *Jedediah Smith and the Opening of the West*, 208.
52. Quoted in ibid., 208-209.
53. Lieut. Ignacio Martínez to Gov. José María Echeandía, San Jose, May 21, 1827, Doc. 3048, Archives of the Archdiocese of San Francisco, photostat copy on file at Mission Santa Barbara Archives, Santa Barbara, Calif.
54. Sullivan, ed., *The Travels of Jedediah Smith,* 35-36.
55. Morgan, *Jedediah Smith and the Opening of the West*, 209. The letter is published in Appendix A, 333.
56. Ibid., 209-10.
57. Weber, *The Californios versus Jedediah Smith*, 27-28.
58. Luís Antonio Argüello to Harrison G. Rogers, Mission San José, May

31, 1827, quoted in ibid., 28-29.
59. Harrison G. Rogers to Capt. Luís Antonio Argüello, n.p., June 3, 1827, quoted in ibid., 32- 34.
60. Luís Antonio Argüello to Gov. José María Echeandía, quoted in ibid., 35-36.
61. Morgan, *Jedediah Smith and the Opening of the West*, 236-55.
62. Sullivan, *The Travels*, 45.
63. Garner, *Letters from California, 1846-1847*, 103.
64. Sebastian Rodriguez, Diary, April 20 to May 6, 1828, in Cook, trans. and ed., "Expeditions," 184-85.
65. Ibid., 185. The following year, Californios again attacked the Hovima, killing forty men and eight women. See Gov. José María Echeandía to the Minister of War, San Diego, May 22, 1829, in ibid., 187.
66. Rodríguez, Diary, 185.
67. Sebastian Rodríguez, Report, May 26 to June 9, 1828, in Cook, trans. and ed., "Expeditions," 185-86.
68. Ibid., 186.
69. Ibid.
70. Ibid.
71. Fr. Narciso Duran to Ignacio Martínez, San José, November 9, 1828 in ibid., 169.
72. Milliken, *Native Americans at Mission San Jose*, 62.
73. Quoted in Lothrop, "The Indian Campaigns of General M.G. Vallejo, Defender of the Northern Frontier of California," 165n.
74. Osio, *The History of Alta California*, 89.
75. Duran to Martinez, November 9, 1828, 169.
76. Osio, *The History of Alta California*, 89.
77. Fr. Narciso Duran to Ignacio Martínez, San Jose, March 1, 1829, in Cook, trans. and ed., "Expeditions," 169.
78. José Sánchez, Diary, May 1-10, 1829, in ibid., 173.
79. Ibid., 174.
80. Ibid.
81. Juan Bojorques, "Recuerdos sobre la Historia de California," in ibid., 172.
82. Ignacio Martínez to Mariano Guadalupe Vallejo, San Francisco, May 76, 1829, in ibid., 175-76.
83. Joaquin Pina, Diary, May 26 to June 1, in ibid., 177-78.
84. Ibid., 178-79.
85. Ibid., 179.
86. Ibid.
87. Mariano Guadalupe Vallejo to Commandant Ignacio Martínez, San José, June 4, 1829, in ibid., 176.
88. Gov. José María Echeandía to Commandant Ignacio Martínez, San

Diego, August 7, 1829, in ibid., 180.

89. Commandant Ignacio Martínez, Report of the Fiscal, San Francisco, October 31, 1829, in ibid., 190.
90. Lothrop, "The Indian Campaigns," 170.
91. McCarthy, *The History of Mission San Jose*, 217.
92. Jose Berreyesa, Statement, San José, July 15, 1830, in Cook, "Expeditions to the Interior of California," 180.
93. Entry No. 6513, December 31, 1829, Mission Santa Clara Register of Burials, June 22, 1777- December 22, 1866, Orradre Library, University of Santa Clara, Santa Clara, Calif.
94. Antonio Armijo, "Diary," in Hafen and Hafen, *Old Spanish Trail: Santa Fe to Los Angeles*, 159-65.
95. Garner, *Letters from California, 1846-1847*, 103.
96. Armijo, "Diary," 165; Hill, "The Old Spanish Trail: A Study of Spanish and Mexican Trade and Exploration Northwest from New Mexico to the Great Basin and California," 464-66.
97. Warner, Hayes, and Widney, *An Historical Sketch of Los Angeles County, California*, 34. Warner wrote chapter 1 which covers the years 1771 to 1847.
98. Ibid., 33.
99. José Berreyesa, statement, San José, July 15, 1830, in Cook, trans. and ed., "Expeditions," 187. Huyunhepa is mentioned in a list of chiefs compiled on October 1, 1828; see Documentos para la Historia de California, Archivo Particular de Sr. Don Mariano Guadalupe Vallejo, C-B 14, no. 251, Bancroft Library, Berkeley, Calif.
100. Berreyesa, statement, in Cook, "Expeditions," 187.
101. Carson, *Kit Carson's Autobiography*, 15-16.
102. Hill, "Ewing Young in the Fur Trade of the Far Southwest, 1824-1834," 25-26.
103. Carson, *Kit Carson's Autobiography*, 16-17.
104. Gov. Manuel Victoria to Commanders at Santa Barbara and San Diego, Monterey, March 10, 1831, in Cook, trans. and ed., "Expeditions," 162.
105. Garner, *Letters from California, 1846-1847*, 103.
106. Lawrence, "Mexican Trade between Santa Fe and Los Angeles, 1830-1848," 29.
107. Fr. Vicente Pasqual Oliva to Gov. Jose Figueroa, San Gabriel, February 17, 1833, in Cook, "Expeditions," 162-63.
108. *Honolulu Sandwich Island Gazette and Journal of Commerce*, December 2, 1837.
109. Lawrence, "Mexican Trade between Santa Fe and Los Angeles, 1830-1848," 29-30.
110. Lawrence, "The Old Spanish Trail from Santa Fe to California," 73-

74. See also Oliva to Figueroa in Cook trans. and ed., "Expeditions," 162-63.

111. Gov. José Figueroa to Commandant of Santa Bárbara, February 26, 1833, appendix in Lawrence, "Old Spanish Trail," 133.
112. Ibid., 134-35.
113. Lawrence, "Old Spanish Trail," 75.
114. Lawrence, "Mexican Trade," 30-31.
115. Robert E. Elwell to Jim__, Santa Barbara, February 4, 1834, Documentos Para la Histora de California, C-B 31, pt. 1, Bancroft Library, Berkeley, Calif.
116. Lawrence, "Mexican Trade," 30-31.
117. Gov. José Figueroa to Minister of War and Navy, Monterey, April 12, 1833, in Cook, "Expeditions," 188.
118. Work, *Fur Brigade to Bonaventura: John Work's California Expedition of 1832-33 for the Hudson Bay Company*, 42-43.
119. Ibid., 64.
120. Ibid., 65.
121. Ibid., 66-67.
122. Ibid., 68.
123. Leonard, *Narrative of the Adventures of Zenas Leonard*, 142-43.
124. Ibid., 196, 197.
125. Ibid., 185.
126. Thomas Beall, "Recollections of Wm. Craig," *Lewiston Morning Tribune*, March 3, 1918.
127. Alcalde of San José to Political Chief of the Territory, San José, November 10, 1833, in Cook, trans. and ed.,"Expeditions," 188.
128. Gov. José Figueroa, Order and decree concerning robbers of horses and other livestock, Monterey, November 18, 1833, in ibid., 188-89.
129. Ibid.
130. Leonard, *Narrative*, 189-91.
131. Warner, "Reminiscences of Early California," 188.
132. Kelley, *Hall J. Kelley on Oregon*, 351-52.
133. Ibid., 352-53.
134. Holmes, *Ewing Young: Master Trapper*, 97.
135. Gov. José Figueroa to John McLoughlin, n.p., n.d., quoted in ibid., 106-107.

Chapter V: Cultural Modification

1. Of the many studies of the secularization of the missions, consult Hutchinson, "The Mexican Government and the Mission Indians of Upper California, 1821- 1835," 335-62; Garr, "Planning, Politics and Plunder: The Missions and Indian Pueblos of Hispanic California," 291-312; Phillips, *Vineyards and Vaqueros: Indian Labor and the Economic*

Expansion of Southern California, 1771-1877, 159-181; Jackson and Castillo, *Indians, Franciscans, and Spanish Colonization*, 87-106; Hackel, *Children of Coyote, Missionaries of Saint Francis: Indian-Spanish Relations in Colonial California, 1769-1850*, 369-419.

2. The emergence of the rancho system is discussed in Robinson, *Land in California*, 45-90; Hornbeck, "Land Tenure and Rancho Expansion in Alta California, 1784-1846," 371-90; Phillips, *Vineyards and Vaqueros*, 279-32, 297-320.
3. Ibid.
4. Beechey, Narrative of a Voyage to the Pacific and Bering's Strait, vol. 2, 19.
5. Garner, *Letters from California, 1846- 1847*, 171.
6. Pilling, "The Archaeological Implications of an Annual Coastal Visit for Certain Yokuts Groups," 440.
7. Unidentified newspaper article reprinted in *Santa Barbara Gazette*, n.d.; and unidentified newspaper article, November 1861, in Hayes, Scrapbooks, "Indians of Santa Barbara, vol., 39.
8. Librado, *Eye of the Flute*, 45.
9. Dana, "Ten Decades on a California Rancho," 19.
10. James H. Carson, "Tulare Plains," *San Joaquin Republican*, March 17, 1852.
11. Leonard, *Narrative*, 200.
12. Ibid., 201.
13. Lieut. N. H. McLean to Maj. H. W. Wessels, Fort Miller, July 12, 1853, Letters Received by the Office of the Adjutant General, 1822-1860 (Main Series), RG 94, Microcopy 567, role 483, U.S. National Archives. Hereafter cited as NA.
14. For a discussion of post-contact trade relations established between California and other Indians, see Layton, "Traders and Raiders: Aspects of Trans-Basin and California-Plateau Commerce, 1800-1880," 124-37.
15. Capt. Francis J. Lippsitt to Lieut. William T. Sherman, Santa Barbara, March 9, 1848, Pacific Division, Records of the 10th Military Department, Letters Received, 1846-1851, RG 98, Microcopy 210, NA.
16. Eugene Upton, "Letter from California," Merced River, June 12, 1850, unidentified newspaper article, Eugene Upton Scrapbook No. 7, California Historical Society Library, San Francisco, Calif.
17. *Daily Alta California*, December 9, 1851.
18. José Francisco Palomares, "Memoria," in Cook, trans. and ed., "Expeditions," 202.
19. Brig. Gen. Bennett Riley to Gen. R. Jones, Monterey, October 15, 1949, Pacific Division, Records of the 10th Military Department,

Letters Received, 1846-1851, RG 98, Microcopy 210, roll 1, NA.

20. John Marvin, "Some Account of the Tulare Valley, and the Indians from Fresno River to Tihone Pass," *San Francisco Morning Post*, July 28, 1851.
21. Lieut. George H. Derby to Maj. Edward R. S. Canby. Monterey, July 10, 1850, Report of the Secretary of War, U.S. Congress, Senate, 32d Cong., lst sess., Exec. Doc. 110, 7-11.
22. Jackson, "Gentile Recruitment and Population Movement in the San Francisco Bay Area Missions," 233-35. See also Gook and Borah, *Essays in Population History: Mexico and California*, vol. 3, 194-95.
23. Fr. Marcelino Marquinez to Gov. Pablo Vicente de Solá, Santa Cruz, December 13, 1816, in Sherburne Cook, trans. and ed., "Expeditions," 273.
24. Gifford, "Miwok Lineages and the Political Unit in Aboriginal California," 391-92.
25. Gayton, "Yokuts-Mono Chiefs and Shamans," 401-402.
26. Cook, trans. and ed., "Expeditions to the Interior of California," 207.
27. Duhaut-Cilly, "Duhaut-Cilly's Account of California in the Years 1827-28," 313.
28. Sebastian Rodríguez, Report, May 26 to June 9, 1828, in Cook, trans. and ed., "Expeditions," 186.
29. Leonard, *Narrative*, 201.
30. Cook, "American Invasion," 322.
31. Bidwell, *In California before the Gold Rush*, 65-66.
32. Marvin, "Some Account."
33. Upton, "Letter from California."
34. Uldall and Shipley, *Nisenan Texts and Dictionary*, 247, 260, 263.
35. Broadbent, *The Southern Sierra Miwok Language*, 242, 248, 260, 265, 266.
36. Shipley, "Spanish Elements in the Indigenous Languages of Central California," 17-21.
37. Broadbent, *Southern Sierra Miwok*, 229, 243, 258, 263, 269.
38. Uldall and Shipley, *Nisenan Texts*, 251, 257, 266, 271, 272, 275.
39. Shipley, "Spanish Elements," 17-21.
40. Broadbent, *Southern Sierra Miwok*, 231, 238, 240, 247, 248, 256.
41. Uldall and Shipley, *Nisenan Texts*, 267.
42. Beeler, "Noptinte Yokuts," in Jesse Sawyer, 35.
43. Broadbent, *Southern Sierra Miwok*, 243.
44. Ibid., 281; Uldall and Shipley, *Nisenan Texts*, 253; Shipley, "Spanish Elements," 17-21.
45. Broadbent, *Southern Sierra Miwok*, 250.
46. Wilkes, *Narrative of the United States Exploring Expedition*, vol. 5, 180.

47. Townsend, *The California Diary of General E. D. Townsend*, ed. Malcolm Edwards, 129.
48. Kip, *The Early Days of My Episcopate*, 226.
49. Belcher, *Narrative of a Voyagge Round the World*, vol. 1, 125-26.
50. Bryant, *What I Saw in California*, 239.
51. Fr. Junípero Serra to Fr. Fermin Francisco de Lasuén, Monterey, January 12, 1780, in *Writings of Junípero Serra*, trans. and ed. Antonine Tibesar, vol. 3, 421.
52. Fr. Antonio Ripoll, "Fray Antonio Ripoll's Description of the Chumash Revolt at Santa Barbara in 1824," 352.
53. Waseurtz af Sandels, *A Sojourn in California by the King's Orphan*, 76-77.
54. T. F. W., "Letters from California," Yerba Buena, June 25, 1846, *Honolulu Friend*, December 1, 1846.
55. Riley to Jones, October 15, 1849.
56. Marvin, "Some Account."
57. Revere, *Tour of Duty in California*, 124.
58. Garner, *Letters from California, 1846-1847*, 161-63. For another account of how Indians stole horses, see Hartnell, "An Indian Ruse," 27.
59. Garner, *Letters from California*, 162.
60. Ibid., 163-64.
61. Fr. Narciso Duran, "Notes on the Circular or Bando of Don José María Echeandía Addressed to the Missionaries of the Four Missions in the South on November 18th, 1832," quoted in Engelhardt, *The Missions and Missionaries of California*, vol. 3, 437.
62. Gov. José Figueroa, Order and decree concerning robbers of horses and other livestock, Monterey, November 18, 1833, in Cook, trans. and ed., "Expeditions," 189.
63. Gov. José Figueroa to Alcalde of San Jose, Monterey, January 24, 1835, in ibid.
64. Quoted in Winther, "The Story of San Jose, 1777-1869: California's First Pueblo," 23.
65. Jose Manuel Pinto, et al., to the Ayuntamiento of San José, August 21, Doc. 3616, Archives of the Archdiocese of San Francisco, photostat copy on file at Mission Santa Barbara Archives, Santa Barbara, Calif.
66. Francisco Arucho to Mariano Guadalupe Vallejo, Valle de San Leandro, August 20, 1837, in Cook, trans. and ed., "Expeditions," 190.
67. Ignacio Martinez to Mariano Guadalupe Vallejo, San Francisco, September 9, 1837, in ibid., 190.
68. Mariano Guadalupe Vallejo, "Historical and Personal Memoirs Relating to Alta California," vol. 4, trans. Earl R. Hewitt, C-D 21, 117, Bancroft Library, Berkeley, Calif.
69. Lyman, *John Marsh, Pioneer*, 206-207, 213.

70. John Marsh, Draft of a Military Proposal, n.p., January 22, 1838, John Marsh Family Papers, C-B 879, Box 1, Bancroft Library, Berkeley, Calif.
71. Lyman, *John Marsh, Pioneer*, 213, 219-20.
72. Vallejo, "Historical and Personal Memoirs," 23.
73. Davis, *Seventy-five Years in California*, 45-46.
74. Lyman, *John Marsh, Pioneer*, 221, 228-29.
75. Ibid., 228-29.
76. Vallejo, "Historical and Personal Memoirs," 22.
77. José de Jesús Vallejo, Statement, San José, August 16, 1838, in Cook, trans. and ed., "Expeditions," 191; Engelhardt, *The Missions and Missionaries of California*, vol. 4, 311-12.
78. José Francisco Palomares. "The Death of Yoscolo," 313-14.
79. Ibid., 314.
80. Capt. Santiago Estrada to Prefect of the First District, San Juan de Castro, July 7, 1839, in Cook, trans. and ed.,"Expeditions," 191.
81. Mariano Guadalupe Vallejo to José Castro, July 7, 1839, Documentos para la Historia de California, Archivo Particular de Sr. Don Mariano Guadalupe Vallejo, C-B 7, 330-330b, Bancroft Library, Berkeley, Calif.
82. Prado Mesa to Mariano Guadalupe Vallejo, San José, August 1, 1839, in Cook, trans. and ed., "Expeditions," 191.
83. José de Jesús Vallejo to Mariano Guadalupe Vallejo, San José, December 10, 1839, in ibid., 191.
84. Gov. Juan Bautista Alvarado to Mariano Guadalupe Vallejo, Monterey, December 13, 1839, in ibid., 191.
85. Davis, *Seventy-five Years in California*, 63-64. Davis's claim that the raid took place in 1839 is incorrect.
86. Juan José Vallejo to Mariano Guadalupe Vallejo, San José, January 15, in Cook, "Expeditions," 192.
87. Gov. Juan B. Alvarado, Decree, San Juan de Castro, July 4, 1840, in ibid., 192. This plan resembles that proposed by John Marsh in January 1838.
88. Manuel Jimeno to Secretary of Communications, San Juan de Castro, January 24, 1841, in ibid., 193.
89. Phelps, *Alta California, 1840-1842: The Journal and Observations of William Dane Phelps*, 142-43.
90. Ignacio Alviso to Justice of the Peace of San José, Santa Clara, March 12, Calendar and Catalogue, Archives of the Pueblo of San Jose, 266, San José Public Library, San José, Calif.
91. Wilkes, *Narrative of the United States Exploring Expedition*, vol. 5, 173-74.
92. Ibid., 208.
93. Ibid., 174.

94. Phelps, *Alta California, 1840-1842*, 114.
95. Duflot de Mofras, *Duflot de Mofras' Travels on the Pacific Coast*, vol. 1, 254.
96. Esteban Munras et al., Petition to Gov. Manuel Micheltorena, Monterey, June 4, 1843, in Vallejo, "Historical and Personal Memoirs," 271-72.
97. José Rafael Gonzales, deposition, San Francisco, January 30, 1857, in Transcript of the Proceedings in Case no. 255. 98. "Pro Bono Puplico" to editors, Kings River, December 6, 1859, *Visalia Delta*, December 10, 1859; Smith, *Garden of the Sun*, 90-92.
99. Juan B. Alvarado, deposition, San Francisco, December 12, 1856, in Transcript of the Proceedings in Case no. 255.
100. Vincente Prefecto Gomez, deposition, San Francisco, January 30, 1857, in Transcript of the Proceedings in Case no. 255.
101. Garner, *Letters from California, 1846-1847*, 104.
102. Carson, *Recollections of the California Mines*, 104. For other descriptions of the wild horses, see Harris, *The Gila Trail: The Texas Argonauts and the California Gold Rush*, 102, and Bryant, *What I Saw in California*, 302. The horse's impact on the environment is briefly discussed in Preston, *Vanishing Landscapes: Land and Life in the Tulare Basin*, 59-60.
103. John A. Sutter, "Personal Reminiscences of General John Augustus Sutter," 7876, C-D 14, 126, Bancroft Library, Berkeley, Calif.
104. Garner, *Letters from California, 1846-1847*, 104.
105. Carson, *Recollections of the California Mines*, 104-105.
106. Leonard, *Narrative*, 191.
107. Davis, *Seventv-five Years in California*, ed. Douglas S. Watson, 63.
108. Sutter, "Personal Reminiscences," 67.
109. Garner, *Letters from California, 1846-1847*, 164.
110. Jose Berreyesa, Statement, San José, July 15, 1830, in Cook, "Expeditions," 187.
111. For a description of how Indians trapped horses, see Baker, *San Joaquin Vignettes*, 41-42.
112. Johnson and Winter, *Route across the Rocky Mountains*, ed. 115-16.
113. James H. Carson, "Tulare Plains," *San Joaquin Republican*, March 17, 1852.
114. Bidwell, *In California before the Gold Rush*, 48.
115. Frémont, *Memoirs of My Life*, vol. 1, 445.
116. *San Francisco California Star*, April 10, 1847. For discussion of the dietary changes Indians underwent after white contact, see Cook, "The Mechanism and Extent of Dietary Adaptation Among Certain Groups of California and Nevada Indians," 447-507.
117. Caughey, ed., *Indians of Southern California*, 5. The author of the report, Benjamin Hayes, used the term "Tularenos" when describing the

Tejonenos. In this study, "Tejoneños" is applied to the Indians residing in five settlements on Tejón, El Paso, and Tunis Creek in June 1851 when they signed a treaty with the United States. See "Treaty Made and Concluded at Camp Persifer F. Smith, at the Texan Pass, State of California, June 10, 1851, between George W. Barbour, United States Commissioner, and the Chiefs, Captains and Head Men of 'Castake,' 'Texon,' &tc., Tribes of Indians," Kappler, ed., *Indian Treaties*, 4, 1102.

118. Sutton. "Kitanemuk Prehistory," 214.
119. Bancroft, *History of California*, 2: 536-37n.
120. Leonard, *Narrative of the Adventures of Zenas Leonard*, 199-201.
121. Beeler and Klar, "Interior Chumash," 295; Grant, "Interior Chumash," 533-34; Hudson, "Alliklik-Tataviam Problem," 230-31. See also McLendon and Johnson, *Chumash Peoples*, 1: 156-64.
122. Beeler and Klar, "Interior Chumash," 300-301.
123. Juan Coluco, deposition, Tule River Indian Agency, February 23, 1922, Harrington Papers, vol. 2.
124. Juan Dionisio, deposition, Tule River Indian Agency, February 23, 1922, Harrington Papers, vol. 2.
125. Johnson, "Visual Images of the Tejón Indian Community."
126. Capt. Henry W. Wessells to Asst. Adj. Gen. E. D. Townsend, Fort Miller, August 2, 1853, Message from the President of the United States, transmitting Report in regard to Indian affairs on the Pacific, U.S. Congress, House, 34th Cong., 3d sess., Exec. Doc. 76, Serial 906, 31.
127. John R. Johnson, "Indians of Mission San Fernando," 262-63. Acording to Johnson, Vicente's full name was Vicente Kawana and Francisco's was Francisco Tinoki. In the historical documentation Francisco is usually referred to as Chico. Zapatero's first name was either Antonio or José, but he was commonly known as just Zapatero, a convention followed in this study. According to the *Population Schedule of the Eight Census of the United States, 1860, California*, vol. 3, p. 14, his first name was "Jose."
128. Information about Martin (except that his full name might have been Mateo Martin), Francisco, and José Antonio have not been found.
129. Correspondent to editors, n.p., n,d., *San Joaquin Republican*, n.d.; reprinted in *San Francisco Daily Herald*, May 13, 1855.
130. Dionisio, deposition, February 23, 1922.
131. Guadalupe Isidro, deposition, February 23, 1922, Harrington Papers, vol. 2.
132. Maria Chololo, deposition, February 19, 1922, Harrington Papers, vol. 2.
133. Coluco, deposition, February 23, 1922.

134. Abel Stearns, deposition, January 7, 1858, in Transcript of the Proceedings in Case No. 240.
135. Harris, *Gila Trail*, 100. Harris stated that he met Zapatero at the foot of Canada de las Uvas, but the Indian lived much closer to the Tejón Pass.
136. Bunnwell, *Discovery of the Yosemite*, 262, 268.
137. *San Francisco Daily Herald*, August 8, 1853.
138. Blake, *Report of a Geological Reconnaissance in California: Made in Connection with the Expedition to Survey Routes of California, to connect with the Survey*, 39-40.
139. Lieut. Nathaniel H. McLean to Maj. Henry W. Wessells, Fort Miller, July 12, 1853, Office of the Adjutant General, Letters Received, 1822-1860.
140. Dionisio, deposition, February 23, 1922, Harrington Papers, vol. 2.
141. Blake, Geological Reconnaissance, 39-40.
142. Dionisio, deposition, February 22, 1922.
143. Chololo, deposition, February 19, 1922.
144. "The Tejon Reservation—Superintendent Beale," *Los Angeles Star*, June 24, 1854. A white man described the same technique among Indians in the Southern Mines. See Eccleston, *Mariposa Indian War*, 129.
145. McLean to Wessells, July 12, 1853. For a discussion of the role of the bear in California Indian culture, see Heizer and Hewes, "Animal Ceremonialism in Central California in the light of Archeology," 587-603.
146. Blake, Geological Reconnaissance, 46.
147. Coluco, deposition, February 23, 1922; Thomas Henley to George W. Manypenny, Tejón Military Reserve, February 8, 1854, *Annual Report of the Commissioner of Indian Affairs for the Year 1854*, 302.
148. For a thorough description of the construction techniques used by the Indians in the Tulare Valley, consult Latta, *Yokuts Indians*, 350-58.
149. Merriam, *California Indians*, 77-83. Gayton, "Culture-Environment Integration." 257. Firsthand descriptions of the ceremony can be found in Kip, *The Early Days of My Episcopate*, 224-25; and in Townsend, *California Diary*, 127-29.
150. Magruder, *Upper San Joaquin Valley, 1772-1870*, 42.
151. Ibid., 60.
152. Tomas Valle, deposition, San Francisco, September 28, 1854, in Transcript of the 623 Proceedings in Case No. 536.
153. "The Tejón Rancho," *Los Angeles Star*, October 12, 1854. The article summarizes the case brought before a federal land commission and includes synopses of testimonies.
154. José Maria Covarrubias, deposition, Los Angeles, November 5, 1853,

in Transcript of the Proceedings in Case No. 240.
155. Manuel Jacinto Fogo, deposition, Los Angeles, October 19, 1852, in Transcript of the Proceedings in Case No. 240.
156. Juan Gullardo, deposition, Los Angeles, November 25, 1853, in Transcript of the Proceedings in Case No. 240; *Los Angeles Star*, October 12, 1854.
157. Magruder, *Upper San Joaquin Valley*, 60.

Chapter VI: Foreigners Establish a Foothold

1. *Sutter: The Man and His Empire*, 66-67. In late 1837 smallpox struck northern California. The disease spread from Fort Ross, a Russian trading post established on the coast north of San Francisco Bay in 1812, to Sonoma and then into the interior, decimating Indian societies in the Sacramento Valley. See Cook, "Smallpox in Spanish and Mexican California, 1770-1845," 184- 87.
2. *Sacramento Daily Union*, September 29, 1862.
3. Davis, *Seventy-five Years in California*, 19.
4. Lienhard, *I Knew Sutter*, 16-17.
5. Phelps, *Alta California, 1840-1842*, 10.
6. Mariano Guadalupe Vallejo, "Historical and Personal Memoirs Relating to Alta California," vol. 4, trans. Earl R. Hewitt, C-D 21, 28, Bancroft Library, Berkeley. Calif.; Zollinger, *Sutter, The Man and His Empire, A Biography*, 68-69.
7. John Sutter to Gov. Juan B. Alvarado, n.p., 1841, Departmental State Papers, vol. 17, CA-33, Bancroft Library, Berkeley, Calif.
8. See Chapter 4, 88-89.
9. Entry No. 6362, January, 18, 1831, Mission San Jose Register of Baptisms, September 2, 1797-May 8, 1859, Chancery Office, Archdiocese of San Francisco, San Francisco, Calif. (I thank Randy Milliken for this source.)
10. Merriam, "California Mission Baptismal Records," 222.
11. Jackson, "Gentile Recruitment and Population Movements in the San Francisco Bay Area Missions," 238.
12. Ibid.
13. McCarthy, *The History of Mission San Jose*, 217.
14. Juan Bautista Alvarado, "History of California," vol. 4, trans. Earl R. Hewitt, C-D 4, 211, Bancroft Library, Berkeley, Calif.
15. Lienhard, *A Pioneer at Sutter's Fort, 1846-1850: The Adventures of Heinrich Lienhard*, 7.
16. Sutter, *The Diary of Johann August Sutter*, 6.
17. Wilkes, *Narrative*, 182-83.
18. John A. Sutter, "Personal Reminiscences of General John Augustus Sutter," 1876, C-D 14, 40, Bancroft Library, Berkeley, Calif.

19. Sutter, *Diary*, 9.
20. Sutter, "Personal Reminiscences," 41.
21. Frémont, *Memoirs of My Life*, vol. 1, 442.
22. Lienhard, *Pioneer*, 7.
23. Cordua, "The Memoirs of Theodor Cordua, the Pioneer of New Mecklenburg in the Sacramento Valley," 309.
24. John A. Sutter to José de Jesús Vallejo, New Helvetia, October 15, 1840, Sutter Collection, 9 Letters, Misc. Box 312, California State Library, Sacramento.
25. Ibid.
26. Ibid.
27. Sutter, "Personal Reminiscences," 44-46.
28. Sutter to Vallejo, October 15, 1840.
29. Bancroft, *History of California*, vol. 4, 1840-1895, 136-37.
30. Zollinger, *Sutter*, 89.
31. Quoted in anonymous, *History of Sacramento County California*, 182.
32. Alvarado, "History of California," 213.
33. Sutter, *Diary*, 17.
34. Sutter to Alvarado, 1841.
35. Ibid.
36. Ibid.
37. Salvador Vallejo, "History of California," 1874, C-D 22, 112-13, Bancroft Library, Berkeley, Calif.
38. Zollinger, *Sutter*, 102.
39. Phelps, *Alta California, 1840-1842*, 194.
40. Sutter to Alvarado, n.p., 1841.
41. Bryant, *What I Saw in California*, 344.
42. Frémont, *Memoirs of My Life*, vol. 1, 442.
43. Willard Buzzell, Deposition, San Francisco, California, September 6, 1853, Transcript of the Proceedings in Case No. 523, Hicks and Martin Claimants vs. the United States, Defendant, for the Place Named "Cosumnes," U.S. Land Claims 240 ND, 23, Bancroft Library, Berkeley, Calif. The Indians were Muqueleme Miwok.
44. John A. Sutter, deposition, San Francisco, September 14, 1853 in ibid.
45. George F. Wyman, deposition, San Francisco, September 6, 1853, in ibid., 28.
46. Sutter, deposition, ibid., 34.
47. Sutter et al., *New Helvetia Diary*, 96, 98, 111, 124-25, 128.
48. Ibid., 25, 43, 61-62, 90.
49. John A. Sutter to_____, New Helvetia, May 18, 1845, published in the *San Francisco California Farmer*, March 13, 1857.
50. Phelps, *Alta California*, 208.

51. Frémont, *Memoirs of My Life*, 351.
52. Lienhard, *Pioneer*, 68.
53. Waseurtz af Sandels, *A Sojourn in California*, 72-73.
54. Lienhard, *Pioneer*, 68.
55. Waseurtz af Sandels, A Sojourn in California. 58. Other visitors presented similar accounts; see Bryant, *What I Saw in California: By Wagon from Missouri to California in 1847-48*, 267-68; Lienhard, *Pioneer*, 68; and Johnson, *Sights in the Gold Region and Scenes by the Way*, 743.
56. Phelps, *Alta California, 1840-1842*, 208.
57. Frémont, *Memoirs of My Life*, 351.
58. Sutter, "Personal Reminiscences," 41; Bryant, *What I Saw in California*, 267-68.
59. Lienhard, *Pioneer*, 89.
60. Sutter et al., *New Helvetia Diary*, 2, 10; Lienhard, *Pioneer*, 89-90.
61. Wilkes, *Narrative*, 178.
62. Lienhard, *Pioneer*, 77.
63. Sutter, "Personal Reminiscences," 47.
64. Lienhard, *Pioneer*, 76-77.
65. Ibid., 76.
66. Ibid., 78.
67. Alvarado, "History of California," 274.
68. Cordua, "Memoirs," 309.
69. For a discussion of this aspect of Sutter's Indian labor policy, see Hurtado, *Indian Survival on the California Frontier*, 55-71.
70. Wilkes, *Narrative*, 178, 180.
71. Lothrop, "The Indian Campaigns of General M.G. Vallejo, Defender of the Northern Frontier of California," 794.
72. Alvarado, "History of California," 225.
73. Sutter, "Personal Reminiscences," 42.
74. Sutter, deposition, September 14, 1853.
75. Sutter, "Personal Reminiscences," 42.
76. Sutter, *Diary*, 18-19.
77. Sutter, "Personal Reminiscences," 77-78.
78. Johnson and Winter, *Route Across the Rocky Mountains*, 115-16.
79. John A. Sutter to John Marsh, New Helvetia, June 28, 1844, John Marsh Collection, Box 240, California State Library, Sacramento.
80. Clyman, *James Clyman: American Frontiersman, 1792-1881*, 174.
81. John A. Sutter to Thomas O. Larkin, New Helvetia, July 21, 1845, in George P. Hammond, ed., *The Larkin Papers*, vol. 3, 278-80.
82. Ibid.
83. James Douglas to Sir George Simpson, Fort Vancouver, March 5, 1845, Rich, ed., *The Letters of John McLoughlin*, 183. For an overview of this incident, see Heizer, "Walla Walla Indian Expeditions to the

Sacramento Valley," l-7.
84. Sutter, *Diary*, 21-22.
85. Thomas O. Larkin to William Hooper, Monterey, March 22, 1845, in Hammond, ed., *The Larkin Papers*, 83.
86. Sutter, *Diary*, 24-25.
87. Sutter, *Diary*, 25.
88. Sutter, "Personal Reminiscences," 127.
89. John A. Sutter to Thomas O. Larkin, New Helvetia, April 21, 1845, in Alvarado, "History of California," 215. Sutter's claim that only immigrants could conquer the horse thieves was repeated six months later. See John A. Sutter to Thomas O. Larkin, New Helvetia, October 8, 1845, in Hammond, ed., *The Larkin Papers*, vol. 4, 11.
90. Bancroft, *History of California*, vol. 5, 1846-1848, 524.
91. Contract between the Government and John Marsh and John Gantt in regard to the pursuit of the Indian Robbers, Los Angeles, February 27, 1845, John Marsh Family Papers, C-B 879, Bancroft Library, Berkeley, Calif.; Hittell, *History of California*, vol. 2, 388-89.
92. José Castro, Instructions to John Gantt, Los Angeles, February 27, 1845, Sherburne Cook Papers, 79/21c, G-4, Bancroft Library, Berkeley, Calif.
93. John A. Sutter to Antonio Sunol, New Helvetia, June 14, 1845, John A. Sutter Collection,
Misc. Box 311, California State Library, Sacramento.
94. Peter Lausen. deposition, San Francisco, September 1, 1853, Transcript of the Proceedings in Case No. 255, Charles M. Weber, Claimant, vs. the United States, Defendant, for the Place Named "Campo de los Franceses." U.S. Land Claims 298 ND, 24, Bancroft Library, Berkeley, Calif.
95. On August 16, 1843, a justice of the peace, Isadoro Guillen, granted Weber a safe-conduct passport to travel to New Helvetia. See Weber Family Papers, 1788-1981, C-B 829, Bancroft Library, Berkeley, Calif.
96. "California Indian Chiefs," *Sacramento Daily Union*, January 31, 1857.
97. Gilbert, *History of San Joaquin County, California*, 12-13, 16.
98. *Stockton Daily Independent*, May 7, 1881; Gilbert, *History of San Joaquin County, California*, 16.
99. Tinkham, *A History of Stockton*, 66-68.
100. Sutter, "Personal Reminiscences," 69-70.
101. Alpheces Flech, Deposition, San Francisco, September 1, 1853, Transcript of the Proceedings in Case No. 255 for the Place Named "Campo de los Franceses." U S. Land Claims 298 ND, 19, Bancroft Library, Berkeley, Calif.
102. Sutter to Sunol, June 14, 1845.
103. Sutter to Larkin, July 21, 1845.

104. Thomas O. Larkin to Joseph B. Hull, Monterey, August 20, 1845, in Hammond, ed., *The Larkin Papers*, vol. 3, 319.
105. José María Covarrubias to the Prefect of the District of Monterev, Monterey, September 24, 1845, in ibid., 363-64.
106. Sutter et al., *New Helvetia Diary*, 2.
107. Sutter, deposition, U.S. Land Claims, 240 ND, 34-35.
108. On several occasions, Heleno visited New Helvetia; see Sutter et al., *New Helvetia Diary*, 53, 75, 134.
109. Ibid., 19.
110. John A. Sutter to John Marsh, New Helvetia, April 3, 1846, John Marsh Collection, Box 240, California State Library, Sacramento; John Marsh to ___, New Helvetia, March 2, 1846, in Mayo Elizabeth Wheeler, "John A. Sutter, a California Pioneer; an Historical Sketch and Collection of Correspondence," 426.
111. Sutter et al., *New Helvetia Diary*, 52, 57, 62, 67, 68, 71, 73, 81, 105, 112, 717-18. Information about Polo is sketchy and not very reliable. A visitor to California claimed Polo had been educated at one of the missions and was fluent in Spanish. Supposedly, he took four wives but insisted his followers remain monogamous. See Downey. *Filings from an Old Saw*, 19.
112. "Letters from California, 1846," Yerba Buena, June 25, 1846, *Honolulu Friend*, December 1, 1846.
113. Sutter, *Diary*, 32.
114. John A. Sutter to William A. Leidesdorff, New Helvetia, July 22, 1846, Leidesdorff Papers, LE 164, Huntington Library, San Marino, California.
115. John A. Sutter to William A. Leidesdorff, New Helvetia, June 1, 1846, Leidesdorff Papers, LE 137, Huntington Library, San Marino, California.
116. Sutter, *Diary*, 33-34.
117. John A. Sutter to Mariano Guadalupe Vallejo, New Helvetia, June 1, 1846, 185.
118. Sutter, *Diary*, 33-34.
119. Sutter to Leidesdorff, July 22, 1846.
120. Revere, *Tour of Duty in California*, 155.
121. Duvall, *A Navy Surgeon in California*, 17.

Chapter VII: Americans Intervene

1. Thomas O. Larkin to editor, *Journal of Commerce*, Monterey, July 1845, in Hammond, ed., *The Larkin Papers*, vol. 3, 294.
2. Thomas O. Larkin to F. M. Dimond, Monterey, March 1, 1846, in ibid., vol.4, 216.
3. Thomas O. Larkin, "Description of California," Monterey, April

20, 1846, in ibid., 307-308.

4. The American conquest of coastal California is described in detail in Harlow, *California Conquered.*
5. Larkin, "Description," 306.
6. "Letters from California, 1846," Yerba Buena, June 25, 1846, *Honolulu Friend*, December 1, 1846.
7. Duvall, *A Navy Surgeon in California*, 42.
8. *Monterey Californian*, August 15, 1846, Job. F. Dye, "Recollections of California, 1877," C-D 69, 18- 19, Bancroft Library, Berkeley, Calif.
9. *Monterey Californian,* August 22, 1846.
10. Ibid., September 26, 1846.
11. Ibid., October 10, 1846.
12. Hussey and Ames, Jr., "California Preparations to Meet the Walla Walla Invasion, 1846," 9-21.
13. Bryant, *What I Saw in California*, 267.
14. Ibid., 273-74.
15. Revere, *Tour of Duty in California,* 157.
16. Mariano Guadalupe Vallejo to Thomas O. Larkin, Sonoma, September 15, 1846, in Hammond, ed., *Larkin Papers*, vol. 5, 237.
17. Harlow, *California Conquered*, 159-73.
18. Bryant, *What I Saw*, 347n.
19. Janssens, *The Life and Adventures in California of Don Augustín Janssens, 1834-1856*, 127.
20. William A. Maddox to Charles Weber, San Juan Bautista, October 28, 1846, Weber Family Papers, C-B 829, Bancroft Library, Berkeley, Calif.
21. Garner, *Letters from California, 1846-1847*, 118.
22. Bryant, *What I Saw in California*, 347.
23. John Sutter, "Personal Reminiscences of General John Augustus Sutter," 1876, C-D 14, 153-54, Bancroft Library, Berkeley, Calif.
24. Swasey, *The Early Days and Men of California*, 70.
25. Sutter, "Personal Reminiscences," 153-54.
26. Frémont, *Memoirs of My Life*, vol. 2, 229-30.
27. Bryant, *What I Saw in California*, 359-60.
28. Jacob R. Snyder to Edward M. Kern, Los Angeles, February 11, 1847, in Spence and Jackson, eds., *The Expeditions of John Charles Frémont,* vol. 2, 302.
29. Sutter, "Personal Reminiscences," 153-54.
30. *Monterey Californian*, December 23, 1846.
31. Garner, *Letters from California, 1846-1847*, 164.
32. *Monterey Californian*, December 23, 1846. Because Indian raiding continued long after the uprising had been crushed, Garner's and the *Californian's* claims lack merit.

33. Janssens, *The Life and Adventures in California*, 127.
34. See Harlow, *California Conquered*, 193-218.
35. Grivas, *Military Governments in California*, 80-81.
36. Col. Richard B. Mason to Gen. Stephen Watts Kearny, n.p., March 20, 1847, Archives of California, Unbound Documents, CA-63, 146-47, Bancroft Library, Berkeley, Calif.
37. José María Sánchez to Gen. Stephen Watts Kearny, San Juan Bautista March 19, 1847, Pacific Division, Records of the 10th Military Department, Letters Received, RG 98, Microcopy 210, Roll 2, NA.
38. Gen. Stephen Watts Kearny to W. L. Marcy, Monterey, California, April 28, 1847. U.S. Congress, House, 3lst Cong., lst sess., Exec. Doc. 17, 286.
39. Davis, *Seventy-five Years in California*, 386. The history of the regiment is described in Biggs, *Conquer and Colonize: Stevenson's Regiment and California.*
40. *San Francisco California Star,* April 10, 1847.
41. Wierzbicki, *California As It Is And As It May Be*, 16.
42. Garner, *Letters from California,1846-1847,* 164.
43. *San Francisco California Star*, April 10, 1847.
44. Ibid., May 7, 1847.
45. Ibid.
46. Ibid. Also challenging Marsh's contention that a party of whites intended to join the horse-thief Indians was an individual using the initials R. T. See ibid., August 14, 1847.
47. Gen. Stephen Watts Kearny to John A. Sutter, Monterey, April 7, 1847, U.S. Congress, House, 31st Cong., lst sess., Exec. Doc. 17, 294.
48. John A. Sutter to Gen. Stephen Watts Kearny, New Helvetia, May 18, 1847, Archives of California, Unbound Documents, CA-63, Bancroft Library, Berkeley, Calif.
49. Sutter et al., *New Helvetia Diary*, 45.
50. John Sutter, Statement, New Helvetia, May 22, 1847, T. Perceval Gerson Collection, 100/51, Department of Special Collections, University of California, Los Angeles.
51. John A. Sutter to Gen. Stephen Watts Kearny, New Helvetia, May 27, 1847, Archives of California, Unbound Documents, CA-63, Bancroft Library, Berkeley, Calif.
52. Thomas O. Larkin to Robert Field Stockton, Monterey, April 26, 1847, in Hammond, ed., *The Larkin Papers*, vol. 6, 126.
53. Mariano Guadalupe Vallejo to Gen. Stephen Watts Kearny, Santa Clara, April 18, 1847, Pacific Division, RG 393, U.S. Army Continental Commands, 182l-1920, Microcopy 210, Roll 2. NA.
54. Capt. Henry Naglee, Journal, May 24-June 20, 1847, Naglee Family Collection, MR-116, Bancroft Library, Berkeley, Calif.

55. Ibid., 9-13.
56. Ibid., 19-24.
57. Sutter et al., *New Helvetia Diary*, 49-51.
58. Frémont, *Memoirs*, 2, 231n.
59. *Monterey Californian*, June 19, 1847.
60. An individual who kept a journal of the journey made no mention of Indian raids. See Turner, *The Original Journals of Henry Smith Turner*, 126.
61. For an account of the transfer of power to Mason, see Harlow, *California Conquered*, 280-81.
62. William Dana to Gen. Stephen Watts Kearny, San Luis Obispo, June 6, 1847, Archives of California, Unbound Documents, CA 63, Bancroft Library, Berkeley, Calif.
63. Col. Richard B. Mason to Gen. R. Jones, Monterey, July 19, 184, Pacific Division, Records of the 10th Military Department, Letters Received, 1846-1851, RG 98, Microcopy 210, Roll 1, NA.
64. John A. Sutter to Col. Richard B. Mason, New Helvetia, July 12, 1847, U.S. Congress, House, 31st Cong., lst sess., Exec. Doc. 17, 374.
65. Ibid.
66. Extracted from a letter, New Helvetia, July 10, 1847, in the *San Francisco California Star*, July 24, 1847.
67. Sutter to Mason, July 12, 1847.
68. Col. Richard B. Mason to John A. Sutter, Monterey, July 21, 1847, U.S. Congress, House, 3 1st Cong., lst sess., Exec. Doc. 17, 76-77.
69. Col. Richard B. Mason to Lieut. Charles Anderson, Monterey, July 21, 1847, in ibid., 343-44.
70. Col. Richard B. Mason to Mariano Guadalupe Vallejo and John A. Sutter, August 19, 1847, in ibid., 384; Lieut. H. W. Halleck to John A. Sutter, Monterey, August 16, 1847, in ibid., 38-83.
71. Gen. Stephen Watts Kearny to Mariano Guadalupe Vallejo, Monterey, April 14, 1847, in ibid., 296-91 .
72. Lieut. H. W. Halleck to Mariano Guadalupe Vallejo, Monterey, September 15, 1847, in ibid., 395.
73. Bancroft, *History of California*, vol. 5, 1846-1848, 610.
74. Halleck to Sutter, August 16, 1847.
75. Ibid.
76. John A. Sutter to Lieut. H. W. Halleck, New Helvetia, December 20, 1847, 94-95. See also Hurtado, *Indian Survival on the California Frontier*, 65-69.
77. John A. Sutter to William A. Leidesdorff, New Helvetia, September 10, 1847. William A. Leidesdorff Papers, LE 321, Huntington Library, San Marino, Calif.
78. John A. Sutter to William Leidesdorff, New Helvetia, October 13,

1847, LE 340, in ibid.

79. Lieut. William T. Sherman to John Burton, Monterey, September 6, 1847, U.S. Congress, House, 31st Cong., lst sess., Exec. Doc. 17, 355.
80. Lieut. William T. Sherman to Capt. Henry Naglee, Monterey, September 9, 1847, PacificDivision, Records of the 10th Military Department, Letters Received, 1846- 1851, RG 98, Microcopy 210, Roll 1, NA.
81. Ryan, *Personal Adventures in Upper and Lower California*, vol. 1, 130-34.
82. Oliver M. Wozencraft, "Indian Affairs, 1849-50," 1877, C-D 204, Bancroft Library, Berkeley, Calif.
83. Ryan, *Personal Adventures*, vol. 1, 134.
84. Ibid., 107-108. During a military operation in Baja California, Naglee also executed two Mexican prisoners. See Col. Richard B. Mason to Gen. R. Jones, Monterey, August 16, 1848, U.S. Congress, House, 3lst Cong., lst sess., Exec. Doc. 17, 512-13.
85. Gilbert, *History of San Joaquin County*, California, 20.
86. Sutter et al., *New Helvetia Diary*, 115.
87. James Weeks to Charles Weber, San Jose, December 28, 1847, Weber Family Papers, C-B 829, Bancroft Library, Berkeley, Calif.
88. Gilbert, *History of San Joaquin County, California*, 20. Charles Weber, Deposition, San Francisco, April 3, 1855, Transcript of the proceedings in Case No. 767, Francisco Rico et al., Claimants, vs. the United States, Defendant, for the Place Named Rio Estanislao, U.S. Land Claims 413 ND, 13-14, Bancroft Library, Berkeley, Calif.
89. "California Indian Chiefs," *Sacramento Daily Union*, January 31, 1857.
90. Col. Jonathan D. Stevenson to Andres Pico, Los Angeles, February 14, 1848, Pacific Division, U.S. Army Continental Commands, 182l-1920, RG 393. Microcopy 210, Roll 3, NA.
91. Capt. Francis J. Lippsitt to Lieut. William T. Sherman, Santa Barbara, February 25, 1848, in ibid.
92. Lieut. John M. Huddart to Capt. Francis J. Lippsitt, Santa Barbara, February 25, 1848, in ibid.
93. Lippsitt to Sherman, February 25, 1848.
94. Col. Richard B. Mason to Juan Price, Monterey, March 21, 1848, U.S. Congress, House, 31st Cong., lst sess., Exec. Doc. 17, 496-97.
95. Capt. Francis J. Lippsitt to Lieut. William T. Sherman, Santa Barbara, March 9, 1848, Pacific Division, Records of the l0th Military Department, Letters Received, 1846-1851, RG 98, Microcopy 210, Roll 3, NA. The village may have been Pohalin Tinleu of the Hometwoli (Yokuts), which was located on Kern Lake.
96. Ibid.
97. Lieut. J. L. Bonnycastle to Capt. Francis J. Lippsitt, Los Angeles,

April 2, 1848, Pacific Division, U.S. Army Continental Commands 1821-1920, RG 393, Microcopy 210, Roll 3, NA.

98. Capt. Francis J. Lippsitt, Statement, Santa Bárbara, April 18, 1848, Roll 6, in ibid.

99. Charles White to Col. Richard B. Mason, San José, April 29, 1848, Archives of California, Unbound Documents CA-63, Bancroft Library, Berkeley. Calif.

100. Charles White to Col. Richard B. Mason, San José, July 16, 1848, in ibid.

101. Ibid.

102. Zollinger, *Sutter: The Man and His Empire*, 221.

103. "The Sutter-Marshall Lease with the Yalesumney Indians, 1848," 109-10.

104. Ibid.

105. Henry Bigler, Notes from his diary, January-February, 1848, C-D 45, 66, Bancroft Library, Berkeley. Caiif.

106. James W. Marshall to Charles E. Pickett, n.p., January 28, 1856, in Hittell, *Mining in the Pacific States of North America*, 11-12.

107. John A. Sutter to Col. Richard B. Mason, New Helvetia, February 22, 1848, Pioneer
Manuscript Collection, 236, California State Library, Sacramento.

108. Col. Richard B. Mason to John A. Sutter, Monterey, March 5, 1848, U.S. Congress, House, 31st Cong., lst sess., Exec. Doc. 17, 490.

109. Caughey, *The California Gold Rush*, 20.

110. Col. Richard B. Mason to Gen. R. Jones, Monterey, August 17, 1848, U.S. Congress, House, 31 st Cong., lst sess., Exec. Doc. 17, 533.

111. Col. Richard B. Mason to Gen. R. Jones, San Francisco, November 24, 1848, ibid., 648-49.

112. William Garner to Col. Richard B. Mason, San Luis Obispo, March 15, Pacific Division, Records of the 10th Military Department, Letters Received, 1846-1851, RG 98, Microcopy 210, Roll 3, NA.

113. Ibid.

114. Gen. Bennett Riley to Lieut. William T. Sherman, Monterey, April 16, 1849, U.S. Congress, House, 31st Cong., lst sess., Exec. Doc. 17, 900.

115. *San José Pioneer*, April 27, 1878.

116. Ibid.

117. Quoted in Carson, *Recollections of the California Mines*, 13.

118. *San José Pioneer*, April 27, 1878. The individual who escaped took Garner's journal to the coast; see Carson, *Recollections of the California Mines*, 12-13.

119. Asst. Adj. Gen. Edward R. S. Canby to Maj. Anthony S. Miller, Monterey, May 4, 1849, U.S. Congress, House, 3lst Cong., lst sess.,

Exec. Doc. 17, 904-905.

120. Asst. Adj. Gen. Edward R. S. Canby to Maj. Anthony S. Miller. Monterey, May 7, 1849, in ibid., 906-907.
121. Asst. Adj. Gen. Edward R. S. Canby to Lieut. Clarendon J. L. Wilson, Monterey, June 2, 1849, in ibid., 913-14.
122. Lieut. Clarendon J. L. Wilson to Asst. Adj. Gen. Edward R. S. Canby, Camp Stanislaus, August 20, 1849, Pacific Division, Records of the 10th Military Department, Letters Received, 1846-1851, RG 98, Microcopy 210, Roll 4, NA.
123. Ibid.
124. Gen. Bennett Riley to Gen. R. Jones, Monterey, June 11, 1849, U.S. Congress, House, 31st Cong., lst sess., Exec. Doc. 17, 977.
125. *San Francisco Weekly, Alta California*, May 3, 1849.
126. Gen. Bennett Riley to Col. W. G. Freeman, Monterey, September 20, 1849, U.S. Congress, House, 31st Cong, lst sess., Exec. Doc. 17, 941-43.
127. Gen. Bennett Riley to Col. J. Hooker, Sacramento City, July 22, 1849 in ibid., 925-26.
128. Gen. Bennett Riley to Gen. R. Jones, Monterey, October 15, 1849, Pacific Division, Records of the 10th Military Department, Letters Received, 1846-1851, RG 98, Microcopy 210, Roll 1, NA.
129. Ibid.
130. Ibid.
131. Asst. Adj. Gen. Edward R. S. Canby to 1st Lieut. George H. Derby, Monterey, April 9, 1850, Report of the Secretary of War communicating, in compliance with a resolution of the Senate, a report of the Tulare Valley, made by Lieutenant Derby, U.S. Congress, Senate, 32d Cong., 1st sess., Exec. Doc. 110, Serial 621, 2-3.
132. 1st Lieut. George H. Derby to Asst. Adj. Gen. Edward R. S. Canby, Monterey, July 10, 1850, in U.S. Congress, Senate, 32d Cong., 1st sess., Exec. Doc. 110, Serial 621, 4-7.
133. Ibid., 7-8.
134. Ibid., 10-11. Although Derby called the Indian "De-e-jah," he probably was Echa, chief of the Yokod.
135. Derby to Canby, July 10, 1850, 11-12.
136. B. Oscar Field, deposition, Mariposa County, December 23, 1851, U.S. Congress, Senate, 33d Cong., sp. sess., Exec. Doc. 4, Serial 688, 236-37.
137. Derby to Canby, July 10, 1850, 12.
138. Joseph T. Hamm, deposition, December 31, 1851, U.S. Congress, Senate, 33d Cong., sp. sess., Exec. Doc. 4, Serial 688, 238.
139. Lewis Thorp, deposition, December 23, 1851, U.S. Congress, Senate, 33d Cong., sp. sess., Exec. Doc. 4, Serial 688, 238.

140. Derby to Canby, July 10, 1850, 12.
141. Ibid., 12-13.
142. Ibid.
143. Letter to editors, "The Tulare Lakes," n.d., *San Francisco Picayune*, November 15, 1851. Also published in Heizer, ed., *Ethnographical Articles*, 57-60. An Indian informant told an anthropologist in the late 1920s that the earliest chief remembered was named K'anti; he was succeeded by a son of the same name. Either the father or the son might have been the Quintin mentioned in the historical documentation. See Gayton. "Yokuts and Western Mono Ethnography," l: 26.
144. Derby to Canby, July 10, 1850, 15.
145. Ibid, 16.
146. "Motu" to editors, Merced River, June 12, 1850, unidentified newspaper, Upton, Scrapbook no.7, California Historical Society Library, San Francisco California.
147. John Marvin, "Some Account of the Tulare Valley, and the Indians from the Fresno River to Tihone Pass," no. 2, *San Francisco Morning Post*, n.d, in Marvin, Scrapbooks, vol. 1; Lewis Granger to Abel Stearns, Los Angeles, February 4, 1851, in Hafen, ed., *Letters of Lewis Granger*, 30-31. The original letter is in the Abel Stearns Collection in the Huntington Library, San Marino, Cal.
148. Marvin, "Some Account," no. 2. The *San Joaquin Republican* of May 6, 1856 stated that Francisco led the attack on the settlement in the Four Creeks. Written ten years after the attack, a significantly different and less trustworthy version is Abraham Hillard to editors, n.p., n.d., *San Francisco Mirror*, n.d.; reprinted in *Visalia Sun*, September 5, 1860.
149. P. to editors, n.p., n.d., *Stockton Times*, March 5, 1851; Granger to Stearns, February 4, 1851.
150. Granger to Steams, February 4, 1851.
151. Marvin, "Some Account," no. 2.
152. Granger to Stearns, February 4, 1851.
153. [Rasey Biven] to editors, Sebastian Military Reserve, September 22, 1854, *San Francisco Times and Transcript*, n.d., in Thomas Henley to George W. Manypenny, San Francisco, December 29, 1854, Office of Indian Affairs, Letters Received, 1824-81, roll 54. Rasey Biven identified himself as the author of the article in a letter to Thomas Henley and Edward F. Beale published in the *San Francisco Daily Herald*, August 20, 1855.
154. Marvin, "Some Account," no. 2.
155. Benjamin Hayes, letter, n.p., n.d., in Letter Received by B. D. Wilson, January 15, 1851, from Gov. H. Smith, in Hayes, *Scrapbooks*, vol. 39.
156. Wolcott, ed., *Pioneer Notes*, 95-96.
157. Marvin, "Some Account," no. 2.

158. Wessells to Townsend, August 2, 1853, 31; *San Francisco Daily Herald*, August 8, 1853; Blake, *Geological Reconnaissance*, 47; *Los Angeles Star*, June 17, 1854. Because Zapatero was living in an adobe house when visited by white men, it has been assumed that he built it. The Tejoneños did not build in adobe until after the founding of a reservation in the area. See Thomas Henley to George W. Manypenny, San Francisco, December 18, 1855. Office of Indian Affairs, Letters Received, 1824-81, roll 35.
159. [Biven] to editors, September 22, 1854.
160. Williamson, *Explorations and Surveys*, 21; Blake, *Geological Reconnaissance*, 38.

PART II: RELOCATION

Chapter VIII: Inventing a New Indian Policy

1. Prucha, *The Great Father: The United States Government and the American Indians*, 1:232-33.
2. For a discussion of the removal policy, see Satz, *American Indian Policy in the Jacksonian Era*.
3. Mahon, "Indian-United States Military Situation, 1775-1848," 159-60.
4. Satz, *American Indian Policy*, 42-43.
5. Trennent, Jr., *Alternative to Extinction: Federal Indian Policy and the Beginning of the Reservation System, 1846-1851*, 3.
6. Hoopes, *Indian Affairs and Their Administration*, 1.
7. Trennent, *Alternative to Extinction*, 29-30.
8. William Medill, "Report of the Commissioner of Indian Affairs," November 30, 1848, U.S. Congress, House, 30th Cong., 2d sess., Exec. Doc. 1, Serial 537, 386.
9. Ibid., 397.
10. Prucha, *Indian Policy in the United States: Historical Essays*, 154.
11. Luke Lea, *Report of the Commissioner of Indian Affairs*, Washington, D.C., November 27, 1850, U.S. Congress, Senate, 3lst Cong., 2d sess., Exec. Doc. 1, Serial 587, 35-36.
12. Luke Lea, *Report of the Commissioner of Indian Affairs*, November 27, 1851, U.S. Congress, Senate, 32d Cong., last sess., Exec. Doc. 1, Serial 613, 274.
13. A. H. H. Stuart, *Report of the Secretary of the Interior*, November 29, 1851, U.S. Congress, Senate, 32d Cong., last sess., Exec. Doc. 1, Serial 612, 502-503.
14. Ward, *Sam Ward in the Gold Rush*, ed., Carvel Collins, 41.
15. Sylvester Woodbridge to Zachary Taylor, Benicia, January 23, 1850, Letters Received by the Office of Indian Affairs, California Superintendence, 1849-1880, RG 75, Microscopy 234, Roll 32, NA.

16. William Medill to Adam Johnston, Washington, D.C., April 14, 1849, U.S. Congress, House, 31st Cong., last sess., Exec. Doc. 17, Serial 573, 187.
17. Whig members of the Ohio Legislature to Zachary Taylor, Columbus, December 18, 1848, Interior Department Appointment Papers, State of California, 1849-1907, RG 48, Microscopy 732, NA.
18. Adam Johnston, deposition, March 31, 1858, in United States Court of Claims, Felix Aragonite vs. The United States, George W. Right Manuscript, California Historical Society Library, San Francisco, Calif., 63.
19. Whig Members to Taylor, December 18, 1848; Redick McKee to Thomas King, Washington, D.C., March 29, 1849, Interior Department Appointment Papers, State of California, 1849-1907, RG 48, Microscopy 732, NA.
20. Medill to Johnston, April 14, 1849, 187-88.
21. Adam Johnston to Orlando Brown, San Francisco, January 31, 1850, U.S. Congress, Senate, 33d Cong., sp. sess., Exec. Doc. 4, Serial 688, 34-35.
22. Adam Johnston to Orlando Brown, San Francisco, March 1, 1850, ibid., 36-37.
23. John Sutter to Orlando Brown, Sacramento, May 23, 1850, ibid., 37.
24. Adam Johnston to Orlando Brown, Chico, July 6, 1850, ibid., 38.
25. "Treaty between Thomas T. Green and Weimar, Buccaneer, and Poll, May 25, 1850," *Sacramento Transcript*, May 30, 1850; *Daily Alta California*, May 3l, 1850.
26. Johnston to Brown, July 6, 1850, 38-41, *Sacramento Transcript*, August 30, 1850.
27. *Sacramento Transcript*, August 17, 1850.
28. Adam Johnston to Orlando Brown, September 16, 1850, U.S Congress, Senate, 33d Cong., sp. sess., Exec. Doc. 4, Serial 688, 44-45.
29. John C. Frémont to Orlando Brown, Washington, D.C., June 17, 1850, Letters Received by the Office of Indian Affairs, California Superintendency, 1849-1880, RG 75, Microscopy 234, Roll 32, NA.
30. U.S. Congress, *Journal of the Senate*, 31st Cong. last sess., September 11, 1850, 622.
31. John C. Frémont, Senate Bill No. 332, U.S. Congress, Senate, 31st Cong., last sess., September 11, 1850. Records of the U.S. Senate, RG 46, NA. See also Kelsey, "The California Indian Treaty Myth," 227-28.
32. U.S. Congress, Senate, Congressional Globe, 31st Cong., last sess., September 14, 1850, 1816.
33. Ibid.

34. U.S. Congress, *Journal of the Senate*, 3lst Cong., last sess., September 16, 1850, 336.
35. U.S. Congress. House, *Congressional Globe*, 3lst Cong., last sess., September 17, 1850, 1038, 2023.
36. *Statutes At Large*, vol. 9, 519.
37. U.S. Congress, House, *Congressional Globe*, 3lst Cong., last sess., August 31, 1850, 1124; U.S. Congress, Senate, *Congressional Globe,* 31st Cong., last sess., September 2, 1850, 1731.
38. U.S. Congress, Senate, Appendix to the *Congressional Globe*, 31st Cong., last sess., September 25, 1850, 1706.
39. U.S. Congress, House, *Congressional Globe*, 31st Cong., last sess., September 28, 1850, 2016, 2018-19.
40. *Statutes at Large*, vol. 9, 519, 558.
41. Luke Lea, *Report of the Commissioner of Indian Affairs*, November 27, 1850, 42.
42. Kelsey, "The California Indian Treaty Myth," 229-30.
43. A.S. Loughery to Redick McKee, Washington, D.C., October 10, 1850, U.S. Congress, Senate, 33d Cong., sp. sess., Exec. Doc. 4, Serial 688, 7. The same letter was sent to George W. Barbour and O. M. Wozencraft.
44. A.S. Loughery to Redick McKee, George W. Barbour, and O. M. Wozencraft Washington, D.C., October 15, 1850, ibid., 8-9.
45. Hoopes, *Domesticate or Exterminate*, 62, 71.
46. Rafael, *Little White Father*, 15-16.
47. James E. Whatnot to President Zachary Taylor, Wheeling, Virginia, March 1, 1849, Interior Department Appointment Papers, State of California 1849-1907, RG 48, Microscopy 732, NA.
48. Joshua Russell, et al., to Thomas S. Raymond, Sistersville, Virginia. September 12, 1850, ibid.
49. Loughery to McKee, Barbour, and Wozencraft, October 15, 1850.
50. Charles E. Mix to Redick McKee, Washington, D.C., August 9. 1851. U.S. Congress, Senate, 33d Cong., sp. sess., Exec. Doc. 4, Serial 688, 19-20.
51. Kelsey, "Charles E. Mix," in Kvasnicka and Viola, eds., *The Commissioners of Indian Affairs, 1827 -1977*, 77 -78.
52. Redick McKee to A. S. Loughery, Pittsburgh, November 1, 1850, U.S. Congress, Senate, 33d Cong., sp. sess., Exec. Doc. 4, Serial 688, 48.
53. Luke Lea to Redick McKee, Washington, D.C., November 9, 1850, ibid., 12.
54. Loughery to McKee, Barbour, and Wozencraft, October 15, 1850, ibid., 9.
55. Redick McKee to Luke Lea, New York, November 9, 1850, ibid.,

49.

56. Redick McKee to Luke Lea, Panama, December 6, 1850, ibid., 53.

Chapter IX: Conflict in the Southern Mines

1. Bunnell, *Discovery of the Yosemite and the Indian War of 1851 Which Led to that Event*, 70, 72-73, 297-98.
2. Ibid., 75-76, 297.
3. Lafayette Houghton Bunnell, "How the Yo-Semite Valley was Discovered and Named, *Hutchings' California Magazine*, 3, no. 11 (May 1859): 503.
4. Bunnell, *Discovery of the Yosemite*, 74, 176-7, 298.
5. Ibid., 70-72, 74, 79-80, 86. The origin and derivation of "Yosemite" is discussed in Barrett, "The Geography and Dialects of the Miwok Indians," 68.
6. Bunnell, *Discovery of the Yosemite*, 79.
7. "Huge Paw" to editors, Stanislaus County Weekly, News, January 22, 1875; Bunnell, *Discovery of the Yosemite*, 2-3.
8. William Penn Abrams, "Diary," 1849-1851, C-F 65:1, Bancroft Library, Berkeley, Calif. See also Heald, "The Forgotten Pioneer,"
7. Heald is baffled why historians have not acknowledged Abrams as perhaps the first white man to enter Yosemite.
9. Woods, *Sixteen Months at the Gold Diggings*, 82-83.
10. Bunnell, *Discovery of the Yosemite*, 3.
11. Samuel Kip to editors, Cunningham's Ranch, June 9, 1850, *San Francisco Daily, Alta California*, June 18, 1850; "San Joaquin Intelligence," Stockton, June 17, 1850, *San Francisco Daily, Alta California*, June 19, 1950; "San Joaquin Intelligence," Stockton, June 29, 1850, *San Francisco Daily, Alta California*, July 3, 1850.
12. Mitchell, *Jim Savage and the Tulareno Indians*, 16; Mitchell, "Major James D. Savage and the Tularenos," 223-24.
13. Lorenzo Vinsonhaler to Maj. George W. Patten, Fresno Reservation, September 20,1852, in Maj. George W. Patten to Lieut. W. M. Gardner, Fort Miller, September 16, 1852, Records of the U.S. Army Continental Commands, 1821- 1920, RG 393, NA.; *San Francisco Courier*, February 29, 1851.
14. Downey, *Filings from an Old Saw*, 68-69.
15. Swasey, "California, 1845-6," C-D 200, Bancroft Library, Berkeley, Calif.
16. Eccleston, *The Mariposa Indian War*, 106.
17. O'Meara, "A White Medicine Man," 150.
18. Harris, *The Gila Trail*, 146.
19. Ward, *Sam Ward in the Cold Rush*, 60-61.
20. Downey, *Filings From an Old Saw*, 68-69.

21. Harris, *The Gila Trail*, 746.
22. T. G. Palmer to Father, Hart's Ranch, January 16, 1851, quoted in Bunnell, *Discovery of the Yosemite*, 30.
23. *San Francisco Courier*, February 29, 1851.
24. Ward, *Sam Ward in the Gold Rush*, 62.
25. R. W. to editors, Castoria, January 27, 1851, *San Francisco Daily, Alta California*, January 29, 1851.
26. O'Meara, "White Medicine Man," 151.
27. Sutter, et a1., *New Helvetia Diary*, 47, 55, 57, 58, 80, 81 ; Eccleston, *The Mariposa Indian War*, 106; Vinsonhaler to Patten, September 20, 1852.
28. Vinsonhaler to Patten, September 20, 1852.
29. Hittell, *Mining in the Pacific States of North America*, 71.
30. *San Francisco Daily, Alta California,* August 22, 1852.
31. Anonymous to editors, n.p., n.d., *Daily True Standard*, n.d., John G. Marvin, Scrapbooks, vol. 1, 1840-1853, HM 51846, Huntington Library, San Marino, Calif.
32. Abrams, "Diary," 1849-1851.
33. Brownlee, *An American Odyssey: the Autobiography of a 19th Century Scotsman, Robert Brownlee, at the request of his children: Napa County, California, October 1892*, 127.
34. *San Francisco Courier*, February 29, 1851; *San Francisco Daily, Alta California*, August 20, 1852; Derbec, *A French Journalist in the California Gold Rush*, 148.
35. Brownlee, *An American Odyssey*, 127.
36. Harris, *The Gila Trail*, 146-47
37. Bell, *Reminiscences of a Ranger Or Early Times in Southern California,* 299.
38. Harris, *The Gila Trail,* 146.
39. Ibid., 127.
40. Bunnell, *Discovery of the Yosemite,* 4-5.
41. Ibid., 5-7, 9. Bunnell called Bautista "Vow-ches-ter." a corruption of "Bautista."
42. Ibid., 7.
43. Ibid., 8-9. José Rey's Indian name may have been Powitich. See John Marvin, "Mariposa Indian War," *Sacramento Democratic State Journal*, n.p., n.d., John G. Marvin, Scrapbooks, vol. 2, 1852-1854, HM 51847, Huntington Library, San Marino. Calif.
44. Adam Johnston to Luke Lea, March 7, 1851, U.S. Congress, Senate, 33d Cong., sp. sess., Exec. Doc. 4, Serial 688, 64-65.
45. Adam Johnston to Gov. Peter H. Burnett, San José, January 2, 1851, California Legislature, Journal of the Senate, 2d sess., 564; Eccleston, *The Mariposa Indian War*, 15.
46. J. E. D. to editors, Little Mariposa, March 16, 1851, *San Francisco*

Daily, Alta California, March 24, 1851; J. M. Hutchings, *In the Heart of the Sierras*, 49-50; Ward, *Sam Ward in the Gold Rush*, 86.

47. *Stockton Times*, March 26, 1851.
48. J. E. D. to editors, March 16, 1851.
49. The execution is described in Chapter 7.
50. Johnston to Burnett, January 2, 1851.
51. *Stockton Times*, January 1, 1851: Vinsonhaler to Patten, September 20, 1852.
52. Johnston to Burnett, January 2, 1851; Eccleston, *The Mariposa Indian War*, 15; "Arpad" to editors, San Francisco, January 2, 1851, *San Francisco Daily, Alta California*, January 3, 1851; James Burney to J. M. Hutchings, Modesto, March 20, 1885, Yosemite Museum Library, Yosemite National Park, Calif.
53. James D. Savage to Adam Johnston, Valley of San Joaquin, October 21, 1851, U.S. Congress, Senate, 33d Cong., sp. sess., Exec. Doc. 4 Serial 688, 231-32. Included in his claim of $25,150 was $1,600 worth of property Indians stole from his Mariposa post.
54. *Stockton Times*, January 22, 1851; *Sacramento Transcript*, February 1, 1851; Harris, *The Gila Trail*, 147-48.
55. C. D. Gibbes to editors, Washington City, December 23, 1850, *Stockton Times*, January 4, 1851.
56. Burney to Hutchings, March 20, 1885.
57. Gibbes to editors, December 23, 1850.
58. Burney to Hutchings, March 20, 1885.
59. *Mariposa Gazette*, January 18, 1879.
60. C. D. Gibbes to editors, Washington City, December 29, 1850, *Stockton Times*, January 11, 1851.
61. Unidentified newspaper article, n.d. Marvin, Scrapbooks, vol. 1.
62. Perkins, *Three Years in California*, 198. Only a few months before, the residents of Sonora feared not Indians but "the Peons of Mexico, the renegades of South America, and the convicts of the British Empire." See *Sonora Herald*, July 27, 1850.
63. *Stockton Times*, January 8, 25, 1851.
64. *San Francisco Daily, Alta California*, January l, 1851.
65. Ibid., January 6, 1851.
66. *Stockton Times*, January 25, 1851.
67. *Stockton Journal*, January 25, 1851.
68. *Stockton Times*, February 5, 1851.
69. C. D. Gibbes to editors, Stockton, February 15, 1851, *Stockton Times*, February 19, 1851.
70. William J. Howard to editors, Howard's Ranch, March 17, 1905, *Gazette-Mariposan*, April 15, 1905.
71. Eccleston, *The Mariposa Indian War*, 16.

72. Howard to editors, March 17, 1905.
73. Palmer to Father, January 16, 1851, 30-31.
74. Unidentified newspaper article, n.d., Marvin, Scrapbooks, vol. 1.
75. R. W. to editors, January 27, 1851.
76. Palmer to Father, January 16, 1851, 31 .
77. Ibid.
78. R. W. to editors, January 27, 1851.
79. J. M. Hogan, interview, *Stockton Journal*, January 29, 1851; E.C. to editors, Empire City, January 19, 1851, *San Francisco Daily Herald*, January 25, 1851; *Sacramento Transcript*, February 1, 1851.
80. R. W. to editors, January 27, 1851.
81. Unidentified newspaper article, n.d., Marvin, Scrapbooks, vol. 1.
82. R. W. to editors, January 27, 1851; James Burney to editors, Agua Fría, January 13, 1851, *Stockton Journal*, January 18, 1851.
83. Palmer to Father, January 16, 1851, 33.
84. John G. Marvin, "Some Account of the Tulare Valley, and the Indians from the Fresno River to Tihone Pass," no. 5, *San Francisco Morning Post*, n.d., Marvin, Scrapbooks, vol. 1.
85. James Burney to Peter Burnett, Agua Fría, January 13, 1851, California Legislature, *Journal of the Senate*, 2d sess., 605; *San Francisco Daily, Alta California*, January 21, 1851.
86. Eccleston, *The Mariposa Indian War*, 17-18.
87. Bunnell, *Discovery of the Yosemite*, 13-14.
88. Howard to editors, March 17, 1905. In 1857, Bautista guided six white men to the scene of the battle and bragged about defeating Savage. See O'Meara, "White Medicine Man," 156.
89. Eccleston, *The Mariposa Indian War*, 18-19; R.W to editors, Castoria, February 4, 1851, *San Francisco Daily, Alta California*, February 7, 1851.
90. *Sacramento Transcript*, February 1, 1851.
91. Eccleston, *The Mariposa Indian War*, 18; R. W. to editors, Castoria, January 22, 1851, *San Francisco Daily, Alta California*, January 26, 1851.
92. R. W. to editors, January 27, 1851.
93. R. W. to editors, February 4, 1851.
94. C. to editors, Mariposa, February 8, 1851, *Stockton Journal*, February 15, 1851; A. to editors, Agua Fría, February 14, 1851, *Stockton Times*, February 22, 1851. The fight is described in Marvin, "Some Account of the Tulare Valley," no. 2, *San Francisco Morning Post*, n.d., Marvin, Scrapbooks, vol. 1; Bunnell, *Discovery of the Yosemite*, 11-12; and Granger, *Letters of Lewis Granger*, 30-31.
95. Bunnell, *Discovery of the Yosemite*, 14-15.
96. Ibid., 15-16.
97. J. R. W. to editors, Quartzburg, January 26, 1851, *San Francisco Pacific News*, February 7, 1851.

98. "Mountaineer" to editors, Oak Flat, February 16, 1851, *Stockton Times*, February 26, 1851.
99. B. to editors, Agua Fría, February 11, 1851, *Stockton Times*, February 19, 1851.
100. Anonymous to editors, Stockton, February 11, 1851, *San Francisco Daily, Alta California*, February 13, 1851.
101. Anonymous to editors, Sonora, n,d., *San Francisco Daily, Alta California*, February 15, 1851.
102. C. D. Gibbes to editors, Stockton, March 7, 1851, *Stockton Times*, March 8, 12, 1851.
103. Capt. E. D. Keyes to Asst. Adj. Gen. Edward R. S. Canby, Camp McKee, March 2, 1851, Pacific Division, Records of the 10th Military Department, Letters Received, 1846-1851, RG 98, Microcopy 210, Roll 5, NA. For a description of the fight, see. E. D. to editors, Little Mariposa River, March 2, 1851, *San Francisco Daily, Alta California*, March 8, 1851.
104. *Sacramento Transcript*, March 14, 1851.
105. James D. Savage to Gov. John McDougal, Mariposa, March 9, 1851, California Legislature, *Journal of the Assembly*, 2d sess., 1369. Excerpts of the letter were published in the *Stockton Times* of March 26, 1851.
106. Anonymous to editors, Mariposa, March 6, 1851, unidentified newspaper article, Marvin, Scrapbooks, vol. 1; *San Francisco Courier*, March 10, 1851.
107. *San Francisco Daily, Alta California*, March 17, 1851.
108. John G. Marvin, "Mariposa Indian 'War," no. 4, *Sacramento Democratic State Journal*, n.d., Marvin, Scrapbooks, vol. 2.
109. *Stockton Times*, March 15, 1851.

Chapter X: State Interposition

1. J. M. Bondurant and Richard H. Daly to Gov. Peter Burnett, Agua Fría, January 13, 1851, California Legislature, *Journal of the Senate*, 2d sess., 603.
2. James Burney to Gov. Peter Bumett, Agua Fría, January 13, 1851, ibid., 605.
3. Message from the Governor in relation to El Dorado, Mariposa, Bear Creek, and Gila Expeditions, San José, January 18, 1851, ibid., 599-600.
4. Gov. John McDougal to J. Neely Johnson, San José, January 25, 1851, ibid., 672.
5. Special Message of the Governor of the State of California to the Legislature, in Relation to the Indian Hostilities in Mariposa County, with Accompanying Documents, San José, January 20, 1851, ibid., 601-602.

6. *San Francisco Daily, Alta California,* January 23, 1851; *Sacramento Transcript,* January 25, 1851.
7. *San Francisco Daily, Alta California,* January 24, 1851, *Stockton Journal,* January 25, 1851.
8. D. P. Baldwin, Minority Report, January 22, 1851, California Legislature, *Journal of the Assembly,* 2d sess., 966-67.
9. *San Francisco Daily, Alta California,* January 24, 1851.
10. Ibid.
11. "Nous Verrous" to editors, Stockton, January 25, 1851, *San Francisco Pacific News,* n.d., John G. Marvin, Scrapbooks, vol. 1, 1840-1853, HM 51846, Huntington Library, San Marino, Calif.
12. *San Francisco Daily, Alta California,* January 26, 1851.
13. *Journal of the Assembly,* 2d sess., January 25, 1851, 1013-14; *San Francisco Daily, Alta California,* January 17, 1851.
14. *Journal of the Assembly,* 2d sess., January 27, 1851, 1018-19.
15. *San Francisco Daily, Alta California,* January 26, 1851.
16. Ibid., January 24, 1851.
17. Report of the Finance Committee on Indian Affairs, January 28, 1851, *Journal of the Senate,* 2d sess., 678.
18. *San Jose Daily Argus,* January 31, 1851.
19. Gov. John McDougal to Gen. Persifer F. Smith, San José, January 28, 1851, *Journal of the Senate,* 2d sess., 670-71.
20. Gen. Persifer F. Smith to Gen. R. Jones, Sonoma, March 13, 1851. U.S. Congress, House, 33d Cong., lst sess., Exec. Doc. 2, Serial 634, 137-38.
21. McDougal to Johnson, January 25, 672-75.
22. *Stockton Transcript,* February 28, 1851.
23. C. to editors, Mariposa, February 8, 1851, *Stockton Journal,* February 15, 1851.
24. B. to editors, Agua Fría, February 11, 1851, *Stockton Times,* February 19, 1851. In March or April 1851, one of the volunteers discovered in the Yosemite Valley a bridle and part of a riata which had been attached to the mule Indians had stolen while he was waiting for the Indian commissioners to conduct a treaty. See Bunnell, *Discovery of the Yosemite,* 86.
25. J. E. D. to editors, Camp Winn, February 21, 1851, *San Francisco Daily, Alta California,* February 28, 1851.
26. Bunnell, *Discovery of the Yosemite,* 44-45; *Sacramento Transcript,* February 28, 1851.
27. The name, rank, age, and home state of each volunteer in each company are listed in an appendix in Eccleston, *The Mariposa Indian War,* 131-41.
28. J. E. D. to editors, February 21, 1851; C. to editors, February 8, 1851.

29. James Burney to J. M. Hutchings, Modesto, March 20, 1885, Yosemite Museum Library, Yosemite National Park, Calif.
30. "An Act Authorizing the Governor to Call Out Troops to Defend Our Frontier, and Providing for Their Pay and Compensation," March 11, 1851, *The Statutes of California*, 402-403.
31. J. Neely Johnson to John G. Marvin, Agua Fría, February 14, 1851, California Legislature, *Journal of the Assembly*, 3d sess., 375-76.
32. Brownlee, *An American Odyssey*, 125, 145n.
33. J. Neely Johnson to James Savage, Agua Fría, February 15, 1851, in John G. Marvin, "Mariposa Indian War," no. 9, *Sacramento Democratic State Journal*, n.d., John G. Marvin, Scrapbooks, vol. 2, 1852-1854, HM 51847, Huntington Library, San Marino, Calif.; *Sacramento Transcript*, February 21, 1851 .
34. James Savage to Gov. John McDougal, Agua Fría, February 16, 1851 in Marvin, "Mariposa Indian War," no. 10. Savage may have been illiterate. If so, colleagues wrote his letters for him.
35. *The San Francisco Courier*, February 19, 1851.
36. The Statutes of California, 1851, 520-21; *San Francisco Herald*, February 12, 1851; *Sacramento Transcript*, February 14, 1851.
37. *California State Journal*, March 26, 1851.
38. Unidentified newspaper article, Marvin, Scrapbooks, vol. 1.
39. John G. Marvin to Gov. John McDougal, Vallejo, July 19, 1851, Governors Papers, Miscellaneous Communications Received, 1851, GP1:118, California State Archives, Sacramento, Calif.; *San Francisco Daily, Alta California*, March 10, 1851.
40. Marvin, "Mariposa Indian War," no. 11.
41. John G. Marvin to Gov. John McDougal, Benicia, March 11, 1851, California Legislature, *Journal of the Assembly*, 3d sess., 376-77.
42. Ibid.
43. Marvin, "Mariposa Indian War," no. 9
44. Message of the Governor, March 15, 1851, *Journal of the Assembly*, 2d sess.
45. Ibid., 1371-73.
46. "An Act Authorizing the Governor to Call Out Troops," 402-403.
47. Gov. John McDougal to President Millard Fillmore, San José, March 1, 1851, U.S. Congress, House, 32d Cong., lst sess., Exec. Doc. 2, Serial 634, 138-40.
48. C.M. Conrad to Gov. John McDougal, Washington, D.C., April 30, 1851, ibid., 140-42.
49. James Savage to John Kuykendall, Mariposa, March 1, 1851, quoted in Elliot, *History of Fresno County, California*, 178.
50. J. E. D. to editors, Little Mariposa, March 17, 18, 1851, *San Francisco Daily, Alta California*, March 24, 1851; Capt. E. D. Keyes to Asst. Adj.

Gen. Edward R. S. Canby, Camp Fremont, March 19, 1851, Pacific Division, Records of the 10th Military Department, Letters Received, 1846-1851, RG 98, Microcopy 210 Roll 5, NA. Keyes identified the Indians as Pitkachi and Chukchansi.

51. James Savage to John Kuykendall, Camp no. 3, March 18, 1851, quoted in Elliot, *History of Fresno County*, 179.

Chapter XI: Negotiations Begin

1. Redick McKee to Luke Lea, San Francisco, January 13, 1851, U.S. Congress, Senate, 33d Cong., sp. sess., Exec. Doc. 4, Serial 688, 53-54.
2. George Barbour, Redick McKee, and O. M. Wozencraft to Luke Lea Graysonville, February 17, 1851, ibid., 56.
3. Redick McKee to Luke Lea, Stockton, February 11, 1851, ibid.; *San Francisco Daily, Alta California*, February 12, 1851.
4. Asst. Adj. Gen. Edward R. S. Canby to Capt. E. D. Keyes, San Francisco February 1, 1851, Pacific Division, Records of the 10th Military Department Letters Received, 1846-1851, RG 98, Microcopy 210, Roll 1, NA.
5. McKee to Lea, February 11, 1851.
6. Barbour, McKee, and Wozencraft to Lea, February 17, 1851, 57; *San Francisco Daily, Alta California*, February 13, 1851 .
7. George Barbour to Luke Lea, n.d., Received in the Indian Office on the 2d February, 1852, U.S. Congress, Senate, 33d Cong., sp. sess., Exec. Doc. 4, Serial 688, 250-51.
8. J. E. D. to editors, Graysonville, February 15, 1851, *San Francisco Daily, Alta California*, February 20, 1851.
9. Barbour, McKee, and Wozencraft to Lea, February 17, 1851-58.
10. J. E. D. to editors, February 15, 1851.
11. Barbour, McKee, and Wozencraft to Lea, February 17, 1851-59.
12. J. E. D. to editors, Tuolumne River, February 21, 1851, *San Francisco Daily, Alta California*, February 28, 1851.
13. J. M. H. to editors, Tuolumne River, February 20, 1851, *Stockton Journal*, February 26, 1851.
14. J. E. D. to editors, Tuolumne River, February 24, 1851, *San Francisco Daily, Alta California*, March 1, 1851.
15. George Barbour and O. M. Wozencraft to Luke Lea, Mariposa River, March 5, 1851, U.S. Congress, Senate, 33d Cong., sp. sess., Exec. Doc. 4, Serial 688, 60-61.
16. Ibid., 61-62.
17. Ibid.
18. J. E. D. to editors, Little Mariposa, March 2, 1851, *San Francisco Daily, Alta California*, March 8, 1851.

19. George Barbour and Redick McKee to Luke Lea, Camp Gibson, March 25, 1851, U.S. Congress, Senate, 33d Cong., sp. sess., Exec. Doc. 4, Serial 688, 69.
20. Bunnell, *Discovery of the Yosemite*, 42.
21. Barbour and McKee to Lea, March 25, 1851.
22. J. E. D. to editors, Little Mariposa, March 16, 1851, *San Francisco Daily, Alta California*, March 24, 1851.
23. Barbour and McKee to Lea, March 25, 1851, 69-70.
24. Ibid., 70.
25. Capt. E. D. Keyes to Act. Asst. Adj. Gen. E. Steele, San Francisco [sic], May 10, 1851, Pacific Division, Records of the 10th Military Department, Letters Received, 1846-1851, RG 98, Microcopy 210, Roll 5.
26. Barbour and McKee to Lea, March 25, 1851, 70.
27. "Treaty Made and Concluded at Camp Frémont, State of California, March 19, 1851, Between Redick McKee and Others, Commissioners on the Part of the United States, and the Chiefs, Captains, and Head Men of the Si-yan-te, etc., Tribes of Indians," in Kappler, ed., *Indian Affairs: Laws and Treaties*, vol. 4, 1081-82.
28. Ibid., 1082-83.
29. Ibid., 1083.
30. Ibid., 1083-85.
31. Perlot, *Gold Seeker*, 224.
32. Luke Lea to Redick McKee, George Barbour, and O. M. Wozencraft, Washington, D.C., May 22, 1851, U.S. Congress, Senate, 33d Cong., sp. sess., Exec. Doc. 4, Serial 688, 15.
33. Redick McKee to Luke Lea, Camp Gibson, March 24, 1851, ibid., 67. McKee's emphasis.
34. Charles E. Mix to Redick McKee, Washington, D.C., August 9, 1851, ibid., 19.
35. *Office Copy of the Laws, Regulation, Etc., of the Indian Bureau, 1850,* 23-24.
36. Ibid., 17-19.
37. Luke Lea to Redick McKee, Washington, D.C., November 9, 1850, U.S. Congress, Senate, 33d Cong., sp. sess., Exec. Doc. 4, Serial 688, 12.
38. See, for example, the treaty with the Florida Indians in *Treaties between the United States of America and the Several Indian Tribes, from 1778 to 1837*, 307-13. For a history of treaties, see Prucha, *American Indian Treaties: The History of a Political Anomaly*.
39. O. M. Wozencraft, "Indian Affairs, 1849-50," D-D 204, Bancroft Library, Berkeley, Calif.
40. *Stockton Times*, March 26, 1851.
41. Wozencraft, "Indian Affairs. "

42. *San Francisco Daily, Alta California,* March 25, 1851.
43. Wozencraft, "Indian Affairs."
44. Capt. E. D. Keyes to Asst. Adj. Gen. Edward R. S. Canbv, Camp McLean, April 11, 1851, Pacific Division, Records of the 10th Military Department, Letters Received, 1846-1851, RG 98, Microcopy 210, Roll 3, NA; Wozencraft, "Indian Affairs," *San Francisco Daily, Alta California,* June 18, 1852.

Chapter XII: Yosemite and Chauchila Defiance

1. M. to editors, San José, April 22, 1851, *San Francisco Daily, Alta California*, April 23, 1851.
2. Bunnell, *Discovery of the Yosemite,* 51-52.
3. M. to editors, April 22, 1851.
4. Bunnell, *Discovery of the Yosemite*, 52.
5. Ibid., 54.
6. Bunnell, "How the Yo-semite Valley Was Discovered and Named," 499.
7. Bunnell, *Discovery of the Yosemite*, 54.
8. Ibid., 54-55.
9. Ibid., 56-59.
10. M. to editors, April 22, 1851.
11. Bunnell, *Discovery of the Yosemite*, 60.
12. Carl Russell, "Interview with Maria Lebrado at Bear Creek," February 1928, Yosemite Museum Library, Yosemite National Park, Calif.
13. Bunnell, *Discovery of the Yosemite*, 60-62.
14. In one publication, Bunnell stated that the battalion entered the valley about March 21. See Bunnel, *Discovery of the Yosemite,* 78. That date, however, is too early. In another publication, he identified March as the month the valley was "discovered" but did not say which day. See Bunnell, "The Date of the Discovery of the Yosemite," 796.
15. Bunnell, *Discovery of the Yosemite*, 81-83.
16. Bunnell, "How the Yo-semite Valley was Discovered and Named," 500. A slightly different version of the encounter is provided by M. to editors, April 22, 1851.
17. Bunnell, *Discovery of the Yosemite*, 84-88.
18. M. to editors, April 22, 1851.
19. Bunnell, *Discovery of the Yosemite,* 98-100.
20. Eccleston, *The Mariposa Indian War*, 50.
21. Bunnell, *Discovery of the Yosemite,* 107.
22. John McKee, "Journal of the United States Indian Commissioners for California, Camp McLean, April 5, 1851," U.S. Congress, Senate, 33d Cong., sp. sess., Exec. Doc. 4, Serial 688, 88-89.
23. Ibid., 89-91.

24. Bunnell, *Discovery of the Yosemite*, 110.
25. M. to editors, April 22, 1851.
26. Bunnell, *Discovery of the Yosemite*, 110.
27. Redick McKee, "Journal of the United States Indian Commissioners, April 27, 1851," 92.
28. Bunnell, *Discovery of the Yosemite*, 717.
29. John Bowling to James Savage, San Joaquin River, April 29, 1851, *San Francisco Daily, Alta California*, June 11, 1851.
30. Bunnell, *Discovery of the Yosemite*, 122-23.
31. Bowling to Savage, April 29, 1851.
32. Ibid.
33. Eccleston, *The Mariposa Indian War*, 71.
34. Bunnell, *Discovery of the Yosemite*, 128-29. Bunnell's emphasis.
35. Ibid., 142-44.
36. James Savage to John Bowling, Camp Fresno, May 4, 1851, quoted in Elliott, *History of Fresno County*, 179-80.
37. R. E. Russell to M. B. Lewis, Camp Fresno, May 17, 1851, *San Francisco Daily, Alta California*, June 12, 1851.
38. Ibid.
39. John Bowling to James Savage, Merced River, May 15, 1851, ibid.
40. Bunnell, *Discovery of the Yosemite*, 151-52.
41. Bowling to Savage, May 15, 1851.
42. Bunnell, *Discovery of the Yosemite*, 168.
43. Ibid., 167-70. In John Bowling's account of the events, only one of the five Indians captured was Tenaya's son and two Indians were killed while attempting to escape. See Bowling to Savage May 15, 1851.
44. Bowling to Savage, April 29, 1851.
45. Bunnel, *Discovery of the Yosemite*, 156-58.
46. Ibid., 173.
41. Ibid., 176-78.
48. Ibid., 192-93.
49. Ibid., 194.
50. Bowling to Savage, May 15, 1851.
51. Bunnell, *Discovery of the Yosemite*, 195-97.
52. Ibid., 197-98.
53. John Bowling to George Barbour, Fresno River, May 29, 1851, *San Francisco Daily, Alta California*, June 14, 1851. Bowling identified Panwatchee as the leader of the Nukchu scouts.
54. Bunnell, *Discovery of the Yosemite*, 225-28.
55. Ibid., 230-31.
56. Ibid., 231-34.
57. Bunnell, "How the Yo-semite Valley was Discovered and Named,"

502.
58. Bunnell, *Discovery of the Yosemite*, 237, 241.
59. Bowling to Barbour, May 29, 1851.
60. Bunnell, *Discovery of the Yosemite*, 242.

Chapter XIII: Negotiations Conclude

1. Capt. E. D. Keyes to Capt. L. Steele, Camp Barbour, April 22, 1851, Pacific Division, Records of the 10th Military Department, Letters Received, 1846-1851, RG 98, Microcopy 210, Roll 7, NA.
2. Redick McKee, George Barbour, and O. M. Wozencraft to Luke Lea, Camp Barbour, May 1, 1851, U.S. Congress, Senate, 33d Cong, sp. sess, Exec. Doc. 4, Serial 688, 74-75.
3. John McKee, "Journal of the United States Indian Commissioners for California," Camp Barbour, April 26, 1851, ibid., 93-94.
4. Ibid., 94-95.
5. Ibid., April 28, 1851, 95-96.
6. Ibid., April 29, 1851, 97.
7. "Treaty Made and Concluded at Camp Barbour, on the San Joaquin River, State of California, April 29, 1851, Between Redick McKee and Others, Commissioners on the Part of the United States, and the Chiefs, Captains and Head Men of the How-ech-ees, &tc., Tribes of Indians," in Kappler, ed., *Indian Affairs*, vol. 4, 1087-88.
8. Keyes, *Fiftv Years' Observation*, 237.
9. McKee, "Journal," May 1, 1851, 97-98. The activities of Redick McKee in northern California are discussed in Anderson, "The Hoopa Valley Indian Reservation in Northwestern California: A Study of its Origins," 28-66; Hoopes, "Redick McKee and the Humboldt Bay Region, 1851-1852," 195-219; and Raphael, *Little White Father: Redick McKee on the California Frontier*. Regarding the northern activities of O. M. Wozencraft, see Knoop, "The Federal Indian Policy in the Sacramento Valley, 1846-1860," 61-94.
10. Redick McKee, George Barbour, and O. M. Wozencraft to Luke Lea, Camp Barbour, May 1, 1851, U.S. Congress, Senate, 33d Cong., sp. sess., Exec. Doc. 4, Serial 688, 74-76.
11. Ibid., 76.
12. Redick McKee to Luke Lea, San Francisco, May 13, 1851, ibid., 77.
13. Redick McKee to George W. Barbour, San Francisco, May 13, 1851, ibid.,79.
14. Redick McKee to O. M. Wozencraft, San Francisco, May 13, 1851, ibid., 80.
15. O. M. Wozencraft to Luke Lea, San Francisco, May 14, 1851, ibid., 83-84.
16. George Barbour, "The Journal of George W. Barbour, May 1 to

October 4, 1851," pt. 1, Camp Belt, May 5-11, 1851," 148-49.

17. "Treaty Made and Concluded at Camp Belt, on King's River, in the State of California, May 13, 1851, Between George W. Barbour, Commissioner on the Part of the United States, and the Chiefs, Captains, and Head Men of the Taches, Cah-Wai, etc., etc., Tribes of Indians," in Kappler, ed., *Indian Affairs*, vol. 4, 1093.
18. George Barbour to Luke Lea, Camp Belt, May 14, 1851, U.S. Congress, Senate, 33d Cong., sp. sess., Exec. Doc. 4, Serial 688, 81.
19. John G. Marvin, "Some Account of the Tulare Valley, and the Indians from the Fresno River to Tihone Pass," no. 2, *Sacramento Democratic State Journal*, n.d., John G. Marvin, Scrapbooks, vol. 1, 1840-1853, HM 51846, Huntington Library, San Marino, Calif. See also Granger, *Letters of Lewis Granger*, 30-31.
20. Thomas Paine to editors, Stockton, March 3, 1851, *Stockton Times*, March 5, 1851; *Sacramento Daily Union*, May 7, 1856.
21. Barbour, "The Journal," pt. 1, Camp Belt, May 12, 1851, 149-50.
22. Ibid., 150.
23. "Treaty Made and Concluded at Camp Belt," 1092.
24. Barbour, "The Journal," pt. 1, May 12, 1851, 150-51.
25. "Treaty Made and Concluded at Camp Belt," 1093-94.
26. Barbour, "The Journal," pt. 1, May 12, 1851, 151.
27. Barbour to Lea, May 14, 1851, 81.
28. Capt. E. D. Keyes to Capt. E Steele, Camp Barbour, April 22, 1851, Pacific Division, Records of the 10th Military Department, Letters Received, 1846-1851, RG 98, Microcopy 210, Roll 7, NA.
29. Capt. E. D. Keyes to Capt. F. Steele, Camp Barbour, May 1, 1851, ibid.
30. Capt. E. D. Keyes to George Barbour, Camp Belt, May 21, 1851, U.S. Congress, Senate, 33d Cong., sp. sess., Exec. Doc. 4, Serial 688, 264.
31. George Barborn to Capt. E. D. Keyes, Camp Belt, May 21, 1851,35., ibid., 265.
32. Capt. E. D. Keyes to Capt. E. Steele, Camp Belt, May 25, 1851, Pacific Division, Records of the l0th Military Department, Letters Received, 1846-1851, RG 98, Microcopy 210, Roll 7, NA.
33. Col. George A. McCall to Maj. Gen. Winfield Scott, Fort Miller, July 29, 1852, Records of the Adjutant General's Office, 1780s-1917, Letters Received, 1822-1860, RG 94, Microcopy 56Z, Roll 483, NA. For a history of the fort, see Richter, *Fort Miller, California, 1851-1865.*
34. Latta, *Handbook of Yokuts Indians*, 662.
35. "Treaty Made and Concluded at Dent & Vantine's Crossing," May 28, 1851, Between O. M. Wozencraft, United States Commissioner, and the Chiefs and Head Men of Iou-ol-Umnes, Wethillas, &tc.,

Tribes of Indians," in Kappler, ed., *Indian Affairs*, 1096-98.

36. O. M. Wozencraft to Luke Lea, Dent and Vantine's Ferry, May 28, 1851, U.S. Congress, Senate, 33d Cong., sp. sess., Exec. Doc. 4, Serial 688, 84.
37. O. M. Wozencraft to editors, n.d., n.p., *San Francisco Daily, Alta California*, October 10, 1851.
38. "Treaty Made and Concluded at Dent & Vantine's Crossing," 1098-99; *San Francisco Daily, Alta California*, May 31, 1851.
39. J. E. D. to editors, Graysonville, February 15, 1851, *San Francisco Daily, Alta California*, February 20, 1851.
40. In an article entitled "California Indian Chiefs," the *Sacramento Union* of January 31, 1857 stated that José Jesús was poisoned at a store run by a Frenchman on the Mokelumne River. A miner, however, claimed that he was shot near Stockton by the son of a New York clergyman. See Alfred A. Green, "Life and Adventures of a 47-er of California," 1878, C-D 94, Bancroft Library, Berkeley, Calif
41. "Treaty Made and Concluded at Dent & Vantine's Crossing," 1099.
42. George Barbour, "The Journal of George W. Barbour, May 1, to October 4, 1851," pt. 2, Camp Keyes, May 29, 1851, 247.
43. George Barbour to Luke Lea, San Francisco, July 28, 1851, U.S. Congress, Senate, 33d Cong., sp. sess., Exec. Doc. 4, Serial 688, 122-23.
44. "Treaty Made and Concluded at Camp Keyes, on the Cah-wai River, in the State of
California, May 30, 1851, Between George W. Barbour, United States Commissioner, and the Chiefs, Captains and Head Men of the Ko-ya-te, Wo-a-si, etc., Tribes of Indians," Kappler, ed., *Indian Affairs*, vol. 4, 1094-95.
45. Barbour to Lea, July 28, 1851, 123.
46. "Treaty Made and Conducted at Camp Keyes," 1095.
47. Barbour, "The Journal," pt. 2, Camp Keyes, May 29, 1851, 247-48.
48. "Treaty Made and Conducted at Camp Keyes," 1096.
49. H. to editors, Camp Belt, May 23, 1851, *San Francisco Daily, Alta California*, May 29, 1851.
50. Barbour, "The Journal" pt. 2, Paint Creek, May 30-31, June 1-2, 1851," 248. Paint Creek is now known as Deer Creek.
51. "Treaty Made and Concluded at Camp Burton, on Paint Creek, State of California, June 3, 1851, Between George W. Barbour, United States Commissioner, and the Chiefs, Captains and Head Men of the Chu-nute, Wo-wol, &., Tribes of Indians," in Kappler, ed., *Indian Affairs*, vol. 4, 1099-1100.
52. George Barbour to Luke Lea, n.p., n.d., Received at Indian Office on the 2d February, 1852. U.S. Congress, Senate, 33d Cong., sp.

sess., Exec. Doc. 4, Serial 688, 256.

53. Barbour, "The Journal" pt. 2, Camp Burton, June 3, 1851, 248-49.
54. "Treaty Made and Concluded al Camp Burton," 1100.
55. George Barbour to Luke Lea, Princeton, Kentucky, January 5, 1852, Report of the Secretary of the Interior, U.S. Congress, Senate, 32d Cong., lst sess., Exec. Doc. 61, Serial 620, 4.
56. Barbour, "The Journal," pt. 2, Camp Burton, June 4, 1851, 249.
57. Barbour to Lea, Received at Indian Office on the 2d February 1852, 256.
58. Barbour, "Journal," pt. 2, Camp Persifer F. Smith, June 7, 8, 1851, 249; Keyes, *Fifty Years' Observation*, 236.
59. Barbour, "Journal," pt. 2, June to, 1851, 249.
60. Keyes, *Fifty Years' Observation*, 236.
61. Barbour, "Journal," pt. 2, June to, 1851, 249-50.
62. "Treaty Made and Concluded at Camp Persifer F. Smith at the Texan [sic] Pass, State of California, June 10, 1851, Between George W. Barbour, United States Commissioner, and the Chiefs, Captains and Head Men of 'Castake,' 'Texon,' &tc., Tribes of Indians," in Kappler, ed., *Indian Affairs*, vol. 4, 1102. Rafael Maria's full name was Rafael Jvlaria Aguinamogihuason. In the treaty, Mat'apxwelxwel was called Uvas. The Yokuts called it Lapnaw. See Johnson, "Indians of Mission San Fernando," 263-64; and Johnson, "Trail to Kashtiq," 190.
63. Barbour, "Journal," pt. 2, June to 1851, 250.
64. Johnson, "Chumash Social Organization," 238. According to Merriam, "Carises," the area Raymundo represented and identified by Barbour in his journal, was an Indian name for Kern Lake, the homeland of the Hometwoli. See Merriam, "So-Called Tribes," and Heizer, "Analysis of 'Tribes'."
65. Latta, "Alexis Godey," 42.
66. Juan Coluco, deposition, Tule River Indian Agency, February 23, 1922, and José Juan, testimony, n.d., in Harrington Papers, vol. 2.
67. Barbour, "Journal," pt. 2, June 10, 1851, 250.
68. Johnson, "Indians of Mission San Fernando," 263.
69. "Treaty Made and Concluded at Camp Persifer F. Smith," June 10, 1851, 1101.
70. Ibid., 1101-2.
71. Barbour. "Journal," pt. 2, June 10, 1851, 250.
72. Ibid., 250-51.
73. Ibid., 251; Luke Lea to Redick McKee, George Barbour and O. M. Wozencraft, Washington, D.C., April 72, 1851, U.S. Congress, Senate, 33d Cong., sp. sess.," Exec. Doc 4. Serial 688, 14.
74. Capt. E. D. Keyes to George Barbour, Camp Magruder, June 17,

1851, ibid., 127.

75. Barbour to Lea, July 28, 1851, 124-25.
76. Barbour, "The Journal," pt. 2, Tejón Pass, July 6, 1857, 251-52.
77. Ibid., Fort Miller, July 16, 1851, 253.
78. Barbour to Lea, Received at Indian Office on 2d February, 1852, 260
79. Barbour to Lea, July 28, 1851, 125.
80. Barbour, "The Journal," pt. 2, Fort Miller, August 23, 25, 1851, 255.
81. Barbour to Lea, Received at Indian Office on 2d February, 1852, 260.
82. Barbour, "The Journal," pt. 2, San Francisco, September 8, 1851, 255.
83. Ibid., 256-57
84. Barbour to Lea, Received at Indian Office on 2d February, 1952, 264.
85. George Barbour to President Millard Fillmore, Washington, D.C., February 2, 1852, U.S. Congress, Senate, 33d Cong., sp. sess., Exec. Doc. 4, Serial 688, 268.
86. "Treaty Made and Concluded at the Fork of the Cosumnes River, September 18, 1851, between O. M. Wozencraft, United States Indian Agent, and the Chiefs, Captains, and Head Men of the Cu-lu, Yas-si, etc., Tribes of Indians," in Kappler, ed., *Indian Affairs*, 1115-17.
87. "California Indian Chiefs," *Sacramento Union*, January 31, 1857.
88. "Treaty Made and Concluded at the Fork of the Cosumnes River," 1117.
89. O. M. Wozencraft to Luke Lea, San Francisco, December 1, 1851, U.S. Congress, Senate, 33d Cong., sp. sess., Exec. Doc. 4, Serial 688, 230.
90. For a discussion of the uprising and the activities of Wozencraft in Southern California see George Harwood Phillips, *Chiefs and Challengers: Indian Resistance and Cooperation in Southern California, 1769-1906*, 99-130.
91. O. M. Wozencraft to Luke Lea, n.d., n.p., Letters Received by the Office of Indian Affairs, 1824-1881, California Superintendency, 1849-1852, Microcopy 234, Roll 32, NA; *Sacramento Daily Union*, January 8, 1852.
92. *Los Angeles Star*, November 8, 1851.
93. Wozencraft to Lea, n.d., Letters Received by the office of Indian Affairs.
94. Ellison, *A Self-governing Dominion*, 149. According to an anthropologist, of the 139 signatory groups, 67 were tribelets (distinct political groups), 45 villages, 14 duplicates spelled differently and 13 either unidentifiable or personal names. See Heizer, "Treaties," 703.

Chapter XIV: Administering to the Indians

1. George Barbour and Redick McKee to Luke Lea, Camp Gibson, March 25, 1851, U.S. Congress, Senate, 33d Cong., sp. sess., Exec. Doc. 4, Serial 688, 70.
2. Redick McKee, George Barbour, and O. M. Wozencraft to Luke Lea, Camp Barbour, May 1, 1851, ibid., 75.
3. Adam Johnston to Luke Lea, Merced Indian Reservation, June 24, 1851, ibid., 105; Adam Johnston, deposition, March 31, 1858, in United States Court of Claims, Felix Argenti vs. The United States, George W. Wright Manuscript, California Historical Society Library, San Francisco, Calif., 66.
4. Agreement between Adam Johnston and Isaac H. Marks and Samuel Stone, Mariposa County, June 4, 1851, U.S. Congress, Senate, 33d Cong, sp. sess., Exec. Doc. 4, Serial 688, 110-11.
5. Adam Johnston to Luke Lea, Merced Indian Reservation, April 11, 1851, ibid., 72-74.
6. Ibid., 73-74.
7. Johnston to Lea, June 24, 1851, 108.
8. Redick McKee to Luke Lea, San Francisco, June 30, 1851, ibid., 109.
9. George G. Belt to Adam Johnston, Merced River, May 8, 1851, ibid., 103-104.
10. Ibid.
11. Adam Johnston to Luke Lea, Merced River, June 24, 1851, ibid., 103. Although written on the same day, this is a different letter than the one cited in notes 3 and 7 above.
12. Adam Johnston, voucher, Merced Reservation, n.d., in George G. Belt's Executrix vs. The United States, Cases Decided in the Court of Claims at the December Term, 1879, vol. 15, 99.
13. Ward, *Sam Ward in the Gold Rush*, 46-47.
14. Anderson, *The Mystery of "A Public Man"*, 146-50.
15. Thomas, *Sam Ward: "King of the Lobby,"* 158-69, 175-77.
16. Ibid., 179-80.
17. Ward, *Sam Ward in the Gold Rush*, 22.
18. Ibid., 24-25.
19. Samuel Ward to Julia Ward Howe, Merced Reservation, February 2, 1852, quoted in Elliott, *Uncle Sam Ward and His Circle*, 431.
20. Ward, *Sam Ward in the Gold Rush,* 44-45.
21. Ibid., 45.
22. Ward to Howe, February 2, 1852.
23. Samuel Ward, statement, n.p., n.d., in Ward, *Sam Ward in the Gold Rush*, 47n.
24. Ibid., 51-52n.

25. William J. Howard, Testimony Government Relations with the Mariposa Indians, Copy of Reporter's Transcript, vol. 4, September 27, 1890, Mary Corcoran Papers, Bancroft Library, Berkeley, Calif., 20-21, 27.
26. Ward, *Sam Ward in the Gold Rush*, 51-52n.
27. Ibid., 56-57. Tripoxi is also described in Powers, *Tribes of California,* 353-54.
28. Ward, *Sam Ward in the Gold Rush*, 59-63.
29. Ibid., 63-64.
30. Ibid., 64.
31. Ward to Howe, February 2, 1852, 429-30.
32. Ward, *Sam Ward in the Gold Rush*, 63, 127.
33. Ibid., 68-69.
34. Ibid., 109-12.
35. "Notice," Stanislaus River, May 29, 1851, LP2:1399, California State Archives, Sacramento. Calif.; *San Joaquin Republican*, September 8, 1851.
36. Johnston to Lea, Merced River, June 24, 1851, 102.
37. Adam Johnston to Lewis Dent and James Vantine, Knight's Ferry, May 29, 1851, LP2: 1683, May 30, 1851, LP2: 1684, California State Archives, Sacramento, Calif.
38. Abstract of disbursements made by O. M. Wozencraft, United States Indian agent, from the 1st of May, 1851, to the 30th of August, 1852, inclusive, U.S. Congress, Senate, 33d Cong., sp. sess., Exec. Doc. 4, Serial 688, 399.
39. Johnston to Lea, June 24, 1851, 102.
40. Charles Mix to Adam Johnston, Washington, D.C., August 12, 1851, ibid., 21.
41. W. M. Ryer to Adam Johnston, Merced River, June 1, 1851, ibid., 198.
42. Contract between Adam Johnston and W. M. Ryer, Merced Indian Reservation, June 11, 1851, ibid., 199.
43. W. M. Ryer to Adam Johnston, Stanislaus River, July 1, 1851, ibid., 199.
44. W. M. Ryer to Adam Johnston, Kaweah River, September 26, 1851, ibid., 202.
45. Adam Johnston to Luke Lea, Merced Indian Reservation, October 8, 1851, ibid., 198.
46. W. M. Ryer, Bills for Services Rendered, June 30, July 1, July 31, August 31, September 26, 1851, Report of the Secretary of the Interior, 32d Cong., 1st sess., Exec. Doc. 61, Serial 620, 20-23.
47. Johnston to Lea, June 24, 1851, 107.
48. Mix to Johnston, August 12, 1851, 21.

49. Johnston to Lea, June 24, 1851, 105-106.
50. John C. Frémont to O. M. Wozencraft, San Francisco, May 12, 1851, U.S. Congress, Senate, 33d Cong., 1st sess., Exec. Doc. 87, Serial 702, 2-3.
51. O. M. Wozencraft to John C. Frémont, n.p., n.d., ibid., 3.
52. Redick McKee, deposition, 1858, Argenti vs. The United States, 111-12.
53. John C. Frémont to George Barbour, Mariposa, May 19, 1851, U.S. Congress, Senate, 33d Cong., sp. sess., Exec. Doc. 4, Serial 688, 267.
54. "Treaty Made and Concluded at Camp Keyes, on the Cah-wai River, in the State of California, May 30, 1851, Between George W. Barbour, United States Commissioner, and the Chiefs, Captains and Head Men of the Ko-ya-te, Wo-a-si, etc., Tribes of Indians;" and "Treaty Made and Conducted at Camp Burton, on Paint Creek, State of California, June 3, 1851, Between George W. Barbour, United States Commissioner, and the Chiefs, Captains and Head Men of the Chu-nule, Wo-wol, &tc., Tribes of Indians," in Kappler, *Indian Affairs*, vol. 4, 1096, 1100.
55. George Barbour to Luke Lea, Princeton, Kentucky, January 5, 1852, Report of the Secretary of the Interior, U.S. Congress, 32d Cong., lst sess., Exec. Doc. 61, Serial 620, 2.
56. George Barbour to John C. Frémont, Camp Keyes, May 28, 1851, U.S. Congress, Senate, 33d Cong., sp. sess., Exec. Doc. 4, Serial 688, 267-70.
57. Joel Brooks, deposition, March 10, 1858, Argenti vs. The United States 11-13; *Los Angeles Star*, July 19, 1851.
58. Alexander Godey, deposition, June 24, 1858, Argenti vs. The United States 133, 135, 136.
59. George Barbour to Luke Lea, San Francisco, July 28, 1851, U.S. Congress, Senate, 33d Cong., sp. sess., Exec. Doc. 4, Serial 688, 125.
60. George Barbour to John C. Frémont, Tejón Pass, July 7, 1851, in Spence, ed., *The Expeditions of John Charles Frémont*, vol. 3, 241.
61. George Barbour to John C. Frémont, Kaweah River, July 15, 1851, ibid., 242.
62. Brooks, deposition, March 10, 1858, 13.
63. Godey, deposition, June 24, 1858, 143.
64. Barbour to Lea, January 5, 1854, 4.
65. Henry B. Edwards, Statement, Washington, D.C., January 24, 1852, Report of the Secretary of the Interior, U.S. Congress, Senate, 32d Cong., 1st sess., Exec. Doc. 61, Serial 620, 16-17.
66. "Frémont's Indian Beef Contract–Receipt 1," August 28, 1851, in Spence, ed., *The Expeditions of John Charles Fremont*, vol. 3, 260-61.
67. "Frémont's Indian Beef Contract–Receipt 2," August 28, 1851,

ibid., 261-62.

68. Brooks, deposition, June 24, 1858, 11.
69. Edwards, statement, January 24, 1852, 17; Godey, deposition, June 24, 1858, 146.
70. "Frémont's Indian Beef Contract–Receipt 1," August 28, 1851, 261-62 and notes, 262.
71. "Frémont's Indian Beef Contract–Receipt 2," August 28, 1851, 261-62. Because Frémont received separate drafts for providing cattle on the hoof and beef by the pound, either live animals and butchered beef had been delivered separately at the six reservations or he charged the United States twice for the same number of cattle. The truth is difficult, perhaps impossible, to uncover. Henry Edwards, a Frémont employee, stated in 1852 that he joined the drive before it reached its destination and that 551 animals had been delivered to the Indians residing between the Tejon Pass and the Fresno River. That number, however, is suspiciously precise, the exact sum of the number of animals Frémont claimed were delivered on the hoof (270) and by the pound (281). In a legal case conducted in 1858, Joel Brooks, an unsavory character and notorious liar who was not on the drive, swore that only one delivery had taken place at each reservation. Frémont's trail boss, Alexis Godey, however, testified in the same case that the cattle had been delivered to the reservations, although he could not recall how many. See Edwards, Statement, January 24, 1852, 16-17; Brooks, Deposition, March 10, 1858, 24-25; Godey, deposition, June 24, 1859, 133-34.
72. Adam Johnston, Statement, Fort Miller, August 28, 1851, U.S. Congress, Senate, 33d Cong., sp. sess., Exec. Doc. 4, Serial 688, 268.
73. Adam Johnston, deposition, March 31, 1858, Argenti vs. The United States, 71, 78-79.
74. Johnston to Lea, June 24, 1852, 106.
75. *Daily Alta California*, December 8, 1851. In a deposition given in 1858, Joel Brooks swore that James Savage ordered him to take twice as many receipts for the number of animals actually delivered to the San Joaquin, Kings River, and other reservations to the south and to get three receipts for each head delivered to Fresno Reservation. Brooks's vaqueros would run the cattle until they were hot and mad before turning them over to the Indians on the reservations. Some of the wild steers and bulls would break away from the Indians and make their way back to the main herd. None, Brooks claimed, was returned to the Indians. From the herd of 1,900, the southern Indians received about 250 head. In September 1852, Brooks stated that in October 1851, under orders from Savage, he turned over 78 head of cattle to Alexis Godey to sell to miners, and the following

month he delivered an additional 450 head to Godey for the same purpose. A short time later, Brooks presented over 800 head to an employee of Savage who herded them to the Fresno Reservation. Supposedly Savage gave some of the animals to his Indian workers but kept most of the herd for himself. Brooks insisted that none of the animals were delivered to Indians on the other reservations. At the time he made his statement, Brooks recently had left the employ of Savage under strained circumstances. His claims, therefore, may be highly exaggerated or blatantly false. Adam Johnston, in his 1858 deposition, said they were untrue. See Brooks, deposition, March 10, 1858, 30-31; Brooks, statement, San Francisco, September 21, 1852, U.S. Congress, Senate, 33d Cong., sp. sess., Exec. Doc. 4, Serial 688, 369; Joel Brooks, Official Statement, Sebastian Military Reserve, November 4, 1854, Report of J. Ross Brown and Accompanying Documents, concerning accounts of Supt. Beale, Washington, D.C., January 22, 1855, RG 46, Records of the U.S. Senate, Sen 35A-F2, NA; Adam Johnston, deposition, March 31, 1858, 97.

76. Johnston, deposition, March 31, 1858, 71.
77. Adam Johnston to Gen. E. A. Hitchcock, Merced Indian Reservation, August 4, 1851, U.S. Congress, Senate, 33d Cong., sp. sess., Exec. Doc. 4, Serial 688, 200.
78. Adam Johnston to Luke Lea, Merced Indian Reservation, October 8, 185l, ibid., 197.
79. Johnston to Hitchcock, August 4, 1851, ibid., 200.
80. Johnston to Lea, October 8, 1851, ibid., 196.
81. Gen. E. A. Hitchcock to Gov. John McDougal, Benicia, August 6, 1851, in unidentified newspaper, John G. Marvin, Scrapbooks, Vol. 1, 1840-1853, HM 51846, Huntington Library, San Marino, Calif.
82. V. Van Voorhies to Gen. E. A. Hitchcock, August 14, 1851, in unidentified newspaper, ibid.
83. Johnston to Lea, October 8, 1851, 195-96.
84. Lieut. Treadwell Moore to Adam Johnston, Fort Miller, August 20, 1851, Letters Received by the Office of Indian Affairs, California Superintendency 1849-1880, Microcopy 234, Roll 34.
85. Johnston to Lea, October 8, 1851, 195-96.
86. William Stewart and John C. Dent, Statement, n.p., October 14, 1851. LP2: 1398, California State Archives, Sacramento, Calif.
87. George Keeler and L.D. Chapman and Adam Johnston, Agreement n.p., October 14, 1851, LP2: 1398, California State Archives, Sacramento, Calif.
88. Adam Johnston to George Keeler and L. D. Chapman, Knight's Ferry October 15, 1851, LP2: 1400. California State Archives, Sacramento, Calif.

89. *San Francisco Daily, Alta California*, October 31, 1851.
90. *San Francisco Evening Picayune*, November 25, 1851.
91. Adam Johnston to A. H. H. Stuart, San Francisco, December 4, 1851, U.S. Congress, Senate, 33d Cong., sp. sess., Exec. Doc. 4, Serial 688, 233-34.
92. Adam Johnston to A. H. H. Stuart, San Francisco, December 3, 1851, Special Files of the Office of Indian Affairs, 1807-1904, Special File 266, Micro-copy 574, Roll 73, NA.
93. Frémont and George W. Wright's Contract with Adam Johnston, n.p., November 1, 1851, Spence, ed., *The Expeditions of John Charles Frémont*, vol. 3, 274, 275n; *San Francisco Daily Evening Picayune*, November 25, 1851.
94. Johnston, deposition, March 31, 1858, 67, 73-74.
95. Adam Johnston, receipt, November 11, 1851, in Spence, ed., *The Expeditions of John Charles Frémont*, vol. 3, 274.
96. Johnston, deposition, March 31, 1858, 67-68, 105-106.
97. John C. Frémont to George W. Wright, San Francisco, December 26, 1851, *The Expeditions*, ed., Spence, 297.
98. O. M. Wozencraft to Samuel J. Hensley, San Francisco, February 11, U.S. Congress, Senate, 33d Cong., sp. sess., Exec. Doc. 4, Serial 688, 363; Samuel J. Hensley, receipt, San Francisco, February 11, 1852, ibid.
99. Reports of the Committees, no 111, 1860, U.S. Congress, Senate 36th Cong., 1st sess., Serial 1039, 9-10.
100. Gen. E. A. Hitchcock to A. H. H. Stuart, Benicia, December 3l, 1851, *San Francisco Daily Herald*, April 25, 1853.
101. Adam Johnston to Luke Lea, Merced Indian Reservation, January 30, 1852, U.S. Congress, Senate, 33d Cong., sp. sess., Exec. Doc. 4, Serial 688, 244.
102. Ibid., 244-46.
103. Ibid., 246-47
104. Luke Lea to Adam Johnston, Washington, D.C., January 9, 1852, ibid., 24.
105. Adam Johnston to Luke Lea, San Francisco, March 4, 1852, ibid., 295.
106. United States Indian Department, on Account United States Indian Commissioners and Agents for California, to Dent, Vantine, & Co., United States Indian Traders for the Stanislaus River Reserve, ibid., 394-97.
107. George G. Belt's Executrix vs. The United States, Cases Decided in the Court of Claims at the December Term, 1879, Vol. 15, 99, 111.
108. Ward, *Sam Ward in the Gold Rush*, 72-74
109. *San Francisco Daily, Alta California,* March 16, 1852.

110. Ward, *Sam Ward in the Gold Rush*, 80-82
111. Ibid., 82-94.
112. Ibid., 86.
113. "Treaty Made and Concluded at Camp Frémont, State of California," March 19, 1851, Between Redick McKee and Others, Commissioners on the Part of the United States, and the Chiefs, Captains and Head Men of the Si-yan-te, etc., Tribes of Indians," in Kappler, ed., *Indian Affairs*, vol. 4, 1084.
114. Ward, *Sam Ward in the Gold Rush*, 86-87.
115. Ibid., 87-88.
116. Ibid., 88-91.
117. Ibid., 92-93.
118. Ibid., 136-40.
119. Ibid., 136, 143.
120. Ibid., 159-60.
121. *Stockton Journal* (Steamer Edition), June 11, 1852.
122. Howard, testimony, September 27, 1890, 24.
123. *Stockton Journal* (Steamer Edition), June 11, 1852.
124. Thomas, *Sam Ward: King of the Lobby*, 190-95.
125. Howard, Testimony, September 27, 1890, 28-29.
126. Abstract of the Census of 1852, of the State of California, 24, 34.

Chapter XV: James Savage and the Fresno Reservation

1. Adam Johnston to Luke Lea, Fresno River, June 20, 1851, U.S. Congress, Senate, 33d Cong., sp. sess., Exec. Doc. 4, Serial 688, 100-101.
2. Adam Johnston to James Savage, Fresno River, June 20, 1851, ibid., 101.
3. Adj. Gen. E. H. McKinstry, General Orders No. 1, San José, May 3, 1851, California Legislature, *Journal of the Assembly*, 3d sess., 1852, 378.
4. Accounts for Major Burney's Battalion, 1851, Brownlee, Clark & Company, Agua Fría, California, 81-82, C-G 197, Bancroft Library, Berkeley, Calif. See also Brownlee, *An American Odyssey*, 145n.
5. McKinstry, General Orders, May 3, 1851.
6. John G. Marvin to Quarter-Master General of the State of California, W. H. Richardson, Vallejo, July 19, 1851, *Journal of the Assembly*, 3d sess., 38d.
7. Eccleston, *The Mariposa Indian War*, 105; M. B. Lewis, Statement of Disbandment of the Mariposa Battalion, Buckeye Creek, July 1, 1851, in Elliott, *History of Fresno County, California*, 181; Brownlee, *An American Odyssey*, 128; Report of the Committee on Indian Affairs Relative to the Claim of James Birney [sic], California Legislature,

Journal of the Senate, 4th sess., 1853, Appendix, Doc. 67. Between March 17, 1851 and May 3,1852, Burney issued $230,000 in warrants to the volunteers.

8. McKinstry, General Orders No. 1, May 3, 1851; Eccleston, *The Mariposa Indian War*, 105; Accounts for Major Burney's Battalion, 1851.
9. James D. Savage, Store Record Cash Book, California, 1851-1855, Fresno City and County Historical Society, Fresno, Calif.
10. John G. Marvin, Account Book, McHenry Museum, Modesto, Calif. See also Ferris, *Judge Marvin*, 45-46.
11. Eccleston, *The Mariposa Indian War*, 107, 115.
12. Ibid., 100.
13. Corporal Trim to editors, Rootville, September 15, 1851, *San Francisco Daily, Alta California*, September 26, 1851.
14. Correspondent to editors, Minersville, October 3, 1851, *San Joaquin Republican*, n.d., reprinted in *San Francisco Daily, Alta California*, October 10, 1851.
15. Eccleston, *The Mariposa Indian War*, 120.
16. John G. Marvin to William Gwin, San Francisco, October 3, 1851, Interior Department Appointment Papers, State of California, 1849-1907, RG 48, Microcopy 732, Roll 26, NA.
17. W. B. Dameron to William Gwin, San Francisco, October 3, 1851, ibid.
18. Joel Brooks, Samuel A. Bishop, depositions, March 10, June 22, 1858, respectively, in the United States Court of Claims, Felix Argenti vs. The United States, George W. Wright Manuscript, California Historical Society Library, San Francisco, Calif., 37, 118, 135.
19. *San Francisco Daily Herald*, November 2, 1851.
20. Unidentified newspaper article, n.d., reprinted in *San Francisco Daily, Alta California*, November 17, 1851.
21. *San Joaquin Republican*, November 22, 1851.
22. "Careless" to editors, San Joaquin, December 18, 1851, *San Joaquin Republican*, December 24, 1851.
23. Redick McKee, Deposition, n.d., 1858, Argenti vs. The United States, 110.
24. Correspondent to editors, Fort Miller, November 22, 1851, *Stockton Journal*, n.d., reprinted in *San Francisco Daily California*, December 11, 1851.
25. "Careless" to editors, San Joaquin, January 26, 1852, *San Joaquin Republican*, February 4, 1852.
26. Ibid.
27. Bishop, Deposition, June 22, 1858; "Responsible" to editors, *San*

Joaquin Republican, February 14, 1852.

28. *San Francisco Daily Herald*, January 25, 1852; *Daily Alta California*, January 25, 1852.
29. J. R. W. to editors, San Joaquin River, February 22, 1852, *San Joaquin Republican*, March 3, 1852.
30. Abstract of disbursements made by O. M. Wozencraft, Indian Agent, from lst of May, 1851, to the 30th of August, 1852, inclusive, U.S. Congress, Senate, 33d Cong., sp. sess., Exec. Doc. 4, Serial 688, 398.
31. Samuel A. Bishop, deposition, June 22, 1858, 129-30.
32. Felix Argenti to the Senate and Assembly of the State of California, San Francisco, May, 1853, in the United States Court of Claims, Samuel J. Henley vs. The United States, n.d., George W. Wright Manuscript, California Historical Society, San Francisco, Calif., 1-2; Adam Johnston, Alexander Godey, Edward J. Stearns, depositions, San Francisco, March 31, June 24, June 26, 1858 respectively, in Argenti vs. The United States, 105-106; 135, 147-48, 151-52, 167. See also Spence, ed., *The Expeditions of John Charles Frémont*, vol. 3, 275n, 353n.
33. Reports of the Committees, no. 111, 1860, U.S. Congress, Senate 36th Cong., lst sess., Serial 1039, 9-10; Edward F. Beale, M. B. Lewis, Lewis Leach Lorenzo D. Vinsonhaler, depositions, n.d., *Henley vs. The United States*, 4, 4-6, 6-7, 7-9; List of cattle delivered to the Indians in the San Joaquin Valley, Papers of the Beale Family, Manuscript Division, Box 4, General Correspondence 1856-1859, Library of Congress, Washington, D.C.
34. Anonymous to O. M. Wozencraft, Fresno Indian Reservation, May 9, 1852, *San Francisco Alta California* (Steamer Edition), May 31, 1852.
35. "Observer" to editors, Fort Miller, April 30, 1852, *San Joaquin Republican*, May 8, 1852.
36. Anonymous to editors, Fort Miller, May 1, 1852, *San Joaquin Republican*, May 15, 1852.
37. Ibid., *San Francisco Daily Herald,* May 17, 1852.
38. *San Francisco Alta California* (Steamer Edition), May 31, 1852.
39. *San Francisco Daily, Alta California*, July 9, 1852.
40. Col. George A. McCall to Maj. Gen. Winfield Scott, Fort Miller, July 29, 1852, Records of the Adjutant General's Office, 1780s-1917, Letters Received 1822-1860, Microcopy 567, Roll 483, RG 94, NA.
41. *San Francisco Daily, Alta California*, July 9, 1852.
42. "Observer" to editors, Fort Miller, April 30, 1852, *San Joaquin Republican*, May 8, 1852.
43. J. R. W. to editors, Fort Miller, May 5, 1852, *San Joaquin Republican*, May 15, 1852.
44. Anonymous to editors, Fort Miller, July 18, 1852, *San Joaquin Republican*,

July 28, 1852.

45. "Observer" to editors, April 30, 1852.
46. Anonymous to O. M. Wozencraft, Fresno Indian Reservation, May 31, 1852, *San Francisco Alta California* (Steamer Edition), May 31, 1852.
47. Johnston to Lea, June 20, 1851, 101.
48. J. R. W. to editors, Fort Miller, n.d., *San Joaquin Republican*, July 3, 1852.
49. *Stockton Journal*, August 27, 1852.
50. Lorenzo Vinsonhaler to Maj. George W. Patten, Fresno Reservation, September 20, 1852, in Maj. George W. Patten to Lieut. W. M. Gardner, Fort Miller September 26, 1852, Records of the U.S. Army Continental Commands,1821-1920, RG 393, NA. The influence Savage exerted over the Indians is discussed but exaggerated in James O'Meara, "A White Medicine Man," *Californian* 5, no. 26 (February 1882): 150-57.
51. *Sacramento Daily Union*, August 12, 1852.
52. *Los Angeles Star*, May 14, 1852.
53. J. R. W to editors, Fort Miller, July 18, 1852, *San Joaquin Republican*, July 28, 1852.
54. Bunnell, *Discovery of the Yosemite*, 276-77.
55. Carl Russell, "Interview with Maria Lebrado at Bear Creek," February 1928, Yosemite Museum Library, Yosemite National Park, Calif.
56. Bunnell, *Discovery of the Yosemite*, 277-78.
57. Stephen F. Grover, "Grover's Narrative--A Reminiscence," in Russell, *One Hundred Years in Yosemite*, 52-54.
58. Ibid., 54-57.
59. Ibid., *San Francisco Daily, Alta California*, June 10, 1852.
60. Grover, "Grover's Narrative," 57.
61. *San Francisco Daily, Alta California*, June 18, 1852.
62. Lieut. Treadwell Moore to Capt. E. D. Townsend, Fort Miller, June 12, 1852, Records of the U.S. Army Continental Commands, 1821-1920, Letters Received, 1849-1853, RG 393, NA.
63. McCall to Scott, July 29, 1852.
64. *San Francisco Daily, Alta California*, July 2, 1852.
65. Lieut. Treadwell Moore to Capt. E. D. Townsend, Camp Steele, July 8, 1852, Records of the U.S. Army Continental Commands,1821-1920, Letters Received, 1849-1853, RG 393, NA; *San Francisco Daily, Alta California*, July 2, 1852; J. R. W to editors, Fort Miller, n.d., *San Joaquin Republican*, July 3, 1852.
66. Moore to Townsend, July 8, 1852.
67. J. R. W to editors, July 18, 1852.
68. Moore to Townsend, July 8, 1852.
69. Bunnell, *Discovery of the Yosemite*, 279-80.

70. J. R. W to editors, July 18, 1852.
71. Moore to Townsend, July 8, 1852. For a slightly different version of the campaign, see "Careless" to editors, Headwaters of the San Joaquin, September 11, 1852, *San Joaquin Republican*, September 15, 1852.
72. Bunnell, *Discovery of the Yosemite*, 280-81; *San Joaquin Republican*, August 21, September 1, 15, 1852; *San Francisco Daily Herald*, August 28, 1852.
73. Bunnell, *Discovery of the Yosemite*, 272-73.
74. J. R. W to editors, San Joaquin River, February 22, 1852, *San Joaquin Republican*, March 3, 1852.
75. *San Francisco Alta California* (Steamer Edition), May 31, 1852.
76. List of cattle delivered to the Indians in the San Joaquin Valley, Papers of the Beale Family.
77. *San Francisco Daily, Alta California*, June 18, 1852.
78. *San Francisco Daily Herald*, July 25, 1852.
79. John Marvin, "Some Account of the Tulare Valley and the Indians from the Fresno River to Tihone Pass," no. 2, *Sacramento Democratic State Journal*, n.d., Marvin, Scrapbooks, vol. 1.
80. "An Act Creating Tulare County and to Provide for Its Organization," published in the *San Joaquin Republican*, May 15, 1852. See also Bancroft, *History of California*, vol. 7, 1860-1890, 209-10; and Mitchell, *Jim Savage and the Tulareno Indian*, 11-72.
81. Bunnell, *Discovery of the Yosemite*, 284.
82. James D. Savage, Proclamation, Fresno River, June 17, 1852, in John G. McBe, et al., to editors, Kings River, July 8, 1852, *San Joaquin Republican*, July 24, 1852.
83. Joel Brooks, Deposition, March 10, 1858, 57.
84. McBe, et al., to editors, July 8, 1852.
85. Ibid.
86. William F. Edgar to Gen. E. A. Hitchcock, Fort Miller, July 5, 1852, Records of the U.S. Army Continental Commands, 1821-1920, Letters Received, 1849-1853, RG 393, NA.
87. McBe, et al., to editors, July 8, 1852.
88. W. A. A. to editors, San Joaquin River, July 4, 1852, *San Francisco Daily, Alta California*, July 11, 1852.
89. T.H. to editors, Kings River, July 13, 1852, *San Joaquin Republican*, July 21, 1852.
90. Walter H. Harvey to editors, Kings River, July 10, 1852, *San Joaquin Republican*, July 17, 1852.
91. "Amigo" to editors, Fresno Reservation, July 16, 1852, *San Joaquin Republican*, July 21, 1852.

92. Patten to Gardner, September 26, 1852.
93. "Amigo" to editors, July 16, 1852.
94. *Stockton Journal*, August 27, 1852.
95. "Amigo" to editors, July 16, 1852.
96. W. A. A. to editors, San Joaquin River, July 4, 1852, *San Francisco Daily, Alta California*, July 17, 1852.
97. Edgar to Hitchcock, July 5, 1852; *Stockton Journal*, July 13, 1852.
98. "Amigo" to editors, July 16, 1852.
99. S. to editors, Four Creeks, July 9, 1852, *San Joaquin Republican*, July 17, 1852.
100. *San Francisco Daily Herald*, July 25, 1852.
101. Ibid., July 15, 1852.
102. *San Francisco Daily, Alta California*, July 19, 1852.
103. W. A. A. to editors, July 4, 1852.
104. *Stockton Journal*, July 13, 1852.
105. Maj. George W. Patten to Asst. Adj. Gen. E. D. Townsend, Benicia, July 26, 1852, F3753: 225, California State Archives, Sacramento, Calif.
106. O. M. Wozencraft to Gov. John Bigler, Fresno River, July 13, 1852 in the Report of Edward F. Beale, Superintendent of Indian Affairs in California Respecting the Condition of Indian Affairs in That State, U.S. Congress Senate, 33d Cong., 2d sess., Exec. Doc. 57, Serial 665, 13.
107. Extract of a communication from Agent Wozencraft to Superintendent Beale, dated San Francisco, September 9, 1852, ibid., 13.
108. *San Francisco Daily, Alta California*, August 7, 1852.
109. Patten to Gardner, September 26, 1852.
110. Ibid., *San Francisco Daily, Alta California*, August 25, 1852; *San Joaquin Republican*, August 21, September 1, 1852; *Stockton Journal*, August 24, 1852. Although an inquest found Walter Harvey innocent of murder, apparently he spent the rest of his life fearing that Indians would take revenge for his killing of Savage. See the *Mariposa Gazette*, January 18, 1879. For a brief summary of Harvey's later life, see Mitchell, *Jim Savage and the Tulareno Indians*, 83-84.
111. Patten to Gardner, September 26, 1852.
112. Maj. George W. Patten to Asst. Adj. Gen. E. D. Townsend, Fort Miller, August 26, 1852,
Pacific Division, Records of the 10th Military Department, Letters Received, 1846-1851, RG 98, Microcopy 210, Roll 7, NA.
113. Patten to Gardner, September 26, 1852.
114. Maj. George W. Patten to Asst. Adj. Gen. E. D. Townsend, Fort Miller, August 23,1852, Records of the U.S. Army Continental Commands, 1821-1920, Letters Received, 1849-1853, RG 393, NA; *San Francisco*

Daily Herald, August 24, 1852.
115. Patten to Gardner, September 26, 1852.
116. Patten to Townsend, August 23, 1852.
117. *Stockton Journal*, August 27, 1852.
118. Patten to Townsend, August 23, 1852.
119. Patten to Townsend, August 26, 1852.
120. Petitioners to Gen. E. A. Hitchcock, Woodville, August 28, 1852, Pacific Division, Records of the 10th Military Department, Letters Received, 1846-1851, RG 98, Microcopy 210, Roll 3. NA.
121. Vinsonhaler to Patten, September 20, 1852. Vinsonhaler's emphasis.
122. Anonymous to editors, Fresno Reservation, August 31, 1852, *Stockton Journal*, September 10, 1852.
123. J. R. W to editors, Fort Miller, September 1, 1852, *San Joaquin Republican*, September 11, 1852.
124. *San Francisco Daily, Alta California*, August 25, 1852; *San Francisco Herald*, August 21, 1852; *San Joaquin Republican*, August 21, September 1, 1852; *Stockton Journal*, August 24, 1852.
125. *San Francisco Daily, Alta California*, August 22, 1852.
126. Russell, "Interview with Maria Lebrado."

Chapter XVI: Public Debate

1. Redick McKee, George Barbour, and O. M. Wozencraft to the people of California residing in the vicinity of the Indian troubles, San Francisco, January 13, 1851, *San Francisco Daily, Alta California*, January 14, 1851. The proclamation was also published in the *San Francisco Daily Herald* of January 22, 1851.
2. Ibid.
3. Ibid., January 15, 1851.
4. *Stockton Journal*, January 25, 1851.
5. C. D. Gibbes to editors, Stockton, February 15, 1851, *Stockton Times*, February 19, 1851.
6. Thomas Paine to editors, March 3, 1851, *Stockton Times*, March 5, 1851.
7. *San Francisco Daily, Alta California*, April 2, 1851.
8. Ibid., May 31, 1851.
9. Ibid., June 19, 1851.
10. Ibid., July 7, 1851.
11. Ibid., July 26, 1851.
12. Ibid.
13. Redick McKee to editors, San Francisco, July 30, 1851, unidentified newspaper article, n.d., John G. Marvin, Scrapbooks, vol. 1, 1840-1853, HM 51846. Huntington Library, San Marino, Calif.
14. Anonymous to editors, n.p., n.d., *San Francisco Daily, Alta California*,

August 2, 1851.
15. *Sacramento Placer Times & Transcript*, July 30, 1851.
16. George Barbour to editors, n.p., n.d., *San Francisco Daily, Alta California*, September 9, 1851.
17. Ibid., September 10, 1851.
18. Ibid., September 16, 1851.
19. Ibid., September 20, 1851.
20. *Sacramento Placer Times & Transcript*, September 24, 1851.
21. *San Francisco Daily, Alta California*, September 26, 1851.
22. Gen. E. A. Hitchcock to editors, Benicia, October 3, 1851, *San Francisco Daily, Alta California*, October 6, 1851.
23. Ibid., October 10, 1851.
24. In Senate, January 16, 1852, California Legislature, *Journal of the Senate*, 3d sess., 44-45.
25. In Senate, January 19, 1852, ibid., 46-47.
26. *Sacramento Daily Union*, January 27, 1852.
27. Ibid.
28. "Address of Dr. Wozencraft, Delivered at the Capitol on Friday Evening, January 30," *Sacramento Daily Union*, February 2, 1852.
29. Ibid.
30. O. M. Wozencraft to editors, *San Francisco Daily Evening Picayune*, n.p., n.d., John G. Marvin, Scrapbooks, vol. 1.
31. *Stockton Journal* (Steamer Edition), March 12, 1852.
32. John Bigler, Special Message to the Senate and Assembly of the State of California, *San Francisco Daily, Alta California*, January 31, 1852.
33. Shasta [Redick McKee] to editors, February 9, 1852, ibid., Shasta's emphasis.
34. *San Jose Weekly Visitor*, February 13, 1852.
35. In Senate, February 12, 1852, California Legislature, 109.
36. Winslow S. Pierce to Senate, February 14, 1852, ibid., 114.
37. In Senate, February 14, 1852, ibid., 114.
38. *San Francisco Daily, Alta California*, February 13, 1852.
39. Majority Report, February 11, 1852, California Legislature, *Journal of the Senate*, 3d sess., 597-600.
40. Ibid., 599-601.
41. Unidentified newspaper article, n.d., Marvin Scrapbooks, vol. 1. During the 1830s some Indians were settled on reservations within states. The Potawatomi, for example, received small reservations in Michigan, Indiana, and Illinois. See Prucha, *American Indian Treaties*, 188-87.
42. Unidentified newspaper article, n.d., Marvin, Scrapbooks, vol. 1.
43. *San Joaquin Republican*, February 18, 1852.
44. Ibid. The figures of five million dollars and seven million dollars

presented in the article are misprints.

45. Unidentified newspaper article, Marvin, Scrapbooks, vol. 1.
46. "Shasta" [Redick McKee] to editors, n.p., n.d., *San Francisco Daily, Alta California*, February 24, 1852.
47. Minority Report, February 13, 1852, California Legislature, *Journal of the Senate*, 3d sess., 602-604.
48. Unidentified newspaper article, n.d., Marvin, Scrapbooks, vol. 1. In a treaty he negotiated with Indians in Southern California, Wozencraft reserved for J. J. Warner one square league within the land set aside for a reservation. See Treaty Made and Conducted at the Village of Santa Ysabel, California, Between O. M. Wozencraft, United States Indian Agent and the Captains and Head Men of the Nation of Dieguino Indians, January 7, 1852, in Kappler, ed., *Indian Affairs*, vol. 4, 1128.
49. In Senate, February 14, 1852, California Legislature, 111.
50. Memorial of the People of California to the Congress of the United States February 12, 1852, ibid., 588-89.
51. *Sacramento Daily Union*, February 13, 1852.
52. In Senate, March 18, California Legislature, 198.
53. Report of the California Assembly Committee to Inquire into the Treaties Made by the United States Indian Commissioners with the Indians of California, February 16, 1852, California Legislature, *Journal of the Assembly*, 3d sess., 202-204.
54. Ibid., 205.
55. "Shasta" [Redick McKee] to editors, February 24, 1852.
56. Redick McKee to William H. Lyons, Sacramento, March 4, 1852, *Sacramento Daily Union*, March 13, 1852.
57. Unidentified newspaper article, n.p., n.d., Marvin, Scrapbooks, vol. 1.
58. Ibid.
59. Redick McKee to editors, n.p., n.d., *Sacramento Daily Union*, March 13, 1852.
60. *Sacramento Daily Union*, March 20, 1852.
61. "Address of Col. Redick McKee, before the Committee on 'Indian Reservations' at the Capitol, Sacramento City, Saturday Evening, March 20, 1852," *Sacramento Daily Union*, March 25, 1852.
62. Ibid.
63. Ibid.
64. Ibid.
65. Ibid.
66. Ibid.
67. California Legislature, *Journal of the Assembly*, 3d sess., March 22, 1851, 396-97; *San Francisco Daily Herald*, March 23, 1852. Ironically,

Indians killed Coats and two other men while they were guarding a wagon train in Northern California. They had journeyed north to assist immigrants against hostile Indians. See *San Francisco Daily Herald*, September 21, 1852.

68. John Bigler to Redick McKee, Sacramento, April 15, 1852, U.S. Congress, Senate, 33d Cong., sp. sess., Exec. Doc. 4, Serial 688, 320.
69. Redick McKee to John Bigler, San Francisco, April 16, 1852, Letters Received by the Office of Indian Affairs, California Superintendency, 1849-1880, Microcopy 234, Roll 32, NA.
70. *Statutes at Large and Treaties of the United States of America from December 1851 to March 3, 1855*, 10:2-3.
71. Petitioners to President Millard Fillmore, San Francisco, March 31, 1852, Interior Department Appointment Papers, State of California, 1849-1907, RG 48, Microcopy 732, NA.
72. Redick McKee to President Millard Fillmore, San Francisco, April 3, 1852, U.S. Congress, Senate, 33d Cong., sp. sess., Exec. Doc. 4, Serial 688, 308.

PART III: SUBJUGATION

Chapter XVII: A Superintendent for California

1. Thompson, *Edward F. Beale*, 2-3.
2. Ibid., 3.
3. Ibid., 3-5.
4. Ibid., 5-7.
5. Quoted in Thompson, *Edward F. Beale*, 5.
6. Quoted in ibid., 8-9. Beale's emphasis.
7. Ibid., 16-17.
8. Ibid., 18-22.
9. Ibid., 22-27.
10. Ibid., 29-31.
11. Ibid., 34-35.
12. Ibid., 39-40.
13. Ibid., 41-42.
14. Ibid., 42-43.
15. "California Measures in the U.S. Senate," unidentified newspaper article, Marvin, Scrapbooks, vol. 1. Included in the article is "A Bill to provide for the appointment of a Superintendent of Indian Affairs in California."
16. William M. Gwin, Joseph W. McCorkle, and Edward G. Marshall to President Millard Fillmore, n.p., n.d., Interior Department, Appointment Papers, roll 20.
17. "An Act to provide for the Appointment of a Superintendent of Indian affairs in California," March 3, 1852, *U.S. Statutes at Large*,

vol. 10, 2-3.

18. Ellison, "The Indian Federal Indian Policy in California, 1846-1860," 59.
19. Alexander H. H. Stuart to Luke Lea, Washington, D.C., March 11, 1852, Office of Indian Affairs, Letters Received, 1824-81, roll 32.
20. Mark to editors, n.p.. n.d., *Sacramento Daily Union*, May 4, 1852.
21. Harry Edwards, statement, Washington, D.C., January 24, 1852, Report of the Secretary of the Interior, U.S. Congress, Senate, 32d Cong., 1st sess., Exec. Doc. 61, Serial 620, 16-17.
22. In October 1855, when the drafts were honored, Beale's share amounted to $29,376. See John C. Frémont, deposition, September 18, 1851, "Law Report," *San Francisco Daily, Alta California*, October 2, 1855. The deposition entitled "Frémont's Agreement with Edward F. Beale," is in Spence, ed., *The Expeditions of John Charles Frémont*, vol. 3: 264.
23. John C. Frémont to Edward F. Beale, New York, March 8, 1852, Office of Indian Affairs, Letters Received, 1824-81, roll 32.
24. Edward F. Beale to Luke Lea, Washington, D.C., April 7, 1852, U.S. Congress, Senate, 33d Cong., sp. sess., Exec. Doc. 4, Serial 688, 308-9.
25. Mark to editors, New York, March 24, 1852, *Sacramento Daily Union*, May 1, 1852.
26. *Stockton Journal*, June 15, 1852.
27. Mark to editors, Washington, D.C., March 5, 1852, *Sacramento Daily Union*, April 15, 1852.
28. *Sacramento Daily Union*, April 16, 1852.
29. "Amicus" to editors, n.p., n.d., *San Francisco Evening Picayune*; reprinted in the *Sacramento Daily Union*, April 21, 1852.
30. "Manhatan" to editors, n.p., n.d., *Sacramento Daily Union*, May 3, 1852.
31. *Sacramento Daily Union*, May 4, 1852. Editor's emphasis.
32. Luke Lea to Edward F. Beale, Washington, D.C., May, 1852, U.S. Congress, Senate, 33d Cong., sp. sess, Exec. Doc. 4, Serial 688, 26.
33. Edward F. Beale to Luke Lea, Washington, D.C., May 11, 1852, U.S. Congress, Senate, 33d Cong., sp. sess., Exec. Doc. 4, Serial 688, 327-28.
34. Ibid., 328-29.
35. Ibid., 329.
36. Luke Lea to Alexander H. H. Stuart, Washington, D.C., May 14, 1852, in Kappler, ed., *Indian Affairs*, vol. 4, 1087-88n. Lea's emphasis.
37. Alexander H. H. Stuart to President Millard Fillmore, Washington, D.C., May 22, 1852, in Kappler, ed., *Indian Affairs*, vol. 4; 1085n.
38. President Millard Fillmore to the United States Senate, June 1, 1852,

in Kappler, ed., *Indian Affairs*, vol. 4, 1085n.

39. Eighteen Treaties Rejected, June 8, 1852, in Kappler, ed., *Indian Affairs*, vol. 4, 1018-1085n. The deliberations taking place in the Senate were not recorded, and the titles of each treaty and names of those voting were not published until 1887. See *Senate Executive Journal*, vol. 8, 417-20.
40. Edward F. Beale to Luke Lea, Washington, D.C., July 14, 1852, Office of Indian Affairs, Special Files, File 159.
41. J. J. Crittenden to Alexander H. H. Stuart, Washington, D.C., July 21, 1852, in Alexander H. H. Stuart to Luke Lea, Washington, D.C., July 27, 1852, Office of Indian Affairs, Letters Received, 1824-81, roll 32.
42. Alexander H. H. Stuart to Luke Lea, Washington, D.C., July 26, 1852, Office of Indian Affairs, Letters Received, 1824-81, roll 32.
43. Edward F. Beale to Luke Lea, Chester, Penn., August 31, 1852, U.S. Congress, Senate, 33d Cong., sp. sess., Exec. Doc. 4, Serial 635, 358.
44. *San Francisco Daily, Alta California*, September 6, 1852.
45. O. M. Wozencraft to Luke Lea, San Francisco, October, to, 1851, and Redick McKee to President Millard Fillmore, San Francisco, April 3, 1852. U.S. Congress, Senate, 33d Cong., sp. sess., Exec. Doc. 4, Serial 688, 203 and 308 respectively.
46. O. M. Wozencraft to Edward F. Beale, San Francisco, September 9, 1852, U.S. Congress, Senate, 33d Cong., sp. sess., Exec. Doc. 4, Serial 688, 400-403.
47. O. M. Wozencraft to Edward F. Beale, San Francisco, September 14, 1852, U.S. Congress, Senate, 33d Cong., sp. sess., Exec. Doc. 4, Serial 688, 403.
48. Memorandum of conversation of Superintendent Beale with Agent O. M. Wozencraft, San Francisco, September 14, 1852, in The report of Edward F. Beale, Superintendent of Indian Affairs in California, respecting the condition of Indian affairs in that State, March 3, 1853, U.S. Congress, Senate, 32d Cong., 2d sess., Exec. Doc. 57, Serial 665, 3.
49. Official statement of Joel H. Brooks to Superintendent Beale, dated San Francisco, September 27, 1852, U.S. Congress, Senate, 32d Cong., 2d sess., Exec. Doc. 57, Serial 665, 4-5.
50. Edward F. Beale to Luke Lea, San Francisco, September 30, 1852, U.S. Congress, Senate, 33d Cong., sp. sess., Exec. Doc. 4, Serial 688, 404.
51. O. M. Wozencraft to Luke Lea, San Francisco, September 30, 1852, ibid., 404.
52. Luke Lea to O. M. Wozencraft, Washington, D.C., September 2, 1852, ibid., 29.

53. O. M. Wozencraft to Edward F. Beale, San Francisco, October 1, 1852, ibid.,404.
54. O. M. Wozencraft to Edward F. Beale, San Francisco, November 20, 1852, ibid., 405.
55. Redick McKee to Luke Lea, San Francisco, April 17, 1852, ibid., 310.
56. Redick McKee to Luke Lea, San Francisco, May 1, 1852, ibid., 324.
57. Edward F. Beale to Redick McKee, San Francisco, October 8, 1852, Office of Indian Affairs, Letters Received, 1824-81, roll 34.
58. Redick McKee to Luke Lea, San Francisco, October 14, 1852, U.S. Cong., Senate, 33d Cong., sp. sess., Exec. Doc. 4, Serial 688, 373.
59. Extract from a letter of R. McKee, Indian Agent, to E. F. Beale Superintendent of Indian Affairs, Nevada, November 22, 1852, ibid., 386.
60. Ibid., 386-88. McKee's emphasis.
61. Ibid., 388, McKee's emphasis.
62. Edward F. Beale to Redick McKee, San Francisco, November 30, 1852, ibid., 389.
63. Edward F. Beale to Luke Lea, San Francisco, November 28, 1852, ibid., 382-84.
64. Luke Lea to Edward F. Beale, Washington, D.C., January 18, 1853, ibid., 33.
65. Edward F. Beale to Redick McKee, Washington, D.C., March 31, 1853, Office of Indian Affairs, Letters Received, 1824-81, roll 33.

Chapter XVIII: Formulating Plans

1. Brig. Gen. E. A. Hitchcock to Edward F. Beale, San Francisco, September 21, 1852, U.S. Congress, Senate, 33d Cong., sp. sess., Exec. Doc. 4, Serial 688, 367.
2. Edward F. Beale to Luke Lea, Washington, D.C., San Francisco, October 29, 1852, U.S. Congress, Senate, 33d Cong., sp. sess., Exec. Doc. 4, Serial 688, 374.
3. Brig. Gen. E. A. Hitchcock, statement, San Francisco, October 31, 1852, U.S. Congress, Senate, 33d Cong., sp. sess., Exec. Doc. 4, Serial 688, 374-75. The editors of a California newspaper claimed that "the basis of the plan was furnished by Lieut. Beale and Gen. Hitchcock." See *Sacramento Democratic State Journal*, January 24, 1853.
4. Brig. Gen. E. A. Hitchcock to Adj. Gen. Samuel Cooper, San Francisco, November 29, 1852, in *San Joaquin Republican*, May 7, 1853– A condensed version of the letter is in Bonsal, *Edward Fitzgerald Beale*, 182-84.
5. *San Francisco Daily Herald*, December 1, 1852.
6. *Sacramento Democratic State Journal*, December 4, 1852.

7. *San Joaquin Republican,* January 22, 1853.
8. *Sacramento Democratic State Journal,* January 27, 1853.
9. President Millard Fillmore and Daniel Webster, Appointment of Benjamin Wilson as agent for the Indians of California, September 1, 1852; and Edward F. Beale to B. D. Wilson, San Francisco, October 8, 1852, Wilson Collection, WN 1282 and WN 105 respectively, Huntington Library, San Marino, Calif.
10. Luke Lea to Edward F. Beale, Washington, D.C., September 4, 1852, U.S. Congress, Senate 33d Cong., sp. sess., Exec. Doc. 4, Serial 688, 28.
11. Edward F. Beale to Luke Lea. San Francisco, October 1, 1852, U.S. Congress, Senate, 33d Cong., sp. sess., Exec. Doc. 4, Serial 688, 371. Wilson's life is discussed in Caughey, "Don Benito Wilson," 285-300.
12. *Los Angeles Star*, October 16, 1852.
13. Edward F. Beale to B. D. Wilson, San Francisco, November 11, 1852, U.S. Congress, Senate, 33d Cong., sp. sess., Exec. Doc. 4, Serial 688, 376.
14. Pearson B. Reading to Luke Lea, Washington, D.C., September 10, 1852, U.S. Congress, Senate, 33d Cong., sp. sess., Exec. Doc. 4, Serial 688, 360.
15. B. D. Wilson to Edward F. Beale, San Francisco, November 11, 1852, U.S. Congress, Senate, 33d Cong., sp. sess., Exec. Doc. 4, Serial 688, 376-77.
16. Edward F. Beale to B. D. Wilson, San Francisco, November 22, 1852, Wilson Collection, WN 106, Huntington Library, San Marino, Calif.
17. B. D. Wilson to Edward F. Beale, San Francisco, November 22, 1852, Wilson Collection, WN 1017, Huntington Library, San Marino, Calif.
18. Edward F. Beale to Luke Lea, San Francisco, November 22, 1852, U.S. Congress, Senate, 33d Cong., sp. sess., Exec. Doc. 4, Serial 688, 377-18.
19. Ibid., 379. Beale probably spoke with or showed his letter to the editors of the *San Francisco Daily Herald*, because on December 1, 1852, they presented similar calculations regarding Indian labor.
20. Beale to Lea, November 22, 1852, 380.
21. [B. D. Wilson] to Edward F. Beale, n.p., December 20, 1852, Bancroft Collection, C-E 165, Bancroft Library, Berkeley, California.
22. Wolcott, "Foreword," in Wolcott, ed., *Pioneer Notes*, ix-xi. The Bancroft Library in Berkeley, California houses the voluminous papers of Benjamin Hayes.
23. See Hayes, Scrapbooks, especially vol. 39.
24. Benjamin Hayes, "Diary, January 1, 1853," in Wolcott, ed., *Pioneer Notes*, 94.

25. Caughey, ed., *Indians of Southern California*, 1-32. At the end of the report, almost as an afterthought, Hayes added a short section on the Mohave and the Quechan (then called Yumas) of the Colorado River. See pp. 61-66.
26. Ibid., 32-34. Hayes' emphasis.
27. Ibid., 38-39.
28. Ibid., 49-50.
29. Ibid., 50-51.
30. Ibid., 52-57.
31. Ibid., 58.
32. Ibid., 59.
33. Benjamin Hayes to David R. Atchison, Los Angeles, January 14, 1853, in Caughey, ed., *Indians of Southern California*, 82-83.
34. *Los Angeles Star*, January 15, 1853.
35. *San Francisco Daily Herald*, February 15, 1853. From July 18 to September 19, 1868, the *Los Angeles Star* published the report in ten installments. John Caughey assembled these installments for *Indians of Southern California*, apparently unaware that the original draft of the report is in the Benjamin Hayes Collection, C-E 165, Bancroft Library, Berkeley, Calif. Except for an introduction by Albert L. Hurtado, the University of Nebraska Press reprinted Caughey's book verbatim in 1995.
36. Edward F. Beale to Luke Lea, Fresno River, December 14, 1852, U.S. Congress, Senate, 33d Cong., sp. sess., Exec. Doc. 4. Serial 688, 392. See also C. to editors, Fresno River, January 1, 1853, *San Francisco Daily Herald*, January 11, 1853.
37. *Los Angeles Star*, January 8, 1853.
38. Beale to Lea, December 14, 1852.
39. C. to editors, Fresno River, January 1, 1853, *San Francisco Daily Herald*, January 11, 1853.
40. "Treaty Made and Concluded at Camp Barbour, on the San Joaquin River, State of California, April 29, 1851, Between Redick McKee and Others, Commissioners on the Part of the United States, and the Chiefs, Captains and Head Men of the How-ech-ees, &tc., Tribes of Indians," in Kappler, ed., *Indian Affairs*, vol. 4. 1090.
41. C. to editors, January 1, 1853.
42. Ibid.
43. Lewis Leach, receipt, Fresno River, January 7, 1853, Office of Indian Affairs, Special Files, File 159.
44. Lorenzo Vinsonhaler, receipt, Fresno River, January 10, 1853, Office of Indian Affairs, Special Files, File 159.
45. Samuel Bishop, testimony, June 22, 1858, in the United States Court of Claims, Felix Argenti vs. The United States, Wright Manuscript,

124; "Operations of the Late Major Savage," *San Francisco Daily Herald*, September 11, 1852; J. Ross Browne to George W. Manypenny, Washington, D.C., January 22, 1855, in Browne, Report and accompanying documents, concerning accounts, &tc. of Supt Beale.

46. Edward F. Beale to Luke Lea, Fresno River, December 14, 1852, U.S. Congress, Senate, 33d Cong., sp. sess., Exec. Doc. 4, Serial 688, 391-92.
47. Edward F. Beale to Luke Lea, Fresno River, December 23, 1852, U.S. Congress, Senate, 33d Cong., sp. sess., Exec. Doc. 4, Serial 688, 392.
48. *Los Angeles Star*, January, 1853, in "Tularenos and Edward E Beale," Hayes, Scrapbooks, vol. 39. The day of the month is not cited.
49. *Los Angeles Star*, January 8, 1853.
50. Edward F. Beale, statement, n.p., n.d., U.S. Congress, Senate, Records of the Senate.
51. Edward F. Beale, The report of Edward F. Beale, Superintendent of Indian Affairs in California, respecting the condition of Indian Affairs in that State, Washington, D.C., February 25, 1853, U.S. Congress, Senate, 32n Cong., 2d sess., Exec. Doc. 57, Serial 665, 2-18.
52. Luke Lea to Alexander H. H. Stuart, Washington, D.C., March 3, 1853, and Alexander H. H. Stuart to William K. Sebastian, March 3, 1853., U.S. Congress, Senate, 32n Cong., 2d sess., Exec. Doc. 57, Serial 665, 1.
53. Beale, report, February 25, 1853, U.S. Congress, Senate, 32n Cong., 2d sess., Exec. Doc. 57, Serial 665, 2.
54. Ibid., 2-8.
55. Ibid., 12-14.
56. Ibid., 18.
57. Ellison, "Indian Policy," 212.
58. "Policy of Congress for the treatment of California Indians.–Debate in the U.S. Senate," *San Francisco Daily Herald*, May 13, 1853.
59. Ibid.
60. Ellison, "Indian Policy," 213.
61. Robert McClelland to Edward F. Beale, Washington, D.C., April 13, 1853, U.S. Congress, House, 33d Cong., lst sess., Exec. Doc. 1, Serial 710, 465-66.
62. J. E. L. to editors, n.p., n.d., *San Francisco Daily Placer Times and Transcript*, April 22, 1853.
63. *San Francisco Daily Herald*, April 22, 1853.
64. *San Joaquin Republican*, April 23, 27, 30, May 7, 1853. Editors' emphasis.
65. O. M. Wozencraft to editors, San Francisco, April 29, 1853, *San Francisco Daily Placer Times and Transcript*, April 30, 1853.
66. Bunnell, *Discovery of the Yosemite*, 287.

67. "Citizens of Mariposa and vicinity, Resolutions, Mariposa, October 25, 1853," *San Francisco Daily Placer Times and Transcript*, November 17, 1853.
68. *San Francisco Daily Placer Times and Transcript,* November 19, 1853.

Chapter XIX: Founding a Reservation

1. Thompson, *Edward F. Beale*, 59-60.
2. Robert McClelland to Edward E Beale, Washington, D.C., April 13, 1853. U.S. Congress, House, 33d Cong., lst sess., Exec. Doc. 1, Serial 710, 465.
3. Thompson, *Edward F. Beale*, 61.
4. Frederick Kerlin to B. D. Wilson, San Francisco, May 26, 1853, Wilson Collection WN 1424. The route of the trail is traced in Crampton and Madsen, *Spanish Trail.*
5. Adj. Gen. Samuel Cooper to Maj. Gen. John E. Wool, Washington, D.C., October 28, 1854, U.S. Congress, House, 35th Cong., lst sess., Exec. Doc. 88, Serial 956, 117; *Los Angeles Star*, July 16, 1853.
6. Lieut. Nathaniel H. McLean to Maj. Henry W. Wessells, Fort Miller, July 12, 1853, Office of the Adjutant General, Letters Received, 1822-1860; "Army Intelligence," *San Francisco Daily, Alta California*, July 21, 1853.
7. McLean to Wessells, July 12, 1853.
8. *Los Angeles Star*, June 12, 1852; Latta, *Rancho el Tejon*, 128. For oral accounts of Zapatero's Role in the capture, consult Latta, *Joaquin Murrieta*, 106, 368, 375-77, 388-97. An in depth discussion of Murrieta can be found in Johnson, *Roaring Camp*, 25-53.
9. *Los Angeles Star*, June 12, 1852. See also Antonio Rodriguez to Don Joaquin Carrillo, May 9, 1852 and comment in unidentified newspaper article, probably in *La Estrella*, in Hayes, Scrapbooks, vol. 39. *La Estrella* was the Spanish language section of the *Los Angeles Star.*
10. S. Barney to editors, Santa Barbara, May 12, 1851, *Los Angeles Star*, n.d.; reprinted in *San Francisco Daily, Alta California*, June 8, 1852.
11. *Los Angeles Star*, June 12, 1852.
12. *Los Angeles Star,* n.d.; reprinted in *San Francisco Daily, Alta California*, June 8, 1852.
13. Ibid.
14. *Los Angeles Star*, June 12, 1852.
15. *Los Angeles Star*, n.d.; reprinted in *San Francisco Daily, Alta California*, June 8, 1852.
16. *Los Angeles Star*, June 12, 1852.
17. Vouchers for Supplies Furnished the Tejón Indians, March 22, April 2, 1853; T. S. Hereford, receipt, Los Angeles, April 9, 1853; Samuel Arbuckle, receipt, Los Angeles, June 1, 1853, Wilson Collection, WN

1805.

18. San Francisco Daily Herald, August 8, 1853; Col. Joseph K.F. Mansfield to Maj. Gen. John E. Wool, Merced River, July 1, 1854, in Frazer, ed., *Mansfield on the Condition of the Western Forts*, 189.
19. *Los Angeles Star*, February 26, 1853.
20. B. D. Wilson to editors, n.p., n.d., *Los Angeles Star*, May 7, 1853.
21. Joel Brooks to editors, Tejón, August 15, 1853, *San Francisco Daily Alta California*, August 24, 1853. The following year, Vicente told a newspaper editor that once he had visited the Paiutes at Owens Lake. See the *Los Angeles Star*, June 17, 1854.
22. Brooks to editors, August 15, 1853.
23. Edward F. Beale, Messages suggesting legislation and transmitting specific information, May 19, 1858--February 1859, voucher no. 41, U.S. Congress, Senate, Records of the Senate.
24. J. Ross Browne to George W. Manypenny, Washington, D.C., January 22, 1855, in Browne, Report and accompanying documents, concerning accounts, &tc. of Supt Beale.
25. Harry Edwards to Edward F. Beale, San Joaquin River, September 20, 1853, U.S. Congress. House, 33rd Cong., lst sess., Exec. Doc. 1, Serial 110, 472-73.
26. Ibid., 474.
27. Capt. Thomas Jordan to Maj. Osborne A. Cross, Fort Miller, August 15, 1853, Office of the Quartermaster General, Consolidated File on Fort Miller, 1853-58.
28. Edwards to Beale, September 20, 1853.
29. Lewis Leach, receipt, Fresno River, March 31, 1853; Leach and Company, receipt, Fresno River, June 30, 1853; Samuel Bishop, statement, n.d., Office of Indian Affairs, Special Files, File 159.
30. Charles F. Janis, receipt, San Francisco, March 1, 1853, Office of Indian Affairs, Letters Received, 1824-81, roll 33.
31. Frederick Kerlin to Thomas Henley, An approximate statement, showing the issues of Provisions to Indians on the San Joaquin Reserve, n.p., n.d., U.S. Congress, Senate, Records of the Senate.
32. Edward F. Beale, "Diary, August 22, 1853," in Bonsal, *Edward Fitzgerald Beale*, 165. Had the superintendent departed by ship for California immediately upon receiving his orders, he would have arrived about the middle of May. See Browne to Manypenny, January 22, 1855.
33. Edward. F. Beale to George W. Manypenny, Los Angeles, August 22, 1853. U.S. Congress, House, 33d Cong., lst sess., Exec. Doc. 1, Serial 710, 467-68.
34. B. D. Wilson to Edward F. Beale, Los Angeles, August 28, 1853, Wilson Collection, WN 1018.
35. *Los Angeles Star*, September 3, 1853.

36. Edward F. Beale to George W. Manypenny, San Francisco, September 30, 1853, U.S. Congress, House, 33d Cong., 1st sess., Exec. Doc. 1, Serial 710, 469.
37. *San Francisco Daily, Alta California*, September 22, 1853.
38. Beale to Manypenny, September 30, 1853, 469-70.
39. *San Francisco Daily, Alta California*, September 22, 1853; J. A. L. to editors, Los Angeles, November 11, 1853, *San Francisco Daily, Alta California*, November 23, 1853.
40. Beale to Manypenny, September 30, 1853, 470.
41. Lieut. George Stoneman, Lieut. Robert S. Williamson, and Lieut. John G. Parke to Edward F. Beale, Tejón Pass, September 4, 1853, U.S. Congress, House, 33d Cong., 1st sess., Exec. Doc. 1, Serial 710, 478-79.
42. *San Francisco Daily, Alta California*, September 22, 1853.
43. *San Francisco Daily Herald*, September 22, 1853.
44. Beale to Manypenny, September 30, 1853, 470-72.
45. Edward F. Beale, vouchers to J. W. Johnston, October 5, 1853, and to Simon P. Storms, November 1853, U.S. Congress, Senate, Records of the Senate.
46. Letter to editors, n. p., October 7, 1853, *San Francisco Daily Herald*, October 9, 1853.
47. "Treaty Made and Concluded at Camp Union, near Yuba River," July 18, 1851, Between O. M. Wozencraft, United States Indian Agent, and the Chiefs, Captains, and head men of the Das-Pia, Ya-Ma-Do, etc., Tribes of Indians," in Kappler, ed., *Indian Affairs*, vol. 4, 1103-5.
48. Letter to editors, October 7, 1853.
49. Ibid.
50. Contract between Edward F. Beale and Nathaniel Blackstone, San Francisco, October 10, 1854, U.S. Congress, Senate, Records of the Senate.
51. *San Francisco Daily, Alta California*, October 17, 1853.
52. Edward F. Beale to B. D. Wilson, San Francisco, October 17, 1853, Wilson Collection, WN 108; "Potomac," to editors, San Pedro, November 12, 1853, *San Francisco Daily Placer Times and Transcript*, November 23, 1853.
53. Contract between Beale and Blackstone, October 10, 1854.
54. Simon P. Storms, receipt, Tejón Reservation, November 5, 1853, U.S. Congress, Senate, Records of the Senate.
55. Edward E. Chevers, Estimate of expense of removing five hundred Indians from Yuba (Feather River) to the Indian Reserve by land, Office of Indian Affairs, Special Files, File 159.
56. Edward F. Beale to George W. Manypenny, San Francisco, October

10, 1853, U.S. Congress, House, 33d Cong., lst sess., Exec. Doc. 1, Serial 710, 474-75.

57. Ibid.
58. Edward F. Beale to William M. Gwin and M. S. Latham, September 27, 1853, U.S. Congress, House, 33d Cong., lst sess., Exec. Doc. 1, Serial 710, 475-76. The same day, Beale sent a similar letter to Senator John B. Weller.
59. John B. Weller to Edward F. Beale, San Francisco, October 2, 1853, U.S. Congress, House, 33d Cong., lst sess., Exec. Doc. 1, Serial 710, 476-77.
60. George W. Manypenny to Edward F. Beale, Washington, D.C., November 18, 1853, U.S. Congress, House, 33d Cong., lst sess., Exec. Doc. 1, Serial 710, 480-81.
61. Ignacio del Valle to Edward E Beale, Los Angeles, November 1853, Office of Indian Affair Letters Received, 1824-81, roll 36. The day of the month is not cited.
62. Edward F. Beale to Ignacio del Valle, Tejón, December 28, 1853. Office of Indian Affairs, Letters Received, 1824-81, roll 36.

Chapter XX: Auspicious Beginning

1. Nathaniel Blackstone to editors, Los Angeles, November 18, 1853, *San Francisco Daily, Alta California*, November 23, 1853; "Potomac," to editors, San Pedro, November 12, 1853, *San Francisco Daily Placer Times and Transcript*, November 23, 1853; Juan Coluco, deposition, Tule River Indian Agency, February 23, 1922, Harrington Papers, vol. 2.
2. A. C. Bradford. statement, Washington, D.C., April 6, 1855, U.S. Congress, Senate, Records of the Senate.
3. Receipt, November 10, 1853, U.S. Congress, Senate, Records of the Senate.
4. Charles E. Janis, receipt, November 20, 1853, U.S. Congress, Senate, Records of the Senate.
5. Edward F. Beale, statement, December 5, 1853, U.S. Congress, Senate, Records of the Senate; G. W. Bradford, receipt, Tejón, December 5, 1853, Office of Indian Affairs, Special Files, File 159.
6. B. D. Wilson to Edward F. Beale, Los Angeles, November 8, 1853, Wilson Collection, WN 1020.
7. W. T. B. Sanford, receipt, December 20, 1853, U.S. Congress, Senate, Records of the Senate.
8. W. T. B. Sanford, receipt, Los Angeles, February 8, 1854, Office of Indian Affairs, Special Files, File 159.
9. Francisco María Felis, receipt, Tejón, December 12, 1853, Office of Indian Affairs, Special Files, File 159. The receipt erroneously stated

that 999, instead of 1,499 head of cattle were delivered. Beale's clerk corrected the error.

10. B. D. Wilson to Edward F. Beale, Los Angeles, October 4, 1853, Wilson Collection, WN 1019.
11. Edward F. Beale to B. D. Wilson, San Francisco, October 10, Wilson Collection, WN 1168.
12. Andrew Sublette and James Thompson, receipt of $22,594.00, Los Angeles, June 30, 1854, Office of Indian Affairs, Special Files, File 159.
13. Harry Edwards, receipt, San Francisco, January 20, 1854, Office of Indian Affairs, Special Files, File 159.
14. Andrew Sublette and James Thompson, receipt of $20,450.95, Los Angeles, June 30, 1854, Office of Indian Affairs, Special Files, File 159.
15. Samuel F. Dummer, deposition, San Francisco, September 7, U.S. Congress, Records of the Senate.
16. "Notice to Travelers and Emigrants," Tejon Military Reserve, November 25, 1853, *Los Angeles Star*, December 3, 1853. On December 8, 1853, the *San Francisco Daily, Alta California*, in a section called "From Los Angeles," paraphrased the notice and alerted its readers to the full advertisement in another part of the paper.
17. *San Francisco Daily Herald*, December 30, 1853, January 9, 22, 1854.
18. Edward F. Beale to George W. Manypenny, Tejon, December 28, 1853, Office of Indian Affairs, Special Files, File 159.
19. Edward F. Beale to George W. Manypenny, Tejon Reservation, February 8, 1854, *Annual Report of the Commissioner of Indian Affairs for the Year 1854*, 299.
20. *San Joaquin Republican*, n.d.; reprinted in the *San Francisco Daily Herald*, January 23, 1854.
21. Thomas Henley to George W. Manypenny, San Francisco, August 28, 1854, *Annual Report of the Commissioner of Indian Affairs for the Year 1854*, 302-303.
22. Capt. P. Edward Connor to Janus W. Segfield, Tejon Military Reserve, February 22, 1854, Office of Indian Affairs, Letters Received, 1824-81, roll 33.
23. Beale to Manypenny, February 8, 1854, 298-99.
24. Capt. Thomas Jordan to Edward F. Beale, Fort Miller, October 6, 1854, U.S. Congress, Senate, Records of the Senate.
25. Beale to Manypenny, February 8, 1854, 300.
26. Connor to Segfield, February 22, 1854.
27. Employment Records, Sebastian Military Reserve, July 20, August 7, 1854, U.S. Congress, Senate, Records of the Senate.
28. Edward F. Beale, voucher, March 31, 1853, U.S. Congress, Senate,

Records of the Senate. The voucher stated that Beale paid Godey $1500 for six months' work beginning on October 1, 1852.

29. Edward F. Beale, statement, n.p., n.d., U.S. Congress, Senate, Records of the Senate. Beale's emphasis.
30. Edward F. Beale to Thomas Henley, San Francisco, August 30, 1854, U.S. Congress, Senate, Records of the Senate; J. Ross Browne to George W. Manypenny, Washington, D.C., January 22, 1855, in Browne, Report and accompanying documents, concerning accounts, &tc. of Supt. Beale.
31. Browne to Manypenny, January 22, 1855.
32. Johnson, "Indians of Mission San Fernando," 264; Johnson and Earle, "Tataviam Geography," 205.
33. Browne to Manypenny, January 22, 1855.
34. H. Storrs Washburn to Thomas Henley, San Francisco, December 14, 1854, in Thomas Henley to George W. Manypenny, San Francisco, December 15, 1854, Office of Indian Affairs, Letters Received, 1824-81, roll 34.
35. Ibid. Map of the Sebastian Military Reserve as surveyed by H.S. Washburn, under the direction of E. F. Beale, Superintendent of Indian Affairs, Approved by Maj. Gen. J.W. Wool, Com. Pac. Div. U.S.A, Cont. 49,928,7355/1000 Acres, Map 184, RG. 75. NA.
36. Edward F. Beale to George W. Manypenny, San Francisco, October 10, 1853; Executive Documents, House of Representative 33d Cong., lst sess., Ex. Doc. 1, 475.
37. Washburn to Henley, December 14, 1854.
38. Washburn, Field notes of survey of Sebastian Military Reserve and Santa Remelia or Wool Military Reserve.
39. [Rasey Biven] to editors, Sebastian Military Reserve, September 22, 1854, *San Francisco Daily Placer Times and Transcript*, n.d., in Thomas Henley to George W. Manypenny, San Francisco, December 29, 1854. Office of Indian Affairs, Letters Received, 1824-81, roll 34; Joel Brooks, statement, Mariposa, July 8, 1854, in Browne to Manypenny, January 22, 1855.
40. Beale to Manypenny, December 28, 1853.
41. *San Francisco Daily Herald*, January 9, 1854.
42. *San Francisco Daily Herald*, January 22, 1854.
43. "Superintendent Beale—The Tejon Reservation," *Los Angeles Star*, June 17, 1854.
44. Beale to Manypenny, February 8, 1854, 300.
45. "Treaty Made and Concluded at Camp Burton, on Paint Creek, State of California, June 3, 1851, Between George W Barbour, United States Commissioner, and the Chiefs, Captains and head men of the Chunute,Wo-wol, &tc., Tribes of Indians," in Kappler. ed., *Indian*

Affairs, 4:1099-100.

46. Barbour, "Journal," pt. 2, Camp Burton, June 3, 1851, 248-49.
47. Beale to Manypenny, February 8, 1854, 300. See also *San Francisco Daily Herald*, May 1, 1854.
48. *Mariposa Chronicle*, May 5, 1854.
49. [Biven] to editors, September 22, 1854.
50. Johnston, "Visual Images of the Tejon Indian Community," Paper presented at the California Indian Conference, University of California, Los Angeles, October 7, 1995.
51. Ibid.; Latta, "Alexis Godey," 42; Barbour, "Journal," pt. 2, Camp Persifer F. Smith, June 10, 1851; "Treaty Made and Concluded at Camp Persifer F. Smith at the Texan Pass, State of California, June 10, 1851, Between George W. Barbour, United States Commissioner, and the Chiefs, Captains and Head Men of the 'Castake,' 'Texon,' &tc., Tribes of Indians," in Kappler, ed., *Indian Affairs*, 4: 1102.
52. Raymundo and Jesús José, receipt, February 28, 1854, U.S. Congress, Senate, Records of the Senate. Jesús José may have been a neophyte from Mission Santa Barbara who settled in the Four Creeks. He fits the description given by S. C. Brown of a Juan José who lived near Visalia and who had once visited San Francisco. See Stewart, "Interview with S. C. Brown," Stewart Collection.
53. "Superintendent Beale—The Tejon Reservation," *Los Angeles Star*, June 17, 1854.
54. "Treaty Made and Concluded at Camp Persifer F. Smith, June 10, 1851," 1102.
55. "Superintendent Beale—The Tejon Reservation," *Los Angeles Star*, June 17, 1854.
56. Capt. P. Edward Connor to editors, Tejon Reservation, July 1, 1854. *Stockton Journal*, n.d.; reprinted in *Southern Californian*, July 14, 1854.
57. In June 1854, William Howard encountered Alexander Godey and Indian teamsters on their way to Tulare Lake to bring in some Indians. See William J. Howard, to editors, Tejón Pass, June 24, 1854, *San Joaquin Republican*, n.d.; reprinted in *San Francisco Daily, Alta California*, July 10, 1854.
58. Jose M. Soto, receipt, February 12, 1854, U.S. Congress, Senate, Records of the Senate.
59. Gabriel Allen, receipt, Tejón Reservation, March 15, 1854, U.S. Congress, Senate, Records of the Senate.
60. Pay schedule, Tejon Reservation, June 16, 1854, U.S. Congress, Senate, Records of the Senate.
61. N. M. Dubois, receipt, June 30, 1854, U.S. Congress, Senate, Records of the Senate.

62. *San Francisco Daily Herald*, May 1, 1854.
63. "Superintendent Beale-The Tejon Reservation," *Los Angeles Star*, June 17, 1854.
64. Ibid.
65. Connor to editors, July 1, 1854.
66. "Superintendent Beale-The Tejon Reservation," June 17, 1854.
67. Lieut. Col. Benjamin L. Beall to Asst. Adj. Gen. W. W. Mackall, Fort Tejon, September 29, 1856, Message from the President of the United States, transmitting Report in regard to Indian Affairs on the Pacific, U.S. Congress, House, 34th Cong., 3d sess., Exec. Doc. 76, Serial 906, 139-40.
68. Johnson, "Mat'apxwelxwel Ethnohistory," 28.
69. Browne to Manypenny, January 22, 1855.
70. Edward F. Beale to George W. Manypenny, Washington, D.C., December 14, 1854, U.S. Congress, Senate, Records of the Senate.
71. *Mariposa Chronicle*, May 5, 1854; Juan Coluco, deposition, Tule River Indian Agency, February 23, 1922, Harrington Papers, vol. 2.
72. Howard to editors, June 24, 1854.
73. Col. Joseph K. E. Mansfield to Lieut. Gen. Winfield Scott, Middletown, Connecticut, March 1, 1855, in Frazer, ed., Mansfield, 149; Coluco, deposition, February 23, 1922.
74. Col. Joseph K. E Mansfield to Maj. Gen. John E. Wool, Merced River, July 1, 1854, in Frazer, ed., *Mansfield on the Condition of the Western Forts*, 190-91.
75. Maj. Gen. John E. Wool, Special orders no. 60, San Francisco, June 24, 1854, Office of the Quartermaster General, Consolidated Correspondence File, 1794 -1915.
76. Maj. James L. Donaldson to Gen. T. S. Jesup, Baltimore, Maryland, June 28, 1855, Office of the Quartermaster General, Consolidated Correspondence File, 1794-1915.
77. Removal of California Indians, July 31, 1854, *U.S. Statutes at Large*, vol. 10, 332.
78. Maj. Gen. John E. Wool to Asst. Adj. Gen. L. Thomas, San Francisco, September 14, 1854, U.S. Congress, House, 35th Cong., 1st sess., 1857-58, Exec. Doc. 88, Serial 956.
79. Crowe, *Men of Tejon*, Appendix, 155.

Chapter XXI: Politics and Policies

1. "The Tejon Reservation-Superintendent Beale," *Los Angeles Star*, June 24, 1854.
2. J. Ross Browne to George W. Manypenny, January 22, 1855, in Browne, Report and accompanying documents, concerning accounts, &tc. of Supt. Beale; Thompson, *Edward F. Beale*, 72; Michael A. Sievers,

"Malfeasance or Indirection?" 280-81.
3. *San Francisco Daily California Chronicle*, July 11, 1854.
4. *San Francisco Chronicle*, n.d., reprinted in *Mariposa Chronicle*, September 1, 1854.
5. J. Ross Browne to George W. Manypenny, January 22, 1855, in Browne, Report and accompanying documents, concerning accounts, &tc. of Supt. Beale.
6. San Francisco Daily, Alta California, October 13, 1855. According to the editors, by late 1855 the Spanish mission already had become romanticized. A historian has argued, however, that early American views of the mission largely were negative and that the romanticization did not come until late in the nineteenth century. See Rawls, "California Mission," 343-60.
7. Thomas Henley to editors, San Francisco, October 13, 1855, *San Francisco Daily, Alta California*, October 15, 1855.
8. *San Francisco Daily, Alta California,* October 15, 1855.
9. *San Francisco Golden Era*, September 4, 1856.
10. Maj. Gen. John E. Wool to John B. Weller, Benicia, October 5, 1856, Message from the President of the United States, transmitting Report in regard to Indian affairs on the Pacific, U.S. Congress, House, 34th Cong., 3d sess., Exec. Doc. 76, Serial 946, 144.
11. Maj. Gen. John E. Wool to D.C. Broderick and William M. Gwin, Benicia, January 28,
1857, U.S. Congress, House, 34th Cong., 3d sess., Exec. Doc. 88, Serial 956, 211. Wool's emphasis.
12. The topographical memoir and report of Captain T. J. Cram, relative to the Territories of Oregon and Washington, in the military department of the Pacific, March 3, 1859. U.S. Congress. House, 35th Cong., 2d sess., Exec. Doc. 11, 123.
13. *San Jose Semi-Weekly Tribune*, July 28, 1854.
14. *Los Angeles Star,* a.d., reprinted in the *San Francisco Daily, Alta California*, August 8, 1854.
15. *San Francisco Daily California Chronicle*,. July 11, 1854.
16. *Southern Californian*, August 17, 1854.
17. Ibid., November 16, 1854.
18. Ibid., December 28, 1854. The building of the road is discussed in Robinson, "Taming of San Fernando Pass," 44-55; and in Ripley, "San Fernando Pass," 39-48.
19. "For Kern River Gold Mines via San Pedro," *San Francisco Daily, Alta California*, January 23, 1855.
20. *Southern Californian*, June 20, 1855.
21. Ibid.
22. Browne to Manypenny, January 22, 1855.

23. Townsend, *California Diary*, 126.
24. *Los Angeles Star,* November 9, 1854.
25. *Southern Californian,* June 13, 1855. The physical environment of the fort is discussed in Stammerjohan et al., *Fort Tejon State Historic Park*, 25-35.
26. *Southern Californian,* June 20, 1855. For a discussion of Indian life in Los Angeles, consult Phillips, *Vineyards and Vaqueros*, 81-86, 115-127, 259-295.
27. *Los Angeles Star,* June 30, 1855.
28. Ibid. For the original report, see Thomas Henley to George W. Manypenny, San Francisco, April 14, 1855, Office of Indian Affairs, Letters Received, 1824-81, roll 34.
29. Samuel Bishop to editors, Los Angeles, July 5, 1855, *Southern Californian*, July 18, 1855. See also the *Southern Californian,* July 4, 1855.
30. Thomas Henley to Charles E. Mix, San Francisco, September 19, 1855, Office of Indian Affairs, Letters Received, 1824-81, roll 34.
31. John R. Grice to George W. Manypenny, Sebastian Indian Reservation, November 30, 1855, Office of Indian Affairs, Letters Received, 1824-81, roll 35.
32. Walter H. Harvey to Gen. James W. Denver, Los Angeles, October 31, 1855. Office of Indian Affairs, Letters Received, 1824-81, roll 34.
33. *Los Angeles Star*, September 15, 1855.
34. *Southern Californian*, late September 1855, in Hayes, Scrapbooks, vol. 39.
35. Edward F. Beale to B. D. Wilson, Washington, D.C., January 18, 1855, Wilson Collection, WN 1169.
36. Pitt, *Los Angeles A to Z: An Encyclopedia of the City and County*, 20.
37. "Notes on a Trip to Los Angeles—No. 2;" *San Francisco Daily, Alta California*, October 7, n.y..
38. Thompson, *Edward F. Beale*, 89-90; Crowe, *Men of El Tejon*, 49.
39. Samuel Bishop, deposition, December 21, 1855, in Transcript of the Proceedings in Case No. 170. According to the *Los Angeles Star* of June 28, 1856, between two and three thousand head of cattle grazed on the rancho.
40. Bonsal, *Edward Fitzgerald Beale*, 277.
41. Johnson and Earle, "Tataviam Geography and Ethnohistory," 195, 201.
42. Kip, *The Early Days of My Episcopate*, 219.
43. Townsend, *The California Diary of General E. D. Townsend*, 115.
44. *Los Angeles Star*, October 20, 1855. On one occasion, Beale supposedly told an employee that cattle, with the brand La Cachora, were grazing on the rancho when he bought it. See Latta, *The Saga of Rancho El*

Tejón, 193. This book consists of a long interview by Latta with José Jesús López, the narration being in words of López.

45. Juan Coluco, testimony, Tule River Indian Agency. February 23, 1922, Papers of John P. Harrington in the Smithsonian Institution, Northern and Central California, Records Relating to the Tejón Case, 690510-100, Microfilm 100 and 525m, vol. 2, and 4.
46. J. Ross Browne, Report and accompanying documents, concerning account &tc. of Supt. Beale, Washington, D.C., January 22, 1855, Records of the U.S. Senate, Sen. 35A-F2, RG 46, NA.
47. *Population Schedules of the Eighth Census of the United States, 1860*, vol. 3, Fresno, Humboldt, Klamath, and Los Angeles Counties, Microcopy 653, Roll 59, NA, 2.
48. Thomas Henley to George W. Manypenny, San Francisco, October 19, 1855, including a copy of Memorial of Citizens of Los Angeles City & County, protesting against the removal of the Sebastian Military Reservation, October 6, 1855, Office of Indian Affairs, Letters Received, 1824-81, roll 34.
49. Thomas Henley to George W. Manypenny, San Francisco, November 15, 1855, including a copy of a protest from the Citizens of Santa Barbara County, against the removal of the Sebastian Military Reserve, Santa Barbara, October 8, 1855, Office of Indian Affairs, Letters Received, 1824-81, roll 34.
50. *Los Angeles Star*, October 20, 1855.
51. *Southern Californian*, October 24, 1855.
52. *Los Angeles Star*, October 27, 1855.
53. Ibid., November 10, 1855.
54. Ibid.
55. "The Sebastian Indian Reserve," *Santa Barbara Gazette*, November 15, 1855.
56. *Los Angeles Star*, November 24, 1855.
57. John B. Weller to B. D. Wilson, Washington, D.C., January 17, 1856, Wilson Collection, WN 928.
58. Concurrent Resolutions, March 20, 1856, California Legislature, *Journal of the Assembly*, 7th sess., 521-22.
59. John B. Weller and P. T. Herbert to Robert McClelland, Washington, D.C., May 28, 1856, Office of Indian Affairs, Letters Received, 1824-81, roll 34.
60. Letter on the Condition of the Indian Reservations in California from J. Ross Browne, n.p., n.d., 1857, Office of Indian Affairs, Letters Received, 1824-81, roll 35.
61. J. Ross Browne to James W. Denver, San Francisco, January 14, 1858, Office of Indian Affairs, Letters Received, 1824-81, roll 36.
62. Ibid.

63. *San Francisco Daily Morning Call*, February 19, 1858.
64. Godard Bailey to Charles E. Mix, Washington, D.C., October 27, 1858. Office of Indian Affairs, Letters Received, 1824-81, roll 36.
65. J. Ross Browne to Charles E. Mix, San Francisco, September 4, 1858, Office of Indian Affairs, Letters Received, 1824-81, roll 36.
66. Godard Bailey to Charles E. Mix, Washington, D.C., November 4, 1858, *Annual Report of the Commissioner of Indian Affairs for the Year 1858*, 298.
67. Ibid., 302.
68. Ibid., 303-4.
69. Ibid., 304-5.
70. Ibid., 305.
71. Charles E. Mix to Jacob Thompson, Washington, D.C., November 6, 1858, *Annual Report of the Commissioner of Indian Affairs for the Year 1858*, 10-ll.
72. Report of the Secretary of the Interior, December 2, 1858, in Message of the President of the United States to the Two Houses of Congress at the Commencement of the Second Session of the Thirty-fifth Congress, 83.
73. *San Francisco Weekly National*, January 13, 1859. Editor's emphasis.
74. O. M. Wozencraft to editors, January 6, 1859, *San Francisco Weekly National*, January 6, 1858.
75. *San Francisco Daily Herald*, January 25, 1859.
76. "The Purchase of Lower California as an Indian Reservation," *San Diego Herald*, May 23, 1859. The idea of expelling the Indians of California to Santa Cruz and Santa Rosa Islands was discussed respectively in the *Marysville Daily Appeal*, February 21, 1862, and in the *Visalia Weekly Delta*, December 17, 1863.

Chapter XXII: The Indian Farms

1. "Messenger" to editors, Fort Miller, October 27, 1853, *San Francisco Daily, Alta California*, November 2, 1853.
2. *Mariposa Chronicle*, October 6, 1854.
3. Thomas Henley to George W. Manypenny, San Francisco, October 14, 1854, Office of Indian Affairs, Letters Received, 1824-81, roll 33; *San Francisco Daily Herald*, October 12, 1854.
4. Thomas Henley, A Statement of Mechanics Laborers & Employed on the Fresno Indian Farm, California, Commencing September 12, 1854 and ending June 30, 1855, Office of Indian Affairs, Letters Received, 1824-81, rolell 34.
5. J. Ross Browne to George W. Manypenny, Washington, D.C., January 22, 1855, in Browne, Report and accompanying documents, concerning accounts, &tc. of Supt. Beale.

6. Lieut. Lucien Loeser to Asst. Adj. Gen. E. D. Townsend, Fort Miller, October 6, 1854, U.S. Army Continental Commands, Letters Received, 1821-1920.
7. Edward F. Beale to Luke Lea, Fresno River, December 14, 1852, U.S. Congress, Senate, 33d Cong., sp. Sess., Exec. Doc, 4, Serial 688, 391.
8. D. A. Enyart to Thomas Henley, Fresno Reservation, November 3, 1854, Office of Indian Affairs, Letters Received, 1824-81, rolel1 34.
9. D. A. Enyart, labor report, January 1 to February 1, 1855, Fresno Indian Farm, February 1, 1855, in Thomas Henley to George W. Manypenny, San Francisco, February 20, 1855, Office of Indian Affairs, Letters Received, 1824-81, roll 34.
10. D. A. Enyart to Thomas Henley, Fresno Indian Farm, January 25, 1855, Office of Indian Affairs, Letters Received, 1824-81, rolel1 34.
11. Ibid.
12. D. A. Enyart, Daily Journal of Fresno Indian Farm for the Months of February & March, February 1, 11, 30, 1855, Office of Indian Affairs, Letters Received, 1824-81, roll 34.
13. Thomas Henley to George W. Manypenny, San Francisco, April 14, 1855, Office of Indian Affairs, Letters Received, 1824-81, roll 34. Most likely, the chief was Naiyakqua.
14. D. A. Enyart to Thomas Henley, Fresno Indian Farm, May 16, 1855, Office of Indian Affairs, Letters Received, 1824-8l, roll 34.
15. D A. Enyart to Thomas Henley, Fresno Farm, June 1, 1855, Office of Indian Affairs, Letters Received, 1824-81, roll 34; D. A. Enyart to editors, Fresno Indian Farm, June 14, 1855, *San Joaquin Republican*, June: 19, 1855.
16. Enyart to Henley, June 1, 1855; Enyart to editors, June 14, 1855.
17. Enyart to Henley, June l, 1855.
18. Enyart to editors, June 14, 1855.
19. Henley to Manypenny, April 14, 1855.
20. A Statement of Mechanics, laborers etc. employed on the Fresno Indian Farm, Cal'a during the Quarter Ending December 31st 1855, Office of Indian Affairs, Letters Received, 824-81, roll 35.
21. William Campbell to Thomas Henley, Kings River, May 3, 1855, Office of Indian Affairs, Letters Received, 1824-81, roll 34.
22. Ibid; William Campbell to Thomas Henley, Kings River, July 23, 1855, in Thomas Henley to George W. Manypenny, August 14, 1855, Office of Indian Affairs, Letters Received, 1824-81, roll 34.
23. D. A. Enyart to Thomas Henley, Fresno Indian Farm, August 22, 1855, Office of Indian Affairs, Letters Received, 1824-81, ro1l 34.
24. E. P. Hart, statement, Visalia, January 2, 1859, *Mariposa Star*, February 1, 1859.

25. M. B. Lewis to Thomas Henley, Fresno Farm, December 13, 1855, Office of Indian Affairs, Letters Received, 1824-81, roll 35.
26. Ibid.
27. William Welby and Samuel Brooks to M. B. Lewis, Fresno River, February 22, 1856, Office of Indian Affairs, Letters Received, 1824-81, roll 35.
28. M. B. Lewis to Thomas Henley, Fresno Indian Farm, March 24, 1856, Office of Indian Affairs, Letters Received, 1824-81, roll 35.
29. Ibid., January 19, 1856.
30. Ibid., March 22, 1856.
31. Ibid., April 11, 1856.
32. Ibid., April 19, 1856.
33. Ibid., May 2, 1856.
34. Ibid., May 16, 1856.
35. Ibid., May 23, 1856.
36. M. B. Lewis to Thomas Henley, Fresno Indian Farm, July 22, *Annual Report of the Commissioner of Indian Affairs for the Year 1856*, 252-54.
37. M. B. Lewis to Thomas Henley, Statement of Indians belonging to and recognizing the Fresno Indian Agency on 30th September 1856, in Thomas Henley to George W. Manypenny, San Francisco, November 5, 1856, Office of Indian Affairs, Letters Received, 1824-81, roll 35.
38. Thomas Henley to M. B. Lewis, San Francisco, August 7, 1856, Office of Indian Affairs, Letters Received, 1824-81, roll 35.
39. M. B. Lewis to Thomas Henley, Fresno Indian Farm, September 28, 1856, Office of Indian Affairs, Letters Received, 1824-81, roll 35.
40. Thomas Henley to George W. Manypenny, San Francisco, September 4, 1856, *Annual Report of the Commissioner of Indian Affairs for the Year 1856*, 226-27.
41. "The Indian Tribes of the Tulare Valley," *San Francisco Daily Herald*, December 19, 1853, typed version in Cohen, Scrapbooks, vol. 1. For an overview of Indian burning, consult Lewis, *Indian Burning*.
42. M. B. Lewis to Thomas Henley, Fresno Farm, July 22, 1856, *Annual Report of the Commissioner of Indian Affairs for the Year 1856*, 254-55.
43. *Sacramento Daily Union*, August 27, 1856.
44. Ibid.
45. Lieut. LaRhett L. Livingston to Asst. Adj. Gen. W. W. Mackall, Fort Miller, August 17, 1856, in Message from the President of the United States, transmitting Report in regard to Indian Affairs on the Pacific, February 16, 1857, U.S. Congress, House, 34th Cong., 3d sess., Exec. Doc. 76, 136.
46. William Campbell to Thomas Henley, Millerton, September 12, 1856, Office of Indian Affairs, Letters Received, 1824-81, roll 35.

47. Ibid.
48. Lieut. Lucien Loeser to Asst. Adj. Gen. W. W. Mackall, Fort Miller, October 28, 1856, in Message from the President, 141.
49. When Indians began stealing stock along the lower Kings River is not known, but stockmen claimed it was soon after they arrived. See Justin Esrey et al., to M. B. Lewis, Fresno Indian Agency, November 14, 1858, Office of Indian Affairs, Letters Received, 1824-81, roll 36.
50. Citizens of the lower Kings River to M. B. Lewis, Kings River, October 25, 1857, Office of Indian Affairs, Letters Received, 1824-81, roll 36.
51. M. B. Lewis to Thomas Henley, Fresno Indian Farm, December 7, 1857, Office of Indian Affairs, Letters Received, 1824-81, roll 36.
52. Thomas Henley to M. B. Lewis, San Francisco, December 19, 1857, Office of Indian Affairs, Letters Received, 1824-81, roll 36.
53. Thomas Henley to James W. Denver, San Francisco, December 18, 1857, Office of Indian Affairs, Letters Received, 1824-81, roll 36.
54. Thomas P. Madden to Thomas Henley, Tejón Agency, June 22, 1857, Office of Indian Affairs, Letters Received, 1824-81, roll 35.
55. M. B. Lewis to Thomas Henley, Fresno Indian Farm, August 4, 1857, *Annual Report of the Commissioner of Indian Affairs for the Year 1857*, 400-401.
56. Lieut. LaRhett L. Livingston to M. B. Lewis, Fort Miller, November 30, 1857, Office of Indian Affairs, Letters Received, 1824-81, roll 36.
57. M. B. Lewis to Lieut. LaRhett L. Livingston, Fresno Indian Farm, December 7, 1857, Office of Indian Affairs, Letters Received, 1824-81, roll 36.
58. M. B. Lewis to Thomas Henley, Fresno Indian Farm, January 4, 1858, Office of Indian Affairs, Letters Received, 1824-8l, roll 36.
59. M. B. Lewis to Thomas Henley, Fresno Farm, May 8, 1858, Office of Indian Affairs, Letters Received, 1824-81, roll 36.
60. M. B. Lewis to Thomas Henley, Fresno Indian Agency, August 18, 1858, *Annual Report of the Commissioner of Indian Affairs for the Year 1858*, 291-92.
61. M. B. Lewis to Thomas Henley, Fresno Indian Agency, September 26, 1858, Office of Indian Affairs, Letters Received, 1824-81, roll 36.
62. Thomas Henley to Charles E. Mix, San Francisco, September 4, 1858, *Annual Report of the Commissioner of Indian Affairs for the Year 1858*, 283 .
63. J. Ross Browne to Charles E. Mix, San Francisco, November 1, 1858, Office of Indian Affairs, Letters Received, 1824-81, roll 36.

64. W. G. to editors, King's River, November 12, 1858, *San Joaquin Republican*, November 27, 1858.
65. William F. Edgar to J. Ross Browne, San Francisco, July 18, 1858, Office of Indian Affairs, Letters Received, 1824-81, roll 36. See also Richter, *Fort Miller*, 70.
66. According to a settler, M. B. Lewis spread the rumor. Whether true or not (and probably not), it might have motivated the settlers to take the law into their own hands, See W. G. to editors, Fresno, December 20, 1858, *San Joaquin Republican*, December 31, 1858.
67. M. B. Lewis to Thomas Henley, Fresno Indian Agency, November 14, 1858, Office of Indian Affairs, Letters Received, 1824-81, roll 36.
68. Ibid.
69. M. B. Lewis to Thomas Henley, Fresno Indian Agency, November 21, 1858, Office of Indian Affairs, Letters Received, 1824-81, roll 36.
70. M. B. Lewis to L.A. Whitmore, Fresno Indian Agency, November 11, 1858, Office of Indian Affairs, Letters Received, 1824-81, roll 36. Evidently, L.A. Whitmore paid dearly for his assistance. The *San Joaquin Republican* reported on February 17, 1859 that a dozen settlers, all of whom supported the relocation, broke into his house, and a Dr. Workman shot him dead. Supposedly the violence erupted over an argument involving the loss of a pig, but it probably resulted from Whitmore's support of the Indians.
71. Lewis to Henley, November 14, 1858.
72. P. to editors, Fresno Indian Agency, November 15, 1858, *Mariposa Gazette*, December 3, 1858.
73. Esrey et al., to Lewis, November 14, 1858.
74. W. G. to editors, Fresno, December 20, 1858, *San Joaquin Republican*, December 31, 1858.
75. Ibid.
76. M. B. Lewis to Thomas Henley, Fresno Indian Agency, December 27, 1858, Office of Indian Affairs, Letters Received, 1824-8l, roll 37.
77. Ibid.
78. M. B. Lewis to Thomas Henley, Fresno Indian Agency, January 1859, Office of Indian Affairs, Letters Received, 1824-81, roll 37.
79. Lewis to Henley, December 27, 1858.
80. M. B. Lewis to Alfred B. Greenwood, Fresno Farm, August 30, 1859, Office of Indian Affairs, Letters Received, 1824-81, roll 37.

Chapter XXIII: Cross Purposes

1. *San Jose Telegraph* and *Santa Clara County Register*, July 27, 1854.
2. Frederick Kerlin to B. D. Wilson, Tejón, July 16, 1854, Wilson Collection, WN 498.
3. *San Jose Telegraph* and *Santa Clara County Resister*, July 27, 1854.
4. Kerlin to Wilson, July 16, 1854. A newspaper reported that only fifty Indians had fled to the east side of the Sierra Nevada. See *Southern Californian*, July 27, 1854.
5. Frederick Kerlin, statement, Washington, D.C., December 14, 1854, in Edward F. Beale to George W. Manypenny, Washington, D.C., December 14, 1854, U.S. Congress, Senate, Records of the Senate; *San Jose Telegraph* and *Santa Clara County Register*, July 27, 1854.
6. H. to editors, Yuba County, April 17, 1855, *San Francisco Daily, Alta California*, April 20, 1 855.
7. Thomas Henley to George W. Manypenny, San Francisco, July 23, 1855, Office of Indian Affairs, Letters Received, 1824-81, roll 34.
8. [Rasey Biven] to editors, Sebastian Military Reserve, September 22, 1854, *San Francisco Daily Placer Times and Transcript*, n.d., in Thomas Henley to George W. Manypenny, December 29, 1854. Office of Indian Affairs, Letters Received 1824-8l, roll 34. Raymundo is identified as Beale's interpreter in Thomas Henley to George W. Manypenny, San Francisco, October 20, 1855, Office of Indian Affairs, Letters Received, 1824-81, roll 34.
9. [Biven] to editors, September 22, 1854.
10. Thomas Henley to Samuel Bishop, San Francisco, September 26, 1854, Office of Indian Affairs, Letters Received, 1824-81, roll 36.
11. Thomas Henley to George W. Manypenny, San Francisco, August 28, 1854, *Annual Report of the Commissioner of Indian Affairs for the Year 1854*, 302; [Biven] to editors, September 22, 1854.
12. Invoice of Public Property, Tejon Reservation, August 7, 1854, Office of Indian Affairs, Letters Received, 1824-81, roll 33.
13. [Biven] to editors, September 22, 1854. Biven's emphasis.
14. Benjamin Wilson et al., deposition, Los Angeles, October l, 1854, Office of Indian Affairs, Letters Received, 1824-81, roll 33.
15. Thomas Henley to George W. Manypenny, San Francisco, December 8, 1854, Office of Indian Affairs, Letters Received, 1824-81, roll 34.
16. Edward F. Beale, deposition, Washington, D.C., January 20, 1855, Office of Indian Affairs, Letters Received, 1824-81, rol l 34; Edward F. Beale, M. B. Lewis, Lewis Leach, Lorenzo Vinsonhaler, testimonies, n.d., n.p., in the United States Court of Claims, Samuel J. Hensley vs. The United States, Wright Manuscript, 4-8.
17. J. Ross Browne to George W. Manypenny, Washington, D.C., January 22, 1855, in Browne, Report and accompanying documents,

concerning accounts, &tc. of Supt. Beale; Pay Schedule, Tejon Reservation, November 13, 1853, U.S. Congress, Senate, Records of the Senate.

18. Thomas Henley to George W. Manypenny, San Francisco, December 8, 1854, Office of Indian Affairs, Letters Received, 1824-81, roll 34.
19. Ibid.; Beale, deposition, January 20, 1855, Browne to Manypenny, January 22, 1855. On one occasion Samuel Dummer acknowledged raising his own sheep on the reservation. See Samuel Dummer to B. D. Wilson, Tejon, April 4, 1854, Wilson Collection, WN 245.
20. Browne to Manypenny, January 22, 1855.
21. J. Ross Browne to Charles E. Mix, San Francisco, October 8, 1858, Office of Indian Affairs, Letters Received, 1824-81, roll 36.
22. [Biven] to editors, September 22, 1854. Biven's emphasis.
23. Thomas Henley to George W. Manypenny, San Francisco, August 28, 1854, Office of Indian Affairs, Letters Received, 1824-81, roll 33.
24. Thomas Henley to George W. Manypenny, San Francisco, September 1, 1854, Office of Indian Affairs, Letters Received, 1824-81, roll 33.
25. Thomas Henley to George W. Manypenny, August 28, 1854, *Annual Report of the Commissioner of Indian Affairs for the Year 1854*, 303-304. This is a different letter from the one cited in note 23.
26. Ibid., 301, 304. John Sutter's use of Indian labor is discussed in Hurtado, *Indian Survival*, 55-71.
27. Thomas Henley to Edward F. Beale, San Francisco, September 15, 1854, Office of Indian Affairs, Letters Received, 1824-81, roll 33.
28. Thomas Henley to Samuel Bishop, San Francisco, September 26, 1854, Office of Indian Affairs, Letters Received, 1824-81, roll 34.
29. A Statement of Mechanics, Laborers, etc., employed on the Sebastian Military Reservation, California, commencing July 30, 1854, and ending June 30, 1855, Office of Indian Affairs, Letters Received, 1824-81, roll 34.
30. Alonzo Ridley to Thomas Henley, Sebastian Military Reserve, September 30, 1855, Office of Indian Affairs, Letters Received, 1824-81, roll 34.
31. Thomas Henley and J. Ross Browne to George W. Manypenny, San Francisco, October 15, 1854, Office of Indian Affairs, Special Files, File 159.
32. *San Francisco Daily Herald*, October 16, 1854.
33. Browne to Manypenny, January 22, 1855.
34. Ibid.
35. Ibid.
36. J. Ross Browne to George W. Manypenny, San Francisco, November 14, 1854, Office of Indian Affairs, Special Files, File 159.

37. Edward F. Beale to B. D. Wilson, San Francisco, October 14, 1854. Wilson Collection, WN 114.
38. Browne to Manypenny, January 22, 1855.
39. Edward F. Beale to B. D. Wilson, Washington, D.C., January 18, 1855, Wilson Collection, WN 1169.
40. Frederick Kerlin to B. D. Wilson, Washington, D.C., March 7, 1855, Wilson Collection, WN 499.
41. Thomas Henley to George W. Manypenny, San Francisco, December 7, 1854, Office of Indian Affairs, Letters Received, 1824-81, roll 34.
42. Thomas Henley to George W. Manypenny, San Francisco, January 29, 1855, Office of Indian Affairs, Letters Received, 1824-81, roll 34.
43. Saunder Ranson to J. Ross Browne, San Francisco, December 9, 1854, U.S. Congress, Senate, Records of the Senate.
44. Henley to Manypenny, December 7, 1854.
45. Thomas Henley to George W. Manypenny, San Francisco, April 14, 1855, Office of Indian Affairs, Letters Received, 1824-81, roll 34.
46. *San Francisco Daily Herald*, May 13, 1855.
47. *Southern Californian*, July 18, 1855.
48. Browne to Mix, October 8, 1858; *Los Angeles Star*, February 8, 1855.
49. A Statement of Mechanics, Laborers, &tc., employed on the Sebastian Military Reservation, during the 3d Quarter ending 30th September 1855, Office of Indian Affairs, Letters Received, 1824-81, roll 34.
50. *Los Angeles Star*, August 11, 1855.
51. Copy of Instructions to Subagent Alonzo Ridley, in Thomas Henley to George W. Manypenny, San Francisco, July 16, 1855, Office of Indian Affairs, Letters Received, 1824-Bl, roll 34; Statement of Mechanics, Laborers &tc. employed on the Sebastian Military Reserve, during the 4th quarter 1855, Office of Indian Affairs, Letters Received, 1824-81, roll 35
52. Copy of instructions to Ridley.
53. Report of Labor ending October 1, 1855, Tejon Reservation, in Thomas Henley to George W Manypenny, San Francisco, October 20, 1855, Office of Indian Affairs, Letters Received, 1824-81, roll 34.
54. Report of Labor, December 11, 1854, Tejon Reservation, in Thomas Henley to George W. Manypenny, San Francisco, October 20, 1855, Office of Indian Affairs, Letters Received, 1824- 81, roll 34.
55. Alonzo Ridley, Report of Labor, October 8, 1855, Tejon Reservation, in Thomas Henley to George W. Manypenny, San Francisco, November 17, 1855, Office of Indian Affairs, Letters Received, 1824-81, roll 34.
56. Townsend, *California Diary*, 127.

57. Ibid., 127-29.
58. Ibid., 129.
59. In his report to Henley of January 22, 1855, J. Ross Browne warned that whites might divide into factions.
60. *Los Angeles Star*, October 19, 1854.
61. Ibid., October 26, 1854.
62. Lieut. Col. Benjamin L. Beall to Judge Ord, Fort Tejon, November 21, 1854, unidentified newspaper article, n.d., in "Tejón Reservation," Hayes, Scrapbooks, vol. 39. Redman's employment ended shortly before the incident. See A Statement of Mechanics, Laborers & Employed on Sebastian Military Reservation Commencing July 20, 1854 and ending June 1855, Office of Indian Affairs, Letters Received, 1824-81, roll 34.
63. *Southern Californian*, December 7, 1854, in "Tejon Reservation," Hayes, Scrapbooks, vol. 39. The newspaper article was copied by hand from the original.
64. Thomas Henley to George W. Manypenny, San Francisco, May 1855, Office of Indian Affairs, Letters Received, 1824-81, roll 34.
65. Report of labor done at the Sebastian Military Reserve from June 21, 1855 to June 27, 1855, in Thomas Henley to George W. Manypenny, San Francisco, July 16, 1855, Office of Indian Affairs, Letters Received, 1824-81, roll 34.
66. Thomas Henley to Maj. Gen. John Wool, San Francisco, October 15, 1855, in Thomas Henley to George W. Manypenny, San Francisco, October 20, 1855, Office of Indian Affairs, Letters Received, 1824-81, roll 34. See also, Hinton, "John Ellis Wool," 294-95.
67. Henley to Wool, October 15, 1855.
68. Thomas Henley to George W. Manypenny, October 20, 1855, Office of Indian Affairs, Letters Received, 1824-81, roll 34.
69. John Grice to George W. Manypenny, November 10, 1855, Tejon Reservation, Office of Indian Affairs, Letters Received, 1824-81, roll 35.
70. Thomas Henley to J. Neely Johnson, San Francisco, June 24, 1856, Secretary of State Office, Indian War Papers.
71. "Law Intelligence," May 8, 1855, *San Francisco Daily Herald*, May 9, 1855.
72. Thomas Henley to George W. Manypenny, San Francisco, July 12, 1855, Office of Indian Affairs, Letters Received, 1824-81, roll 34.
73. J. Lancaster Brent to Thomas Henley, Sacramento, February 2, 1856, Office of Indian Affairs, Letters Received, 1824-81, roll 35.
74. George W. Manypenny to Robert McClelland, Washington, D.C., June 21, 1856, U.S. Congress, House, Records of the House of Representatives.

75. The secretary of the interior appointed Vineyard Indian agent in early 1855, but as of May he had not been assigned to the Tejon Reservation. See Robert McClelland to Thomas Henley, Washington, D.C., March 16, 1855, and Statement of Employees engaged in the Indian Service in California and not located upon Indian Reservations during the 3rd Quarter ending 30th September 1855, Office of Indian Affairs, Letters Received, 1824-81, roll 34.
76. J. R. Vineyard, Report of Labor on Tejon Reserve for the week ending August 23, 1856, Office of Indian Affairs, Letters Received, 1824-81, roll 35; Porte Monnaie to editors, Sebastian Reservation, n.d., *Los Angeles Star*, May 22, 1858.
77. J. R. Vineyard to Thomas Henley, Sebastian Military Reserve, July [?], 1856, *Annual Report of the Commissioner of Indian Affairs for the Year 1856*, 246.
78. Ibid., 248.
79. "Treaty Made and Concluded at Camp Persifer F. Smith, at the Texan Pass, State of California, June 10, 1851, Between George W. Barbour, United States Commissioner, and the Chiefs, Captains and Head Men of the 'Castake,' 'Texon,' &tc., Tribes of Indians," in Kappler, ed., *Indian Affairs*, vol. 4, 1102.
80. Vineyard to Henley, July [?] 1856, 247.
81. Thomas Henley to J. R. Vineyard, San Francisco, August 7, 1856, Office of Indian Affairs, Letters Received, 1824-81, roll 35.
82. Vineyard, Report of Labor ending August 23, 1856.
83. Thomas Henley to George W. Manypenny, San Francisco, November 13, 1856, Office of Indian Affairs, Letters Received, 1824-81, roll 35.
84. J. R. Vineyard, Report of Labor on Sebastian Military Reserve commencing September 15 and ending October 25, 1856, in Thomas Henley to George W. Manypenny, San Francisco, November 13, 1856, Office of Indian Affairs, Letters Received 1824-81, roll 35.
85. Thomas Henley to George W. Manypenny, San Francisco, September 4, 1856, *Annual Report of the Commissioner of Indian Affairs for the Year 1856*, 236. The paraphrased version of Henley's letter, originally published in the *Christian Advocate*, n.d., was reprinted in *San Francisco Daily, Alta California* on January 9, 1857.
86. Thomas Henley to George W. Manypenny, San Francisco, February 18, 1857, Office of Indian Affairs, Letters Received, 1824-81, roll 35.
87. J. R. Vineyard to Thomas Henley, Sebastian Military Reserve, August 15, 1857; *Annual Report of the Commissioner of Indian Affairs for the Year 1857*, 401-402.
88. Thomas Madden to Thomas Henley, Office of Tejón Agency, June

25, 1857, Office of Indian Affairs, Letters Received, 1824- 81, roll 35.

89. Ibid.
90. Thomas Henley to R. Vineyard, San Francisco, July 10, 1857, Office of Indian Affairs, Letters Received, 1824-81, roll 35.
91. Thomas Madden to Thomas Henley, San Francisco, September 20, 1857, in Thomas Henley to James W. Denver, San Francisco, October 2, 1857, Office of Indian Affairs, Letters Received, 1824-8l, roll 35.
92. Ibid.
93. Ibid.
94. Vineyard to Henley, August 15, 1857, 402.
95. Madden to Henley, September 20, 1857.
96. *Los Angeles Star*, February 20, 1858.
97. John Temple to Charles E. Mix, Washington, D.C., January 30, 1858, Office of Indian Affairs, Letters Received, 1824-81, ro11 36.
98. J. Lancaster Brent to Charles E. Mix, Washington, D.C., March 25, 1858, Office of Indian Affairs, Letters Received, 1824-81, roll 36.
99. J. R. Vineyard to Thomas Henley, Tejón Agency, August 20, *Annual Report of the Commissioner of Indian Affairs for the Year 1858*, 294-96. Evidently, the Indians traded or sold some of their handiwork, because at least two of their garments reached Northern California. "We have seen some specimens of sewing by Indian women of the Tejón Reservation," reported a newspaper. "It is most elegant and beautiful work. The specimens which we saw were a little girl's dress and a lady's undergarment, embroidered. It is as nice as any work ever done by white hands." See *Red Bluff Beacon*, n.d. reprinted in *Sacramento Daily Union*, October 11, 1858.
100. Vineyard to Henley, August 20, 1858.
101. Inventory of public property remaining on hand at Tejon Indian Reservation (James R. Vineyard, agent), on 13th of June, 1859. Report of the Secretary of the Interior, 36th Cong., 1st Sess. Senate, Exec. Doc. 45, 35-37.
102. Letter to editors, Fort Tejón, June 22, 1859, *Los Angeles Star*, June 25, 1859.
103. Benjamin Hayes, Diary, January 5, 1860, in Wolcott, ed., *Pioneer Notes*, 184-85. See also the *Los Angeles Star*, September 3, 1859 and February 4, 1860.
104. Vineyard to Henley, August 15, 1857.
105. J. R. Vineyard to James McDuffie, Tejon Agency, August 12, *Annual Report of the Commissioner of Indian Affairs for the Year 1859*, 443-44.
106. Ibid.

Chapter XXIV: Resistance and Retaliation in the Tulare Valley

1. Capt. Thomas Jordan to Maj. Osborn A. Cross, Fort Miller, August 15, 1853, Office of the Quartermaster General, Consolidated File on Fort Miller, 1853-58. The California State Census of 1852 put the number of Indians in Tulare County at 8,400. The county then encompassed most of the Tulare Valley. See Governor's Message, and the Abstract of the Census of 1852 of the State of California appendix of the *Journal of the Senate*, 4th sess., 1853, 53. At least one contemporary challenged the validity of the census, claiming that only 1,000 to 1,500 Indians resided in the valley. See J. H. B. [Joel Brooks] to editors, Tehon Pass, August 2, 1852, *San Francisco Daily Alta California*, August 9, 1852, 2; Lieut. John Nugen to Lieut. Thomas Wright, Camp Wessells, December 31, 1853, U.S. Army Continental Command, Letters Received, 1821-1920.
3. "Tripod" to editors, n.p., n.d., *San Joaquin Republican*, December 11, 1853.
4. Lieut. Nathaniel H. McLean to Maj. Henry W. Wessells, Fort Miller, July 12, 1853, Office of the Adjutant General, Letters Received, 1822-1860.
5. The attack is described in Chapter 7.
6. McLean to Wessells, July 12, 1853.
7. *San Francisco Daily Herald*, July 25, 1852.
8. Stewart, "Interview with S. C. Brown," Stewart Collection.
9. McLean to Wessells, July 12, 1853.
10. Abraham Hillard to editors, n.p., n.d., *San Francisco Mirror*, n.d., reprinted in the *Visalia Sun*, September 5, 1860; Nugen to Wright, December 31, 1851. See also Stewart, "Indian War," 47.
11. Nugen to Wright, December 31, 1853.
12. Maj. Henry W. Wessells to Asst. Adj. Gen. E. D. Townsend, March 7, 1854, U.S. Army Continental Commands, Letters Received, 1821-1920.
13. W.R. Davis to editors, Posy Creek, May 11, 1855, *San Jose Semi-Weekly Tribune*, May 25, 1855; Hillard to editors, n.d.; Stewart, "Indian War," 48.
14. Townsend, *California Diary*, 135.
15. William P. Lewis et al., to Thomas Henley, Visalia, August 28, 1855, Office of Indian Affairs, Letters Received, 1824-81, roll 34.
16. Thomas Henley to Samuel Jennings, San Francisco, September 20, 1855, Office of Indian Affairs, Letters Received, 1824-81, roll 35.
17. Samuel Jennings to Thomas Henley, Visalia, February 5, 1856, in Thomas Henley to George W. Manypenny, San Francisco, June 3, 1856, Office of Indian Affairs, Letters Received, 1824-81, roll 35.
18. Hittell, *Mining*, 27-28.

19. Boyd, *California Middle Border*, 49.
20. Thomas Henley to Charles E. Mix, San Francisco, February 9, 1858, Office of Indian Affairs, Letters Received, 1824-81, roll 36.
21. "Superintendent Beale—The Tejon Reservation," *Los Angeles Star*, June 17, 1854. Urbano had signed the treaty with George Barbour at Tejon. See "Treaty Made and Concluded at Camp presider F. Smith, at the Texan Pass, State of California. June 10, 1851. Between George W. Barbour United States Commissioner, and the Chiefs. Captains, and Head Men of the 'Castake,' 'Texon.' &tc., Tribes of Indians," in Kappler, ed., *Indian Affairs*, vol. 4, 1102.
22. Thomas Maltby to Thomas Henley, Kern River, December 13, 1857, in Henley to Mix, February 9, 1858.
23. Ibid. Maltby thought the Indians who attacked Urbano's people were "Tulare Indians" (Tulareños), but they most likely were Paiutes. See also Joseph Daniels to Thomas Henley, San Francisco, May 25, 1856, in Henley to Manypenny, June 3, 1856. The early years of Keysville are discussed in Boyd, *California Middle Border*, 49-55.
24. Maltby to Henley, December 13, 1857; Daniels to Henley, May 25, 1856.
25. Hugh A. Carrolel to Thomas Henley, Visalia, April 30, 1856, in Henley to Manypenny, June 3, 1856. The incident ignited what has been called the Tule River War. See Stewart, "Indian War," 46-53; Mitchell, "Tule River Indian'War," 1-3; Gorenfeld and Gorenfeld, "Tule River War," 48- 52, 80; and Frank and Goldberg, *Defying the Odds*, 37-40.
26. *San Francisco Daily Evening Bulletin*, May 5, 1856.
27. *San Joaquin Republican*, May 6, 1856.
28. Daniels to Henley, May 25, 1856; Robert Murray to editors, Fort Miller, May 18, 1856, *San Francisco Daily Evening Bulletin*, May 23, 1856.
29. Carrolel to Henley, April 30, 1856.
30. *San Joaquin Republican*, May 5, 1856; *Sacramento Daily Union*, May 7, 1856.
31. J. R. Vineyard to Thomas Henley, Tejon Reservation, May 22, 1856, Office of Indian Affairs, Letters Received, 1824-81, roll 35.
32. Lieut. Col. Benjamin L. Beall to Asst. Adj. Gen. D.R. Jones, Fort Tejon, May 3, 1856, in Message from the President, February 16, 1857, 119; J. R. Vineyard to Thomas Henley, Report of Labor on Sebastian Military Reservation commencing April 1st and ending May 3rd, 1856, Office of Indian Affairs, Letters Received 1824-81, rolel1 35.
33. J. R. Vineyard to Thomas Henley, May 22, 1856, Office of Indian Affairs, Letters Received, 1824-81, roll 35.

34. Correspondent to editors, n.p., n.d., *Volcano Ledger*, n.d., reprinted in *Sacramento Daily Union*, May 21, 1856.
35. Asst. Adj. Gen. D. R. Jones to Adj. Gen. of California William D. Kibbe, Benicia, May 15, 1856, in Message from the President of the United States, transmitting Report in regard to Indian affairs on the Pacific, February 16, 1857, U.S. Congress, House, 34th Cong., 3d sess., Exec. Doc. 76, Serial 906, 123.
36. *Sacramento Daily Union*, May 10, 1856.
37. Maj. Gen. John E. Wool to Asst. Adj. Gen. L. Thomas, Benicia, May 17, 1856, in Message from the President, February 16, 1857, 118.
38. J. Neely Johnson to Samuel Charles George, Sacramento, May 8, 1856, Secretary of State Office, Indian War Papers.
39. J. Struggles to editors, Fort Miller, May 9, 1856, *San Francisco Daily Evening Bulletin*, May 16, 1856. Another letter by Struggles, dated May 7, was published in the same edition.
40. Citizens of Kern River Mines to Mr. Alexander, Keysville, Kern River, May 2, 1856, in *Los Angeles Star*, May 10, 1856.
41. *San Joaquin Republican*, May 6, 1856.
42. *Sacramento Daily Union*, May 10, 1856.
43. J. Struggles to editors, Fort Miller, May 1856, *San Francisco Daily Evening Bulletin*, May 16, 1856; *San Joaquin Republican*, July 26, 1853; "Treaty Made and Concluded at Camp Belt, on King's River, in the State of California, May 13, 1851, Between George W. Barbour, Commissioner on the Part of the United States, and the Chiefs, Captains, and Head Men of the Taches, Cah-Wai, etc., etc., Tribes of Indians," in Kappler, ed., *Indian Affairs*, vol. 4, 1093.
44. Struggles to editors, May 9, 1856.
45. Lieut. Col. Benjamin L. Beall to J. R. Vineyard, Fort Tejon, May 5, 1856, in *Los Angeles Star*, May 10, 1856.
46. Lieut. Col. Benjamin L. Beall, Orders, Fort Tejon, May 5, 1856, Office of the Quartermaster General, Consolidated Correspondence File.
47. Daniels to Henley, May 25, 1856.
48. Lieut. Joseph Stewart to Asst. Adj. Gen. D. R. Jones, Fort Miller, May 1, 1856, in Message from the President, February 16, 1857, 121.
49. Daniels to Henley, May 25, 1856.
50. Letter, Fort Miller, May 25, 1856, in *San Joaquin Republican*, June 1, 1856. By whom and to whom the letter was written was not stated.
51. John Barker and W. R. Bower, "Indian War in Tulare in 1856," *Bakersfield Daily Californian*, January 29, 1904, reprinted in Boyd and Rodger, eds., *San Joaquin Vignettes*, 12.
52. *Stockton Argus*, n.d; reprinted in *San Francisco Daily Evening Bulletin*, June 12, 1856, Daniels to Henley, May 25, 1856; "Skirmish with

the Tulare Indians-Parley with the Indians," unidentified newspaper article, n.d., in "Kings River War," Hayes, Scrapbooks, vol. 39.
53. Barker and Bower, "Indian War," 13.
54. Letter, Fort Miller, May 25, 1856.
55. *Stockton Argus*, n.d.; reprinted in *San Francisco Daily Evening Bulletin*, June 12, 1856.
56. David B. James to George W. Stewart, San Francisco, November 17, 1902, Notes of Conversation concerning Yokut[s] Indians, Stewart Collection, Folder 9.
57. Daniels to Henley, May 25, 1856.
58. Letter, May 25, 1856.
59. Correspondent to editors, Visalia, May 30, 1856, *Stockton Argus*, n.d.; reprinted in *Sacramento Daily Union*, June 5, 1856.
60. *Sacramento Daily Union*, June 1856.
61. J. Neely Johnson, statement, April 19, 1858, Secretary of State Office, Indian War Papers, 263.
62. *Los Angeles Star*, June 28, 1856.
63. Edward F. Beale to J. Neely Johnson, San Francisco, July 12, 1856, Secretary of State Office, Indian War Papers, 263.
64. "Skirmish with the Tulare Indians-Parley with the Indians," n.d, *Stockton Argus*, n.d.; reprinted in *San Francisco Daily Bulletin*, June 12, 1856.
65. M. B. Lewis to Thomas Henley, Fresno Indian Farm, June 14, 1856, Secretary of State Office, Indian War Papers, 263.
66. Beale to Johnston, July 12, 1856.
67. Ibid; *Sacramento Daily Union*, July 1, 1856.
68. Sacramento Daily Union, June 1856; Beale to Johnston, July 12, 1856.
69. Ibid.
70. William Campbell to Thomas Henley, Fresno Farm, June 14, 1856, Secretary of State Office, Indian War Papers, 251.
71. William Campbell to M. B. Lewis, Fresno Farm, June 14, 1856, Secretary of State Office, Indian War Papers, 251.
72. M. B. Lewis to Thomas Henley, Fresno Farm, June 31, 1856, Secretary of State Office, Indian War Papers, 263.
73. Thomas Henley to J. Neely Johnson, San Francisco, June 24, 1856, Secretary of State Office, Indian War Papers.
74. Thomas Henley to Edward F. Beale, San Francisco, June 27, 1856, Secretary of State Office, Indian War Papers.
75. *Los Angeles Star*, June 28, 1856.
76. Ibid., August 30, 1856.
77. *San Joaquin Republican*, September 12, 1856.
78. Alonzo Ridley to Thomas J. Henley, Tule River, September 23, 1856,

Office of Indian Affairs, Letters Received, 1824-81, roll 35.

79. J. Ross Browne to Charles E. Mix, San Francisco, November 1858, Office of Indian Affairs, Letters Received, 1824-81, roll 36.
80. Thomas P. Madden, September 30, 1857, Record of Applications for School Land Warrants, in Browne to Mix, November 1, 1858, 6; Royce, ed., "Indian Land Cessions," pt. 2, 815, 1. On May 3, 1852 the California legislature passed an act opening up 500,000 acres of school lands for sale. To obtain the school land warrants, an individual had to obtain an affidavit from a notary pubic, a clerk or judge of a county, a district judge, or judge of the supreme court stating the fact for permanent settlement of land not exceeding 640 acres. The affidavit would then be forwarded to the comptroller; payment of two dollars an acre would be sent to the Treasurer. School lands were the sixteenth and thirty-six sections of each townships which were to be set aside for school purposes, Shasta Courier, July 24, 1852. See also Ellison, *A Self-governing Dominion,* 131-33.
81. Alonzo Ridley to Thomas J. Henley, Tule River, September 24, 1856, in Thomas J. Henley to James Denver, San Francisco, October 2, 1857, Office of Indian Affairs, Letters Received, 1824-81, roll 35; Thomas P. Madden to Thomas Henley Tejhon [sic] Agency, September 20, 1855, ibid.; Ridley to Henley, September 24, 1856, B. C. Whiting to N. G. Taylor, San Francisco, August 19, 1867, *Annual Report on Indian Affairs by the Acting Commissioner*, 105.
82. Alonzo Ridley to Thomas J. Henley, Tule River, September 24, in Thomas Henley to James W. Denver, San Francisco, October 2, 1857, Office of Indian Affairs, Letters Received, 1824-8l, roll 35; Thomas P. Madden to Thomas Henley, Tejhon [sic] Agency, September 20, 1855, Office of Indian Affairs, Letters Received, 1824-81, roll 35.
83. J. R. Vineyard to Thomas Henley, Fresno Indian Agency, August 1858, *Report of the* Commissioner of India Affairs Accompanying the Annual Report of the Secretary of the *Interior for the Year 1858*, 648.
84. Affidavits of J. S. Clapp, H. A. Bostwick, and Henry G. Sears in J. Ross Browne to Charles E. Mix, San Francisco, November 1, 1858, Office of Indian Affairs, Letters Received, 1821-81, roll 36.
85. J. Ross Browne to Charles E. Mix, San Francisco, November 1, 1858, ibid.
86. J. Y. McDuffie, to A.B. Greenwood, San Francisco, September 19, 1859, Report of the Secretary of the Interior, Senate, 36 Cong, lst sess., Ex. Doc. 46, 29-31.
87. *Visalia Weekly Delta*, April 21, 1866.
88. John P. H. Wentworth to William P. Dole, San Francisco, July 14, 1861, *Report of the Commissioner of Indian Affairs Accompanying the Annual Report of the Secretary of the Interior for the Year 1861*, 142; *Los Angeles Star*,

November 30, 1961.

89. *The Daily Appeal*, May 16, 1862.
90. John P. Wentworth, "List of Employees in the Southern Indian District of California," Letters Received of the Office of Indian Affairs, San Francisco, September 30, 1862.
91. John P. H. Wentworth to William P. Dole, San Francisco, August 30, 1862, *Report of the Commissioner of Indian Affairs for the Year 1862*, Washington, D.C., Government Printing Office, 1863, 328.
92. John P. H. Wentworth to William P. Dole, San Francisco, August 11, 1863, *Report of the Commissioner of Indian Affairs for the Year 1863*, 104.
93. *Visalia Delta*, May 5, 1864.
94. Charles Maltby to Thomas D. W. Cooley, San Francisco, December 6, 1865, Letters Received by the Office of Indian Affairs, microcopy 234, roll 41.
95. Austin Wiley to William P. Dole, San Francisco, July 11, 1864, *Report of the Commissioner of Indian Affairs for the Year 1864*, 131.

Chapter XXV: Defiance And Degradation in the Southern Mines

1. Borthwick, *Three Years*, 306. For a discussion of the ethnic and cultural diversity in the Southern Mines, consult Johnson, Roaring Camp. The Northern Mines, located north of the Mokelumne River, received their supplies from Sacramento, whereas the Southern Mines got theirs from Stockton. See Hittell, *Mining*, 71.
2. Abstract of the Census of 1852, of the State of California, appendix of the *Journal of the Senate*, 4th sess., 23-24, 52.
3. See Chapter l0 for an account of the conflict.
4. "Ichabod" to editors, Mariposa, January 31, 1853, *San Francisco Daily Herald*, February 3, 1853; Extract of a letter from Frederick Kerin, Stockton, dated February 11, 1853, Office of Indian Affairs, Letters Received, 1824-81, roll 33.
5. "Ichabod" to editors, January 31, 1853.
6. Extract of a letter from Kerlin, February 11, 1853.
7. A. J. L. to editors, Aqua Friá, April 23, 1853, *San Joaquin Republican*, April 27, 1853.
8. K. to Editors, n.p., n.d., *San Joaquin Republican*, February 5, 1853.
9. *Sacramento Daily Union*, February 3, 1853.
10. Ibid.
11. Ibid.
12. Ibid. Copied from other newspapers, the fight was reported in the *San Francisco Daily, Alta California*, February 4, 1853, and in the *Columbia Gazette*, February 12, 1853. For a more detailed assessment of the fight, consult Farris, "'Indian Rancherie on Dry Creek': An Early 1850s Indian Village on the Sacramento and San Joaquin County

Line," 63-74.
13. *San Francisco Daily, Alta California*, April 28, 1853.
14. *San Joaquin Republican*, May 24, 1853.
15. *Sacramento Daily Union*, June 6, 1853.
16. *San Francisco Daily, Alta California*, July 18, 1853. See also "Doctor" to editors, Sonora, July 10, 1853, *San Joaquin Republican*, July 12, 1853; and "Mephistopheles" to editors, n.p., n.d., *San Joaquin Republican*, July 14, 1853.
17. R. to editors, Sonora, July 10, 1853, *San Francisco Daily, Alta California*, July 14, 1853.
18. P. S. to editors, Sonora, n.d., *San Joaquin Republican*, July 21, 1853.
19. P. S. to editors, Sonora, July 22, 1853, *San Joaquin Republican*, July 23, 1853.
20. "Mariposa" to editors, Mariposa, August 1, 1853, *San Joaquin Republican*, August 6, 1853.
21. Letter to editors, Mariposa, July 31, 1853, *San Joaquin Republican*, August 4, 1853. Writer's emphasis.
22. Bunnell, *Discovery of the Yosemite*, 296-99. According to one source, the Yosemite were reduced to eight young and a few old men. See Bunnell, "How the Yosemite Valley was Discovered," 503.
23. Bunnell, *Discovery of the Yosemite*, 301.
24. Ibid., 301-4
25. *Mariposa Chronicle*, July 28, 1854.
26. "Treaty Made and Concluded at Camp Fremont, State of California March 19, 1851, Between Redick McKee and Others, Commissioners on the Part of the United States, and the Chiefs, Captains, and Head Men of the Si-yan-te, etc., Tribes of Indians," in Kappler, ed., *Indian Affairs*, vol. 4, 1084.
27. B. to editors, n.p., n.d., *San Joaquin Republican*, July 7, 1853.
28. *Mariposa Chronicle*, July 28, 1854.
29. "Volunteer" to editors, n.p., n.d., *Mariposa Chronicle*, September 15, 1854.
30. Perlot, *Gold Seeker*, 223-24. Perlot erroneously called Cypriano a Yosemite.
31. Ibid., 225-27.
32. Ibid., 228-29.
33. Indian raiding in Southern California is discussed in Phillips, *Vineyards and Vaqueros*, 201, 218.
34. The utilization of horses and mules by California Indians is discussed in Chapter 5.
35. M. B. Lewis, "Mariposa County-Valuable Statistics," *San Francisco Daily, Alta California*, November 12, 1852.
36. *San Joaquin Republican*, January 15, 1853.

37. John Barker, "Wild Horses of the San Joaquin Valley," *Bakersfield Daily Californian*, March 11-12, 14, 1904. Reprinted in Boyd and Rodgers, eds., *San Joaquin Vignettes*, 38.
38. *San Francisco Golden Era*, January 23, 1853.
39. Lewis, "Mariposa County-Valuable Statistics."
40. M. B. Lewis to Thomas Henley, Fresno Indian Farm, July 22, 1856, *Annual Report of the Commissioner of Indian Affairs for the Year 1856*, 254-55.
41. *Mariposa Gazette*, November 12, 1856.
42. James H. Carson, "Tulare Plains," *San Joaquin Republican*, January 28, 1852. Carson's letters are published in Browning, ed., *Bright Gem.*
43. *San Joaquin Republican*, March 17, 1852.
44. Borthwick, *Three Years in California*, 289.
45. General Ogle to editors, n.p., n.d., *San Francisco Golden Era*, July 31, 1853.
46. "Don Cypriano's Speech." Mariposa County, May 20, 1853, *San Joaquin Republican*, July 7, 1853. Present was a white man who took notes and translated the speech from Spanish to English.
47. Ibid.
48. Lewis to Henley, July 22, 1856, 253. For a discussion of the plight of Indian women mainly in northern California during the 1850s, consult Hurtado, *Indian Survival*, 169-92.
49. "The Last of the Yachicumnes," *San Joaquin Republican*, January 4, 1852.
50. Capt. Thomas Jordan to Maj. Osborn A. Cross, Fort Miller, August 15, 1853, Office of the Quartermaster General, Consolidated File on Fort Miller, 1853-58.
51. Thomas Henley to George W. Manypenny, San Francisco, August 29, 1854, *Annual Report of the Commissioner of Indian Affairs for the Year 1854*, 304.
52. Asst. Surgeon William Edgar to J. Ross Browne, San Francisco, July 18, 1858, Office of Indian Affairs, Letters Received, 1824-81, roll 36.
53. Lieut. LaRhett L. Livingston to Asst. Adj. Gen. W. W. Mackall, Fort Miller, March 9, 1857, U.S. Army Continental Commands, Letters Received, 1821-1920.
54. Keyes, *Fifty Years' Observation*, 263-64.
55. *Tuolumne Courier*, n.d., reprinted in *San Francisco Daily Evening Bulletin*, September 23, 1858.
56. *Sacramento Daily Union*, September 20, 1858.
57. Newspapers accounts of Indians abusing Chinese are published in Heizer, ed., *The Destruction of California Indians*, 287-90; and in Heizer, ed., *They Were Only Diggers*, 99-103. Because many of the documents

in the two collections are erroneously cited and carelessly transcribed, they should be used with caution.

58. *San Francisco Daily Herald*, August 8, 1853.
59. Maj. Henry W. Wessells, to Asst. Adj. Gen. E. D. Townsend, Fort Miller, March 7, 1854, U.S. Army Continental Commands, Letters Received, 1821-1920.
60. Lewis to Henley, July 22, 1856, 253.
61. Scavenging as an adaptive strategy is discussed in Downs, "Differential Response," 115-37.
62. G. W. Patrick to Thomas Henley, Tuolumne County, July 24, 1856, in Thomas Henley to George W. Manypenny, September 4, 1856, *Annual Report of the Commissioner of Indian Affairs in the Year 1856*, 240-41.
63. Borthwick, *Three Years in California*, 289.
64. Perlot, *Gold Seeker*, 261-62.
65. Camp, ed., *John Doble's Journal*, 55-56.
66. Gerstaecker, *California Gold Mines*, 77.
67. Borlhwick, *Three Years*, 312.
68. Perlot, *Gold Seeker*, 262.
69. Ibid.
70. Gerstaecker, *California Gold Mines*, 77.
71. Heizer, ed., *They Were Only Diggers*, 67. Heizer cites the *San Joaquin Republican* (no day or month, 1858) as the source, when, in fact, it was another newspaper quoting the *Republican*.
72. *San Joaquin Republican*, August 6, 1858.
73. *San Joaquin Republican*, September 9, 1858.
74. *San Joaquin Republican*, September 16, 1858.
76. Quoted in Graig B. Bates, "Miwok Dancers of 1856: Stereographic Images from Sonora, California," 13.
77. M. B. Lewis to Alfred B. Greenwood, Fresno Farm, August 30, 1859, Office of Indian Affairs, Letters Received, 1824-81, roll 37. Although his figures clearly indicate the steep decline the Indians had undergone, Lewis probably underestimated the number of Indians in the Southern Mines, because he counted only those associated with the Fresno Indian Agency. Lewis also estimated the numbers of the Indians residing south of the San Joaquin River" in particular those residing on the Kings River, whom he considered to be under the jurisdiction of the agency.
78. Abstract of the Census of 1852, 23-24.
79. *Visalia Delta*, November 14, 1861.

Chapter XXVI: Closure

1. M. B. Lewis to Thomas Henley, Fresno Indian Agency, January 15, 1859, Office of Indian Affairs, Letters Received, 1824-81, roll 37.
2. M. B. Lewis to Thomas Henley, Fresno Indian Agency, April, 1859, Office of Indian Affairs, Letters Received, 1824-81, roll 37.
3. M. B. Lewis to Thomas Henley, Fresno Indian Agency, May 12, 1859, Office of Indian Affairs, Letters Received, 1824-81, roll 37.
4. M. B. Lewis to Alfred B. Greenwood, Fresno Indian Agency, August 30, 1859, Office of Indian Affairs, Letters Received, 1824-81, roll 37.
5. James Y. McDuffie to Jacob Thompson, Tejon Indian Reservation, August 9, 1859, Office of Indian Affairs, Letters Received, 1824-81, roll 37.
6. James Y. McDuffie to Alfred B. Greenwood, San Francisco, September 4, 1859. Report of the Secretary of the Interior, May 17, 1860, U.S. Congress, Senate, 36th Cong. 1st sess., Exec. Doc. 46, 8.
7. Ibid., 8-10.
8. J. Ross Browne to Alfred B. Greenwood, San Francisco, November 4. 1859, Report of the Secretary of the Interior, May 17, 1860, U.S. Congress, Senate, 36th Cong. 1st sess., Exec. Doc. 46, 16-17.
9. Ibid.; J. Ross Browne to Alfred B. Greenwood, San Francisco, November 5, 1859, Office of Indian Affairs, Letters Received, 1824-81, roll 37.
10. James Y. McDuffie to Alfred B. Greenwood. San Francisco. November 19. 1859, Office of Indian Affairs, Letters Received, 1824-81, roll 37.
11. John P. H. Wentworth to William P. Dole, San Francisco, July 14, 1861, *Annual Report of the Commissioner of Indian Affairs for the Year 1861*, 142.
12. J. Elias & Co. to William P. Dole, Fresno County, July 15, 1863, Office of Indian Affairs, Letters Received, 1824-81, roll 39.
13. John P. H Wentworth to William P. Dole, San Francisco, January 2, 1862, Office of Indian Affairs, Letters Received, 1824-81, roll 38; *Los Angeles Star*, November 30, 1861.
14. *Visalia Delta*, November 21, 1861.
15. Extract from the Annual report of the Secretary of the Interior to Congress, of December 1, 1859, *Annual Report of the Commissioner of Indian Affairs for the Year 1859*, 6-7.
16. Dale, *Indians of the Southwest*, 41.
17. John P. H. Wentworth to William P. Dole, San Francisco, July 14, 1861, *Annual Report of the Commissioner of Indian Affairs for the Year 1861*, 141.
18. *San Francisco Daily Herald*, a.d., reprinted in *Los Angeles Star*, January 26, 1861.

19. Samuel Bishop, Edward F. Beale, Frederick Kerlin et al. to Gen. Albert S. Johnston, Fort Tejón, February, 1861, *War of the Rebellion*, 437.
20. Stammejohan, "Fort Tejón Historic Park: Part 3," 20.
21. Population Schedules of the Eighth Census.
22. *Visalia Delta*, July 11, 1861; Giffen and Woodward, *El Tejón*, 123.
23. Lieut. B.F. Davis to Maj. James H. Carleton, Los Angeles, July 23, 1861, *War of Rebellion*, 542-43.
24. Lieut. M. T. Carr to Maj. James H. Carleton Fort Tejón, June 21, 1861, *War of Rebellion*, 520; *Visalia Delta*, July 11, 1861.
25. Maj. James H. Carleton to Lieut. M. T. Carr, Los Angeles, June 21, 1861, *War of Rebellion*, 520.
26. Davis to Carleton, July 23, 1861.
27. List of Employees in the Southern Indian District of California, Jno. P. H. Wentworth, Spt. Agent, from January 1, 1862 to March 31, 1862, Office of Indian Affairs, Letters Received, 1824-81, roll 38.
28. John P. H. Wentworth to William P. Dole, San Francisco, July 14, 1861, *Annual Report ofthe Commissioner of Indian Affairs for the Year 1861*, 143-44.
29. John P. H. Wentworth to William P. Dole, San Francisco, October 10, 1861, *Annual Report of the Commissioner of Indian Affairs for the Year 1861*, 145-46.
30. *Los Angeles Star*, November 30, 1861.
31. John P. H. Wentworth to William P. Dole, San Francisco, January 2, 1862, Office of Indian Affairs, Letters Received, 1824- 81, roll 38.
32. *Los Angeles Star*, November 30, 1861.
33. *Semi-Weekly Southern News*, November 29, 1861.
34. Caleb B. Smith to John P. H. Wentworth, Washington, D.C., January 31, 1862, Office of Indian Affairs, Letters Received, 1824-81, roll 38; *Semi-Weekly Southern News*, February 14, 1862.
35. John P. H. Wentworth to William P. Dole, Washington, D.C., March 20, April 29, 1862, Office of Indian Affairs, Letters Received, 1824-81, roll 38.
36. John P. H. Wentworth to William P. Dole, San Francisco, August 30, 1862, *Annual Report of the Commissioner of Indian Affairs for the Year 1862*, 325.
37. Ibid., 324-25; Boschulte, *Statement of Farms*, March 31, 1862.
38. Wentworth to Dole, August 30, 1862, 325.
39. Boschulte, *Statement of Farms*, March 31, 1862.
40. *Havilah Weekly Courier*, March l, 1870.
41. George L. Hoffman, Statements taken at Tule Farm Indian reservation California, July 14 and 15, 1865, *The Reports of the Committees of the Senate of the United States for the Second Session, Thirty-ninth Congress, 1866-*

67, no. 156, 495.

42. *Los Angeles Tri-Weekly News*, February 18, 1863.
43. Ibild., May 8, 1863.
44. John P. H. Wentworth to William P. Dole, San Francisco, September 1, 1853, *Annual Report of the Commissioner of Indian Affairs for the Year 1863*, 104, 750.
45. Capt. Moses A. McLaughlin to Asst. Adj. Gen. R. C. Drum, Owens River Valley, April 24, 1863, *War of Rebellion*, 209.
46. Letter to editors, Keysville, April 1, 1863, *Visalia Delta*, April 16, 1863.
47. Lieut. Col. William Jones to Asst. Adj. Gen. R. C. Drum, Visalia, April 8, 1863, *War of Rebellion*, 386.
48. The California Volunteers are discussed in Lewis, *The War in the Far West*.
49. Jones to Drum, April 8, 1863, 386.
50. McLaughlin to Drum, April 24, 1863, 209.
51. Wilke and Lawton, eds., *Expedition*, 17.
52. José Pacheco [Chico] to Gen. George Wright, Fort Tejón, April 16, 1864, in *Visalia Delta*, May 19, 1864.
53. Captain Moses A. McLaughlin to John Middleton, Owens Valley, May [?] 1863, *San Francisco Daily, Alta California*, June 9, 1863.
54. José Pacheco to Wright, April 16, 1864.
55. Nanna Rankin, "Impressions of Early Days," quoted in Powers, North Fork Country, 54.
56. McLaughlin to Middleton, May, 1863.
57. José Pacheco to Wright, April 16, 1864.
58. McLaughlin to Middleton, May, 1863.
59. McLaughlin to Drum, April 24, 1863, 209; Pacheco to Wright, April 16, 1864; Letter to editors, April 19, 1863, *Visalia Delta*, April 23, 1863; Correspondent to editors, n.p., n.d., *Visalia Delta*, April 23, 1863. José Chico and the massacre are discussed in Chandler, "José Chico," 54-60; Walker, "Judas," 10- 11; Chandler, "Failure of Indian Reform," 290-91; and Powers, *North Fork Country*, 54-58.
60. McLaughlin to Drum, April 24, 1863, 209. Evidently, José Chico settled in the same village or the same area as that occupied by Urbano, the chief who faced difficulties with settlers and hostile Paiutes in 1855-1856. See Letter to editors, April 19, 1863.
61. E. P., statement, n.p., n.d., in Voegelin, *Tubatulabal Ethnograpy*, 72. E. P. also claimed that one man survived the massacre.
62. Correspondent to editors, n.p., n.d., *Visalia Delta*, April 23, 1863.
63. Mclaughlin to Drum, April 24, 209.
64. Mclaughlin to Middleton, May 1863.
65. Wentworth to Dole, September 1, 1863, 99.

66. Robert Daley, Statements taken at Tule River Farm reservation, California, July 14 and 15, 1865, *Reports of the Committees of the Senate of the United States, for the Second Session, Thirty- ninth Congress, 1866-67*, no. 156, 496; Report of Employees in the Indian Dist., Cal, Southern Agency for the Third Quarter, 1863, Office of Indian Affairs, Letters Received, 1824-81, roll 39.
67. *San Francisco Daily, Alta California*, July 26, 1863.
68. On September 13, 1862, Beale officially stated that Rancho El Tejón had been surveyed and that the survey and plat had been approved by the U.S. Surveyor. See Office of the Surveyor General of the United States, for California, Case No. 327
69. A map of the reservation produced in 1862, clearly identifies Beale's house. See Theodore Boschulte, Statement of Farms and acres worked by Government for the Indians on Tejón Reservation, March 31, 1862. Archives of the Society of California Pioneers, Bancroft Library, Berkeley, California.
70. Crowe, *Men of El Tej*ón, 754; Giffen and Woodward, *El Tej*ón, 45.
71. Edward F. Beale to John P. H. Wentworth, San Francisco, July 24, 1863, in Wentworth to Dole, September 1, 1863, 102.
72. John P. H. Wentworth to Edward F. Beale, Southern District, July 29, 1863, in Wentworth to Dole, September 1, 1863, 102, *Annual Report of the Commissioner of Indian Affairs for the Year 1863*, 102, and Wentworth to Dole, September 1, 1863, 101-102. See also *Los Angeles Tri- Weekly News*, July 29, 1863.
73. Edward F. Beale to John P. H. Wentworth, San Francisco, July 24, 1863, in Wentworth to Dole, September 1, 1863, 102.
74. Wentworth to Beale, July 29, 1863.
75. Edward F. Beale to John P. H. Wentworth, San Francisco, July 29, 1863, in J. Wentworth to Dole, September 1, 1863, 102-103.
76. John P. H. Wentworth to Edward F. Beale, San Francisco, August 10, 1863, in Wentworth to Dole, September 1, 1863, 103.
77. Edward F. Beale to John P. H. Wentworth, San Francisco, August 11, 1863, in Wentworth to Dole, September 1, 1863, 103-4.
78. Nordhoff, *California*, 236; Bonsal, *Edward Fitzgerald Beale*, 274.
79. John P. H. Wentworth to William P. Dole, San Francisco, September 14, 1863. Office of Indian Affairs, Letters Received, 1824-81, roll 39.
80. John P. H. Wentworth to William P. Dole, September 12, 1863, Office of Indian Affairs, Letters Received, 1824-81, roll 39.
81. Wentworth to Dole, September 14, 1863.
82. Asst. Adj. Gen. E. Sparrow Purdy to Capt. Moses A. McLaughlin, Fort Tejón, October 27, 1863, *War of Rebellion*, pt. 2, 558.
83. Daley, Statements, July 14 and 15, 1865, 496.

84. John P. H. Wentworth to Capt. Moses A. McLaughlin, El Tejón, September 30, 1863, *War of Rebellion*, pt. 2, 658.
85. Asst. Adj. Gen. E. Sparrow Purdy to Capt. Moses A. McLaughlin, San Francisco, October 13, 1 863, *War of Rebellion*, pt. 2, 645.
86. "Practical" to editors, Visalia, May 17, 1864, *Visalia Delta*, May 19, 1864.
87. *Visalia Delta,* May 5, 1864.
88. Capt. John C. Schmidt to Asst. Adj. Gen. R.C. Drum, Fort Tejón, January 26, 1864, *War of Rebellion*, pt. 2, 733-34.
89. Jose Pacheco to Wright, April 16, 1864.
90. "Practical" to editors, May 17, 1864.
91. "Veritus" to editors, Fort Tejón, May 26, 1864, *Visalia Delta*, June 2, 1864.
92. Report of Employees in the Southern Indian District of California, Southern Agency, for the 2d Quarter 1864, Office of Indian Affairs, Letters Received, 1824-81- roll 39. Wentworth had appointed Godey supervisor of the Colorado District on February 1, 1862. See John P. H. Wentworth to William P. Dole, Washington, D.C., April 3, 1862, Office of Indian Affairs, Letters Received, 1824-81, roll 39. See also *Semi-Weekly Southern News*, February 12, 1862. The editors erroneously claimed that Godey had been appointed Superintendent of Indian Affairs for the Southern District of California.
93. A Bill to provide for the better organization of Indian affairs in California, and for other purposes, Reported with an amendment, March 17, 1864, U.S. Congress, Senate, 38th Cong., 1st sess.
94. The superintending agents for the northern and southern districts discussed the five reservations in their respective areas in *Annual Report of the Commissioner of Indian Affairs for the Year 1863*, 89, 107.
95. Austin Wiley to Charles E. Mix, San Francisco, June 1, 1864, *Annual Report of the Commissioner of Indian Affairs for the Year 1864*, 125.
96. Austin Wiley to William P. Dole, San Francisco, July 11, 1864, ibid., 131; Pacheco to Wright, April 16, 1864.
97. Giffen and Woodward, *El Tejón*, 133-34.

Chapter XXVII: From Farm to Reservation

1. Austin Wiley to William P. Dole, San Francisco, September 1, 1864, *Report of the Commissioner of Indian Affairs for the Year 1864*, 118-20.
2. *Visalia Delta*, January 10, 1866.
3. Charles Maltby to D. W. Cooley [sic], San Francisco, September 15, 1865, *Report of the Commissioner of Indian Affairs for the Year 1865*, 114-15.
4. Thomas Madden to Charles Maltby, San Francisco, April 16, 1866, Letters Received from the Office of Indian Affairs, microcopy 234,

roll 41.

5. Charles Maltby to D. N. Cooley, San Francisco, September 15, 1866, *Report of the Commissioner of Indian Affairs for the Year 1866*, 93-94.
6. *Visalia Delta*, July 18, 1866.
7. Charles Maltby to D. N. Cooley, San Francisco, September 15, 1866, *Report of the Commissioner of Indian Affairs for the Year 1866*, 93.
8. Ina Stiner, "Jose Vera Recalls Incidents of His Life on Original Indian Reservation East of Porterville."
9. Powers, *Tribes of California*, 394-96. Further evidence that Jose Chico was the Paiute assisting the Americans on the Kern River in 163 [sic] comes from an anthropologist who visited the Tule River Reservation in 1902. He mentioned that a Chico, a Kern Valley Indian, had once lived on the reservation and that thirty years ago, Juan Immeterio had married his daughter. See Merriam, "Ethnographic Notes on California Indian Tribes III," 412, 413. Frank and Goldberg, however, claim that there were two José Chicos, contending that one on the farm must have been a Koyeti because a chief could only come from a group indigenous to the area where the farm was located. See *Defying the Odds*, 322, 22n. In different articles Robert J. Chandler and Ardis Walker state there was only one José Chico.
10. Maltby to Cooley, September 15, 1866.
11. George J. Hoffman to D. N. Cooley, Tule River Farm, August 17, 1866, ibid., 98.
12. Robert J. Stevens to Lewis Bogy, Washington, D.C. January 1, 1867, *Report on Indian Affairs by the Acting Commissioner, 1867*, 131-32.
13. Ibid.
14. B. C. Whiting to N. G. Taylor, San Francisco, August 19, 1867, ibid., 105.
15. Charles Maltby to N. G. Taylor, Tule River, August 20, 1868, *Report of the Commissioner of Indian Affairs for the Year 1868*, 134.
16. Ibid., 135-36.
17. Ibid., 136.
18. Charles Maltby to E. S. Parker, Tule River, August 7, 1869, *Report of the Commissioner of Indian Affairs for the Year 1869*, 191. Ironically, after all the time, effort, and money spent on removing the Paiutes from Owens Valley to Fort Tejón, then to the Tejón Reservation, and finally to the Tule River Farm, no effort was made to bring them back. The white settlers in the Owens Valley now needed their labor.
19. Ibid., 192.
20. John H. Purcell to E. S. Parker, Tule River, September 9, 1869 ibid., 193. The change in policy is explained in Charles Berdan Leonard, "The Federal Indian Policy in the San Joaquin Valley, its Application and Results," 398.

21. Gen J. B. McIntosh to E. S. Parker, San Francisco, November 8, 1869, Letter Received by the Office of Indian Affairs, microcopy 234, roll 43.
22. John H. Purcell to J. B. McIntosh, Tule River, February 1, 1870, Letters Received by the Office of Indian Affairs, microcopy 234, roll 43.
23. John H. Purcell to E. S. Parker, Tule River, August 5, 1870, *Report of the Commissioner of Indian Affairs for the Year, 1870*, 87.
24. Ibid., 88.
25. J. B. McIntosh to E. S. Parker, May 27, 1870, Letters Received by the Office of Indian Affairs, microcopy 234, roll 43.
26. J. B. McIntosh to E. S. Parker, June 6, 1870, ibid.
27. Citizens of Porterville to the Secretary of the Interior, Porterville, June 2, 1870, ibid.
28. N. G. Turney to the Secretary of the Interior, Vandalia, June 4, 1870, ibid.
29. McIntosh, to Parker, June 6, 1870, ibid.
30. John H. Purcell to B. C. Whiting, Tule River, August 31, 1870, ibid.
31. John W. Miller to E. S. Parker, Tule River, September 30, 1870, *Report of the Commissioner of Indian Affairs for the Year 1870*, 89.
32. Dale, *The Indians of the Southwest,* 82.
33. J. B. McIntosh to E. S. Parker, San Francisco, July 13, 1870, *Report of the Commissioner of Indian Affairs for the Year 1870*, 78-79.
34. John W. Miller to E. S. Parker, Tule River, September 30, 1870, ibid., 89-90.
35. Cook, *The Population of the California Indians, 1769-1970*, 55-56.
36. *Fresno Expositor*, August 24, 1870 in Leonard, "The Federal Indian Policy in the San Joaquin Valley," 404.
37. Gayton, "The Ghost Dance of 1870 in South-Central California," 75-76.
38. Miller to Parker, September 30, 1870, 89.
39. Latta, *Tailholt Tales*, 108-09. Latta's account is supported in a letter written to him by the daughter of the murdered woman. See Flora B. Seligman to F. F. Latta, Venice, California, March 20, 1931, in ibid., 110-112.
40. *Visalia Weekly Delta*, December 7, 1870.
41. Ibid., December 14, 1870.
42. Ibid., December 14, 1870.
43. Ibid., December 21, 1870.
44. Ibid., December 21, 1870.
45. Citizens and Property Owners of Tulare County, California to E. S. Parker, December 19, 1870, Letters Received by the Office of Indian Affairs, microcopy 234, roll 44.

46. E. D. Thompson to J. M. Schofield, Washington, D.C., January 24, 1871, ibid., B. C. Whiting to H. R. Clum, San Francisco, September 1, 1871, *Report of the Commissioner of Indian Affairs for the Year 1871*, 327
47. Gayton, "The Ghost Dance of 1870," 60-61.
48. Ibid., 68-69.
49. Ibid., 70-71.
50. Latta, *Handbook of Yokuts Indians*, 695-97.
51. Enos Barton, "Great Ghost Dance," 2.
52. Latta, *Handbook of the Yokuts Indians*, 699-700.
53. Barton, "Great Ghost Dance," 2.
54. Latta, *Handbook of Yokuts Indians*, 699-700.
55. Gayton, "The Ghost Dance of 1870," 61.
56. C. G. Belknap to the commissioner of Indian affairs, Tule River Indian Agency, August 20, 1877, *Annual Report of the Commissioner of Indian Affairs for the Year 1877*, 42.
57. Latta, *Handbook of the Yokuts Indians*, 674, 682.
58. Ibid., 700.
59. Charles Maltby to E. S. Parker, Tule River, September 1, 1871, *Report of the Commissioner of Indian Affairs for the Year 1871*, 339.
60. Ibid., 339-40.
61. Flora J. Saxe to Charles Maltby, Tule River, June 30, 1871, ibid., 341.
62. Charles Maltby to B. C. Whitting, Tule River, September 7, 1872, *Annual Report of the Commissioner of Indian Affairs for the Year 1872*, 381.
63. Ibid.
64. Charles Maltby to E. P. Smith, Tule River, September 10, 1873, *Report of the Commissioner of Indian Affairs for the year 1873*, 326-27.
65. Ibid.
66. José Chico et al. Certificate of Delivery of Goods During the Winter Quarter Ending March 31, 1874, Tule River, March 31, 1874, Letters Received by the Office of Indian Affairs, microcopy 234, roll 46.
67. For a discussion of this act, see Frank and Goldberg, *Defying the Odds*, 48-50.
68. Maltby to Smith, 327.
69. J. B. Vosburgh to E. P. Smith, Tule River, September 9, 1874, *Report of the Commissioner of Indian Affairs for the Year 1874*, 315.
70. Ibid., 315-16
71. Ibid., 316.
72. Ibid.
73. J. B. Vosburgh to E. P. Smith, Porterville, September 4, 1875, *Report of the Commissioner of Indian Affairs for the year 1875*, 228-29.
74. Ibid., 229.
75. Ibid.

76. Ibid., 229.
77. C. G. Belknap to Commissioner of Indian Affairs, Porterville, August 21, 1876, *Report of the Commissioner of Indian Affairs for the year 1876*, 17.
78. C. G. Belknap to Commissioner of Indian Affairs, Tule River, August 20, 1877, *Report of the Commissioner of Indian Affairs for the Year 1877*, 41.
79. Frank and Goldberg, *Defying the Odds*, 321-22.
80. Belknap to Commissioner of Indian Affairs, August 20, 1876.
81. Ibid., 42.
82. Ibid.
83. C. G. Belknap to Commissioner of Indian Affairs, Tule River, August 20, 1878, *Report of the Commissioner of Indian Affairs for the Year 1878*, 13-14.

Chapter XXVIII: From Reservation to Rancho

1. Thompson, *Edward F. Beale*, 130.
2. Ibid., 32. "Map of Public Surveys in California to accompany the Report of the Surveyor General, 1859 and 1862."
3. Thompson, *Edward F. Beale*, 741.
4. Correspondent to editors, Visalia, July 19, 1862, *Evening Bulletin*, San Francisco, August 15, 1862.
5. Ibid.
6. Thompson, *Edward F. Beale*, 142.
7. William H. Brewer, *Up and Down California*, 287-88; Thompson, *Edward F. Beale*, 146.
8. Quoted in Bonsal, *Edward Fitzgerald Beale*, 274-75.
9. Earl Crowe, "Appendix," in *Men of El Tejon*, 54.
10. Ibid.
11. Brewer, *Up and Down California*, 384.
12. Crowe, "Appendix," in *Men of Tejon*, 157.
13. *San Jose Evening News*, June 3, 1893.
14. John P. H. Wentworth, "List of Employés in the Southern Indian District, from January 1st 1862 to March 31st 1862," Office of Indian Affairs, Letters Received, 1824-81, roll 38.
15. John P. H. Wentworth to William P. Dole, Washington, D.C., April 4, 1862, Office of Indian Affairs. Letters Received, 1824-81, roll 38.
16. John P. H. Wentworth, "List of Employés in the Southern Indian District of California, During the Quarter Ending December 31, 1862," Office of Indian Affairs, Letters Received, 1824, 81, roll 39.
17. Thompson, *Edward F. Beale*, 151.
18. *Kern County Weekly Courier,* March 1, 1870. Godey's controversial life in the Cuyama Valley has been discussed by Harrington, "Alexander

Godev: Hero Villain?;" Skinner, "More Re. Godey;" Lafra, "Alexis Godey in Kern County;" Cowles, "The Man Behind the Cuyama Valley Indian Massacre;" and Glover, "Alexis Godey: Forgotten Frontiersman."

19. Latta, "Alexis Godey," 43 -44; Magruder, *The Upper San Joaquin Valley*, 43-46.
20. Brewer, *Up and Down California*, 385.
21. *Kern County Weekly Courier*, March 1, 1870.
22. Latta, "Alexis Godey," 51-52.
23. Crowe, "Appendix."
24. Thompson, *Edward F. Beale,* 178.
25. Magruder, *The Upper San Joaquin Valley,* 43.
26. Theodore Boschulte, "Statement of Farms and acres worked by Government for the Indians on Tejon Reservation, March 31st, 1862." For the transitions of missions to ranchos, consult Phillips, *Vineyards and Vaqueros*, 219-32.
27. Brewer, *Up and Down California*, 387.
28. Veritus to editors, Fort Tejon, May 26, 1864, *Visalia Weekly Delta*, June 2, 1864.
29. Austin Whiley to Charles E. Mix, San Francisco, June 1, 1864, *Annual Report of the Commissioner of Indian Affairs for the Year 1864*, 125-26.
30. *Los Angeles Tri-Weekly News*, July 9, 1864.
31. Giffen and Woodward, *The Storv of El Tejon*, 49-50.
32. Thompson, *Edward F. Beale*, 178.
33. Giffen and Woodward, *The Story of El Tejon,* 49.
34. Thompson, *Edward F. Beale*, 193; Crowe, *Men of El Tejon*, 77.
35. Latta, *Handbook of the Yokuts Indians*, 723-24.
36. Ricardo Francisco, testimony, Tule River Agency, February 23, 1922, Papers of John P. Harrington.
37. Mary Austin, *The Flock*, 233.
38. Juan Coluco, testimony.
39. Ibid.
40. Testimony of Guadalupe Isidro, Tule River Agency, February 23, 1922, ibid.
41. Testimony of Juan Dionisi, Tule River Agency, February 23, 1922, ibid. Removal to one settlement is briefly mentioned in Johnson and Earl, "Tataviam Geography and Ethnohistory," 205.
42. Latta, *The Saga of Rancho El Tejón*, 129.
43. John Hayes, "Sheep Farming in California," *The Overland Monthly*, vol. 8, no. 6 (June 1872): 495.
44. Latta, *The Saga of Rancho El Tejón*, 193.
45. Nordhoff, *California: for Health, Pleasure, and Residence*, 234-35.
46. Ibid., 235-36.

47. Latta, *Rancho El Tejón*, 144.
48. Austin, *The Flock*, 238-39.
49. In 1918 sixty Indians remained on their plots of land, but forty resided at the ranch headquarters. The special status of the vaquero in Southern California is discussed in Phillips, *Vineyards and Vaqueros*, 72, 210-27, 144, 136-37.
50. Latta, *The Saga of Rancho El Tejón*, 93, 96, 99.
51. Mora, *Californios*, 114.
52. Nordhoff, *California*, 240.
53. Ibid., 240-41.
54. Rojas, *The Vaquero,* 148-49.
55. Ibid., 24.
56. Latta, *The Saga of Rancho El Tejón*, 88. Latta asserted that Acuña was an Indian by noting that he was not buried with the the other Indians in the Indian cemetery. See p. 91.
57. Ibid., 130.
58. For a Discussion of the role of stores on ranchos, see Phillips, *Vineyards and Vaqueros*, 231-32.
59. Marie Beale, "Spain in California," talk prepared for radio, n.d. Papers of the Beale Family, Manuscript Division, L.G. Box 8, Speeches and Writings Files by Mrs. Truxton Beale, 1928-48, Library of Congress.
60. Coluco, testimony.
61. Latta, *The Saga of Rancho El Tejón*, 144.
62. Ibid., 128.
63. *Population Schedules for the Eighth Census*, 8. The age is based on the 1860 census that put his age at 62.
64. Latta, *The Saga of Rancho El Tejón*, 128.
65. *Population Schedules of the Eighth Census*, 14. The age is based on the 1860 census that put his age at 38.
66. Latta, *The Saga of Rancho El Tejón*, 128-31.
67. Kappler, ed., *Indian Affairs,* vol. 4, 1102.
68. Latta, *The Saga of Rancho El Tejón*, 133. Lopez called him Francisco Cota.
69. *San Francisco Evening Bulletin*, September 2, 1891.
70. Austin, *The Flock*, 224-25.
71. Thompson, *Edward F. Beale*, 197.
72. Ibid., 214-15. The drive from Tejon to Wyoming is described in detail in Latta, *The Saga of Rancho El Tejón*, 249-71.
73. Latta, *The Saga of Rancho El Tejón*, 193.
74. Thompson, *Edward F. Beale*, 216.
75. Elliott, *History of Tulare County, California,* 95.
76. Thompson, *Edward F. Beale*, 178.
77. Coluco, testimony.

78. Latta, *The Saga of Rancho El Tejón*, 187.
79. Edward F. Beale to Mary Beale, Tejón, Cal. October 21, 1886, quoted in Bonsal, *Edward Fitzgerald Beale*, 290.
80. Austin, *Earth Horizon: Autobiography*, 195-98.
81. Crowe, *Men of El Tejon*, 86.
82. Coluco, testimony.
83. Thompson, *Edward F. Beale*, 235.
84. Coluco, testimony.
85. Ibid. In 1905 anthropologist noted that all the Indians on the ranch resided at the village at the entrance to Tejon Canyon. See Merriam, "Ethnographic Notes on California Indian Tribes, III," 429.
86. M. K. Sniffern, *Thirty-fourth Annual Report of the Executive Committee of the Indian Rights Association for the Year Ending December 14, 1916*, 53.
87. H. V. Clotts, "Report of Tejon Indians, Kern County, California, January 15, 1918," 3-4; Cutts, "Tejon Indians," 5.
88. In his pamphlet, "The Story of Tejon Rancho," published in 1955, Hillinger claims that time and earthquakes destroyed the Indian homes. Residing on the rancho were few people, "members of a tiny community," and one family had a vegetable garden and poultry and lived in many ways as did their ancestors: "No TV or automatic machines here."

Conclusion: Historical Reconsiderations

1. See for example, Hurtado, *Indian Survival on the California Frontier.*
2. Sherburne F. Cook claimed that Indian raids peaked in 1845, but in fact they intensified after that time. See Cook, "The Physical and Demographic Reaction of the Non-Mission Indians in Colonial and Provincial California," in Cook, *The Conflict between the California Indians and White Civilization*, 232.
3. For a counter argument, see Phillips, *Vineyards and Vaqueros,* 201-232.
4. For an account of Indian life in the pueblo of Los Angeles, see ibid., 183-199, 259-295.
5. Anna Gayton. "Chukchansi–field Notes" June-July 1938, 79/6c, Bancroft Library, Berkeley, Calif.
6. Lowie, *An Introduction to Anthropology*, 221-22.
7. See, for example, Jablow, *The Cheyenne in Plains Indian Trade Relations*, 1195-1840; Kenner, *A History of New Mexico-Plains Indian Relations*, and Newcomb, Jr., "A Reexamination of the Causes of Plains Warfare," 317-30. See also, James F. Brooks, *Captives & Cousins: Slavery, Kinship, and Community in the Southwest Borderlands*.
8. Cook, "The Mechanism and Extent of Dietary Adaptation Among Certain Groups of California and Nevada Indians," in Cook, "The Conflict between the California Indians and White Civilization,"

477-507.

9. See, for example, Ray, *Indians in the Fur Trade: Their Role as Hunters, Trappers, and Middlemen in the Lands Southwest of Hudson Bay, 1660-1870.*
10. David J. Weber, "American Westward Expansion and the Breakdown of Relations between Pobladores and 'Indios Barbaros' on Mexico's Far Northern Frontier, 1821-1846," 221-38.
11. The classic study of the Santa Fe Trail is Gregg, *The Commerce of the Prairies*.
12. In early 1848, the last major caravan to use the Old Spanish Trail left California with 4,582 animals. See Hussey, "The New Mexico-California Caravan of 1847-1848," 1-16.
13. Hafen and Hafen, *Old Spanish Trail: Santa Fe to Los Angeles*, 232.
14. *San Francisco Daily, Alta California*, July 7, 1851.
15. Zollinger, *Sutter: The Man and His Empire*, 76.
16. Dillon, *Fool's Gold*, 200.
17. See, for example, Bancroft, *California Pastoral*, 1769-1848: and Van de Grift Sanchez, *Spanish Arcadia*. The disjointed nature of California historiography is examined by Earl Pomeroy, "Old Lamps for New: The Cultural Lag in Pacific Coast Historiography," 105-26; and by Weber, "Mexico's Far Northern Frontier, l821-1854: Historiography Askew," 279-93.
18. Juan Bautista Alvarado, "History of California," vol. 4, 1838-1842, trans. Earl R. Hewitt, C-D4, Bancroft Library, Berkeley, Calif.
19. Edward Kemble, "Yerba Buena, 1846," *Sacramento Daily Union*, January 6, 1872.
20. Broadbent, "Conflict at Monterey: Indian Horse Raiding, 1820-1850," 86-101; Charles Hughes, "The Decline of the Californios: The Case of San Diego, 1846- 1856," 1-31.
21. Pitt, *The Decline of the Californios*, 12-13.
22. The law is discussed by Hornbeck, "The Patenting of California's Private Land Claims, 1851-1885," 434-48; and by Gates, "The California Land Act of 1851," 395-430.
23. See, for example, Harlow, *California Conquered*, 50-51.
24. Indirect rule is discussed in John E. Flint, "Nigeria: the Colonial Experience from 1880 to 1914," 220-60.
25. *San Francisco Daily, Alta California*, January 12, 1851.
26. See Bennett, "Settlers and Politics in Kenya," 265-332.
27. Heizer, ed., "Preface," *They Were Only Diggers*, viii.
28. Raphael, *Little White Father*, 202.
29. Ellison, "Rejection of California Indian Treaties: A Study in Local Influence on National Policy," 63.
30. Johnson, *K-344 or the Indians of California vs. the United States*, 53.
31. Heizer, "Introduction," *The Eighteen Unratified Treaties of 1852 between*

the California Indians and the United States Government, 5.
32. Hoopes, "Preface," *Domesticate or Exterminate*.
33. Kelsey, "The California Indian Treaty Myth," 225-38.
34. Leonard, "The Federal Indian Policy in the San Joaquin Valley, its Application and Results," 258-59.
35. Crouter and Rolle, "Edward Fitzgerald Beale and the Indian Peace Commissioners in California, 1851-1854," 120.
36. Phillips, *Chiefs and Challengers* (first edition), 334-35.
37. Hurtado, *Indian Survival*, 141.
38. Rawls, *Indians of California: The Changing Image*, 146.
39. See Ellison, "Federal Indian Policy," 67; Hoopes, "Indian Affairs," 68; Caughey, *California*, 2d ed., 326-27; Crouter and Rolle, "Edward Fitzgerald Beale," 125; Thompson, *Edward F. Beale*, 79.
40. See Prucha, *American Indian Treaties*, 235-60.
41. Col. Joseph K. F. Mansfield to Asst. Adj. Gen. Erwin McDowell, Fort Tejón, February 18, 1859, Office of the Adjutant General, Letters Received, 1822-1860.
42. Thompson, *The Army and the Navajo*, 12-14.
43. Eugenia Mendez, deposition, probably Tule River Indian Agency, February 23, 1922, Harrington Papers, vol. 2.
44. Juan Coluco, deposition, Tule River Indian Agency, February 23, 1922, Harrington Papers, vol. 2.
45. Leonard, "Federal Indian Policy," 364-65.
46. Nordhoff, *California*, 216-37.
47. Elliott, *History of Tulare County, California*, 95.
48. Barker, "The Sorceress of the Tejón Mountains: True Tale of Indian Tribe," *Daily California*, July 20, 1904, reprinted in Boyd and Rodgers, eds., *San Joaquin Vignettes*, 92, 94.
49. Mary Austin, *The Flock*, 220.
50. Bonsal, *Edward Fitzgerald Beale*, 194-95.

Bibliography

Government Documents

National Archives

Brown. J. Ross. Report of J. Ross Brown and Accompanying Documents, concerning accounts of Supt. Beale. Washington, D.C., January 22, 1855. Record Group 46, Records of the U.S. Senate, Sen. 35A-F2.

Clotts. H. V. "Report on Tejón Indians." Kern County. California. January 14, 1918. Department of the Interior. United States Indian Irrigation Service, Smithsonian Institution, Washington, D.C.

Fremont, John C. Congress. Senate. Bill No. 332. 31st Cong., 1st sess., 1850. Record Group 46, Records of the U.S. Senate, Sen. 31A-Bl.

Interior Department. Appointment Papers. State of California, 1849-1907. Microcopy 732, Rolls 20, 21, 25, 26. Record Group 48.

Office of the Adjutant General, Letters Received (Main series), 1822-60. Microcopy 567, Roll 483, Record Group 94.

Office of Indian Affairs, 1824-81. Letter Received. California Superintendency, 1849-52. Microcopy 234, Rolls 32-49, Record Group 75.

Office of Indian Affairs, Special Files 1807-1904. Files 158-59, Special File 159, Microcopy 574, Roll 33. Files 258-66. Special File 266, Microcopy No. 574, Roll 73. Office of the Quartermaster General. Department of the Pacific. Consolidated Correspondence File, 1794-1915. Box 1110. Record Group 92.

Office of the Quartermaster General. Department of the Pacific. Consolidated File on Fort Miller, 1853-58. Record Group 92.

Office of the Quartermaster General. Department of the Pacific. Map of Public Surveys in California to Accompany Report of Surveyor General, 1862. Consolidated File, 1794- 1915. Record Group 92.

Office of the Surveyor General of the United States for California. José Antonio Aguirre, claimant. Tejón Grant Land Claims 327, Southern District. Bancroft Library, Berkeley, California.

Population Schedules of the Eight Census of the United States, 1860. vol.3. Fresno, Humboldt, Klamath, and Los Angeles Counties. Microcopy 653, Roll 59. Vol. 5: San Bernardino, San Diego, San Joaquin Counties. Microcopy 653, Roll 64. Records of the Adjutant General's Office, 1780s-1917. Letters Received 1822-60, Microcopy 567, Roll 483. Record Group 94.

Records of U.S. Army, Continental Commands, 1821-1920. Letters Received 1849-53. Record Group 393. Records of the 10th Military Department. Pacific Division. Letters Received, 1846-51. Microcopy 210, Rolls 1, 2, 3, 4, 5, 6, 7. Record Group 98.

U.S. Army Continental Commands. Department of the Pacific. Records. Letters Received, 1821-1920. Record Group 393.

U.S. Army Continental Commands. 1821-1920. Pacific Division. Microcopy 210, Rolls 2, 3, 5, 6. Record Group 393.

Washburn, H. Storrs. Field Notes of Surveys of Sebastian Military Reserve and Santa Remelia or Wool Military Reserve, April 18, 1854. "Ancient and Miscellaneous Surveys." Vol. 4. *United States*.

Abstract of the Census of 1852, of the State of California. *Journal of the Senate*, 4th sess., Doc. 14, 1853.

Annual Reports of the Commissioner of Indian Affairs, 1854-1878.

Blake, William P. *Report of a Geological Reconnaissance in California*. New York: H. Balliere, 1858.

Cases Decided in the Court of Claims of the December Term, 1879. vol. 15.

Congressional Globe.

____.31st Cong., 1st sess., pts. 1 and 2, 1850.

____.32d Cong., 1st. sess., pt 1, 1852.

____.33d Cong., 1st sess., pt 1, 1853.

House of Representatives. 35A-D8.5 Record Group 233

____.30th Cong., 2d sess., Exec. Doc. 1, 1848 (Serial 537).

____.31st Cong., lst sess., Exec. Doc. 17, 1850 (Serial 573).

____.32d Cong., 1st sess., Exec. Doc. 2, 1851-52 (Serial 634).

____.33rd Cong., 1st sess., Exec. Doc. 1, pt. 1, 1853 (Serial 710).

____.34th Cong., 3d sess., Exec. Doc. 76, 1857 (Serial 906).

____.35th Cong., lst sess., Exec. Doc. 88, 1857-58 (Serial 956).

____.35th Cong., 2d sess., Exec. Doc. 114, 1859 (Serial 1120).

Senate. Senate. Records. Senate 35a-F2. Record Group 46

____.31st Cong., 2d sess., Exec. Doc. 1, 1850 (Serial 587).

____.32d Cong., 1st sess., Exec. Docs. 61, 110. 1852 (Serials 620, 621).

____.32d Cong., 1st sess., Exec. Doc. 110.

____.32d Cong., 2d sess., Exec. Doc. 57. 1852-53 (Serial 665).

____.33d Cong., sp. sess., Exec. Doc. 4, 1853 (Serial 688).

____.33d Cons., 1st sess., Exec. Doc. 87, 1854 (Serial 702).

____.33d Cong., 1st sess., Misc. Doc. 69, 1853-54 (Serial 705).

____.33d Cong., 2d sess., Exec Doc. 41, 1855 (Serial 752).

____.34th Cong., 3d sess., Exec. Doc. 69, 1857 (Serial 881).

____.36th Cong., 1st sess., Reports of the Committees, no. 111, 1860 (1039).

____.36th Cong., 1st sess., Report of the Secretary of the Interior, Exec. Doc. 46, 1860 (Serial 1033).

____.39th Cong., 2d sess., Report of the Committees, no. 156, 1967 (Serial 1279). *Senate Executive Journal*, vol 8. Washington, D.C.: Government Printing Office, 1887.

Kappler, Charles J., ed. *Indian Affairs: Laws and Treaties*, vol. 4., Washington, D.C.: Government Printing Office, 1929.

Office Copy of the Laws, Regulations, Etc., of the Indian Bureau, 1850. Washington, D.C.: Gideon & Co,. Primers, 1850.

"Report of the Secretary of the Interior," December 2, 1858. In *Message of the President of the United States to the Two Houses of Congress at the Commencement of the Second Session of the Thirty-fifth Congress.* Washington, D.C.: William A. Harris, 1858.

Royce, Charles C., ed. *Indian Land Cessions in the United States*. Eighteenth Annual Report of the Bureau of American Ethnology, pt. 2. Washington, D.C.: Government Printing Office, 1899.

Statutes at Large and Treaties of the United States of America from December 1, 1845, to March 3, 1851. Vol. 9, 1851.

Statutes at Large. Vol. 10. 32d Cong., 1st sess., 1855.

The War of the Rebellion: Official Records of the Union and Confederate Armies. Series 1, vol. 50, 2 parts.

Treaties between the United States of America. and the Several Indian Tribes, from 1778 to 1837. Washington, D.C.: Langree and O'Sullivan, 1837. Kraus Reprint Co., Millwood. New York, 1975.

Williamson, R.S. *Reports of Explorations and Surveys to Ascertain the Most Practicable and Economical Route for a Railroad from the Mississippi River to the Pacific Ocean, 1853-4.* 33d Cong., 2d sess., Senate Exec. Doc. 91.

California

Abstract of the Census of 1852 of the State of California, *Journal of the Senate*, 4th sess,. 1853. Governors' Papers. Miscellaneous Communications Received, 1851. F3753: 179, 180, 182, 183, 184. California State Archives, Sacramento, California.

Governors' Papers. Miscellaneous Communications Received, 1851. F3753:179, 180, 182, 183, 184. California State Archives, Sacramento,

California.
Journal of the Assembly, 3d sess., 1852.
Journal of the Assembly, 7th sess., 1856.
Journal of the Senate, 2d sess., 1851; 3d sess., 1852.
Secretary of State Office. Military Records—Adjutant General. Indian War Papers. F3753:179- 286. California State Archives, Sacramento, California. Statutes of California, 7th sess., 1856; 8th sess., 1857.
Statutes of California, 2d sess., 1851.

Newspapers

Bakersfield Daily Californian, 1901.
California State Journal, 1851.
Daily Appeal, 1862.
Daily California Chronicle, n.d.
Daily True Standard, n.d.
Evening News, 1893.
Fresno Morning Republican, 1922.
Gazette Mariposan, 1905.
Havilah Weekly Delta, 1866.
Honolulu Friend, 1846.
Honolulu Sandwich Island Gazette and Journal of Commerce, 1837.
Kern County Weekly Courier, 1870.
Lewiston Morning Tribune, 1918.
Los Angeles Semi-Weekly Southern News, 1861-1862.
Los Angeles Star, 1851-1861, 1868, 1874.
Los Angeles Tri-Weekly News, 1863-1864.
Mariposa Chronicle, 1854.
Mariposa Gazette, 1877, 1889.
Mariposa Star, 1859.
Marysville Daily Appeal, 1862.
Monterey Californian, 1846, 1847, 1848.
Monterey Sentinel, 1856.
Sacramento Daily Union, 1852-1853, 1855-1858, 1862, 1867, 1872.
Sacramento Democratic State Journal, 1852-1853.
Sacramento Placer Times, 1849, 1850.
Sacramento Placer Times & Transcript, 1851, 1852.
Sacramento Transcript, 1850, 1851.
San Diego Herald, 1852, 1859.
San Francisco Alta (Steamer Edition), 1852, 1858.
San Francisco California Farmer, 1857, 1867.
San Francisco California Star, 1847.
San Francisco Courier, 1851.
San Francisco Daily Alta California, 1851-1855, 1857- 1859.
San Francisco Daily California Chronicle, 1854.

San Francisco Daily Evening Bulletin, 1851, 1856, 1864.
San Francisco Daily Evening Picayune, 1851.
San Francisco Daily Herald, 1851-1856, 1859.
San Francisco Daily Morning Call, 1858.
San Francisco Daily Placer Times and Transcript, 1853-1 854.
San Francisco Golden Era, 1853, 1854, 1856.
San Francisco Morning Post, 1851.
San Francisco Pacific News, 1851.
San Francisco Weekly Alta California, 1854.
San Francisco Weekly Chronicle, 1855.
San Francisco Weekly National, 1859.
San Joaquin Intelligence, 1851.
San Joaquin Republican, 1852, 1853, 1855, 1856, 1858.
San Jose California State Journal, 1851.
San Jose Daily Argus, 1851.
San Jose Pioneer, 1878.
San Jose Semi-Weekly Tribune, 1854, 1855.
San Jose Telegraph and Santa Clara County Register, 1854.
San Jose Weekly Visitor, 1852.
Santa Barbara Gazette, 1855.
Shasta Courier, 1852.
Sonoma Herald, 1850.
Southern Californian, 1854, 1855.
Stanislaus County Weekly News, 1875.
Stockton Daily Independent, 1851.
Stockton Journal, 1851, 1852.
Stockton Journal (Steamer Edition), 1852.
Stockton Times, 1851.
Tulare County Times, 1852.
Visalia Delta, 1859, 1860, 1861, 1862, 1863, 1864.
Visalia Sun, 1860.

Unpublished Primary sources

Abrams, William Penn. Diary, 1849-1851. C-F 65:1. Bancroft Library, Berkeley, California.

Alvarado, Juan Bautista. "History of California." Vols. 2,4, translated by Earl R. Hewitt. C-D 2, 4. Bancroft Library, Berkeley, California.

Archives of California. Unbound documents. CA-63. Bancroft Library, Berkeley, California.

Archives of the Archdiocese of San Francisco. Documents 735, 1135, 1137, 1139, 1143, 1531, 1535, 1797, 2065, 2593, 2609, 2651, 2652, 2656, 2812, 3047, 3048, 3616, 3988. Mission Santa Barbara Archives, Santa Barbara, California. Photostats.

Bancroft, Hubert Howe. H. H. Bancroft Collection. C-E 165. Bancroft

Library, Berkeley, California.
Boschulte, Theodore. Statement of Farms and Acres Worked by Government for the Indians on Tejon Reservation, March 31, 1862. Society of the California Pioneers. Copies of the Archives. C-E 71. Bancroft Library, Berkeley, California.
Bowman, J.N. Index of the Spanish-Mexican Private Land Grant Records and Cases of California, C-R, vol. 1, pt. 2, 1958. Bancroft Library, Berkeley, California.
Bigler, Henry. "Diary of a Morman," January-February, 1848. C-D 45, Bancroft Library, Berkeley, California.
Bowers, Stephen. "The Santa Barbara Indians." 1879. Ms. 532. Southwest Museum Library, Los Angeles, California.
Brown, S.C. Interview. Box 802, Folder 6. George W. Stewart Collection, California State Library, Sacramento.
Brownlee, Clark & Company, Agua Fria, California. Accounts for Major Savage's Battalion, 1851. C-G 191. Bancroft Library, Berkeley, California.
Burney, James. Letter to J. M. Hutchings. Modesto, California, March 10, 1885. Yosemite Museum Library, Yosemite National Park, California.
Buzzel, William. Deposition. San Francisco, September , 1853. Transcript of the Proceedings in Case No. 523, Hicks and Martin, Claimants, vs. the United States. Defendant, for the Place Named "Cosumnes." U.S. Land Claims, 2110 ND. Bancroft Library, Berkeley, California.
Calendar and Catalogue of Spanish and Mexican Archives (1792-1859) of the Pueblo of San Jose de Guadalupe. San Jose Public Library, San Jose, California.
Cohen, William. Scrapbooks, vols. 1 and 74. Huntington Library, San Marino, California.
Cook, Sherburne F. Papers. 79/21lc, G-4. Bancroft Library, Berkeley, California. Departmental State Papers. Vol. 17, CA-33. Bancroft Library, Berkeley, California.
Documentos para la Historia de California. Archivo Particular de Sr. Don Mariano Guadalupe Vallejo, C-B 7, 14. 3L. Bancroft Library, Berkeley, California.
Dossier regarding the killing of two soldiers by gentile Indians (1790 and 1791). Translated by Maureen Campión de la Necochea, Archivo General de la Nacion-Californias, vol. 46, Mexico City. Transcript on file in U.S. Forest Service, Goleta, California.
Dye, Francis Job. "Recollections of California." 1877. C-D 69. Bancroft Library, Berkeley, California.
Flech, Alpheces. Deposition. San Francisco, September 1, 1853. Transcript of the Proceedings in Case No. 255. Charles M. Weber, Claimant, vs. the United States, Defendant, for the Place Named "Campo de los

Franceses." U.S. Land Claims 298 ND. Bancroft Library, Berkeley, California.

Fort Sutter Papers. Vol. 20, Manuscript no. 81. Huntington Library, San Marino, California.

Gayton, Anna H. Chukchansi—Field Notes, June-July, 1938. 79/6c Bancroft Library, Berkeley, California.

Green, Alfred A. "Life and Adventures of a 47-er of California." C-D 94. Bancroft Library, Berkeley, California.

Harrington, John P. Papers, 1916-17. National Anthropological Archives, Smithsonian Institution, Washington, D.C.

Harrington, John P. Letters Received and Sent, 1904-1950. Box 40. National Anthropological Archives, Smithsonian Institution, Washington, D.C.

____.Papers of John P. Harrington in the Smithsonian Institution 1907-1957, Northern and Central California. Records Relating to the Tejon Case, 690510-100. Microfilm 100 and 52,. vols. 2 and 4.

Hayes, Benjamin. Scrapbooks, vols. 38, 39, 42. Bancroft Library, Berkeley, California.

Heizer, Robert, "Analysis of 'Tribes' Signing the 1851/1852 Treaties." Archaeological Research Faculty ms 443. Department of Anthropology, University of California, Berkeley, California.

Hayes, Beniamin. "Missions of Alta California." C-C21, pt. 1. Bancroft Library, Berkeley, California.

____.Scrapbooks. Indians of Santa Barbara, vol. 39. Bancroft Library, Berkeley, California.

Howard, William J. Testimony Government Relations with Mariposa Indians. Copy of Reporter's Transcript, vol. 4, September 27, 1890, Mariposa County, California. Mary Corcoran Papers. Bancroft Library, Berkeley, California.

Hicks and Martin, Claimants, vs. the United States, Defendant, for the Place Named "Cosumnes." Transcript of the Proceedings in Case No 523. U.S. Land Claims 240 ND. Bancroft Library, Berkeley, California.

Latta, Frank. Papers. Yosemite Research Library, Yosemite National Park, California.

Lausen, Peter. Deposition, San Francisco. September 1, 1853. Transcript of the Proceedings in Case No. 255, Charles M. Weber. Claimant, vs the United States, Defendant. for the Place named "Campo de los Franceses." U.S. Land Claims 298 ND. Bancroft Library, Berkeley, California.

Leidesdorff, William A. Papers. LE 22, 32, 74, 122, 129, 137, 138, 164, 321, 340. Huntington Library, San Marino, California.

Marsh, John, Claimant, vs. the United States, Defendant, for the Place Named "Los Meganos." Transcript of the Proceedings in Case No 213. U.S. Land Claims 107 ND. Bancroft Library, Berkeley, California.

Marsh, John. Collection. Box 240. California State Library,. Sacramento Family Papers. C- 879. Bancroft Library, Berkeley, California.

Marvin, John G. Account Book. McHenry Museum, Modesto, California.

____.Scrapbooks, vol. 1, 1840-1853, HM 51846; vol. 2, 1852-1854, HM 51847. Huntington Library, San Marino, California.

Marvin, John G. Scrapbooks. vol. 1, 1840-1853, HM 51846; vol. 2, 1852-1854, HM 51847. Huntington Library, San Marino, California.

Merriam, C. Hart. "List of So-Called Tribes Mentioned in the Eighteen Treaties of 1851-52." C. Hart Merriam Collection 8o/i8c, Bancroft Library, Berkeley, California.

Mission San Jose Register of Baptisms, September 2, 1797-May 8, 1859, Chancery Office. Archdioceses of San Francisco, San Francisco, California.

Mission Santa Clara Register of Burials, June 22, 1777-December 22, 1866. Orradre Library, University of Santa Clara, Santa Clara, California.

Naglee, Henry. Journal, May 24-June 20, 1847. Naglee Family Collection, MR-116. Bancroft Library, Berkeley, California.

Papers of the Beale Family Manuscript Division. Box 4. General Correspondence, 1856-69. Library of Congress, Washington, D.C.

Pioneer Manuscript Collection. Box 236. California State Library, Sacramento, California.

Reading, Pierson B. Collection. Box 285, 286. California State Library, Sacramento, California.

Russell, Carl P. "Interview with Maria Lebrado, February 1928." Yosemite Museum Library Yosemite National Park, California.

Savage, James D. Store Record Cash Book, California, 1851-1855. Fresno City and County Historical Society, Fresno, California.

Stewart, George W. "Interview with S.C. Brown, October 8, 1902." George W. Stewart Collection. Box 802. California State Library, Sacramento, California.

____. Stewart, George W. "Notes of Conservation concerning Yokut Indians." George W. Stewart Collection. Box 802. California State Library, Sacramento, California.

Sutter, John A. Collection. Miscellaneous Boxes 311, 312. California State Library, Sacramento, California.

____. Deposition, San Francisco, September 14, 1853. Transcript of the Proceedings in Case No. 523, Hicks and Martin, Claimants. vs. the United States, Defendant, for the Place Named "Cosumnes." U.S. Land Claims, 240 ND. Bancroft Library, Berkeley, California.

____. Papers. C-B 63L. Bancroft Library, Berkeley, California.

____. "Personal Reminiscences of General John Augustus Sutter." 1876. C-D 14. Bancroft Library, Berkeley, California.

____. Statement. 1847. T. Perceval Gerson Collection. 100/5L. Department of Special Collections, University of California, Los Angeles, California.

Swasey, William F. "California, 1845-6." C-D 200. Bancroft Library, Berkeley, California.

Transcript of the Proceedings in Case No. 170, Jose Maria Flores, Appellants vs. The United States, Appellees, for a Place Named "La Liebre." Land Claims 429. Southern District. Bancroft Library, Berkeley, California.

Transcript of the Proceedings in Case No. 240, Jose Antonio Aguirre et al., Claimants vs. The United States, Defendant, for the Place named "Tejon." Land Claims 327, Southern District. Bancroft Library, Berkeley, California.

Transcript of the Proceedings in Case No. 255, Manuel Castro, Claimant vs. The United States, for a Place Named "Laguna de Tache." Land Claims, 189. Southern District. Bancroft Library, Berkeley, California.

Transcript of the Proceedings in Case No. 536, Jose Maria Covarrubias, Claimant vs. the United States, Defendant, for the Place Named "Castec." Land Claims 349, Southern District. Bancroft Library, Berkeley, California.

Upton, Eugene. Scrapbook no. 7. California Historical Society Library, San Francisco, California.

Vallejo, Mariano Guadalupe. "Historical and Personal Memoirs Relating to Alta California." Translated by Earl R. Hewitt. Vols. 1, 4. C-D 18, 2L. Bancroft Library, Berkeley, California.

Vallejo, Salvador. "Notas historicas sobre California." 1874. C-D 21. Bancroft Library, Berkeley, California.

Vineyard, James. Tejon Record and Account Book, August 14, 1854-November 2, 1861. Special Collection, 170/95. University of California at Los Angeles, Los Angeles, California.

Warner, Juan Jose. "Reminiscences of Early Life in California." Unidentified newspaper article in *Missions of Alta California*. Benjamin Hayes Collection. C-C 21, pt. 1. Bancroft Library, Berkeley, California.

Weber, Charles M. Claimant, vs. the United States, Defendant, for the Place Named "Campo de los Franceses." Transcript of the Proceedings in Case No. 255. U.S. Land Claims 298, ND. Bancroft Library, Berkeley, California.

_____.Deposition, San Francisco, April 3, 1855. Transcript of the Proceedings in Case No. 767, Francisco Rico, et al., Claimants, vs. the United States, Defendant, for the Place Named "Rio Estanislao." U.S. Land Claims 413 ND. Bancroft Library, Berkeley, California.

Weber Family Papers. C-B 829. Bancroft Library, Berkeley, California.

Wilson, Benjamin D. Benjamin Wilson Collection, WN 104, 105,106, 107, 108, 110, 112, 136, 244, 245, 283, 286, 49, 498,499, 1017, 1018,

1019, 1020, 1029, 1168, 1169, 1240, 1282, 1289, 1423, 1425, 1721, 1805. Huntington Library, San Marino, California.

Wozencraft, O. A. "Indian Affair,. 1849-1850," 1877. C-D 204. Bancroft Library, Berkeley, California.

Wright, George W. Manuscript. In the United States Court of Claims. *Samuel J. Hensley vs. The United States. Felix Argenti vs. The United States.* California Historical Society, San Francisco, California.

Wyman, George F. Deposition, San Francisco, September 6, 1853. Transcript of the Proceeding in Case No. 523, Hicks and Martin, Claimants, vs. the United States, Defendant, for the Place Named "Cosumnes." U.S. Land Claims 240 ND. Bancroft Library, Berkeley, California.

_____.Deposition, San Francisco, April 3, 1855. Transcript of the Proceedings in Case No. 767, Francisco Rico. et al., Claimants, vs. the United States, Defendant. for the Place Named "Rio Estanislao." U.S. Land Claims 413 ND. Bancroft Library, Berkeley, California.

<u>Theses, Dissertation, and Unpublished Secondary Sources</u>

Anderson, George Esborne. "The Hoopa Valley Indian Reservation Northwestern California: A Study of Its Origins." M.A. thesis, University of California, Berkeley, 1956.

Beale, Marie. "Spain in California." The Papers of the Beale Family. Manuscript Division. L.G. Box 8. Speeches and Writings File by Mrs. Truxton Beale, 1928-48. Library of Congress.

Bean, Lowell John. and Sylvia Brakke Vane. "Petition to the Government of the United States from the American Indian Council of Mariposa County for Acknowledgment as the Yosemite Indian Tribe." Menlo Park: Cultural Systems Research, Inc., 1984.

Crampton, C. Gregory. "The Opening of the Mariposa Mining District, 1849-1859, with Particular Reference to the Mexican Land Grant of John Charles Fremont." Ph.D. diss., University of California, Berkeley, 1941.

Cutter, Donald Colgett. "Spanish Exploration of California's Central Valley." Ph.D. diss., University of California, Berkeley, 1950.

Ellison, William Henry. "The Federal Indian Policy in California, 1846-1860," Ph.D. diss., University of California, Berkeley, 1919.

Fort Tejon State Historic Park General Plan. Sacramento, Cal.: Department of Parks and Recreation, 1992.

Hinton, Harwood Perry. "Military Career of John Ellis Wool." Ph.D. diss., University of Wisconsin, 1960.

Johnson, John. "Chumash Social Organization: An Ethnohistorical Perspective." Ph.D. diss., University of California, Santa Barbara, 1988.

____. "Visual Images of the Tejon Indian Community," Paper presented at the California Indian Conference, University of California, Los Angeles, October, 1995.

Knoop, Anna Marie. "The Federal Indian Policy in the Sacramento Valley, 1846-1860." M.A. thesis, University of California, Berkeley, 1941.

Lawrence, Eleanor. "The Old Spanish Trail: From Santa Fe to California." M.A. thesis, University of California, Berkeley, 1930.

Leonard, Charles Berdan. "The Federal Indian Policy in the San Joaquin Valley: Its Application and Results." Ph.D. diss., University of California, Berkeley, 1928.

Munoz, Neva Jeanne Harkins. "Political Middlemanship and the Double Bind: James Savage and the Fresno River Reservation." Ph.D. diss., University of California, Riverside, 1980.

Stammejohan, George R., et al., Fort Tejon State Historic Park General Plan, Sacramento. State of California, Department of Parks and Recreation, 1992.

Stiner, Ira H. "Porterville, California: An Appreciation of the Past". Porterville City Library.

Wheeler, Mayo Elizabeth. "John A. Sutter, a California Pioneer: An Historical Sketch and Collection of Correspondence." M.A. thesis, University of California, Berkeley, 1924.

Published Primary Sources

Barbour, George W. "The Journal of George W. Barbour, May 1, to October 4, 1851," pts. 1 and 2, Edited by Alban W. Hoopes. *Southwestern Historical Quarterly* 40, nos. 2 and 3 (October 1936 and January 1937):145-53, 247-61.

Barker, John. *San Joaquin Vignettes: The Reminiscences of Captain John Barker*. Edited by William Harland Boyd and Glendon J. Rodgers. Bakersfield: Kern County Historical Society, 1955.

Barton, Enos. "Great Ghost Dance." *Los Tulares*, 14 (March 1953): 2.

Beechey, F. W. *Narrative of a Voyage to the Pacific and Beering's Strait*. vol. 2. London: Henry Colburn and Richard Bentley, 1831.

Belcher, Edward. *Narrative of a Voyage Round the World, performed in Her Majesty's Ship, Sulphur, During the Years 1836-1842*. vol. 1. London: Henry Colburn Publisher, 1843.

Belden, Joseph. "Pastoral California through Gringo Eyes." *Touring Topics* 22, no.8 (August 1930): 40-47, 53-54.

Bell, Major Horace. *Reminiscences of a Ranger or, Early Times in Southern California*. Los Angeles: Yarnell, Castile & Mathes, Printers, 1881.

Bidwell, John. *In California before the Gold Rush*. Los Angeles: Ward Ritchie Press, 1948.

Borthwick, J. D. *Three Years in California*. Edinburgh: Wiiliam Blackwood and Sons, 1857.

Brewer, William H. *Up and Down California in 1860-1864*. Edited by Francis

P. Farquhar. Berkeley: University of California Press, 1966.

Browning, Peter. ed. *Bright Gem of the Western Seas: California 1846-1852, Early Recollections of the Mines, Tulare Plains, Life in California by James H. Carson, and a Report of the Tulare Valley by Lieutenant George H. Derby* Lafayette, Cal.: Great West Books, 1991.

Brownlee, Robert. An American Odyssey: The Autobiography of a 19th Century Scotsman, Robert Brownlee. Edited by Patricia A. Etter. Fayetteville: University of Arkansas Press, 1986.

Bryant, Edwin. *What I Saw in California*. Philadelphia: D. Appleton & Company, 1848.

Bunnell, Lafayette Houghton. *Discovery of the Yosemite and the Indian War of 1851 which Led to that Event*. Fourth edition. Los Angeles: G. W. Gedicher, 1911.

____. "How the Yo-semite Valley was Discovered and Named." *'Hutchings' California Magazine* 3, no. 11 (May 1859): 498-505.

____. "The Date of the Discovery of the Yosemite." *The Century Illustrated Monthly Magazine* 40, no. 5 (September 1890): 795-97.

Camp, Charles L., ed. *John Doble's Journal and Letters from the Mines: Mokelumne Hill, Jackson, Volcano, and San Francisco, 1851-1865*. Denver: Old West Publishing, 1962.

Carson, James H. *Recollections of the California Mines*. Stockton: privately printed, 1852. Edited by Joseph A. Sullivan. Reprint, Oakland: Biobooks, 1950.

Carson, Kit. *Kit Carson's Autobiography*. Edited by Milo Milton Quaife. Lincoln: University of Nebraska Press, 1935.

Caughey, John Walton, ed. *The Indians of Southern California in 1852: The B. D. Wilson Report and a Selection of Contemporary Comment*. San Marino, Cal.: Huntington Library, 1952.

Christman, Enos. One Man's Gold: *The Letters & Journal of a Forty-Niner*. Edited by Florence Morrow Christman. New York: McGraw-Hill Book Company, 1930.

Clark, Walter van Tilburg. ed. *The Journals of Alfred Doten, 1849-1903*, vol. 1, Reno: University of Nevada Press, 1973.

Clyman, James. *James Clyman: American Frontiersman, 1792-1881*. Edited by Charles L. Camp. San Francisco: California Historical Society, 1928.

Cook, Sherburne F., trans. and ed. "Colonial Expeditions to the Interior of California: Central Valley, 1800-1820." *Anthropological Records* 16. no. 6 (May 1960): 239-92.

____. trans. and ed. "Expeditions to the Interior of California: Central Valley, 1820-1840." *Anthropological Records* 20, no. 5 (February 1962): 151-213.

Cordua, Theodor. "The Memoirs of Theodor Cordua, the Pioneer of New Mecklenburg in the Sacramento Valley." ed. and trans. by

Erwin Gustav Gudde. *Quarterly of the California Historical Society*, 12, no. 4 (December 1933): 279-311.

Cox, Ross. *The Columbia River*. vol. 2. London: Henry Colbum and Richard Bentley, 1832.

Crespi, Juan. "Diary Kept During the Exploration that was Made of the Harbor of our Father San Francisco." In Herbert Eugene Bolton, *Fray Juan Crespi: Missionary Explorer on the Pacific Coast, 1769-1774*. Berkeley: University of California Press, 1927.

Cutter, Donald, ed. and trans. *Writings of Mariano Payeras*. Santa Barbara, Bellerophon Books, 1995.

Dana, Juan Francisco. "Ten Decades on a California Rancho; Random Memories of Stirring Events in the Golden State under Three Flags." ed. by John Edwin Hogg, *Touring Topics* 2-3, no. 11 (November 1931): 16- 19, 44.

Davis, William Heath. *Seventy-Five Years in California*. ed. by Douglas S. Watson. San Francisco: John Howell, 1929.

De Anza, Juan Bautista. "Anza's Diary of the Second Anza Expedition, 1775-1776." *In Anza's California Expeditions, vol. 3. The San Francisco Colony, Diaries of Anza, Font and Eixarch, and Narratives of Palou and Moraga*. trans. and ed. by Herbert Eugene Bolton. Berkeley: University of California Press, 1930.

De la Guerra Ord, Agustias. *Occurrences in Hispanic California*. trans. and ed. by Francis Price and William H. Ellison. Washington: Academy of American Franciscan History, 1956.

Derbec, Elienne. *A French Journalist in the California Gold Rush*. ed. by A.P. Nasatir. Georgetown. Calif.: The Talisman Press, 1961.

Downey, Joseph T. *Filings from an Old Saw: Reminiscences of San Francisco and California's Conquest*. ed. by Fred Blackburn Rogers. San Francisco: John Howell, 1956.

Duflot de Mofras. *M. Duflot de Mofras' Travels on the Pacific Coast*. vol. 1, trans. and ed. by Marguerite Eyer Wilbur. Santa Ana: The Fine Arts Press, 1937.

Duhaut-Cilly, A. "Duhaut-Cilly's Account of California in the Years 1827-28." trans. by Charles Franklin Carter. *Quarterly of the California Historical Society* 8, no. 4 (December 1929): 306-36.

Duran, Narciso. "Expedition on the Sacramento and San Joaquin Rivers in 1817: Diary of Fray Narciso Duran." ed. by Charles Edward Chapman. *Publications of the Academy of Pacific Coast History* 2, no. 5 (December 1911): 329-49.

Duvall, Marius. *A Navy Surgeon in California 1846- 1847: The Journal of Marius Duvall*. ed. by Fred Blackburn Rogers. San Francisco: John Howell, 1957.

Eccleston, Robert. *The Mariposa Indian War, Diaries of Robert Eccleston: The*

California Gold Rush, Yosemite, and the High Sierra. ed. by C. Gregory Crampton. Salt Lake City: University of Utah Press, 1975.

Estudillo, José Maria. "Estudillo among the Yokuts: 1819." trans. and ed. by Anna H. Gayton. In Robert Lowie, ed., *Essays in Anthropology*, 67-85. Berkeley: University of California Press, 1936.

Fages, Pedro. "Fages's Note to his Diary of 1772." In Herbert Eugene Bolton, "In the South San Joaquin Ahead of Garces." *Quarterly of the California Historical Society*, 10. no. 3 (September 1931): 211-19.

Font, Pedro. *Font's Complete Diary: A Chronicle of the Founding of San Francisco*. trans. and ed. by Herbert Eugene Bolton. Berkeley: University of California Press, 1933.

Fremont, John Charles. *Memoirs of My Life*. 2 vols. Chicago and New York: Belford, Clark & Company, 1887.

Frazer, Robert W., ed. *Mansfield on the Condition of the Western Forts, 1853-54*. Norman: University of Oklahoma Press, 1963.

Garces, Francisco. *On the Trail of a Spanish Pioneer: The Diary and Itinerary of Francisco Garces in his Travels through Sonora, Arizona, and California*, 1775-1776, vol. 1. trans. and ed. by Elliott Coues. New York: Francis P. Harper, 1900.

Garner, William Robert. *Letters from California, 1846-1847*. ed. by Donald Munro Craig. Berkeley, Los Angeles, and London: University of California Press, 1970.

Gerstaecker, Friedrich. *California Gold Mines*. Oakland, Cal.: Biobooks, 1946.

Gregg, Josiah. *The Commerce of the Prairies*. ed. by Milo Milton Quaife. Chicago: R. R. Donnelley & Sons Company, 1926.

Granger, Lewis. *Letters of Lewis Granger: Reports of the Journey from Salt Lake to Los Angeles in 1849 and of Conditions in Southern California*. ed. by LeRoy R. Hafen. Los Angeles: Glen Dawson, 1959.

Hammond, George P., ed. *The Larkin Papers: Personal, Business, and Official Correspondence of Thomas Oliver Larkin, Merchant and United States Consul in California*, 4 vols., Berkeley and Los Angeles: University of California Press, 1951-53.

Harris, Benjamin Butler. *The Gila Trail: The Texas Argonauts and the California Gold Rush*. ed. by Richard H. Dillon. Norman: University of Oklahoma Press, 1960.

Hartnell, Ella S. "An Indian Ruse." *The Land of Sunshine* 6, no. 1 (December 1896): 27.

Heap, Gwin Harris. *Central Route to the Pacific by Gwin Harris Heap*. ed. by LeRoy R. Hafen and Ann W. Hafen. Glendale, Cal.: The Arthur H. Clark Company, 1957.

Heizer, Robert F., ed. *The Eighteen Unratified Treaties of 1851-1852 between the California Indians and the United States Government*. Berkeley: Archaeological Research Facility, Department of Anthropology,

University of California, 1972.

____. ed. *They were Only Diggers: A Collection of Articles from California Newspapers, 1851-1866, on Indian and White Relations*. Ramona, California: Ballena Press, 1975.

Hittell, John S. *Mining in the Pacific States of North America*. San Francisco: H. H. Bancroft and Company, 1861.

Hutchings, J. M. In the Heart of the Yo-semite Valley. Oakland: Pacific Press Publishing House, 1888.

____. *Scenes of Wonder and Curiosity in California: A Tourist's Guide to the Yo-Semite Valley*. New York and San Francisco: A. Roman and Com pany, Publishers, 1871.

Janssens, Agustín. *The Life and Adventures in California of Don Agustin Janssen, 1834-1856*. ed. by William H. Ellison and Francis Price. San Marino: Huntington Library, 1953.

Johnson, Overton, and William H. Winter. *Route Across the Rocky Mountains*. Lafayette, Ind.: John B. Semans, Printers, 1846. ed. by Carl L. Cannon. Reprint. Princeton: Princeton University Press, 1932.

Johnson, Theodore T. *Sights in the Gold Region and Scenes by the Way*. New York: Baker and Scribner, 1849.

Kelley, Hall J. *Hall J. Kelley on Oregon*. ed. by Fred Wilbur Powell. Princeton: Princeton University Press, 1932.

Keyes, E. D. *Fifty Years' Observation of Men and Events, Civil and Military*. New York: Charles Scribner's Sons, 1884.

Kip, William Ingraham. *The Early Days of My Episcopate*. New York: Thomas Whittaker, 1892.

Kuykendall, Ralph S. "Early History of Yosemite Valley, California." *Grizzly Bear*) July 1919). Reprint. Washington, D.C.: Government Printing Office, 1919, 3-12.

Leonard, Zenas. *Adventures of a Mountain Man: The Narrative of Zenas Leonard*. First Published in 1839. ed. by Milo Milton Quaife. Lincoln: University of Nebraska Press, 1978.

Librado, Femando. *Breath of the Sun: Life in Early California as Told by a Chumash Indian, Fernando Librado, to John P. Harrington*. ed. by Travis Hudson. Banning, Cal.: Museum Press, 1980.

____. *The Eye of the Flute: Chumash Traditional History and Ritual As Told by Fernando Librado Kitsepawit to John P. Harrington*. ed. by Travis Hudson, Thomas Blackbum, Rosario Curletti, and Janice Timbrook. Second edition. Banning: The Malki Museum Press, 1981.

Lienhard, Heinrich. *A Pioneer at Sutter's Fort, 1846-1850: The Adventures of Heinrich Lienhard*. trans. and ed. by Marguerite Eyer Wilbur. Los Angeles: The Calafia Society, 1941.

____. *I Knew Sutter*. trans. by George T. Smisor. Sacramento: The Nugget Press, 1939.

Lynch, James. *With Stevenson to California*. Oakland: Biobooks, 1954. Manly, William Lewis. *Death Valley in '49*. New York: Wallace Nebberd, 1894.

Martin, Thomas S. *With Fremont to California and the Southwest, 1845-1849*. ed. by Ferol Egan. Ashland, Ore.: Lewis Osborne, 1975.

Martinez, José Longinos. *California in 1792: The Expedition of Jose Longinos Martinez*. trans. by Lesley Byrd Simpson. San Marino: Huntington Library, 1938.

Marryat, Frank. *Mountains and Molehills or Recollections of a Burnt Journal*. NewYork: Harper & Brothers, Publishers, 1855.

Merriam, C. Hart. "California Mission Baptismal Records." Chapter in *Studies of California Indians*, ed. by the staff of the Department of Anthropology of the University of California, 188-225. Berkeley and Los Angeles: University of California Press, 1962.

____. "Ethnographic Notes on California Indian Tribes III: Ethnological Notes on Central California Indian Tribes." ed. by Robert F. Heizer. *Reports of the University of California Archaeological Survey* no. 68, pt. 3, 257- 448.

Nordhoff, Charles. *California for Health, Pleasure, and Residence: A Book for Travelers and Settlers*. New York: Harper and Brothers, 1872. Reprint, Ten Speed Press, 1973.

O'Meara, James. "A White Medicine Man." *Californian* 5, n 26 (February 1882): 150-57.

Osio, Antonio María. *The History of Alta California: A Memoir of Mexican California*. ed. by Rose Marie Beebe and Robert M. Senkewicz. Madison: University of Wisconsin Press, 1996.

Palomares, José Francisco. "The Death of Yoscolo." ed. by Robert L. Hoover. *Pacific Historical Review* 51, no. 3 (August 1982): 312-14.

Peard, George. *To the Pacific and Arctic with Beechey: the Journal of Lieutenant George Peard of H.M.S. Blossom, 1825-1828*. ed. by Barry M. Gough. Cambridge: Cambridge University Press, 1973.

Perkins, William. *Three Years in California: William Perkins' Journal of Life at Sonora, 1849-1852*. ed. by Dale L. Morgan and James R. Scobie. Berkeley and Los Angeles: University of California Press, 1964.

Perlot, Jean-Nicolas. *Gold Seeker: Adventures of a Belgian Argonaut during the Gold Rush Years*. trans. by Helen Harding Bretnor and ed. by Howard R. Lamar. New Haven and London: Yale University Press, 1985.

Phelps, William Dane. *Alta California 1840-1842: The Journal and Observations of William Dane Phelps, Master of the Ship "Alert."* ed. by Briton Cooper Busch. Glendale: The Arthur H. Clark Company, 1983.

Powers, Stephen. *Tribes of California*. Washington, D.C.: Government Printing Office, 1877. Reprint. Berkeley, Los Angeles, and London: University of California Press, 1976.

Revere, Joseph Warren. *Tour of Duty in California*. New York: C.S. Francis

& Co., 1849.

Rich, E. E., ed. *The Letters of John McLoughlin From Fort Vancouver to the Governor of Committee*. Third Series, 1844-46. Toronto: The Champlain Society, 1944.

Ripoll, Antonio. "Fray Antonio Ripoll's Description of the Chumash Revolt at Santa Barbara in 1824." trans. and ed. by Maynard Geiger. *Southern California Quarterly*, 52, no.4 (December 1970): 345-64.

Ryan, William Redmond. *Personal Adventures in Upper and Lower California in 1848-9*. 2 vols. London: William Shoberl, Publisher, 1850.

Smith, Jedediah. *The Southwest Expedition of Jedediah S. Smith: His Personal Account of the Journey to California, 1826-1827*. ed. by George R. Brooks. Glendale: Arthur H. Clark Company, 1977.

Spence, Mary Lee, and Donald Jackson. eds. *The Expeditions of John Charles Fremont, vol. 2, The Bear Flag Revolt and the Court Martial*. Urbana, Chicago, and London: University of Illinois Press, 1973.

Spence, Mary Lee. ed. *The Expeditions of John Charles Fremont. vol. 3. Travels From 1848 to 1854*. Urbana and Chicago: University of Illinois Press, 1984.

Steiner, Ira. "Jose Vera Recalls Incidents of His Life on Original Indian Reservation East of Porterville." *Historical Bulletin*, October 1940.

Sullivan, Maurice S. *The Travels of Jedediah Smith: A Documentary Outline, Including the Journal of the Great American Pathfinder*. Santa Ana: The Fine Arts Press, 1934.

Sutter, John A. Letter to H. W. Halleck, New Helvetia, December 20, 1847. "Document la." *Contributions of the University of California Archaeological Research Facility*, no. 9 (July 1970): 94-95.

____. Letter to Mariano Guadalupe Vallejo, New Helvetia, June 1, 1846. "Documentary: The Fremont Episode." *California Historical Society Quarterly* 6, no. 2 (June 1927): 181-91.

____. *The Diary of Johann August Sutter*. San Francisco: The Grabhorn Press, 1932.

____. et al. *New Helvetia Diary: A Record of Events Kept by John A. Sutter and his Clerks New Helvetia, California, From September 9, 1845 to May 25, 1848*. San Francisco: The Grabhorn Press, 1939.

Swasey, F. W. *The Early Days and Men of California*. Oakland, Cal.: Pacific Press Publishing Company, 1891.

____. "The Sutter-Marshall Lease with the Yalesumney Indians, 1848." "Document 3b." *Contributions of the University of California Research Facility*, no. 9, (July 1970): 109-10.

Taylor, Alexander. "The Indianology of California." *The California Farmer and Journal of Useful Silences*. March 23, 1860.

Thirty-fourth Annual Report of the Executive Committee of the Indian Rights Association for the Year Ending in 1916. Philadelphia: Office of the Indian Rights

Association, 1916.

Taylor, Bayard. *Eldorado*. ed. by Richard H. Dillon. Palo Alto, Cal.: Lewis Osborne, 1968.

Tibesar, Antonine. trans. and ed. *Writings of Junipero Serra*, vol. 3. Washington, D.C.: Academy of American Franciscan History, 1956.

Townsend, E. D. *The California Diary of General E. D. Townsend*. ed. by Malcolm Edwards. Los Angeles: The Ward Ritchie Press, 1970.

Turner, Henry Smith. *The Original Journals of Henry Smith Turner with Stephen Watts Kearny to New Mexico and California, 1846-1847*. ed. by Dwight L. Clark. Norman: University of Oklahoma Press, 1966.

Vischer, Edward. "Edward Vischer's First Visit to California." trans. and ed. by Erwin Gustav Gudde. *California Historical Society Quarterly*, 19. no. 2 (September. 1940): 193-216.

Ward, Samuel. *Sam Ward in the Gold Rush*. ed. by Carvel Collins. Stanford. Cal.: Stanford University Press, 1949.

Warner, Juan Jose. "Reminiscences of Early California from 1831 to 1846." *Annual Publications of the Historical Society of Southern California*, 1 (1907-1908): 176-93.

____. Benjamin Hayes, and J. P. Widney. *An Historical Sketch of Los Angeles County, California*. Los Angeles: Louis Lewin and Co., 1876. Reprint. Los Angeles: O. W. Smith, Publisher, 1936.

Waseurtz af Sandels, G. M. *A Sojourn in California by the King's Orphan: The Travels and Sketches of G.M. Waseurtz af Sandels, a Swedish gentleman who visited California in 1812-1843*. ed. by Helen Putnam Van Sicklen. San Francisco: The Book Club of California, 1945.

Waters, Willard O., ed. *Glances at California, 1847-1853: Diaries and Letters of William Rich Hutton, Surveyor*. San Marino, Cal.: Huntington Library, 1942.

Weber, David. *The Californios versus Jedediah Smith, 1826-1827: A New Cache of Documents*. Spokane: The Arthur H. Clark Company, 1990.

Wierzbicki, Felix Paul. *California As It Is and As It May Be*. San Francisco: Washington Bartlett, 1849. Reprint. New York: Burt Franklin, 1970.

Wilkes, Charles. *Narrative of the United States Exploring Expedition during the Years 1838, 1839, 1840, 1841, 1842*, vol. 5. Philadelphia: Lea and Blanchard, 1845.

Wilke, Philip J., and Harry W. Lawton, eds. *The Expedition of Capt. J. W Davidson from Fort Tejón to the Owens Valley in 1859*. Socorro, N. M.: Ballena Press, 1976.

Wolcott, Magorie Tisdale, ed. *Pioneer Notes: From the Diaries of Judge Benjamin Hayes, 1849-1875*. Los Angeles: Privately printed, 1929. Reprint. New York: Arno Press, 1976.

Woodward, Arthur, ed. "Benjamin David Wilson's Observations on Early Days in California and New Mexico." Dictated December 6, 1877.

Annual *Publications of the Historical Society of Southern California* (1934): 74-150.

Woods, Daniel B. *Sixteen Months at the Gold Diggings*. New York: Harper and Brothers, Publishers, 1851.

Work, John. *Fur Brigade to Bonaventura: John Work's California Expedition of 1832-1833 for the Hudson's Bay Company*. ed. by Alice Bay Maloney. San Francisco: California Historical Society, 1945.

Wozencraft, Oliver M. "Oration." *Twenty-Fifth Anniversary of the Corporate Society of California Pioneers*, 3 (San Francisco: 1875): 7-14.

Secondary Sources

Austin, Mary. *Earth Horizon: Autobiography*. Boston and New York: Houghton Mifflin Company, 1932.

____. *The Flock*. Boston: Houghton Mifflin, 1906.

Anderson, Frank Maloy. *The Mystery of A Public Man: A Historical Detective Story*. Minneapolis and London: University of Minnesota Press, 1948.

Anderson, George E. and Robert F. Heizer. "Treaty Making by the Federal Government in California 1851-1852." *In Treaty Making and Treaty Rejection by the Federal Government in California, 1850-1852*, 1-36. ed. by Robert F. Heizer. Socorro, N.M.: Ballena Press, 1978.

Anderson, Robert T. "Anthropology and History." *Bucknell Review* 15, no. 1 (March 1967): 1-8.

Anonymous. *History of Sacramento County, California*. Oakland: Thompson and West, 1880.

Anonymous. "Sebastian Indian Reservation," *Historic Kern* 37. no. 1 (March 1988): 1-3.

Applegate, Richard B. "The Datura Cult among the Chumash." *Journal of California Anthropology* 2, no. 1 (Summer 1975): 7-17.

Axtell, James. "Ethnohistory: An Historian's Viewpoint." Chapter in *The European and the Indian: Essays in the Ethnohistory of Colonial North America*, 3-15. New York, Toronto, and Melbourne: Oxford University Press, 1981.

Bancroft, Hubert Howe. *California Pastoral, 1769-1848*. San Francisco: The History Company, Publishers, 1888.

____. *History of California*. 7 vols. San Francisco: The History Company, Publishers, 1885-1890.

Barrett, Samuel A. "The Geography and Dialects of the Miwok Indians." *University of California Publications in American Archaeology and Ethnology* 6, no. 2 (1908): 343-68.

____. and Edward W. Gifford. "Indian Life of the Yosemite Region: Miwok Material Culture." *Bulletin of the Public Museum of the City of Milwaukee* 2, no. 2 (March): 117-376.

Bates, Craig D. "Miwok Dancers of 1856: Stereographic Images from Sonora, California." *Journal of California and Great Basin Anthropology*

6, no. 1 (1984): 6-18.

Bauer, William J., Jr. *We Were All Like Migrant Workers Here: Work, Community, and Memory on California's Round Valley Reservation, 1850-1941*. Chapel Hill: University of North Carolina Press, 2009.

Baumhoff, Martin A. "Ecological Determinants of Aboriginal California Populations." *University of California Publications in American Archaeology and Ethnology* 49, no. 2 (May 1963): 155-236.

Beals, Ralph L., and Joseph A. Hester, Jr. "A New Ecological Typology of the California Indians." In *Men and Cultures*. ed. by Anthony F.C. Wallace, 411-19. Philadelphia: University of Pennsylvania Press, 1960.

Beattie, George William. "California's Unbuilt Missions: Spanish Plans for an Inland Chain." *Historical Society of Southern California Annual Publications* 14, pt. 2 (1929): 243-64.

Becker, Robert H. *Designs on the Land: Disenos of California Ranchos and Their Makers*. San Francisco: Book Club of California, 1969.

Beeler, Madison S. "Noptinte Yokuts." *In Studies in American Indian Languages*. University of California Publications in Linguistics, vol. 65, 11-76. ed. by Jesse Sawyer. Berkeley: University of California Press, 1971.

____. and Kathryn A. Klar. "Interior Chumash." *Journal of California Anthropology* 4, no. 2 (Winter 1977): 287-305.

Bennett, George. "Settlers and Politics in Kenya." In *History of East Africa*, vol. 2, ed. by Vincent Hadow and E.M. Chilver, 265-332. Oxford: Clarendon Press, 1965.

Bennyhoff, James A. *Ethnogeography of the Plains Miwok*. Center for Archaeological Research at Davis, Publication No. 5. Davis; University of California, 1977.

Berkhofer, Robert F., Jr. "The Political Context of a New Indian History." *Pacific Historical Review* 15, no. 3 (August 1971): 357-82.

Biggs, Donald C. *Conquer and Colonize: Stevenson's Regiment and California*. San Rafael: Presidio Press, 1977.

Bonsal, Stephen. *Edward Fitzgerald Beale: A Pioneer in the Path of Empire*, 1822-1903. New York and London: G.P. Putnam's Sons, 1912.

Bolton, Herbert Eugene. "In the South San Joaquin Ahead of Garces." *Quarterly of the California Historical Society* 10, no. 3 (September 1931): 211-19.

Bowman. J. N. "The Resident Neophytes (Existentes) of the California Missions, 1769-1834." *Southern California Quarterly* 40, no. 2 June (1958): 138- 48.

Boyd, William Harland. *A California Middle Border: The Kern River Country, 1772-1880*. Richardson, Tex.: The Havilah Press, 1972.

Broadbent, Sylvia M. "Conflict at Monterey: Indian Horse Raiding, 1820-1850." *Journal of California Anthropology* 1, no. 1 (Spring 1974): 86-101.

____. *The Southern Sierra Miwok Language*. University of California Publications in Linguistics, vol. 38. Berkeley and Los Angeles: University of California Press, 1964.

Chandler, Robert. "Jose Chico: Bearing a Bi-Cultural Burden." *Dogtown Territorial Quarterly*, no.32 (Winter 1997): 54-63.

____. "The Failure of Indian Reform: White Attitudes and Indian Response in California during the Civil War Era." *Pacific Historian* 24, no. 3 (Fall 1980): 284-94.

Caughey, John Walton. *California*, 2nd ed. Englewood Cliffs, N.J.: Prentice-Hall, 1953.

____. "Don Benito Wilson, an Average Southern Californian." *Huntington Library Quarterly* 2 (1939): 285- 300.

____. *The California Gold Rush*. First Published in 1948. Berkeley, Los Angeles, and London: University of California Press, 1975.

Chartkoff, Joseph L., and Kerry Kona Chartkoff. *The Archaeology of California*. Stanford: Stanford University Press, 1984.

Colwes, Theresa. "The Man Behind the Cuyama Valley Indian Massacre." *Californians* 12. no. 3 (1995): 29-35.

Cook, Sherburne F. "Smallpox in Spanish and Mexican California, 1710-1845." *Bulletin of the History of Medicine* 7, no. 2 (February 1939); 153-91.

____. "The Aboriginal Population of Alameda and Contra Costa Counties, California." *Anthropological Records* 16, no. 4 (June 1957): 131-55.

____. "The Aboriginal Population of the San Joaquin Valley, California." *Anthropological Records* 16, no. 2. (July 1955): 31-78.

____."The American Invasion, 1848-1870." *Ibero-Americana* 23 (1943). Part Three in Sherburne F. Cook, *The Conflict Between the California Indian and White Civilization*, 252-361. Berkeley and Los Angeles: University of California Press, 1976.

____. "The Epidemic of 1830-1833 in California and Oregon." *University of California Publications in American Archaeology and Ethnology* 43, no. 3 (1955): 303-25.

____. "The Indian versus the Spanish Mission." *Ibero-Americana* 21 (1943). Part One in *The Conflict Between the California Indian and White Civilization*, 1-194. Berkeley and Los Angeles: University of California Press, 1976.

____. "The Mechanism and Extent of Dietary Adaptation Among Certain Groups of California and Nevada Indians." *Ibero-Americana* 18 (1941). Part Six in *The Conflict Between California Indian and White Civilization*, 447-507. Berkeley and Los Angeles: University of California Press, 1976.

____. "The Physical and Demographic Reaction of the Nonmission Indians in Colonial and Provincial California." *Ibero-Americana* 21 (1943). Part Two in *The Conflict Between the California Indian and White Civilization*,"195-251. Berkeley and Los Angeles: University of California Press, 1976.

____. *The Population of the California Indians, 1769-1970*. Berkeley, Los Angeles, and London: University of California Press, 1976.

Cook, Sherburne F., and Woodrow Borah. *Essays in Population History: Mexico and California*. Berkeley, Los Angeles. and London: University of California Press, 1979.

Coombs, Gary B. "With What God Will Provide: A Reexamination of the Chumash Revolt of 1824." *Noticias* 26, no. 2 (Summer 1980): 21-29.

Crampton, C. Gregory, and Stephen K. Madsen. *In Search of the Spanish Trail: Santa Fe to Los Angeles, 1829-1848*. Salt Lake City. Ut: Gribbs-Smith, 1994.

Crouter, Richard E. and Andrew F. Rolle. "Edward Fitzgerald Beale and the Indian Peace Commissioners in California, 1851-1854." *Southern California Quarterly* 42 (June 1960): 107-32.

Crowe, Earle. *Men of El Tejon: Empire in the Tehachapis*. Los Angeles: Ward Ritchie Press, 1957.

Cullimore, Clarence. *Old Adobes of Forgotten Fort Tejon*. Second Edition. Bakersfield, Cal.: Kern County Historical Society, 1949.

Dale, Edward Everett. *The Indians of the Southwest: A Century of Development under the United States*. First published in 1949. Norman: University of Oklahoma Press. 1976.

Davis, James T. *Trade Routes and Economic Exchange among the Indians of California*. University of California Archaeological Ethnology Report No. 54 (1961). Reprint. Ballena Press Publications in Archaeology Ethnology and History, No. 3. Ramona, Cal.: Ballena Press, 1974.

Dening, Gregory. "Ethnohistory in Polynesia: The Value of Ethnohistorical Evindence." *Journal of Pacific History* 1 (1966): 23-42.

____. *Islands and Beaches: Discourse on a Silent Land, Marquesas, 1774-1880*. Honolulu: University Press of Hawaii, 1980.

Downs, James E. "Differential Response to White Contact: Paiute and Washo." *University of Utah Anthropological Papers* 67 (August 1963): 115-37.

Dillon, Richard H. *Fool's Gold: The Decline and Fall of Captain John Sutter of California*. New York: Coward-McCann, 1967.

____. *J. Ross Browne: Confidential Agent in Old California*. Norman: University of Oklahoma Press, 1965.

Du Bois, Cora. "The 1870 Ghost Dance." *Anthropological Records* 3, no. 1 (1939): 1-139.

Elliott, Maud Howe. *Uncle Sam Ward and His Circle*. New York: The MacMillan Company, 1938.

Elliot, Wallace W. *History of Fresno County, California*. San Francisco: Wallace W. Elliot & Co., Publishers, 1882.

____. *History of Tulare County California*. San Francisco: Wallace W. Elliot & Co., Publishers, 1883.

Ellison, William Henry. "The Federal Indian Policy in California, 1846-1860." *Mississippi Historical Review* 9, no. 1 (1922): 37-67.

____. *A Self-Governing Dominion: California, 1849-1960*. First Published in 1950. Reprint. Berkeley: University of California Press, 1978.

____. "Rejection of California Indian Treaties: A Study in Local Influences on National Policy," *Grizzly Bear* (May, June, July, 1925). Reprinted in *Treaty Making and Treaty Rejection by the Federal Government in California, 1850-1852*, 50-70. ed. by Robert F. Heizer. Socoro, New Mexico: Ballena Press, 1978.

____. "The Federal Indian Policy in California, 1846-1860." *Mississippi Historical Review* 9, no. 27 (1922): 37-67.

Engelhardt, Zephyrin. *The Missions and Missionaries of California*. 4 vols. San Francisco: James H. Barry Company, 1908-1915.

____. *Mission San Luis Obispo in the Valley of the Bears*. Santa Barbara: Mission Santa Barbara, 1933.

____. *San Miguel, Arcangel, The Mission on the Highway*. Santa Barbara: Mission Santa Barbara, 1929.

Evans-Pritchard, E.E. "Anthropology and History." In *Social Anthropology and Other Essays*, 172-91. New York: The Free Press of Glencoe, 1962.

Farquhar, Francis R. *History of the Sierra Nevada*. Berkeley and Los Angeles: University of California Press, 1969.

Farris, Glenn. "'Indian Rancherie' on Dry Creek: An Early 1850s Indian Village on the Sacramento and San Joaquin County Line." *Journal of California* and *Great Basin Anthropology* 28, no. 1 (2008): 63-74.

Fenton, William N. "Ethnohistory and Its Problems." *Ethnohistory* 9, no. 1 (Winter 1962): 1-23.

Ferris, David Frederic. *Judge Marvin and the Founding of the California Public School System*. Berkeley and Los Angeles: University of California Press, 1962.

Fisher, Nora, ed. *Spanish Textile Tradition of New Mexico and Colorado*. Santa Fe: Museum of New Mexico Press, 1979.

Flint, John E. "Nigeria: The Colonial Experience from 1880 to 1914." *In Colonialism in Africa, 1870-1960*, vol. 1, 220-60. *The History and Politics of Colonialism*, 1870-1914, ed. by L. H. Gann and Peter Duignan, Cambridge: The University Press, 1969.

Forbes, Jack D. "Frontiers in American History and the Role of the Frontier Historian." *Ethnohistory* 15. no. 2 (Spring 1968): 203-35.

____. "Indian Horticulture West and Northwest of the Colorado River." *Journal of the West* 2, no. 1 (January 1963): 1-14.

Frank, Gelya and Carole Goldberg. *Defying then Odds: The Tule River Tribe's Struggle for Sovereignty in Three Centuries*. New Haven and London: Yale University Press, 2010.

Garr, Daniel. "Planning, Politics and Plunder: The Missions and Indian

Pueblos of Hispanic California." *Southern California Quarterly* 54, no. 4 (Winter 1972): 291-312.

Gates, Paul. "The California Land Act of 1851." *California Historical Society Quarterly* 5, no. 4 (December 1971): 395-430.

Gayton, Anna H. "Culture-Environment Integration: External References in Yokuts Life." *Southwestern Journal of Anthropology* 2, no. 3 (Autumn 1946): 252-68.

____. "Yokuts and Western Mono Ethnography I: Tulare Lake, Southern Valley, and Central Foothill Yokuts." *Anthropological Records* 10, no. 1 (1948): 1-142.

____. "Yokuts and Western Mono Ethnography II: Northern Foothill Yokuts and Western Mono." *Anthropological Records* 10, no. 2 (1948): 143-302.

____. "Yokuts and Western Mono Social Organization." *American Anthropologist* 41, no. 3 July-September 1945): 409-26.

____. "Yokuts-Mono Chiefs and Shamans." *University of California Publications in American Archaeology and Ethnology* 24, no. 8 (October 1930): 361-420.

____. and Stanley S. Newman. "Yokuts and Western Mono Myths." *Anthropological Records* 5, no. 1 (October 1940): 1-110.

Giffen, Helen S., and Arthur Woodward. *The Story of El Tejon*. Los Angeles: Dawson's Book Shop, 1942.

Gifford, Edward Winslow. "Miwok Lineages and the Political Unit in Aboriginal California." *American Anthropologist* (28, no. 2 (April 1926): 389-401.

Gilbert, Frank T. *History of San Joaquin County, California, with Illustrations Descriptive of its Scenery*. Oakland. Cal.: Thompson and West, 1879.

Glover, Jeffrey. "Alexis Godey: Forgotten Frontiersman," *Historic Kern* 45, no. 3 (September 1995): 1-4.

Goldschtnidt, Walter. "Social Organization in Native California and the Origin of Clans." *American Anthropologist* 50, no. 3 (July-September 1948): 444-56.

Goodman, David Michael. *A Western Panorama, 1849-1875: The Travels, Writings, and Influence of J. Ross Browne*. Glendale, Cal.: Arthur H. Clark. 1966.

Gorenfeld, William, and John Gorenfeld. "The Tule River War." *Wild West* (June 1999): 48-49, 52, 80.

Grant, Campbell. "Interior Chumash." In *California*, ed. by Robert Heizer, vol. 8, 530-34. *Handbook of North American Indians*. ed. by William C. Sturtevant. Washington: Smithsonian Institution, 1978.

Gray, Barbara B. "The Story of San Emigdio Rancho." *Historic Kern* 8, no. 1 (September 1957): 1-2.

Gray, Thorne B. *The Stanislaus Indian Wars: The Last of the California Northern Yokuts*. Modesto: The McHenry Museum Press, 1993.

Grivas, Theodore. *Military Governments in California, 1846-1850*. Glendale: The Arthur H. Clark Company, 1963.

Guest, Francis F. *Fermin Francisco de Lasuen (1736-1803): A Biography.* Washington: Academy of American Franciscan History, 1973.

____. "Junipero Serra and His Approach to the Indians." *Southern California Quarterly* 67, no. 3 (Fall 1985): 223-61

Gutierrez, Ramón A. *When Jesus Came, the Corn Mothers Went Away: Marriage, Sexuality, and Power in New Mexico, 1500-1846*. Stanford: Stanford University Press, 1991.

Hackel, Steven W. Children of Coyote, *Missionaries of Saint Francis: Indian-Spanish Relations in Colonial California, 1769-1850*. Chapel Hill: Published for the Omohundro institute of Early America History and Culture. Williamsburg, Virginia, by the University of North Carolina Press, 2005.

____. "The Staff of Leadership: Indian Authority in the Missions of Alta California." *William and Mary Quarterly* 54, no 2, 1997: 347-76.

Hafen, LeRoy R. "The Old Spanish Trail, Santa Fe to Los Angeles." *Huntington Library Quarterly* 1l, no. 2 (February 1948): 149-60.

____. and Ann W. Hafen. *Old Spanish Trail: Santa Fe to Los Angeles*. Glendale: The Arthur H. Clark Company, 1954.

Hall, Frederic. *The History of San Jose and Surroundings with Biographical Sketches of the Early Settlers*. San Francisco: A. L. Bancroft and Company, 1871.

Hammond, George P., and Dale L. Morgan. *Captain Charles M. Weber Pioneer of the San Joaquin and Founder of Stockton, California*. Berkeley Friends of the Bancroft Library, 1966.

Harlow, Neal. *California Conquered: The Annexation of a Mexican Province, 1846-1850*. Berkeley, Los Angeles and London: University of California Press, 1982.

Harrington, M. R. "Alexander Godey: Hero or Villain?" *Touring Topics* 25, no. 7. pt. 1 (June 1933): 14-15, 33-34.

Hathaway, Martha N. *The Little Story of The Indian Board of Co-operation and the Indians of El Tejon*. The Indian Board of Co-operation, nd.

Hayes, John. "Sheep Farming in California." *The Overland Monthly* 8, no. 6 (June,1972): 489- 495.

Heald, Weldon F. "The Forgotten Pioneer," *Westways* 46, no. 3 (March, 1954): 7.

Heap, Gwinn Harris. *Central Route to the Pacific*. ed. by LeRoy R. Hafen and Ann W. Hafen. The Arthur H. Clark Company, Glendale Cal.: 1957.

Heizer, Robert F., ed. "A Collection of Ethnographical Articles on the California Indians." *Ballena Press Publications in Archaeology, Ethnology, and History*, no. 7. Ramona, Cal.: Ballena Press, 1976.

____. "The Direct-Historical Approach in California Archaeology." *American Antiquity* 7, no. 2 (October 1941): 98-122.

____. "Treaties." In *California*, ed. by Robert R. Heizer. vol. 8, 701-704. *Handbook of North American Indians*, ed. by William C. Sturtevant. Washington, D.C.: Smithsonian Institution, 1978.

____. "Walla Walla Indian Expeditions to the Sacramento Valley." *California Historical Society Quarterly* 21, no. 1 (March 1942): 1-7.

____. and Albert B. Elasser. *The Natural World of the California Indians*. Berkeley, Los Angeles, and London: University of California Press, 1980.

____. and Gordon W. Hewes. "Animal Ceremonialism in Central California in the Light of Archeology." *American Anthropologist* 40 (1940): 587-603.

Hill, Joseph J. "Ewing Young in the Fur Trade of the Far Southwest, 1822-1834." *Quarterly of the Oregon Historical Society* 24 no. 1 (March 1923): 1-35.

____. "The Old Spanish Trail: A Study of Spanish and Mexican Trade and Exploration Northwest from New Mexico to the Great Basin and California." *Hispanic American Historical Review* 4, no. 3 (August 1921): 444-73.

Hillinger, Charles. "The Story of Tejon Ranch." Reprinted from the *Los Angeles Times*. December 1955. No place, no date.

Hittell, Theodore H. *History of California*, vol. 3. San Francisco: N.J. Stone and Company, 1897.

Holmes, Kenneth L. *Ewing Young: Master Trapper*. Portland Binfords & Mort, 1967.

Holterman, Jack. "The Revolt of Estanislao." *The Indian Historian* 3 no. 1 (Winter 1970): 43-54.

Hornbeck, David. "Land Tenure and Rancho Expansion in Alta California, 1784-1846." *Journal of Historical Geography* 4, no. 4 (1978): 371-90.

____. "The Patenting of California's Private Land Claims, 1851-1885." *Geographical Review* 69 no. 4 (October 1979): 434-48.

Hoopes, Alban W. *Indian Affairs and Their Administration with Special Reference to the Far West, 1849-1860*. Philadelphia: University of Pennsylvania Press, 1932.

____. "Redick McKee and the Humboldt Bay Region, 1851-1852." *California Historical Society Quarterly* 49, no. 3 (September 1970): 195 219.

Hoopes, Chad L. *Domesticate or Exterminate: California Indian Treaties Unratified and Made Secret in 1852*. Eureka: Redwood Coast Publications, 1975.

Horsman, Reginald. *Expansion and American Indian Policy, 1783-1812*. East Lansing: Michigan State University Press, 1967.

____. "Redick McKee and the Humboldt Bay Region, 1851-1852." California *Historical Quarterly* 49, no. 3 (September 1970): 195-219.

Hudson, Travis, and Thomas Blackburn. "The Integration of Myth and Ritual in South-Central California: The 'Northern Complex.'" *Journal of California Anthropology* 5, no. 2 (Winter 1978): 225-50.

Hughes, Charles. "The Decline of the Californios: The Case of San Diego. 1846-1856." *Journal of San Diego History* 21, no. 3 (Summer 1975): 1-31.

Hurtado, Albert L. "California Indians and the Workaday West: Labor, Assimilation, and Survival." *California History* 69, no. 1 (Spring 1990): 2-11.

____. *Indian Survival on the California Frontier*. New Haven: Yale University Press, 1988.

Hudson, Travis. "The Alliklik-Tataviam Problem." *Journal of California and Great Basin Anthropology* 21, no. 2 (Winter 1982): 222-32.

____. "Kitanemuk." In *Native America in the Twentieth Century: An Encyclopedia*, 290-91. ed. by Mary B. Davis. New York: Garland, 1994.

Hunt, Aurora. *The Army of the Pacific: Its Operations in California, Texas, Arizona, New Mexico, Utah, Nevada, Oregon, Washington, Plains Region, Mexico, etc., 1860- 1866*. Glendale, Cal.: Arthur H. Clark, 1951.

Hussey, John Adam. "The New Mexico-California Caravan of 1847-1848." *New Mexico Historical Review* 18, no. 1 (January 1943): 1-16.

____. and George Walcott Ames. Jr. "California Preparations to Meet the Walla Walla Invasion, 1846." *California Historical Society Quarterly* 21, no. 1 (March 1942): 9-21.

Hutchinson, C. Alan. "The Mexican Government and the Mission Indians of Upper California, 1821-1835." *The Americas* 21, no. 4 (April 1965): 335-62.

Jablow, Joseph. *The Cheyenne in Plains Indian Trade Relations, 1795-1840*. Monographs of the American Ethnological Society, 19. New York: J. J. Augustin Publisher, 1950.

Jackson, Robert H. "Gentile Recruitment and Population Movements in the San Francisco Bay Area Missions." *Journal of California and Great Basin Anthropology* 6, no. 2 (1980): 225-39.

James, Steven R., and Suzanne Graziani. "California Indian Warfare." *Contributions of the University of California Archaeological Research Facility*, no. 23 (March 1975): 47-109.

Jennings, Francis. "A Growing Partnership: Historians, Anthropologists and American Indian History." *Ethnohistory* 29, no. 1 (1982): 21-34.

Johnson, Kenneth M. *K-344 or the Indians of California vs. the United States*. Los Angeles: Dawson's Book Shop, 1966.

Johnson, Susan Lee. *Roaring Camp: The Social World of the California Gold Rush*. New York: W. W. Norton, 2000.

Johnson, John R. "Indian History in the Santa Barbara Back Country." *Los Padres Notes* 3 (Spring 1984): 1-23.

____. "Mission Registers as Anthropological Questionnaires: Understanding the Limitations of the Data." *American Indian Culture and Research Journal* 12, no. 2 (1988): 9-30.

____. "Mat'apxwelxwel Ethnohistory." In *Archaeological Passages: A Volume in Honor of Claude Nelson Warren*, 24-39. ed. by Joan S. Schneider, Robert M. Yohe II, and Jill K. Gardner. Western Center for Archaeology & Paleontology. Publications in Archaeology, 2000.

____. "The Indians of Mission San Fernando." Southern California Quarterly 79, no. 3 (1998): 249-90.

____. "The Trail to Kashtiq." *Journal of California Anthropology* 5, no. 2 (Winter 1978): 188-98

____. and David D. Earle. "Vegetation Burning by the Chumash." *Journal of California and Great Basin Anthropology* 4, no. 2 (Winter 1982): 163-86.

____. and David D. Earle. "Tataviam Geography and Ethnohistory." *Journal of California and Great Basin Anthropology* 12, no. 2 (1990): 191-214.

Jones, Oakah L., Jr. *Pueblo Warriors and Spanish Conquest.* Norman: University of Oklahoma Press, 1966.

Kelsey, Harry. "Charles E. Mix." in *The Commissioners of Indian Affairs 1827-1972*. ed. by Robert M. Kvasnicka and Herman J. Viola, 77-79. Lincoln and London: University of Nebraska Press, 1979.

____. "The California Indian Treaty Myth." *Southern California Quarterly* 55, no. 3 (Fall 1973): 225-38.

Kenner, Charles L. *A History of New Mexico-Plains Indian Relations*. Norman: University of Oklahoma Press, 1969.

Klein, Kerwin Lee. *Frontiers of Historical Imagination: Narrating the European Conquest of Native America, 1890-1900*. Berkeley, Los Angeles, and London: University of California press, 1997.

Kroeber, Alfred L. *An Anthropologist Looks at History*. ed. by Theodora Kroeber. Berkeley and Los Angeles: University of California Press, 1966.

____. "California Place Names of Indian Origins." *University of California Publications in American Archaeology and Ethnology* 12, no. 2 (June 15, 1916): 31-68.

____. "Culture Element Distributions. Volume 15: Salt, Dogs, Tobacco." *University of California Publications in Anthropological Records* 6 (1941-1942): 1-20.

____. *Handbook of the Indians of California*. Smithsonian Institution Bureau of American Ethnology Bulletin 78. Washington: Government Printing Office, 1925.

Kunkel, P. H. "The Pomo Kin Group and the Political Unit in Aboriginal California." *Journal of California Anthropology* 1, no. 1 (Spring 1974), 7-18.

Kvasnicka, Robert M., and Herman J. Viola, eds. *The Commissioners of Indian Affairs, 1824-1977*. Lincoln: University of Nebraska Press, 1979.

Latta, Frank F. "Alexis Godey in Kern County." *Kern County Historical Society*, (1939): 23-52.

____. *Handbook of Yokuts Indians*. Second Edition. Santa Cruz, Cal.: Bear

State Books, 1977.

____. *Joaquin Murrieta and His Horse Gangs*. Santa Cruz, Cal.: Bear State Books, 1980.

____. *The Saga of Rancho El Tejon*. Santa Cruz, Cal.: Bear State Books, 1976.

Lawrence, Eleanor. "Mexican Trade between Santa Fe and Los Angeles, 1830-1848." *California Historical Society Quarterly* 10, no. 1 (1931): 27-39.

Layton, Thomas N. "Traders and Raiders: Aspects of Trans-Basin and California-Plateau Commerce, 1800-1830." *Journal of California and Great Basin Anthropology* 3, no. 1 (Summer 1981), 127-37.

Lee, Gaylen D. *Walking Where We Lived*. Norman: University of Oklahoma Press, 1998.

Levi-Strauss, Claude. "Introduction: History and Anthropology." Chapter in *Structural Anthropology*, l-28. trans. by Claire Jacobson and Brooke Grundfest Schoepf. Garden City, N.Y.: Anchor Books, Doubleday and Company, 1967.

Lewis, Henry T. *Patterns of Indian Burning in California: Ecology and Ethnohistory*. Ballena Press Anthropological Papers, no. 1. Ramona Calif.: Ballena Press, 1973.

Lewis, I. M. "Introduction." In *History and Social Anthropology*, ix-xxvii. ed. by I. M. Lewis. London, New York, Sidney, Toronto, and Wellington: Tavistock Publications, 1968.

Lewis, Oscar. *The War in the Far West, 1861-1865*. Garden City, N.Y.: Doubleday, 1961.

Lothrop, Marion Lydia. "The Indian Campaigns of General M. G. Vallejo, Defender of the Northern Frontier of California." *Quarterly of the Society of California Pioneers* 9, no. 3 (September 1932): 161-205.

Lowie, Robert, H. *An introduction to Cultural Anthropology*. New York: Farrar and Rinehart, 1934.

Lyman, George D. *John Marsh, Pioneer: The Life Story of a Trail-Blazer on Six Frontiers*. San Francisco: The Chatauqua Press, 1931.

Magruder, Genevieve Kratka. *The Upper San Joaquin Valley, 1772-1870*. Bakersfield, Cal.: Kern County Historical Society, 1950.

Mahon, John K. "Indian-United States Military Situation, 1775-1848." In *History of Indian White Relations*. ed. by Wilcomb E. Washburn, vol. 4, 144-62. *Handbook of North American Indians*. ed. by William C. Sturtevant. Washington, D.C.: Smithsonian Institution, 1988.

Martin, Calvin, ed. *The American Indian and the Problem of History*. New York and Oxford: Oxford University Press, 1987.

McCarthy, Francis Florence. *The History of Mission San Jose, California 1797-1835*. Fresno: Academy Library Guild, 1958.

McCawley, William. *The First Angelinos: The Gabrielino Indians of Los Angeles*. Banning, Cal.: Malki Museum Press, with Novato, Calif.: Ballena Press, 1996.

McLendon, Sally, and John R. Johnson. *Cultural Affiliation and Lineal Descent of Chumash Peoples in the Channel Islands and the Santa Monica Mountains.* vols. 1 and 2. Santa Barbara, Cal.: Santa Barbara Museum of Natural History, 1999.

Merrell, James H. *The Indians' New World: Catawbas and their Neighbors from European Contact through the Era of Removal.* Chapel Hill: University of North Carolina Press, 1989.

Merriam, C. Hart. "Distribution of Indian Tribes in the Southern Sierra and Adjacent Parts of the San Joaquin Valley, California." *Science* 19, no. 494 (June 7, 1904): 912-17.

____. "Ethnographic Notes on California Indian Tribes III: Ethnographic Notes on Central California Indian Tribes." ed. by Robert E. Heizer. *Reports of the University of California Survey*, no. 68, pt. 3 (December 1967): 429-36.

____. *Studies of California Indians.* ed. by the Staff of the Department of Anthropology of the University of California. Berkeley: University of California Press, 1955.

Meyer, Melisa L., and Kerwin Lee Klein, "Native American Studies and the End of Ethnohistory." In Russell Thornton, ed., *Studying Native America: Problems and Prospects.* The University of Wisconsin Press, 1988.

Milliken, Randall. *A Time of Little Choice: The Disintegration of Tribal Culture in the San Francisco Bay Area, 1769- 1810.* Menlo Park. Cal.: Ballena Press, 1995.

____. *Native Americans at Mission San Jose.* Banning, Cal.: Malki-Ballena Press, 2008.

Mitchell, Annie R. *Jim Savage and the Tulareno Indians*, Los Angeles: Westernlore Press, 1957.

____. *King of the Tulares and Other Tales from the San Joaquin Valley, 1772 1852.* Visalia, Cal.: privately published, 1941.

____. "Major James D. Savage and the Tulareños." *California Historical Society Quarterly 28*, no. 4 (December 1949): 323-41.

____. "Tule Indian War of 1856." *Los Tulares: Quarterly Bulletin of the Tulare County Historical Society*, no. 68 (March 1966): 1-3.

Mora, Jo. *Californios: The Saga of the Hard Riding Vaqueros, America's First Cowboys.* Garden City, New York: Doubleday & Company, Inc., 1946.

Morgan, Wallace M. *History of Kern County, California with Biographical Sketches of the Leading Men and Women of the County.* Los Angeles: Historic Record Company, 1914.

Morgan, Dale L. *Jedediah Smith and the Opening of the West.* Lincoln: University of Nebraska Press, 1953.

Morrow, William W. *Spanish and Mexican Private Land Grants.* San Francisco: Bancroft-Whitney, 1923. Newcomb, W. W., Jr. "A Re-examination of the Causes of Plains Warfare." *American Anthropologist* 52, no. 3

(July-September 1950): 317- 30.

Ortiz, Alfonso. "Indian-White Relations: A View from the Other Side of the Frontier." In *Indians in American History: An introduction*, 1-16. ed. by Frederick E. Hoxie. Arlington Heights, III.: Harlan Davidson, 1988.

Paul, Rodman W. *California Gold: The Beginning of Mining in the Far West*. First published in 1947. Lincoln: University of Nebraska Press, 1965.

Phillips, George Harwood. *Chiefs and Challengers: Indian Resistance and Cooperation in Southern California*. Berkeley and Los Angeles: University of California Press. 1975.

____. *Chiefs and Challengers: Indian Resistance and Cooperation in Southern California, 1769-1906* (second edition). Norman: University of Oklahoma Press, 2014.

____. "Indians and the Breakdown of the Spanish Mission System in California." Ethnohistory 21, no. 4 (Fall 1974): 291-302.

____. "Indians in Los Angeles, 1781-1875: Economic Integration, Social Disintegration." *Pacific Historical Review* 49, no. 5 (August 1980); 427- 51.

____. "The Alcaldes: Indian Leadership in the Spanish Missions of California." *In The Struggle for Political Autonomy: Papers and Comments from the Second Newberry Library Conference on Themes in American History*. Occasional Papers in Curriculum Series, no. 11, 83-87. Chicago: The Newberry Library, 1989.

____. *Vineyards and Vaqueros: Indian Labor and the Economic Expansion of Southern California*. Norman, Oklahoma: The Arthur H. Clark Company, 2010.

Phillips, Michael James. *History of Santa Barbara County, California, From Its Earliest Settlement to the Present Time*. Chicago: S. J. Clarke, 1927.

Pilling, Arnold R. "The Archaeological Implications of an Annual Coastal Visit for Certain Yokuts Groups." *American Anthropologist* 52, no. 3 (July-September 1950): 438-40.

Pitt, Leonard. *The Decline of the Californios: A Social History of the Spanish-Speaking Californian, 1846-1890*. Berkeley and Los Angeles: University of California Press, 1968.

____. and Dale Pitt. *Los Angeles A to Z: An Encyclopedia of the City and County*. Los Angeles and London: University of California Press, 1997.

Pomeroy, Earl. "Old Lamps for New: The Cultural Lag in Pacific Coast Historiography." *Arizona and the West* 2, no. 2 (Summer 1960): 105-26.

Powers, Bob. *North Fork Country*. Los Angeles: Westernlore Press, 1974.

Powers, Stephen. *Tribes of California*. Washington, D.C.: Government Printing Office, 1877. Reprint. ed. by Robert F. Heizer. Berkeley: University of California Press, 1976.

Preston, William L. *Vanishing Landscapes: Land and Life in the Tulare Lake Basin*. Berkeley, Los Angeles and London: University of California Press, 1981.

Prucha, Francis Paul. *American Indian Policy in the Formative Years: The Trade and Intercourse Acts, 1790-1834*. First published in 1962. Lincoln: University of Nebraska Press, 1970.

____. *American Indian Treaties: The History of a Political Anomaly*. Berkeley, Los Angeles, London: University of California Press, 1994.

____. *Indian Policy in the United States: Historical Essays*. Lincoln and London: University of Nebraska Press, 1981.

____. *The Great Father: The United States Government and the American Indians*, 2 vols. Lincoln and London: University of Nebraska Press, 1984.

Raphael, Ray. *Little White Father: Redick McKee on the California Frontier*. Eureka, California: Humboldt County Historical Society, 1993.

Rawls, James. *Indians of California: The Changing Image*. Norman: University of Oklahoma Press, 1984.

____. "The California Mission as Symbol and Myth." *California History* 71, no. 2 (Fall 1992): 343-60.

Ray, Arthur J. *Indians in the Fur Trade: Their Role as Hunters, Trappers, and Middlemen in the Lands Southwest of Hudson Bay, 1660-1870*. Toronto and Buffalo: University of Toronto Press, 1974.

Richtler, Bertina. *Fort Miller, California, 1851-1856*. New York, Bern, Frankfurt am Main, Paris: Peter Lang Publishing, 1988.

Richman, Irving Berdine. *California Under Spain and Mexico, 1535-1847*. Boston and New York: Houghton Mifflin Company, 1911.

Ripley, Vernette Snyder. "The San Fernando Pass and the Pioneer Traffic That Went over It." *Historical Society of Southern California Quarterly* 29, no. 1 (March 1947): 9-48; nos. 3, 4 (September-December 1947): 137-42; vol. 30, no. 1 (March 1948): 13-64; no. 2 (June 1948): 111-60.

Robinson, John W. "Tejon Pass and Those Who Crossed It" *Dogtown Territorial Quarterly*, no. 30 (Summer 1997): 4-5, 12-15, 17-25, 31-45.

____. "The Taming of San Fernando Pass." *Dogtown Territorial Quarterly*, no. 39 (Fall 1999): 44-45.

Robinson, W. W. *Land in California*. Berkeley and Los Angeles: University of California Press, 1948.

Rojas, Arnold R. *The Vaquero*. Charlotte and Santa Barbara: McNally and Loftin, 1964.

Russell, Cari P. *One Hundred Years in Yosemite: The Romantic Story of Early Human Affairs in the Central Sierra Nevada*. Stanford, London, and Oxford: Stanford University Press. 1931.

____. "The Geography of the Mariposa Indian War." *Yosemite Nature Notes* 30, nos. 3, 4, 6, 7 (March, April, June, July, 1951): 23-30, 32-35, 52-56, 62-71.

Satz, Ronald N. *American Indian Policy in the Jacksonian Era*. Lincoln: University of Nebraska Press, 1975.

Secrest, William B. ed., "From the Frontier: Eyewitness Accounts of

Fresno County's Beginnings," pt. 1. *Fresno Past and Present* 36, no. 1 (Spring 1994): 1-11.

____. "From the Frontier: Eyewitness Accounts of Fresno County's Beginnings." pt. 2. *Fresno Past and Present* 37, no. 1 (Spring 1995); 1-11.

Sahlins, Marshall. "Other Times, Other Customs: The Anthropology of History." *American Anthropologist* 85, no. 3 (September 1983): 517-44.

Sample, L. L. "Trade and Trails in Aboriginal California." *Reports of the University of California Archaeological Survey*, no. 8 (September 1950): 1-30.

Sanchez, Nellie Van de Grift. *Spanish Arcadia*. San Francisco, Los Angeles, and Chicago: Powell Publishing Company, 1929.

Sandos, James, A. *Converting California: Indians and Franciscans in the Missions*. New Haven and London: Yale University Press, 2004.

____. "Levantamiento!: The 1824 Chumash Uprising Reconsidered." *Southern California Quarterly* 67, no. 2 (Summer 1985): 109-33.

Schapera, L. "Should Anthropologists be Historians?" *Journal of the Royal Anthropological Institute of Great Britain and Ireland* 92, pt. 2 (July-December 1962): 143-56.

Schenk, W. Egbert. "Historic Aboriginal Groups of the California Delta Region." *University of California Publications in American Archaeology and Ethnology* 23,. no. 2 (1926) , 123-46.

Shipley, William F. "Native Languages of California." In California, ed. by Robert Heizer. vol 8. In *Handbook of North American Indians*, 80-90, ed. by William C. Sturtevant. Washington, D.C.: Smithsonian Institution, 1978.

____. "Spanish Elements in the Indigenous Languages of Central California." *Romance Philology* 16, no. 1 (August 1962): 1-21.

Shoup, Laurence H., and Randall T. Milliken. *Inigo of Rancho Posolmi: The Life and Times of a Mission Indian*. Novato, Cal.: 1999.

Stewart, George W. "The Yokut Indians of the Kaweah Region." *Sierra Club Bulletin* 12, no. 4 (1927): 385-400.

Steward, Julian H. "Ethnography of the Owens Valley Paiute." *University of California Publications in American Archaeology and Ethnology* 33, no. 3 (September 1933): 233-350.

Sturtevant, William C. "Anthropology, Historical, and Ethnohistory." *Ethnohistory* 13, nos. 1 and 2 (Winter-Spring 1966): 1-51.

Sievers, Michael A. "Malfeasance or Indirection? Administration of the California Indian Superintendency's Business Affairs." *Historical Society of Southern California Quarterly* 56, no. 3 (Fall 1974): 273-94.

Smith, Wallace. *Garden of the Sun*. n.p.: first published in 1939; privately published, 1960.

Stammerjohan, George R. "Fort Tejon State Historic Park: An Interpretive History." *Dogtown Territorial Quarterly*, no. 31 (Fall 1997): 54-63; pt. 2, no. 32 (Winter 1997): 4-6, 8-25, 31-37; pt. 3, no. 33 (Spring 1998):

16-25, 61-62.

Stewart, George W. "The Indian War on Tule River." *The Overland Monthly* 3 (January 1884): 46-53.

Sutton, Mark Q. "Some Aspects of Kitanemuk Prehistory." *Journal of California and Great Basin Anthropology* 2, no. 2 (Winter 1980): 214-25.

Thomas, Lately. *Sam Ward: "King of the Lobby."* Boston: Houghton Mifflin Company, 1965.

Thompson, Gerald. *Edward F. Beale and the American West.* Albuquerque: University of New Mexico Press, 1983.

Traywick, Ben T. *Big Jim Savage: Blond King of the Indians and Discoverer of Yosemite.* Privately published, 1972.

Trennent, Robert A. *Alternative to Extinction: Federal Indian Policy and the Beginnings of the Reservation System, 1846-51.* Philadelphia: Temple University Press, 1975.

Taylor, George Rogers. ed. *The Turner Thesis Concerning the Role of the Frontier in American History.* Lexington, Mass., Toronto, and London: D.C. Heath and Company, 1972.

Teilman, I., and W. H. Shafer. *The Historical Story of Irrigation in Fresno and Kings Counties in Central California.* Fresno: Williams and Son, 1943.

Thomas, Keith. "History and Anthropology." *Past and Present: A Journal of Historical Studies*, no. 24 (April 1963): 3-24.

Thompson, Joseph A. *El Gran Capitan, Jose de la Guerra: A Historical Biographical Study.* Los Angeles: Cabrera and Sons, 1961.

Thompson, Leonard, and Howard Lamar. "Comparative Frontier History." In *The Frontier in History: North America and South Africa Compared*, 3-13. ed. by Howard Lamar and Leonard Thompson. New Haven and London: Yale University Press, 1981.

Timbrook, Jan. "Virtuous Herbs: Plants in Chumash Medicine." *Journal of Ethnobiology* 7, no. 2 (Winter 1987): 171-80.

Tinkham, George H. *A History of Stockton.* San Francisco: W. M. Hinton & Co., Printers, 1880.

____. *History of San Joaquin County.* Los Angeles: Historic Record Company, 1923.

Trigger, Bruce G. "Ethnohistory: Problems and Prospects." *Ethnohistory* 29, no. 1 (Winter 1982): l-19.

____. *The Children of Aataentsic 1: A History of the Huron People to 1660.* Montreal and London: McGill-Queen's University Press, 1976.

Thompson, Gerald. *Edward F. Beale and the American West.* Albuquerque: University of New-Mexico Press, 1983.

____. *The Army and the Navajo: The Bosque Redondo Reservation Experiment, 1863-1868.* Tucson: University of Arizona Press, 1976. "Tule River Indian Reservation: One of the Oldest in California." *Tulare County Historical Society Historical Bulletin*, no. 4 (October 1949): 1, 3.

Tyler, S. Lyman. *Indian Affairs: A Study of the Changes in Policy of the United States toward the Indians*. Salt Lake City: Brigham Young University Press, 1964.

Uldall, Hans Jorgen, and William Shipley, *Nisenan Texts and Dictionary*. University of California Publications in Linguistics, vol. 46. Berkeley and Los Angeles: University of California Press, 1966.

Voegelin, Ermine W. "Tiibatulabal Ethnography." *Anthropological Records* 2, no. 1 (1938- 1940): 1-84.

Wallace, W. Elliott. *History of Tulare County, California*. San Francisco: Wallace W. Elliott & Co., 1883.

Wallace, William J. "Southern Valley Yokuts." In California, ed. by Robert Heizer. vol. 8 in *Handbook of North American Indians*, 448-67. ed. by William C. Sturtevant. Washington, D.C.: Smithsonian Institution, 1978.

Weber. David J. "American Westward Expansion and the Breakdown of Relations between 'Pobladores and Indios Barbaros' on Mexico's Far Northern Frontier, 1821-1846." *New Mexico Historical Review* 56, no. 3 (1981): 221-38.

____. "Mexico's Far Northern Frontier, 1821-1854: Historiography Askew." *Western Historical Quarterly* 7, no. 3 (July 1976): 279-93.

Wells, Robin F. "Frontier Systems as a Sociocultural Type." *Papers in Anthropology* 14, no. 1 (Spring 1973): 6-15.

Wells, K. P. "Ethnohistory and Material Culture of the Southern Sierra Miwok: 1852-1880." *Yosemite Museum Library*, Yosemite National Park, California, 1982.

White, Richard. "Using the Past: History and Native American Studies." In Russell Thornton, ed., *Studying Native America: Problems and Prospects*. The University of Wisconsin Press, 1988, 217-243.

Winther, Oscar Osburn. "The Story of San Jose, 1777-1869: California's First Pueblo." pt. 1. *California Historical Society Quarterly* 14, no. 1 (1935): 3-27.

Wyman, Walker D., and Clifton B. Kroeber. "Introduction." In The *Frontier in Perspective*, xiii- xx. ed. by Walker D. Wyman and Clifton B. Kroeber. Madison: University of Wisconsin Press, 1957.

Walker, Ardis. "Judas of the Kern." *Westways* 50, no. 3 (March 1958): 10-11.

Wood, Raymond F. *California's Agua Fria: The Early History of Mariposa County*. Fresno, Cal.: Academy Library Guild, 1954.

Zollinger, James Peter. *Sutter: The Man and His Empire*. New York. London, and Toronto: Oxford University Press, 1939.

Index